Four Years in the Saddle

Charge of the First Ohio Volunteer Cavalry at the Battle of Stone's River, Tennessee, December 31, 1862

Four Years in the Saddle
The History of the First Regiment
Ohio Volunteer Cavalry in the
American Civil War

W. L. Curry

Four Years in the Saddle: the History of the First Regiment Ohio Volunteer Cavalry in the American Civil War
by W. L. Curry

Leonaur is an imprint of Oakpast Ltd

Text in this form and material original to this edition
copyright © 2008 Oakpast Ltd

ISBN: 978-1-84677-542-0 (hardcover)
ISBN: 978-1-84677-541-3 (softcover)

http://www.leonaur.com

Publisher's Notes

The opinions expressed in this book are those of the author and are not necessarily those of the publisher.

Contents

Preface	9
First Ohio Volunteer Cavalry	13
Organizing Our Army in 1861	17
From Columbia to Pittsburgh Landing	46
Battle of Pittsburg Landing	53
Battle of Pittsburg Landing	64
From Pittsburg Landing to Corinth	71
From Corinth to Decherd, Tenn.	79
From Northern Alabama to Louisville, Kentucky	87
Perryville Campaign	95
Battle of Perryville	101
Stone River Campaign	109
Battle of Stone River	117
After the Battle of Stone River	130
From Murfreesborough to Chattanooga.	138
Chickamauga Campaign	158
Raid of the Rebel Cavalry Through Tennessee	186
Campaigns	207
Demonstration on Dalton	224
Atlanta Campaign	235
Kilpatrick's Raid Around Atlanta	242
Atlanta Battles and Losses	267
The Nashville Campaign	291
Companies A & C First Ohio Cavalry	326
The Capture of Jefferson Davis	344
Reminiscences & Incidents	374
Biographies	510
The End	538
Roster of Troops	547

Sketch of Badge of Cavalry Corps
Army of the Cumberland

To our comrades of the First Ohio Volunteer Cavalry,
who sleep on the battlefields of the Republic
this feeble tribute is affectionately dedicated
by the author.

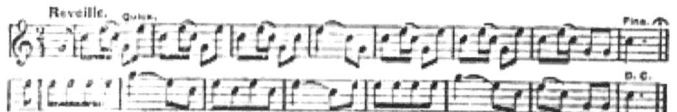

Preface

For a number of years short sketches of some of the campaigns of the regiment, written by comrades, have been read at our reunions and afterwards were published in the proceedings.

As these articles proved interesting to the survivors, the matter of writing a history of the campaigns of the regiment was suggested and discussed at the reunions and W. L. Curry, who had been elected historian for several years, was urged to begin the work at once. At the reunion held at Galloway, Ohio, September 15, 1892, the plan was outlined and J. W. Chapin was appointed to assist in compiling the history, and other comrades volunteered their services to give all the aid possible in the good work. A large amount of material had already been accumulated and a systematic effort was then made to correct the roster by writing letters to comrades of every company and by sending copies of the company roster to them for examination, and many corrections in names and dates were made by them.

The diary kept by W. L. Curry during his services has been depended on very largely for data, as the distance of our daily marches with names of towns and rivers were noted, as well as dates of battles and skirmishes and many incidents of historic interest.

Neither time nor pains have been spared to get information on all points of interest; many months have been devoted to the preparation of the manuscript. After careful corrections the manuscript was all typewritten before it was placed in the hands of the publisher.

More than one hundred volumes of the *Records of the Rebellion* published by the War Department have been carefully examined, and all orders, reports of officers of the regiment, brigade and division have been copied, and many of them are published in the history. From this mass of material the story has been written without any attempt to embellish the history with high flown language or graphic and romantic descriptions that in so many histories have a tinge of fiction, it is only the plain story of the regiment

Official reports and statistics may seem a little dry in some instances, but it is the history of our campaigns recorded on the field, and cannot be refuted; and the fact that our history is fortified by these reports made at the time, is what adds to its value.

From the time the regiment entered Kentucky in the fall of 1861 until the battle of Perryville, October 8, 1862, we were not brigaded as cavalry, but were attached to brigades or divisions of infantry, temporarily. After that date the cavalry was organized into brigades and divisions and acted independent of the infantry, and for the last three years of the war the history of the regiment must necessarily be blended with that of the brigade and division. We are greatly indebted to many of the comrades, who responded to every call, for intelligent assistance in all parts of the work, and in the chapter of "Incidents and Reminiscences" they are given full credit for their contributions.

The roster of the regiment, published in the back part of the book, was purchased from the firm that published the cavalry roster of the state for the Adjutant-General's Department. In this roster many errors in spelling names, also in dates and casualties, appear. Many of these mistakes have been corrected, and are published on a separate page; but no doubt errors have crept in, notwithstanding every effort has been made to make the roster correct During the month of March, 1898, alone, nearly one hundred letters were written to members of the regiment to correct dates of enlistment, discharge, etc. We have studiously avoided indulging in fulsome praise of any officer or soldier now living, and have only tried to give credit where credit was due; but to those who died on the field too much praise cannot be given. In addition to the story of the regiment, the history has been somewhat widened by short histories of battles in which the regiment participated, with losses in the two armies, which cannot fail to be of absorbing interest to every reader. Biographies of deceased officers, published in the history, were furnished by their families, and all cuts for portraits were paid for by the families of these officers, and cuts for portraits of surviving soldiers were paid for by the soldiers themselves. All other cuts, maps and illustrations were furnished and paid for by the author. We are under obligations to the following gentlemen for the use of cuts kindly loaned: General H. V. Boynton, for several cuts made for his book, *The Chickamauga National Military Park*, and also for giving us permission to copy from his book the strength and losses of the Union and Confederate armies at the battle of Chickamauga Colonel N. D. Preston, of the Tenth N.Y. Volunteer Cavalry, for cut of Cavalryman, *Going to the Front* and *Forward*; and to Captain C. T. Clark, of Columbus, and Major J. C. McElroy for the use of cuts.

And now, when the story of the regiment is completed, written as it was in the intervals of pressing business and official duties, the pen is laid aside, regretting that the history could not have been written by some other member of the regiment better qualified to wield the pen, and who could have devoted more time to the work. If the brief history of the services of the regiment meets with the approval of the boys with whom we have "marched many a weary day and watched many a frosty night," the author will feel amply repaid for the time devoted to preparing the manuscript for publication.

W. L. Curry
J. W. Chapin
Committee

First Ohio Volunteer Cavalry

The first notice of the organization of the First Ohio Cavalry, is found in a report of the Adjutant-General of Ohio for 1861. In his report for that year the Adjutant-General states that:

.... on July 21, 1861, after earnest solicitation, authority was received from Washington for raising eight companies, or a regiment of cavalry, directly for the service of the Federal Government. It was determined that this regiment should be one of maximum size, to consist of twelve companies. This was raised without difficulty, and rendezvoused at Camp Chase, in July, August and September."

Official List of Battles

Liberty, Ky., Co. B	November, 1861
Siege of Corinth	April and May, 1862
Farmington, Miss	May 28, 1862
Booneville, Miss	May 30, 1862
Blackland, Miss	June 4, 1862
Russellville, Ala	July 1, 1862
Courtland, Ala	July 25, 1862
Bardstown, Ky	October 4, 1862
Perryville, Ky	October 8, 1862
Franklin, Tenn	December 12, 1862
Nolensville, Tenn	December 26, 1862
Stone's River, Tenn	December 31, 1862; January 1, 2, 3, 1863

Tullahoma, Tenn	July 1, 1863
Elk River, Tenn	July 2, 1863
Alpine, Ga	September 11, 1863
Chickamauga, Ga	September 19 and 20, 1863
Wheeler's Raid through Tennessee	October 1 to 9, 1863
Cotton Port, Tenn	September 30, 1863
McMinnville, Tenn	October 4, 1863
Murfreesboro, Tenn	October 5, 1863
Shelbyville, Tenn	October 7, 1863
Farmington, Tenn	October 7, 1863
Sugar Creek, Tenn	October 9, 1863
Paint Rock, Ala	October 30, 1863
Missionary Ridge, Tenn	November 25, 1863
Cleveland, Tenn	November 27, 1863
Charleston and Calhoun, Tenn	December 28, 1863
Tunnel Hill, Ga	February 25, 1864
Buzzard Roost, Ga	February 27, 1864
Decatur, Ala	May 26, 1864
Moulton, Ala	May 29, 1864
McAfees Cross Roads, Ga	June 12, 1864
Noon Day Creek, Ga	June 15, 1864
Kenesaw Mountain, Ga	June 21, 1864
Chattahoochie River	July 12, 1864
Peach Tree Creek, Ga	July 19 & 20, 1864
Atlanta, Ga	July and August, 1864
Kilpatrick's Raid around Atlanta	August 18, 19, 20, 21, 22, 1864
Fairburn, Ga	August 19, 1864
Jonesboro, Ga	August 19, 1864
Lovejoy Station, Ga	August 20, 1864
Rome, Ga	October 13, 1864
Snake Creek Gap	October 15, 1864
Little River, Ga	October 20, 1864
Coosa River, Ga	October 25, 1864

The Wilson raid through Alabama and Georgia
March and April, 1865

Montevallo, Ala	March 20, 1865
Ebenezer Church, Ala	April 1, 1865
Selma, Ala	April 2, 1865
Montgomery, Ala	April 12, 1865
Columbus Ga	April 16, 1865
West Point, Ga	April 16, 1865
Surrender — Macon, Ga	April 20, 1865
Irwinsville, Ga.	Capture of Jeff Davis May 10, 1865

Every battle in the above table is published in the official list of battles by the War Department excepting Cotton Port, Tenn October 1, 1863, and Farmington, Tenn, October 7, 1863. The fight at Cotton Port was the day Wheeler crossed the Tennessee River and we had several soldiers wounded and captured. October 7, 1863, we drove the rebel cavalry from Shelbyville to Farmington, and in the official list it is given as Shelbyville, but it was always known in the regiment as Farmington, as we captured a battery at that place.

CHAPTER 1

Organizing Our Army in 1861

It was no ordinary task to organize an army, either north or south, from raw citizens that had absolutely no knowledge of military affairs at the beginning of the war in 1861.

The war came like a thunder-clap in the North and the Union army at the beginning was but a crowd of brave and patriotic citizens. The officers and men all stood on a common level so far as knowledge of military affairs went, for not one in a hundred knew the difference between a corporal and a brigadier-general and hardly knew a right face from a left face.

One instance is recalled of an Ohio regiment that had a noted lawyer for their first colonel, and the members of the regiment and their friends predicted a brilliant military career for this promising officer. But he proved to be a dismal failure, as he was too lazy to drill or even study the tactics. In time the regiment took the field and was soon in front of the enemy. This colonel was ordered to take a certain position on the line. He marched his regiment out in columns of fours, and was ordered to "feel the enemy carefully" which he proceeded to do in the most approved military style in favour of the enemy, as it was soon demonstrated. As the regiment neared the battle line, they passed an old veteran regiment, supporting a battery, and this veteran regiment was hugging the ground closely, expecting an attack every moment. Some of the members of the new regiment sung out, "Where are the rebels? Just show them to us!"

And the response from the veterans, hugging the ground still more closely, was: "You will find them on the other side of that cornfield." And into the cornfield the brave, but new recruits marched, and as one of the boys afterwards stated, they went in "slaunch ways." In a few moments the rebel line raised up and gave them one enfilading volley, and the regiment was soon in full retreat, for no veterans could have stood such a withering fire in an open field. As they passed back through the lines of the veterans still hugging the ground, some of the boys could not refrain from asking them if "they found the rebels."

This is referred to as one instance of scores in which some of our best regiments were in the beginning commanded by incompetent officers who were appointed by political influence. The regiment referred to proved to be one of the fighting regiments and had a long and honourable record in the field.

The first year's service tested the qualities of the rank and file. A few months exposure and hardship sent the physically incapable to hospital to die or be discharged for disability, while in that time those who had the physique but not the spirit of soldiers found means to be detached from their commands and, though still carried on the muster rolls, to be detailed as clerks in bureaus or headquarters, hospital nurses, or in some other non-combatant capacity. Those soldiers, who after a year's service, were still in the field with their commands were really the "army" that fought the war. They were physically, at least, the flower of the American people.

During the months of May, June and July, 1861, the appearance of the camps of instruction would look grotesque to the militia of to-day where thousands of soldiers were encamped without arms or uniforms. Think of a regiment manoeuvring almost like clock-work and yet no two men dressed alike; for many regiments were well drilled in company and battalion drill before arms and clothing were issued. It was common to see a sentinel walking his beat with a stick at a "support," and the officer of the guard in making his rounds would return the salute of the sentinel with a flourish of his wooden sword. Though not soldiers, they were actually "playing soldier," and played it seri-

Col. B. B. Eggleston.

Lieut. Col. Valentine Cupp.

Gen'l. T. C. H. Smith.

Maj. D. A. B. Moore.

Col. Minor Millikin.

Col. T. J. Pattin.

Maj. Martin Buck.

Maj. James N. Scott.

Maj. J. C. Frankeberger.

Our Heroic Dead

ously. This was the situation in 1861, and out of this rustic mob in a few months was moulded an army of boys as brave as the old Guard that followed the eagles of Napoleon.

The regiments that were so fortunate as to get a regular officer for a colonel were usually well organized, and that was the case in the First Ohio. We had a great contempt for our colonel in the beginning as he was a regular martinet, but when we got into the field, we had a very high regard for him, as at once inaugurated strict military discipline and, as the boys said "brought the officers to time," organised an officers' school and looked after the smallest details of clothing, rations and all things that pertained to the comfort of his men, systematically examined for himself all clothing equipments and food before allowing them to be issued, and whatever was poor in quality or short in quantity, he rejected with good round oaths and with a savage threat of arrest to the quartermaster or commissary. It was amusing to observe that the company officers soon adopted his careful system of looking out for his mens' rights and even imitated his oaths.

When we were at Camp Chase, Ohio, in the fall of 1861, I remember of being down at the quartermaster's tent when we had just received an invoice of blankets, and was opening up the boxes, and it proved that the blankets were of all kinds and colours, some red, some gray, and others striped. Just then the colonel, an officer of the regular army, as before mentioned, stepped in, and, taking a survey of the situation, commenced swearing, and in a moment the blankets and air were all of the same colour "blue." Said he, "Box them up, send them back, for I'll be d—d if I propose to have my regiment decked out in blankets with as many different colours as 'Joseph's Coat.'"

It struck me, a raw, verdant country boy, as being extremely funny and ridiculous, and I never forgot it. I presume the blankets were sent back. The writer was orderly sergeant at that time, and when the orderly's call would sound in the morning, I remember we always went up to headquarters with our morning reports with "fear and trembling," for if there was anything in the least degree wrong, he would always send us back to our quarters to correct it, and some of us can testify today that we were sent back at least three times in one morning. He never reprimanded the Sergeants, but would say: "Tell your captain so and so"; and it was not an unusual thing for the captain to be summoned into his presence, where he usually got a scoring.

At the beginning of the war the Cavalry arm of the service had no separate organization as an army. Yet raw and undisciplined as they were, they were of the same blood and had the same soldierly qualities of dash, vim and independence of all other arms of the service, and never failed to respond to any and every duty they were called upon to perform.

The tramp of their triumphant steeds shook the ground all along the line, and their bugle calls rang out alike from every valley and mountain that marked the great battles of the war.

Under the military regime of the old army during the interval between the war with Mexico and the breaking out of the war of the Rebellion, the *esprit de corps* of the Cavalry arm of the service had been sadly neglected.

In the campaigns of the Revolution, the war of 1812, and more especially, the war with Mexico, which consisted very largely in the besieging of fortifications, and the country being so unfavourable to successful cavalry operations, hence the importance of a well mounted and well equipped cavalry force was not fully realized by General Scott and his lieutenants.

We had very few regiments of cavalry at the beginning of the war, and they were broken up in squadrons and companies, and were scattered along our western frontier fighting Indians, patrolling and doing courier duty between the outposts. But in the first battles of the war the importance of raising and equipping a strong cavalry force, and placing them under command of dashing young leaders, was fully demonstrated to the officers of the old army.

In the early part of the war, our cavalry was badly handled by the officers in command. While the volunteer officers knew nothing more of the service than the rank and file of their commands, it seemed that the officers assigned to duty in the cavalry service from the regular army did not understand that cavalry to be effective must be kept on the move, and should never receive an attack from the enemy at a halt. Not until the battle of Stone's River was the effectiveness of the cavalry demonstrated in the army of the Cumberland, when the First Ohio, led by their intrepid young commander, Colonel Minor Millikin, made their first sabre charge, holding at bay a large force of the left wing of the rebel army by their bold charge.

As will be remembered by all members of the regiment, in the early part of our service it was usual to halt to receive the attack of the enemy, and attempt to fire from our horses, instead of dismounting to fight on foot, or drawing sabre and charging him; all of which we learned before the close of the war. During the siege of Corinth, in 1862, the regiment did picket duty in front of the infantry lines during the greater part of that siege of two months; and it was no unusual occurrence to have from a half dozen to a dozen alarms during each night, and at each alarm the reserve was mounted with "advance carbine" ready to receive the attack.

During the last days of the siege we were in such close proximity to the main entrenched lines of the enemy that our pickets, put on duty at dark, were required to keep their posts until daybreak without being relieved, as it was not possible to change the guard on the outposts without drawing the fire of the enemy. Had we been required to do this kind of duty during the late years of the war, the picket would have been dismounted, thus saving the horses, and giving the picket guard a much better opportunity of watching the movements of the enemy, and also keeping himself concealed and not drawing the fire of the enemy by the champing of bits and neighing of horses. These are mentioned as a few of the abuses of the cavalry service before even our best generals had learned the art of war.

Nor were our officers of high rank entitled to all the credit for the efficiency of our arm of the service, but the credit belongs largely to the rank and file, to the non-commissioned and line officers, who did the hard service, and was each one a general unto himself, and daily made suggestions to his superiors who profiting by them, took all the honour to themselves.

The life of a cavalryman in time of war is one of constant activity hard and dangerous service. During the winter season, when the main army is snugly ensconced in winter quarters, the cavalry are the most active and have the hardest service to perform, as they are kept constantly patrolling and scouting. It was a very usual occurrence, as is well remembered by every trooper of the regiment, that just as we would get comfortably tucked in our dog tents, after "taps," on a stormy winter's night, to hear the bugle ring out from headquarters, sounding "Boots and saddles!" and in fifteen minutes a company, squadron, or perhaps a regiment, would be in the saddle, booted and spurred ready for duty. And the order be to make a reconnaissance twenty miles to the right or left flank of the army to watch some reported movement of the enemy, and off we dashed through darkness, rain and mud, to find our way the best we could, along the miry and unfrequented roads, not knowing at what moment we would run into an ambuscade of the enemy of thrice our own number, reaching our destination perhaps at daybreak to find that it was a "contraband report." The cavalry outpost duty was a hard and dangerous service and they were required to furnish the advance sentinels, when not confronted by entrenched lines. As grand guards are chiefly to watch the enemy in the front, they are never entrenched, except by barricades hastily thrown up, to repel the attack of cavalry; and it is not only the duty of the grand guard to watch the movements of the enemy, but to reconnoitre his position, and to determine the force and position of the advance posts. Small posts of picked men are sent forward to ascertain if the enemy is advancing, and we all remember well what a perilous duty this was. Marching always in silence and on the approach of the enemy to fire and fall back on the reserve, by routes selected during the day. In the day time the cavalry videttes are placed on high grounds and as much under cover as possible, and always required to carry the carbine in the hand; but, day or night, the sentinel must be sure of the presence of the enemy before firing, and then he must fire, even if surrounded, as the safety of thousands may depend upon one man. Reconnoitring parties were sent out day and night, and just before daybreak the advance guards and scouts were drawn close together, as this was the hour of danger, when an attack was anticipated.

All these movements of the cavalry arm of the service required vigilance, secrecy, energy, promptness and dash; and whether the command was composed of a Brigade, Regiment, Squadron, Company or Platoon, the commander must not halt or hesitate, but act immediately and supply by strategy what he lacks in numbers. During the second, third and fourth years of the war, cavalry officers were largely composed of young men who at the beginning of the war were privates or non-commissioned officers. The older men could not, but with rare exceptions, endure the hard picket duty, routes and raids of fifty or sixty miles a day, which was of usual occurrence. Some of the most dangerous expeditions were under command of corporals and sergeants, penetrating the enemy's lines, capturing outposts and couriers with dispatches that were of vital importance to our army. Many instances of bravery and heroism in the rank and file could be related that would do honour to a Kilpatrick or a Custer, and instances of individual adventure and heroic deeds in the cavalry service could be multiplied by the score that would be of intense interest to every reader of this history.

The First Ohio Cavalry was organized under the first call for the three years' service in 1861, and as the companies were recruited they rendezvoused at Camp Chase, near Columbus, Ohio, and were mustered in as a regiment on the fifth day of October, 1861. The first commission issued was to Captain J. H. Robinson, of Company A, and was dated August 16, 1861. Company A was recruited in Fayette county; Company B in Guernsey and Muskingum counties; Company C in Fayette, Pickaway, Hamilton and Highland counties; Company D in Licking and Union counties; Company E in Pickaway county; Company F in Franklin, Fairfield and Licking counties; Company G in Clermont, Warren and Hamilton counties; Company H in Highland county; Company I in Miami county; Company K in Union, Madison and Franklin counties; Company L in Washington county; and Company M in Ross county. The members of the regiment were composed largely of farmers boys, and many of them furnished their own horses and equipments, and as they were accustomed to riding and training horses, they were well adapted to the cavalry arm of the service.

Of the commissioned officers of the regiment, four attained the grade of colonel, five of lieutenant-colonel, sixteen of major, four of surgeon, two assistant surgeon, one chaplain, forty-six of captain, and one hundred and twenty-nine of lieutenant — making in all two hundred and seven commissions. There being originally twelve captains, thirty-four lieutenants were promoted to the rank of captain. There were but four officers in the regiment at the close of the war that were commissioned at, the organization of the regiment; all the other officers remaining in the regiment at the close of the war, having been promoted from the ranks. Of the colonels of the regiment, Ransom resigned, Millikin was killed at Stone River, Smith was promoted to Brigadier-General, and Eggleston was also promoted to Brigadier-General, and died since the war, was mustered out with the regiment. Colonel Cupp was killed at Chickamauga. Major Moore and Lieutenant Condit were killed at Stone River; Colonel Patten has died since the war, as has also Major Scott. Major Frankeberger, Major Buck, and Major Robinson died during the war. Captains Emery and Scott were killed in action, as was Lieutenant Allen, Lieutenant Stevens, and Lieutenant Rennick died in the service. Surgeon Cannan, Captain Pickering, Lieutenants Overly, Scott, L'Hommedien, Ferguson, Bryson, Goodrich, Captain Conn, Captain Lawder, Lieutenant Leib, Lieutenant Hall and Captain Siverd have died since the war, and scores of our comrades of the rank and file have answered their last roll-call and passed to the camping ground on the other shore.

Colonel O. P. Ransom was a regular army officer and he at once commenced drilling the regiment dismounted, and issued the strictest orders for all routine camp duty. But few of the officers knew anything about the cavalry tactics, or any other tactics; but an officer's school was soon organized and every officer was required to get a set of cavalry tactics and devote his time to study and drill, and the company officers were required to organize a school for the non-commissioned officers and give them instructions every night.

We denounced Colonel Ransom as an "old martinet and tyrant" then, but we soon learned to respect him as a disciplinarian, and before the end of our service blessed his memory for the strict discipline inaugurated when we first went into camp.

One of our historians of the war speaks very highly of the personnel of the regiment at the organization, and uses the following language:

"It being the first organization of its class raised in the State, there was at once manifested a great anxiety to join its ranks. This fact enabled the recruiting officers and the surgeon of the regiment to discriminate largely in the selection of men. It may well be doubted whether more applicants were ever rejected from a similar organization in the service, or if a nobler band of men in physical development could possibly have been selected from the yeomanry of Ohio."[1]

During the month of September, 1861, and before the regiment was fully organized, Companies A and C, having been mounted and equipped, were ordered to Western Virginia, where they were destined to campaign in the Army of the Potomac for the next three years, participating in some of the hardest battles and some of the most daring raids of the cavalry service. Company B having been mounted and fully equipped, about the first of October was ordered to report to General Mitchell's Headquarters in Cincinnati, and in a few days it was sent on an expedition into Kentucky. At West Liberty they met the command of Colonel Humphrey Marshall and had a lively fight.

---

1. Reid's *Ohio in the War.*

Lieutenant Samuel Fordyce and a few men of the company were wounded, being the first blood shed in the regiment. The company remained in this section of Kentucky until December and joined the regiment at Louisville in the same month. As will be remembered by all members of the regiment, our camp was along the National Road at the extreme west end of Camp Chase, and we were quartered in tents, while all the other troops in camp were quartered in wooden barracks.

The 40th Regiment, O. V. I., and 42nd Regiment, O. V. I., were in camp— the 42nd being Garfield's regiment— and with this regiment we had a lively skirmish at one time, and after that we did not have any particular love for each other. The 40th and 42nd boys got into a fight something about post sutler's quarters. The guards of the 42nd refused to allow the 40th boys to pass the guard lines to go to the sutlers, and this resulted in a big racket between the two regiments and a large number of soldiers of both regiments assembled at the guard line. Before the officer of the day arrived hostilities had commenced, and the First Ohio re-enforced the 40th and took a hand and there were many knock-downs and bloody noses on both sides, and the 42nd was "knocked out in the first round," at least it was so claimed by the boys of the First and Fortieth. This was the "baptism of blood" for these three regiments, that were destined to fight on so many bloody fields within the next four years, and it was a little episode well remembered by every soldier of these regiments present at the time.

During our stay in Camp Chase we had a very enjoyable time, as the fall weather was beautiful, and we had hundreds of visitors from the city and surrounding country, and we were I very much in love with "playing soldier." The company's in the facings and marching were kept up regularly, two drills each day, until the regiment had become quite proficient in the dismounted drill before the horses were issued. We received our horses in the month of October, and then the cavalryman was in his glory, for through all the hard work of "setting up" and the many weeks of dismounted drill he had been cheered by the promise and the bright hope that he would soon be mounted on his good steed and ready to meet the enemy in his chosen arm of the service. The dismounted drill, while distasteful to the trooper, was very important, as we learned, after the field, that it was necessary to often dismount to light foot, and had our horses been furnished immediately after we went into camp, much of the dismounted drill would have been omitted, and we also had more time to devote to sabre and manual of carbine and revolver. When the horses were issued, they proved to be very fine mounts, as but few cavalry horses had been purchased in that section of the state, and such a large number of fine horses to select from, many were condemned and rejected. Those were the handsomest and most serviceable lot of horses we had during our service— no horse being accepted if he was less than five years of age, and at least one horse of that number was in service to the end of the war, and was turned in at Hilton Head, S. C., when the regiment was discharged. The horses were issued to the companies and the company commanders then had two numbers made out for each horse, one was tied to the head of the halter, and the other put in a hat from which each soldier drew a number and then started on a double quick for the picket line to find his horse. It is safe to say that there was more horse trading done in one day, after we received our horses, than was ever done in the State of Ohio in the same time, as every soldier was anxious to get a good mount, and if his horse did not suit him on the first trial, he exchanged with the first trooper that was willing to trade, and this was kept up for some weeks.

The average cavalryman has reached the height of his ambition when he is mounted and equipped, and we commenced mounted drills at once, and kept it up continuously, at least two drills each day, as long as we remained in Camp Chase. We frequently made practice marches along the National Road and into the city, with drawn sabres, and our new uniforms, fine, gaily-caparisoned horses and clanking spurs attracted a great deal of attention, especially from the fair maidens. The flirtations of these dashing troopers no doubt caused the hearts of the "girls we left behind" to sigh for their cavaliers when we were ordered to the front. As the large per cent of the boys recruited in the regiment were farmers, and as in that day a great deal of horseback riding was done, a large majority of our men were, as the saying goes, "raised on a horse's back," and were fine horsemen. To be an accomplished rider, it must be learned when the person is young and at the age when he has a certain amount of recklessness and has no fear, for a person that is timid and has no confidence in his ability to control his horse never can become a good rider.

The First Ohio had a great advantage in this regard over many cavalry regiments that were recruited in cities and in localities where there was little horseback riding, as the men were accustomed to caring for horses and understood feeding, grooming and saddling, and did not have these duties to learn after enlisting. Many of the men brought their own horses to camp and owned them throughout the war, and received forty cents a day from the Government for their service. The men who owned their own mounts usually had the best horses and cared for them the best, as they had a pecuniary interest and also understood the care of horses. With all these advantages, the regiment took up the mounted drill readily, and before we left Camp Chase in December, 1861, had become quite proficient in mounted battalion and regimental drill, which attracted large crowds of visitors, and was viewed with admiration and envy by the infantry soldiers, in camp. The manoeuvres of a thousand horsemen at a trot, gallop and charge is a magnificent sight, and, once seen, is always remembered, and has a great attraction for the average young American, and we were all soon imbued with the dash and exciting attractions of the cavalry service.

While no soldier can become a good cavalryman unless he is a good horseman, we soon learned that the service of a cavalryman, with all its many attractions, was at all times laborious, and while he might be a good rider he had many other duties to learn and perform. The trooper has his carbine to care for and keep in order, which evens him up with the infantryman in care of arms and equipments, and in addition to this he has his revolver, sabre and horse equipments to keep in order and his horse to water, feed and groom every day, and the soldier who enlists in the cavalry service expecting a "soft snap" will soon learn, to his sorrow, that he has been labouring under a grievous mistake.

On a campaign or march in good weather, when it is not necessary to pitch tents at night, the infantry stack arms, get supper and are soon at rest or asleep; but not so with the cavalryman the company must first put up the picket rope and then the horses must be watered, fed and groomed. If there is no forage in the wagon train, he must then hunt forage for his horse, and perhaps go a mile or two for that. Then he unsaddles, gets his coffee, grooms his horse, and is ready to lie down an hour after the infantryman is asleep. In the morning, if the cavalry are to move at the same hour the infantry are to march, they must have reveille an hour earlier than the infantry, to have time to feed, groom and water their horses; and while he has the advantage on the march, it would not be considered by the average citizen a very easy task to march forty, fifty or even sixty miles a day mounted, which was a usual occurrence on our scouts and raids. We did not know all of these things when we were drilling in Camp Chase in the fall of 1861, but before the regiment was mustered out— September 13, 1865 — we learned by experience that it was a reality.

On the eighth day of December the long looked for order to "march to the front" was received, and it took a full day and night to pack up and cook rations for the anticipated campaign.

All day of the eighth was consumed in writing letters to the dear ones at home and sending a last loving message to the "girl we left behind." But little sleep was had that night by anyone, as many of the boys took advantage of the last night in camp to visit the city, and, as a result, came into camp all hours of the night, many of them in a hilarious and boisterous condition, much to the disgust of the infantry boys doing duty along the National Road, as squads of cavalrymen of from six to a dozen would dash through the guard lines under the spur yelling like a lot of savages. Thus the night of the eighth passed in a whirl of excitement, and just after day-break of the ninth the "general" was sounded, tents were struck, and the straw and debris that had accumulated during over three months encampment was fired, and for two or three hours we were almost suffocated with the black, dense smoke from the many fires all over the camp. Each soldier of the regiment had been presented by the Sanitary Commission with a large cotton comforter in camp, but very uncomfortable to pack, as they were so large and cumbersome. Imagine a cavalry saddle with the following load mailed on the pommel and the cantel and you see the saddle of a trooper of the First Ohio Cavalry as it appeared when packed for the first time: One double blanket, one rubber *talma*, one overcoat, one shirt, an extra suit of underwear, socks, etc., one feed sack, one lariat rope, curry-comb and brush, and one cotton comforter. When the saddle was packed and ready for putting on the horse's back, it was a fair rival in appearance to a Pennsylvania moving wagon.

Each trooper had sufficient baggage for three, and it took two of the boys to lift a saddle up on a horse's back in saddling, and when he mounted, the horses groaned under their heavy load. Here we had our first experience in "waiting for orders," and we had to wait two or three hours after saddling, but finally, much to our delight, we took up our line of march for the city. It was a beautiful, sunshiny December day, and every soldier who was in the regiment at that time will well remember that march from Camp Chase. One thousand cavalrymen, armed and equipped in heavy marching orders, marching by fours along the old National Road and through the streets of Columbus, was a grand spectacle and one never to be forgotten. The boys were all in high spirits and as we passed the old Four Mile House, the genial landlord of that famed hostelry, with his family, were out on the long porch waving us good-bye, and the boys were singing the "Girl I left behind me," little thinking that many of them were leaving their sweethearts for the last time on earth.

Many of the boys in the regiment had enlisted from Columbus and from Franklin, Madison, Union, Licking, Fairfield,

Pickaway and other adjoining counties, and as the word had gone forth that we were to march on that day, scores of relatives and friends had been attracted to the camp to bid their fathers, brothers, sons and sweethearts good-bye and to see them off for the war, and as was usual in all regiments that left for the "front," there were many sad farewells, and "Good-bye, God bless and protect you" came from many a bleeding heart.

There were some amusing and exciting incidents, even in this quiet march to the city, as the loads were so heavy that many of the saddles turned and the horses would become frightened and run, and in some instances broke away from their riders, after they were thrown or dismounted, and some of the well packed saddles were kicked to pieces by the frightened horses, and the big cotton comforters were badly demoralized.

The streets were lined by thousands of people, and as we marched across High Street and out Broadway the regiment was greeted by shouts and by waving of flags and handkerchiefs all along the line, and hundreds of people followed to the stock yards, east of the depot, to see us on board the train.

It took all the afternoon to load horses and baggage aboard the cars, and we were ready to pull out just about dark, and the men were marched down to the depot to take the passenger coaches in waiting, and we were soon steaming toward the Queen City with long trains of freight cars loaded with horses and baggage following close behind. We arrived in Cincinnati about daybreak on the morning of the tenth sleepy, tired and hungry. The work of unloading horses and baggage was commenced at once and consumed the greater part of the forenoon, and, as will be remembered, we marched through the market, and the boys both amused themselves and replenished their haversacks by running their sabres into the piles of fruit exhibited for sale, much to the anxiety of the market vendors. We marched to the wharf, where several transports were steamed up waiting, and by 3 o'clock p. m. we were all safely on board, with horses on the lower decks, ready to start down the beautiful Ohio for Louisville.

The horses were closely crowded together, and the hissing

of the steam, the noise of the machinery, and the dashing of the waves against the sides of the boat frightened the horses so that some of them became almost wild and unmanageable, and it was necessary to keep a very strong stable guard on all the time to look after them. The floors were very slippery and at times the swaying of the boat would cause them to slip and fall it was almost worth a man's life to go in among those wild, stamping horses, and we were all very happy when we landed at Louisville, Ky., on the morning of the eleventh the first cavalry regiment to enter that department excepting Wolford's Kentucky regiment.

Reid says in his *Ohio in the War*: "The First Ohio was the nucleus of that host of cavalry which, under the leadership of Stanley, Crook, Long, Kilpatrick, Minty, Millikin, Garrard, Mitchell and Wilson achieved such triumphs for the country and fame for themselves."

We went into camp at Oakland, a fine park just outside of the city limits, south west, and named it Camp Buell, in honour of General Don Carlos Buell, Commander of the Army of Ohio

It was a beautiful camp with good drill grounds, and we resumed drills and regular camp duties at once, with mounted "dress parades" and practice marches on the pikes leading out from the city. Soon after our arrival at Camp Buell measles, that disease much more to be dreaded among soldiers than smallpox, broke out in the regiment, and as it was quite severe winter weather, many of those taken down with the disease caught cold and died, and with many others disease of throat and lungs resulted, which followed them through their army service, and in some cases through life.

The regiment remained at Camp Buell, with nothing to break the monotony of camp-life, only one incident, that many members of the regiment will recall with a smile. By the order of some one in authority, and we understood at the time that it was from Lieutenant-Colonel T. C. H. Smith in the absence of Colonel Ransom, we were directed to have our sabres ground, and we marched into the city, one company at a time, to a machine shop, and had a razor edge put on our sabres, and we then imagined that we were ready to go to chopping off heads in the most approved order of modern warfare. Colonel Ransom, on his return, was very indignant, and ordered us to dull the edges by sabre exercise and fencing, as they were very dangerous in drilling with the sabre when mounted, and besides it was against the rules of civilized warfare. During the service of the regiment we had many a laugh over our experience with our razor-edged sabres at Camp Buell.

We remained at Camp Buell drilling until the sixteenth day of January, 1862, when we were ordered to join General Thomas at Mill Springs, and marched out seven miles on the afternoon of the sixteenth, and on the seventeenth we marched twenty-five miles and camped on the banks of Salt River in a cornfield, and as it had rained all day the mud was about boot-top deep, and we passed a very uncomfortable night. On the eighteenth we marched about twenty-five miles and camped on the banks of "Rolling Fork," and as the rain had poured down in torrents all day we were drenched to the skin and chilled to the bone.

The site selected for the camp was on the side of a very steep hill, so steep that it was not possible for a mule team to pull a wagon up, and it was all we could do to climb up dismounted, leading our horses. The wagons did not arrive until after dark, and as we had no cooking utensils we could not make any coffee, and all the supper we had was a cracker and a slice of cold pork. But few tents were pitched, as it was so stony that tent pins could not be driven, and the majority of the boys stood around the fires or sat on their saddles beside a tree all night. Two or three companies pitched their tents down in the flat along the stream, and during the night the stream raised very suddenly and the water came down like a mountain torrent with such force that it washed off some of the saddles and equipments before they could be taken to a place of safety.

I do not think there is a soldier of the regiment now living that was on that march but will remember it very distinctly, and will unanimously agree that it was one of the most disagreeable day's marches, and that we passed in Camp Frankenberger (as it was named in honour of our quartermaster) one of the most uncomfortable nights of our service during the war.

On the nineteenth we marched about sixteen miles and camped near Lebanon, Camp Smith, and received the news of the battle of Mills Springs, fought that day and a great victory for our army General Zollicoffer of the rebel army killed. On the twenty-first marched through Lebanon and out on the Somersett Pike about two miles, Camp McCook. Here the regiment resumed drill, and January 24 John Morgan made a dash on our pickets and burned a church that was used as a telegraph office on the line from Lebanon to General Thomas' head quarters at Mill Springs. Three companies of the regiment were sent in pursuit and drove the rebel cavalry to Green River, taking a number prisoners. After crossing the river the rebels cut the bridge, and as the stream could not be forded, the pursuit was abandoned and the battalion returned to camp on the twenty-fifth, and on the twenty-sixth another company was sent out on a scout and to guard the telegraph line, and they captured a few more prisoners.

This was our first campaign against Morgan's bold riders, who were destined to give our regiment so much trouble during the next four years. We remained in camp near Lebanon until February 14 and kept up mounted drill every day with the usual parades and guard mounting, with but one or two incidents to break in on the monotony of camp life, and one was the dedicating of the regimental colours, just received, to the cause of the Union by appropriate ceremonies and a prayer by the regimental Chaplain, Drake, and it was an impressive and beautiful service.

Colonel Ransom having resigned while the regiment was in camp at Louisville, in January the command devolved on Lieutenant-Colonel T. C. H. Smith, who commanded the regiment up to February 14, when he was relieved by Colonel Minor Millikin who had been promoted to the Colonelcy from the Senior Major of the regiment. There was much dissatisfaction the Promotion of Colonel Millikin over Lieutenant-Colonel

Smith, and the officers waited on him in a body on his arrival —and requested him to resign, as it was thought by many of them who were his warm, personal friends, that it would work great harm to the organization, and many of the officers threatened to resign, but Colonel Millikin, by his soldierly conduct at all times and by his acknowledged merit and ability and his gallantry upon the field, outlived all this prejudice and died upon the battle-field "booted and spurred," the idol of the regiment.

On February 14 we broke camp at Lebanon, and as it had snowed the night before, we had a very cold day's march and that night camped near the village of Fredricktown — about fifteen miles distant and pitched our tents on the snow.

At that time we had the old round Sibley tents and each tent was provided with a Sibley stove made of sheet iron, running up funnel-shaped about three feet high, and as there was no bottom, it was set on the ground, and about two joints of pipe completed the outfit. It was five or six feet from the top of the pipe to the top of the tent, where there was a hole around the centre pole for the smoke to escape. Many times the tent would be so full of smoke that we would all be compelled to leave the tent to keep from smothering and put the fire out, and all winter the boys looked like a band of red-eyed, smoked savages, and they prayed that they might be forever after delivered from the curse of living in Sibley tents with Sibley stoves. That cold evening of February 14 our wagon train had been delayed and did not come up until dark, and we were cold and shivering around a little camp-fire for two or three hours, and I think this is the first evening the boys ever confiscated any hay, but as there were a number of haystacks in sight, some venturesome fellow made a break, and in a few minutes the hay was all in bundles, either to be fed to the horses or put in the tents for beds, "as the case might be," according to the tactics.

On the fifteenth we marched to Bardstown and went into "Camp Lytle," and remained here until the twenty-fourth, and during this time learned of the fall of Fort Henry and Fort Donaldson, and some of the officers of the regiment were very much worried and exercised for fear the war would close before we got into a fight, but it proved that their fears were groundless, as we learned within the next three and a half years by testing steel with a worthy foe on many a hard-contested field.

February 24 broke camp and started on the march for Louisville, which we reached on the twenty-fifth, and lay in camp until the twenty-seventh, then marched through the city and took boats at Portland and sailed down the Ohio and reached Smithland, at the mouth of the Cumberland River, on the second of March without any incident of note. We steamed up the Cumberland and passed Fort Donaldson on the fourth, and from the boats had a fine view of the rebel batteries. This was our first view of a battle-field, and was a scene long to be remembered, as the timber along the river below the Fort was almost mowed down by shot and shell from the gun-boats and batteries. We also took a look at the old long, low white house, near the river bank, where the rebel General, Floyd, took a last look at the scenes of his former glory and then said to himself, "He that fights and runs away, will live to fight another day," and then ran. Here were the wreck and ravages of war in reality, and it made a profound impression on the members of the regiment that has never been forgotten.

We arrived at Nashville on the seventh and went into camp about two miles out from the city on the Charlotte pike, adjoining a deer park, with many of these fleet-footed animals skipping over the snow, as it had snowed a light skift and was quite cold. On the ninth a raiding party of Texan Rangers made a dash on our pickets and captured a number of men and horses. Our cavalry made chase and captured the men and horses and several prisoners, and among the prisoners captured was a brother of John Morgan, and on the eleventh our pickets had another brush with the rebel cavalry. We remained in camp, drilling mounted every day until the fifteenth inst., when we received marching orders. We started at 10 o'clock p. m. and made a dash, as the advance of Buell's Army, to save the bridge across Duck River at Columbia, marched all night and reached Franklin just after day-break on the sixteenth Sunday morning and aroused the citizens of that quiet town by galloping across the bridge and up the main street, and the citizens rushed to their doors and windows to view for the first time the "Yankee" cavalry. The ladies were all in negligee, with uncombed hair, and were very much frightened at the early morning raiders, and we galloped on through the town without halting to give a Sunday morning salute to these fair Southern daughters. We halted a mile or two from Franklin, fed our horses, loosed up saddle girths, had a quick cup of coffee, and in an hour were again in the saddle, moving rapidly forward.

About 10 o'clock passed through Spring Hill, just as the Sunday worshippers were assembling at their churches, and there was a general stampede across lots for their houses. Just on the outskirts of the town we passed several omnibuses and stages filled with an august and badly-scared body of citizens, who proved to be members of the Tennessee Legislature hurrying to their homes. But we had no time to waste on the worshippers or the harmless members of the defunct Legislature of Tennessee, and we moved rapidly forward. We arrived at Duck River at about 2 o'clock, just in time to give the rear guard of the rebel cavalry a parting salute and to find the bridge in flames. The bridge burned down, and we did not attempt to cross that evening, but exchanged a few shots with the rebel pickets and went into camp.

On the seventeenth the advance of McCook's Division arrived and went into camp near our Brigade. On the evening of the nineteenth Company K was called "to horse" at 10 o'clock and were ordered to make a reconnaissance back toward Spring Hill. The company moved out in a hurry and two or three miles from camp ran into the pickets of an Indiana cavalry regiment, the advance guard of General Nelson's Division. We charged the pickets on the full gallop and drove them back on the reserve, and the reserve opened fire at once and thirty or forty shots were fired, but fortunately no one was hurt, but two or three horses were wounded, and we captured a number of prisoners before we learned that they were our own men.

The officer in command of the picket was very angry and threatened to arrest our officers, but explanations were soon made and Company K took the pike and moved on into Spring Hill, and on a hint from a Union man searched a furniture establishment and found a large number of rebel uniforms in coffins, which they proceeded to confiscate and took them back to camp.

We remained in camp, sending out scouting parties every day patrolling the river and found all bridges burned, and on the twenty-sixth the Third Battalion, composed of Companies E, F, I and K, forded the river at Columbia by swimming their horses across the stream, and took possession of that beautiful town, renowned for its pretty girls, who, notwithstanding they were hot-headed and bitter rebels, were soon flirting with the gay cavalry boys. We were kept busy scouting after Jackson's and Scott's cavalry until Nelson's Division commenced crossing on the twenty-ninth by wading the stream, and on the thirtieth the pontoon bridge was completed and the balance of the troops commenced crossing rapidly. It was here that we first saw General Willich, who by his army experience and knowledge of military matters, rendered valuable service when we forded the stream. We had never had any experience in swimming our horses and when we started into the stream marching by fours and as the horses began to swim the fours were soon broken, and just at this time our attention was attracted by an officer standing on the bank with long hair thrown back over his shoulders, gesticulating and shouting loudly, "Do not break the fours." We did not know what reason there was for this, but we endeavoured to keep our fours together the best we could, and soon learned that this was the only safe way to ford a stream by swimming horses, as in that manner the horses support each other, and they can swim much easier and it is more safe for the men than to become scattered. Also when the infantry commenced crossing the pontoons a few days later, a regiment was marching down to the bridge lead by a band keeping the step, and as they struck the bridge it commenced swaying and would have soon broken down had it not been that General Willich again came to the rescue, as he was standing on the bank and shouted to the band to "stop playing" and for the "soldiers to break the step." It is well known among military men that a bridge that would stand the test of a large body of cavalry or artillery would break down under the step of a regiment of infantry with a band to keep the time.

We took a great many lessons in swimming our horses during our service and soon learned that to swim a horse successfully the reins must not be touched and that a horse must be given free head and guided by splashing water against the side of his head with the hand.

We were on the move, scouting every day during our stay at Columbia, and one of the most daring and hardest rides ever made by any members of the regiment, was made by Sergeant Joseph T. Reynolds and David Ault, of Company F, who were detailed to carry dispatches from General Buell to General Grant at Savannah, Tennessee, which is best told in the words of Captain Reynolds himself:

> On Sunday, March 30, 1862, the regiment was camped at Columbia, Tenn., being the advance of General Buell's Army, on its way to form a junction with that of General Grant's at Pittsburg Landing, Tenn. I had fallen asleep in my tent about eleven o'clock that night and was awakened by some person shaking me. It proved to be Captain Cupp, and he told me to put on my clothes and come out as quickly as possible. We walked to a distance from the company quarters out of earshot of any other person, and he then informed me that there was a dispatch from General Buell sent to the regiment and that it was to be carried to General Grant, somewhere on the Tennessee River, and that he had orders to furnish two men to carry it; that he had chosen me to go, and honoured me by giving me the privilege of choosing my companion. I chose David Ault, and he then ordered us to go and pick our horses from the eighty or ninety horses that belonged to the company, to carry only our carbines and revolvers, and report to the

colonel's quarters as quickly as possible. On entering the tent we found Colonel T. C. H. Smith, Captain Cupp and one or two others, whose names I do not recollect now, were present. They had a common state map of Tennessee spread out, and by the dim light of a tallow candle they tried to give us some idea of where we were to go and the route we were to take, and the knowledge we gained was very indefinite and unsatisfactory. The orders from General Buell, under which we were to go were read to us, and with the dispatch handed over to us. Briefly, the orders were to ride as fast as horses could go, and if those we were riding gave out, to secure others by any means in our power; If fired on, not to stop; to return the fire, but to ride on; and if cut off from the road, to abandon the horses and take to the woods; and under no circumstances, whatever, to allow the dispatch to fall into the enemy's hands. We rode out just about midnight and took the pike, passed the plantations of the Polks and Pillows to the little town of Mount Pleasant. The night was balmy and pleasant as a night in the latter part of May in Ohio. The moon, at about her second quarter, was shining brightly in the west. Just out of Mt. Pleasant the road formed a Y and we were at a loss to know which one to take, but we took the right hand one and determined to make inquiry at the first opportunity. I should have stated that in the orders read to us at the colonel's tent we were to go by New Market and to pass that town, if possible, before daylight. After riding on the right hand road for half or three-quarters of a mile, we discovered a cabin on the other side of a high fence in the edge of some woods. Giving Dave my horse and telling him to signal me if anything unusual occurred, I climbed the fence, went to the cabin and called out to the occupants, and after some delay had just ascertained that we should have taken the other road, when Dave gave a signal of danger. I rushed to the fence, clambered over, and quickly mounted, wheeled around, and we galloped back and took the other road, Dave in the meantime telling me that there were mounted men approaching from the direction that we had been travelling. Urging our horses to a brisk speed we travelled mile after mile, without having any idea of time or distance, through a country broken and rough, with a large part of it covered with timber, over ordinary country roads. At one time the road was so indistinct that we lost it and spent some time in regaining it. After riding for what appeared to be a long time, we discovered fires to our left about half a mile away, and we were in doubt whether they were the camp-fires of a body of troops or whether it was only fires from burning the timber land that was being cleaned, but from the regularity of their appearance judged that it was a camp. After riding perhaps two miles, in crossing a small water course, we allowed our horses a moment to get a little water, the moon having by this time set, and it was quite dark. Dave touched me on the arm, and as I raised my eyes to look at him I saw what was a mere coal of fire and indistinctly what appeared to be horses. Without a word we spurred our tired horses forward, and as we dashed past them we saw four cavalrymen with their horses tied to the fence. They appeared to be confused and frightened and did not fire on us. Whether they pursued us or fled, we had no time to ascertain. Sometime afterward my horse failed, and after searching three or four stables in the dark, I secured a horse and we pushed on. Soon after this we passed a collection of cabins which we vainly hoped was New Market. But as it became day-light we passed a cabin, the owner of which was standing on his doorstep, and we passed ourselves on him as belonging to Rody's rebel cavalry, and found that Rody had left New Market the day before, and was then satisfied that it was his camp that we had passed. We soon reached Pointer's charcoal iron furnace, and in his barn we found two good horses, but were compelled to stand Mr. Pointer and two other white men,

Our Heroic Dead.

CO. F.

Capt. Lafayette Pickering.

CO. B.

Capt. Geo. F. Conn.

CO. F.

Lieut. A. D. Lieb.

Maj. John G. Robinson.

CO. B.

Capt. H. H. Siverd.

CO. D.

Lieut. Harvey Ferguson.

CO. K.

Lieut. Frank P. Allen.

CO. D.

Lieut. Chas. H. Goodrich.

all armed with pistols, backed by perhaps eighty or a hundred coloured people, with cocked carbines. The country here was quite thickly settled and a town of two or three hundred inhabitants a couple of miles away. Remember, this was in 1862, these people had never seen a U. S. soldier, and knowing full well, that after taking these horses by force, that capture meant death by a rope, we hesitated about riding through New Market. But knowing that delays were dangerous, we decided to dash through and take the chances. Our horses were fine and we rode very fast until within two or three miles of Savannah, when I became so ill that I was compelled to dismount and lie down. Dave carried the dispatch in and delivered it at General Grant's headquarters. General Grant was absent, and we were ordered to report them at 7 o'clock that evening. It was then about 10 o'clock a. m., as near as I can recollect. Dave came back and assisted me into town, and at 7 o'clock in the evening we reported, as ordered, and were admitted into General Grant's presence. After asking us many questions about General Buell's army, where it was, etc., he ordered us to report the next morning to carry a dispatch to the general commanding the advance of Buell's army. I informed him that I was not able to ride; but he did not change his order, and we received the dispatch the next morning and carried it back beyond New Market and met the 2nd Indiana Cavalry, and, being completely worn out, we turned it over to the colonel of that regiment. We were taken before General Nelson that evening for stealing Pointer's horses, but on hearing the circumstances, complimented us and discharged us after compelling us to give up the horses. There had been heavy artillery firing that day in the direction of the Tennessee Elver, and he appeared to be very uneasy and asked us many questions about matters there, although we were able to give him very little information. How much the delivery of these dispatches had to do with the timely arrival of General Nelson's Division at Pittsburg Landing Sunday evening i n time to save General Grant's army from being driven into the Tennessee River, is locked in the breasts of the dead and will probably never be known, as I have since learned the distance was eighty-eight miles, which we rode in about ten hours.

That Columbia had more bewitching and pretty girls to the number of inhabitants than any other town the First Ohio was ever stationed at, "goes without saying," and there were flirtations during our short stay, and we left that fair the home of the Polks and the Pillows and other prominent families — with many regrets.

CHAPTER 2

From Columbia to Pittsburgh Landing

On the first day of April the rear guard of the army crossed Duck River and the regiment received marching orders. Early on the morning of the second we left our pretty camp in the east suburb of Columbia and marched out on the Mt. Pleasant pike two or three miles, and went into camp to wait for the infantry column of General Thomas' division, to which we had been attached, to pass.

The next day we passed through a beautiful country, passing the plantations of the Pillow's and Ex-president James K. Polk, the Polk homestead being the most beautiful and picturesque in its surroundings of any we had ever seen in Tennessee, and as the day was warm and balmy, all enjoyed the scenery very much. We passed Mt. Pleasant, and here the pike ended, and with it the fine country, and the country became poor, rough and barren wooded mostly with scrubby oak timber and a poor and uncultivated farming country. We passed some iron and charcoal furnaces, which seemed to be about the only industry of the country, the roads were miserable, and we were compelled to march very slowly on account of the wagon trains and artillery. The regiment reached Waynesboro about noon, Sunday, the sixth, and went into camp near this little village of two or three hundred inhabitants. Here we first heard the cannonading of the first day's battle of Pittsburg Landing, about thirty miles distant, which continued with one steady roar all the afternoon, and during all of that night we could hear the regular boom of cannon, which we afterwards learned was the gun-boats, *Tyler* and *Lexington*, throwing shot and shell into the rebel lines, while Buell's army was disembarking from the transports and forming their line of battle for the next day's victory. It rained very hard that night, and we marched at day break of the seventh on toward the roar of battle, that was getting more distinct each moment as we toiled on through mud and slough, for the roads were now almost impassable, and we began to overtake the wagon trains of Buell's advance. We made frequent halts for the wagon trains and artillery horses to rest a few minutes, and during these halts General Thomas would ride back along the column with anxious looks and would speak earnestly to some commander of a regiment or battery and then move to the front again; but little did we know, as did that brave old soldier, of the great disaster of the day before, and how anxiously Grant was looking for his division. Some of the infantry regiments had thrown their knapsacks down, making a forced march. When night came on we did not halt, but marched on in the darkness, and the further we marched, the worse the roads became. Teams were becoming exhausted, wagon tongues, single trees, and double trees were breaking, and here and there we would pass a wagon piled up just in the edge of the woods, so the columns could pass, with mules unhitched eating, and drivers trying to repair their wagons by the light of a little camp-fire, or improvising a pole for a wagon tongue. On we marched over that narrow road, mud knee deep, cavalry, infantry, artillery, wagons, ambulances, all floundering through the mud that inky dark night, and we could scarcely distinguish a white wagon cover, mule drivers yelling and swearing, quartermasters striving to keep their trains closed up, and officers urging the men forward.

About midnight a terrible rain storm came up, and the lightning flashed, the thunder roared, and it seemed that the artillery of the heavens were vying with the artillery of the battle-field of Shiloh, which had been roaring all day. Still on we marched, and it seemed a perfect "bedlam" until finally we halted, and whether by order or from sheer exhaustion, is very uncertain. The men were ordered to make themselves as comfortable as they could in any way, and a number made a rush for a double log stable, which could be seen near the road by the flashes of lightning, and, tying our horses to the logs on the outside, climbed up into the hay-mow—found no hay, but lay down on the pole floor, glad to get out of the rain. The lightning continued in a perfect blaze until about daybreak, and we got but little rest, as the horses were pawing and snorting all the time, and this, with the roar of the storm, made it impossible to sleep. We were glad to see daylight dawn again, and it can be safely said that this was one of the hardest marches and one of the most disagreeable nights the regiment ever passed through in the service.

We found, on the morning of the eighth, that we were near Savannah, and we marched in early and bivouacked in the suburbs, and learned of the great victory of the day before and saw many wounded soldiers who had made their way down from the battle-field. Our wagons and sick men were sent down to Clifton, a small town on the Tennessee River a few miles below Savannah, and the regiment was ordered to march up on the north side of the river to Pittsburg Landing, distant about eight miles, and the infantry and artillery of Thomas division were taken up on the transports. The rain had been so heavy that the streams were very much swollen, and the flat country along the river was covered with water.

We came to one stream with high banks, the current running very swift, and as there was no ford, it seemed at first that we could not make the crossing at that point. After a short halt, a few of the more venturesome plunged in and swam their horses across, but as the banks were steep on the opposite side, they had hard work getting up, and there was great danger of the horses falling back and injuring or drowning their riders. A rude foot bridge was found a short distance down the stream, and it was decided to let the horses swim across without their riders. Bridle reins were tied up, and carbines taken off the saddles, the column was led by two or three reckless fellows, and the other horses were urged over the bank as rapidly as possible, and soon a column of riderless horses were swimming the stream, following each other like a flock of sheep, and the men crossed rapidly on the foot bridge, caught their horses on the other side, and in this manner the stream was safely forded.

That night we went into camp on the north side of the river, immediately opposite Pittsburg Landing, right on the river bank and only a few yards from the gun boats, *Tyler* and *Lexington*, anchored on the north side, with their black-mouthed guns glaring out from the port-holes. Our camp was in an old cane-field, without any tents, as they were all with the wagon trains. The sky had cleared up during the day, and the sun came out warm and everything seemed favourable for a good night's rest. Most of the men made their beds in the old furrows of the plowed field, first gathering and throwing down some old cane stocks. During the night another rain storm came up, and it poured down in torrents. The furrows were soon flooded, the men completely soaked, and for the balance of the night all they could do was to stand or sit against the trees along the river bank.

The next morning, the ninth, we were a well drenched and sorry-looking set, and how we envied the gun-boat boys as they came out on the decks in their neat, clean, jaunty uniforms and polished shoes!

During the forenoon we boarded the transports and were transferred across the river to Pittsburg Landing, which consisted of two or three old houses, of which one was log, and it was simply a landing for loading cotton, and the high bank was cut down to an easy incline, and as soon as the regiment commenced landing, we could begin to see some of the effects of the battle of the two previous days. Wounded and dead men were lying along the bank, and some of them almost to the edge of the water, just as they had been carried down with hundreds of the other wounded to be loaded on the hospital boats, and many had died of their wounds before they could be transferred to the boats. Around the landing there was a broad plateau, clear and bare, of several acres, and here stood a few pieces of artillery with blackened muzzles toward the battle-field, where they had been belching forth shot and shell for two days. It was a busy scene around the landing, many transports and hospital boats were in the river, thousands of rations and tons of supplies were being unloaded from the boats, and loaded into the hundreds of wagons from the front. Ambulances were still bringing in the wounded, wagons were hauling in the dead, and they were being piled up like cord wood beside the long trenches being dug, in which they were to be buried in their coats of blue, many of them not even wrapped in their army blankets. Such was the scene that greeted us as we marched across the plateau at Pittsburg Landing that April day in 1862, the first, and it may be truly said, one of the worst battle-fields we saw during the war, as the rear of any army after a battle always looks demoralized and has all the sickening and depressing scenes.

As we moved out a few hundred yards to the edge of the timber, we began to see the effects of the shells from the gun boats and batteries. Limbs from the trees, in some instances a foot or more in diameter, were cut off, some low down and others in the tops of the trees, while the bodies of the large trees were pierced with solid shot, and some of them split and torn and almost ready to fall. Broken guns, carriages, caissons and wheels were scattered thick, and on every side could be seen the results of the carnage and wreck of battle.

The regiment marched out about a mile and bivouacked, as we had no tents, and out that distance it was a regular sea of mud. Teams made no pretence of following a road, as there was no road to be seen, and a team of four horses hitched to a caisson loaded with one bale of hay, weighing from three to four hundred pounds, would sometimes mire down and stick fast.

Dead horses were to be seen everywhere, swollen up and giving out a terrible stench, as the sun was coming down hot, and as the ground was wet, wherever the ground was cleared a hot and sickening steam was rising. All the water we had for drinking and cooking was from the ravines, Bullies and rivulets, all being fed by water from the ground covered by dead soldiers, mules and horses.

We bivouacked on the battle-field until the seventeenth of April, under those conditions, before our tents arrived, as we had not seen them since the sixth, and there were not twenty-four hours passed during those twelve days but that there was a soaking rain, and our blankets and clothing were never dry.

We kept big fires of logs burning almost continuously to dry our clothing, blankets and equipments, and devised all kinds of plans to keep our blankets up off the wet ground, and to keep our arms and ammunition dry. Many of the soldiers cut poles with their hatchets about ten or twelve feet long, and put about three of them together, one end of them on a log and the other on the ground. On these poles they would first lay their saddle blankets, and then their sleeping blankets, and if it was not too cold their overcoats, and at the head of the bed, next to the log, lay their carbines, sabres, revolvers, cross-wise, and then the ammunition, and on top of this their saddles for a pillow, and, as is well known, a cavalry saddle is a wooden tree covered with raw hide, so it is not a very downy pillow. His bed was soon all ready, and, lying down and covering himself with his rubber blanket or talma , he was ready for the rain, and if he was a six-footer, he had to keep himself pretty well curled up or his feet or head would be out in the rain.

One of the first things a soldier must learn is to take care of himself, make the best of everything and no grumbling, and, as the "Yankees" say, "be shifty."

During the two weeks we were on the battle-field in rainy and miserable weather, without our tents, the soldier learned many things about caring for himself that was of good service to him throughout the war.

The first few days the members of the regiment put in much of the time in looking over the battle-field, and as there were many soldiers yet unburied, they saw, in some places, the dead lying so near each other that they could step from one to the other. In a spot of about three acres of cleared ground we counted seventy dead rebels who had been killed while making a charge across this little space of ground against a thicket of small trees, the bushes of which were riddled and almost mowed down by musket balls.

The regiment was put on picket duty at once, and each day, as the line advanced, we could see fresh evidence of the rout and stampede of the rebel army, by the wreck and debris left behind in their hurried retreat. Tents were here and there standing with hundreds of stands of small arms scattered over their camps, with flour meal and camp equipage. At one place was about half a wagon load of Bowie knives, made out of old files, butcher knives, with leather scabbards and sheaths.

About ten days after the battle, when the regiment was on picket, some of the boys discovered twenty-four dead rebels lying near together in two rows, with feet towards each other, and a space of a yard or two between, as if they had been in a hospital tent and died of their wounds, and then the tent had been removed. Some of them had haversacks and others canteens strung across their shoulders, and they were swollen and their faces blackened beyond recognition.

Word was sent back to the camps and a detail of infantry was sent out to bury them, which was certainly a very disagreeable duty.

CHAPTER 3
Battle of Pittsburg Landing
April 6 & 7, 1862

The First Ohio Cavalry was not under fire in the battle of Pittsburg Landing, yet it was a part of the army of Ohio which, under General Buell, contributed very largely to the victory of our army in the second day's battle, and the members of the regiment take a just pride in that fact.

The regiment occupied the field the day after the battle and was actively engaged with the advance of the army during the siege of Corinth from April 8 until May 30, the date of the evacuation of that stronghold. For that reason I have thought best to publish some extracts from the pens of prominent commanders of both the Union and Confederate army, as it will be a subject of interest to every soldier who participated in that campaign. It is not unjust to any commander; then let each reader study the history of that great battle carefully and draw his own conclusions as to the much discussed question, "Was Grant's army surprised on the morning of April 6, 1862?"

It was the third greatest battle of the war and was fought without rifle pit, earth works or barricades of any kind an open field fight between the flower of the Northern and Southern armies.

The rebel army, under Johnson, had 49,444 men with twenty batteries of artillery, making about eighty pieces, while Grant in the first day's battle had 37,335 men and fifty pieces of artillery. In the second day's fight General Lew Wallace came up with his division of 7,564 men and twelve pieces of artillery, and Buell arrived with

the army of Ohio, with about 20,000, making a grand total in both armies of 114,343 soldiers who took part in the battle, making 258 organizations, and the losses aggregated nearly 30,000.

In the National Cemetery at Pittsburg Landing there are buried nearly 4,000 Union Soldiers, and on the battle-field 4,000 Confederate soldiers are buried; besides these, many of the dead of both armies were taken north and south by their friends and buried at home. No great battle of the war has been so much discussed as the battle of Shiloh, the great question being: was Grant's army surprised, and would his army have been defeated and driven into the Tennessee River, had it not been for the timely arrival of the Army of Ohio, commanded by General Buell, on the evening of the first day's battle?

Whether or not it was a surprise, it is not the province of the writer of a regimental history to discuss. A historian, in writing of the battle of Shiloh, says: "We cannot find infallibility in mortal man, to err is human. Our Generals were then struggling with the theories of war, and it was necessary, as it now seems, at Shiloh to go through the red hot, boiling, seething cauldron of disaster, which would be such a bitter experience that forever after no enemy caught them napping."

Johnson's line of battle was formed one and one-half miles in front of Sherman's camp at 3 o'clock Saturday afternoon, April 5, 1862, and the attack would have been made that evening, but Bragg's corps did not get into position until 6 o'clock. About this time Sherman was sending dispatches to Grant, in which he said, "All is quiet along my lines, I do not apprehend anything like an attack upon our position." The army did not seem to have any thought of danger at that time, yet the whole Confederate army was in line of battle only a mile and one-half in front of our camps at 6 o'clock Saturday evening, and at 5 o'clock the next morning the battle was opened.

An officer who was on the field all day and saw Grant, writes thus of the battle: "No great battle was fought under such peculiar circumstances, no battle ever had so much history, and of no battle was so little truth known after it was over." "All was ignorance before the battle; all was confusion during the battle; all was conjecture and rumour after the battle."

The bone of contention has been not only as to the surprise at Shiloh, but also whether Grant gave full credit to the Army of Ohio, commanded by General Buell, for the victory in the last day's battle.

The following communications from Buell to Grant a few days before the battle show how Buell was making every effort to reach Savannah before Grant's army was attacked.

> Camp near Columbia. Tenn. *via* Nashville.
> March 27, 1862, 9 a. m.

Major-General Halleck

I arrived here yesterday. The progress of the bridge over Duck River has been much slower than I expected, but the difficulties have been greater than I supposed. I find that the bridge cannot be ready for crossing until Monday. I shall then move rapidly forward. My messenger returned last night from General Grant with a communication dated the twenty-fourth and verbal information that he is cutting a road. No information of interest.

D. C. *Buell,* Major-General.

> Camp
> 3 Miles West of Waynesborough
> 4. 4. 1862

General Grant
Savannah

I shall be in Savannah myself to-morrow with one, perhaps two, divisions. Can I meet you there? Have you any information for me that should affect my movements? What of your enemy and your relative positions; what force at Florence or Corinth? We will require forage as soon as we arrive and provisions in two or three days after. Has a steamer arrived with a bridge for me?

D. C. *Buell,* Commanding

Also the following dispatch from Grant to Halleck is of interest:

Savannah
March 26, 1862

Major-General H. W. Halleck
St. Louis, Mo.

My scouts are just in with a letter from General Buell. The three divisions coming this way are yet on the east side of Duck River, detained bridge building. Rebel cavalry are scattered through from here to Nashville gathering supplies. Through citizens I learn that a large quantity of pork for the Southern army is in store forty miles below here. I have boat and detail now getting it. No news from Corinth.

U. S. Grant, Major-General

The following extract from the reports of General Grant shows that at that time he appreciated very highly the efficient service of the Army of the Ohio, whatever may have been written or said by him since the war.

REPORTS OF GEN. U. S. GRANT, U. S. ARMY
COMMANDING ARMY OF THE TENNESSEE

Pittsburg
April 7, 1862

Yesterday the rebels attacked us here with an overwhelming force, driving our troops in from their advance position to near the Landing, General Wallace was immediately ordered up from Crump's Landing, and in the evening one division of General Buell's army and General Buell in person arrived. During the night one other division arrived, and still another today. This morning, at the break of day, I ordered an attack, which resulted in a fight which continued until late this afternoon, with severe loss on both sides, but a complete repulse of the enemy. I shall follow tomorrow far enough to see that no immediate renewal of an attack is contemplated.

U. S. Grant, Major-General
Major-General H. W. Halleck
St. Louis Mo.

Pittsburg, Tenn.
via Savannah
April 8, 1862

Enemy badly routed and fleeing towards Corinth. Our cavalry, supported by infantry, are now pursuing him, with instructions to pursue to the swampy grounds near Pea Ridge. I want transports here for our wounded.
U. S. Grant

EXTRACT FROM REPORT OF U. S. GRANT

Pittsburg
Tenn.
April 8, 1862

Captain:— It becomes my duty again to report another battle fought between two great armies, one contending for the maintenance of the best Government ever devised, the other for its destruction. It is pleasant to record the success of the army contending for the former principle.

On Sunday morning our pickets were attacked and driven in by the enemy. Immediately the five divisions stationed at this place were drawn up in line of battle, ready to meet them. The battle soon waxed warm on the left and centre, varying at times to all parts of the line. The most continuous firing of musketry and artillery ever heard on this continent was kept up until night-fall, the enemy having forced the entire line to fall back nearly half way from their camps to the Landing.

At a late hour in the afternoon a desperate attempt was made by the enemy to turn our left and get possession of the Landing, transports, etc. This point was guarded by the gun boats *Tyler* and *Lexington*, Captains Gwin and Shirk, U. S. Navy, commanding, four 20-pounder Parrot guns and battery of rifled guns. As there is a deep and impassable ravine for artillery or cavalry, and very difficult for infantry, at this point, no troops were stationed here, except the necessary artilleries and a small infantry force for their support. Just at this moment the advance of Major-General Buell's column (a part of the division under General Nelson) arrived, the two Generals named both being present. An advance was immediately made upon the point of attack and the enemy soon driven back. In this repulse much is due to the presence of the gun-boats *Tyler* and *Lexington*, and their able commanders, Captains Gwin and Shirk.

During the night the divisions under Generals Crittenden and McCook arrived. General Lewis Wallace, at Crump's Landing, six miles below, was ordered at an early hour in the morning to hold his division in readiness to be moved in any direction to which it might be ordered. At about 11 o'clock the order was delivered to move up to Pittsburg, but owing to its being led a circuitous route did not arrive in time to take part in Sunday's action.

During the night all was quiet, and feeling that a great moral advantage would be gained by becoming the attacking party, an advance was ordered as soon as the day dawned. The result was a gradual repulse of the enemy at all parts of the line from morning until probably 5 o'clock in the afternoon, when it became evident the enemy was retreating. Before the close of the action the advance of General T. J. Wood's division arrived in time to take part in the action.

My force was too much fatigued from two days hard fighting and exposure in the open air to a drenching rain during the intervening night to pursue immediately.

Night closed in cloudy and with heavy rain, making the roads impracticable for artillery by the next morning. General Sherman, however, followed the enemy, finding that the main part of the army had retreated in good order.

Hospitals of the enemy's wounded were found all along the road as far as pursuit was made. Dead bodies of the enemy and many graves were also found.

General Buell, coming on the field with a distinct army

long under his command, and which did such efficient service, commanded by himself in person on the field, will be much better able to notice those of his command who particularly distinguished themselves than I possibly can.

The country will have to mourn the loss of many brave men who fell at the battle of Pittsburg, or Shiloh, more properly. The exact loss in killed and wounded will be known in a day or two. At present I can only give it approximately at 1,500 killed and 3,500 wounded.

The loss of artillery was great, many pieces being disabled by the enemy's shots and some losing all their horses and many men. There were probably not less than 200 horses killed.

The loss of the enemy in killed and left upon the field was greater than ours. In wounded the estimate cannot be made, as many of them must have been sent back to Corinth and other points. The enemy suffered terribly from demoralization.

General Orders No. 34

Headquarters
District of West Tennessee
Pittsburg
April 8, 1862

The General commanding congratulates the troops who so gallantly maintained, repulsed and routed a numerically superior force of the enemy, composed of the flower of the Southern army, commanded by their ablest Generals, and fought by them with all the desperation of despair.

In numbers engaged, no such contest ever took place on this continent; in importance of results, but few such have taken place in the history of the world.

Whilst congratulating the brave and gallant soldiers, it becomes the duty of the General commanding to make special notice of the brave wounded and those killed upon the field. Whilst they leave friends and relatives to mourn

their loss, they have won a nation's gratitude and undying laurels, not to be forgotten by future generations, who will enjoy the blessings of the best government the sun ever shone upon, preserved by their valour.
By order of Major-General U. S. Grant:
John A. Rawlins, Asst. Adjutant-General

Gen. Alfred Roman, in his history of *The Military Operations of General Beauregard, during the War,* writes very entertainingly, and the following extracts from his history give a view of the beginning of the battle of Shiloh from the Confederate side. He says:

> Our forces could not get into position for battle until late on the afternoon of the fifth too late to commence the action on that day. As soon as it had become evident that the day was too far advanced for a decisive engagement, General Johnston called the corps and reserve commanders together in an informal council, on the roadway, near his temporary headquarters, within less than two miles of those of General Sherman, at the Shiloh meeting-house. Our plan of operations had been foiled by the tardiness of our troops in starting from Corinth, followed by such delayed and noisy demonstrations on the march, that a surprise, which was the basis of his plan, was now scarcely to be hoped for; that ample notice of our proximity for an aggressive movement must have been given through the conflict of our cavalry, on the preceding day, with the enemy's reconnoitring force, and the prolongation of our presence in front of their positions before the hour for battle, next morning; that the Federal army would, no doubt, be found entrenched to the eyes, and ready for our attack. We knew from the careful examination of Colonel Crocket, the Federal officer captured on the fourth, that up to the evening of that day there were no breastworks; but the several warnings given by the conflict in which he was captured, the noisy incidents of the next day's march and reconnaissance, and our presence in full force on the for fifteen hours before the attack, were facts which forced

Beauregard to believe the Federals would surely use the ample time they had, during that night, to throw up entrenchments sufficient for the repulse of our raw troops.

Our forces, as they had arrived on the afternoon of the fifth, at the intersection of the Griersford (Lick Creek) and Ridge Roads, from Corinth to Pittsburg, less than two miles from the Shiloh meeting-house, were formed into three lines of battle; the first, under General Hardee, extended from near Owl Creek, on the left, to near Lick Creek, on the right, a distance of less than three miles, and somewhat oblique to the Federal front line of encampments, being separated from it, on the right, by about one and a half miles, and on the left, about two miles. General Hardee's command not being sufficiently strong to occupy the whole front, it was extended on the right by Gladden's brigade, of General Bragg's corps, and his artillery was formed immediately in his rear, on the main Pittsburg road. His cavalry protected and supported his flanks. The second line, about five hundred yards in rear of the first, was composed of the rest of General Bragg's troops, arranged in the same order. General Polk's corps, formed in column of brigades, deployed on the left of the Pittsburg road, between the latter and Owl Creek. The front of the column was about eight hundred yards in rear of the centre of General Bragg's left wing, and each brigade was followed immediately by its battery.

General Polk's cavalry supported and protected his left flank. Breckenridge's command occupied a corresponding position behind General Bragg's right wing, between the Pittsburg road and Lick Creek. His cavalry protected and supported his right flank. The two latter commands constituted the reserve, and were to support the front lines of battle by being deployed, when required on the right and left of the Pittsburg road, or otherwise, according to exigencies.

Our pickets had been thrown out well in advance of our first line of battle, not far from the enemy's position, without seeing or discovering any of his pickets or outposts. Such an oversight on the part of the Federal commanders is really unaccountable, unless they chose to overlook that important maxim of war: Never despise an enemy, however weak and insignificant he may appear.

So near to each other were the opposing forces, that, hearing a loud beating of drums about the hour of tattoo, and believing it proceeded from our lines, General Beauregard immediately dispatched a staff officer with orders to suppress such thoughtless and imprudent sounds. The staff officer returned shortly afterwards and reported that the noise General Beauregard had heard, and was desirous of quieting, came not from our troops, but from the enemy's encampment in our front. Later in the evening, a Federal Assistant Surgeon and his orderly, riding out on some night excursion, crossed our picket lines and were captured. They were speechless with astonishment when brought to Generals Johnston and Beauregard, at beholding so large a force within striking distance of their own camps, where all was now silent and repose, and where none suspected the approaching storm. From them we learned that General Grant had returned for the night to Savannah.

Before 5 o'clock a. m. on the sixth of April, General Hardee's pickets, driving in those of General Prentiss, encountered some companies of the Federal advance guard, and a desultory firing began.

Notwithstanding the bold movements of the Confederate cavalry on the previous evening, and the noise of the conflict since dawn, General Sherman remained under the belief that no more than a strong demonstration was intended, until nearly eight o'clock, when, seeing the Confederate bayonets moving in the woods beyond his front, he became satisfied, for the first time, that the enemy designed a determined attack on the entire Federal camp.

CHAPTER 4

Battle of Pittsburg Landing

Grant in his *Memoirs* has this to say of Buell and the Army of Ohio and the battle of Shiloh:

> On one occasion during the day I rode back as far as the river and met Buell, who had just arrived; I do not remember the hour, but at that time there probably were as many as four or five thousand stragglers lying under cover of the river bluff, panic-stricken, most of whom would have been shot where they lay, without resistance, before they would have taken muskets and marched to the front to protect themselves. This meeting between General Buell and myself was on the dispatch-boat, used to run between the landing and Savannah. It was brief and related especially to his getting his troops over the river. As we left the boat together, Buell's attention was attracted by the men lying under cover of the river bank. I saw him berating them and trying to shame them into joining their regiments, he even threatened them with shells from the gun-boats near by, but it was all to no effect. I have no doubt that this sight impressed General Buell with the idea that a line of retreat would be a good thing just then. Before any of Buell's troops had reached the west bank of the Tennessee, firing had almost entirely ceased; anything like an attempt on the part of the enemy to advance had ceased. There was some artillery firing from an unseen enemy, some of his shells passing

beyond us; but I do not remember that there was the whistle of a single musket-ball heard. As his troops arrived in the dusk, General Buell marched several of his regiments part way down the face of the hill, where they fired briskly for some minutes, but I do not think a single man engaged in this firing received an injury.

Victory was assured when Wallace arrived, even if there had been no other support. I was glad however to see the reinforcements of Buell and credit them with doing all there was for them to do. During the night of the sixth the remainder of Nelson's division, Buell's army, crossed the river and were ready to advance in the morning, forming the left wing. Two other divisions, Crittenden's and McCook's, came up the river from Savannah in the transports and were on the west bank early on the seventh, Buell commanding them in person. We had now become the attacking party, the enemy was driven back all day, as we had been the day before, until finally he beat a precipitate retreat.

The criticism has often been made that the Union troops should have been entrenched at Shiloh. Up to that time the pick and spade had been but little resorted to at the West. I had, however, taken this subject under consideration soon after re-assuming command in the field, and, as already stated, my only military engineer reported unfavourably. Besides this, the troops with me, officers and men, needed discipline and drill more than they did experience with the pick, shovel and axe.

The admissions of the highest Confederate officers engaged at Shiloh make the claim of the victory for them absurd. The victory was not to either party until the battle was over. It was then a Union victory, in which the Armies of the Tennessee and the Ohio both participated. But the Army of the Tennessee fought the entire rebel army on the sixth and held it at bay until near night; the night alone closed the conflict and not the three regiments of Nelson's division.

The following extracts from General W. T. Sherman's *Memoirs* will be of interest:

I always acted on the supposition that we were an invading enemy; that our purpose was to move forward in force, make a lodgement on tactics of Fort Donelson, by separating the rebels in the interior from those at Memphis and on the Mississippi River. We did not fortify our camps against an attack, because we had no orders to do so and because such a course would have made our raw men timid. At a later period of the war, we could have rendered this position impregnable in one night, but at this time we did not do it, and it may be it is well we did not. But thus far we had not positively detected the presence of infantry, for cavalry regiments generally had two guns along, and I supposed the guns that opened on us on the evening of Friday, April 4, belonged to the cavalry that was hovering along our whole front. On Saturday, April 5, the enemy's cavalry was again very bold, coming well down to our front; yet I did not believe they designed anything but strong demonstration. On Sunday morning early, the sixth inst, the enemy drove our advance guard back on the main body, when I ordered under arms all my division. About 8 a. m. I saw the glistening bayonets of heavy masses of infantry to our left front in the woods beyond the small stream alluded to, and became satisfied for the first time that the enemy designed a determined attack on our whole camp. The battle opened by the enemy's battery, in the woods to our front, throwing shells into our camp. Here I saw for the first time, April 7, the well ordered and compact columns of General Buell's Kentucky forces, whose soldierly movements at once gave confidence to our newer and less disciplined men. Here I saw Willich's regiment advance upon a point of water-oaks and thicket, and behind which I knew the enemy was in great strength, and enter it in beautiful style. Then arose the severest musketry-fire I ever heard, and lasted some twenty minutes.

The enemy had one battery close by Shiloh, and another near the Hamburg road, both pouring grape and canister upon any column of troops that advanced upon the green point of water-oaks. Willich's regiment had been repulsed, but a whole brigade of McCook's division advanced beautifully, deployed and entered this dreaded wood. I ordered my second brigade (then commanded by Colonel T. Kilby Smith, Colonel Stuart being wounded) to form on its right, and my fourth brigade, Colonel Buckland, on its right, all to advance abreast with this Kentucky brigade before mentioned, which I afterwards found to be Rousseau's brigade of McCook's division.

"I am ordered by General Grant to give personal credit when I think it is due, and censure where I think it is merited. I concede that General McCook's splendid division from Kentucky drove back the enemy along the Corinth road, which was the great centre of this field of battle, where Beauregard commanded in person, supported by Bragg's, Polk's and Breckenridge's divisions. Probably no other battle of the war gave rise to such wild and damaging reports. It was publicly asserted at the North that our army was taken by surprise; that the rebels caught us in our tents, bayoneted the men in their beds, that General Grant was drunk; that Buell's opportune arrival saved the Army of the Tennessee from utter annihilation, etc. These reports were in a measure sustained by the published opinions of Generals Buell, Nelson and others, who had reached the steam boat landing from the east, just before night-fall of the sixth, when there was a large crowd of frightened, stampeded men, who clamoured and declared that our army was all destroyed and beaten. General Grant also explained to me that General Buell had reached the bank of the Tennessee River opposite Pittsburg Landing, and was in the act of ferrying his troops across at the time he was speaking to me. About an hour afterward, just before dark, General Buell himself rode up to where

I was, accompanied by Colonels Fry, Michler, and others of his staff. I was dismounted at the time, and General Buell made of me a good many significant inquiries, matters and things generally. By the aid of a manuscript map made by myself, I pointed out to him our positions as they had been in the morning, and our then positions; I also explained to him that my right then covered the bridge over Lick Creek by which we had all day been expecting Lew Wallace; that McClernand was on my left, Hurlbut on his left, and so on. But Buell said he had come up from the landing and had not seen our men, of whose existence in fact he seemed to doubt. Buell said that Nelson's, McCook's and Crittenden's divisions of his army, containing eighteen thousand men, could cross over in the night, and be ready for next day's battle. I argued that with these reinforcements we could sweep the field. Buell seemed to mistrust me and repeatedly said he did not like the looks of things, especially about the boat-landing, and I really feared he would not cross over his army that night, lest he should become involved in our great disaster. Buell did cross that night, and the next day we assumed the offensive and swept the field, thus gaining the battle decisively. The enemy having forced the centre line to fall back nearly half way from their camps to the landing, at a late hour in the afternoon a desperate effort was made by the enemy to turn our left and get possession of the landing, transports, etc. The point was guarded by the gun-boats *Tyler* and *Lexington*, Captains Given and Shirk commanding, with four twenty-one pounder Parrott guns, and a battery of rifled guns. As there is a deep, but impassable ravine for artillery or cavalry, and very difficult for infantry at this point, no troops were stationed here except necessary artillerists and a small infantry force for their support. Just at this moment the advance of Major-General Buell's column and part of the division of General Nelson's arrived, the two generals named both being present. An advance was immediately made upon the point of attack, and the enemy soon driven back. During all of that day we fought, and night found us a mile to the rear of our camp, which was in possession of the enemy. The next day we regained the grounds steadily and about 4 p. m. I was again on horse-back near our old camp. The tents were still standing, though riddled with bullets. At the picket rope in front lay two of my horses dead. The dead bodies of men in blue and gray lay around thick, side by side, and scraps of paper showed what was a fact, that Beauregard, Breckenridge and Bragg, old personal friends, had slept the night before in my camp, and had carried away my scant bedding.

CHAPTER 5

From Pittsburg Landing to Corinth
April and May, 1862

After the battle of Pittsburg Landing the army was reorganized and the regiment was attached to the 7th Division, composed of the following organizations.

Seventh Division
(First Division, Army of the Ohio)
Brigadier Geo. H. Thomas

First Brigade	**Second Brigade**
17th Ohio	4th Kentucky
12th Kentucky	10th Kentucky
31st Ohio	10th Indiana
38th Ohio	14th Ohio
Third Brigade	**Artillery**
2nd Minnesota	1st Michigan, Battery D
9th Ohio	1st Ohio
35th Ohio	4th U. S. (1 battery)
18th U. S.	**Cavalry**
	1st Ohio

The movement of the army from Pittsburg Landing commenced at once and during the siege of Corinth the regiment was on duty almost continuously picketing or scouting until Corinth was evacuated by the enemy on the night of May 29.

The country between the landing and Corinth, twenty miles

distant, was miserable, and usually the farms were small, buildings poor, and the water was very bad, as the streams were small, well water bitter, and in some parts of the country the only water for use was from ponds and swamps. The timber was generally small and scrubby, with a few acres cleared around the houses, and the whole country presented a general forsaken and forlorn appearance, as the people had nearly all abandoned their homes.

The heavy siege guns were dragged through the mud by oxen, as many as ten yoke were hitched to one gun, and the progress on the march was very slow, as in many places corduroy bridges had to be built across the swamps and low ground, and until about the tenth of May the whole country was a sea of mud, and for some days the army would be at a standstill, as the roads were impassable. The regiment had a great deal of picket duty to do, and that too, in front of the infantry, and it was a very hard, dangerous service, as we were at times in such close proximity to the enemy that the pickets could not be changed during the night, so they were compelled to stand on post from dark till daylight.

Some nights there would be a great deal of firing on the picket lines, and it was not an unusual occurrence for the reserve to be called to horse and mount a half dozen times during the night.

As there was so much timber, it was a very hard place for cavalry to operate, and the reserve would lay in line all night holding their horses ready to mount at a moment's notice. One instance is recalled of an alarm on the picket line one evening when a battalion of the regiment was on picket not far from the Driver House. The reserve was stationed at the forks in a road and the videttes were thrown out on the roads a few hundred yards in advance of the reserve. It was after sunset, the shadows had begun to grow long, the relief had just been posted, and everything was as quiet as if there was not an armed enemy within ten miles.

The reserve had their horses unbridled and feed sacks out, and some of the men were making coffee, little thinking of the foe in the thicket.

All at once *bang, bang* cracked the carbines out on the picket line, there was a "mounting in hot haste" and the reserve was soon mounted, and drawn up in line at an advance carbine. Hot coffee was spilled, and there was a general hurry and excitement all along the lines, until Scotty went out to the front and made reconnaissance among the pickets. The firing soon ceased and Scotty reported all "quiet in front," and said as he rode back to the reserve that he was "momentarily expecting a volley from them as they had their carbines at an advance, before he started to the front" but he was happily disappointed.

The reserve lay in line all night holding their horses, and there were several alarms and some picket firing, but this is only one instance of many similar ones that happened almost every night on some part of the line.

During the siege of Corinth, General A. J. Smith, an officer of the regular army, was made chief of cavalry, and this was the first movement of the cavalry in this department, as a separate and independent organization, and after a careful inspection by the chief, several expeditions were planned and executed by the cavalry entirely independent of the infantry arm of the service.

The cavalry regiments were still attached to and camped with the different infantry divisions, but were concentrated when any independent movement of the cavalry was contemplated.

Our first reconnaissance in force was on the fifteenth of April, in which we had a skirmish and a few of our men wounded, and again on the eighteenth the rebels made a reconnaissance and we were called out and lay in line of battle all day, but no fighting. On the thirteenth of May there was another strong demonstration by the cavalry and a brisk skirmish, and on the seventeenth of May all the cavalry of the army was concentrated and made a raid on the extreme right of the army, burned a railroad bridge and had a skirmish with the enemy's cavalry with but little loss. This was the first raid in which the regiment participated, and was the largest body of cavalry that had ever marched together in this department.

From the tenth of April until the evacuation of Corinth the regiment was on duty almost constantly, either on picket or scouting, and while we had many skirmishes, the losses were very small in action, but from sicknesses it was very heavy. On account of the bad water many of the men were taken sick with camp fever, and while the death rate was not so large in the regiment, yet many of the men became unfit for service were sent to hospitals, and large numbers of them drifted back home, and by the time the army entered Corinth, June 1, the strength of the regiment was reduced at least one-half.

Many men and officers had been detailed for escort duty with General Thomas, General T. W. Sherman, General Fry, General Shoef and others, and it seemed that we had but a skeleton of the thousand sabres with which we marched out of Camp Chase only six months before. Almost every regiment in that army had the same experience, and it is safe to say that there was no two months during the balance of the war that so many men were placed *hors de comba*t in the regiment as during the months of April and May, 1862.

Among those of the many who died on the campaign was Lieutenant John M. Rennick, of Company M, who died of disease May 28. He was the first officer of the regiment who died, and he was universally respected as a gentleman of high character and an excellent officer.

On the night of May 29 the Confederate army evacuated Corinth, and the first convincing evidence we had of that fact was about six o'clock on the morning of the thirtieth by hearing the heavy explosions from the powder magazines blown up by the retreating army.

We were called to horse and, mounting, moved rapidly to the left toward Farmington.

Passing through that village we moved out on the Danville road and soon struck the rear guard of the rebel army, which we attacked vigorously, and they were soon retreating rapidly. About noon we halted, and after a brief rest passed to the right and commenced pushing the rear guard on another road, had a skirmish and kept picking up prisoners all the after noon, and lay on our arms all night and did not unsaddle our horses.

All day Saturday, the thirty-first, we kept feeling the enemy's lines on two or three different roads, taking some prisoners, and found the enemy making stronger resistance, but drove them steadily all day.

Late in the evening they burned a bridge across a small stream and masked a battery on the other side, and as our advance reached the bank just at dark the battery opened up with grape and cannister and the first volley killed several men and wounded many more.

As it had now become dark, we fell back out of the range of the guns and lay on our arms in line of battle, holding our horses the second night. Sunday morning, June 1, our line advanced, and one of our batteries opened up on the position of the masked battery at the bridge and soon routed them. A bridge was hastily constructed across the stream and we were soon in hot pursuit, and during the day took a large number of prisoners. On the second we had several skirmishes with the rear guard, and on the third the regiment was detached and made a reconnaissance to Ripley, and at Blackland had a sharp engagement, charging the enemy, wounding and killing several, taking a number of prisoners, a large lot of small arms, wagons and mules.

On the fourth Captain Pattin, with Companies D and I, was on outpost duty near Booneville with about fifty men when a large force of rebel cavalry attacked him, and after a severe fight the enemy was repulsed with heavy loss, the loss in the First being ten men wounded.

The regiment was specially mentioned for gallantry in these two fights by General Rosecrans and General Gordon Granger in their reports hereto attached.

EXTRACT FROM REPORT OF W. S. ROSECRANS
BRIGADIER-GENERAL, U. S. A.

Headquarters
Army of Mississippi
June 28, 1862

About 8 p. m. a messenger came to me from the front with information from Brigadier-General A. J. Smith, and thus

I ascertained that the cavalry was in advance on our road, and that it had overtaken a rebel force up the Tuscumbia four miles to the front, was fighting, and in some danger of losing part of a battery.

The rebel rear guard fled from a small battery they had constructed 150 yards north of the bridge, and, crossing, fired and destroyed the bridge. Bisell's engineers cut away the timber felled to obstruct the road, and, with the sharp shooters, occupied the ground during the night. General Smith not having been placed under my orders, I gave him the infantry asked for and went into bivouac with the remaining troops at 11 p. m.

A squadron of cavalry, supported by a regiment of infantry and one section of artillery, took the right-hand fork of that same road forward to a point on the bluff overlooking the bottom of Twenty Mile Creek and drove in the enemy's cavalry pickets, and saw a column of infantry on the march and filing eastwardly for one hour. At the same time General Smith sent a cavalry reconnaissance toward Carrollville, on the right of the railroad, and drove in their cavalry pickets and infantry at Twenty Mile Creek. Another, by Crockett's encountered their pickets near Brownlett's Spring, while the First Ohio Cavalry went to Blackland, a single company charging eighty rebel cavalry and driving them from the place.

Colonel Smith deserves special mention for a reconnaissance which he made with his cavalry the First Ohio in the direction of Blackland.

Extract of report of C. Granger
Brigadier-General, commanding cavalry division
Army of the Mississippi

Near Corinth
June 19, 1862

Lieutenant-Colonel Smith, who had joined me at Rienzi with the First Ohio, and Colonel Ingersoll, with one battalion of the 11th Illinois, rendered most valuable assistance in reconnoitering.

June 3. Lieutenant-Colonel Smith, First Ohio Cavalry, with seven companies, made a reconnaissance toward Ripley. At Blackland he encountered the enemy, 100 strong, whom he charged and drove in, wounding several, taking prisoners, and capturing their animals, wagons, and several guns dropped by the enemy in his flight. Colonel Smith reports Sergeant-Major Scott as having been in this affair particularly distinguished for coolness and daring.

Lieutenant-Colonel Smith, First Ohio Cavalry, who had reported to Colonel Elliott with Companies E, I and M, was directed to act as a support to Lieutenant Barnett's section of artillery, which duty was gallantly done, although exposed to a fire from the enemy. His position not being tenable, Colonel Elliott retired his force in good order across the bridge. His loss was two killed, eight wounded and two missing. The list would have been largely increased had not the enemy fired too high. A prisoner reports the loss in killed and wounded of the enemy at thirty.

On June 4 Captain Pattin, First Ohio Cavalry, on outpost duty four miles west of Booneville with Companies L and D, forty-eight men, was attacked, and after a sharp action of three-fourths of an hour succeeded by coolness and discipline in repulsing two hundred and fifty of the enemy's cavalry with serious loss. Our loss, seven wounded.

Lieutenant-Colonel Smith and Captain Pattin, First Ohio, have well and faithfully performed their whole duty and merit the highest consideration from their General and their country.

The regiment was scouting and reconnoitring in the vicinity of Booneville and Blackland until the tenth and then marched back through Rienzi and Danville to within five or six miles of Corinth.

Colonel T. C. H. Smith was promoted to Brigadier-General and assigned duty on the staff of General Pope as Inspector-General.

After the cavalry fight at Booneville and Blackland the First Ohio was in great demand and it seems from the following communication that there was a clash of authority between Generals Buell and Pope.

Buell's Headquarters
Corinth
June 11, 1862

General Halleck

The First Regiment of the Ohio Cavalry belongs properly to Thomas division, and when I left Booneville I directed it to come in with the division. General Pope has detained it. My cavalry force is limited, and where I am going the services of this regiment are imperatively necessary. The little cavalry I now have in Tennessee is broken down by constant and hard work. I request that the regiment be brought in and accompany Thomas division.

D. C. Buell, Major-General

On the twelfth of June the regiment returned to Corinth and went into camp inside the fortifications. On the fourteenth Company K was sent back to Pittsburg Landing as guard to one hundred and seventy prisoners, and all along the roads back to the Landing could be seen, now and then, a foot or hand and arm protruding out of the ground of soldiers who had been buried, by digging a shallow trench along the roadside, as the rebel army retreated after the battle of Pittsburg Landing, and they were only buried deep enough in the mud to hide their bodies from sight.

The grounds inside the fortifications at Corinth were in a miserable filthy condition and many more men were added to the already long sick roll, but under the supervision of General Thomas the camp soon presented a very different appearance for the better.

CHAPTER 6

From Corinth to Decherd, Tenn.
June and July, 1862

The regiment remained in camp at Corinth until June 17, and on that date took up the line of march east along the Memphis and Charleston Railroad for the purpose of guarding the railroad from the raids of the rebel cavalry, before Buell's army commenced their movement to the east, toward Chattanooga.

Companies L and M were stationed at Bear Creek near Iuka, Ala., under command of Captain T. J. Pattin; Companies B, D, G and H at Tuscumbia under Colonel Millikin; Companies E, F and K at Town Creek and Courtland under Captain Eggleston, and Company I at Decatur under Captain Writer.

The whole country was swarming with rebel cavalry and the different companies were kept on the move almost continuously on outpost duty and scouting in the direction of General Bragg's headquarters at Tupalo, Miss., watching the movements of the enemy, and skirmishes were of almost daily occurrence.

Company G had a severe engagement at Russellville, Ala., July 1, in which Captain Emery was mortally wounded and several men of the company were killed and wounded. Captain Emery was an efficient, brave officer, and his loss so early in the war was a severe blow to his company and the regiment as well.

On the fifteenth day of July Company I, stationed at Decatur with a part of the 15th Indiana Infantry, made a reconnaissance and had a sharp engagement with General Armstrong's brigade of rebel cavalry, in which Captain Writer, of Company

I, was severely wounded, the loss in Company I being two captured and four wounded.

On the nineteenth of July the following order was issued for the concentration of the detachments and proposed movement of the regiment.

EXTRACT FROM SPECIAL ORDERS OF GEO. E. FLYNT
ASSISTANT ADJUTANT-GENERAL
TUSCUMBIA, ALABAMA, JULY 19, 1802.:

7. The battalion of the First Ohio Cavalry, Colonel Minor Millikin commanding, and the two batteries commanded by Captain R. Loder, will cross the Tennessee River at Florence on Friday, the twenty-fifth instant, and march with the Third Brigade to Huntsville, Ala., leaving Florence with five days rations and forage, two days rations cooked and carried in haversacks.

8. The battalion of the First Ohio Cavalry, Captain Pattin commanding, on being relieved at Iuka, Miss., will march with two days rations and forage to Tuscumbia, Ala., and report to Colonel Minor Millikin.

9. The battalion of the First Ohio Cavalry, Captain Eggleston commanding, on being relieved from Town Creek, Courtland and Decatur, will march to Huntsville, Ala., crossing the Tennessee River at Decatur, and report to Colonel Millikin. Five days rations and forage will be required.

But the movement was delayed a few days by reason of the attack made by a brigade of rebel cavalry, commanded by General Armstrong, on the garrison at Courtland, July 25.

On the twenty-third day of July, B. F. Lucas, of Company K, was carrying a dispatch from Town Creek to Courtland, distant about five miles, and when about midway between the two posts, at a point where the woods were thick on either side of the road, he ran into an ambush of rebel cavalry waiting to capture a wagon train loaded with supplies going from Courtland to Town Creek.

The rebels were mounted and concealed in the woods on both sides of the road, and when Lucas rode in between the lines the rebels rose up out of the brush and ordered him to halt. Lucas was mounted on a very fine spirited bay horse, and he was a brave and rather reckless soldier, and instead of halting, he stuck the spurs into his horse, laid down on one side of his flying steed, and made an effort to run the gauntlet of the gleaming gun barrels.

As the rebel cavalry was there for the purpose of capturing the wagon train, they did not wish to fire, and Lucas had almost reached the end of the line, when the order was given to fire, a score of muskets were levelled at him, and he was pierced with six balls and instantly killed, and his horse was riddled with musket balls.

The particulars were learned from a trooper who was riding a short distance in advance of Lucas, who surrendered, was paroled, and came into the lines the next day.

The guard with the wagon train heard the firing and halted, thus saving the wagons and supplies from being captured, as the rebels, knowing that the troops at both posts would soon be aroused, beat a hasty retreat. Lucas was buried with military honours at Courtland, just within bounds of the camp, on the evening of the twenty-third.

Courtland was a beautiful town, situated about midway between Tuscumbia and Decatur, Ala., about twenty-five miles from each, on the Memphis and Charleston railroad. It was a lazy little town of fifteen hundred to two thousand inhabitants, noted for the beautiful shade trees that lined the streets, and pretty Southern girls who would insist on making mashes on must continue true and loyal to the "Girl they left behind them" among the hills and valleys of the bonny Buckeye state. We had been stationed here from about the first of July, our camp being in a beautiful grove, along a creek, distant about one-half mile from town, and the camp was supplied with water from several fine springs within a stone's throw from headquarters. The duty of the detachment was guarding the railroad bridges and pickets were thrown out on all of the roads, about a mile from camp, to guard against a surprise from the enemy's cavalry who were making frequent dashes against these small detachments.

Compared with the campaign of the siege of Corinth during the months of April and May this was considered a soft snap, as rations were of the best and duty light. Our camp was on the plantation of an old fellow by the name of Bynam, who professed to be intensely loyal to the old flag, and his cornfields along one side of our camp, just in good roasting ears, were carefully guarded, and a soldier that even plucked one ear had the guard-house staring him in the face, and visions of extra duty—policing the quarters with a pine-brush broom. This was in the early days of the war, before the emancipation proclamation and before any property had been confiscated, but we got bravely over such fastidious ideas before another year rolled around, and learned, as Sherman said, "that war was cruelty and we could not refine it," and required as well the destruction of the sinews of war as the destruction of life.

On the morning of July 25, after guard mount, the weather being very warm, the men were scattered over the camp taking it quiet and easy and many of them sitting in the shade in front of their tents, or on the piles of forage sacks, having a game of old sledge or poker with a 10 cent ante, while others were writing letters to the dear ones at home, or to their best girls, which was more often the case, little dreaming that the enemy, in large force, was rapidly marching and preparing to pounce down upon our little handful of men like a hurricane.

Lieutenant James Cutler, being a physician, had charge of the sick at the post, and had established a temporary hospital over in the town in a brick church, and he was making his usual morning visit to the sick, and I being next in rank, had command of the company. Just as I had settled down on my cot for a little rest, as I was sick with malaria and camp fever, Captain Eggleston, commanding Company E, came running to my tent in his shirt sleeves and bare head, and shouted to me

| CO. D. | CO. A. | CO. K. |

Capt. J. W. Kirkendall.   Capt. J. A. O. Yeoman.   Capt. W. L. Curry.

| CO. G. | | CO. I. |

Capt. Leonard Irwin.   Serg. Rudolph Wirth.   Capt. J. P. Rea.

| CO. K | | CO. K |

Capt. James Cutler.   Adjt. M. H. Neil.   Lieut. Robert K. Reese.

that the rebels were advancing upon our camp. I called to the bugler to sound "boots and saddles" and ran down through the quarters, directing the men to saddle their horses and mount as rapidly as possible.

Looking across the camp and toward old Bynam's house, I saw a cloud of dust raising and in five minutes time the advance of the rebel column came down the road within three hundred yards of our camp and gave the rebel yell that would have raised the hair on the head of a Comanche Indian.

The command that attacked us was General Armstrong's brigade of cavalry, consisting of about 1700 men, and including Colonel Roddy's regiment, that had been recruited in Northern Alabama, in and around Courtland, Tuscumbia and Decatur.

General Armstrong was an officer of the old army and a fine-looking soldier, and became quite a cavalry leader during the war.

The rebel commander attacked our camp on three sides, simultaneously, and he had been piloted through woods and mountains on by-roads by citizens of the vicinity, who knew every cow-path in the country and knew the position of every picket, as they passed in and out of the camp at will. They had reached a position near our camp before daybreak, and when the picket guard was relieved in the morning they were in plain view of the rebel advance, concealed in the woods and ravines, and passed two or three of the picket posts unobserved, cut the pickets off from camp, but I think all of these pickets made their escape after the camp was attacked, and they found themselves cut off from the command.

The total number of men in our command in the two companies of infantry and the two companies of cavalry was about one hundred and sixty, and when they took position behind the railroad embankment, they made it lively for the rebel brigade for a short time, and in the fight the rebels lost seventeen killed and twenty-seven wounded; but the rebels closed in on three sides and it seemed useless and hopeless to prolong the fight, and Captain Davidson, of the Tenth Kentucky Infantry, the senior officer, raised the white flag and surrendered.

When this was done our cavalry charged out through the lines and all escaped but twenty-five, Captain B. B. Eggleston and Lieutenant Alkire, of Company E, and Lieutenant Cutler, of Company K, First O. V. C., were taken prisoners. The total number of prisoners taken was one hundred and thirty-four, including the writer, with all the wagons, mule teams and camp equipage. The prisoners were put under a regular guard commanded by Major Smith, of Missouri, Provost Marshall, who proved to be a good soldier and gentleman as well, as he protected the prisoners from insult, and we were soon travelling southward on the road to Tupalo, Miss., General Bragg's headquarters. The first day we marched to Moulton, Ala., about twenty miles distant. Here the commissioned officers were separated from the enlisted men and went on south in ambulances and wagons, while the enlisted men had to "hoof it,"" much to the disgust of the prisoners who were cavalrymen. As the rebels had no stockades or prisons in that part of the south that were safe, and nothing for us to eat excepting green corn, and that without salt, they became alarmed for fear we would escape, and we were soon paroled.

The prisoners were sent to parole camp and were not exchanged until February, 1863, about six months after being captured.

On the twenty-seventh General Thomas dispatched General Buell from Florence as follows:

Florence
Ala.
July 27, 1862

Major-General D. C. Buell

Telegram to General Morgan received and forwarded. The attack on the guard at Courtland delayed me one day, but shall be able to get the troops across today and start tomorrow for Athens. Two battalions First Ohio Cavalry are here and one company at Decatur for duty.

Geo. H. Thomas, General

At the time of the Courtland fight the headquarters of the

regiment was at Tuscumbia, but on the twenty-sixth the companies at headquarters, under Colonel Millikin, marched east with General Thomas division and the whole regiment was concentrated at Athens, Ala., July 30, and marched to Decherd, Tenn., where it arrived August 5.

CHAPTER 7

From Northern Alabama to Louisville, Kentucky

August and September, 1862

This was the beginning of the retrograde movement of our army and the great race between Buell and Bragg through Tennessee and Kentucky, ending up at Louisville, Ky., about the first of October. This proved to be a very hard campaign, as the weather was extremely hot and dry, and both men and horses suffered greatly from heat and thirst. The air was filled with dust almost to suffocation continuously when the army was moving, water was very scarce, and in many places the only water to be had for men, horses and mules was from stagnant ponds, and hundreds of animals famished on the march. The regiment had very hard service throughout the campaign, as they were kept continuously on the move on courier duty and scouting, watching the movements of the enemy and harassing their flanks.

The regiment was immediately assigned to important and hard service, as shown by the following order from General Thomas, who had determined, after the murder of General Bob McCook by guerillas under command of Captain Gurley, to put a stop to these outrages.

General McCook was sick and riding in an ambulance in advance of his brigade near New Market, when Gurley's band of marauders surrounded the ambulance in a lonely spot and deliberately murdered him. McCook's regiment, the 9th O.V. I, on learning of his death, were so incensed that they burned all the houses and buildings for miles along the road. Gurley was captured near Huntsvile, Ala., about a year afterwards by our regiment and turned over to General Rosencrans.

EXTRACT FROM ORDERS OF JAMES B. FRY
COLONEL AND ASSISTANT ADJUTANT-GENERAL
CHIEF OF STAFF:

Huntsville
August 8, 1802

A battalion of the First Ohio Cavalry will move on the morning of the tenth instant for the same point as the above, about three or four miles from New Market. The object of the move is, first, to destroy guerillas, and no pains must be spared to accomplish this object. If negroes can be found who will act as guides to guerilla parties or camps, they must be used for the purpose, and brought in.

Second, to produce an effect upon the community, by arresting all men of bad characters in the vicinity where General McCook was shot, and let them see such outrages cannot be unnoticed. But do this in such a way that they will understand it is by authority and not the acts of individuals; every able-bodied man of suspicious character or suspicious loyalty or hostility, within a circuit of ten miles around the place where McCook was shot, three miles east of New Market, will be arrested and brought to Huntsville; and all horses fit for service within that circuit will be taken by the officer in command and brought in with the men, receipts being given in due form in each case and payment to be determined on hereafter.

When the troops get together near New Market the senior officer will take command and see that the orders are executed and that the men behave in an orderly and soldierly manner. As soon as the arrests are made, the companies of the First Ohio will return to Decherd.

Headquarters
First Division
District of Ohio
Decherd
Tenn.
August 10, 1862

Colonel Minor Millikin
Commanding First Ohio Cavalry
Colonel: Enclosed please find orders from headquarters Army of Ohio for cavalry expedition in the direction of New Market.

Your instructions are very explicit concerning the ground over which you are to march. The General directs that in all matters connected with the expedition you carry out the instructions of the commanding general.

Geo. E. Flint, Assistant Adjutant-General and Chief of Staff

The regiment lay in camp at Decherd until August 17, and on that date Colonel Millikin, with six companies, marched to McMinnville and the other four companies, under command of Captain Pattin, made a reconnaissance to Fayetteville. On the nineteenth Lieutenant Rea, of Company I, while on a scout got into a sharp fight and he and six of his company were captured by the rebel cavalry. When Captain Pattin joined the main column a few days later, he and his battalion were assigned to duty at General Crittenden's headquarters, and marched through to Louisville with Buell's army, scouting and skirmishing continuously on the flanks and in the advance. Major Laughlin with a squadron—Companies F and K—was with Shoepf's brigade and were at Altamont and Pelham, and at the first named town the enemy was concentrated in strong force and a fight was expected to take place at that point, as shown by the attached order from General Buell.

> Headquarters
> Decherd
> August 24, 1862, 3:30 p. m.
>
> General Thomas
> McMinnville
>
> McCook is ordered to be at Pelham to-night. In case you should hear that the enemy has concentrated in superior force at Altamont, you must force yourself through to Hillsborough tonight. If, on the other hand, you have reason to believe that he is not in too great force, push through and attack him tomorrow morning.
>
> McCook will have a long and rough road, but Shoepf and Sill can be up. In case you fail, fall back on Hillsborough or Manchester. Report all your movements by courier. I shall be with Shoepf.
>
> *D. C. Buell*

They were kept continuously on the move doing courier duty and scouting through Tennessee, and joined Captain Pattin's battalion at Bowling Green, Ky.

The first battalion, under Colonel Millikin, was attached to General Thomas headquarters doing escort and courier duty, until they reached Louisville, about the last of September, and some days in advance of the other companies of the regiment.

The armies of Buell and Bragg marched on parallel lines and it was a neck and neck race for the Ohio River, and so intent was each commander to reach the goal first, that there was but little time for fighting. It is remarkable that these two armies marched through the states of Tennessee and Kentucky and during a greater part of the time the two columns were separated but a few miles, and yet during all of this campaign there was no general engagement.

During the month of July Buell's army was actively employed in repairing the railroad from Nashville to Decatur, Alabama, and also the line from Nashville to Stevenson, Ala., as these were the two lines over which all of his supplies were to be transported in his proposed advance on Chattanooga.

About the middle of July the enemy's cavalry, in the rear of Buell's army, became very active. Railroad guards were captured in Tennessee and Kentucky, and Buell was soon convinced that his communication was endangered and he became satisfied that Bragg had determined to assume the offensive. General John Morgan made a bold dash from Knoxville, Tennessee, with a cavalry force of fifteen hundred men, announcing that he was leading the advance of a great army moving to liberate Kentucky. General Forrest swept up from Chattanooga through Tennessee to Murfreesboro, cutting the railroad and creating consternation among the railroad guards; still, as no column of the enemy's infantry appeared, it was at first thought this was only a cavalry raid to cut our communication.

Forrest captured, at Murfreesboro, the 9th Michigan Infantry and a large amount of ammunition and supplies, besides doing great damage to the railroad. Morgan swept over into Kentucky and dashed up through Glasgow to Lebanon and captured a detachment under Colonel A. Y. Johnson at that place, and destroyed the railroad between Louisville and Lexington.

General Buell did not have sufficient cavalry to cope with Forrest and Morgan and protect his communication, and about this time he made earnest request for more cavalry, but without avail.

About the twentieth of August it was evident that Bragg had assumed the offensive; his army had passed to the north bank of the Tennessee River, and Buell abandoned his plan of advancing on Chattanooga and prepared to meet his wily adversary.

On the thirtieth General Buell gave orders for the movement of his whole army to Murfreesboro; he made no halt here, but moved directly on to Nashville. While at Murfreesboro Buell was apprised of the battle between our forces under General Nelson and the army of Kirby Smith at Richmond, Kentucky, and he then decided to make a rapid march to Louisville, Kentucky. About the seventh of September he left Nashville, leaving General Thomas in command with his own division and the division of Negley and Palmer, but Thomas was in a few days ordered to join the main army with his division.

On the twelfth the head of Bragg's column, with a brigade of cavalry under Scott, tore up the railroad near Bowling Green, then made a bold dash for Mumfordsville, but were repulsed by the garrison in a two days fight. On the seventeenth the garrison surrendered, after being surrounded by an overwhelming force of the enemy. Bragg then moved eastward and Buell marched rapidly toward Louisville, and the last division reached that city September 29, and at about the same date Bragg's army arrived at Bardstown.

During all of this campaign of two months the First Ohio was kept in continuous hard service— on courier duty, scouting and skirmishing with the enemy, as the enemy had a much stronger cavalry force than we had.

The following dispatch from Buell to Halleck will give the situation during the last days of July:

Headquarters
Huntsvile
July 23, 1862

General Halleck or General Thomas
Washington, D. C.

I cannot err in repeating to you the urgent importance of a larger cavalry force in this district. The enemy is throwing an immense cavalry force on the four hundred miles of railroad communication upon which this army is dependent for its supplies. I am building stockades to hold from thirty to one hundred men at all bridges, but such guards, at least, only give security to certain points and against a small force. There can be no safety without cavalry enough to pursue the enemy in large bodies. Twice already our roads have been broken up by these formidable raids, causing great delays and embarrassment, so that we were scarcely able to subsist from day to day. I am concentrating all the cavalry I can spare, to operate actively in force. I do not pretend to know whether you have cavalry that you can spare elsewhere, but if so, it can find abundant and very important service here.

D. C. Buell

>Headquarters
>First Division
>Army of Ohio
>McMinnville
>Tenn.
>August 24, 1862

Major-General Buell
Decherd
A reconnoitering party under Major Laughlin, First Ohio Cavalry, sent by me toward Pikeville day before yesterday, has just returned. Major Laughlin reports that he reconnoitered (?) the enemy's advance scouts at Spencer, and gained reliable intelligence from one or two citizens that a force of two or three thousand infantry and some artillery was then at Pikeville, and that the enemy intended advancing on this place by two or three routes.
G. H. Thomas

>Headquarters
>First Division
>Army of Ohio
>McMinnville
>August 28, 1862

Major-General Buell
Decherd
Saturday, three regiments of cavalry were at Pikeville, but fell back to Robinson Cross Roads, hearing that I was advancing on that road. I have sent a brigade of infantry on the Murfreesboro road after Forrest, who is at Woodbury with something over one thousand men. Please send the First Ohio Cavalry here. It is very much needed.
G. H. Thomas

>September 13, 1862, 8 p. m.

Major-General Thomas
You must reach Bowling Green in three days and a half at most and will march directly on from there.
Leave the siege artillery and most of the cavalry with Ne-

gley. Post Negley at the defensible works and position and at the capitol and at the bridge, and direct him to leave twenty days rations at each point for its garrison. He must defend his position to the last extremity. Explain the urgency of the matter to Governor Johnson. If Bragg's army is defeated, Nashville is safe; if not, it is lost.
Fry

From the dispatches copied above, it will be seen that the regiment was in great demand.

CHAPTER 8

Perryville Campaign

October 1- November 15, 1862

On arriving at Louisville, General Buell found a large force of recruits in the works around the city, and he lost no time in commencing reorganization and getting his army fully equipped for a campaign against the Confederates, now boldly confronting him in Kentucky. His army was organized into three corps, and Major-Generals A. Mc. D. McCook, T. L. Crittenden and C. C. Gilbert were assigned to command the three corps.

An order, bearing date September 29, designated Major-General Thomas as the commander of the Army of the Ohio, but Thomas entered an earnest protest against this order, and through his influence General Buell was again assigned to the command, and October 1 his army began their advance against General Bragg's army.

The hard service of the past two months, with scarcity of water and forage, had played sad havoc with the horses of the First Ohio and new mounts were very much needed. Horses were in great demand, and the short time allowed for mounting and equipping the men was improved to the best advantage, but by no means to the satisfaction of Colonel Millikin, as he was very anxious to have his regiment the best mounted and equipped in the department.

During the campaign through Tennessee and Kentucky in August and September the regiment had been divided up into battalions, one commanded by Colonel Millikin, one by Major Laughlin, and the other by Captain Pattin, and the duties, as before stated, were very arduous, as the different battalions were distributed so that at times they covered the whole front of Buell's army and did not have a moment's rest.

The battalion of six companies commanded by Colonel Millikin marched from Louisville October 2, in advance of General Shoepf's division, and on the third had a sharp fight with the enemy at Shepherdstown, repulsing them and capturing about thirty prisoners. This battalion had the advance on the Perryville road and had some sharp skirmishing, driving the enemy at every point, and were continuously at the front during all of the manoeuvring up to the battle of Perryville, October 8, and Colonel Millikin was highly complimented for his vigorous and aggressive dashes against the lines of the enemy.

Major Laughlin's battalion of the regiment left Louisville October 2 and moved out on the Bardstown pike, marching rapidly, and about ten miles from Bardstown struck the enemy's cavalry, drove them back gradually until within about a mile of Bardstown. Here a regiment of Confederate cavalry drew the battalion into an ambuscade at the fair grounds, by forming their main line behind a high, close board fence surrounding the grounds. Their skirmishers fell back slowly and when they reached the grounds the rebels charged out through the gates and openings, yelling like demons, almost creating a stampede, but Major Laughlin soon rallied his men, making a furious charge which sent the rebel cavalry whirling back through the town with a loss of about twenty-five of his men. He captured a number of prisoners, with a large amount of army supplies. A flag of truce was sent into our line near Bardstown, and the escort was under command of a Major Prentice, and at the time it was understood that he was the son of Geo. D. Prentice, editor of the Louisville Courier Journal and a strong Union man. The escort was halted at the outpost and the communication was sent in to the commanding officer, while the escort and the reserve picket mingled together in a very friendly manner, and finally some of the boys became engaged in the "vet's" old reliable game of "draw poker."

Maj. Gen. Emery Upton.

Maj. Gen. Kenner Garrard.

CO. D.

Guidon, Co. H.

Capt. Samuel Hamilton.

Soon the game became intensely interesting and earnest, and George Pearl, of Company K, and one of the escort got into a quarrel, hot words were exchanged, both men jumped to their feet, and had it not been for the interference of the officers on both sides, there might have been a regular *mêlée*. The troopers on both sides were ordered to their horses and there was no more poker playing that day. When the messenger returned and the escort mounted, a long haired Texan Ranger dropped his hat to the ground, whether accidentally or purposely, is not known, but as if to show the "Yanks" the superior horsemanship of the Texan, he turned his horse quickly about and attempted to pick up his hat with out dismounting, but his foot slipped and off he fell, much to the amusement of our boys and chagrin of the Ranger. Ned Garner, a wild, reckless trooper, of Company K, as if in contempt of the exhibition made by the Texan, threw his hat on the ground and, galloping along, picked it up easily, and the escort joined our boys in a loud laugh at the expense of the discomfited rebel trooper.

Poor George and Ned both sleep in the sunny south land. Pearl was killed at Lovejoy, Ga., August 20, 1864, after his time was out, and Garner was taken prisoner at Washington, Tenn., September 30, 1863, and died in Andersonville prison. They were both good soldiers and had a most intense hatred and contempt for all rebels, and when an opportunity offered expressed themselves in language more emphatic than elegant. When in a fight, Pearl was always in a towering rage, and with a contemptuous smile he would swear every time he fired a shot, never failing to take deliberate aim and was perfectly cool, never throwing away a shot.

In this dash among the Confederate prisoners captured was a Major Moore, of the 12th Alabama Mounted Infantry. His horse fell and Charley Welch, the regimental saddler, captured him and delivered him over to Major Pattin, and he remained in the tent with Pattin and Welch over night. The next morning he stated, that if he was paroled, he would go home to Mobile and would not enter the Confederate service again, as he was sick of it. He was paroled and the incident was almost forgotten. During the Wilson raid, in the spring of 1865, Welch was taken prisoner by Forrest's Confederate cavalry at Ebenezer Church, Ala., and was sent to Mobile. There, much to his surprise, he met this same Major Moore and found that he was a citizen of high standing, and he entertained Welch royally in return for the kindness shown by Pattin and Welch when he was a prisoner with the First Ohio. True to his promise, Moore had not entered the Confederate service again after he was paroled.

The battalion under Major Laughlin was on the flanks and had some skirmishing during the battle of Perryville, October 8, and at one time they supported a battery dismounted. Sergeant John Lucas, now gone to his reward, told a very amusing incident in connection with the support of that battery. It seems that the battery was in position with a cornfield in front, and on the opposite side of the cornfield the infantry skirmishers were having a hot time with the enemy and the minnie balls were zipping through the corn, passing most uncomfortably near the heads of the cavalry boys, and consequently they were hugging the ground very close. A regiment of recruits from Illinois came marching along in column of fours, tall, fine looking, sturdy farmer boys, who had just arrived and had never been under fire. They seemed anxious to get into a fight. As they passed to the right of the cavalrymen, lying very low on the ground, some tall young "sucker" yelled out, as if in contempt, "Just show us where the Johnnies are and we will give them Hades," to which some of the cavalry boys replied, "You will find them over there." On they marched into the cornfield in column of fours towards the rebel line at an angle, so that the enemy could get a good enfilading fire. There was one volley from the rebel line in the woods, and in about twenty minutes back came the regiment of recruits through the cornfield pell mell, almost tramping the artillery support into the ground, and as they hurried to the rear the boys shouted after them: "Did you find the Johnnies over there?" The recruits were not at fault, for no veteran regiment could have withstood that withering enfilading fire. It was the fault of the officers, who, unsuspectingly, led them in, and not the rank and file who carried the muskets.

The other battalions of the regiment were on the flanks and were engaged in several skirmishes, and there were several men wounded; among others was Captain Kirkendall, wounded severely in the arm.

CHAPTER 9

Battle of Perryville

The battle of Perryville was fought almost exclusively by General A. McD. McCook's corps, although the corps of both Gilbert and Crittenden were in easy supporting distance. McCook called on General Buell repeatedly for reinforcements, but for some unaccountable reason none were sent until after 4 p. m., although the battle opened at half past 12 p. m. While Buell had given orders to advance and was momentarily expecting the battle to open, yet it seems that he did not know that McCook's corps was seriously engaged until 4 p. m.

It appears from official reports that neither Buell nor Bragg understood the number nor disposition of the troops in their fronts. Buell had in position eight divisions and Bragg had but three divisions when he attacked Buell's left, still he out numbered McCook's two divisions, on which the brunt of the battle fell, very largely. Bragg evidently did not wish to fight a battle at Perryville, but was forced into it by the pressure on his rear divisions, and then thought he was only fighting the advance of Buell's army. The fighting was very severe and losses heavy for the number of troops engaged and were principally from McCook's two divisions and Gooding's brigade from Mitchell's division. This brigade lost nearly 500 men out of 2000. The total loss in Buell's army was 916 killed, 2943 wounded, and 489 missing a total loss of 4348. The loss in Bragg's army is not known, but Buell claims that he captured about 4500 prisoners.

The enemy withdrew during the night and Buell did not advance until the morning of the eleventh, when he found the enemy in force near Harrodsburg, and Bragg's army fell back after a sharp skirmish with our cavalry under Colonel Minor Millikin, which is mentioned in a dispatch from General Thomas.

General Buell went back to Louisville in a few days, where he got into a controversy with the authorities at Washington regarding the conduct of the campaign, which caused his removal from the command of, the Army of Ohio, October 30, 1862, and General Rosecrans was put in command of the "Department of the Cumberland," designated as the "14th Army Corps," but soon after as the "Army of the Cumberland."

When General Rosecrans assumed command, the army was concentrated around Bowling Green, and the army commenced the advance on Nashville November 4.

On the day of the battle of Perryville the regiment was again united, after having been cut up in detachments for more than two months, in the campaign through Tennessee and Kentucky, and here Captain B. B. Eggleston, Captain James Cutler and Lieutenant A. Alkire, who had been taken prisoners at Courtland, Ala., joined the regiment.

The day after the battle of Perryville, October 9, Colonel Millikin was assigned to the command of the 3rd brigade of cavalry, composed of the First Ohio Cavalry, First Kentucky Cavalry and Fourth Michigan Cavalry, in all about 1200 men. General John Morgan was marauding with his freebooters through Kentucky and was giving General Buell's army no end of trouble by cutting rail roads and destroying supplies. With this small force of cavalry, and without any artillery, Colonel Millikin was ordered to drive Morgan out of the country. On the eleventh Millikin moved out toward Harrodsburg and Crab Orchard and on the same day he struck the enemy and had a brisk fight, and as shown by the following dispatches he was making a vigorous campaign against Bragg's retreating army.

Headquarters
Harlan House
October 11, 1862, 9:30 a. m.

General Buell

Colonel Millikin is now skirmishing with about 1200 of the enemy's cavalry about two or three miles this side of Harrodsburg, on the left of the Perryville pike. He reports they have two pieces of artillery. I have directed him to attract their attention to enable the reconnoitering party to flank them on the Harrodsburg and Danville pike, by which move I may succeed in capturing some, if not all. Has General Gilbert's party marched yet?

Respectfully,

Geo. H. Thomas, Major-General, U. S. Volunteers

October 11, 1862

General Thomas

My men have had no rest or food since yesterday morning. They came in last night at nine and went out this morning at twelve, and have been in the advance, skirmishing (on foot) all the way from Danville.

Can we not have a few hours relief after coming back from this reconnaissance? They are unfit to fight. Colonel McCook's brigade is in advance of me, having relieved my line this morning.

Very respectfully,

Minor Millikin, Colonel Commanding.

October 12, 1862

Colonel Zahm
Commanding Cavalry
Danville

Has Millikin's cavalry reached Danville? If so, did he get my instruction before leaving Crab Orchard? His command must go to Bardstown and watch and try to intercept Morgan from that point and prevent his making a descent on the Lebanon Railroad.

James B. Fry, Colonel and Chief of Staff

After driving the enemy's cavalry through Harrodsburg, Sanford and Crab Orchard with some sharp skirmishing every day, Millikin was ordered with his brigade to Bardstown and Lebanon, where Morgan was threatening the railroad, and on the twentieth he was at Springfield, on the twenty-first at Lebanon, on the twenty-second at Mumfordsville, on the twenty-fourth at Brownsville, on the twenty-fifth at Woodsonville, and then back to Mumfordsville, having been on the move almost continuously day and night from October 9 chasing Morgan and intercepting him at every point.

Colonel Millikin's report of this campaign is herewith appended and speaks for itself in plain language, so characteristic of that brave, conscientious officer. Among the losses mentioned was Albert Nicely, Company F, died of wound at Nashville, Tenn., October 16, 1862.

Headquarters
Third Brigade Cavalry
Camp near Mumfordsville
Ky.
October 27, 1862

Colonel J. B. Fry
Chief of Staff

Colonel: Because of the somewhat unintelligible and apparently unreasonable movements made by the forces under my command in the recent pursuit of Morgan and the fruitless result of the whole affair, I suppose it proper, both in justice to myself and because some wholesome inferences may be drawn from them, to state a few disconnected facts: I was on my way to Bardstown (agreeably to your first order) and had reached a point five miles west of Springfield at 2 a. m. Monday morning (October 20); I had marched 48 miles since Sunday morning, and had only 23 miles to march in eight hours in order to reach Bardstown at 10 a. m. This I had fully intended to do, having given the men three hours sleep at Perryville. But at this point I run into General Gay's column. Sending forward to know what caused the delay I received an order to remain where I was until morning. Supposing him to have met the enemy or to have received (as the general's staff officer) other information, and greatly desiring to co-operate, I obeyed. When morning came I was ordered on by General Gay, and we reached Springfield at 10 a. m. Monday, twentieth. From the time I reached him (Gay) until the morning I left Lebanon (Tuesday, twenty-first) the same anxiety to co-operate and the same inference as to his better acquaintance with the general's intentions led me to obey his orders.

On the morning of twenty-first, having expected orders all night, I was incidentally informed that my command was an independent one, and that I was expected to "catch Morgan" in my own way. Failing to get any information or suggestions from General Gay or any one else, I started as soon as possible to Mumfordsville, Gay promising to go to Glasgow *via* Campbellsville. Of this I advised you, but the telegraph not working, you did not receive it promptly.

Reaching Mumfordsville on Wednesday night (October 22), having marched 18 miles Tuesday afternoon and 33 miles on Wednesday, I left on Thursday morning, as soon as I had opened communication with Colonel Bruce at Bowling Green, for Brownsville.

I had proceeded five miles when the order disbanding my brigade and ordering the regiments to remain at Mumfordsville turned me back. I left again pursuant to subsequent orders received from you, for the same place at 2 a. m. of Friday, and was within four miles of Brownsville at 3 p.m. same day. I there learned definitely where Morgan had gone, and returned next day (*via* Dipping Springs) to within three miles of Woodsonville, where I stopped for forage and sent on to Mumfordsville for rations. I would have gone on to Woodbury without rations or rest if any result had suggested itself. Morgan having, by all the testimony of soldiers, scouts, and citizens, left my track, I returned.

Morgan was at Bardstown Sunday morning (nineteenth) at daylight. By unexampled marching I could only have reached there at 10 o'clock a. m., and then in such an exhausted condition as would have made me no match for his greatly superior force and would have entirely unfitted me for pursuit. I should have reached him in that time and in that condition too if I had not been ordered differently.

Morgan was at Elizabethtown on Sunday night and at Litchfield Monday night (twentieth), He did not finally leave Litchfield until the morning of the twenty-third and did not reach Morgantown until the twenty-fourth, or leave it until the day of Colonel Bruce's skirmish with him, the twenty-fifth. He was in no sort of haste. When at Springfield I urged General Gay to divide the forces, a part keeping higher up through New Haven, Hodgensville, Millerstown and Litchfield, pressing Morgan rapidly down, and another part sent to Brownsville or Glasgow. This, with the disposition of Colonel Bruce's force at Bowling Green and Russellville, Colonel Craddock remaining at this point, would have made an excellent trap to catch Morgan. If executed, this would certainly have hastened and perhaps destroyed him.

There were 300 of Morgan's men at Brownsville on Thursday, and remained during the day. At 8 o'clock of that day I was five miles toward B., and would certainly have struck him there had I not been ordered to return. Arriving at B., I might have pushed on to Litchfield or Woodbury, cutting off Morgan's stragglers, or with Bruce's forces attacked his main body. Starting when I did I knew every step was useless.

At no time has my force been sufficient to cope successfully with Morgan. He is known to have had Duke's and Gano's regiments and Breckenridge's battalion, aggregating, by all accounts, 2,000 men, and two pieces of artillery. Against this I had 575 seasoned troops (375 First Ohio and 200 First Kentucky), and 600 green troops, never under fire (Fourth Michigan), aggregating but 1175 men, and not a single piece of artillery. In whatever way I might have met Morgan, had he had his back against the wall and shown fight, the result would have been doubtful and could not have been else than partial and unsatisfactory.

I have the honour to be, very respectfully, your obedient servant,

Minor Millikin, Colonel Commanding

General Thomas held Colonel Millikin in high esteem; it was for this reason that he was given command of this provisional brigade and assigned to this hard campaign, as it required an officer of energy and dash. His brigade was disbanded at Mumfordsville, and about the first of November a brigade was organized at Bowling Green, Ky., composed of the First Ohio Cavalry, Third Ohio Cavalry, Second Kentucky Cavalry, Fifth Kentucky Cavalry, and Colonel Lewis Zahm, of the Third O.V. C., being the ranking officer, was assigned to command.

Early in November the brigade left Bowling Green for Nashville, and at Gallatin, Tennessee, they again encountered John Morgan with a force of 2500 men. The brigade attacked him, with great impetuosity, driving Morgan's men out of Gallatin and capturing nearly 100 prisoners.

Bowling Green
November 7, 1862

Colonel Zahm
(*via* Mitchellsville and courier lines)
The General commanding has received your dispatch, and approves your course. General Crittenden was in Scottsville last night; moves on Gallatin this morning. Inform him of all you know, and keep up communications with him. Act on the principle that the cavalry are the eyes of the army. Take orders for co-operation from General Crittenden. Always keep up your communication with headquarters.

Arthur C. Ducat, Lieutenant-Colonel & Acting Chief of Staff

The brigade marched *via* Hartsville to Nashville and went into camp about the fifteenth of November near that city. By the following order Brigadier-General D. S. Stanley was announced as Chief of Cavalry, Army of the Cumberland.

GENERAL ORDERS NO. 22

Headquarters
Fourteenth Army Corps,
Department of the Cumberland
Nashville
Tenn.
November 24, 1862

I. Brigadier-General D. S. Stanley having reported for duty, in accordance with the orders of the Secretary of War, is announced as Chief of Cavalry, and assigned to command of all the cavalry in this department.

J. P. Garesche, Assistant Adjutant-General & Chief of Staff.

After three and a half months continuous hard service, beginning with the crossing of the Tennessee River about the last days of July, and ending with their arrival at Nashville about the middle of November, a brief rest of a few days was welcomed by both officers, soldiers and horses. The losses in the regiment during the campaign, killed, wounded and prisoners, were about seventy-five, and a large number of men had been placed *hors de combat*, as many horses had given out on the hard marches and scouts, and those that were still in service required rest, care and shoeing to prepare them for the winter campaign, soon to be inaugurated by General Rosecrans, the newly-appointed commander of the Army of the Cumberland.

CHAPTER 10

Stone River Campaign
December, 1862

General Negley with two divisions had held Nashville for two months, and his troops had seen some hard service during that time. He had not only to hold the city with the two divisions as a garrison, but he was compelled to gather his supplies from the surrounding country, and detachments of the enemy's cavalry and infantry were hovering on all sides ready to pounce down upon foraging parties, and all forage trains were protected by strong guards.

The troops in the vicinity of Nashville that were continually threatening Negley were under command of Breckenridge, but Negley kept them off at arm's length, so that they could not invest the city, and starve the garrison out.

He made several demands for the surrender of Negley's forces, but Negley met these demands by dashing outside of the fortification and attacking the enemy, and at one time he routed Breckenridge's forces near Lavergne with a loss to the enemy of about eighty killed and wounded, two hundred prisoners, and a battery of three field guns.

It soon became evident that Bragg was concentrating his army in middle Tennessee, and Rosecrans immediately moved his whole army to Nashville, and arrived there in person November 9. As soon as the First Ohio went into camp at Nashville, Colonel Millikin went to work with great energy to remount and equip his command for the campaign against Bragg's army concentrating at Murfreesboro.

Requisitions were made for horses, many jaded and worn-out horses were condemned and turned in to the post quartermaster, and a general reorganization was commenced. Colonel Millikin had always been very strongly in favour of organizing the cavalry into brigades and divisions, as he always claimed they could be of much more service massed than by cutting them up into detachments and having them attached to divisions of infantry by regiments or battalions.

Up to the time of the battle of Perryville, the cavalry of Buell's army had all been used in this manner, and with the exception of one or two raids during the siege of Corinth and the pursuit of Bragg's army after the evacuation of Corinth by a large force of cavalry under command of General A. J. Smith, the cavalry of this department had not operated as independent organizations in large numbers.

Colonel Millikin was a born cavalry leader, and he entered into the spirit of the new movement with great enthusiasm, which was imparted to the officers and soldiers of his command. He at once inaugurated strict discipline and resumed both mounted and dismounted drill, which was very much needed, as there had been but little, if any, drilling since the evacuation of Corinth. From the middle of November until the last days of December, the regiment was encamped with the brigade, now composed of the First, Third and Fourth Ohio and Fifth Kentucky Cavalry, and designated the Second Cavalry Brigade, near Nashville, and in addition to the regular camp duties, the command was sent out on many scouts and reconnaissances, as Rosecrans believed in the old maxim that "the cavalry was the eyes of the army," and he proposed to use his cavalry for the purpose of observation and to keep at all times well advised as to the movements of the enemy.

General D. S. Stanley, a cavalry officer of long, active service in the regular army, had just been assigned to duty as Chief of Cavalry, Army of the Cumberland, and as he was very active and aggressive, a long felt want in that arm of the service seemed to have been supplied. He was always on the alert for any duty

MAJOR-GENERAL D. S. STANLEY
CHIEF OF CAVALRY, STONE RIVER CAMPAIGN.

required of his command, and he did not propose to settle down and wait for the enemy to come to him, but he went after the enemy, and usually found him, as Forrest, Wheeler and Morgan were tireless riders and were making raids on the railroads almost daily.

About the twenty-first of December, Stanley moved out on the Franklin pike to make a reconnaissance, and, striking the enemy near Franklin, had a sharp fight, routed the enemy, killing, wounding and capturing a number of cavalrymen, including one commissioned officer, with a large number of horses and other valuable supplies.

The First Ohio was sent out on a number of scouts during the month of December, in several of which they had sharp skirmishes with the enemy, and under the leadership of their fearless commander never failed to rout the enemy.

Rosecrans determined to attack Bragg's army, now strongly

posted at Murfreesboro, with his advance divisions thrown forward to Franklin, Triune and Lavergne. On the morning of December 26 the advance was begun, McCook commanding the right wing, Thomas the centre, and Crittenden the left wing.

Colonel Zahm's brigade moved on the Franklin pike, with three days rations in their haversacks and one wagon to the regiment, reaching Franklin the afternoon of December 26, where they struck the enemy's cavalry, and after a sharp fight routed them, killing four and wounding a large number, some of whom fell into our hands, with a number of prisoners, including several officers, and he then pushed on to Petersburg the same evening. On the twenty-seventh the brigade advanced toward Triune, skirmishing all day, and at Triune they attacked Wharton's brigade of cavalry, and had a lively fight, routing the enemy, and on the twenty-eighth still advanced, pushing the enemy back slowly with severe loss.

On the twenty-ninth they attacked Wharton's brigade with great vigour, driving them back to the main battle line, until a battery opened up on the brigade from the opposite side of Stone's River.

The same evening the brigade was put in position on the extreme right of our army and held this position until the close of the battle. On the thirtieth there was fighting all along the line, as both armies were manoeuvring for position, and the brigade was skirmishing and on the alert, watching the movements of the enemy all day.

On the morning of the thirty-first Hardee made an impetuous attack on McCook's right division, driving it back in great confusion and with heavy loss in both officers and soldiers. The pickets of the brigade were attacked about daybreak by Wheeler's division of cavalry and a hot fight was kept up for two hours.

When Johnson's division was driven from the field, the brigade covered the retreat and fought stubbornly for every inch of ground. Colonel Millikin acted with great bravery and coolness, encouraging his officers and soldiers and handling his regiment with great skill to prevent them from partaking of the general panic on the right. But the brigade was pushed slowly until the rebel cavalry were so close that they were using their revolvers.

The very acme of Colonel Millikin's ambition had been to have the regiment make a sabre charge, and now the supreme opportunity had arrived. His officers and soldiers were falling around him rapidly, Major Moore had been mortally wounded early in the day by a shell while the regiment was manoeuvring for position, and Adjutant W. H. Scott had been severely wounded in attempting to capture a rebel flag, and Lieutenant Sam Fordyce, of Company B, was also wounded. Joel Harris, of Company H, and Wesley Poling, of Company D, were also among the killed.

He must act at once, or his regiment would be stampeded and driven from the field, as they were being pushed and crushed by an overwhelming force of the enemy, flushed with victory. No officer of the brigade seemed to grasp the situation, no orders were given by the brigade commander, then Colonel Millikin, sending word to the commanders of the other regiments of the brigade to support his regiment in a charge, wheeled his regiment by fours to the rear giving the command, "Draw sabre." There was no time to tighten girths or to look after the condition of revolvers, but tightening the reins on his noble bay "Archie" and raising in his stirrups, gave the command, "Charge!" which was repeated to right and left along the line.

With sharp ring of bugle the sabres all clank
And the spurs are pressed to each horse's hot flank.

"Commending their souls to God, they charged home." Dashing forward under the spur, with a cheer they followed their brave and peerless leader to his death in that awful carnage.

On, on they go, striking the rebel lines, cutting right and left, leaving a swathe behind of wounded and killed intermingled the blue and the gray. On they went, cutting a line the full length of the regiment, sweeping everything before them, penetrating clear through the rebel line, and there was a fearful struggle when the shock came and the mêlée was on, with its confusion, fighting, yelling, cursing, horses and men falling, sabres flashing, revolvers cracking, horses and men struggling in a confused mass and going down together.

Colonel Millikin was in the midst of the fray, which lasted but a few minutes, and in a hand to hand fight he was shot through the neck with a revolver, fell from his horse with sabre in hand, and died without a struggle. General John A. Wharton, who commanded a brigade in Wheeler's cavalry, claims in his report that a cavalryman of his command, a private named John Bowers, Company K, Texas Rangers, killed Colonel Millikin.

The rebels soon rallied and commenced firing from both flanks and closed up the gap in the rear, and it was just at this critical moment that Colonel Millikin fell.

The regiment at this time was completely surrounded, and they again cut their way back to our lines, with many wounded and killed and a loss of about one hundred taken prisoners. The Fourth U. S. Cavalry then charged the rebel line and a majority of the prisoners were recaptured.

Whitelaw Reid, in his history, *Ohio in the War,* writes as follows of this charge:

> When the disaster of the thirty-first occurred, the brigade covered the retreat of our infantry, falling back slowly," contending for the ground until near the Murfreesboro and Nashville pike. It was then perceived that to permit the enemy to pass that point would prove ruinous. Colonel Millikin, having received no orders from his brigade commander, took the responsibility of sending orderlies to the various regimental commanders of the brigade, requesting them to support him in a sabre charge upon the advancing foe. Seeing that instant action was necessary, and without waiting for a response, Colonel Millikin wheeled his regiment into line and threw it with irresistible power upon the enemy, driving those in his immediate front a distance of a quarter of a mile. Not receiving the expected support, the enemy rallied and closed in on his rear, making his position one of extreme peril. He was absolutely

fighting the victorious left wing of the rebel army with a force not exceeding three hundred men. Perceiving that the safety of his men demanded their immediate extrication, the 'about' was sounded, and the chivalrous little band cut its way through the lines formed across its rear.

The First Cavalry fell back from the field of its glory, where it had made one of the most heroic charges of the war, with saddened heart, for, weltering in his life's blood in the midst of that carnage, lay its young and gallant commander, Colonel Minor Millikin. Justice never lost a more faithful champion, nor his country a more promising genius or heroic son. Fame, on the list of her favoured ones, has few younger and no brighter names. Had Minor Millikin's life been spared but we dare not say it! He lived long enough to die for his country, and who would or who could ask a more glorious destiny? He was mourned by his comrades as the brave mourn for the brave.

The loss of the regiment in this charge was thirty-one killed and wounded, with a number of prisoners, including Colonel Millikin, Major Moore and Lieutenant Condit, killed, and Adjutant Scott and Lieutenant Fordyce, wounded.

On the first day of the battle, Surgeon Wirth and Hospital Steward Doty, when on the field caring for the wounded, were both taken prisoners and taken to Murfreesboro, where they assisted in caring for the wounded of both armies for four days, and until Bragg retreated and our army occupied the town. Dr. Wirth had two hundred of our wounded in a large store room with floor covered with straw, no cots or beds, and but few blankets. The weather was cold and freezing, and the only means of heating the room was by a large fire-place, in which a blazing fire of pine knots was kept burning. The coals from the fire kept flying continuously, igniting the straw, and it kept one or two soldiers busy day and night putting out the fire to keep the wounded from burning. One night Dr. Wirth and Hospital Steward Doty dressed wounds and amputated limbs from dark to daylight, and the only light they had was a tallow candle held by a soldier. They had no chloroform and but little morphine or stimulants, and the suffering of the wounded men was most excruciating. Surgeon Wirth appealed to the Medical Director in charge of the Confederate hospitals for medicine and chloroform, and was informed that they had none, but he gave Surgeon Wirth free access to all his supplies, and he helped himself to such medicines as were in stock.

During all the time Wirth and Doty were prisoners they were told by the rebels that Rosecrans' army had been completely annihilated, and of course they had no good reason for disputing it, and as may be well imagined, they were overjoyed when Bragg's army commenced retreating and they were left with the wounded of our army.

When Rosecrans' army entered Murfreesboro, the first troops to discover the Surgeon and Hospital Steward was the First Ohio Cavalry. Major Moore, who had been mortally wounded by a shell, was taken to Murfreesboro by the Confederates, and his body was found in a cellar and sent home about the same time Colonel Millikin's body was sent.

After the charge of the regiment, December 31, Major Martin Buck, the senior Major present, took command until the next day, and on that day Major Laughlin, having come up from Nashville, assumed command, as he was the senior officer present. The regiment continued at the front during the fighting of the next two days, but only participated in some light skirmishes, with but few casualties.

CHAPTER 11

Battle of Stone River

From the twenty-sixth to the thirtieth day of December, 1862, General Rosecrans was feeling the lines of the enemy very carefully, manoeuvring for position, and on the evening of the thirtieth the two armies were in close proximity to each other.

There had been considerable of fighting on different parts of the line, but no general engagement; the right, under Sheridan and Davis, had done pretty sharp fighting on the thirtieth, and the two divisions lost about three hundred men. McCook commanded the right wing, Thomas the centre, and Crittenden the left wing, resting on Stone's River, and McCook's right near the Franklin pike. It seems, by the reports of both Rosencrans and Bragg, that their plan of battle was identical, that is, each decided to make the attack from their left flank.

On the night of the thirtieth fires were built for a long distance to the right of McCook's line, to make the impression that the Union army was massing on the right to cover the intended attack on the left. Vancleve and Wood, who held the extreme left of the Union line, were to attack the enemy and force a crossing at the upper and lower fords of Stone's River, and Thomas was to advance in the centre and McCook was to "hold the enemy on the right if attacked, and if the enemy did not attack him, he was to attack the enemy." The principal part of the ground in front of both armies was open, still there were some strong defensive positions along both battle fronts. The left wing of Bragg's army, under Hardee, attacked McCook early on the morning of the thirty-first, thus taking the initiative, putting the Union army on the defensive.

The enemy attacked furiously, and McCook's right was pressed back, for some distance, after a very stubborn resistance and great slaughter in both armies. McCook was very largely outnumbered, as Hardee commanded at least three-fifths of Bragg's army. Bragg's army continued to wheel to the right, the battle extended to the Union left, and the whole Confederate army was soon involved, excepting Breckenridge's division, which was on the east side of the river.

There was but little fighting on the left of the Union army during the early part of the day, and by 10 o'clock the advance by Bragg's army had been checked both on the right wing and centre. Bragg then commenced the transfer of Breckenridge's division across the river to attack Crittenden's left, and there was a lull from the centre to the right of the Union army.

Breckenridge attacked our left and the assault fell on Hazen near the railroad, in a heavy wood, afterward named by the Confederate commander as the "Round Forest," and the fighting at this point in the line was very severe, but the repeated attacks were repulsed, and our left persistently held the "Round Forest" to the end of the battle. The losses to the enemy on the left by their repeated assaults was very heavy, and some of the regiments engaged were almost annihilated.

The enemy had now been fully checked all along the line, and there was but little fighting during the balance of the day, both armies were well exhausted, rested on their arms all night within rifle shot of each other, waiting the dawn of the New Year. The forenoon of that New Year's day, 1863, was a day of great anxiety to the two army commanders, as each hoped the other would retreat, and there was little fighting up to noon, excepting some artillery firing and manoeuvring by both armies for position. Breckenridge withdrew to the east side of the river, and Beatty's division and Grose's brigade of the Union army crossed the river, took position in front of Breckenridge, and the day passed without any general engagement.

During the morning of the second there was some skirmishing and artillery firing, and at noon Breckenridge massed his forces and made a vigorous attack on the Union left. The Union line was at first pushed back to the river, but Crittenden's Chief of Artillery, massed fifty-eight guns, opened up against the enemy, and drove him back with great slaughter. There was no fighting on the third, and during the night Bragg retreated. The fourth was spent in burying the dead, and on the fifth Rosecrans' army occupied Murfreesboro. When General Rosecrans left Nashville he had in round numbers 47,000 men, and he fought the battle with about 43,500, consisting of 38,000 infantry, 3000 cavalry and 2220 artillery. His losses were 1533 killed, 7244 wounded and 2800 missing; total loss, 11,577, an aggregate loss of more than twenty per cent.

Bragg reported his strength at 35,000, while Rosecrans estimated Bragg's army at 60,000. The enemy's losses were reported 9000 killed and wounded, and 1000 missing, but it is fair to presume that his losses were at least equal to that of the Union army.

The Union army held the field, and the enemy retreated to Duck River.

Nashville
December 26, 1862, 1:40 a. m.

Brigadier-General Stanley
Chief of Cavalry

General: Your dispatch is just received. The general's directions are that your right wing shall move along the Franklin pike, your left along the Murfreesborough, the reserve along the Nolensville, with the exception of the Fourth (U. S.) Cavalry, which will accompany the General on the Murfreesborough. There are some 700 of the enemy in Franklin. The General wishes a dash made at them, and when driven out, he wants the cavalry to sweep over in the direction of Nolensville, picketing the Wilson pike leading toward Petersburg, with one or two regiments, according as the enemy shall prove to be in greater or less force along our front.

J. P. Garesche, Assistant Adjutant-General & Chief of Staff

Extract from report of Assistant Adjutant-General J. P. Garesche

>Headquarters
>Department of the Cumberland
>Camp near Murfreesborough Pike
>December 27, 1862

Major-General Crittenden
Commanding Left Wing

Stanley says cavalry acted well; dislodged enemy from Franklin last night; took some prisoners, among them commissioned officers. Things work well so far. Enemy under impression our advance was a feint. The distance from Triune to Murfreesborough being seventeen miles, and the direction of Hardee's retreat uncertain, he will not order an advance tonight on Murfreesborough.

J. P. Garesche

>Camp near Nolensville
>December 27, 1862

Colonel Zahm drove the enemy from Franklin yesterday; established a strong picket at Petersburg, and is camped tonight on the Wilson pike. I shall move the balance of my command to Stewartsborough tomorrow, unless otherwise ordered.

Very respectfully,
Geo. H. Thomas, Major-General
U. S. Volunteers, Commanding

>Nolensville
>December 27, 1862

Lieutenant-Colonel J. P. Garesche

Colonel Zahm entered Franklin yesterday, and drove their pickets from that place, killing four. He has gone today toward Petersburg to observe. Will leave his pickets there tonight and come to this place with his main force.

Geo. H. Thomas

Headquarters
Department of the Cumberland
Camp 3½ miles north of La Vergne
December 28th 1862, 12:10 p. m.

Brigadier-General Stanley
Chief of Cavalry, Triune

General: The General commanding desires me to inform you that there is every prospect of the enemy's fighting a battle between Stewart's Creek and Murfreesborough. General McCook will give you the substance of the information we have on this point. Act in concert with him, and cover his movements.

J. P. Garesche, Chief of Staff

Wilkinson's Cross Roads
December 29, 1862

Major-General McCook

General: Our cavalry are about two miles beyond this. Zahm is abreast with us; he has been fighting some. The burning going on seems to be the Nashville pike bridge over Stone River. The prisoners and negroes say the rebels are in line of battle from the Franklin to the Nashville pike. They have moved all their camps. I will arrange to bivouac if you have no orders.

D. S. Stanley, Brigadier-General

EXTRACT FROM REPORT OF
MAJOR-GENERAL A. D. MCCOOK

December 29, 1862

Colonel Garesche
Chief of Staff

Zahm drove the rebels in within sight of Murfreesborough, when he was shelled from the other side of Stone River. How will I communicate with you now, as the courier .line is with drawn? Stanley will attend to the roads south.

A. McD. McCook

Camp
First Ohio Volunteer Cavalry
Near Murfreesborough
Tenn.
January 6, 1863

Sir: I have the honour to submit the following report of the First Ohio Volunteer Cavalry:

On the morning of January 1 I was ordered to take command of the regiment, and was immediately ordered in the rear of Stewart's Creek and on the right, on picket or outpost duty. In the evening I was ordered back in front of Stewart's Creek and on the right to stand on picket for the night.

On the morning of the second I was ordered to advance my regiment forward on the right, which I did, and found the enemy in my front and skirmished with them until dark.

On the morning of the third I was ordered to march my regiment to the rear of Stewart's Creek, which I did. In the evening I was ordered to join my command with the Fourth Ohio Cavalry and make a reconnaissance on our left, which was done, and we returned to camp the same night.

Remained in camp on the fourth until evening; was ordered to the front and left to guard the railroad bridge for the night. On the morning of the fifth went on scout beyond Murfreesborough on the Shelbyville pike and returned.
Your most obedient
James Laughlin, Major, Commanding First O.V. C.

Headquarters
First Ohio Volunteer Cavalry
January 6, 1863

Colonel L. Zahm
Commanding Second Cavalry Brigade

December 26 left Nashville for Franklin; arrived at Franklin at 3 p. m.; found the enemy occupying the town; drove them from it and proceeded to Wilson's Creek pike, and encamped for the night.

December 27 left camp at 8 o'clock; proceeded toward Triune; struck the enemy's pickets within five miles of Triune; drove in their pickets, captured six, and returned to the camp occupied the previous night.

December 28 left camp at 8 o'clock for Triune, where we encamped.

December 29 left camp at 9 o'clock on a reconnaissance toward Murfreesborough. Struck the enemy's scouts when within one mile of Stewart's creek, when active skirmishing commenced and continued until sundown, having driven the enemy's cavalry at least three and a half miles.

December 30, skirmished with the enemy all day on the right of General Johnson's division, driving the enemy's cavalry wherever they made their appearance.

December 31. At 7 a. m. I was ordered by you to take two companies and make a thorough reconnaissance up the creek in the woods on our right. After throwing out skirmishers into the woods, I received orders from you to withdraw my command as soon as possible, for the enemy were advancing in force on my left. I immediately withdrew at full speed and passed the enemy's left (infantry) within 150 yards under heavy fire slightly wounding one man and two horses. After passing their flank half a mile, I discovered your brigade formed in line of battle in the cornfield on the opposite side of the creek. Being unable to join my regiment at this point, I proceeded down the creek and crossed, joining my brigade on the right, retiring slowly in column of fours. After retiring half a mile, we were again formed in line of battle, and remained until we were under heavy fire from the enemy's artillery, when we were compelled to retire. Here the brave and heroic Major D. A. B. Moore fell, mortally wounded. We then retired across a cornfield, the enemy in full and fast pursuit, with at least three times our number, when we again formed, receiving three heavy charges from the enemy's cavalry, but repulsed them every time with a fire from our carbines. Their artillery was still open on us. The enemy (cavalry and infantry) immediately appearing, our noble commander, Colonel Minor Millikin, ordered our regiment, five companies, to charge them. Being unable to hold his position after the charge, he ordered the regiment to retire, when he received the fatal shot that killed him instantly. About this time, Second Lieutenant Condit was killed, and our Adjutant, First Lieutenant Wm. Scott, fell seriously wounded. The companies then returned to the pike and crossed Stewart Creek on the pike. I found myself in command and repulsed the enemy, who had pursued to the creek and taken possession of our wagon train, killing two and wounding four.

January 1, at 9 a. m., Major Laughlin reported for duty and took command of the regiment.

Total loss, thirty-one.

Valentine Cupp, Captain
Commanding First Ohio Volunteer Cavalry

Extract from report of Colonel Zahm

>Headquarters Second Cavalry Brigade
>In camp near Murfreesborough
>Tenn.
>January 6, 1863

I herewith have the honour to report the part taken and the work performed by my brigade since our departure from Nashville until the close of the battle before Murfreesborough.

I left Nashville on the morning of the twenty-sixth *ultimo*, with three regiments of my brigade, *viz.*: the First, Third and Fourth Ohio Cavalry, the Fifth Kentucky remaining at Nashville. My force numbered 950 men. When within two miles of Franklin, drove in the rebel pickets, skirmished all the way down to Franklin, drove the enemy out, and pursued him some two miles. From the best information received the enemy was 900 strong (all cavalry), part of Wharton's brigade. We killed four, wounded several and took ten prisoners, among them a Lieutenant of Bragg's escort, several horses and mules, and destroyed their camps, with some tents standing thereon.

On the twenty-seventh sent the First Ohio and most of the Fourth Ohio under the command of Colonel Millikin, on the Wilson Creek pike, to reconnoitre toward Triune. They proceeded within two miles of Triune, captured six of the rebel pickets, when the enemy opened on them with shells; threw some fifty without damaging us any.

On the twenty-eighth moved with the command to Triune, without anything occurring worth mentioning.

On the twenty-ninth proceeded toward Murfreesborough, moving between the Franklin road and the road called Bole Jack road, which General McCook's corps moved on. I divided my brigade into three columns, marching parallel with one another and with the main force, the right (the Fourth Ohio), moving on the Franklin road, the Third in centre, and the First on the left, the columns being from one to one and a half miles apart, throwing out skirmishers, connecting one column with the other, and connecting on the left with the main column. We thus proceeded for five miles, when the centre column encountered the enemy's pickets, which they drove in, the different columns steadily advancing.

Shortly after, both the right and the left encountered pickets, driving them in before them. After proceeding about one mile farther we came upon the enemy's cavalry (Wharton's brigade), engaged them for three hours, sometimes the right wing, then the left, then the centre, receiving several charges, which were repulsed, driving the enemy some two miles, when the brigade concentrated, repelling a heavy charge from the enemy, driving him back under his guns, which were only a short distance from us.

Some few causalities occurred this day. The officers and men behaved admirably during the whole day.

On the morning of the thirtieth was ordered to proceed on the Franklin road toward Murfreesborough, to push the enemy hard.

I proceeded that morning with my command and the Second East Tennessee, which reported to me via that road to the Franklin road, at which crossing we encountered the enemy's pickets and drove them in. I increased the number of skirmishers, especially to the left, skirmished with the enemy for an hour or more.

In the meantime, I had ascertained, likewise, that a heavy force of the enemy was encamped some little distance south of the Franklin road, and east of where my column halted. I did not think it prudent to advance, and owing to the bad grounds (being all timber), where my force halted, I retired to my camping-ground, near where were large open fields, well adapted for cavalry movements. I soon formed a line of battle. The enemy made his appearance. Skirmishers engaged him pretty briskly.

The enemy manoeuvred with the design to outflank me, but did not succeed.

At daybreak of the morning of the thirty-first I had my command drawn up in line of battle in the rear of my camp, sent out two squadrons to the front and to the right to reconnoitre.

Had been in the line about half an hour, when I heard heavy firing—cannon and musketry— to my left and a little to the front. Soon after, I beheld our infantry scattered all over the field, running toward my line, when I learned that General Johnson's division was repulsed. At about the same time, my skirmishers engaged the enemy, when they were driven in, reporting that the enemy were approaching in heavy force. To my right the enemy's cavalry were coming in long columns, with the evident design to outflank us.

I retired slowly toward the main body of our army, the enemy pressing hard on me; kept him at bay with my skirmishers. I retired this wise for a mile, when I formed a line of battle with the First and Third, when the enemy charged on them with their cavalry, but were repulsed by our men. The first shell that landed mortally wounded

Major Moore, of the First Ohio. I formed a new line, received the enemy's charge, repulsed them, and made many of the rebels bite the dust.

When we arrived on the open ground, General McCook's aide told me that the whole of General McCook's ammunition train was close by on a dirt road running by that point, and that I must try to save it. I soon formed my command in line, when the enemy made his appearance in a position occupying two-thirds of a circle. They prepared to charge upon us, like wise commenced throwing shells. The First had been ordered to proceed farther on to form and to receive a charge from another line of the enemy's cavalry. The First charged upon the enemy; did not succeed in driving them back. On returning from said charge, the gallant Colonel Millikin and one lieutenant were killed, and another Lieutenant severely wounded.

Lewis Zahm, Colonel
Commanding Second Cavalry Brigade

Extract from report of
Brigadier-General John A. Wharton, C. S. Army,
Commanding Cavalry Brigade at Stone River

Headquarters
Wharton's Cavalry Brigade
Shelbyville Pike
Tenn.
January 22, 1803

About three hundred of the enemy's cavalry, not over four hundred yards distant, were bearing down upon the battery with a speed that evinced a determination to take it at all hazards. A few men, with Colonel Smith, were promptly formed, and the battery unlimbered and ordered to fire upon the approaching enemy. Several shells were exploded in their ranks and they retired in confusion. The command that had captured the wagons, thinking that they had driven the entire force of the enemy's cavalry across Overalls

Creek and apprehending danger alone from that quarter, were prepared to meet it only from that direction. Besides, many were scattered along the entire length of the wagon train, directing its movements and guarding the many prisoners taken. In this condition they were attacked by the same party of cavalry from the direction of Murfreesborough, that I had repulsed with the artillery, the enemy's cavalry that we had driven across Overall's Creek being in condition likewise to attack them in the rear
In this engagement the enemy suffered severely, losing many officers and men, both killed and captured. Among the former was Colonel Minor Millikin, who was killed by Private John Bowers, of Company K, Texas Rangers, in single combat.

EXTRACT FROM REPORTS OF
COLONEL JOHN M. HARLAN, TENTH KENTUCKY INFANTRY
COMMANDING BRIGADE

La Vergne
January 25, 1863
A train of cars were attacked one-half mile this side of Antioch this morning; two cars were burned; fifty-six prisoners were captured and paroled by the enemy a cavalry force under command of Forrest. The force at Mill Creek Abridge came to relieve the train and succeeded in saving the locomotive and several cars. This force is estimated at about two thousand and it is supposed that they had returned toward Franklin.
V. Cupp, Captain, First Ohio Volunteer Cavalry

Department of the Cumberland
Murfreesborough
January 5, 1863
Major-General Rosecrans
General: I occupy Murfreesborough with General Negley and Rousseau's divisions. General Stanley has followed up the enemy with his cavalry on his two routes of retreat, Shelbyville

and Manchester pikes. From the best information I can obtain, the main body of their infantry and artillery went out by the Manchester pike, both columns well covered by a heavy body of cavalry. As yet, I have not heard of any public property, but will make the necessary inquiries. Colonel Zahm has just sent me word that he is engaging the enemy's rear guard on the Shelbyville pike, about five miles from town. They have three pieces of artillery. I have ordered a brigade of infantry and a battery of artillery to go to Zahm's support.
Geo. H. Thomas

Extract from a number of the Richmond Dispatch January, 1863

General Bragg has certainly retreated to Shelbyville, thirty miles from his victory at Murfreesborough, as he did last fall from his victory at Perryville. On this occasion, he has saved his prisoners, captured guns, stores, et. But, if he has retired (that is the fashionable phrase on our side, as "change of base" is on the other) to Shelbyville with his whole army, he has thrown East Tennessee entirely open to the Yankees. There is a very strong position, beginning with Shelbyville on the left, extending across the railroad running from Nashville to Chattanooga, at or near its junction with the Shelbyville road, with its centre at a place called Decherd's, and its right terminating in the Cumberland Mountains, the whole distance being twenty-five miles from left to right, which, we understand, military men thought last summer ought to be the place to defend East Tennessee. It may be that Bragg has fallen back to this position. If he has, all is right. But if he has merely gotten out of the way, with the design to go to re-enforce the army facing Grant, which is three hundred miles off, then East Tennessee is in great danger, if Rosecrans wishes to take it. And East Tennessee is precisely the very portion of the Confederacy which it is most inconvenient for us to lose, since it cuts it completely in two.

CHAPTER 12

After the Battle of Stone River
January 1, 1863- June 24, 1863

After the death of Colonel Millikin, the command of the regiment devolved on Major James Laughlin, and soon after the battle of Stone's River, the regiment went into camp at Lavergne, Tenn., a station on the Nashville and Chattanooga Railroad, about ten miles north from Murfreesborough. Companies B and D were stationed at Stewart's Creek, about midway between Lavergne and Murfreesborough. During the winter and spring months of 1863, the service of the regiment was very arduous, as the First was the only cavalry regiment on duty between Nashville and Murfreesborough to guard the communication along a railroad line of thirty miles, in addition to guarding the fords along Stone's River for many miles.

One brigade of infantry was stationed at Lavergne, commanded by General Ward, of Kentucky, but their service as compared with that of the cavalry was very light. The infantry was only called out when a reconnaissance was made in force or when a large wagon train was sent out some distance to forage for two or three days.

Buchanan's Mills, Dr. Charlton's ford and Dobson's on Stone's River are all names familiar to the members of the First Ohio, and with each of these familiar names some incident of interest can be recalled. The night march from Lavergne through dark cedars to Buchanan's Mills, and the burning of the mills at midnight can be recalled, and in imagination we can see the bright flames leaping high above the old mill, lighting up the dark forest along the banks of the stream. Another night is remembered, when a company of the Fourteenth Ohio Infantry and a platoon of Company K, First O.V. C. made a night march to the river for the purpose of capturing a squad of rebel cavalry who were in that vicinity, and a coloured man had come into our camp about dark and reported that a supper was being prepared for them at a house on the east side of the river. The detachment of our command arrived at the river about eleven o'clock, and cavalry and infantry were rowed over in a rickety boat by a faithful old coloured man, taking six at a load. Guided by this old darkey, the command marched to the house designated, but did not find any enemy, as they had no doubt been apprised of the movement of our men by some citizen on the alert, and they had made good their escape. A fine supper had been prepared, with covers for about twenty-five, and our boys proceeded at once to partake of the good things spread, to which they done ample justice. The only thing they contributed to the supper was coffee, of which they had an abundance, and which was made under the direction of the good lady of the house. There might have been a few crumbs left when the repast was finished, but it is doubtful whether or not twelve baskets could have been gathered from the table. It was a hard night's march and devoid of results from a military standpoint, but the boys thought there was a little glory in capturing the supper prepared for the enemy, and so there was. The captain in command thanked the lady of the house in a neat little speech for her hospitality to the defenders of the old flag, and became quite eloquent as he warmed up to his subject, but his eloquence fell on deaf ears, so far as any outward indications appeared. Quite a number of neighbouring ladies were present, and all were treated with the greatest respect and gallantry by the chivalric cavalrymen.

 We were kept on the move almost continuously, day and night, scouting and patrolling the river, and the many miles traversed over the by-roads among the cedars became as familiar as our neighbouring roads near our homes in Ohio.

Major-General Eli Long

During the months of April and May, a platoon, and some times a company was sent out each morning, leaving camp about three o'clock, so as to reach the fords along Stone's River about daybreak, sometimes striking the river at Buchanan's Mills, then patrolling up the river past Charlton's, leaving a squad at each ford to watch the movements of the enemy, and "report if any thing unusual was discovered." This kind of service was very monotonous, but now and then the monotony was relieved by a little skirmish. The roads were narrow, and the woods were very thick. Frequently scouting parties were fired upon by guerillas, who usually made their escape easily. One of our outposts was at Antioch Church, about three miles from Lavergne on the railroad, in the direction of Nashville. The home of Dick McCann, the notorious bushwhacker and guerila leader, was near this church, and he made a number of raids, capturing trains in this vicinity in spite of the vigilance of our troops.

At one time he piloted a large force of rebel cavalry to this point on the railroad and captured a train with a large amount of money in the express car. Our troops at Murfreesborough had just been paid off and the boys were expressing their money home, and whether or not the rebels were aware of that fact, they got a rich haul. Colonel Cupp, Lieutenant Leib and several other soldiers of the regiment were on the train en route for Nashville, all of whom were captured. They were paroled and returned to the regiment in a few days, and reported that some of the rebel cavalrymen had their haversacks full of greenbacks. We were kept on the alert all the time watching the movements of the enemy, and scarcely a day or night passed without some part of the regiment was called out to make a scout to ascertain whether or not some reported movement of the enemy was true or was only a "grape vine" reported by some frightened contraband. One day we would be hurried out on a gallop toward Triune or Eagleville, on the right flank; perhaps the same night we would be called out to reconnoitre along the fords of Stone's River, on the left flank, to check some movement of the enemy reported at headquarters. Thus we were kept continuously on the move, while the main body of the army was lying in camp having comparatively little, or in fact, no hard service. The cavalry are the eyes of the army, so to speak, and when two armies are lying in close proximity to each other, as were the armies of Rosecrans and Bragg, from January 1 to June 24, 1863, glaring at each other like two gladiators, watching for any advantage he may take over his antagonist from some weak place in his lines, by some movement of his troops, then it is that the commander appreciates the good service of his cavalry, handled by daring and intelligent young officers, for on their audacity and dash, when reconnoitering the enemy's position to get information, often the safety of the whole army depends. These two astute commanders of the Union and rebel armies seemed to be equally watchful and enterprising, and each was determined that the other should not get any advantage by movements on the flanks or rear, consequently the clashes between the cavalry of the two armies were frequent and some times lively. During the winter and early spring months there was a great deal of rain, and this continuous service in mud, sleet and rain, disabled many of the horses by "scratches" and cracked heels, as we had no shelter for them at any time, and they were covered with mud and water night and day, and it was impossible to keep them clean and dry, so that many horses were totally disabled. In some instances the disease was so bad that the hoofs would almost come off, and it was not possible to move horses in this condition. When the weather became warm and the roads dried up, these horses were soon cured, and the troops were all well mounted, adding quite a good many horses pressed into the service from the surrounding country. I think it is safe to say that at no time during our service were so many horses totally disabled as during the time we were stationed at Lavergne.

Some of the daring exploits of small scouting parties, often commanded by non-commissioned officers, would have done honour to an officer of high rank, notably the affair at Dobson's Ford, which appears in the official published list of the battles and skirmishes of the war. A patrol was sent out one morning under command of Sergeant Chapin, of Company K, and after patrolling up the river, halted at Dobson's to watch the ford for the day. The widow Dobson's house stood on the east bank of the river near the ford, and the patrol was stationed on the west side, directly opposite the house.

The Dobson family consisted of the widow and three hand some daughters, all bitter rebels, still they would smile sweetly on the gay cavalry boys now and then. Although their house was known to be the favourite rendezvous of the bushwhackers and rebel cavalry, still our boys would take the chance of visiting the girls, notwithstanding it was always attended with danger, and taking heed that "faint heart ne'er won fair lady," they would cross the ford to talk with the southern beauties over the garden wall.

On this particular morning, as usual, a couple of the troopers crossed the ford to have a chat with the girls, whom they found in an unusually friendly mood, and gave the troopers a very cordial invitation to go over and eat dinner, as they would have fried chicken and many other tempting dishes.

The boys were delighted and accepted as a matter of course, but when they joined the patrol and reported, the sergeant in command said, "Nay, there is a nigger in the wood-pile; those girls are entirely too friendly, so we will wait and watch developments."

The pickets were placed at a proper distance from the ford to watch for any scouting party of the enemy that might appear on the opposite bank of the river. All through the morning the girls could be seen flitting about the house and often appearing at the front door or yard, watching longingly for their tardy lovers who did not come, and the boys were swearing through their teeth, because the Sergeant had seen fit to exercise his authority and cut short the promised pleasures of the day. All day they watched, but no enemy appeared, and as the patrol usually started for camp about sun down, orders were given to ride down to the ford and water the horses before taking up the march.

Just as the platoon rode into the river and threw the reins down on their horses necks to allow them to drink, bang! bang! bang! came a volley from the high bank near the Dobson house, shot guns, yaugers, and revolvers, all joining in a general medley, as can only be given by a squad of bushwhackers, armed with all kinds of weapons. The platoon galloped back to the position they had occupied during the day, and then opened up on the enemy with their carbines, and, after a few volleys, routed them from their ambuscade and took possession of the ford, which they held until satisfied that the rebels had beat a hasty retreat from their ambuscade. The bank was so high on the opposite side of the river that the first volley went over the heads of our men, and not a man was touched, but as it was a complete surprise, and, under the circumstances, rallying as they did and holding the position with a little squad of less than a score of men, shows what discipline will do under the most trying crisis.

It was the intention of the Dobson family to induce the boys to take dinner, and at the proper time, when they were in the house, a signal would have been given, and this band of bushwhackers would have pounced down upon them, capturing their horses and equipments, and either killing or wounding all of the men before the detachment on the other side of the river could have rallied to their support. But the scheme failed, much to the disgust of the fair southern girls, as was learned a few days later by some of the same detachment, who crossed the ford to reconnoitre the situation and ascertain if any damage had resulted from the fusillade of their carbines. The girls were in the front door and did not meet the boys with the same sweet smiles as of old, but berated them in very severe and indignant language, pointing at a bullet hole just above the door made by one of our carbine balls.

The troopers retorted, that if they proposed to take a hand in the war by intriguing to have our troops, who had been kind to them and had protected their property and protected them as ladies, captured and murdered by bushwhackers, they must take the chances of war. This argument seemed to have the desired effect, and we were never after troubled by bushwhackers at Dobson's. They refused to give any information as to the loss of the rebels in the skirmish, but it was afterwards ascertained that a Lieutenant Buchanan and several of the band that infested the fords along Stone's Elver were wounded, and Buchanan was afterwards captured at his home.

This is only one of many similar incidents that were occurring almost daily in the cavalry service, testing the courage and coolness of our troopers under fire very often against great odds.

During the months of May and June, in addition to the regular scouting, patrol and picket duty, the regiment resumed mounted drill, and devoted much of the time to remounting and equipping for the coming campaign. The whole cavalry force was reorganized, and by the middle of June we were fully equipped and ready for the hard campaign soon to commence. The regiment remained in camp at Lavergne until June 18, and then joined the brigade at Murfreesborough, the Second Brigade, Second Cavalry Division, commanded by that ideal soldier, Colonel Eli Long, who, before the close of the war, was promoted to a Major-General "for gallant and conspicuous service on the field."

The Second Cavalry Division was now commanded by General Turchin, and General David S. Stanley was Chief of the Cavalry. The Third and Fourth Ohio Cavalry, belonging to the same brigade as the First, after the battle of Stone's River were encamped near Murfreesborough, and during the winter they were frequently engaged in skirmishing near Liberty, Lebanon and Alexandria. They at one time routed John Morgan's command, taking one hundred prisoners, and on April 3, at Snow's Hill, defeated a brigade of rebel cavalry arid cut the railroad in the rear of Bragg's army, near McMinnville, Tenn.

CHAPTER 13

From Murfreesborough to Chattanooga.
June 24-September 22, 1863

Cavalry Organization, June, 1863

Cavalry corps
Major-General David S Stanley, Commanding
Second Cavalry Division
Brigadier-General John B Turchin, Commanding
Second Brigade
Colonel Eli Long

Second Kentucky	Colonel Thomas P Nicholas
First Ohio	Colonel Beroth B Eggleston
Third Ohio	Lieutenant-Colonel Chas B Seidel
Fourth Ohio	Lieutenant-Colonel Oliver P Robie
Tenth Ohio	Colonel Chas Smith
Stokes Chicago Board of Trade	Captain James H Stokes

On the morning of June 24, 1863, the Army of the Cumberland struck tents and moved out with banners flying and drums beating, glad to break the monotony of camp life for the excitement and dangers of an active campaign.

This army was well uniformed, splendidly armed, and it may well be doubted if a better equipped or more confident army ever struck tents at the sound of the "general" or moved to the inspiring strains of martial music with a prouder step. "Reveille" sounded at early dawn; an hour later the "general" and "boots and saddles" and "to horse" followed in quick succession, and at six o'clock we were "booted and spurred," mounted and off to the front.

The Second Cavalry Division took the Readyville pike east, passing the gallows on which a few days before several bushwhackers had been hanged by the direction of General Rosecrans. A short time after we moved out a heavy rainstorm set in, which lasted for seventeen days in succession, and during all this time our blankets were never dried out, and our rations in our old greasy haversacks were a conglomerated mass of coffee, salt, sugar, sow-belly, and hard-tack. We moved on the extreme left of the army, passed through Readyville and, on the evening of the first day's advance, reached Bradyville, where our advance had a brisk skirmish, routed a detachment of rebel cavalry, taking a few prisoners, and got into camp wet, hungry, and patriotic, as only soldiers can be who fight for $13 a month and no questions asked.

I will now copy from my diary, kept daily during the war, the incidents of each day, which may not be of interest to the general reader, but which will be of absorbing interest to every soldier of the Second Cavalry Division who was in that memorable campaign, from Murfreesboro to Chickamauga.

June 25. Move at daybreak, march five miles and encounter a brigade of rebel cavalry, taking twenty prisoners. No loss on our side. Go into camp.

June 26. Advance three miles, but do not strike the enemy. Heavy cannonading on the right. Receive news this evening that General Thomas has taken "Hoover's Gap."

June 27. Moved out on the McMinnville pike, but all quiet in front. A heavy cavalry fight on the right at Shelbyville. Many rebels were crowded off bridges and drowned in Duck River, and many prisoners brought in with sabre cuts, which is ample proof of a hard hand-to-hand fight.

June 28. Strike tents at 3 a. m., and march fifteen miles

1. Gen. Wm. S. Rosecrans.
2. Gen. Geo. H. Thomas.
3. Gen. Braxton Bragg, C. S. A.
4. Gen. James Longstreet, C. S. A.

to Manchester, which is evacuated by the rebels with but little resistance. Manchester is a very pretty little town of about 1,000 inhabitants, situated on Duck River.

June 29. Remain here all day. Rain pouring down in torrents, and, just as we get snugly ensconced under "dog tents" and "gum blankets," with a prospect of a little sleep, an orderly passes along the line of tents at 7 p. m., singing out the unwelcome order, "Strike tents and be ready to march in half an hour!" We feel much more inclined to strike that orderly than striking tents; and, with a few adjectives in the superlative degree, consigning the fellow who issued the order to a very warm climate, we tumble out in the rain, pack up, and in half an hour we are in the saddle.

This is one of the interesting experiences of the cavalry man packing up all his worldly effects, dark as pitch, raining in torrents, no light not even so much as a coal of fire. First, find your horse, then your saddle, bridle, saddle-blanket, feed-sack, spurs, dog-tent, blanket, poncho, haversack, canteen, carbine, revolver, sabre all to be packed up according to the "rules and regulations." Try this, and if you do not admit that a soldier who can practice this kind of gymnastics for three or four years and always keep his temper, and still "stand by the old flag," is not an angel (barring the wings), then I will set up a canteen of apple jack for the crowd.

We took the road leading toward Tullahoma and marched through mud and rain all night. It seemed as if the whole army was on this road and spread out through woods and fields, vying with each other to see who could throw the most mud. I am confident that every comrade will agree that that was the softest night's march we had ever made during our term of service.

June 30. We are now but a few miles from Tullahoma, and a battle is imminent at any moment. Our company on picket, and this evening we have a brisk skirmish all along the lines.

Movements in McLemore's Cove

July 1. One of the boys of our company shot and wounded a soldier, in front of our lines, this morning, who proved to be a deserter from the rebel army at Tullahoma, but who the soldier that fired the shot mistook for a rebel picket slipping up to our lines. As he shouted to us that he was badly wounded, three of us moved cautiously down through the woods, picked him up and carried him back to the reserve. He was an old man, dressed in the usual Confederate gray, but he was not armed and had nothing about his person to indicate that he was a soldier, except that an old haversack hung over his shoulder. He was badly wounded and, on being interrogated, declared emphatically that Tullahoma was evacuated at daybreak that morning. His voice was so earnest and his face so impressive, that we could not doubt his statement. He also said that his name was S. H. D. Duncan, and that he was then trying to make his way to his home in Manchester, Tenn. Immediately on receiving the news of the evacuation of Tullahoma, which I knew, if true, was very important to the commanding General, I mounted my horse and galloped rapidly back to General Thomas headquarters and gave him the news of the evacuation of Tullahoma, as given by Duncan. Thomas at once called his Adjutant-General, Flint, and ordered an immediate forward movement of the army.

We were on picket in front of General Reynold's division, and as they advanced we moved out, and, as will be well remembered, rode into the works in front of Tullahoma without firing a shot. We all supposed that the man Duncan would die of his wounds in a few hours, but he recovered, and a few years ago, by writing to the postmaster at Manchester, I learned his address, and, on writing and receiving an answer, learned that he had always suffered from the wound and that one side of his body was paralysed.

On entering the works at Tullahoma we found that the rebels had abandoned much of their camp equipage, and the cornmeal was strewn over the ground so thickly that it looked like snow. We followed up the retreat rapidly toward Elk River, and overtook their rear guard at Beaver Fork, and here our regiment had a sharp fight, with a loss of several men wounded and one killed, Jack Hickman, of Company H. We captured quite a number of prisoners, and on the third a detachment of our regiment was sent to the rear with the prisoners and delivered them over to General Beatty, at Manchester, and I still have in my possession the receipt given by him for the safe delivery of the prisoners.

July 4. The regiment had a fight to-day and drove the rebels at every point on the line and took a number of prisoners. Billy Ball, of Company F, killed. Arrive at Decherd, on the Nashville and Chattanooga Railroad.

July 6. March south-west through Winchester, and all the cavalry of this department, consisting of twenty regiments, encamp together. Sergeant Henry E. Bumgardner, Company B, drowned in crossing Elk River.

July 7, 8, 9. In camp, sending out foraging expeditions every day.

July 10. Move camp to Salem, and on the eleventh send a large foraging party into Alabama.

July 12. Strike tents, and the whole brigade starts on a raid through Northern Alabama, and arrive at Huntsville at 12 o'clock on the thirteenth, having burned a railroad bridge fifteen miles east from here last night.

July 14 and 15. Remain in camp at Huntsville; large foraging and raiding parties sent out and bringing in large numbers of mules and horses.

July 16. March toward Athens and camp on Pine Creek, and on the seventeenth take possession of Athens, and remain here the eighteenth and nineteenth, and on the twentieth take up our march southward and arrive at Elkton, and on the twenty-first reach Pulaski, Tenn.

July 22. The brigade had a lively fight out on the picket line. Remain in camp here until the twenty-fifth, and then march to Faetteville, where our wagon train meets us for the first time since leaving Decherd on the sixth, not having any mail for three weeks, but now we all get letters from the "girl we left behind." We remain here until the first of August, and during our stay about 6,000 persons came in and took the oath of allegiance to save their mules, and then went immediately home, took their shotguns and went to bushwhacking.

We have now confiscated several hundred horses and mules, and the brigade is splendidly mounted. While stationed at Faetteville, the First Ohio published a newspaper called the *Cavalier*, which was edited by William Davis, of Company M, and A. Thompson, of Company D, with T. C. Stevenson and Joe Devreux, of Company D, publishers. The motto of the heading reads: "We Go Where Rebs Await Us." As will be remembered, it was a spicy sheet, and some poetic cavalryman wrote a parody on Morgan's mule, the first verse of which ran thus:

A planter came to camp one day,
His niggars for to find;
His mules had also gone astray,
And stock of every kind.
The planter tried to get them back,
And thus was made a fool,
For every boy in camp he met
Cried; Mister, here's your mule!

Chorus —
Go back, go back, go back old scamp,
And don't be made a fool;
Your niggars they are all in camp,
And Turchin's got your mule.

On the first day of August we struck tents and marched through Salem to Winchester, where we went into camp on the third. We remained at Winchester until the nineteenth, being paid off and the whole army reviewed and inspected. On the morning of the nineteenth we move at early dawn and in the evening camp at the foot of a range of the Cumberland mountains.

August 20. We take the mountain pass at daybreak and pass over the mountain called "The Smoky Range," and descend into the valley after a very hard day's march. We re-crossed the mountain on the twenty-first to assist our wagon train, which we found badly demoralized, many of the wagons being upset and broken to atoms on the rocks. This is a day long to be remembered as the wickedest day on record, as the swearing of the "mule whackers" would rival the demons of Hades and give them a discount of fifty.

August 22. March through Sinking Cove and through Stevenson to the Tennessee River, and on the twenty-third march five miles up the river toward Bridgeport. We picket the river and can plainly see the rebel pickets on the south bank, and Frank Allen, of Company K, with a few more of the boys, take a skiff and row across to pay the Johnnies a visit and trade coffee for "terbacker," while two of the Johnnies come over to visit the "Yanks" and take breakfast. We are on picket duty along the river until the twenty-ninth, when the First Ohio, Third Ohio, and Second Kentucky cross the river, making a successful raid on Trenton, Georgia, capturing many prisoners and a large quantity of stores. On the night of the twenty-eighth pontoons are thrown across the river a few miles below Stevenson and on the morning of the twenty-ninth those of us who are on picket can see the glistening bayonets of our infantry as they are crossing the river about a mile below us.

About this time the rebel pickets across the river rode down to water their horses, when our boys shouted across to them and insisted that they should come over and take breakfast, but the Johnnies, taking in the situation, "stood not upon the order of their going," but putting spurs to their horses went up the mountain pass at a rate of speed that would have put to shame John Gilpin.

We ford the river September 2, and march to the top of Sand Mountain, and on the third descend into the valley between

Sand and Lookout mountains, and on the fourth march through a beautiful cove and camp at the foot of Lookout.

September 5. We take the mountain pass at daybreak, and as the company which I had the honour to command led the advance that day, the boys of Company M will well remember that we had a lively time. My instructions from General Long were that when we "struck the enemy to fire, and then charge him." After reaching the top of the mountain we began to see signs of the enemy, and about noon the first shot was fired by the rebel pickets, and our advance under Corporal McMann raised their carbines, bang! bang! and away we go at a sweeping gallop for a mile or two in pursuit of the rebel pickets. When we reached the pass down the mountain we found our way obstructed by large pine trees cut down across the road along the sides of the mountain, and also by immense rocks rolled down from the ledges hundreds of feet above. Dismounting, we pushed on, the retreating enemy banging away at us from the rocks below, but doing but little damage. We drove them down the mountain into the valley, Generals Crook and Long being up with the skirmish line. As our horses were on top of the mountain further pursuit seemed useless, and only a few companies of the brigade having reached the valley, we were again ordered up the mountain pass, and the boys will bear testimony that we did not make the ascent as rapidly and with as much enthusiasm as we made the descent, with ball and buckshot whizzing through the pine brush and spattering against the rocks. On the top of the mountain we found a large and well cultivated plantation with a peach orchard of about ten acres. We rode into the cornfields to feed our horses, some of the more inquisitive of the boys made a reconnaissance and discovered a still-house where the old planter was engaged in the very laudable business of manufacturing peach brandy. We could then very well understand why the rebel cavalry had made such stubborn resistance for the possession of the top of the mountain, for where was the soldier, "Rebel" or "Yank," who would not fight for territory where there was a prospect of rations, forage for his horse, tobacco or peach brandy? It soon became evident to the officers, from the number of canteens that were being filled, that there was some kind of liquid on that plantation more attractive than spring water or sorghum molasses. General Long sent Captain Scott, of the First Ohio, to reconnoitre the position of the enemy and order every soldier to his command under penalty of arrest. "Scotty" was a brave and gallant soldier, but he was not averse to taking a nip himself for his stomach's sake. General Long soon dispatched an other staff officer to see what Scott was doing and found him standing on a barrel swearing roundly at the boys "not to waste any of the brandy," while two or three fellows were industriously employed boring holes in the barrels with an inch augur. As some of the boys were becoming boisterous and unmanageable, the General declared that the best thing to do was to move out. "To horse" was sounded and the brigade started, and I think I am safe in saying that fully half the horses were without riders. To say that we had a lively time going down the mountain pass that dark night is drawing it very mild. It seemed as if the very Old Nick was in that peach brandy, and I am sure some of the officers will agree with me that they would rather take their chances in a fight than go through the experience of that night again. But we all got to the foot of the mountain by morning, and those that could not ride down or walk down, just fell down.

We drank from the same canteen

It was sometimes water and sometimes milk,
Sometimes apple-jack fine as silk.
But wherever the tipple has been,
We shared it together, in bane or in bliss,
And I warm to you, boys, when I think of this,
We have drank from the same canteen.

Chorus —
The same canteen, my soldier friends,
The same canteen
There's never a bond like this
We have drank from the same canteen.

September 6. We move four miles up the valley and go into camp, and remain until the morning of the eighth, and march to the top of Lookout.

September 9. Descend the mountain on the east and strike the enemy in the evening at Alpine, about 3 o'clock. The whole brigade, with artillery, engaged, and have a sharp fight for an hour. The First is ordered to the right, and Company G, under Captain Frankenberger, and Company M, under Lieutenant Curry, move forward as skirmishers, and, by some misunderstanding, the balance of the regiment is halted, and these two companies are exposed to a heavy fire from the enemy for twenty or thirty minutes. Five men of Company M, and several of Company G wounded. Total loss in the First, thirty. We soon drive the enemy from their position, and learn from prisoners that we are fighting Wheeler's cavalry.

September 10. The brigade made a reconnaissance up the valley on the Chattanooga road, strike the enemy in the evening and have a running fight, drive them a few miles and return to Alpine. Lay in camp all day of the eleventh, and on the morning of the twelfth move out on the Lafayette and Chattanooga road; have a skirmish, take a few prisoners and lay in line of battle all night with horses saddled.

September 13. This is Sabbath morning and we move early; march ten miles and strike the rebel cavalry, drive them and run into a brigade of infantry, charge them and take twenty prisoners, with a loss of three killed and ten wounded. Learn from prisoners that a corps of the rebel army is camped at Lafayette. We move back down the valley to Alpine, our men much worn out, as the weather is very warm and this has surely been the dustiest day's march we have ever had.

The Confederate General, A. D. Hill, in his account of the battle of Chickamauga, published in the *Century Magazine*, April, 1887, says that he was encamped at Lafayette on that day, with his division, and says "that when the attack was made the boldness of the attack by these two regiments of cavalry, the First and Third Ohio, convinced me that an infantry column was not far off. General Polk's brigade was hurried down from Pigeon Mountain, and all preparations were made for a great battle."

September 14. Take the pass and march to the top of Lookout, and on the fifteenth move across the mountain towards Neal's Pass, strike rebel bands and charge them, Companies G and M in advance, taking many prisoners.

September 16. Go down Doherty Pass into McLamoore's Cove after forage. We can see heavy clouds of dust rising to the north-east from the moving armies twenty-five miles distant.

September 17. Lay in camp all day, both armies manoeuvring for position, and a great battle is momentarily expected.

September 18. Make a reconnaissance down Neal's Pass and return to camp.

September 19. Strike tents and march down the mountain into McLamoore's Cove, distance of twenty miles. My company on picket to-night, close to the enemy's lines.

September 20. March at daybreak and form a junction with the right wing of our army near Crawfish Springs, and form our line of battle at 9 o'clock, and before we get into line the rebel batteries are shelling us. Our brigade engages the enemy immediately and soon the rattle of our carbines breaks the stillness of this calm and beautiful Sabbath morning. The battle rages for two hours with dismounted cavalry and our brave boys of the Chicago Board of Trade battery. Our lines were being rapidly pressed back, and by some blunder or misunderstanding in an order the First Ohio was ordered to mount and charge a line of rebel infantry. Lieutenant-Colonel Cupp, commanding the regiment, gave the command, "draw sabre," and led his regiment forward into the cornfield, and had just formed for the charge when the blunder was discovered, and the order countermanded. Had they made this charge, scarcely a man could have escaped, as a solid line of infantry was advancing. Just at this moment Colonel Cupp was killed and almost one fifth of the rank and file were killed and wounded.

The brigade fell back slowly through the woods, keeping up a heavy fire on the advancing columns of Confederate infantry. The Chicago Board of Trade Battery remained with the rear line and kept up a continuous fire from her guns, and sent shot and shell crashing through the rebel lines.

The brigade fell back seven or eight hundred yards to Crawfish Springs and formed in some old fields and awaited with drawn sabres the attack from the enemy, but it seemed that they were not in condition to renew the attack, and skirmishers were immediately advanced from the brigade to reconnoitre the front, and moved forward without any resistance from the enemy and took possession of the field, bringing off many of our wounded, including Colonel Cupp.

Our Surgeons established a hospital in the brick house at Crawfish Springs and left several nurses when we moved back in the woods, and here Colonel Cupp died about 4 o'clock that evening.

We stood in line of battle about two hours, from 2 to 4 o'clock. During all this time the thundering of Thomas artillery was heard on the left, and I have always believed that this was the heaviest artillery firing we heard during the war.

In this battle our brigade lost 145 men out of 900 in line. Of my old Company K, Sergeant J. W. Chapin was severely wounded, and was left on the field and reported dead for three months. Among others wounded were Sergeant C. S. Irwin, John Young, Billy Hiser, and Abe Orr killed. My own horse was shot, and after Sergeant Irwin was put into an ambulance, I mounted his horse, which I think saved me from falling into the hands of the enemy. I remember that Irwin's saddle was covered with blood, and he had bled so profusely that the blood run down both his horse's fore legs and down over the hoofs, and he remained in that condition several days. About 4 o'clock we commenced falling back, and marched until about 2 o'clock in the morning. It was a cold, frosty night, and as the army fell back fences, cotton gins and other buildings were burned and kept a bright light along the route.

We laid in line of battle the balance of the night, and early on the morning of the twenty-first we wheeled our lines and moved out cautiously to meet the advancing lines of the enemy.

After marching down the valley about two miles we struck their skirmishers and we deployed and formed in line of battle. After halting, I remember of looking down the line as the men sat on their horses at an "advance carbine," all intensely watching the advancing columns of the enemy that were plainly in view across some open fields with colours flying and bayonets glistening in the bright September sun. Many faces in our line were pale, but no sign of wavering as we momentarily expected the battle to open, and it impressed me as being the grandest scene I had ever looked upon. Now and then a puff of white smoke would rise and a minnie ball would come zip through the branches over our heads.

An incident occurred just at this time in front of our line that touched the heart of many a grim and sun-bronzed veteran. The First Ohio was formed on the left of the road and just as we moved "front into line," a battery (perhaps the Chicago Board of Trade) came down the road on the gallop and went crashing through the brush and over the logs on the right of the road. Immediately in front of their line and but a few yards distant was a little pine log cabin with a few acres cleared around it. Hearing a piercing cry as if coming from the cabin, and looking in that direction, we saw a woman running from the door and through the yard with a child in her arms and two or three other small children clinging to her dress. The mother and children were all screaming most pitifully. In front of them was the rebel line, in the rear was our line. Halting for a moment at the rail fence around the yard, she looked imploringly around, and after lifting the children over the fence, and with the babe in her arms and another little one clinging to her hand, she started through the little cornfield parallel to our line, while the balls from the skirmish lines of the enemy were cutting the corn blades on every side. But she seemed to have a charmed life and soon disappeared in the woods on the right, and a fervent "thank God" went up from the long line of blue, and not one of these old veterans, that could stand unmoved amid the carnage of battle, but would have risked his life between those two skirmish lines to save that mother and her little ones. This was a very touching incident and I, with many others, no doubt, have often wondered what became of the mother and children.

After a sharp skirmish, the firing ceased, and we lay in line of battle all day. In the evening we moved out and felt the line in front, and found it strong and in very close proximity to ours. Our skirmish lines were so near together that our boys got up a conversation with the Johnnies about dark, one reb singing out, "When's you all going down to Atlanta?" and another asking, "Where is old Granny Burnsides now?" To both of these questions our boys were not able to give a very satisfactory answer. We lay in line all night holding our horses by the bridle and ready to mount at the first gun.

On the morning of the twenty-second General Long came galloping out to the front and directed our Colonel to "Mount his regiment and to order his pickets to join the regiment and fall back rapidly up the Chattanooga Valley." We were soon in the saddle moving to the rear, and after marching two or three miles the rebel skirmishers began firing into our right flank, and a battery soon opened out and the shells came falling thick and fast into our ranks. Companies G and M of the First were ordered by General Long to charge into the woods to the right and check the advance. Captain Frankenberger had command of Company G, and I was in command of Company M, and just as we struck the woods Captain Frankenberger said to me, "Bill, Colonel Long never expects us to get out of this, but I do, and as soon as we strike the advance we will fire a volley and get out of here most devilish quick." We moved forward very cautiously, and had not penetrated the pine woods but a short distance when the rebel skirmish line opened fire on us, which we answered with a volley from our carbines, then moved "twos left about" and fell back rapidly into the valley, which we reached to find that the command was almost out of sight, perhaps a mile distant. Sergeant Young was just coming in with the pickets, and joining our squadron, we all moved up the valley at a brisk gallop.

Just as we overtook the command, the shells commenced falling thick and fast from a rebel battery over the ridge to the right. Our division dismounted, and, forming line, we moved up the ridge, and a division of infantry, that had been sent out from Chattanooga to reinforce us, formed on our left. After a brisk skirmish and driving the rebel line back some distance, we then fell back to our horses, and mounting, marched up the Chattanooga Valley, past the signal station at Somerville, on Lookout Mountain, and into Chattanooga.

The first indication we had that we were nearing Chattanooga was in seeing the black smoke rising from many burning buildings on the outskirts of the city that were in the range of our batteries in the fortifications. We marched through the breastworks and into Chattanooga about 1 o'clock p.m., *Tuesday, September 22*, and as we have always understood, the last troop of Rosecrans array to reach Chattanooga after the battle of Chickamauga.

Thousands of army wagons, ambulances, and mule teams were crowded and jammed in the narrow streets, all anxiously and impatiently awaiting their turn to cross the one pontoon bridge across the Tennessee River. After halting a short time, our command forded the river just within the city limits, to the north-east.

Thus ended the Chickamauga campaign, beginning at Murfreesboro, June 24, and culminating in the hard-fought battle of Chickamauga, September 19 and 20, 1863, being one of the most brilliant campaigns of the war, and General Rosecrans could truly say, as did Sherman after the capture of Atlanta, "Chattanooga is ours, and fairly won."

Monument of the First Ohio Cavalry at Chickamauga

The ground selected for locating the monument of the First, Third and Fourth Ohio Cavalry was near the house of Widow Weather's, but it was afterwards moved further north and east, and the monument is now located about three hundred feet west from the Widow Glen's house, where General Rosecrans had his headquarters, and between Dry Valley Road and the railroad now running from Chattanooga to Rome, about four hundred yards south from Bloody Pond, and a half mile from Battle Station on the Chattanooga and Rome Railroad, and was erected by the State of Ohio at a cost of $1500. The photograph, from which the cut of the monument published in this history, was made, was taken on the field after the monument was erected, the front facing the east and toward the Widow Glen's house, showing the pine trees in the rear, and the forest across Dry Valley, toward the west and south of the Vidito house. The monument is about eleven feet high, and nine feet wide. In the cut published is shown the front of the monument, and on the other side the following inscription appears:

First Ohio Volunteer Cavalry

Organized at Camp Chase, Ohio
August 17 to October 5, 1861
Re-enlisted *January 4, 1864*
Mustered out at Hilton Head, S. C., September 13, 1865

Fought at Glass Mills on Chickamauga Creek, five and one-half miles due S.W. from this point from 10 a. m. to 1 p. m., September 20, 1863. Held second line at Crawfish Springs until 4 p. m., then fell back by road in rear of Lee House, N.W. across ridge to Chattanooga Valley. Colonel Cupp mortally wounded 12 M. September 20; died at Lee House, 4 p. m.

Officers Commanding

Lieutenant-Colonel Valentine Cupp, Commanding Regiment	
Captain G F Conn	Company B
Lieutenant J W Kirkendall	Company D
Lieutenant A D Lutz	Company E
Captain Lafayette Pickering	Company F
Captain J C Frankenberger	Company G
Lieutenant D A Roush	Company H
Captain J P Rea	Company I
Captain W H Woodlief	Company K
Captain J D Barker	Company L
Lieutenant W L Curry	Company M

The First, Third and Fourth are the only monuments of Ohio cavalry regiments erected on the Chickamauga battle-field. Ohio has erected on the battle-field of Chickamauga fifty-five monuments, as follows:

Infantry Regiments

1, 2, 6, 9, 10, 11, 13, 14, 15, 17, 18, 19, 21, 24, 26, 31, 33, 35, 36, 40, 41, 49, 51, 52, 59, 64, 65, 69, 74, 89, 90, 92, 93, 94, 98, 99, 101, 105, 113, 121, 124, 125, regiments.

Cavalry Regiments

First, Third and Fourth Regiments.

First Battalion Ohio Sharp-Shooters Artillery

Independent Batteries Ohio Light Artillery, Sixth, Eighteenth and Twentieth.

Batteries A, B, C, F, G and M, First Regiment, Ohio Light Artillery.

Ohio had a larger representation here than on any other battle-field of the war, and more soldiers here than came from any other state in the Union on the Union side, and more than came from any state on the Confederate side, excepting Tennessee alone.

CHAPTER 14

Chickamauga Campaign
June-September, 1863

When General Rosecrans army advanced from Murfreesboro on the twenty-fourth day of June, 1863, Bragg was strongly entrenched north of Duck River, his line extending from McMinnville on the right to Columbia on his left flank. Rosecrans first made a feint as if he intended attacking Bragg's left, but his objective was the right of Bragg's army. The enemy was driven through Liberty Gap and Hoover's Gap on the twenty-fourth, and on the twenty-fifth a severe battle was fought at Liberty Gap, the Union troops engaged being Johnson's division, and our loss was two hundred and thirty killed and wounded, but that of the enemy was much heavier, as they made the assault against a very strong position held by our troops, and lost, in killed and wounded, eight hundred and fifty. On the twenty-sixth, Thomas made steady advance towards Manchester, and had some sharp fighting, and on the twenty-seventh drove the enemy out of Manchester, taking a number of prisoners. On the same day the cavalry, under Stanley, attacked Wheeler's cavalry at Shelbyville, captured a battery, with five hundred prisoners, drove the enemy across the bridge at Duck River, and about two hundred of the enemy were killed or driven into the river and drowned. There was only one bridge, and as there was a regular stampede, many men and horses were forced off the bridge, and as the stream was deep and rapid, both men and horses were drowned. By the thirtieth Rosecrans whole army was in front of Tullahoma, and as the enemy was strongly fortified, it was expected that he would give battle, but on the night of the thirtieth Bragg evacuated Tullahoma, retreated rapidly across Elk River, with our army in hot pursuit. The cavalry had some sharp fighting at Elk River, but the stream was at high flood, as it had been raining almost continuously since the twenty-fourth, and the waters in all streams were so high that but little progress could be made after Bragg had crossed Elk River. Rosecrans loss in the nine days campaign was about one hundred killed and five hundred wounded. We took one thousand six hundred and twenty nine prisoners, eleven pieces of artillery, and while Bragg's loss in killed is not known, yet it is safe to say that his loss, in killed and wounded, was one thousand, as he lost eight hundred and fifty at Liberty Gap. A brief rest was then given both of our armies, excepting our cavalry. On the twelfth of July, Stanley, with his whole cavalry force, started on a great cavalry raid through Northern Alabama *via* Huntsville. This expedition was gone about two weeks and brought back three hundred prisoners, fifteen hundred horses and mules, twelve hundred cattle and sheep, and six hundred negroes, with a vast amount of provisions. As Rosecrans was getting farther away from his base of supplies, it now required about one-fourth of his effective force to guard his communication back to Louisville, and this important matter gave him great concern in preparing for the next forward movement of his army. Chattanooga was his objective, and his army commenced the movement across the Cumberland Mountains August 16. By the fourth of September our army was all across the Tennessee River, and they began to advance over Sand Mountain. Rosecrans had now decided to move on Bragg's communication through the mountain passes to the south, instead of attacking him at Chattanooga, and the movement was commenced at once.

The cavalry under Stanley, with two brigades from McCook's corps of infantry, crossed the Tennessee River, below Stevenson, and made a reconnaissance toward Lafayette, Ga.

Major-General George Crook

On the eighth Bragg evacuated Chattanooga and Rosecrans took possession of that stronghold without even a skirmish, and General Crittenden's troops were the first to occupy the town. Rosecrans was led to believe that Bragg was retreating, when in fact he was concentrating his army for the purpose of striking Rosecrans army in detail as they emerged from the mountain passes. Rosecrans' army passed over Lookout and Sand Mountains as rapidly as possible, and on the ninth Stanley's cavalry had a sharp fight at Alpine and ascertained that Bragg was not retreating. From the ninth to the nineteenth there was continuous manoeuvring by both armies and several severe engagements. Through the coves, valleys and mountain gaps troops were kept on the march, each wily commander striving for the mastery, and it seems that each commander was completely deceived as to the designs of the other. Stanley's cavalry made a reconnaissance from Alpine toward Lafayette on the thirteenth, had a sharp fight, took some prisoners, and found that Hill's division of Longstreet's corps was at Lafayette, and this was the first intimation we had received that Longstreet's troops had arrived. McCook, with Stanley's cavalry, ascended the mountain on the night of the thirteenth and marched along the mountain road to Stevens' Gap, where they descended and Crook's cavalry division was stationed at Dougherty's Gap. Bragg having failed to crush Rosecrans' army in "detail" decided to give battle by attacking the left of the Union army and concentrated his army for that purpose, but Rosecrans, anticipating his design, moved several divisions to his left during the night of the eighteenth and on the morning of the nineteenth General Thomas confronted Bragg's right ready for battle. The fight opened on our extreme left and the battle was soon raging from left to right. The battle opened at 7:30 near Jay's Mills between Croxton's brigade of the Union army and Forest's cavalry, dismounted, and raged with great fury all day and into the night, and the two armies surged back and forth many times on different parts of the line, with varying success, and when the battle ended on the night of the nineteenth Rosecrans held the roads and passes between Bragg and Chattanooga, and the slaughter in both armies had been fearful. The night of the nineteenth was one of great anxiety to the commanders and a busy night for the troops moving into position for the great struggle which the soldiers of both armies felt assured would take place on the twentieth for the possession of the Lafayette Road. Many changes were made in the formation of the lines and the troops from the right of the Union line were shifted to the left and near the centre of the Union army.

    The battle opened on the morning of the twentieth, about 9:30 o'clock, by Breckenridge's division attacking Baird, and Beatty's brigade of the Union army and Helm's brigade of the Confederate army were so shattered that they were both com-

CRAWFISH SPRINT—THE OLD WHEEL

pelled to withdraw from the field. The fighting on the Union left was terrific, as Breckenridge was desperate in his effort to turn and envelope the left flank of Rosecrans' army. From early morn of that bright September Sabbath day until dark, shot and shell were hissing and screaming through the pine forests along the Chickamauga and mowing great swathes among the ranks of the blue and the gray. The battle lines swayed back and forth, now in the thick woods and again across the open fields, with wounded, dead and dying of both armies mingled together, and when darkness hovered over the field of blood and carnage, both armies were exhausted and there had been but little change in the lines excepting on the right of the Union army. It is not possible in the meagre space that can be used in a regimental history to enter into the details of any great battle, and in writing of the battle of Chickamauga, the author can only skeletonize, and give the strength of the opposing armies with losses. As it is well known to every reader, the Union army was pierced in the centre by Longstreet's forces, and the Union right was swept from the field back through McFarland's Gap, and Rosecrans, with a number of prominent corps and division

commanders, did not halt until they reached Chattanooga, leaving General Thomas to fight the whole Confederate army. From noon until dark, with five divisions, the Bock of Chickamauga held his lines and beat back the fierce assaults of the Confederates for six long hours, and then withdrew his troops in good order, thus saving our army from total defeat. Van Horn, in his history of the Army of the Cumberland, uses the following language regarding the crisis in the battle when Steedman's division of Granger's corps arrived on the field:

> The noise of the conflict had penetrated the murky cloud which overhung the bloody field, and reached General Granger far to the left and rear, suggested the need of his troops where the battle was so hotly raging. Accordingly, he had moved forward rapidly, in disregard of the enemy's effort to arrest his progress, and at the moment of great-

est need reported to General Thomas with two brigades. As the enemy moved down the northern slope of the ridge toward the rear of Brannan and Wood, Whittaker's and Mitchell's brigades of Steedman's division, with a fury born of the impending peril, charged the foe and drove him over the ridge, and then formed a line of battle from Brannan's right to the hill above Viditos, in front of Longstreet's left flank. In gaining this position there was heavy loss, but if the issue of battle has ever given compensation for the loss of valuable lives, it was this action, for the opportune aid of these two brigades saved the army from defeat and rout.

General H. V. Boynton, in his history of the battle of Chickamauga, gives the strength of the two armies and losses as follows:

The battle of Chickamauga, aside from its sanguinary features, was one of the most remarkable of the whole war, inasmuch as neither army was victorious and each withdrew from the field. The pen of the critic has been busy with this memorable engagement for many years, but it is not the province of the writer to say who was or is right, or who wrong; it is sufficient to know that, however the battle was conducted, General Rosecrans obtained his object, the occupation and retention of Chattanooga.

The losses sustained by both armies in this conflict were simply appalling. Each commander claimed he fought superior numbers, and in the absence of official reports dependence is had upon the estimates of officers who were in position to know. General Rosecrans had in action thirty brigades of infantry, five of cavalry, one of mounted infantry and thirty-three batteries, aggregating 50,160 officers and enlisted men. His casualties were 1,656 killed, including General Lytle, 9,749 wounded, among them Generals King, Starkweather and Whittaker, and 4,774 missing, a total of 16,179. General Bragg had on the field thirty-five brigades of infantry, ten of cavalry and about thirty batteries, probably all told, 65,000. He lost in general officers, Brigade Generals Deshler, Helm, Preston and Smith, killed; Major-General Hood and Brigade Generals Adams, Benning, Brown, Bunn, Clayton, Cleburne, Gregg and McNair, wounded; 2,389 officers and enlisted men killed, 13,412 wounded and 2,000 missing, a total of 17,801, and a combined total of 33,980.

All things considered, the battle of Chickamauga, for the forces engaged, was the hardest fought and the bloodiest battle of the Rebellion. Hindman, who fought our right at Horseshoe Ridge, says in his official report that 'he had never known Federal troops to fight so well and that he never saw Confederate soldiers fight better.'

To the enemy the results of the engagement proved a victory barren of any lasting benefits, and produced no adequate results to the immense drain on the resources of his army. In a number of places Bragg's official report shows that his army was so crippled that he was not able to strengthen one portion of his line, when needed, with troops from another part of the field, and after the conflict was over his array was so cut up that it was impossible for him to follow up his apparent success and secure possession of the objective point of the campaign—Chattanooga. This great gateway of the mountains remaining in the possession of the Army of the Cumberland, after Bragg had paid the heavy price he did at Chickamauga, proves that this battle was a victory only in name, and a careful examination of the results and their costs will show how exceedingly small it was to the enemy.

Headquarters
Fourteenth Army Corps
Crumpton's Creek
July 1, 1863

Major-General Reynolds,
Commanding Fourth Division
Orders have been given to General Brannan to send Sted-

man's brigade forward to reconnoitre as near Tullahoma as possible. The general directs that you support his left with your two regiments and what cavalry you have at your disposal. It is believed from pretty good authority that the last of the rebels left Tullahoma last night. You will be prepared to move should this information prove authentic.
Very respectfully, your obedient servant,
Geo. E. Flynt, Assistant Adjutant-General & Chief of Staff.

The above order was issued on the information furnished by Company K, of the First Ohio Cavalry. On the morning of the first a man by the name of Duncan was shot on the picket line in front of Company K and badly wounded, and he stated that Tullahoma was evacuated. This information was immediately transmitted to General Thomas by Lieutenant Curry and the above order was issued at once, and Company K led the advance of Reynolds division into Tullahoma.

<blockquote>
Extracts from report of
D. S. Stanley, Chief of Cavalry
</blockquote>

<blockquote>
Camp near Winchester
July 8, 1863
</blockquote>

We arrived at this place at 1 p. m. and found that the small force under General Turchin's command had been repulsed in their attempt to cross in the forenoon, and immediately measures were taken to force the passage. This was effected with little opposition, a fortunate circumstance, as the current was swift and almost swam a horse. Colonel Long's small brigade crossed first, and was soon engaged in a very heavy skirmish with the enemy's cavalry, driving them in the direction of Decherd.

This skirmish was disastrous to the enemy, one of his colonels being killed and one mortally wounded, who fell into our hands, besides twenty killed and many wounded left on the field.

Camp of First Ohio Cavalry
Near Winchester, Tenn.
July 9, 1863

Sir: I have the honour to report the operations of the four companies, B, D, H and K, detached from the brigade on the thirtieth of June. I was ordered to report to General Brannan on the Winchester road, and from him ordered to report to General Crook for picket duty. The General ordered me to call in my pickets and take position on the right of his advance. My position on the march placed me in a dense thicket. We had more or less skirmishing all the way to Elk River. Late in the afternoon of July 2, the enemy fired on my extreme right from the brush. The three companies were immediately fronted into line, commanded respectively, Captain Conn, of Company B, Captain Erwin, of Company D, and Lieutenant Roush, of Company H, and commenced firing immediately, which lasted for about fifteen or twenty minutes, before the enemy's firing ceased. It is with regret that I have to announce the death of Private Jackson Hickman, of Company H, who was killed instantly while gallantly and faithfully performing his duty.

I had two horses killed and ten men wounded.

James N. Scott, Major
Commanding Detachment First O.V. C.

Report of Major-General David S. Stanley

U. S. Army
Winchester
July 22, 1863

Major-General W. S. Rosecrans

General: I arrived here this morning. Long's brigade is at Pulaski. Long will go to Lawrenceburg and further if I can hear anything from Biffle, and attack him. I brought away in all about 300 contrabands, collected about 500 cattle, and the same number of horses and mules. A force

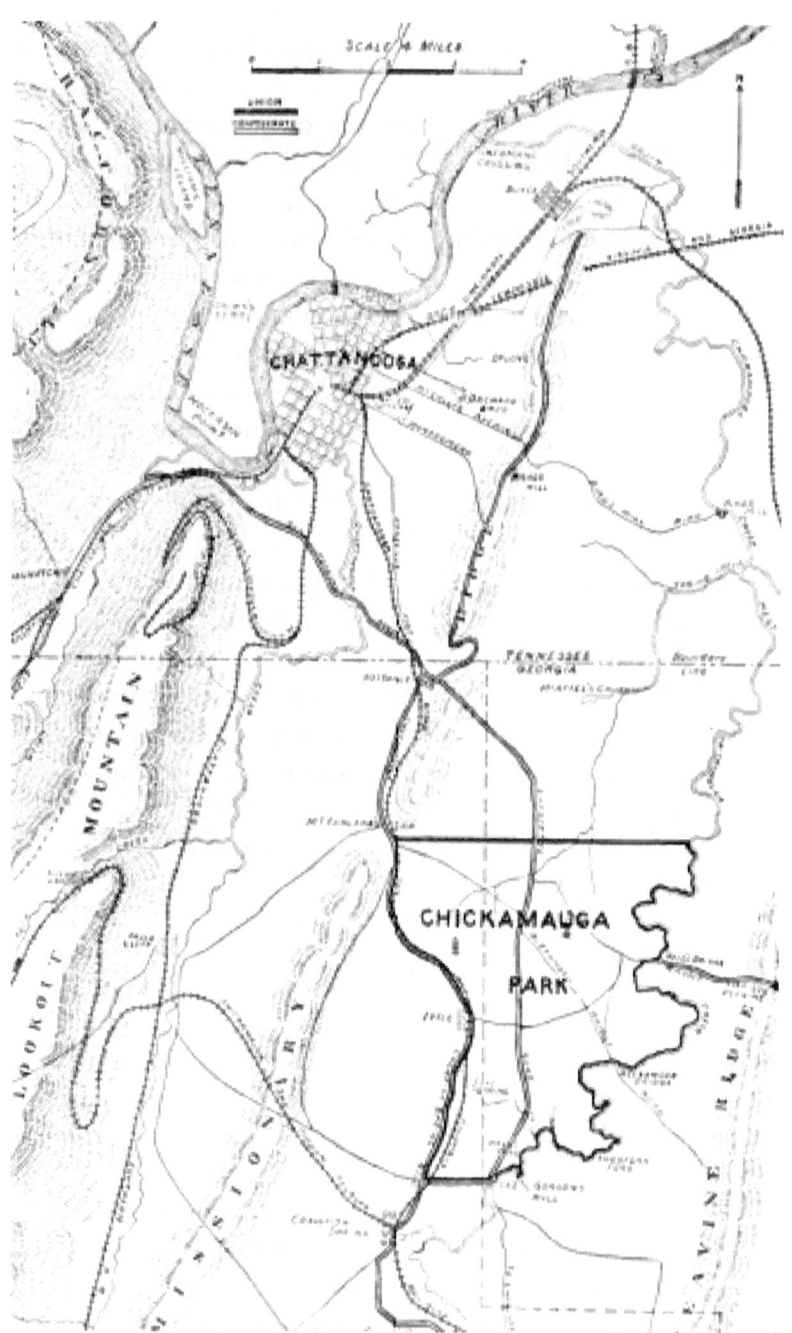

THE NATIONAL PARK AND ITS APPROACHES

of 10,000 could be subsisted in the Huntsville country—plenty of corn, mutton and beef, and if we don t eat, the rebels will.

Extract from report of
Major-General D. S. Stanley

Camp five miles from Winston's
September 3, 1863, 7 p. m.

General: Crook's at Winston's, south of Davis. Wheeler is said to be at Lebanon, which is twenty-four miles from this place; Rawlingsville is twelve miles from. here. We found the march too long to go through today. As soon as I get the cavalry well together, I will move Wheeler.

Headquarters Twentieth Army Corps
Near Winston's
September 7, 1863

General: General Sheridan is encamped at the Narrows, on the Trenton road, about fourteen miles from here. General Stanley starts early tomorrow. From all we can learn it seems quite likely that we may remain hereabouts until his return develops the truth as to the numbers and position of the enemy. General Rosecrans thinks General Johnston has been quite largely re-enforced. A forage party from the First Division was attacked this morning; result not yet ascertained.
G. P. *Thruston,* Chief of Staff

Extract from report of General Crook

Headquarters Second Cavalry Division
Camp Big Will's Valley, Ala.
September 8, 1863

Major: In accordance with orders received from the Major-General commanding cavalry corps, on the morning of the fifth of September I marched from camp at Winston's with two regiments (First and Third Ohio) of the Second Brigade of this division, and proceeded up the mountain at Winston's Gap and then moved forward across the mountain toward Broomtown Valley. From information gained from citizens and residents, it appeared that a body of the enemy's cavalry, supposed to be three companies, had crossed the mountain that evening in the direction of Winston's Gap, for the purpose of blockading the road up the mountain, but upon meeting with our pickets, or learning of their whereabouts, returned upon the road in the direction of Broomtown Valley, with the intention of blockading the road leading down the mountain into the valley. When within three miles of the top and five miles from the valley, our advance guard was fired on by the enemy's pickets. The advance, under Lieutenant Curry of the First Ohio Cavalry, charged the enemy gallantly and drove them back to the pass. Here we found the road down the mountain obstructed by rolling large rocks from the ledges above, and by trees felled across the pass down the mountain. I ordered one hundred to be dismounted and proceed to the foot of the mountain, it being impracticable for horses on account of fallen timber.

Extract from report of
Assistant Adjutant-General G. P. Thurston:

September 8, 1863, 8 p.m.

Major-General P. H. Sheridan
Commanding Third Division

Eight deserters from the Fourth Georgia Cavalry came into our lines today, having left Wharton's division last night near Alpine.

General Stanley starts in the morning with about two-thirds of his effective force. He expects to meet Wheeler's force the first or second day and thinks they will probably fight him. We sent two brigades to Alpine and a third on the mountain for the purpose of protecting their rear. They will be gone four days for the purpose of supporting Stanley and covering his return.

Henderson's Gap
Near Dorsey's Tan-yard
September 9, 1863, 6:30 p. m.

General: I received your dispatch directing me to make a reconnaissance to Summerville, and another by the route General Crook crossed the mountain. At the time I received the dispatch we were near the barricade the enemy had thrown across the gap. We here first struck their pickets, and continued to fight them back through Alpine, where they took the Home road, some going on the Blue Pond road. We took about a dozen prisoners. I send you the dispatches taken from one of Wheeler's couriers. I do not understand their import, excepting that he is concentrating at Lafayette. The labour getting down the mountain today and the fight brought us to nightfall. I occupy Alpine. I have rumours that Bragg is retreating south of the Ostanaula; I have no definite information. The enemy fought stubbornly from the foot of the mountain. The country is well adapted to their mode of warfare. We have had two men killed and seven wounded.

D. S. Stanley, Chief of Cavalry

Extract from dispatch of
Brigadier-General J. A. Garfield

Headquarters
Department of the Cumberland
Chattanooga
September 11, 1863, 10:45 p. m.

Major-General Stanley
Chief of Cavalry

It appears that the enemy has been concentrating a very large force of infantry in the vicinity of Lafayette. If he intends to make a stand, it will be necessary for you to close up your force toward McCook, so as to cover his left flank and operate on the enemy's right. It is now of the utmost importance that the General commanding should be informed as soon as possible of the force and position of the enemy. Take measures to ascertain this as soon as possible.

Headquarters Cavalry
Alpine, Ga.
September 12, 1863, 3 p. m.

Brigadier-General J. A. Garfield
Chief of Staff:

I sent Crook today, with the entire force of cavalry, to drive into Lafayette and see what they have at that place. I shall hear from him in a couple of hours. My belief is that the rebels will not fight at Lafayette, but at Resaca.

D. S. Stanley, Major-General

Henderson's Gap, Ala.
September 13, 1863, 8 p. m.

General: The reconnaissance sent to Lafayette to determine the position of the enemy returned this evening. General Crook went within three miles of there this a. m., and charged and drove their cavalry through their infantry, and captured about twenty of their infantry pickets belonging to the Thirteenth Louisiana. They say they belong to Breckenridge's division and that all of Johnston's army except one division, which has been sent to Charleston, had re-enforced Bragg. As soon as he struck their infantry pickets, they opened upon him with artillery, and he immediately fell back, having accomplished the object for which he was sent.

D. S. Stanley

Extract from report of Major-General McCook

Near Alpine
September 13, 1863, 8:15 a. m.

General Crook sends word, from the information he has, that the enemy have evacuated Lafayette with their infantry. There were immense clouds of dust seen in the direction of Lafayette yesterday.

EXTRACT FROM REPORT OF
ASSISTANT ADJUTANT-GENERAL G. P. THRUSTON

September 14, 1863

General P. H. Sheridan
Commanding Third Division
Crook went within three miles of Lafayette, drove in infantry pickets, captured eighteen infantry (Louisiana Tigers); they say the rebels are going to fight us. Crook says a large force of the enemy is going toward Dirt Town.

Headquarters Chief of Cavalry
Department of the Cumberland
Valley Head
September 15, 1863, 10 p. m.

Brigadier-General Garfield
Chief of Staff
Sir: I have the honour to report that General Crook arrived at Dougherty's Gap at 12 m., driving a small scouting party before him. He is encamped upon the mountain, but has to go down into the valley for forage and water. Has no information of any rebels being near him, but will send an expedition down the cove tomorrow. The gap is clear. Columns of dust could be seen in the valley moving toward Rome.
Robt. M. Mitchell, Brigadier-General

Headquarters Chief of Cavalry
Rodgers House
Near Blue Bird Gap
September 19, 1803, 3:30 a. m.

Brigadier-General Crook, Commanding Second Cavalry Division: General: The General commanding directs that immediately on receipt of the enclosed order you move with your command to Stevens Gap. If you can get your artillery through Dougherty's Gap, come the Valley road and send your train *via* mountain route; if not, come the mountain route. Before coming down the mountain at

Stevens Gap, supply your command with three days rations. Move with all possible dispatch.
William H. Sinclair

Headquarters
Chief of Cavalry
Crawfish Springs
September 20, 1863, 9:35 a. m.

General Garfield
Chief of Staff
General: General Mitchell directs me to say that General Crook is within two miles of here with four regiments of cavalry First, Third and Fourth Ohio, and Second Kentucky Cavalry and five pieces of Stokes battery.
Respectfully yours,
Wm. H. Sinclair

Headquarters Chief of Cavalry
Department of the Cumberland
Crawfish Springs, Ga.
September 20, 1863

Brigadier-General Jas. A. Garfield
Chief of Staff,
Department of the Cumberland
General Crook has arrived and we are warmly engaged at the fords. They are trying to force a passage since I wrote you last in regard to the fight this morning. General Crook says, when he left Stevens Gap, Colonel Post had no orders to leave the gap.
Robt. B. Mitchell

Headquarters Second Cavalry Division
Near McCulloch's Cross-roads
September 21, 1863, 6:30 p. m.

Major William H. Sinclair
Assistant Adjutant-General
Major: I have the honour to report that the officer commanding the pickets reports the enemy in front, at the

junction of the Crawfish Spring and Chattanooga roads, to consist of infantry, cavalry and artillery. The cavalry, supposed to consist of one brigade, is drawn up in line of battle. The infantry is estimated as one division and probably a detachment.
George Crook

Headquarters Chief of Cavalry,
Rock Creek Ford
September, 21, 1863, 8 p. m.

General Garfield
General: I have been in line of battle all day, but have nothing but skirmishing along my front. I enclose reports of this evening from General Crook. We will be wide awake. You can draw your own inference from the report of Crook.
Robt. B. Mitchell

Headquarters
Second Cavalry Division
September 21, 1863

Brigadier-General Mitchell
Commanding Cavalry
General : A messenger from the front reports a heavy body of rebel cavalry moving up the road in this direction three

FRONT OF THE SNODGRASS HOUSE

and one-half miles out, and men escaped from the hospital this morning report infantry moving up the road we came up yesterday.

George Crook

Extract from letter from
Major-General W. S. Rosecrans

September 30, 1863

Brigadier-General Lorenzo Thomas
Adjutant-General,
U. S. Army

As to the cavalry, the accompanying reports are so full that I need only add that, as an arm of the service, it has been equal to its duty on all occasions, and on the eighteenth, nineteenth and twentieth of September it behaved with conspicuous gallantry, covering our shattered right and protected our trains in the valley of Chattanooga Creek on the twentieth.

It was to provide for the security of these trains, which had been sent to that valley on the eighteenth, and that they should be moved into Chattanooga after our right was driven back on the twentieth, that I directed special attention, and it is greatly due to the behaviour of the cavalry on that day that we lost none of our wagons, and that many of our ambulances, and some of our artillery and caissons came safely into place.

The losses of the cavalry appear in the accompanying report, 43 killed, 132 wounded and 283 missing, making a total of 439, instead of 500, as conjecturally stated in my official report.

I cannot forbear calling the special attention of the General in Chief and the War Department to the conspicuous gallantry and laborious service of this arm. Exposed in all weather, almost always moving, even in winter, without tents or wagons, operating in a country poorly supplied with forage, combating, for the most part, very superior numbers, from the feeble beginnings of one year ago, when its operations were mostly within the infantry lines, it has become master of the field and hesitates not to attack the enemy whenever it finds him. This great change, due chiefly to the joint efforts of both officers and men, has been greatly promoted by giving them arms in which they had confidence, and by the adoption of the determined use of the sabre.

Extract from report of General George Crook

September 29, 1863

Arrived at Crawfish Springs on the morning of the twentieth. At this point I found General Mitchell, who ordered me to take post at once in front of the fords of the Chickamauga and hold that point at all hazards. The only point I could occupy was a thick, rocky road woods with heavy underbrush. The enemy was already across the river, occupying a very strong position.

About 11 o'clock I was attacked by Hindman's division of infantry, a battalion of sharpshooters, and a large body of cavalry. They drove us back steadily, contesting every inch of the ground, about two hundred yards, where we held our ground. At this time I received an order from General Mitchell to fall back to the hospital, one and one-half miles distant. Our entire force consisted of Colonel Long's brigade, nine hundred strong. The entire command, both officers and men, behaved very gallantly. Among the list of casualties was Lieutenant-Colonel Cupp, First Ohio Cavalry.

Officers wounded: Lieutenant-Colonel Valentine Cupp, First Ohio Cavalry; First Lieutenant George W. Griffiths, Second Kentucky Cavalry; First Lieutenant Edward B. Ayres, Second Kentucky Cavalry; Captain Charles A. Zachary, Second Kentucky Cavalry; First Lieutenant John Calder, Second Kentucky Cavalry; First Lieutenant Bird P. Brooks, Second Kentucky Cavalry.

Officers missing: First Lieutenant Richard W. Neff, Fourth

Ohio Cavalry; Second Lieutenant Greenleaf Cilley, Fourth Ohio Cavalry; First Lieutenant Charles D. Henry, Fourth Ohio Cavalry.

From this point, we joined the remainder of the cavalry force and fell back to McCulloch's Cross-roads and moved to Chattanooga.

Return of casualties in the Army of the Cumberland, commanded by Major-General W. S. Rosecrans, at the battle of Chickamauga, Ga., September 19 and 20, 1863, Second Cavalry

Brigade, Colonel Eli Long:
Killed: Officers, two; men, seventeen.
Wounded: Officers, five; men, seventy-four.
Missed and captured: Officers, two; men, thirty-six.
Aggregate: One hundred and thirty-six.
Total strength of the brigade : Nine hundred men.

Near Washington
September 30, 1863, 10 a. m.

Major W. H. Sinclair
Assistant Adjutant-General
Commanding Cavalry

Major: The enemy are endeavouring to cross at Cotton Port Ford, three miles from Washington. They are in very heavy force. I am fighting them.

George Crook

Extract from report of
Brigadier-General Robert B. Mitchell
U. S. Army, Chief of Cavalry

Headquarters
Chief of Cavalry
Island Ferry
October 3, 1863

September 9. At daylight the command, First Division, and Second Brigade, Second Division, moved across Lookout

Mountain in the direction of Henderson's Gap, General Crook's command having the advance. As they neared the gap, the advance struck the enemy's pickets, which were easily driven back down the gap. The gap was found to have been obstructed by them by felling timber across the road, which is a narrow pass, and rolling large boulders of rock into it. It took about an hour to clear out the gap, when the command moved into Broomtown Valley.

General Crook's command soon engaged the enemy and a severe skirmish ensued, the enemy resisting stubbornly, having occupied the timber skirting some large fields. However, as soon as Colonel McCook's command came up, by sending strong parties on their flanks, they were forced to retire, fighting us, however, from the time we struck them in the valley until we drove them through Alpine, some retreating on the Rome road, but most of them on the road to Summerville. For the details of the engagement, I refer you to the reports of the division, brigade and regimental commanders. The command, after pursuing until dark, bivouacked at night in the line of battle in the vicinity of Alpine, standing to horse at 3 a. m. in the morning.

September 20. Command was engaged all day in guarding fords on Chickamauga Creek. General Crook, with his command, reported about 10 a. m. from Dougherty's Gap. The enemy attacked the forces at the various fords in strong force, and, after severe fighting, succeeded in effecting a crossing, but gained but little ground afterward, for they were stubbornly resisted at every step, and finally gave up the attempt to get in on our right through the cavalry. About 3 p. m. I received verbal orders from an orderly from General McCook to fall back, as our right had been turned. Not deeming an order of so important nature as that, coming in such a manner, valid, I did not move, as I had been ordered in the morning to hold Crawfish Springs at all hazards, but sent staff officers to ascertain the position of affairs and, if possible, communicate with either General McCook or Rosecrans. From them, I learned that our right had been driven around, and that everything on the right was moving toward Chattanooga up Chattanooga Valley. I therefore, after moving out all trains and loading into ambulances all wounded able to ride from the vicinity of my position, about 5 p. m. commenced falling back up Chattanooga Valley, bringing off on my retreat two pieces of artillery which had been abandoned by General McCook's troops of General McCook's corps, and collecting about a regiment of stragglers from the same command. The command bivouacked on Chattanooga road during the night.

September 21. The whole command stood in line of battle all day in Chattanooga Valley, with frequent skirmishing. The enemy's cavalry was in sight all day, but no severe attack was made.

September 22. In accordance with orders from department headquarters, at daylight, whole force, with the exception of one brigade, which was left to keep up show in front, moved into Chattanooga. The brigade left at the front, fell back about 10 a. m., fighting hard as they came.

I cannot close this report without calling to the attention of the General commanding, the gallantry and daring of the cavalry command during the two days battle, as well as the following two days on our retreat to Chattanooga, each regiment, brigade and division trying to outstrip each other in deeds of daring.

Brigadier-General Crook, commanding Second Division, deserves the gratitude of the country for the gallant manner in which he discharged his duty throughout the entire advance, as well as on the battle-field of Chickamauga.

I must, in conclusion, say that there was never work more opportunely done on the battle-field than the work of the cavalry on the twentieth of September at Chickamauga.

Egbert B. Mitchell, Brigadier-General & Chief of Cavalry

Extract from letter from C. A. Dana

Hon. E. M. Stanton
Secretary of War

All our reports show that Wheeler broke up railroad, destroyed bridges between Wartrace and Murfreesborough. At M(urfreesborough) sacked the town, but did nothing to fortifications. On seventh, Mitchell, with main cavalry force, Crook having joined him, overtook them at Shelbyville and (Farmington), and put them to flight, killing one hundred and capturing two hundred. Butterfield, who came up during this action with Lowe's cavalry and a regiment of Granger's infantry from Wartrace, reports that Mitchell will probably capture and destroy all Wheeler's forces.

Chattanooga
October 8, 1863, 10 a. m.

Circular from Major-General D. S. Stanley

Murfreesborough, Tenn.
November 20, 1863

Soldiers of the Cavalry Command: In parting with you, your late commander takes occasion to express his regrets that the changes of service should separate his fortune from you. For a year we have served together most pleasantly, and I am happy to congratulate the cavalry upon their achievements in that time. My poor efforts to render you efficient have been zealously seconded by both officers and men. As to our success, the testimony of our enemies is the more flattering to us, it being forced from them. They now admit you are dangerous and have left material proof of it upon many a field. Though separated from you, I will serve in the same army with you, and shall always watch your course with confident pride. I leave you, commanded by brave and experienced officers. Give to them the same confidence and cheerful obedience you have given me and your success and glory is assured.

Chattanooga
November 28, 1863, 7 p. m.

Arriving here, I find the results of Colonel Long's cavalry expedition were much more important than was reported at Ringgold. He burned eighty wagons, including Bragg's head quarters train, of which he brought in the mules; tore up the railroad between Cleveland and Charleston and for ten miles south of Cleveland, and captured two hundred and fifty prisoners; would have burned Hiwassee bridge but for the cannon rebels had there.

C. A. Dana

Headquarters
Department & Army of the Tennessee
Bridgeport, Ala.
December 19, 1863

Hon. E. M. Stanton
Secretary of War

Accordingly at Philadelphia, during the night of the second of December, I sent my aid, Captain Audenried, forward to Colonel Long, commanding the brigade of cavalry, to explain to him how all-important it was that General Burnside should have notice within twenty-four hours of our approach, and ordering him to select the best material of his command, to start at once, ford the Little Tennessee, and push into Knoxville, at whatever cost of life and horseflesh. The distance to be travelled was about forty miles, and the road villainous. Before day they were off. Colonel Long arrived at Knoxville with his cavalry, and all was well then.

W. T. Sherman

Extract from report of Major-General U. S. Grant
In field Chattanooga, Tenn.

December 23, 1863

By 3 o'clock of the same day, Colonel Long, with his brigade of cavalry, of Thomas army, crossed to the south side

of the Tennessee and to the mouth of South Chickamauga Creek and made a raid on the enemy's lines of communications. He burned Tyner's Station, with many stores, cut the railroad at Cleveland, captured near a hundred wagons and over two hundred prisoners. His own loss was small.
U. S. *Grant,* Major-General U. S. Army

Report of Colonel Eli Long, Fourth Ohio Cavalry Commanding Second Cavalry Brigade

Headquarters
Second Brigade
Second Cavalry Division
Calhoun, Tenn.
December 28, 1863

General: I have the honour to forward, for the information of the Major-General commanding the department, report of attack made this a. m. upon this place by the rebel General Wheeler. The attack was made about 10 o'clock by a force of from 2100 to 2500 cavalry and mounted infantry, led by General Wheeler in person. Their object was evidently the capture of the supply train, which arrived here last evening under charge of forces commanded by Colonel Laiboldt.

Colonel L(aiboldt) encamped on the Charleston side of the river and his skirmishers were at work with the enemy before I was apprised of their approach. I immediately mounted the small command which remained in camp not on duty (about 150 men), moved across the bridge and found the infantry pretty sharply engaged, the enemy occupying position in the wood. The latter shortly after gave way and I then started rapidly after them. Discovering a small portion of their force now cut off on the right, I ordered a sabre charge, and followed a retreating column of several hundred which had taken out the Chatata road, running up the Hiwassee.

Our rapid pursuit and vigorous use of the sabre completely

demoralized this force, which was thrown into the greatest confusion, and scattered in every direction, their men throwing away large numbers of arms, accoutrements, etc. Several of the enemy (number not known) were killed and wounded, and we captured 121 prisoners, including five commissioned officers. Drove the remainder until I had arrived at a creek, which was scarcely fordable, and deemed it prudent to follow no further. The main rebel column had fled out the Dalton road. I sent a small force out that road, who followed some five miles, and the enemy is still retreating towards Cleveland.

Very respectfully, your obedient servant,
Eli Long, Colonel Commanding, Second Cavalry Brigade

Itinerary of the Second Brigade,
Second Cavalry Division, commanded by
Colonel Eli Long, Fourth Ohio Cavalry
for September, 1863

September 3. Crossed Sand Mountain and arrived in Will's Valley. Remained in camp here until September 8, when the brigade, with one section of Stokes 7 battery, crossed Lookout Mountain and engaged four regiments of rebel cavalry at Alpine, in Broomtown Valley, driving them from the field. Loss: Killed, four; wounded, eight.

September 13. Marched on reconnaissance towards Lafayette in conjunction with Campbell's brigade, First Cavalry Division. Found Bragg's main army entrenched at that place. Falling back, re-ascended Lookout Mountain and proceeded to Dougherty's Gap.

September 19. Marched through Rape's Gap into McLemore's Cove.

September 20. Participated in the battle of Chickamauga, having position on the extreme right of the army at Crawfish Spring. The brigade encountered Hindman's infantry division and a small force of cavalry, and was forced back, after a severe fight, with a loss of one hundred and twenty-two men killed, wounded and missing; seven officers wounded, and Lieutenant-Colonel V. Cupp, First Ohio, and First Lieutenant E. W. Neff, Fourth Ohio, killed.

September 22. Fell back with the army to Chattanooga and recrossed the Tennessee River to the north side.

CHAPTER 15

Raid of the Rebel Cavalry Through Tennessee
October, 1863

Under Command of General Wheeler.

The day we entered Chattanooga after the battle of Chickamauga, I find the following entry in my journal:

> *September 22, 1863.* Reconnoitre in front and find the enemy advancing in force, also flanking us on the left. Fall back toward Chattanooga and have a running fight for five or six miles, our regiment covering the retreat, the enemy pressing us hotly in the rear with both infantry and cavalry and pouring shells into our column from the ridge on the right flank. A heavy force of the enemy having been thrown across the valley in front, we could not see the signal flag from the top of Lookout Mountain, as it was afterwards proved to us, signalling for reinforcements, and after a sharp fight we formed a junction with the right wing of our army, which had fallen back on Chattanooga, and was now fortifying for a desperate struggle. As we came in sight of Chattanooga we seen the black smoke curling up from many burning buildings on the outskirts of the city, to clear them from the range of the batteries being trained on the advancing columns of the enemy. Thousands of men were plying the spade, the pick and the axe on the breastworks, preparing for the attack. General officers, followed

by their escorts, were riding rapidly along the lines, giving stern and hurried orders, while messengers were dashing in all directions under the spur, carrying dispatches. Thousands of army wagons, with mule teams and ambulances, were crowded along the streets, all heading toward the one pontoon bridge across the Tennessee River, and a constant stream of wagons were hurrying to the north bank of the river under directions of the officers of transportation. No pen picture can give but a faint idea of the reality of such a scene as this; to be fully realized, you must be an eye-witness. Here all is excitement, and in many instances confusion. The moaning of the wounded can be heard on all sides as the ambulances are driven rapidly over the stony streets, and mingles with the curses of the "mule whackers," as they recklessly and persistently urge their teams toward the bridge. Such are the scenes in the rear of the army, while in the front the boys are standing to their guns, steadily and anxiously awaiting the onset of the enemy. Rosecrans has been over whelmed by the combined forces of Bragg and Johnson, largely reinforced by Longstreet from the army at Richmond, while our long-promised reinforcements have not yet arrived. After a brief halt, our division was ordered to ford the river at the northern limits of the city. As we got just fairly started across this long and very crooked ford, the rebel batteries were turned on our lines and the shells fell thick and fast in our columns. We went into camp about dark opposite Chattanooga.

September 23. Bivouacked along the river bank all day; cannonading on the right this evening, and our lines advanced a short distance. Our army was busily at work strengthening the fortifications and burning buildings in range of the guns.

September 24. Still in camp. Our wagon trains have all crossed the river. This is the first time we have ever seen our wagon train since September 2. An order issued by General Rosecrans for our quartermasters to be in readi-

Wheeler's Raid

ness to burn all baggage, except rations and ammunition, if he is compelled to evacuate Chattanooga. We take a farewell look at our valises containing our dress suits and love-letters. Tonight at eleven o'clock the rebels made a dash on our lines and a desperate effort to carry the works by storm, and made five charges on the lines, but were repulsed each time with heavy loss; the assault made on Crittenden's lines.

September 25. Go fifteen miles up the river in command of a foraging expedition. All quiet in front.

September 26. Marched up the river toward Washington, twenty-five miles, picketing and patrolling the river on the lookout for the enemy, as our scouts report their cavalry concentrating for the purpose of crossing the river and making a raid in our rear to cut the railroads. Our division is now commanded by General Geo. B. Crook, one of the best cavalry officers in our army, General Stanley having been taken sick a day or two before the battle of Chickamauga.

September 27. March early this morning; we are now getting up in Eastern Tennessee, and there are many Union people here. In many places the stars and stripes were floating from dwelling houses; fine country and plenty of corn; encamped on Richard Creek.

September 28. March through Washington, a small village about fifty miles north-east of Chattanooga. Four companies detached and sent to Cotton Port to picket the river, under command of Major Scott. Encamped on Clear Creek, four miles from Washington.

September 29. Lay in camp all day. An old citizen came into camp today, professing to be a Union man, but excited some suspicion by his actions, and we learned from some coloured men after he left camp that he is a rebel spy. Send a detachment to capture him, but fail.

September 30. The rebels, under General Wheeler, crossed

the river in large force last night; surrounded our pickets at Cotton Port and under a flag of truce demand their surrender. Our boys made a desperate dash through the lines, losing eight boys out of Company K and several of Company B. Rebel battery opened up and General Crook rapidly concentrated his division and moved down the river ten miles. The enemy is now across the river in strong force, and the indications are that we will have a lively time. Several staff officers captured to-day while carrying orders, including Captain Scott and Lieutenant Lieb. Loss in our regiment, twenty men. Rained very hard tonight.

October 1. Take the pass up Raccoon Mountain in hot pursuit of the rebel column. They are some distance in advance, as we have been delayed twenty-four hours in concentrating our division, which is scattered along the river patrolling and picketing. Reach the top of the mountain about dark. Raining in torrents.

October 2. Descend the mountain into Sequatchie Valley and our regiment made a reconnaissance down toward Pikeville and learned that the enemy passed down the valley about five thousand strong. Take Robinson's pass up the Cumberland Mountains at dark and arrive at the top about one o'clock tonight. This is the most difficult mountain pass we have ascended during this campaign.

October 3. March at four o'clock this morning. Move across and down the mountain and strike the enemy in the valley about four o'clock in the evening and drive them about three miles until the darkness prevented our further advance. Killed and wounded a large number of the enemy. We left Chattanooga on the twenty-sixth ult. with five days rations. This is the seventh day out, rations all exhausted, and today as we halted on the mountain the boys cut down many chestnut trees with their hatchets to get the chestnuts to eat. To fight Wheeler's old and tried veterans on empty stomachs, and then to bivouac for a few short hours rest this frosty night supperless, with no prospect of breakfast, but with the assurance that we will have a running fight all day tomorrow is not a very cheering reflection. But it is thirteen dollars a month and plenty of ammunition, so say your prayers, boys, turn in, and no grumbling.

October 4. In the saddle at daybreak, with a breakfast of hard, sour apples, we move on with the determination that if there is anything to eat in this valley we will surround some of it before night, if we have to ride over Wheeler's whole division. A number of our teamsters came into our lines this morning, having made their escape from a wagon train that the rebels attacked at Sequatchie Valley, killing the mules and burning the wagons. We heard the explosion of the shells on the evening of the second and supposed a battle was in progress at Chattanooga. We strike the rebels about noon and charge them about four miles, taking many prisoners. Drive them through McMinnville on the gallop, and recapture some of our prisoners. Have a sharp artillery fight this evening just at dark, using grape and cannister. Halted in an old camp near McMinnville that had been evacuated some weeks, and scraped up some old crackers, blue with mould, and found them to taste delicious. We are getting about desperate enough to eat mule, if we had time to cook one. Distance, twenty miles. Rather a lively Sunday, but we have had a field day of it, driving the rebels at every point they made a stand.

October 5. Take the pike for Murfreesboro and march rapidly, and arrive at Murfreesboro about four o'clock; find the town surrounded and all the troops and citizens in the fortifications; we form and move out, and after a little skirmish the enemy's lines fall back and they are soon in full retreat. The troops and citizens are very much rejoiced and the commissary departments are thrown open, our famishing troopers given the freedom of the city, and many of the boys are up nearly all night cooking and eating. If we had not pressed the enemy hard all day, the city would have been captured and all our rations and quartermaster stores would have been destroyed. The raid on the part of the enemy so far has been a failure, as they have done but little damage to the railroad, and soon they will be compelled to retreat from Tennessee as rapidly as their horses can carry them. In the old veteran, Geo. Crook, the rebel chieftain Wheeler has found a "foeman worthy of his steel."

October 6. Move out on the Shelbyville pike about ten miles, and go into camp and let the men rest all the afternoon, as they are very much exhausted by hard service. We left Murfreesboro with full stomachs and full haversacks, and I think tomorrow we will give the Johnnies a lively racket.

October 7. "Boots and saddles" sounded early, and we are soon in the saddle, eager for the fray that we knew would soon be on. We rode into Shelbyville and found that beautiful little city completely sacked, all the business houses robbed and the citizens terrorized. We move out on the Pulaski pike, and after marching about three miles strike a division of the enemy and immediately charge them, killing and wounding many, and taking hundreds of prisoners. We have a running fight all day, and for fifteen miles it is a stampede, with dead and wounded strewn thickly the whole distance. In the evening, about dusk, the enemy throw up barricades in the streets of the village of Farmington, and prepare for one last desperate stand. They opened on our advance line with grape and cannister, and it seemed that our lines could not stand this raking fire, but two or three regiments are dismounted, and we move into the cedar wood skirting the village, while the balance of the division, mounted, made a flank to the right, and with a shout all along the line, we dash forward on double quick, while grape and cannister are hurled through the thicket like hail. In fifteen or twenty minutes we carried the barricades, capturing a battery of six guns, with mules hitched to the caissons, and seven hundred prisoners. This has been another field day for our divisions. The enemy is now making a desperate effort to escape and only fight when they are compelled to do so. General Crook is adding another star to his straps. Colonel Minty, commanding the First Brigade, having failed to reach a certain point on the field, as ordered today, thereby foiling General Crook's plans, when he reported this evening, he was promptly put under arrest by Crook. The old regular is not to be trifled with. Our regiment bivouacked in the village, tired and hungry, but cheered by the thought that this has been a brilliant victory.

October 8. In the saddle at dawn and march through the villages of Lewisburg and Connellsville and on to Pulaska, where we arrive about sun-down, just in time to see the rebel rear guard dash out on the gallop without firing a shot. The enemy, no doubt, marched all night in order to escape us, and we have had no fighting to-day. Distance, thirty miles. On picket to night; men completely exhausted with this hard service and many horses abandoned. We cannot stand this many days longer.

October 9. Did not close an eye last night and are mounted and on the move by daybreak. Push the rebel rear guard all day; have several skirmishes, killing and wounding several, and taking many prisoners. We charged the enemy about four miles this evening, and those not captured crossed the Tennessee River at Lamb's Ferry. Wheeler's raid has been a failure, as he did but little damage to the railroad and his command is badly demoralized. His loss in killed, wounded and prisoners is up ward of two thousand, with a battery, several hundred stand of small arms and many horses. We go into camp at Rogersville, four miles from the river. We hope to get a few days much needed rest, as both men and horses are very much jaded. Hundreds of camp-fires are burning tonight, and our camp is ringing with shout and song, the boys all feel happy over our grand victory. Wheeler will not trouble us any more this fall.

Headquarters
Chief of Cavalry
Department of Cumberland
Rogersville
October 10, 1863

Sir: The enemy succeeded in crossing the Tennessee River a short distance above Lamb's Ferry. Crook fought them at Farmington the seventh, and has captured five pieces of artillery and about seven hundred prisoners, and their losses, including killed, deserters, stragglers, will amount to two thousand men. My horses are terribly jaded. The enemy crossed the river at a ford unknown before and cut their way down the banks, In order to make a crossing. Your order in regard to Confederate soldiers has been carried out, and thirty-eight men have disappeared. Colonel Minty was arrested by General Crook and sent to the rear for failing to move with his command at the proper time, and not being in time for the battle at Farmington. We have marched, in six days, two hundred and forty-seven miles. Two days, the second out, and yesterday, the First Division marched fifty miles. During the last day's march Wheeler's retreat was a rout and his command were running all day for the river, every man for himself, and hats, canteens, coats, guns and broken-down horses were strewn along the whole road.

We have captured and burned $52,000 worth of cotton belonging to the Confederates States army.

Respectfully, your obedient servant,

D. S. Stanley, Brigadier-General, Chief of Cavalry

Headquarters
Eleventh & Twelfth Army Corps
Stevenson, Ala.
October 17, 1863

Brigadier-General George Crook
Commanding Cavalry
Flint River

General: I am directed by the Major-General command-

ing to inform you that Roddey's cavalry is still on the north side of the Tennessee River, and that he is in your vicinity. A mail to General Bragg, captured to-day from a staff officer of Major-General Wheeler, indicates this, and we know that a rebel force has moved down the south side of the river to aid that force in crossing. The General desires that you will push out in every direction, and, if you can ascertain his whereabouts, strike and destroy him. He has in his command about 1,000 men and is without artillery. From the rebel mail, we learn the full particulars of your fight at Farmington, and it is highly creditable to you and your command.
Very respectfully, your obedient servant,
H. W. Perkins, Assistant Adjutant-General

Headquarters
Second Cavalry Division
Maysville, Ala.
November 5, 1863

Major W. H. Sinclair
Assistant Adjutant-General
Major: I have the honour to report that, on the twenty-third of September I was ordered by the commanding General of the department to proceed to Washington, Tenn., with my command, numbering about two thousand effective men, for the purpose of guarding the fords along the Tennessee River for a distance of some fifty miles. The roads leading to the different fords and ferries were in many cases five miles apart. Between these points there were practicable fords almost every half mile. It was impossible to patrol along the bank of the river between these roads, and to go from one to the other required us, in many instances, to make a detour of ten and even fifteen miles. It was at one of these intermediate points that the enemy, dismounting his men, crossed and established himself on the north bank of the river, with a force far superior to mine, commanded by

Major-General Wheeler. I immediately informed General Rosecrans of the fact, who ordered me to gather all the cavalry and mounted men and pursue the enemy, who had crossed the river for the purpose of making a raid in the rear of our lines. Learning the enemy was crossing Walden's Ridge opposite Smith's Cross-roads, I collected together the First and Second Brigades of my division, commanded respectively by Colonels Minty and Long, and Captain Stokes' Board of Trade Battery, and ascended the mountain some five miles south of Smith's Cross-roads, directing Colonel Miller, commanding brigade of mounted infantry, to join me on top of the mountain that night; but he did not join me until next morning, when I resumed the march, entering the Sequatchie Valley at Pitt's Cross-roads. Learned there that the enemy had divided his force, one portion under General Wharton ascending the Cumberland Mountains at Pikeville, while the remainder, under General Wheeler, had passed down the valley and would ascend the mountain at Dunlap, concentrating at some point beyond the Cumberland Mountains and then move on McMinnville. I also found here that the enemy had fourteen hours the start of me. I took the intermediate road, Robinson's Trace, and, although the mountain was very bad to ascend at this place, I succeeded in getting up my entire command that night. Next morning, after marching some ten miles, I struck Wharton's trail where he came into the Robinson's Trace. I did not meet any of his force, except some stragglers, until I arrived at the descent of the mountain, where he had left some sharpshooters to oppose my advance. I dismounted part of the Fourth Michigan, it being in the advance, and drove them before me, they leaving five of their dead and one wounded on the field. After descending the mountain, I found the country rocky and brushy, no place for cavalry to operate. As soon as I could get my infantry down the mountain, I dismounted them, sending them so as to completely surround their force, holding my cavalry as a support. In this way I had Colonel Crews Texas Brigade completely surrounded, in a space not over ten acres, my men under cover and his exposed. My men poured several volleys into them, but by this time it had become so dark we could not tell friend from foe. Under cover of darkness, they broke through my lines, my men not firing for fear of shooting each other. The light lasted for a couple of hours after night, the remainder of Martin's division coming to Crews' support.

My loss was forty-six killed and wounded. The enemy's loss is not definitely known. We found some ten of their dead close by the road, and a good many of their wounded scattered along the road in houses. I pushed on after them early next morning, and could not ascertain their loss. I left instructions with the citizens to collect them and give them all proper attention. I saw nothing of the enemy until within a couple of miles of McMinnville, where some of his scouts fired into us.

On arriving at McMinnville, I found that the garrison had surrendered without making any resistance. The enemy sacked the place, destroying a great deal of public and private property, and left in the direction of Murfreesborough. I was also informed by an intelligent Union man that he counted four thousand of the enemy, and saw enough more that he was unable to count to make up fully six thousand.

After leaving McMinnville, I became satisfied, from the time occupied by his force in passing a given point, he had between five and six thousand men, my own force at this time numbering about three thousand five hundred effective men. I had not marched more than two miles upon the Murfreesborough road until I came upon his rear guard, posted in the edge of a woods, who commenced skirmishing with my advance. Being satisfied that the guard intended to detain us so that the main body could march unmolested, I ordered Colonel Long to send a regiment ahead to make a sabre charge. The Second Kentucky, Colonel Nicholas commanding, with Colonel Long at their head, made a most gallant charge of some five miles, breaking through his lines, killing and wounding several of his men, capturing eleven prisoners and driving the remainder into the main column, compelling him to turn round and give me fight.

When I arrived with the main column, I found the enemy drawn up in line of battle in the edge of a woods, a large field between us, with high fences intervening. I dismounted my infantry, and with my artillery drove them out of the woods, he forming in another thick jungle a short distance in the rear.

The fight lasted for two hours, until after dark, when I camped in the field. Here again, I was unable to ascertain the number of his killed and wounded, but left instructions for the citizens to collect them. I learned that it was the intention of the enemy to take Murfreesborough and then go to La Vergne, destroying the railroad between these two points, and that he had sent squads of men, who were familiar with the country, to destroy telegraphic communication between Murfreesborough and Nashville, which they succeeded in doing. I tried to get a dispatch through to the commanding officer at Murfreesborough to hold out until I could get there, but the courier could not get through.

At Readyville, I crossed over on to the Liberty pike, so as to get between them and La Vergne, and also to prevent them from ambushing me on the road. By this move, I drove them off in the direction of Shelbyville. I found every person at Murfreesborough in great consternation, and overjoyed to see us. They were momentarily expecting an attack from the enemy, and felt that their force was too weak to repel him. I found here an officer of the Engineer Department who was very kind and energetic, giving me all the assistance in his power. Through the want of proper attention to duty on the part of the assistant quartermaster and Commissary of Subsistence, I was unable to procure anything for my men and horses until nearly morning (although I had marched forty-one miles that day and my men had had no rations for five days), greatly retarding my march. The next night I camped two miles beyond Guy's Gap.

From this point I sent my scouts in different directions, who brought prisoners from the enemy's camp. General Mitchell, with the First Cavalry Division, came up with us here. Next morning I was ordered by him to march on the road to Farmington, south of Duck River. About three miles from Shelbyville I found Davidson's division encamped on Duck River, some two miles north of the road. The brigade of mounted infantry being in the advance, and seeing the enemy's ranks in confusion, I ordered them to charge on horseback. They drove the enemy a short distance into a cedar thicket, and I then dismounted them. At the same time, I ordered Colonel Long's brigade to the front, and, headed by Colonel Long, it made a most gallant sabre charge, driving the enemy three miles, killing and capturing a great many rebels. The enemy made another stand in a cedar thicket, where it was impossible for the cavalry to operate in. I sent the mounted infantry to the front as soon as possible, when they dislodged the enemy, who again made a stand on the main road, and were driven from this point, falling back toward Farmington, skirmishing as they retreated.

About three-fourths of a mile from Farmington I found him posted in force in a dense cedar thicket. I at once dismounted my infantry, deploying them on each side of the road. When I attacked Davidson's division in the morning, breaking through it, part of his column went to the right. Fearing that it would turn my flank, I sent back instructions to Colonel Minty, whose position was in the rear of the column, to move to the right and anticipate them.

I supposed that Colonel Minty had carried out my instructions, but when I arrived at Farmington, I learned from one of my staff that Colonel Minty was not with me.

The absence of Colonel Minty and some five hundred men left at Murfreesborough, having been dismounted during the march, left me but about one thousand five hundred effective men

Finding the enemy vastly superior to me, I left one regiment of cavalry to protect my rear, holding the other two regiments as a support to the infantry, the country being impracticable for the cavalry to operate in. The enemy's battery was posted in the cedar thickets some four hundred yards distant from me, pouring into me a heavy fire of grape, cannister and shell, and made one or two charges on my men, at the same time attempting to turn both of my flanks. At this critical moment I ordered Captain Stokes forward with his battery to operate upon the enemy. He could only find position for one piece, which was in full view of their battery, and not over three hundred and fifty yards distant. They turned their fire from the infantry on to Captain Stokes battery, mowing down his horses and men. The captain sighted his own piece, and in three shots he disabled one of their pieces, blowing up a caisson, and throwing their ranks into confusion.

At this moment my infantry, making a charge, broke through the enemy's line, scattering them to the right and left, capturing four guns, some wagons and several prisoners. The enemy then being in an open country, I ordered Colonel Long to the front to make a sabre charge, but they had the roads barricaded so as to render it impossible. It now getting dark, I went into camp near Farmington.

Had Colonel Minty, with his brigade, been there at the

time the enemy broke, I should have thrown him on the left flank, and, as things turned out since, I would have captured a large portion of his command, together with all his artillery and transportation. I learned here that I fought General Wheeler with his entire command. That night, after the fighting had ceased, Colonel Minty, with his brigade, came up, stating that he had no orders to march with me. From this, together with a disposition manifested during the whole expedition to frustrate my designs in a covert manner, I deprived him of his command and sent him to the rear. I sent my scouts out in different directions that night, and learned that a large portion of the enemy had gone toward Pulaski. Being satisfied that they were making for the Tennessee River, and that the portion cut off would join them by other roads, I the next morning pursued them on the Pulaski road, reaching that point at night, I found today that their retreat, instead of a march, was a rout. Their rear guard left Pulaski as I came in sight of the town.

On this day's march I found that the night before a portion of those cut off came into the road ahead of us at Lewisburg. On the march next day, another portion came into the road six miles south of Pulaski. I found that their men were deserting and scattering over the country, and learned of a great many wounded being left along the road and through the country.

The enemy left some two or three regiments at Sugar Creek, a strong position, to oppose my advance; but instead of fighting them at long range, as they expected, I ordered a sabre charge. The Fifth Iowa, Lieutenant-Colonel Patrick commanding, being in the advance, made a most gallant charge, breaking through their lines, killing ten, wounding nine and capturing some seventy prisoners, and scattering the remainder to the mountains.

From this on I met with only a few stragglers on the road. When within eight miles of the river, although my horses were very tired, I galloped most of the way to the river, and there found that the enemy had crossed at a ford but little known of, and just above Elk River, where twelve could cross abreast. I went into camp at Rogersville, General Mitchell, with the First Division, coming up that night; and from that point I was ordered, with the remainder of the cavalry, to Stevenson, *via* Huntsville.

On arriving at Huntsville, General Mitchell, learning that the rebel General Roddy was passing in the direction of Winchester, went in pursuit of him, but he escaped toward Athens. I was then ordered to Winchester, and thence to this place. I have since learned that General Lee, with five thousand men, reached Courtland the same day that Wheeler crossed the river. Roddy, with about eighteen hundred men, had crossed to the north bank of the river at Guntersville, both he and Lee being ordered to join Wheeler, but the latter was driven out of the state and across the river before a junction could be effected. I have since learned that, at Farmington, the enemy left on the field eighty-six of their dead and one hundred and thirty-seven wounded, while many of their wounded were taken up by citizens through the country, of which I have no account.

The loss of the enemy from the time they crossed the river near Washington until they recrossed near Elk River, judging from the difference in the length of time their column (consumed) in coming in and going out, and other satisfactory evidence, I am fully satisfied is not less than two thousand men. One entire regiment, the Fourth Alabama, deserted and scattered through the mountains.

My loss, during the entire trip, was fourteen killed and ninety-seven wounded. I regret to report the death of the gallant Colonel Monroe, of the One Hundred and Twenty-third Illinois, who fell while bravely leading on his regiment at the battle of Farmington.

It is hard to distinguish individual cases of bravery and gallantry, when all, both officers and men, did so nobly. Not withstanding the fatigue and severe hardships under which the men suffered having but three days rations in twenty days, many of them nearly naked and several times exposed to a cold, drenching rain yet they never complained, but were always cheerful and ever ready to perform all duties required of them.

I am, sir, your obedient servant,
George Crook, Brigadier-General Commanding.

Extract from report of
General R. B. Mitchell, Chief of Cavalry

Decherd, Tenn.
October 20, 1863

I think the record of cavalry service during the entire war cannot show a more severe campaign than the one my command has just closed. There was scarcely an hour during the whole pursuit that the horses were unsaddled; for days and nights together the men were in their saddles, almost constantly on the march, and some days making as high as fifty-three and fifty-seven miles. Take again into consideration the fact that a greater part of the time the troops were out of rations, and our hasty movements giving them little or no time to forage on the country; that the nights were very cold, the men without overcoats, and I think the campaign challenges comparison with any service performed during the war. Yet, with all the severe duty and hardships necessarily devolving upon the men, they made not a murmur, but, on the contrary, seemed only anxious to do everything in their power to accomplish the object for which they had started, *viz.*: to overtake and, if possible, destroy the enemy's cavalry, and whenever we did succeed in reaching them, they proved that they were ready and competent to do this. I only regret that the precipitancy of their movements after the engagement at Farmington prevented us from again overtaking their main body, though on the last day of their fight General Crook captured their rear guard. The damage done the cavalry from the time of their crossing the Tennessee River cannot be definitely stated. We pursued them so closely and vigorously that they had but little time to destroy our communications, and the results of their raid, I think, may be summed up so that when General Wheeler strikes his balance sheet the debits and credits will be on the wrong side of the sheet to give him a very large profit. We captured six pieces of artillery, and, including killed, wounded, prisoners and deserters, I think they recrossed the Tennessee River with between two and three thousand less men than they started out with.

My command is, of course, very badly used up. Hard marches, scarcity of shoes (although each man carried two at starting), and miserable, worthless saddles, that should never have been bought by the Government or put on a horse's back after they were bought, have ruined many of the horses.

It is positively necessary that a large number of horses be had before the command can be again in working con-

BLOODY POND, WIDOW GLENN'S LOOKING EAST

dition. My thanks are due to division and brigade commanders for the interesting energy and zeal they evinced during the entire pursuit.

The troops of their command did all that is possible for troops to do to second the endeavours of their commanders, and when I thank them, as I do, for the fatigues and gallant fighting which they did, I do it in all earnestness and sincerity, realizing and appreciating their labours and sufferings. A simple mention of their marches, of their fighting at Anderson's Cross-roads, at McMinnville and Farmington, is as proud a record as any body of troops need crave.

Very respectfully, your obedient servant,

Egbert B. Mitchell, Brigadier-General Commanding

Loss, Second Division: One hundred and ten.

Congratulatory Order of
Major General Wm. S. Rosecrans, U. S. Army,
Commanding Department of the Cumberland

Special Field Orders No. 279

Headquarters
Department Cumberland
Chattanooga, Tenn.
October 19, 1863

14. The brilliant pursuit of the enemy's cavalry under Wheeler by the cavalry command of this army, especially Crook's division and Stokes Chicago Board of Trade Battery, which were foremost in the fight, deserve honourable mention.

The general commanding thanks the cavalry, and particularly General Crook, with the officers and soldiers of his division, and of Stokes battery, for their valuable services in this pursuit of the enemy, which resulted in driving him in confusion across the Tennessee River. He compliments them for inaugurating the new practice of coming to close quarters without delay. By command of Major-General Rosecrans,

H. M. Cist, Lieutenant &
Acting Assistant Adjutant-General

Extract from report of General G. H. Thomas

This pursuit is unsurpassed for its energy and bravery and endurance of the officers and men engaged in it, and prevented the execution of an extensive plan of destruction of our communications, and plunder, rapine and murder throughout Middle Tennessee and Northern Alabama, in which Roddy and Lee were to cooperate with Wheeler.

CHAPTER 16

Campaigns
October, 1863-March, 1864

The brigade marched from Rogersville on the 11th day of October *via* Pulaski, Fayetteville, Winchester, New Market, and Maysville, and reached Paint Rock on the Memphis and Charleston Railroad, twenty-five miles west of Stevenson, Ala., October 19th. Roddy had crossed the Tennessee River to the north about the time we had driven Wheeler across the river and was moving toward Decherd, and on the march from Rogersville, Crook's division captured some of his scouting parties with a little skirmishing. General Lee, with a brigade of rebel cavalry, had also arrived in the vicinity of Florence, just at the time our forces had sent Wheeler whirling across the river. Both Lee and Roddy were to join Wheeler and assist in the destruction of the Railroad between Nashville and Chattanooga, but when they learned of the defeat of their chief, Lee did not cross the river and Roddy re-crossed to the south side as rapidly as possible. Arriving at Paint Creek, Ala., Crook's division settled down for a little rest so much needed by both men and horses, as the division had been on the move with scarcely a day's rest from June 24th, the date that Rosecrans army made the advance on the Chickamauga Campaign. During that time the regiment had marched nearly if not quite 1200 miles and had participated in more than twenty fights and skirmishes. Our horses were very much in need of shoeing and were in a general run-down and jaded condition, after the hard six months campaign. On the

22nd, a scouting party of the First captured the notorious guerilla, Captain Gurley, who murdered General Robert McCook near Winchester, Tenn., in August, 1862. Our wagon train, which we had not seen since we left Chattanooga, September 22nd, reached us on the twenty-sixth, much to the delight of all, and especially the officers, as their baggage was in the wagons and they had not changed underwear for a month. Scouting parties were sent out every day, and this with outpost and picket duty kept the company busy and the commanding officer seemed to feel so confident that we would spend the winter at Paint Rock that the men were ordered to put up winter-quarters and a great many little huts and cabins were erected with fire-places, mud chimneys and good roofs of boards or any kind of material that would shed the water.

This was an innovation for the regiment, as we had never had anything of the kind before, and the boys began to congratulate themselves that they were going to have a quiet winter campaign. But alas! "the best laid schemes of mice and men gang aft aglee."

On the evening of the seventeenth of November the brigade received marching orders and on the morning of the eighteenth were in the saddle early and off for the front, leaving the wagon-train, unserviceable horses and dismounted men at Paint Rock. The command marched by Stevenson to Bridgeport and crossed the river on a pontoon and went into camp near Brown's Ferry, on the night of the twenty-second, marched up the river along the side of the mountain toward Chattanooga and the enemies camp-fires were in plain view on the mountain. The brigade crossed to the north side of the river at Brown's Ferry and camped opposite to Chattanooga. By order of General Thomas the brigade crossed the river again to the south side above Chattanooga, and marched toward Cleveland and struck the railroad a few miles above Chattanooga, commenced the destruction of telegraph wires and railroad track at once. Having succeeded in securing a copy of Colonel Long's report of the raid on the Georgia Railroad and also the march to Knoxville in advance of Sherman's army and the raid over the Tillico and Unaka Moun-

tains into North Carolina, the report is herewith inserted. This report covers the time from November 17th, 1863, to January 2nd, 1864, and no better history of the service of the regiment could be written than to publish the report in full.

The battle of Chattanooga which includes Orchard Knob, Lookout Mountain and Missionary Ridge, was fought November 23rd, 24th and 25th, 1863. Our losses, as given by General Boynton, were: Killed, 859; wounded, 5,289; total, 6.148.

Confederate Losses

The report of the Confederate losses in these battles are very meagre, but the following losses were reported, but no doubt fall far short of the real losses: Killed, 91; wounded and missing, 1,635.

Report of Colonel Eli Long of raid on the East Tennessee and Georgia Railroad, including operations, November 17, 1863, to January 2, 1864

> Headquarters
> Second Brigade
> Second Cavalry Division
> Calhoun, Tenn.
> January 19, 1864

Brigadier-General William D. Whipple
Assistant Adjutant-General

General: I have the honour to submit detailed account as follows of the operations of my brigade since marching from Woodville, Ala., pursuant to orders received on the night of November 17, 1863. Lieutenant-Colonel Kitchell, Ninety-eighth Illinois Mounted Infantry, and Major Gray, Fourth Michigan Cavalry, having reported to me for orders, with detachments of their regiments, I marched on the morning of the eighteenth with a command of about one thousand strong. Reaching Bridgeport on the evening of the nineteenth, I crossed the river next morning near Kelly's Ford. On the twenty-second, Major Dobb joined me with a battalion of the Fourth Ohio Volunteer Cavalry and Lieutenant-Colonel Jordan reported with a part of the Seventeenth Indiana Mounted Infantry and Fourth Michigan Cavalry, increasing my command to fifteen hundred men. Marched that evening to Brown's Ferry and crossed the Tennessee River to north side, opposite Chattanooga.

On the twenty-fourth, receiving orders from Major-General Thomas to march to Cleveland, Tenn., and destroy, as far as possible, the enemy's lines of communication in that directional crossed by pontoons above Chattanooga and struck the Chattanooga and Cleveland dirt road, running along the railroad. A few miles east of Chattanooga I cut the telegraph wires and at Tyner's Station, burned two rebel caissons. At other points between this and Cleveland, the telegraph was severed and the railroad was destroyed in frequent places by burning and tearing up the track.

On the night of the twenty-fourth I bivouacked thirteen miles from Chattanooga and sent a party forward to Ootewah, who found and destroyed some four thousand pounds of flour. On the following day, I burned two freight cars, together with one hundred cars of tan bark, belonging to the Confederate States of America. Nearing Cleveland, rebel pickets were encountered and driven in. The advance regiment (First Ohio), then charged into the town and drove out Colonel Woodward with the Second Kentucky (rebel) Cavalry Regiment. Next morning I sent a detachment under Colonel Seidel, Third Ohio Volunteer Cavalry, on the East Tennessee and Georgia Railroad with directions to go, if possible, to Hiwassee River and ascertain the enemy's strength at Charleston; also, to tear up the rail road. Major Patten, with the First Ohio Cavalry, was sent down the Dalton road and Major Dobb, with the Fourth Ohio, back on the road we came, each party being directed to damage the railroad. Colonel Seidel went as far as Charleston and found Kelly's Brigade stationed at

Calhoun, with artillery, and drove the cavalry across the river, losing one man wounded. Major Patten destroyed ten miles of the Dalton track and considerable damage was done on the other road. In Cleveland I found a considerable lot of rockets and shells, large quantities of corn and several bales of new grain sacks. Destroyed all that was not appropriated to the use of my command. Burned several railroad cars found here; also, the large copper rolling mill, the only one of the kind, in the Confederacy.

Early on the morning of the twenty-seventh I was attacked by General Kelly with a brigade of cavalry and a section of two pieces of artillery. Started my command out on the Harrison road, sending forward the prisoners under charge of the Fourth Michigan Cavalry. Retired slowly, the enemy pressing us closely and shelling vigorously. A strong line of skirmishers was kept up, till we had passed Candy's Creek, keeping in rear of my column and holding him in check, when the enemy retired. My loss during the action was two killed, fourteen wounded and twelve missing. Most of the latter have since joined. The enemy's loss was not fully known, but he suffered in killed and wounded more severely than we. I moved on, via Harrison, to Chattanooga and reported in person at the headquarters of the Major-General commanding. During this trip I captured two hundred and thirty-three prisoners, including a number of officers, also eighty-five wagons and eleven ambulances, which, together with their contents were burned. Among this number of wagons was the train of General Wright's Brigade.

On the twenty-ninth of November, I again marched for Cleveland, pursuant to orders received at Chattanooga and reported to Major-General Sherman. From there took the road to Benton, sending my ammunition wagons with the infantry column on Charleston road, striking the Federal road, I came upon a drove of about three hundred hogs, belonging to the Confederate Government. Moved on to (Benton) with the main column, sending the Fourth Michigan on reconnaissance to mouth of Ocoee River and the Fourth Ohio down the Federal Road. The latter party captured another drove of about five hundred hogs. *December 1*, 1 marched to Columbus, on the Hiwassee River; then, returning to Benton, detached the Fourth Michigan and Fourth Ohio to go back to Cleveland with captured hogs, and prisoners taken on the twenty-ninth and thirtieth. One regiment was sent to secure the boats at the mouth of the Ocoee and float them down to Charleston and, with the remainder of the command, I proceeded to Charleston. Orders from General Sherman directed me to move on immediately to Athens and I reached there some two hours after midnight. From Athens I sent back one hundred and fifty men under charge of Captain Wade, Ninety-eighth Illinois Mounted Infantry, to garrison the town of Calhoun and hold the bridge at that place; also twenty-five men to be joined by twenty-five others from the two regiments then at Cleveland, to take the captured hogs to Chattanooga. Detachments of the Third U. S. Cavalry and Fifth Ohio Cavalry reported to me for orders and I marched for London in advance of General Sherman's forces. Near London my advance regiment, Third Ohio, was met by a force of rebel cavalry, routed them and took about thirty prisoners, losing one killed and two wounded. General Vaughan with a force of infantry and some artillery occupied the fortifications about the town and opened upon my column with shell. Not being able to dislodge the enemy any other way, I determined to charge the walls. I dismounted my command and moved forward in line, but, on approaching his position, I found him stronger than anticipated, the confronting force being fully equal, if not superior to my own in numbers, besides the advantage of position being greatly in their favour. I then fell back and, after reporting to General Sherman, bivouacked about a mile from London. During the night

Vaughan destroyed his stores, took up his pontoons and, after running into the river four locomotives and forty-four cars, evacuated the place. On the third of December, being ordered to move forward to Knoxville, and open communication with General Burnside that night, if possible, I crossed the Tennessee Elver and marched via Maryville. Travelling from (Maryville) I could get no information as to the position of the forces or condition of affairs at Knoxville. All reports that could be obtained indicated that the town was completely surrounded by Longstreet, but near 2 a. m. I struck Colonel Walferd's pickets some two miles from (Knoxville) and camped within his lines. Reported to General Burnside the following day.

On the night of the sixth, pursuant to orders from General Sherman, I marched to Maryville and was here joined by the two regiments that had been sent back from Maryville to Cleveland. From this point, I was directed to start in pursuit of a train of some three hundred wagons, which had been cut off at London, when we marched on that place and was now making its way into North Carolina. Crossed Little Tennessee River at Motley's Ford and after crossing Tillico and Unaka Mountains and Long Ridge, following up the Hiwassee, I arrived at Murphy, N. C., on the ninth of December. Met no force of the enemy, except a few of Morgan's men and a company of home guards stationed at Murphy. My advance guard had a slight skirmish with these and drove them from the place. Marched six miles from Murphy and camped.

Up to this time, since leaving Chattanooga, I had taken ninety-five prisoners, including seven officers, also a few horses and mules. Found the road from Maryville to Murphy for the most part good. After leaving Tillico Plains the route lies through a mountainous country, but the road over the mountains is well engineered and practicable for wagons. The country is very poor, the fields poorly cultivated and grain and forage more scarce than any locality previously visited during my entire trip. It is well watered, however, by frequent creeks and mountain streams. Frequent incursions have been made in there by rebel cavalry and but few cattle of any kind, horses or mules, were found.

From the best information I could obtain along the route, it appeared that the rebel train was some five or six days march ahead of me and travelling with apprehension of pursuit, so that it was evident that it would be impossible to catch it My horses were all jaded with hard marching and many of them had already given out, leaving a number of men dismounted, and from the scarcity of horses in the country, I could not supply their place. Therefore, after sending a force ten miles further into the country, to get all possible information, I determined to halt The reports of the expedition confirmed previous intelligence. After remaining in camp one day to rest my horses, I started back on the eleventh of December and at Tillico infantry awaiting my return.

Plains found General McL. Smith encamped with his division. Through him, received instructions from General Sherman to rest my horses as long as necessary and then proceed to Chattanooga via Charleston. Remained in camp until the morning of the fourteenth, Major Smith's battalion, Fifth Ohio Volunteer Cavalry, being meanwhile relieved and ordered to Athens. Arriving at Calhoun on the fifteenth, had orders requiring me to remain at that place, guarding the railroad and river as a line looking toward Georgia. The detachment of Third U. S. Cavalry was relieved from duty with my brigade and the Fifth Ohio Volunteer Cavalry, Colonel Heath, temporarily attached. I at once prepared to establish a line of couriers to London and Kingston, communicating with General Elliott, chief of cavalry, and the Fifth Ohio Volunteer Cavalry was assigned to the duty. With the Fourth Michigan, I opened a line of communication to Chattanooga. The Third Ohio

Volunteer Infantry was sent to Columbus on the Hiwassee, to guard the river there and the adjacent fords. On the twenty-second, the courier post at Cleveland was attacked by sixty rebel cavalry and driven out, with the loss of a few horses and arms and one man wounded.

The rebels retired shortly after, leaving two wounded, and the couriers resumed their post.

On the morning of the twenty-eighth, a wagon train which had arrived at Charleston the evening before under escort of convalescents, etc., of General Sheridan's command and commanded by Colonel Laiboldt, was attacked by General Wheeler with about fifteen hundred rebel cavalry. As soon as I was made aware of the attack, I mounted the small portion of my command not on duty (less than one hundred and fifty men), and as soon as the train had crossed the bridges, moved over the river. Colonel Laiboldt was now sharply engaged and soon had the enemy's lines wavering. I then drew sabres and charged, driving before me a force of some four or five hundred, pursued them to Chatata Creek, capturing one hundred and twenty-one prisoners, including five officers and many stand of arms. The enemy lost several killed and quite a number wounded, among the latter two colonels. The main rebel column retreated out the Dalton road. A detachment of my command followed them some five miles and left them in full retreat.

December 30th, the Fifth Ohio, by orders, was relieved from duty with me, and their removal (caused the abandonment) of the courier line to Kingston, as my command was too small to renew it. On the 3rd inst., Captain Beebe reported to me with a section of his battery, the Tenth Wisconsin, and remains here on duty. On the sixth, the Fourth Michigan returned to this camp, the courier line from Cleveland to Chattanooga having been withdrawn, and I then established a line from Calhoun to the Tennessee Elver at Cotton Port, connecting with line at Washington.

A great many of my horses were unshod when we started from Alabama, as some of the regiment had not been able to get any horseshoes since Wheeler's raid into Middle Tennessee, and there were no extra shoes in the command nor could any be obtained at Bridgeport or Chattanooga or anywhere on the whole march. More than one-half the horses of my command were old and not yet recovered from the hard marching after Wheeler. During the three days I was encamped in the vicinity of Kelly's Ford, it was with the utmost difficulty I could get half rations of forage for my animals and during the two days that I lay at Chattanooga I could not draw a grain. On coming to Chattanooga the second time, I was there thirty-six hours and got one feed of corn. On the march to North Carolina, after marching thirty miles, I had to encamp in the mountains with out any forage whatever. Between the time we left Alabama, November 18th, and the time we arrived here, *December 15th,* we travelled (*i. e.* the main column) four hundred and sixty-three miles, and the day we arrived in Knoxville, we had marched on that and the two previous days one hundred and fifteen miles. I have been thus explicit in order to explain to the commanding general the reason why my command decreased with such extraordinary rapidity from dismounted men.

I would respectfully present to the favourable notice of the Major-General commanding, for good conduct under all circumstances and unremitting attention to their duties, all of my staff, *viz.*: Captain Wm. E. Crane, Fourth Ohio Volunteer Cavalry, Acting Assistant Adjutant-General, Lieutenant Wm. H. Scott, First Ohio Volunteer Cavalry, Acting Ordnance Officer and Inspector, Lieutenant C. J. Norton, Second Kentucky Cavalry Aide, Lieutenant H. H. Siverd, First Ohio Volunteer Cavalry, Acting Provost Marshal, Lieutenant J. B. Hayden, Fourth Ohio Volunteer Cavalry, Acting Quartermaster and Commis-

sary of Subsistence and Assistant Surgeon John Cannon, First Ohio Volunteer Cavalry, Acting Brigade Surgeon, also Lieutenant-Colonel Seidel, Third Ohio Volunteer Cavalry, whose regiment was in advance approaching London, for the gallant manner in which they drove the rebels on that occasion, also Major T. J. Patten, First Ohio Volunteer Cavalry, whose regiment, being advance, was led by himself in person in fine style in the fight with Wheeler at this point, and also for good conduct on that occasion, Captains Woodlief and Erwin and Lieutenants Hall, Roush, Riggs and Brison of that regiment. The men all did as well as they could.
Very respectfully, your obedient servant,
Eli Long, Colonel Commanding
Second Brigade, Second Cavalry Division

From the first to the fifteenth of March the regiment lay in camp at Calhoun, resuming routine, camp duty with picket guard and scouting. On the fifteenth the detachment was ordered to Ringgold, Ga., and went into camp near General Baird's infantry division, and here Colonel Long was given leave of absence for a month. On the fifth of April the detachment had a lively skirmish with the rebel cavalry and were kept continuously on duty up to the sixteenth of April, and on that day they started for Nashville to join the regiment of veterans and recruits now being mounted, marching through Chattanooga, Stevenson, Decherd, Winchester, Farmington, Columbia, Franklin, and, arriving at Nashville, the regiment was again reunited, and about this date Lieutenant J. A. O. Yeoman, of Company A, reported with about forty recruits.

This was a campaign of continuous hard service and the First Ohio was particularly distinguished, especially in the fight at Calhoun, December 16, and Colonel Long in his report mentions ten officers of the regiment for meritorious conduct. For the numbers engaged, there was no more brilliant charge by cavalry during the war, and it was a hand to hand combat from the start to finish with sabres, revolvers and clubbed guns, and in addition to the killed and wounded, many of whom were sabred, the regiment took almost as many prisoners as they had soldiers engaged in the fight. Soon after this fight, Colonel Eggleston, who had been home on recruiting service, joined the regiment, and as a large majority of the men were dismounted, they were marched back to Paint Rock, Ala., and thence to Pulaski, Tenn. On the cold New Year's day, 1864, that part of the regiment on the march to Pulaski to re-enlist, was on the road and marched through Athens, Ala., to Prospect, Tenn., and the weather was so intensely cold that the brigade was scattered out along the road for many miles and no effort was made to keep the men in ranks. Many of the men had their ears, hands or feet frozen, and it will always be remembered as the coldest day's march we ever had, and that night we camped near Elk River. The next day the whole command was ferried across Elk River by a rickety old boat, run by a rope and pulley, and one load of men and horses was upset and narrowly escaped drowning. The brigade went into camp at Pulaski, Tenn., January 3, and on the fourth about three hundred men of the regiment re-enlisted for three years more or during the war.

The requirements of this service were that the soldier had "served for two years or more in the same company and regiment," and he was then eligible to re-enlist as a veteran. The inducements were a thirty days furlough and a bounty of $300. About one hundred of the detachment of the regiment stationed at Calhoun, with the balance of the brigade, re-enlisted in February, making the total number of the re-enlistments about four hundred. Whitelaw Reid, in his a *Ohio in the War*, writes of these veteran enlistments as follows:

> The Ohio regiments in the field had dwindled from a thousand to an average of from two to four hundred each. They had been decimated in battle, had languished in hospitals, had borne the manifold sufferings of the camp and the march, had gone through a Red Sea of troubles, and even yet were far from the sight of the promised land. They had left families, unprotected, behind them; they

felt that others at home should be in the ranks besides them; they saw, as yet, little reward for all their toils, privations and wounds.

With such a past and such prospects to contemplate, they heard the demand of the Generals for more troops. Their own terms of enlistment were expiring; and long before the great campaign to which they were then looking forward should be ended, many of them would have the right to turn their faces homeward. But, with a patriotism to which the history of the war furnishes no equal display, they turned from this alluring prospect, resolved that the vacant places by the loved firesides should remain vacant still, perhaps for the war, perhaps for ever, and pledged themselves to the Government once more as its soldiers to the end. Over twenty thousand veterans, the thin remnant of nearly eighty regiments of Ohio soldiers, re-enlisted for the war within a few weeks after the subject was first proposed to them. It was the most inspiring act since the uprising after Sumter.

The brigade remained in camp at Pulaski until the thirteenth of January, and on that day started on the march for Nashville in great spirit at the prospect of going home to see their loved ones so anxiously awaiting their coming. Arrived at Nashville on the sixteenth and remained there making out muster and pay rolls until the twenty-ninth, then took the train for Louisville, reaching there on the thirtieth, where we were paid off. Left the same evening for Cincinnati and on to Columbus, where we arrived on the evening of February 1.

On the second and third the men were all given thirty days furlough and went to their homes with orders to report at Camp Chase, March 4. During their stay the boys were feasted and feted continuously, and the citizens vied with each other in honouring these boys, who had been for more than two years battling for the Union. Again quoting from Reid's history, he says:

> They rekindled the fires of a glowing patriotism throughout the state. They fanned the work of recruiting to a flame. They shamed out the sullen spirit of opposition to

the losses and inconveniences of the war which had culminated in the Vallandigham movement. They secured the devotion anew of the State, and all that it contained, to the great struggle. And for themselves, they found how warm was the popular gratitude, how tender the care of the soldier, how lavish the generous regards of those from whose homes they had been beating back the horrors of war. They were the honoured guests of the State, were feasted at every table, were toasted at every assemblage, were pointed out to the little children wherever they passed as the men who were saving the Nation, were showered with the smiles of beauty and the blessings of age.

The detachment of the regiment that remained at Calhoun, Tenn., and did not re-enlist, seen some hard service during the months of February, March and April, 1864.

Colonel Long was in command of this detachment of the brigade, and the commander of any army in which he served never allowed his command to remain idle very long, if there was any service required of the cavalry. They assisted in building a bridge across the Hiwassee River and constructed two ferries and were out on a number of reconnoitering expeditions, capturing many prisoners.

On the twenty-second of February the mounted men of the brigade, and a detachment of mounted infantry under command of Colonel Long, in all about six hundred men, were ordered out on an expedition to the left of our army and right rear of Bragg's army. On the twenty-third the command struck the enemy and drove them back to within about three miles of Dalton, driving a Mississippi infantry regiment out of their camp, capturing a number of prisoners. On the twenty-fourth the brigade again attacked the rebels, both infantry and cavalry, driving them back toward Dalton, and, dismounting his men, Colonel Long pushed a brigade of infantry back into their camps, where they took position in some log huts, built for winter quarters, and opened up such a strong fusillade, and his force being so small, Colonel Long fell back to the infantry supports.

On the twenty-fifth the brigade again attacked the rebel line, in connection with Colonel Gross brigade of the Fourth Army Corps, and again drove the enemy back and held his position until dark. The fighting on the twenty-third, twenty-fourth and twenty-fifth was all between Varnell's Station and Dalton, and on the twenty-sixth he again drove the rebel cavalry about two and one-half miles back from the Lee House toward Tunnel Hill.

This expedition was only intended as a reconnaissance to develop the enemy's position, but it was a very important demonstration, and Colonel Long was mentioned by the commanding General and very highly commended for his spirited and aggressive attack on the right flank of the rebel army. The total casualties in both cavalry and infantry was about twelve killed and ninety wounded, including Captain Wood, of the Third Ohio Cavalry; also nine horses were killed and a number wounded. Colonel Long reported that he had no means of ascertaining the enemy's loss, but they left eight of their dead on the field and he brought in twenty-three prisoners. A number of dispatches herewith published give a good history of the expedition in brief.

Headquarters
Second Brigade
Second Cavalry Division
Henderson's House
Five miles from Dalton on railroad
February 24, 1864, 6:30 p. m.

Major W. H. Sinclair
Assistant Adjutant-General
Sir: I have just returned from another reconnaissance toward Dalton. Ran into a large infantry cantonment three miles or less from Dalton and ran out again. I had several men wounded. Who is intended to command, Colonel Grose or myself? Please give some directions about it. I don t think they have all left Dalton as much as I did.
Eli Long, Colonel Commanding, Second Brigade

February 24, 1864, 2 p. m.

Major W. H. Sinclair

Sir: I have just driven in, with one squadron, the infantry pickets on the dirt and railroad, three miles from Dalton, and am now in line with pickets skirmishing in front. Their cavalry ran into their infantry support, which they seem to have on all of the roads. I am now five miles from Dalton, and do not think it prudent to go any farther until I hear further from you and the result of your reconnaissance.

Eli Long, Colonel Commanding

> At cross-roads of Benton and Dalton Road and Varnell's Station and King's Lower Bridge Road, six miles south-east of Varnell's Station and nine and one-half miles from Dalton
> February 24, 1864, 1:25 p. m.

Major W. H. Sinclair

At 11:30 this a. m. I attacked and drove out of their camp at least a regiment of rebel infantry, three and one-half miles this side of Dalton. They had winter quarters (log huts), and as they were completely surprised, they had no time to move any plunder out of their huts, and from their appearance and the small amount of plunder in them, I believe they were preparing to leave. The cars were whistling furiously while the skirmish was going on. I have not force enough to cope single-handed with all of their cavalry, but I think you may advance with safety, if you can still keep your supports, Palmer's troops, etc., within supporting distance. I believe they are leaving the place, and they should not be allowed to do (so) undisturbed. I shall be compelled to go somewhere to get some forage. Please let me hear from you as fully in detail as you can. I shall either wait here or move upon the road to Varnell's Station until I hear from you.

Very respectfully, your obedient servant,

Eli Long, Colonel Commanding

Headquarters
Third Brigade
First Division
Fourth Army Corps
Widow Burke's Farm
February 24, 1864, 8 p. m.

Major Sinclair
Assistant Adjutant-General

Major: Colonel Long had the advance, drove their cavalry two miles, when he met what citizens said was Stewart's division in sight of and at the railroad. I advanced the infantry to his support, checked and held the enemy back at a mile from the railroad, until night, when we withdrew to here, leaving Colonel Long and one regiment of infantry to our front.

W. Grose, Colonel Commanding

Chattanooga
February 24, 1864, 4 a. m.

Major-General U. S. Grant

Colonel Long went within three and one-half miles of Dalton, and drove a regiment of infantry out of winter quarters. Our main force encamped within three miles of Tunnel Hill last night, and will be on the road to Dalton tomorrow night.

Geo. H. Thomas

Chapter 16
Demonstration on Dalton

Extract from report by
Brigadier-General Charles Cruft
commanding First Division, First Army Corps

February 22-27, 1864

February 24. Colonel Long took the advance about 3:30 p. m., supported by Colonel Grose, and they drove the enemy's cavalry two miles before them, when they came upon a large infantry force of the infantry near Glaize's house in position on the railroad below Buzzard Roost Gap, and about three miles from Dalton. After considerable musketry and the use of the section of artillery, the enemy, with quite a spirited skirmish, were driven back under cover of their rifle pits and held at the railway until night-fall, when our troops fell back, say two miles, and bivouacked.

In this engagement the casualties fell principally on Colonel Long's command, who is reported to have charged the enemy in splendid style.

Colonel Eli Long, commanding Second Brigade, Second Division of Cavalry, with his command, covered the exposed flank of the division during the entire march, and conformed his movements to those of the division. Though acting under independent orders from department headquarters, he at all times co-operated with me, and by the bravery with which he rushed his column and the care which he took to communicate all the intelligence which he could obtain, contributed largely to attaining the objects of the reconnaissance.

Extract from report of Colonel William Grose

Headquarters
Third Brigade
First Division
Fourth Army Corps
Blue Springs, Tenn.
February 29, 1864

Sir: In this form, we pressed the enemy to within three hundred yards of the railroad, the command of Colonel Long driving the rebel infantry out of their camp immediately in front for some time, when lines of the enemy's infantry commenced an advance upon us. A few well directed rounds from the section of. artillery, with the aid of a heavy skirmish line, brought them to halt and put them under cover.

Extract from report of Colonel Louis H. Walters Eighty-fourth Illinois Infantry

Headquarters
Eighty-Fourth Illinois Infantry
February 29, 1864

Lieutenant J. McC. Preston
Acting Assistant Adjutant-General

Lieutenant: Colonel Long's cavalry having been sent around our left to gain the enemy's rear, soon commenced skirmishing with them also, and in a few minutes the enemy were in retreat.

L. H. *Walters,* Colonel Commanding.

Headquarters
Second Brigade
Second Division Cavalry
Near Lee's House, Ga.
February 27, 1864

Brigadier-General Whippel
Assistant Adjutant-General

General: I have the honour to submit the following report: I left Calhoun, Tenn., Monday, February 22, 1864, in command of six hundred men, three hundred and fifty mounted infantry and two hundred and fifty cavalry, and marched out on the Spring Place road.

I left my encampment near Waterhouse's Tuesday morning, February 23, at 7 a. m., and marched toward Dalton. My advance guard drove in the enemy's vedettes when within four miles of Dalton. I immediately pushed on my column rapidly and attacked a regiment of rebel infantry, which was encamped within three miles of Dalton, driving them from their camp and capturing twelve prisoners belonging to a Mississippi regiment. The enemy then formed and I withdrew my command to Russell's Mills, distance of four miles east of Varnell's Station, and encamped for the night.

I left my encampment at Russell's Mills at 6 a. m., February 24, and reached Varnell's about seven, where I halted until about 10 a. m., in the meantime sending small forces on the different roads leading from Varnell's. They met no enemy and I pushed on toward Dalton, marching on a road running parallel to the Cleveland and Dalton railroad. When within five miles of Dalton, I met with the enemy's pickets. My advance squadron drove them to within three miles of Dalton. I remained in my position, when I was joined by Colonel Grose, commanding a brigade of the First Division, Fourth Army Corps. Soon after the arrival of Colonel Grose, I dismounted my command and advanced in line against the enemy, driving their skirmishers about one mile in the direction of their camp, but there I was compelled to fall back, being attacked by a brigade of rebel infantry who were firing at my men from behind log huts. I fell back to the line of Colonel Grose, and soon afterwards (as it was nearly dark) retired about two miles to the rear, where I encamped for the night.

The next morning, February 25, I took position on the left of our infantry lines and advanced as they did. I moved up about half a mile, when my men Became engaged with the enemy. I was then joined by one hundred men of the Fourth Michigan Cavalry. I pressed on against the enemy until I had gotten a short distance in front of the advance of the left of our infantry lines. I then halted and remained in my position during the remainder of the day.

On the morning of the twenty-sixth, I moved to Lee's House, where our infantry was encamped, and remained there until about 1 p. m., at which time our pickets were fired upon by the enemy's cavalry, when I marched out and drove the enemy off. I followed them about two and one-half miles in the direction of Tunnel Hill.

I had no means of ascertaining the injury done the enemy, but it was reported that eight bodies were left on the field. I took twenty-three prisoners.

Eli Long, Colonel Commanding
Second Brigade, Second Division cavalry

Remounting and Drilling after Re-enlisting as Veterans, March, April and May, 1864

The thirty days veteran furlough having expired, the regiment left Camp Chase for the front on the evening of March 8, 1864, for Cincinnati, and by boat to Louisville, Ky., and then by the L. and N. Railroad, arriving at Nashville, Tenn., on the evening of the eleventh.

The regiment remained in barracks until the eighteenth, and then went into camp out on the Charlotte Pike. A large number of recruits had enlisted in the regiment during the veteran furlough and the regular routine of drill and guard duty was inaugurated with strict discipline, much to the disgust of both veterans and recruits. Dismounted drill, manual of carbine, pistol and sabre, kept up continuously until April 18th, just one month, and at this date the regiment received their horses, much to the delight of men and officers. When the horses arrived, the companies were coloured, three of bay, two of sorrel, one of black, one of iron gray, one of white, one of brown, one of dun, and light sorrel, this was a new departure, and added much to the appearance of the regiment. New saddles and equipments were issued and by the twenty-first the regiment was ready for the field. Mounted drill was the order, the work of bringing the horses down to steady drill was commenced, but before this was accomplished, some of the recruits were hurled to the ground from wild and vicious horses and severely injured. After a few days mounted drill with sabres, the carbine was brought into use, and at first the test of firing would be by fours, then by platoons, and next in company front. A horse will become accustomed to firing about as quick as a man, and after a few drills the majority of horses will quiet down so that they can be easily handled, although they may be excited and nerved up to a high tension. Some horses will never become accustomed to firing, but will be more excited and frightened each drill, and such horses will

Kelly Field, looking north, where Breckinridge gained the Union rear

usually rear or squat, and in some cases will fall flat every time a volley is fired. It was not unusual in first breaking horses, when the company fired a volley, to see a half dozen running away, and the excited trooper would sink his spurs into the sides of his frightened horse in his frantic efforts to stick to his saddle, and this would only tend to increase the speed of the flying charger and the result usually was, that the trooper landed on the ground in the first heat.

There were many laughable incidents of this kind happening every day during our drills at Nashville. On the third day of May the regiment took up the line of march for the front and joined the balance of the brigade under command of Colonel Long at Columbia, Tenn., on the fourth, and went into camp. The regiment remained in camp at Columbia, doing guard and picket duty, and drilling three or four times each day, until the twenty-second of May. The regiment and brigade were better mounted, better armed and equipped, and better drilled than ever before, and when the order was received to march to the front, it was greeted with a shout of joy as every good soldier was ready and anxious to take the field. The brigade left Columbia on the Pulaski Pike on the morning of the twenty-second in high spirits, as it was a beautiful day, and all realized that we were again off for the front. The brigade marched through Pulaski and Athens, and arrived at Decatur, Ala., on the twenty- sixth, crossed the Tennessee River on a pontoon bridge, and joined the Seventeenth Army Corps, also on the march from Memphis, Tenn, to join Sherman's army. The regiment reached Decatur about noon, and went into camp near the town, which had a garrison of two or three regiments, and the Ninth Ohio Cavalry was stationed here. About three o'clock p. m. there was an alarm at the outpost and the First was called to horse and ordered to make a reconnaissance to the west toward Courtland. Reaching the pickets of the Ninth Ohio Cavalry, it was learned that there had been some picket firing, and the regiment moved rapidly out on the Courtland road, and soon struck the enemy's cavalry, driving them pell-mell, capturing twenty prisoners, several wagons, twenty-five mules, and Corporal Samuel Darrah, of Company K., capturing the flag of the Seventh Alabama Cavalry of Roddy's brigade. After driving the enemy about three miles the regiment returned to camp at Decatur.

On the morning of the twenty-seventh the brigade moved out on the Courtland road, and struck Roddy's Cavalry four or five miles from Decatur. After a sharp skirmish the brigade routed them and drove them back slowly all day, reaching Courtland, twenty-five miles distant, about 9 p. m. Our recollections of Courtland were not very pleasant, as about twenty-five men of Companies E and K had been taken prisoners there July 25, 1862. An old planter by the name of Bynum had piloted the Confederate Cavalry under General Armstrong into the camp on that occasion, and the boys of Companies E and K determined to even up on the old man, as he had made great pretence of being loyal when we were camped on his grounds in 1862. Company K marched up to his house the night we entered Courtland, and soon relieved him of many surplus hams with corn and other forage, and then bivouacked on the identical ground they were encamped on in 1862. The coloured folks recognized the boys of the regiment, and were soon busy assisting the boys to the best the plantation afforded, and danced in great glee. The old planter was in a great rage and complained to General Long the next morning, and Lieutenant Curry, who had been prominent in the foraging expedition, as he had been taken prisoner here, was summoned before the general, and after an explanation of Bynum's treachery in assisting in the capture of the detachment of the regiment in 1862, Bynum was dismissed very curtly with an admonition to go and "sin no more." B. F. Lucas, of Company K, was killed here in 1862 and buried near the camp, and some of the boys made a search for his grave, but it could not be found as the hogs had rooted up the ground and the headboard that marked his lonely grave had been knocked down by the stock or carried away. On the morning of the twenty-eighth the brigade moved south on the Moulton road over the same route that about twenty-five of us unhappy prisoners had been taken two years before, and the same brigade of cavalry, commanded by Roddy, was on our flanks and making an effort to obstruct our march. The regiment passed through Moulton and the Old Court House where we had been confined as prisoners of war had been converted into a hospital and a number of sick Confederate soldiers were sitting under the trees and about the doors. This scene brought back vividly to memory the hot July clays of 1862 when we were prisoners of war and the hard night march toward Tupola, Miss., and the threat of the Confederate officer in command, "that a prisoner who fell out of ranks under any pretence should be cut down." But the fortunes of war had changed the situation and we were now masters of the field. We took a grim and justified satisfaction in scowling at the citizens of this town who had greeted us with jeers and insults two years before. The brigade wheeled to the east at Moulton, and marched out about five miles on the Danville Pike and bivouacked. Roddy's command made a few little dashes on the pickets in the evening, and the order was given to unsaddle, feed, water and groom the horses and then saddle again for the night, as General Long anticipated an attack early in the morning. About daybreak Sunday morning the twenty-ninth, Roddy's brigade attacked our pickets dismounted, on two sides of the camp, and the attack was so impetuous that our pickets were driven in before the brigade could be formed to resist the attack and the men were ordered to mount without gathering up their blankets or cooking utensils. The road ran east and west and the First was camped on the south side of the road in a piece of woods, and on the north side of the road was an open field in which the regiment formed, facing the west. The regiment had just swung into line, when it was fairly daylight, and looking across a narrow skirt of woods in our front, a rebel battery was in plain view coming into position on a piece of open ground about half a mile away. In about two minutes the battery opened up on our line with shells, and the gunners could be plainly seen in their shirt sleeves. A shell came screaming over our heads and could be distinctly seen before it reached our line and tore through Company H, cutting down men and horses and the leg of Charley Welche's horse, the regimental saddler, was torn off, and also took Charley's boot heel. The First was ordered to dismount and move to the front across the narrow strip of wood, which movement was executed on the double-quick, and the horses were sent to the rear. When the regiment had crossed the wood, and reached the fence along the line of some old fields, the rebel skirmishers were jumping from tree to tree in an old deadening and were banging away pretty lively. Our whole line laid down behind the fence and opened up with their carbines which soon checked the rebel advance in our immediate front. The shells were flying, knocking up the dirt in front of our line and the rebels were pressing our left flank by a strong dismounted column from the woods south of the road, and our line was pushed back a short distance on the left and the indications were that our left would be turned. At this critical moment a shout was heard on our right and a regiment mounted which proved to be the Third Ohio Cavalry charging the battery. This movement relieved our line and the dismounted men of the brigade dashed forward with a yell, driving the rebels rapidly, capturing a number of prisoners, and Roddy's whole command soon beat a hasty retreat.

As the regiment was lying behind the fence when the fight opened, a shell from the rebel battery struck the ground about a hundred feet in front of the line and made a ricochet, bounced up against the fence, and a recruit in Company K by the name of Strickler or McCormick, reached through the fence and picked the shell up, exclaiming with much delight, "Here it is, boys." There was a lively stampede by the old veterans, as they expected the shell to explode, but fortunately the fuse had gone out and no harm was done. It is safe to say that this recruit never picked up another shell during the service after he fully realized the peril he was in. Another recruit was struck on the shoulder by a spent ball, which whirled him around, and he imagined the ball had gone clear through his shoulder, and it was some moments before he could be convinced that he was not seriously wounded. We had a large number of recruits and they stood up like veterans in this, their first hot fight.

Having driven the enemy in a regular stampede, taking thirty-five prisoners, the brigade fell back to our camp, gathered up quite a number of the enemy's wounded, including two officers. Our loss was about twenty killed and wounded, including Hanibal George, of Company K, a recruit, killed, who had only been under fire once before, and John Click, of Company F, killed. The loss of the enemy must have been much larger, as they made the assault and our troops were protected by woods and fences. The new recruits thought it was a pretty lively scrap before breakfast Sunday morning, and so it was. After getting breakfast we moved east again to join the Seventeenth Army Corps, passing through a very rough, destitute country, and struck the rear of the wagon train of that corps at Summerville on the evening of the same day. We were so delayed by their train that we did not go into camp until two o'clock in the morning, the prisoners marching all that distance on foot. Among the prisoners was a Lieutenant-Colonel of an Alabama regiment, a very jovial, good-natured gentleman, and he related the following incident, much to the amusement of the guards: He said that Roddy called his regimental commanders together before daybreak Sunday morning, and after laying before them his plan of attack, said he "now had the First Ohio just where he wanted them and that he proposed to capture the whole regiment." "But," said the colonel, "instead of Roddy having the First Ohio just where he wants them, it rather strikes me that regiment has got me just where I do not want to be."

The brigade marched with the Seventeenth Corps over Raccoon Mountain through "Valley Pass" and through Warrenton, then up Sand Mountain and down "Rhodes Pass" near Van Buren.

On the second day of June we went into camp in "Will's Valley," unsaddling the first time for four days.

June third, crossed Lookout Mountain, and near the foot of the mountain was large iron works at a place called Blue Pond. A squadron of the First Ohio, I and K, had the advance, and on making inquiry of some citizen, were informed that the rebel cavalry were going to "make a stand at Blue Pond." Thereupon the advance moved very carefully. We also found hand bills, printed on brown paper, tacked to the trees along the road, headed, "Attention, Raid Repelers," and then followed a high-sounding appeal to the citizens to assemble at Blue Pond "to repel the Yankee Vandals." As we approached Blue Pond a city of magnificent distances a cross-road with grocery and post-office, sure enough there were the "repellers" drawn up in line, and they gave us one volley from their shot guns and rifles, then wheeled, and away they went on mules and farm horses. The squadron dashed forward under the spur, and after a chase of about a mile we were gaining so rapidly on them that they began to take to the woods, some of them leaving horses and mules in the road, and taking across the fields, and the squadron captured sixteen prisoners, and the repelers were no more forever.

As we had expected a fight and the affair turned out so ridiculous, it was a by-word during the Atlanta campaign, that the Johnnies would make a stand at Blue Pond.

The same day we passed through Cedar Bluff, where we captured some Confederate uniforms and other stores.

CHAPTER 17

Atlanta Campaign
June-August, 1864

The following troops composed the Second Cavalry Division on the Atlanta campaign:

Second Division — Brigadier-General Kenner Garrard
First Brigade — Colonel Robert H G Minty
Fourth Michigan — Lieutenant-Colonel Josiah B. Park
Seventh Pennsylvania — Colonel William B. Sipes
Fourth United States — Captain James B. McIntyre
Second Brigade — Colonel Eli Long
First Ohio — Colonel Beroth B. Eggleston
Third Ohio — Lieutenant-Colonel Horace N. Howland
Fourth Ohio — Lieutenant-Colonel Oliver P. Robie
Third Brigade
(Mounted Infantry) — Colonel John T Wilder
Ninety-eighth Illinois — Lieutenant-Colonel Edward Kitchell
One Hundred and
Twenty-third Illinois — Lieutenant-Colonel Jonathan Biggs
Seventeenth Indiana — Lieutenant-Colonel Henry Jordan
Seventy-second Indiana — Colonel Abram O. Miller
Artillery
Chicago Board of
Trade Battery — Lieutenant George I. Robinson

Total strength Second Division (K Garrard), 10,293, April, 1864
Total strength Cavalry Corps, 32,485, April, 1864

We reached Rome, Ga., on the fourth of June, where we struck the right of Sherman's army. On the sixth we marched to Kingston, arrived at Alatoona on the eighth, and the brigade was assigned to picket and out-post duty at once in front of Johnston's army.

This was a poor and barren country and forage was very scarce; this soon began to tell very seriously on our mounts, and we were compelled to graze and feed sparingly of wheat, which was just ripening.

We held our camp near Alatoona until the fifteenth and had some skirmishing daily. On the afternoon of the fifteenth the brigade advanced on the extreme left of the army and made an attack, dismounted, on the enemy's lines at Noon Day Creek, driving them back more than a mile and into their works, and here we had a severe engagement, losing about twenty men, killed and wounded. The enemy held the works, and after about one hour the brigade fell back and mounted in some old fields. Here a rebel battery got range on our lines and the shells came rattling down very uncomfortably, killing and wounding several men of the regiment, and we were soon ordered back into the woods and erected barricades of rails and logs. Among the killed was Jerry Griffith, Company K, and Jacob Hendershot, Company H, and among the wounded was Captain Pickering, Company F, John Shultz, Company K, Henry H. Myers, Company G, killed, and Jarratt Johnson, Company H, leg torn off by a shell. Just as Johnson was wounded, the regiment was ordered to fall back into the woods, and when he saw the movement of the regiment he was lying down against a high paling fence in rear of our line, he immediately grasped the fence and commenced hopping and pulling his mangled limb along on the ground. He pleaded with his comrades not to leave him, but under the strict orders then in force, no officer or soldier in the ranks was allowed to fall out to care for a wounded soldier, as General Sherman had said, in issuing this order: "First whip the enemy, and then your wounded are safe." After we fell back into the woods a detail from Company H went back and carried Johnson to the ambulance. His leg was amputated, and he now lives at New Market, Ohio.

We lay in line of battle all night, holding our horses, and on the afternoon of the sixteenth moved to the right, had some skirmishing dismounted, throwing up barricades again. We unsaddled, but as there was heavy cannonading still upon our right, we were ordered to saddle and stood to horse during most of the night.

We lay in our breast-works all day of the seventeenth, with some skirmishing in our front and a continuous artillery duel between a battery just at our right and a rebel battery in our front, at a range of about two miles, and the shells were dropping around uncomfortably near us all day.

We lay in line all day of the eighteenth and had some skirmishing. Heavy fighting on the right and the rebel batteries on Kenesaw Mountain pounded away steadily all day and on into the night. It was a grand sight after night to see the shells exploding, the guns flashing and the signal rockets from both armies.

On the nineteenth our whole division moved to the front and attacked the enemy, driving them into their works across Noon Day Creek. We held our position and lay in line all night. In the morning again attacked the enemy and had a severe fight, and our loss on the twentieth and twenty-first in the division was sixty-five. Attacked the enemy again on the twenty-second and drove them back with considerable loss.

The First was on picket duty on the twenty-third, and in the afternoon the whole division moved up and our pickets were advanced by order of General Garrard, with orders to watch the movements of the enemy very closely, as their pickets were in plain view. In a short time there seemed to be an unusual commotion along the rebel line as mounted men were dashing back and forth, and the General was informed of the movement. In a few moments a dismounted column emerged from a piece of woods in our front on double-quick in column of fours, marching parallel to our line, until a regiment or two was in sight, then wheeled into line and with a yell charged down the hill toward a little creek about half way between the two lines. Our whole division was lying in line dismounted, and at the command they raised up, rushed forward with a yell, opened up with their carbines, and the volleys were deafening for a few minutes. By this time the rebel line had reached the creek and was well sheltered by timber, but volley after volley was poured into them. At this time the Seventeenth Army Corps was advancing on our right, but they had not yet struck the rebel line. General Frank Blair, commander of the Seventeenth Corps, was on the left of his line, and he ordered up a battery, and, under his direction, they opened up on the enemy. Company K, of the First, was on picket and were just falling back to the main line when the battery came up, and the company, being right in front of the battery, was ordered to lie down, and the battery fired over them for several minutes. It was a perilous position, as they were firing very rapidly and there was great danger of the shells exploding soon after leaving the guns. When the boys would look back over their shoulders and see the red flames belching forth from the mouths of the guns, they would then hug the ground a little closer. The rebel advance was soon checked, and we lay in line all night. The next day the rebels asked for an armistice to allow them to bury their dead and care for the wounded. Loss in the division, forty killed and wounded.

From the twenty-fourth of June until the evening of the second of July we lay on the extreme left of the army and were on picket or skirmishing- continuously. During all of this time, day and night, the batteries from both armies were pounding away. The Battle of Kenesaw Mountain was fought June 27th, and in fact the firing was so heavy that it seemed the whole earth was in a tremble all the time. About nine o'clock p. m. of the second, we moved to the right and had a tedious night march, winding around among the breastworks long to be remembered by the regiment. At daybreak of the third we found ourselves direct west from Kenesaw, but instead of the white puffs of smoke rising up from near the lone tree on top of the mountain from the rebel battery as usual, we only saw the bare mountain, gleaming in the hot sunshine that quiet Sunday morning, for Johnson's army had evacuated and were crossing the Chattahoochie.

Headquarters
Cavalry Division
Pace's Ferry
July 5, 1864

Captain Dayton
Acting Assistant Adjutant-General
Captain: I have to report for the information of the Major-General commanding that my command is camped on the Willeyo Creek near Roswell Factory. My advance is at the Factory. I will destroy all buildings. The bridge at this point over the river is burnt by the rebels. The ford is passable; so reported by citizens. I sent a regiment to the paper-mills, burnt the paper-mills, flouring-mills and machine-shops. The citizens report the banks of the river high at Powers Ferry and batteries in position on south bank. They had a pontoon bridge

K. Garrard, Brigadier-General
Commanding Division

July 6, 1864

There were some fine factories here, one woollen factory, capacity 30,000 yards a month, and has furnished up to within a few weeks 15,000 yards per month to the rebel Government, the Government furnishing men and material. Capacity of cotton-factory, 216 looms, 191,086 yards per month, and 51,66 pounds of thread, and 4,229 pounds of cotton rope. This was worked exclusively for the rebel Government. The other cotton-factory, one mile and a half from town, I have no data concerning. There was six months supply of cotton hand, over the woollen factory the French flag was flying, but seeing no Federal flag above it, I had the building burned.

The machinery of the cotton-factory cost, before the war, 400,000. The superintendent estimates that it alone was worth, with its material, etc., when burnt, over a million of our money.

K. Garrard

Chattahoochie
July 7, 1864

General Garrard
Roswell, Ga.

General: Your report is received and is most acceptable. I had no idea that the factories at Roswell remained in operation, but supposed the machinery had all been removed. Their utter destruction is right and meets my entire approval, and to make the matter complete you will arrest the owners and employes and send them, under guard, charged with treason, to Marietta, and I will see to any man in America hoisting the French flag and then devoting his labour and capital in supplying armies in open hostility to our government, and claiming the benefit of his neutral flag. Should you, under the impulse of anger, natural at contemplating such perfidy, hang the wretch, I approve the act beforehand

I do wish to inspire all cavalry with my conviction that caution and prudence should be but a very small element in their characters

I am, with respect, yours truly,

W. T. Sherman
Major-General Commanding

We moved into Marietta on the fourth. On the fifth we marched to the left and burned a large paper mill, and on the sixth burned a large cotton factory at Roswell, employing eight hundred hands. The manager raised the French flag and claimed protection, but the game would not work and the torch was applied. The enemy burned the bridge across the Chattahoochie at this point and our army could not cross until the bridge was rebuilt.

The Army of the Tennessee moved up to Roswell and in a few days erected a bridge out of round poles and logs, and on the tenth some of the infantry commenced crossing the river. Their immense wagon trains were left on the north side of the river and as we were on the extreme left flank, their trains were in great peril and we were kept constantly on the alert watching the movements of the enemy to keep their cavalry at a safe distance from the trains.

From the sixth to the twenty-sixth of July we were encamped in the vicinity of Roswell, scouting, foraging and guarding the fords along the river, and had a number of skirmishes with the enemy's cavalry. On the twenty-sixth the brigade moved down the river and crossed, and on the twenty-eighth and twenty-ninth, thirtieth and thirty-first we were at Marietta, and on the first of August we marched to Buckhead, so named on account of five roads branching off from this point. There was no town here, but. a miserable country, and about three and a half miles north-east from Atlanta.

On the twenty-seventh two brigades of the Second Cavalry division made a raid toward Covington and Stone Mountain and had a severe engagement at Flat Rock, in which the regiment did not participate, as it was on the march from Roswell down the river.

The brigade was in camp at Buckhead from August 1st to the eighteenth, but made a number of scouts and were on out post duty almost all the time, watching the movements of the enemy on the left flank; on the ninth advanced to Decatur and attacked the enemy, driving them about two miles, capturing a number of prisoners.

Again on the fifteenth the brigade made a reconnaissance and developed the enemy in strong force and had a severe engagement again, driving them from the field.

CHAPTER 18

Kilpatrick's Raid Around Atlanta

On the evening of the seventeenth the Brigade was ordered to report to General Kilpatrick on the extreme right of our army at Sandtown by daylight the next morning. After drawing five days rations, we were saddled and mounted by mid night, marched down the Chattahoochie in rear of our army and reached Sandtown early in the morning of the eighteenth. We went into bivouac, watered, fed and groomed our horses and were ordered to take all the rest we could possibly get during the day. The weather was very hot, the flies and insects were swarming and the surroundings were anything but inviting for a good day's rest. The night march had been tedious and tiresome and from sheer exhaustion the men slept some, not withstanding heat, dust and insects. About five o'clock p. m. we were ordered to feed and water our horses and get supper, and be ready to saddle in an hour. By sundown we were again in the saddle and our Brigade was formed in an open field. An order was read, stating that we had been "selected as the last hope of the commanding General to cut the enemy's communication, and we must go forth with the determination to do or die."

General Stoneman and General Ed. McCook with two divisions of cavalry, numbering nine thousand men, General McCook from the right and General Stoneman from the left flank, had made the attempt late in July to cut the railroad south of Atlanta, but had failed to do the work effectively. McCook destroyed a mile or two of the West Point Railroad and reached

Maj. Gen. Judson Kilpatrick.

First Ohio Cavalry watering in Chattanooga Valley, Tenn.

Lovejoy's Station, but was compelled by an overwhelming force of the enemy surrounding his division to fall back to our lines again. General Stoneman was driven back and he, with about one thousand of his command, was captured.

Kilpatrick's command was composed of the First Brigade and Second Brigade of the Second Division, commanded by Colonel Minty and Colonel Long, respectively:

First Brigade, Fourth U. S.	273
Seventh Pennsylvania Cavalry	393
Fourth Michigan Cavalry	250
Headquarters	73
Second Brigade	
First Ohio Cavalry	346
Third Ohio Cavalry	477
Fourth Ohio Cavalry	479
Headquarters	81
Chicago Board of Trade Battery	90
Total	2,398

Third Division, Colonel Murray commanding, 2,400, making a total of 4,798 men, with eight pieces of artillery, and General Kilpatrick in command of the corps. Every officer and soldier in the command realized that the proposed expedition was very perilous and the chances were that many of us would either be killed or wounded or what seemed worse, land in a rebel prison. After the order was read the order was given for the pack train to fall out and all troopers whose horses were lame or exhausted should go to the rear, and some troopers may have dropped out, whose horses were not very lame. In a few minutes and just as the sun was dropping behind the mountain, the command was given "right, forward, fours right", and we were off on what proved to be one of the hardest cavalry raids during our four years service. Soon after dusk we struck the enemy's pickets, which proved to be the advance of Ross and Ferguson's brigades of cavalry, and a brisk skirmish was kept up all night and during a greater part of the time we were dismounted, as the enemy would throw up barricades at every good position at bridges or along the edge of a wood and they gave us so much trouble that instead of reaching the West Point Railroad at midnight, as was intended, we did not strike it until just at daybreak of the nineteenth. The regiment, under orders from Colonel Long, dismounted, commenced tearing up and destroying the railroad track and succeeded in tearing up about a mile of the track near and south-west of Fairburn. Cavalry, when they became accustomed to this kind of work, would tear up a track very rapidly. When the order is given to dismount, number one, two and three dismount, and number four always holds horses, remains mounted and leads the other three horses. Number two hands his reins to number four, number two ties his rein to the bit of number three and number one to rein of number two. The men then form along one side of the track in close order and at command grasp the rails and ties and turn the track over, and sometimes a half mile of track is turned before a joint is broken, the men move along rapidly and many rods of the track will be standing up on edge. If there is time the rails are then torn loose from the ties by picks and axes, carried for that purpose, the ties are piled up and the rails on top of them and then the ties are fired and, thus the rails are heated and bent out of shape by being twisted around trees or telegraph poles, are left there to cool, and no doubt some of them are there yet to mark the trail of the cavalry raiders. The regiment destroyed about half a mile of the track, when the brigade was attacked by the cavalry and artillery of the enemy in both the rear and left flank. We were ordered to mount, and the regiment galloped forward to join the brigade which had crossed the track and had the advance. The brigade formed a line of battle facing toward the left and just as we began to advance a battery galloped into position on a little knoll to the right of our line. The line was advancing at a walk when an officer came dashing down from the battery, who proved to be the dashing dare-devil, Kilpatrick, and he ordered the line forward at a gallop across the field. He was mounted on an Arabian horse and looked the ideal cavalry man as he dashed forward in front of our line, his horse clearing a wide ditch running across the field and into which several horses fell, as they were urged to jump it by their riders. The brigade dashed into the woods and soon routed the enemy, taking a number of prisoners. During all this time Kilpatrick's headquarters band, mounted on white horses, was enlivening the scene by playing some patriotic airs. We soon fell back to the road and the column again moved towards Jonesborough, the Second Brigade having the advance. We struck the enemy in a short time and attacked them at once, pushing them back slowly, but steadily, all day. The country was thickly wooded and a very bad place for cavalry to operate. The enemy would throw up barricades at every favourable position, such as woods, streams or ravines, firing on the advance from ambuscades, the progress of the column was much retarded, and the enemy made every effort to keep our column back from the railroad until re-enforcements could be moved down from Atlanta. About noon the advance halted and dismounted in a thick piece of woods to let the horses rest, and eat a hard-tack raw pork sandwich. The men were all sitting or lying down when all at once the rebels fired a volley and charged the advance guard, driving them back on the reserve before we could mount. Colonel Long ordered the First forward dismounted and on double-quick. A part of the regiment was on the right of the road and advanced across a little field in which there was a melon patch and it was amusing to see the boys grab for the melons regardless of the balls that were knocking up the dust on all sides. As it was very hot and the men were almost famished after the long run, the melons were very refreshing after the rebel rear guard was routed. The rebel force was pushed back steadily until we reached Flint River and on the east side of this stream they had thrown up works, dug rifle-pits and had a strong position. As soon as our advance appeared a rebel battery opened up and the Chicago Board of Trade Battery was put in position and after a lively artillery duel the rebel battery was silenced.

    The First and Second Brigades of the Second Division were dismounted and advanced some distance in the woods on the west side of the stream where we halted and both of our batteries, with eight guns, were put in position on a hill in our rear and at a signal they opened up by volleys for several rounds and as soon as the batteries ceased firing the two brigades rushed forward with a yell and the rebel line left their works and riflepits and fell back rapidly toward Jonesborough. When the bridge was reached the plank had been torn up and there was nothing left but the stringers on which the First and Third Ohio and Fourth Michigan crossed. As we crossed Kilpatrick himself came up, and was ordering the men to jump into the stream after the plank to repair the bridge. The dismounted men moved forward, the First having the right of the line, and reached Jonesborough about sundown. The bridge across the stream was soon repaired and the artillery, mounted men and led horses were closed up by the time we reached the town. We had some skirmishing in the outskirts of the town and to the south on the opposite side of the town a strong force of rebel cavalry was drawn up in line of battle in plain view, and the officers could be seen dashing to and fro forming the lines. Our lines were straightened up and moving forward, the rear guard dismounted, opened up fire on our skirmishes from houses and buildings and a brisk fire was kept up from a brick church. A section of the Chicago Board of Trade Battery came dashing down the street up to the skirmish line unlimbered and sent a few shells into the church, making the bricks and mortar fly, and the church was evacuated in short order. The sound of the guns and scream of the shells was sweet music to the ears of the skirmishers, and they moved forward with a shout and the bang! bang! of their sharp-ringing carbines swelled the chorus as the mayor and a few citizens appeared in the main street with a white flag to surrender the town and claim protection for the citizens. The line advanced rapidly through the town, the rebels fell back along the railroad and we soon had undisputed possession. The shells from the artillery had fired the cotton bales, used as barricades around the railroad buildings, and soon both cotton and buildings were blazing and the water-tank at the station had been shivered by a shell, our men took possession of the telegraph office and it was reported that an old operator in our command caught a dispatch stating that reinforcements were on the way from Atlanta, which was very important news to Kilpatrick. Jonesborough is about twenty five miles south from Atlanta and a considerable amount of clothing and commissary stores were found, with whiskey and other necessary munition of war. All of these supplies that we did not need for immediate use were burned and destroyed.

As Hood's whole army was now between us and Sherman's army, it was not particularly desirable for less than five thousand cavalrymen to remain in this position very long, and the destruction of the railroad, which ran through the main street of the town, was commenced at once; the ties were soon piled up in heaps at a distance from each other of a little less than the length of the rails, then the rails were placed with one end on each bunch of ties, next a pile of ties was built up on top and at the middle of the rails, and then fired. When the rails became hot, the weight of the ties would bend the rails and render them useless. Tearing up the track and destroying the rails and ties was done principally by the Third Division, as they had not been engaged in the fight when we entered the town. The Second Brigade formed a line of battle south of the town and across the railroad, the First Brigade was formed facing Atlanta, and skirmishing was kept up all night. It was a wild night and a most graphic scene, the sky lit up with burning timbers, buildings and cotton bales, the continuous bang of carbines, the galloping of staff officers and orderlies up and down the streets, carrying orders or dispatches, the terrified citizens, peering out of their windows, the constant marching of troops changing position, Kilpatrick's headquarters band discoursing national airs, with the shouts of the men all made up a weird scene never to be forgotten by the troopers who were on that raid.

By midnight about two miles of the road had been effectually destroyed, and in attempting to move farther south along the road, a strong force of infantry was found posted behind barricades, with timber cut in front. This position could not have been taken without a hard fight and heavy loss, and Kilpatrick then determined to withdraw from Jonesborough, make a detour to the east and strike the road again farther south. The movement was commenced about two o'clock in the morning of the twentieth by Kilpatrick's division and Minty's brigade of the Second Division marching on the McDonough road to the east, and the Second Brigade, under Colonel Long, remaining in the barricades to hold the infantry in check. The Second Brigade withdrew just as the first streaks of dawn began to appear in the east, and they were followed up closely by the enemy, both cavalry and infantry, the First Ohio holding the rear. After we had marched about five miles, the advance regiments halted to feed their horses, and the enemy made an impetuous attack on the First, and one battalion was dismounted, throwing up barricades hurriedly of logs and rails, and prepared to give the enemy a warm reception. They attacked the barricades, and as their line was much longer, the battalion was outflanked on both sides, and the balls were soon whizzing from the flanks and, as the Johnnies would say, they took us "end ways." At this critical moment the officer in command of the battalion ran to the rear in a most disgraceful manner, and the line officers took up the fight independent, held the line against the attack until ordered by Colonel Long, who had rode back to the rear, to fall back to the new line formed by the brigade. Colonel Long complimented the line officers of the battalion very highly on the tenacity with which they held the enemy, among whom were Captain Kirkendall, Rea, Woodlief, Yeoman, Curry and others.

The brigade fell back slowly by alternate regiments and Vale, in his history of Minty's Cavalry, says it was one of the prettiest cavalry fights he ever saw, as Minty's brigade was not engaged, and all they had to do was to look on and enjoy the fun.

As soon as the enemy were repulsed, we were ordered to the front on the gallop three or four miles toward Lovejoy Station, where we found that Minty's brigade, on striking the rail road, had been attacked by a heavy force of cavalry and Reynold's division of infantry. The infantry line was concealed in a cut, and as the Seventh Pennsylvania and Fourth U. S. Cavalry dismounted, drove their skirmish line in and were within twenty or thirty rods of the railroad, the infantry line raised up and delivered a very destructive volley, and, rushing from the cut, drove the line of Minty's brigade back in considerable confusion. Just at this opportune moment, the Second Brigade arrived on the field with the Chicago Board of Trade Battery. The brigade was dismounted, formed a line of battle, and by this time many of the dismounted men of the First Brigade came rushing back through our line and it was not safe to fire, as it would endanger the lives of our own men, although the balls from the rebel infantry were whizzing on all sides. The officers of the Second Brigade made every effort to keep their men from firing, and when the First Brigade had passed to the rear, the rebel line was almost upon us, but when our troops did open up, the rebel line was repulsed and driven back with heavy slaughter. The Chicago Board of Trade Battery was up on the front line and did excellent execution, and the rebel infantry fell back into the railroad cut. During this fight the lines were so close together that the officers of the Second Brigade used their revolvers with good execution. Our ammunition in the First was exhausted and a detail was sent back to the ammunition wagons and got a supply in boxes and the boxes were broken open by stones, the cartridges were distributed in a few moments, much to the delight of the troopers. The brigade held this line for an hour, and during this time staff officers were busily engaged forming the led horses in columns of fours facing the rear. One of the guns of the Chicago Board of Trade Battery was disabled in a cornfield just to the left of the First, and it was hauled to the rear by some troopers of the Second Brigade (I think of the Third Ohio).

When the Second Brigade had driven the rebel line back and the firing had about ceased, Colonel Long was ordered to withdraw his brigade and fall back to the led horses a few hundred yards in the rear. We now began to realize that we were surrounded, and the chances began to look desperate, as our ammunition had already been pretty well exhausted, and we must cut our way through the lines. The distance between the two lines of the enemy could not have been more than three-fourths of a mile and the situation was about as follows, quoting from an article written by Lieutenant W. S. Scott, an officer of the First U. S. Cavalry:

> In the rear of the Union troops were two brigades of Cleburne's infantry, Ross and Ferguson's brigades of cavalry, and about a thousand state troops, which had been sent up from below Lovejoy Station; closing in on the right were the remaining brigades of Cleburne's infantry. Martin's and Jackson's divisions of cavalry were in rear of the left. A brigade of infantry and six pieces of artillery had been sent up from Macon, and were at Lovejoy Station. Reynolds' infantry, as before stated, was along the railroad in front. There were also twelve pieces of artillery which had been sent down from Atlanta. It thus seems that there were surrounding the Union troops five brigades of infantry, eighteen pieces of artillery, six brigades of cavalry; in all, a force of twelve thousand men of the three arms. As before stated, Kilpatrick had the Second and Third Divisions, with four pieces of artillery; in all, four thousand seven hundred and ninety-eight cavalrymen and seven guns. Finding himself completely surrounded by such an overwhelming force, he called his division commanders together and instructed them to cut their way out, designating as the point to strike an old deserted plantation. We see that up to this point, although his command was composed exclusively of cavalrymen and field artillery, the cavalry had been fighting almost entirely as infantry; but now his troopers were to be accorded the privilege of a cavalry charge in its true sense, and their sabres, which had been allowed to rust in their scabbards during the expedition, were to be brought into requisition.
> Kilpatrick, a cavalry general, remembering the mistakes which had been made on a former expedition for the same purpose, instead of scattering his troops, massed them.

The Second Division formed on the right of the road and the Third Division on the left of the road, facing toward McDonough, while the artillery, ambulances filled with wounded, and ammunition wagons were formed in the road, with orders to follow up the charging columns as closely as possible. The troops were all formed in columns with the proper intervals, as it was thought best to strike the rebel line and pierce it in several places rather than charge in line, as it was a long distance to charge, and in some places the ground was cut up by ditches and wash-outs, with two or three fences between our forces and the rebel lines. During the time the troops were forming, the surgeons and ambulance corps were busy gathering up the wounded and caring for them as best they could.

The rebels had formed two or three lines with infantry behind barricades of fence rails and logs, as it seems they had anticipated a charge, and they were not disappointed in their expectations. When our troops were forming, two batteries opened up on our lines from the front and the infantry was closing up from our now rear from the railroad. When all was ready every eye was turned intently toward the line of the barricades in front, from whence shells were now coming thick and fast, and through this line and over these barricades we must cut our way out or surrender and perhaps starve in Andersonville! Draw sabre! and forty-five hundred sabres ring out as they are drawn from their scabbards, the reins are tightened, the horses are excited, with nostrils extended as if they "snuffed the battle afar off.

It was a glorious sight, with horses stamping, and champing the bits as if eager for the fray, standards and guidons flung to the breeze, with the dashing here and there of staff officers carrying orders, the serious faces of the commanders, the stern, quick commands of the officers as the squadrons are forming. Many of the boys who witnessed and participated in that wild charge, but whose hair is now silvered with gray, can feel the flush of youth again mount to their cheeks and the blood course more rapidly through their veins as they go back in memory to the day we charged with Kilpatrick, August 20, 1864!

The command "Forward!" is given, the bugles rang out "Trot!" "Gallop!" "Charge!" in quick succession and the columns swept forward under the spur with a yell, scaling fences, jumping ditches in that wild and reckless charge, the shells from the batteries were sweeping the lines, while troopers and horses were falling on every side. The First Brigade struck the rebel line at and just to the right of the road, and Long's brigade struck farther to the right, and Captain W. H. Scott, of the First Ohio, fell mortally wounded in front of one of the guns of a rebel battery. When our columns struck the barricades, the rebels retreated in great confusion, but a lieutenant, commanding a section of artillery, who gave his name as Young, was mortally wounded just in front of where Captain Scott fell, as he was attempting to fire one of his pieces after all of his men had deserted their posts, and all regretted that the life of this young and brave officer, who fell at his post of duty, could not have been spared. Both brigades urged their horses over the barricades, cutting right and left. Many of the prisoners had sabre cuts on their hands, arms and heads, and it is estimated that from six to eight hundred prisoners were sabred.

Infantry, cavalry, led horses and artillery were fleeing in confusion, and at one time we had at least one thousand prisoners, but they nearly all escaped in our rapid march that dark night. A three-gun battery was captured, with horses, and many horses belonging to the cavalry, who were dismounted and in the barricades, were captured.

A dispatch from Atlanta sent to the *Memphis Appeal* and published a few days after the fight is herewith published:

> The newspapers have lately been full of accounts of how Martin's division of cavalry was run over by the Yankees at Lovejoy on the twentieth *ultimo*. The writer was on the field on that occasion and in justice to the much abused cavalry states the facts in the matter: Martin's division, supporting the battery, was formed on the McDonough road. Ross and Ferguson's commands on foot were in front and on each side of the battery, behind rail breastworks. A bri-

gade of Cleburne's infantry was on the left of the road in three lines, the last one in a piece of woods. About one hundred yards in rear of the position of the battery, on the right of the road (east side) the state troops were formed in line. When the Yankees charged they came in a solid column, ten or twelve lines deep, running their horses and yelling like devils. They didn't stop to fight or attempt to keep any kind of order or formation, but each fellow for himself rushed on swinging his sabre over his head. They rode right over Ross and Ferguson's men in the centre, and over and through Cleburne's lines one after another on the left. Cleburne's first line, they say, tried to use their bayonets, but the Yankees cut them to pieces. After the Yankees had cut through all the other forces and captured the battery, Martin, seeing the field was lost, retreated in good order to the east and joined Cleburne's main body, and aided in the final defeat of the enemy on the McDonough road that evening, and pursued them to and through McDonough that night, recapturing nearly five hundred of our men which they took in the charge. The effort to arouse the people against Martin and his brave division is more disgraceful and demoralizing than the Yankees charge itself and should be frowned upon by all who wish well to our cause.

After this long charge over broken ground, ditches, fences and woods, the regiments and brigades were considerably broken up, as many horses had been shot, troopers wounded or killed, and some horses falling in a ditch that we crossed were with great difficulty extricated, so that many of the men were dismounted. Before the Second Brigade could get in position, as Colonel Long had been ordered to cover the retreat, the First Brigade and the Third Division having moved out on the McDonough road, Long's brigade was furiously attacked by Pat Cleburne's division of infantry and a battery of artillery, and this fight lasted about one hour, with a part of the brigade dismounted. In this assault Colonel Long was severely wounded, but rode his horse to the rear, being supported on either side by two mounted orderlies from his escort. The First was forming on some high ground just as Colonel Long rode to the rear, pale and bleeding, and as he passed by the regiment he smiled and bowed and was given a rousing cheer by the boys. The Third Ohio was still fighting dismounted and the brigade was falling back by alternate regiments, and just at this moment the Chicago Board of Trade Battery came galloping back, dashed through a gate and into the dooryard of a plantation house on the opposite side of the road from where the First were forming. On the long porch in front of this house there were twelve or fifteen women and children all running back and forth screaming, and the women wringing their hands, while some were crying, others were praying.

The battery opened up at once, and the rebel battery in our rear soon got range and sent the shells thick and fast, and at least one of which struck the roof of the house, thus adding to the terror of the women and children. While our battery was firing rapidly one of the guns burst, seriously wounding two of the gunners. There was not a grim veteran of our command whose heart was so hardened by the every day scenes of carnage that it did not go out in sympathy for those mothers with their children, and who would not have freely risked his own life to have saved them, but no aid could be rendered those helpless ones, as no soldier could be spared from his post of duty. The enemy were crowding the rear guard and making a desperate effort by shot and shell to create a panic and stampede in our brigade. Never were the words of General Sherman more truthfully demonstrated, that "War is cruelty and you cannot refine it," than by this incident. Lieutenant Bennett, who commanded the section of the battery in this fight, informed the writer the next day that all of the women and children escaped injury, which he considered almost a miracle under the circumstances, as the shells tore up the ground on all sides of the house Bennett added that he did not care to have another such experience, as he expected every moment that a shell from the rebel battery would burst on the porch or in the house, mangling or killing both women and children. The bursting of the gun near this house has a sequel in which every soldier of the command will be interested. In the charge near Lovejoy Station the horse of A. A. Hill, of Company K, was killed, and, in falling, Hill's leg was caught under his body. After he was extricated from this dangerous position, stunned and dazed, instead of throwing up his hands and surrendering, he followed up the charging column on foot, throwing his sabre down, but clinging to his carbine and cartridge box. The ground was soft and in some places muddy, and he next discarded his cavalry boots, and as he had lost his hat in the charge, he was now in light marching order. When the regiment was forming after the charge Hill was counted missing, George Pearl killed and William Hiser seriously wounded, all of Company K. But about the time the company was all accounted for, Hill came up on the left of the company a little blown, but ready for duty, captured one of the horses of a rebel battery, and was in line before the company was ready to move.

In September, 1890, Hill visited the battlefields around Chattanooga and Atlanta and also Jonesboro and Lovejoy Station.

He passed over the ground where the brigade made the charge, and with the assistance of a prominent official of Jonesboro. located the house on the McDonough road where the gun of the battery burst. An old gentleman by the name of Foster, about seventy-five years of age, was living in the house, and he had still retained a piece of the gun, weighing about forty pounds, which he presented to Mr. Hill. He brought it home, had it photographed with his sabre, and the picture is herewith published. After Colonel Long was wounded, the command of the brigade devolved on Colonel Eggleston of the First, and after the brigade fell back from the position occupied on the high ground at the plantation house, above referred to, the rebels followed up and we had some skirmishing during the afternoon, but the rebels seemed to have had all the fight they wanted, and they did not press the rear guard. The command was soon mounted and moving out on the McDonough road before night. Both men and horses were tired out and exhausted, and after the excitement of two days and nights of almost continuous fighting, there was a complete collapse when the firing ceased, and the men had lost so much sleep that they seemed perfectly indifferent to all surroundings.

We marched on all night, but it was utterly impossible to march in any kind of order or to keep out an advance guard, as men and officers would go to sleep. In some instances the horses would halt along the road in fence corners and the riders would either unconsciously dismount or fall off and sleep until dragged out by the rear guard and compelled to mount and move on with the column. Many of them lost their hats, and no doubt others were taken prisoners by the enemy, and the column moved on silently, horses exhausted, half of the men and officers asleep, and the night as dark as pitch. About two or three o'clock in the morning on the twenty-first, the column halted, and at the point where the second brigade halted there was thick woods. We were ordered to unsaddle, as we had not unsaddled since leaving Sandtown on the evening of the eighteenth, and as soon as the saddles were removed the men tumbled down among the trees on the wet ground at their horses heads and were soon sound asleep. We halted there until about six o'clock, about three hours, and then saddled, moving on about half a mile we found ourselves on the banks of a stream called Cotton Indian Creek at high flood, the banks full to over flowing and no bridge. We had to swim our horses across this stream, and as the banks were steep there was a deep cut on either side of the stream, leading to the ford, and it was not possible to get up the bank only at one point, so that the process of crossing the stream was tedious. Picket ropes were stretched across the stream and General Kilpatrick and his division and brigade commanders were on the bank superintending the crossing. Men, horses and mules were floundering around in the stream, and as it was no doubt the first attempt of some of the horses to swim, and in some instances the men would get frightened, pull on the reins, and as a result many of the riders were unhorsed, and they were saved by the ropes. A number of soldiers were drowned and at least one of the First, Emanuel Jones of Company K. His horse had been killed in the charge the day before and he was mounted on a small mule which became unmanageable, and he was thrown from its back and his sabre and carbine carried him down in a moment. Forty or fifty horses and a number of mules were lost, and the dismounted gun hauled in an ammunition wagon was abandoned, but the ambulances, carrying nearly one hundred wounded, were all safely crossed. Having crossed this stream we were not again troubled by the enemy; they did not follow us up, as they were in no better condition for fighting than our own forces. Guns and ammunition were soaked with water, as every man in the command was wet above the waist after fording the creek. After we had marched a short distance the sun came out and the command halted to pour the water out of their boots, and it was very amusing to see three or four thousand troopers engaged in this work for a few minutes. The command marched on all day and about dark reached Lithonia on the Augusta railroad, and went into bivouac for the night, rejoicing to have the opportunity for a much-needed rest, as we had now been out three days and nights, had only unsaddled once and had not had more than two hours sleep, excepting what we had snatched in the saddle. The next day the command marched through Lattimer and Decatur and reached our old camp at Buckhead about sundown of the twenty-second, having marched completely around Hood's army in five days. During that time we destroyed three miles of railroad track, two locomotives and a large number of cars, with a number of railroad buildings, and ware-houses with supplies. The loss in the division was two hundred and sixteen killed, wounded and missing, about equally distributed between the two brigades, but one authority gives the losses in Longs brigade at ten per cent., which would make the loss in that brigade about one hundred and thirty-eight. The enemy's loss was severe, but of course could not be ascertained definitely, yet it was no doubt equal to ours. While at one time we had several hundred prisoners it was not possible to keep them with such rapid marching, and less than one hundred were turned over by the Provost officer on reaching our lines, many of whom had sabre wounds. We also captured a three gun battery and three battle-flags. This was without doubt the five hardest days and nights consecutive service performed by the regiment during the war. The evening we reached Buckhead we received the news that Colonel Long had been promoted to a brigadier-general and the troopers of the brigade gave vent to their enthusiasm by many rousing cheers.

The greatest loss to the First on that raid was Captain William H. Scott, the brave and gallant Irish boy who fell in front of the enemy's batteries, shouting, "Take the guns." No braver soldier nor truer patriot ever drew his sword in defence of the flag, and he was "mourned as the brave mourn for the brave."

A few years ago, December, 1890, General Long wrote a letter correcting some glaring errors in an article written by a cavalry officer, and purporting to be a history of the Kilpatrick Raid. This article charged that General Long had disobeyed orders, when the facts are, first, General Long never received the order as stated, and second, the officer who claimed to have sent the order did not have any authority to give orders to Long, as General Kilpatrick was in command. I herewith copy a few extracts from General Long's letter, as follows:

> The expression, Second Division, is used more than once in the article. Properly speaking, there was no such thing in the command. There were two brigades of that, the Second Division, with the expedition, and the circumstances would have had to be peculiar, while General Kilpatrick was present, to have authorized or warranted the commander of one of these brigades to give an order to the other; it was not done. I have no recollection of said orders being received by me, and of course, of any disobedience on my part or that of my command, and therefore deny

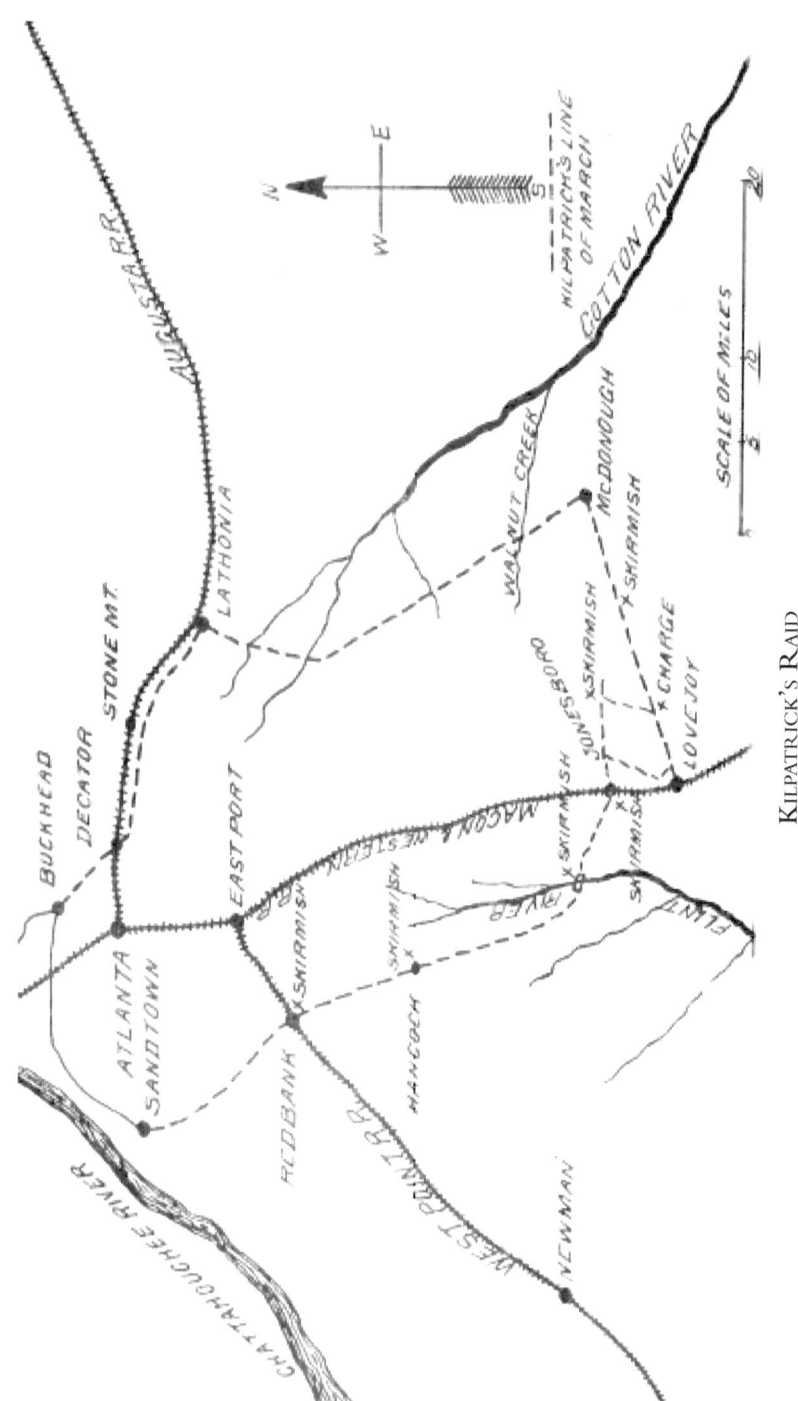

Kilpatrick's Raid

the statement *in toto.* To disobey an order is something I am not conscious of having done during the war.

If there was any confusion or disobedience on the part of the Second Brigade or its commander, it is somewhat singular that something should not have been done or said about it at or about the time it occurred, and that it should be discovered and commented upon only some twenty-six years afterward. As to confusion, considering the time, circumstances and opportunities, I had a good, well-drilled brigade, and during this retreat, fought it when the nature of the ground would permit, as I have never seen done before or since, by bugle commands or signals, retiring alternately one and then another portion of the line, and to me, and to probably most of the men of the brigade, who have seen or heard of it, it is humiliating to have a charge or accusation of this character brought against it at this late day.

The following letters from General Sherman and General Thomas, recommending Colonel Long for promotion to Brigadier-General, shows in what high esteem he was held by those two great commanders, and his commission as Brigadier-General was signed and forwarded by the Secretary of War the very day we started on the Kilpatrick Raid.

> Headquarters
> Military Division of the Mississippi
> In the field near Atlanta, Ga.
> August 16, 1864

Hon. E. M. Stanton
Secretary of War
Washington, D. C.

I need a good cavalry brigadier very much, and recommend Colonel Eli Long, Fourth Ohio Cavalry, now here, and who merited promotion for good service the time I went to Knoxville. He is a junior Colonel now, and the cavalry is not commanded to my satisfaction.

W. T. Sherman, Major-General, Commanding

Headquarters
Department of the Cumberland,
August 16, 1864

Major-General Sherman
Commanding Military Division of the Mississippi
General: I do not know how to overcome the difficulty of finding a commander for the division now commanded by Garrard, unless you could have Colonel Long promoted. I regard Long as a very efficient officer, who, by his services during this war, has dearly earned his promotion, not only for gallantry, but on account of his administrative ability and experience.
Geo. H. Thomas
Major-General U. S. Vol.
Commanding

Washington
August 18, 1864

Major-General Sherman:
The appointment of Colonel Long as Brigadier has been made, and will be forwarded to you by mail immediately.
E. M. Stanton
Secretary of War

No newspaper writer can add to the fame of the command to which he belonged by giving them high sounding names after the war, such as Fighting Brigade, Sabre Brigade, Lightning Brigade, Bayonet Brigade, etc.; neither can he detract from the fair fame of such a brilliant officer as General Eli Long, who won his stars at the front, was severely wounded at least a half dozen times, by any carping criticism, born of jealousy during the war. After the battle of Stone's River the First Ohio was frequently called the Charging First, for the reason that during that battle, in a charge made by the regiment, the colonel, major and a lieutenant were killed and the Adjutant was severely wounded, and the regiment fairly won some distinction on that account. But they did not parade the regiment in the newspapers as the Charging First, for it was considered in bad taste, and is so considered now by good soldiers.

We remained in camp at Buckhead until the twenty-fifth of August, and when Sherman's army commenced the great flank movement to the right, the brigade moved down the Chattahoochie to Sandtown, and encamped there on the twenty-sixth. The next morning we moved to the front and took position on the left of the Twenty-third Army Corps and extreme left of our army. We continued to advance on the left and had more or less skirmishing every day up to the second of September. Atlanta was evacuated on the night of the first, and General Slocum marched into the city with the Twentieth Army Corps on the morning of the second. From the second up to the eighth the brigade watched the left flank of the army as it retired to Atlanta and on the fourth the regiment made a reconnaissance to the east on Cotton Indian Creek near Flat Rock Shoals, took a number of prisoners and learned that there was a heavy cavalry force of the enemy at McDonough. Marched to Cross Keys on the tenth, across roads about fifteen miles north-east of Atlanta, and went into camp. We remained in camp near Cross Keys through the month of September, doing picket duty, scouting and recruiting up our horses, as the hard summer's campaign, with scarcity of forage, had cut the horses down in flesh and rendered many of them unfit for service. During the month there were some changes in the regiment, as the non-veterans started for home to be mustered out on the twenty-first. Captain Erwin and Captain Woodlief resigned September 30, and some of the officers got leave of absence. Lieutenant Curry was detailed as Quartermaster September 12, so that our numbers were not only materially reduced, but there were a number of changes in company commanders. Lieutenant-Colonel Pattin was still in command of the regiment, and Colonel Eggleston in command of the brigade. We left our camp at Cross Keys on the second of October, crossed the Chattahoochie on a pontoon, as the floods had swept all the bridges off, and the pontoon was thrown across for the Twenty-third. A. C. Hood was making his flank movement by the right of our army and had already struck the railroad in our rear, and the day we arrived at Marietta, the fifth, the battle of Alatoona was fought. General French's division of the rebel army attacked a brigade at Alatoona Pass, commanded by General Corse, and was repulsed with heavy loss.

On the day of the fight at Alatoona the regiment bivouacked at the foot of Kenesaw Mountain and the writer, in company with two or three other officers of the regiment, rode to the summit of the mountain. General Sherman, with some members of his staff, was on top of the mountain with the signal corps. We could plainly hear the roar of the guns at Alatoona, fifteen miles away, where the battle was raging, and the smoke could be plainly seen with a field glass, and under the eye of General Sherman, who was very restless and nervous, the signal officer was busily signalling and finally caught the signal that General Corse was in command. Then General Sherman sent the dispatch, "Hold the fort, for I am coming," which furnished the theme for the Sabbath School song, sung by every child in our land, *Hold the Fort*.

The division moved toward New Hope Church on the left flank of the army, now faced toward Chattanooga, and during this retrograde movement and until Hood's army was out of our reach and marched toward Northern Alabama, we were continuously skirmishing with both cavalry and infantry and had some sharp fights. On the seventh the division had a fight at New Hope Church with Armstrong's division of cavalry and drove him back some distance and almost to Dallas. On the twelfth the division, having crossed the river at Rome, attacked Armstrong's division and drove them back toward Cedar Bluff about four miles, with considerable loss to the enemy. The division then fell back toward Rome and bivouacked for the night. On the morning of the thirteenth the enemy's scouts appeared on the hills just east of Rome and in plain view, and the division crossing the Ostenaula River moved to the attack at once with the Second Brigade in advance and the First Ohio, dismounted, as skirmishers. The enemy was rapidly driven back, but soon opened up with artillery. This did not check our line, the boys moved forward with great enthusiasm, as their blood was up and they were anxious for the fray.

They swept everything before them with a whirl, capturing two pieces of artillery, one battle flag of a Texas regiment, about one hundred prisoners, and the enemy was soon routed and in full retreat. General Garrard's report of this fight is herewith attached and gives a good account of the engagement.

Extract from report of Brigadier-General Garrard, Nashville, Tenn., 16 November, 1864

On the thirteenth the enemy's cavalry appeared on the hills west of Rome. The division crossed the Etowah and then the Ostenaula, and drove the enemy away and five miles down the road toward Coosaville. On the thirteenth received orders to find out if the enemy had taken up his pontoon bridge, and if so, on which side of the river. The Twenty-third Corps was ordered to support me. After advancing some four miles struck the enemy. The First Ohio was dismounted as skirmishers, and the Third Ohio was sent out on the flanks mounted, and the Third Brigade, Miller's, was at once dismounted and brought up in line, two regiments on each side of the road.

The enemy, after a little skirmishing, fell back, but our advance continued. Soon after the enemy opened artillery. We were moving through the woods, and could not see his position, but continued to advance, the Third Brigade and First Ohio in line on both sides of the road dismounted, the First Brigade mounted in column of fours in the road, the head of column on line with the dismounted men and two companies of the Third Ohio mounted on each flank. When within long rifle range of their position, the woods ended, and large open corn-fields lay between us and the enemy, who had formed line beyond a creek on a ridge in the edge of some timber. Just as the line was about to emerge from the woods, the charge was ordered. The enemy stood firing his artillery up to the last moment, and the cannoneers used their pistols in defence of their pieces. The artillery, two pieces, was captured just as it was limbered up. The enemy was routed and pursued on several different roads. Their killed, wounded and captured, which fell into our hands, was over seventy, but every pursuing party reported large numbers left wounded and killed on the roads and in the woods. The main body was pursued on the Coosaville road fourteen miles below Rome, and full and complete information was gained in regard to the pontoon bridge. The rebel cavalry was Allen's division of Wheeler's corps. One of the brigades was the Texas brigade. A set of colours of one of the Texas regiments was captured. The loss on our side was fourteen killed and wounded, and between thirty and forty horses. The enemy was completely routed, and I learned afterward it was more than three days before this rebel division of cavalry could be collected together.

On the seventeenth we marched through Snake Creek Gap, which was blockaded by large trees cut by the enemy, and our march was very slow and tedious. Marched down Broomtown Valley through Villanow and to Sublignia at the head of Dirtown Valley, arriving about midnight. On the nineteenth we marched down Dirtown Valley and through the pass of Taylor's Ridge, passed down South Carolina Valley, and on the evening of the eighteenth camped at Chattanooga Creek. The division was on the march continuously, watching the enemy and attacking his flanks and rear guard almost every day. On the twentieth the division crossed Little River and had some skirmishing and followed the enemy's rear guard, Wheeler's cavalry, until dark. In this fight the ammunition of the First was about all exhausted, and as the ammunition wagons did not have cartridges of the right calibre, the regiment was detailed for courier duty at General Sherman's headquarters through Gaylesville to Rome. The headquarters of the regiment was at Coosaville until the thirtieth, and that day we marched to Rome, and Sherman's whole army was moving back toward Atlanta, leaving Hood to be taken care of by General Thomas.

CHAPTER 19

Atlanta Battles and Losses
Summer, 1864

The summer of 1864 was the great battle summer of the war. While Grant was battling his way through the wilderness, Sherman was driving the Confederate army, commanded by General Joe Johnston, steadily through the mountain passes of Northern Georgia. The campaign is generally called the "One hundred days under fire from Chattanooga to Atlanta," but the facts are that the campaign opened May 5 and closed with the taking of Atlanta, September 1, about one hundred and twenty days. It is literally true that from the firing of the first gun, May 5, to the taking of Atlanta, there was fighting on some part of the line every hour. Fighting was the regular daily business of Sherman's army, and the soldiers were aroused from the bivouac each morning to get a hurried breakfast of coffee and hardtack, and the cavalrymen to feed, groom and water their horses, with the full expectation of attacking the enemy at any moment, and they were rarely disappointed.

It is very surprising how quickly young men will adapt themselves to the hardships and perils of war, and so soon be come accustomed to active warfare, that the average soldier goes about it the same as the citizen follows his usual vocation.

The veteran fully realizes that in every battle the chances are against him, but he goes on, never shirking from duty, hoping for the best, and it is rarely the case that a soldier will acknowledge, when a battle opens, that he believes he will be killed.

Lt. Gen. Jos. Wheeler.
C. S. A.

Lt. Gen. N. B. Forrest.
C. S. A.

Piece of the gun of the Chicago Board of Trade Battery that exploded August 20th, 1864, near Lovejoy, Ga.—See page 183.

When Sherman's army commenced the advance, May 5, 1864, he had, in round numbers, 100,000 men present for duty.

Army of the Cumberland
Major-General Thomas

Infantry	54,568
Artillery	2,377
Cavalry	3,828
Total	60,773
Field guns	130

Army of the Tennessee
Major-General McPherson

Infantry	22,437
Artillery	1,404
Cavalry	624
Total	24,465
Field guns	96

Army of Ohio
Major-General Schofield

Infantry	11,183
Artillery	679
Cavalry	1,697
Total	13,559
Field guns	28
Grand total	98,797
Field guns	254

Soon after the campaign began two more divisions of cavalry joined Sherman's army: General Stoneman, 4,000; General Garrard, 4,500.

General Sherman in making an estimate of the number of men and horses to be supplied by his one line of railroad from Louisville to Chattanooga, estimated horses and mules at 35,000, and that it would require one hundred and thirty cars of ten tons each to reach Chattanooga daily to supply his army. He did not calculate to transport any hay, and only five pounds of oats or corn per day for each animal, and expected the cavalry to subsist their horses on grass and wheat for rough forage, and beef cattle were to be driven on the hoof. To transport these supplies it required one hundred locomotives and one thousand freight cars. Before the army moved, orders were issued requiring men and officers to carry their clothing and five days' rations, only one wagon and one ambulance was allowed to each regiment, and the officers of each company one pack mule. Only one tent was allowed each headquarters, and officers and men carried their own shelter tents. A shelter tent, or dog tent, as they were usually called, was composed of two pieces of muslin or tent cloth, about four by six feet, and on one edge of this cloth was a row of buttons, and on the opposite side was a row of button holes. Each soldier carried a half tent and two bunked together. The two pieces of cloth were buttoned together and then stretched over a fence-rail or stick for a ridge pole, driving down about three stakes on each side, and the tent was pitched ready for sleeping. By the time two cavalrymen put their saddles, bridles, carbines, sabres, revolvers, haversacks and canteens under this shelter, there was not an over abundance of room for two soldiers, and the six-footer usually slept with his feet out in the rain. It is safe to say that no army during the war was stripped down to fighting weight and put in better condition for hard campaigning and rapid marching than was Sherman's army when they started on the Atlanta campaign. The army moved May 5 and drove the enemy back steadily from Dalton on to Resaca, and on the fifteenth the opening battle of that great campaign was fought at Resaca. Our loss in that battle was six hundred killed and about thirty-four hundred wounded. Johnson retreated on the night of the fifteenth and did not halt until he reached Cassville, near Alatoona Pass, a very strong position. Instead of attacking Johnston's army at Alatoona, which was a very strong position, Sherman moved his whole army to the right toward Dallas in order to flank Johnston's position and compelled him to evacuate the Pass. Johnston anticipated Sherman, and near Dallas our army, in moving by the flank, struck the Confederates, May 25, and fighting ensued from that date to June 1, with heavy loss to both armies. June 4 Johnston evacuated Alatoona Pass and fell back to Kenesaw Mountain, and Sherman's army moved forward to Big Shanty. The casualties in our army during the month of May was: Killed and missing, 1,863; wounded, 7,436; total, 9,299.

According to the reports of the Confederate army Johnston had 64,465 men in line during the fighting about Dallas and New Hope Church, and his loss in the month of May was: Killed, 721; wounded, 4,672; missing, 3,245; total, 8,638.

By the fourteenth of June Sherman's army was in position in front of Johnston's fortified army with a battle line ten miles long, and there was continuous skirmishing all along the battle front, around Kenesaw Mountain, Little Kenesaw and Pine Mountain.

On the fourteenth Sherman was riding along his lines taking observation and, noticing a rebel battery on Pine Mountain with a group of what he supposed to be a General and his staff observing our lines with glasses, he directed General Howard to have a battery fire three volleys at the group and disperse them. General Polk was killed by a shell fired at this time, and our army learned of his death that afternoon, as one of our signal officers had deciphered their "key" and caught the signal sent from Pine Mountain to Marietta, "Send an ambulance for General Polk's body." It rained in torrents from the fourteenth to about the twenty-fifth, but in spite of the storms, fighting was continued incessantly all the time, our army moving forward steadily, fortifying daily, and Sherman estimated at that time that Johnston had fifty miles of "connected trenches with abatis and finished batteries."

Every soldier in Sherman's army well remembers the great artillery duels that were of daily occurrence along the line, and of the rebel battery on the summit of Kenesaw, that kept booming away day and night for about three weeks, and how the white smoke puffed up near the "Lone Tree," then hear the screaming of the shells and next the report of the guns, and how we would, with watch in hand, calculate the distance.

June 27 Sherman attacked Johnston's fortified army around Kenesaw Mountain, but our army was repulsed with heavy loss, as the Army of the Cumberland lost upward of two thousand killed and wounded, and the Army of the Tennessee about five hundred. Johnston admits his loss in killed and wounded at eight hundred and eight. The fighting was desperate from nine o'clock to eleven a. m., and up to that time it was the hardest fought battle of the campaign. Sherman decided to make another flank to the right to compel Johnston to evacuate Kenesaw. The movement was commenced on the night of July 2, but Johnston anticipated the move and evacuated Kenesaw the same night and fell back to his next line on the Chattahoochie River, where he had strong fortifications. The battle had been almost continuous from June 10 to July 3, and our losses during the month of June were: Killed and missing, 1,790; wounded, 5,740; total, 7,530. Confederate losses for June: Killed, wounded and prisoners, 5,948. On the fourth Thomas attacked Johnston in his works and a hard battle ensued, and there was more or less fighting every day up to the ninth, and that day Schofield crossed the river at Soap's Creek and Garrard's cavalry crossed at Roswell, and that night Johnston evacuated his works on the west side of the river, crossed the river and burned the railroad bridge. Sherman's main army crossed the Chattahoochie on the seventeenth, and the general movement against Atlanta commenced, and our army closed in on Atlanta from the north and north-east by way of Decatur. On the eighteenth Johnston was removed from command of the Confederate army and Hood was given command. On the twentieth Hood left his works and made a sudden and impetuous attack on Thomas army, and the blow was principally against Hooker's corps, the Twentieth. The fighting was very severe and in some places hand to hand, but in two hours the enemy were driven back into their works with heavy loss.

Hooker's loss was about fifteen hundred killed and wounded, and Hood's loss was estimated at four thousand. On the twenty-second was fought what is generally called the battle of Atlanta.

Hood again sallied out of his works and attacked the left and left rear of Sherman's army, commanded by General McPherson. The battle raged from noon until night, and the losses in both armies were very heavy. General McPherson was killed about 11 a. m. and General John A. Logan at once assumed command of the Army of the Tennessee, which he handled with great skill and courage throughout the battle. General Logan reported the total loss of the Army of the Tennessee at 3,521. Hood's loss was: Killed, 3,220; prisoners, 1,017; wounded prisoners, 1,000; total, 5,237.

The losses of the enemy as reported above were those that fell into our hands, and Logan estimated that at least four thousand wounded were kept within the rebel lines. General O. O. Howard was assigned to the command of the Army of the Tennessee July 24.

The cavalry divisions of Stoneman and Garrard were sent to the rear of Hood's army to make a break in the railroad about Jonesboro, and the Army of the Tennessee was ordered to swing around to the extreme right of our army and all of these movements commenced on the twenty-seventh. On the twenty-eighth Hood again sallied out of his trenches and attacked our right flank. The brunt of the battle fell on the Fifteenth Corps, commanded by Logan. Hood's army, the corps of Lee and Hardee, made six successive charges and each time were repulsed with great loss.

The loss of the Fifteenth Corps was five hundred and seventy-two killed and wounded. Logan reported that his command buried five hundred and sixty-five rebels and captured one hundred and seventy-three prisoners, and he estimated the rebel loss at about six thousand, all told, as they were literally slaughtered, our army being protected by barricades.

The campaign during July had been one of constant fighting, and the losses in both armies were heavy. As shown by reports of the Confederate army, Johnston's and Hood's losses were: Killed, 1,341; wounded, 7,500; missing, 1,550. In Sherman's army the losses were: Killed and missing, 3,944; wounded, 5,965; total, 9,909.

The month of August opened with Sherman's army closely

investing Atlanta, and the cavalry expedition under Stoneman had met defeat, lost many prisoners, and General Stoneman himself had been captured with seven or eight hundred men near Clinton, Ga. There was some hard lighting on the right toward West Point on the fifth, sixth and seventh, mostly by the Twenty-third Corps, under Schofield, and a continuous artillery battle was kept up against the fortifications, and into Atlanta shells were tossed daily. Thus the two armies kept pounding away until the eighteenth, and on that date Kilpatrick was dispatched with three divisions of cavalry to make a raid in the rear of Hood's army. He made a successful raid, made a complete circuit of Hood's army, destroyed several miles of railroad track, and reached our lines safely again on the twenty-second. On the night of the twenty-fifth Sherman commenced his great flank movement to the right. There was considerable of fighting during the movement, but the only hard battle fought was at Jonesboro on the evening of September 1. The Fourteenth Corps drove the rebels back and captured in their fortifications Govan's brigade with ten pieces of artillery.

Hood blew up his magazines and evacuated Atlanta on the night of September 1, and "Atlanta was ours and fairly won." The losses in our army during the months of August and September were: Killed and missing, 1,408; wounded, 3,731; total, 5,139. Hood's army: Killed, 482; wounded, 3,223; prisoners, 3,738; total, 7,443.

Johnston and Hood, in reporting their losses in the Atlanta campaign, only reported the killed and wounded, while Sherman reported killed, wounded and missing in his army. Sherman's army captured and sent north during that campaign 12,938 Confederate soldiers, and in compiling Confederate losses these prisoners have been added to the Confederate reports of their losses, stating as near as possible the number captured in each battle.

Total loss in the Atlanta campaign: Union Army: Killed, 4,423; wounded, 22,822; missing, 4,442; total, 31,687. Confederate army: Killed, 3,044; wounded, 18,952; prisoners, 12,983; total, 34,979.

Extract from report of
Major-General Geo. H. Thomas, U. S. Army,
commanding Army of the Cumberland

Headquarters
Army of the Cumberland
In the field near Dallas, Ga.
June 5, 1864

Colonel: General Garrard, commanding Second Cavalry Division, informed me that he was camped on Pumpkin Vine Creek, about three miles from Dallas, and that, in moving on that place, and when within a quarter of a mile from it, he was attacked by what was reported by prisoners to be Bate's division, the advance of Hardee's corps. Garrard repulsed this force and drove it back toward Dallas.

Extract from report of
Major-General Frank P. Blair, Jr., U. S. Army,
commanding Seventeenth Army Corps

Rome, Ga.
June 5, 1864

General: I marched with the Third and Fourth Divisions, commanded respectively by Brigadier-Generals Leggett and Crocker, on the twenty-fifth *ultimo*, in the direction of Decatur, reaching that place on the twenty-sixth, where I was joined by Colonel Long with his brigade of cavalry, twenty-five hundred strong. As Roddy was reported to be encamped near Courtland, fifteen miles distant, I ordered Colonel Long to move on him with his brigade on the morning of the twenty-seventh. In order to give the enemy the impression that this corps was moving in that direction I sent one brigade of infantry, which I obtained from the garrison of Decatur, to support him, with instructions to display the infantry to any force they might meet. This was done successfully, and Roddy's command, after a brief skirmish, fell rapidly back, abandoning his camps. Colonel

Long then, under my instructions, moved in the direction of Moulton, which place he reached without molestation. On the morning of the twenty-ninth he was attacked in camp by Roddy's whole force with four pieces of artillery. After a sharp fight the enemy was routed and driven from the field, leaving his dead, wounded and a number of prisoners in our hands. For particulars I refer you to the enclosed copy of Colonel Long's official report. I desire to call your attention to the very handsome manner in which Colonel Long carried out his instructions and fought his command, by which I am satisfied that our march was relieved from any molestation and Roddy's projected raid on our communications at Athens and Pulaski postponed, if not prevented.

> Headquarters
> Second Cavalry Division
> Crossroads Alabama-Lovegood & Marietta Roads
> June 10, 1864

Major-General McPherson

General: My headquarters are where they were last night. This morning I sent Long's brigade down on the Marietta and Lovegood's bridge road and secured the intersection of that road with the Big Shanty and Roswell Factory road, which is the main road leading from Big Shanty east. I sent a part of Long's brigade, nine hundred men, down the Big Shanty road to come in on the flank of the enemy, but neither Minty or Long could make any headway, though they both charged and took a line of rail breast works. General Wheeler and three divisions of cavalry are said by prisoners to be in my front, and two batteries. I have prisoners from Iverson's, Allen's, Williams' and Ferguson's brigades, and from Martin's division. The fight today was at Doctor McAfee's. I send you a sketch, which please show to General Sherman and also this letter, and say to him that the rebel cavalry is still here. Do you want me to try to hold both the Alabama road and the Big Shanty road, or shall I move down the Marietta road and hold only the Big Shanty road? The roads are over two miles apart, and I may not, if attacked in force, be able to hold both. The Big Shanty guards your flank and, if I lose it and hold only the Alabama road, it would put the enemy between us. Brush Mountain is about twelve miles from the Kenesaw, and in this space are three good roads to Marietta.

K. Garrard, Commanding Division

>Headquarters
>Second Cavalry Division
>In the field near Kenesaw Mountain, Ga.
>June 21, 1864

Respectfully forwarded

Colonel Long had one regiment on picket guarding the crossing of Noonday Creek on the Bell's Ferry road, and two regiments dismounted to meet any emergency. The fight lasted until after dark. From all information received it is just to conclude that the loss of the enemy was very severe, and that two divisions attacked me, supported by other troops.

K. Garrard

>Headquarters
>Second Brigade
>Second Division Cavalry
>Near Roswell, Ga.
>July 12, 1864

Captain J. E. Jacobs
Assistant Adjutant-General

Captain: Please find annexed a report of the operations of the Second Brigade, Second Cavalry Division, since leaving Decatur, Ala., on the twenty-sixth of May, and up to the present month, which I have the honour to forward for the information of the Brigadier-General commanding corps: Leaving Decatur, I proceeded on the Courtland road toward Courtland, Ala., and soon found the enemy, a portion of General Roddy's cavalry command. Attacking them at once, they were thrown into a hasty retreat, and we captured twelve prisoners and two stands of colours, besides wagons, horses, mules, arms.

Next day Roddy's entire command was met near Courtland, and, after an engagement of half an hour, I drove him through the town, taking three prisoners and killing Major Williams. We had one man wounded. On the twenty-eighth we had no fighting, but surprised and captured six of Roddy's men.

May 29, near Moulton, Ala., I was attacked at 4 a. m. by General Roddy with four pieces of artillery. After a severe engagement, lasting two hours, the enemy was completely repulsed on all sides, and compelled to retreat in great disorder toward Moulton, leaving his dead and some wounded on the field. Roddy's loss was twelve to fifteen killed; the number of his wounded not known. We took thirty-six prisoners, including one Lieutenant-Colonel and two Lieutenants. Our own casualties were three killed and fourteen wounded. Marched that morning at eight o'clock, passing through Somerville, Ala., and on the thirtieth of May overtook the Seventeenth Army Corps, Major-General Blair. Remained with this command until the sixth of June, when we arrived at Kingston, Ga. Crossing Raccoon and Sand Mountains was very severe upon our horses, although the roads by this route were generally good and water abundant.

Crossed Lookout Mountain on the third of June and marched toward Rome, Ga., surprising and capturing sixteen rebel soldiers and one Lieutenant-Colonel. June 10 marched from Rome to Kingston, and on the following day to Etowah Bridge, thence toward Marietta. June 11, while encamped ten miles from Marietta, I sent out the First Ohio Cavalry on a reconnaissance toward that town. They met a force of the enemy and drove them some four miles. Our loss here was twelve wounded and two missing. The enemy had several wounded and we took one prisoner. Remained in camp at Noonday Creek, having frequent skirmishing with the rebel pickets, until the fifteenth, when I received marching orders. At 2 p. m. I attacked General Wheeler's cavalry command, and fought him for about an hour, but was at length compelled to fall back, Wheeler being well fortified and entrenched beyond our power to drive him out. In this engagement we lost two killed, sixteen wounded, and two missing. Rebel loss unknown. On the sixteenth of June I moved toward the front and encamped near Kenesaw Mountain, remaining here until the nineteenth, when, upon orders received, I moved my command and drove the enemy to Noonday Creek. The enemy made a stand on the opposite bank of the creek and fought stubbornly for several hours. June 23, crossed Noonday Creek, and was attacked by the enemy some five miles from Marietta. The attack was handsomely repelled, and the enemy driven back, with a loss of one killed and several wounded.

Since leaving Decatur, the brigade has marched (the main column) two hundred and fifteen miles, much of this distance being mountainous country . Besides horses, mules, wagons and arms taken, we captured a total of five officers and fifty-four men, and lost, in killed, five; wounded, forty-five; missing, six.

Eli Long, Colonel, Commanding Brigade

Headquarters
Second Brigade
Second Cavalry Division
Near Roswell, Ga.
July 14, 1804

Captain R. P. Kennedy
Assistant Adjutant-General
Second Cavalry Division

Sir: I have the honour to forward, for the information of the division commander, the following report, showing the movements and operations of the Second Brigade from the first of the present month to date:

Being encamped near Noonday Creek, north of Marietta, I remained there until the evening of the third, then marching to Big Shanty. On the following day I received orders to follow the enemy, who was retreating, and, marching via Marietta, I pursued him some four miles south-east of that town. At 3 a. m. of the fourth I again had marching orders, and on moving out of camp found the rebels in considerable force a short distance in front of the pickets, with strong breast-works thrown up. This was found to be Wheeler's cavalry re-enforced, as nearly as could be ascertained, by a division of infantry. Fighting immediately ensued and was continued at intervals throughout the day with heavy skirmishing, in which my loss was but one killed and seventeen wounded, the men being protected by rail breast-works hastily thrown up. We took two prisoners. Not being able to dislodge the enemy or effect any decided result, the command returned in the evening to camp. On the fifth I marched to within one mile and a half of Chattahoochie River, near the town of Roswell. July 9, upon orders received, I sent the Fourth Ohio Volunteer Cavalry, at 3 a. m., to McAfee's bridge, across the Chattahoochee, eight miles above Roswell, with instructions to hold it and prevent the enemy from crossing or destroying it. The other regiments of my brigade were held as a reserve, saddled and in readiness to move at the shortest notice. The enemy held the further end of the bridge and skirmishing with them was continued until evening, when they fell back.

Eli Long, Colonel, Commanding Brigade

>Headquarters
>Cavalry Division
>July 19, 1864, 10 p. m.

General: I have to report that, owing to the appearance of the enemy in this vicinity last evening, I sent a regiment to the Peach Tree road, one to McAfee's bridge, and ordered Colonel Long with his two regiments up. They met strong

opposition just outside of my pickets and had heavy skirmishing to within a mile of the depot. I then moved up Long and we went into the town. We fought two brigades. We captured one set of colours, which they dropped in their hasty retreat. The depot, containing large amounts of quartermaster and commissary stores, was burned; also about two hundred bales of cotton; also the railroad as fast as we advanced. We had to use artillery to drive them out of the houses. I could only spare five regiments for this duty, and I am to guard such an extended flank it will be impossible for me to do anything else. I would suggest the destruction of McAfee's bridge and that my line be contracted.
K. *Garrard*

Headquarters
Department of the Cumberland
Near Atlanta, Ga.
July 25, 1864

Brigadier-General Garrard, commanding Second Cavalry Division, has just returned from a raid upon the Georgia Railroad, having lost two men and brought in two hundred prisoners and a fair lot of fresh horses and negroes. He destroyed the railroad bridge across the branches of the Ocmulgee and the depots at Conyers, Covington and Social Circle. By command of Major-General Thomas:
Wm. Whipple, Assistant Adjutant-General

In the field near Atlanta, Ga.
July 24, 1864, 2 p. m.

General Garrard
Decatur
General: I am rejoiced to hear that you are back safe and successful. I will give you time to rest and then we must make quick work with Atlanta. I await your report with impatience, and in the meantime tender you assurance of my great consideration.
Your friend,
W. T. Sherman

Headquarters
Second Cavalry Division
Decatur
July 24, 1864

General Sherman
Commanding army

General: I have the honour to report that your instructions have been carried out. Results, three road bridges and one railroad bridge, five hundred and fifty-five feet in length, over the Yellow River, and one road and one railroad bridge, two hundred and fifty feet in length, over the Ulcofauhachee, were burned, six miles of railroad track between the rivers were well destroyed, the depot and considerable quantity of quartermaster and commissary stores at Covington were burned, one train and locomotive captured at Conyers and burnt. One train-platform was burnt at Covington, and a small train, baggage, at station near the Ulcofauhachee, captured and burned. Over two thousand bales of cotton were burnt. A large new hospital at Covington, for the accommodation of ten thousand patients of this army and the Army of the Virginia, composed of over thirty buildings, besides the offices, just finished, were burnt. In the town of Oxford, two miles north of Covington, and in Covington, were over one thousand sick and wounded in buildings used for hospitals. The convalescents able to walk scattered through the woods while the fire was going on in town, and I did not have time to hunt them up before dark. Those in hospitals, together with their surgeons, were not disturbed.

From the two other brigades I have received one hundred and forty prisoners and eleven officers and about two hundred negroes. I cannot mention too highly the zeal and promptness of my whole command, and to their good conduct and earnestness I am indebted for this success. Since leaving Marietta, this division has been so constantly in motion that it is now very much out of condition. I would be pleased to have a few days quiet to shoe horses and repair equipments. I was absent from Decatur less than three days and as a division marched over ninety miles.

K. Garrard

Extract from W.T. Sherman's report

Near Atlanta
July 20, 1804, midnight

General Garrard
Commanding Cavalry Division:

General: Take the road by Lattimar's, touching the rail road at or beyond Lithonia, and thence substantially along the railroad, destroying it effectually all the way, especially the Yellow Elver bridge this side of Covington, as well as the road bridge over the Yellow River, after you have passed. From Covington send detachments to destroy the rail and road bridges east of Covington over the Ulcofauhachee. Try and capture and destroy some locomotives and cars, and the depots and stores at Covington, but of private property only take what is necessary for your own use, except horses and mules, of which you will take all that are fit for service, exercising, of course, some judgement as to the animals belonging to the poor and needy.

It is a matter of vital importance and must be attempted with great vigour. The importance of it will justify the loss of a quarter of your command. Be prepared with axes, hatchets, and bars to tear up sections of track and make bonfires. When the rails are red hot they must be twisted. Burning will do for the bridges and culverts, but not for ordinary track. Let the work be well done.

August 18. No changes on the part of the enemy discovered today. Two p. m. received the following dispatch from General Thomas, dated August 18, as follows:

For the purpose of aiding General Kilpatrick in his operations on the Macon railroad as much as possible, I desire you to concentrate on your left flank as large a force as you can, without weakening your lines too much (by daylight tomorrow morning, nineteenth), and make a strong demonstration and attract the enemy toward you as much as possible, and endeavour to hold him opposite you during the day. It is hoped that General Kilpatrick will be able to reach the Macon road at Jonesboro between 12 m. and 2 p. m. to-morrow, the nineteenth, and if he can have from that time until 10 p. m. to work uninterruptedly, he ought to be able to destroy so much of the road as to make it impossible to operate it for at least ten days, by which time it is supposed Hood will be starved out. Similar instructions have been given to General Garrard, who will operate on the enemy's flank, still farther to your left. It is also desirable for you to make a similar demonstration on the morning of the twentieth, to enable General Kilpatrick to withdraw.

August 20. Ferguson's brigade of cavalry, which was on their right, left at daylight yesterday morning in pursuit of Kilpatrick. One p. m. received from General Garrard, commanding cavalry division, two papers taken from two scouts captured by some of his troops near Decatur. These papers were orders from Hood's chief of scouts, ordering them to be sure and find out where our left flank rests, where the flank joins the main line, and what troops are on our left flank, and to be sure and send in this information and let it be reliable.

August 22. Nothing unusual or of importance occurred during the day. We are closely watching the movements of the enemy and for the effects of General Kilpatrick's raid. Very little artillery firing to-day. Usual picket firing. Two or three men wounded. Five p. m., General Kilpatrick returned from his raid. He destroyed four miles of the Atlanta and Macon Railroad completely, and ten miles at intervals. He had hard fighting; found the enemy's infantry and cavalry on the ground. He was opposed by one division of infantry and one brigade, and three brigades of cavalry.

Near Atlanta, Ga.
August 22, 1864, 10 p. m.

Major-General H. W. Halleck
Washington, D. C.
General Kilpatrick is back. He had pretty hard fighting with a division of infantry and three brigades of cavalry. He broke the cavalry into disorder and captured a battery, which he destroyed, except one gun, which he brought in in addition to all of his own. He also brought in three captured flags and seventy prisoners. He had possession of a large part of Ross brigade, but could not encumber himself with them. He destroyed three miles of the road about Jonesboro, and broke it to pieces for about ten miles more, enough to disable the road for ten days. General Kilpatrick destroyed two locomotives and trains.
W. T. Sherman, Major-General

Extract from report of General Garrard

Jonesboro, Ga.
September 4, 1804

From the commencement to the end of the campaign, this division has been in the front and has, during the whole time, had intrusted to it duties of the highest trust and responsibility. It gives me much pleasure to report that every order it has received has been fully and well executed, and that no accident whatever has occurred, nor has any capture been made on the flank or in the rear where the division has been assigned to duty. The division, though reduced in numbers by the length and severity of the campaign, is still, as an organization, in effective condition. This, in connection with the good service it has rendered, speaks in highest terms of the soldierly qualities of both nay officers and men. All of whom, throughout the campaign, have manifested an earnest and zealous spirit in the performance of duty and have always, with the greatest cheerfulness, under taken any task assigned them. In general terms I cannot say too much in their praise.

K. Garrard, Brigadier-General, Commanding Division.

Special Field Orders No. 64

Headquarters
Military Division of the Mississippi
In the field near Lovejoy's
Sept. 4, 1864

The army having accomplished its undertaking in the complete reduction and occupation of Atlanta, will occupy the place and the country near it until a new campaign is planned in concert with the other grand armies of the United States.

General Kilpatrick's cavalry will cover the left rear of the Army of the Tennessee, and that of General Garrard the right rear of the Army of the Ohio until they reach the positions assigned in this order, when the cavalry commands will move to the points designated, *viz.*: Sandtown and Roswell. The General-in-Chief will give notice when the movement will begin, and after reaching Atlanta will establish headquarters in Atlanta and afford the army an opportunity to have a full month's rest, with every chance to organize, receive pay, replenish clothing and prepare for a fine winter's campaign. By order of Major-General W. T. Sherman:

L. M. Dayton, Aide-de-Camp

EXTRACT FROM REPORT OF GENERAL GEO. H. THOMAS

Headquarters
Department of the Cumberland
Atlanta, Ga.
September 13, 1864

Colonel: On the eighteenth of August Brigadier-General J. Kilpatrick, commanding Third Cavalry Division, was directed to attack and destroy both railroads, and for this purpose he was re-enforced by two brigades taken from Garrard's cavalry division stationed on the left of the army. With this force, numbering in all about four thousand men and two batteries of artillery, General Kilpatrick moved out from Sandtown on the evening of the eighteenth. He met the enemy's cavalry pickets when only a short distance out from Sandtown on the Chattahoochee, and skirmished with them to Jonesboro on the Macon railroad, driving them through that place.

For six hours the command was engaged, destroying the track, etc., until near midnight of the nineteenth, when part of his command was attacked one mile below the town and driven in, but subsequently the enemy was repulsed.

Toward daylight of the twentieth he moved in the direction of McDonough, and thence across country back to the railroad near Lovejoy's Station, reaching that point at about 11 a. m. on the twentieth. There he met a brigade of infantry and, although repulsed at first, finally checked the advantage being gained by the enemy and drove him back with heavy loss.

While thus engaged fighting infantry, a heavy force of cavalry with artillery came up in his rear, and he found he was completely enveloped. Determining at once to break the enemy's line and extricate his command from its delicate position, he decided to ride over the enemy's cavalry and retire on McDonough. The movement was successfully made and resulted in a complete rout of Jackson's cavalry division, numbering four thousand men, leaving in our hands four guns, three battle-flags and all his wagons. Some prisoners were taken and the enemy's loss in killed and wounded is known to be large. Reforming his command, Kilpatrick fought the enemy's infantry for an hour longer, when, finding his men running out of ammunition, he retired in the direction of Lattimar's and Decatur without further molestation, reaching the latter place on the afternoon of the twenty-second.

In the field near Marietta
October 5, 1864

General Elliott

Dear General: I have been up on Kenesaw all day, watching the attack. Since it ceased, we have a signal O. K. Corse wounded. Our infantry can now present a strong front, and if fight we must, so be it. I want to establish communication with Alatoona and have ordered Garrard up.
Yours,
W. T. Sherman

Headquarters
Second Cavalry Division
New Hope Church
October 7, 1864, 4:15 p. m.

Brigadier-General Elliott
Chief of Cavalry
Department of the Cumberland
I have the honour to report that I drove Armstrong from New Hope Church and followed him to the creek near Dallas, where I found him in line across the creek and drew several shots from his artillery. I also explored the Powder Springs, the Lost Mountain road and the Burnt Hickory road.
K. Garrard

Near New Hope Church
October 7, 1864, 11:30 a. m.

General Elliott
Chief of Cavalry

General: I am near New Hope Church, skirmishing with the rear. Armstrong camped where I am now, and French's division at the church. I do not know yet which way they marched, but rumour says toward Dallas. Very conflicting stories are told by citizens and I can determine nothing. I captured the wagon General Sherman wished me to, and in it was a Brigadier-General and a Colonel.
Very respectfully yours,
K. *Garrard*

Headquarters
Second Cavalry Division
October 12, 1864, 6:30 p. m.

General Elliott
Commanding Cavalry
Department of the Cumberland

General: I have driven the rebel cavalry between four and five miles beyond the river. They now have a strong position covering the Cedar Bluff and the Texas Valley roads. I am in camp about a mile and a quarter from the river, covering all roads leading to the bridge.
K. *Garrard*

Headquarters
Army of the Ohio
Five and one-half miles from Rome
October 13, 1864

Major-General Sherman

Garrard is pushing on finely, my division infantry in close support. He has driven Armstrong's cavalry the last two miles. Captured two pieces of artillery and a number of prisoners.

J. D. Cox, Brigadier-General, Commanding.

Headquarters
Second Cavalry Division
On Little River, Ga.
October 20, 1864

General Elliott
Chief of Cavalry

General: I forced a crossing of Little River about 5 p. m. by crossing a mile and a half above and flanking the force at the ford. I have advanced to the cross-roads and can positively state that the infantry on this road turned toward the Coosa River on the Iron-works road. The cavalry this evening fell back toward Blue Pond. Last night Hood's headquarters were at Simm's on the Gadsden road, at the falls of Yellow Creek. Little River is fordable, but quite wide. I was skirmishing and driving the enemy until dark.
K. Garrard

Extract from report of
Brigadier-General Marcus J. Wright,
C. S. Army, commanding brigade

Headquarters Post
Atlanta, Ga.
May 7, 1864

Colonel John B. Sale
Military Secretary

I regret to report that the cavalry of the enemy, commanded by Colonel Long, which crossed near the mouth of the Chickamauga, succeeded in capturing my brigade train, which was en route from Charleston to Chickamauga. Major Elcan, Assistant Quartermaster, and several of the men with him escaped capture. This proved a severe loss to my officers and men, whose personal baggage was in the train as well as a heavy loss to the Government.
Marcus J. Wright, Brigadier-General, Commanding

Chapter 20
The Nashville Campaign

General Wilson, having been appointed Chief of Cavalry, Army of the Cumberland, issued the following special order:

Headquarters
Cavalry Corps
Military Division of the Mississippi,
Borne, Ga.
October 29, 1864

1. Brigadier-General Garrard will immediately organize his division into two brigades, and after furnishing what horses General Kilpatrick requires, mount the Second Brigade of the new organization. As soon as this duty is accomplished, he will proceed to Nashville with the division, taking all horses unfit for field service, and gathering all dismounted men found along its route. Upon his arrival at Nashville, General Garrard will turn over the men and command of his division to Brigadier-General Eli Long.

2. Brigadier-General Eli Long will relieve, at Nashville, Tenn., Brigadier-General K. Garrard from the command of the Second Division, Cavalry Corps, Military Division of the Mississippi. Upon assuming command, General Long will remain in Nashville for the purpose of collecting, remounting and equipping the dismounted men of his division there.

By command of Brevet Major-General Wilson:

E. B. Beaumont, Captain &
Acting Assistant Adjutant-General.

We turned in all of our serviceable horses to General Kilpatrick at Rome, Ga., on the thirty-first of October, and all the equipments were packed up and turned over to the Quartermaster, Lieutenant Curry. On the evening of November 1 we left Rome for Chattanooga, via Calhoun, with the unserviceable horses and wagon train. Our transportation had been so cut down that a large amount of Quartermaster stores had been abandoned, and among other equipments were two hundred and fifty cavalry saddles and horse equipments complete. By order of the brigade commander the quartermaster had these saddles piled up and several hundred rails were piled up on them, and an attempt was made to burn saddles and all other stores that could not be transported, but as we moved at once, no doubt the fire was extinguished by the citizens and the saddles saved. If there is any one thing for which a cavalryman has a supreme disgust over every other thing, it is marching on foot; and as the command was nearly all dismounted, our movement was slow, and we did not reach Chattanooga until the sixth. Here we turned in all of our horses and mules excepting a few regimental teams, and they were driven through to Nashville. We lay in camp at Chattanooga until the twelfth of November and then took the train for Nashville, where we remained one night, and then went on to Louisville, Ky., where we arrived on the tenth and went into camp out on the Preston Pike near Captain Knapp's Garden, long to be remembered by every trooper of the division on account of the many convivial evenings spent in this noted Hostelry with the ever smiling and courteous host. From the time the brigade left Columbia, Tenn., May 22, until we arrived at Louisville, the command had been on the move, marching, scouting, raiding and fighting, with scarcely a day of rest from the most arduous campaigning, and had been under fire no doubt fifty times and had marched many hundreds of miles. The men were sadly in need of clothing, as they looked seedy indeed compared with the dapper soldiers on duty at Louisville. General Long assumed command, and the work of drawing clothing, horses,

MAJOR-GENERAL JAMES H. WILSON

mules, wagons and equipments was commenced at once, and the division was soon equipped and thoroughly reorganized. The government was not able to furnish a sufficient number of horses as rapidly as they were needed to mount the command, and as the battle of Nashville was pending, General Wilson ordered General Long to press in all the serviceable horses in Louisville to mount his command. One morning the citizens of Louisville awakened from their slumbers to find every street and pike leading out of the city picketed by mounted cavalrymen, and the work of pressing in horses commenced and was kept up several days and until the battle of Nashville commenced. There was great consternation among the citizens and every effort was made to secrete their valuable horses. Some were found in cellars and in kitchens, and some in parlours, but they were all brought forth, as the quartermasters were unrelenting and claimed it "was a military necessity," and that settled it. The day the battle of Nashville commenced we were engaged in pressing horses, and as shown by my diary as Quartermaster, the writer drew one hundred and forty-six horses for the First Ohio. Many valuable horses were secured, and the owners were given receipts by the quartermasters, and no doubt the owners received pay in full. While the regiment was encamped at Louisville there were a number of changes among the officers, as the following named officers were mustered out by reason of expiration of term of service: Lieutenant-Colonel Pattin, Major Frankenberger, Lieutenant Ferguson, Lieutenant Lieb, Captain O'Harra, Captain Pickering, Lieutenant Overly, Lieutenant Brison, Lieutenant Roush, Captain Rea, Lieutenant Carr, and Lieutenant High.

Among the officers who left the regiment at this time, as above noted, will be recognized the names of some of the best officers of the regiment, who had been "tried in the fire and were not found wanting, 7 and had been at the front for more than three years. Some of these officers would have resigned on the Atlanta campaign had we not been in the face of the enemy, but on no account would they have left the regiment when we were at the front. The reasons for a number of these officers making request to be mustered out was on account of the troubles growing out of the court martial of the brave and gallant Captain William H. Scott, who fell at Lovejoy, August 20, 1864. All of the facts connected with the persecution of this brave soldier are well known to the old officers of the regiment, and as the chief actors have all answered the last "roll call," we will draw the mantle of charity over their acts. A number of officers were also promoted before we left Louisville, among whom were: Lieutenant J. W. Laughlin to Adjutant Quartermaster Sergeant, David H. Hart to Quartermaster, Hugh H. Siverd to Captain, James W. Kirkendall to Captain, W. L. Curry to Captain, J. M. Sullenberger to Lieutenant, W. G. Lawder to Captain, Thaddeus Scott to Lieutenant, Jonathan Carr to Captain, R. K. Reese to Lieutenant.

Lieutenant Curry was thrown from his horse at Louisville and severely injured December 21, 1864, and was mustered out at Nashville, Tenn., December 30, on account of his injuries.

The division remained at Louisville until December 28 and at that date took up the march for Nashville well mounted, well equipped and anxious to take the field again after a few weeks' rest. Arriving at Nashville, January 8, 1865, joined the cavalry corps commanded by General J. H. Wilson. The division left Nashville on the thirteenth, marching through Franklin, Columbia and to Gravelly Springs, Ala., January 25. In February the cavalry corps was reorganized, and the First was transferred from the Second Brigade, Second Division, and brigaded with the Seventh O.V. C, (Colonel Garrard) and Fifth Iowa (Colonel Young), forming the Second Brigade, Fourth Division, which was placed under the command of Brigadier-General A. J. Alexander. The division remained at Gravelly Springs until the nineteenth of March, drilling and preparing for the great cavalry raid on which they were soon to start. On the nineteenth they crossed the Tennessee and rendezvoused with the balance of the corps at Chickasaw Landing.

Cavalry Corps, Fourth Division, April 30, 1865

Artillery
Brevet Major-General Emory Upton
Illinois Light
Chicago Board of
Trade Battery   Captain George I Robinson

First Brigade
Brevet Brigadier-General Edward F Winslow
Third Iowa   Colonel John W Noble
Fourth Iowa   Lieutenant-Colonel John H Peters
Tenth Missouri   Lieutenant-Colonel Frederick W Benteen

Second Brigade
Brevet Brigadier-General Andrew J Alexander
Fifth Iowa   Colonel J Morris Young
First Ohio   Colonel Beroth B Eggleston
Seventh Ohio   Colonel Israel Garrard

The Wilson Raid through Northern Alabama and Georgia, March and April, 1865
by Captain J. A. O. Yeoman, Company A

The splendid victory achieved by Thomas at Nashville, followed by a vigorous pursuit of Wilson's cavalry, left Hood's army as it crossed the Tennessee but a semblance of that magnificent body that marched around Sherman's flank, struck Alatoona, delivered deadly battle at Franklin, and planted their war-worn colours on the heights around Nashville. As an army it never appeared again; but as broken regiments and divisions drifted toward the east and joined Johnson in a futile attempt to delay the victorious march of Sherman. There still lay in the Southwest several strategic points which had never been threatened by a Union army; there still lay fertile valleys that had received no scars from the war. Selma, Ala., and Columbus, Ga., were among the most strongly fortified towns of the South, and here were vast arsenals that furnished the rebel forces still in the field not only much needed munitions of war, but field and siege ordnance as well. It was the policy of the administration to destroy these, so that there should be no place to rally the broken and defeated regiment that might escape from Grant and Sherman. To this task was assigned Brevet Major-General James H. Wilson, a young man of twenty-seven, an active officer on Grant's staff for two or three years, and unknown as a cavalry officer until he took command of Kilpatrick's division in the spring of 64. He was defeated at Reams Station and came near losing his division; but it has always been believed that it was because of failure of support there promised him by General Grant, and this belief was favoured by the fact that after this defeat he was promoted and sent west and named to the command of the cavalry corps of the Western Department. He arrived in time to remount the dismounted troops that had drifted back from Sherman's army, and with marvellous energy gathered together the odds and ends that were there and welded them into the magnificent cavalry command that turned the flank of Hood's army at Nashville and inflicted the first day's defeat upon this brave but ill-starred General, and then precipitated that defeat into a rout. He was sent to Eastport Landing and Gravelly Springs, Ala., to mass and prepare for the campaign the most magnificent cavalry corps that had ever served under any command since the white plume of Murat carried Napoleon's star to victory on many a fateful field of Europe. The First Ohio had been remounted at Louisville, armed with Spencers, and save the loss of some of its veteran soldiers and some of its idolized subalterns, had a higher morale, and was in better trim for quick, decisive battle than ever before in its history. It marched overland from Louisville to Gravelly Springs in the latter part of December and early January and went into cantonments there, where it drilled as faithfully as if it were a new regiment just taking the field. It was assigned to the brigade of Brevet Brigadier-General A. J. Alexander, with the Seventh Ohio and Fifth Iowa. General Alexander was a regular army officer, a cousin of General Frank Blair, the Adjutant-General of his corps, and the former Adjutant-General of the cavalry corps of the Army of the Potomac under Pleasanton. He was a brave, skillful, efficient and thorough-going officer. These regiments comprised the Second Brigade of the Fourth Division Cavalry Corps, Military Division of the Mississippi. The other brigade consisted of the Third and Fourth Iowa and Tenth Missouri, under the command of Brigadier-General Edward F. Winslow. The division was commanded by General Emery Upton, without doubt the bravest, most untiring, and the greatest natural cavalry soldier the writer ever served under. He was but twenty-seven years of age, a Brevet Major-General, and had received many a brevet on many a hard-fought field of the Army of the Potomac. He was only a boy, just out of West Point, when the war broke out, a Lieutenant of artillery, and became Colonel of the One Hundred and Twenty-first New York, then made a brigade commander. He commanded his brigade at the Bloody Angle in the Wilderness, where Hancock just failed of destroying Lee's army. His brigade lay under the works that they could not carry and fired over four hundred rounds, exchanging their guns with those in the rear in keeping down the rebels from the works. This was where a tree as thick as a man's thigh was cut off by musketry alone. Upton himself was wounded more than once; and of all the splendid soldiers of that magnificent Army of the Potomac there was none to surpass him. He was equally with Wilson the leading spirit and the martial figure of this campaign. It was his division that first crossed the Black Warrior, deemed unfordable. It was his division that first struck Forest's command at Montevallo, drove it back through the pine woods on Randolph, and the next day turned his left at Plantersville and assured the capture of Selma. The First Ohio in its last campaign was fortunate indeed in having such division and brigade Generals.

The Wilson's raid itself stands pre-eminent in the history of mounted raids. No like number of men, infantry or cavalry, ever captured as many guns and cannon, stormed as many fortified towns, and effected as great results in a campaign of thirty days. The reason that it has not received more consideration is because it was made during the latter part of the war, when Lee was surrendering to Grant at Appomattox, and Sherman was striking Johnson unto death in the Carolinas. It was cut off from all communication and outside of its own command nobody knew of the mighty deeds that were being performed by it until the war was over, and then it was lost in the great events that begun with Appomattox and ended with the assassination of Lincoln.

The expedition left the Tennessee River on the twenty-second of March. As the regiment formed at the "call to horse," with a premonition of the brilliant campaign before it, there were hundreds of tried and veteran troopers who longed a little bit for some of their old commanders. Lieutenant-Colonel Pattin, tried and true, hard as a pine knot, and with a sword that always felt for the enemy, had been mustered out at Louisville, and in his place, much to the disadvantage of the regiment, Major Writer was promoted. There were new Captains in command of Companies I, K and G, and while they had not been tried like the old ones, they gave a good account of themselves in the campaign. Yet there was many a soldier who felt, and many an officer, too, that he would have given much to have known that, riding at the head of Company I, was that brilliant, dashing soldier, Captain John P. Rea, who never counted the odds, whose eyes sparkled when the enemy was ahead, and who followed him as the hunter follows the hounds. The First Ohio never had a better and more gallant officer than Rea; and if he had known what fight there was ahead, nothing would have induced him to leave the regiment at that time. There was many a trooper that turned in his saddle and longed to see at the head of Company K, erect as an arrow, cool, confident, tireless and absolutely fearless, Captain Will Curry, who took honours without parade or pomp of any kind, was always as steadfast as the stars in their course, and was always in at the death. Company G would have longed to see, with his sword blazing in their front, old Erwin, the Tipton Slasher, the man whose sabre in hand to hand fight had tasted the blood of the enemy as often as that of any man in the regiment. Also those brave and well tried officers, Captain Woodlief and Captain Pickering, whose courage had been tested on many a hard-fought field. These gallant soldiers had lost the chiefest pleasure of their soldier lives in losing this campaign.

But there was left Kirkendall, another as good man as ever pulled sabre in front of a command; with the brave and dashing Captain Siverd and Captain Lawder, both as true as steel now both mustered out and camping beyond the great river. Also Lieutenants Ward, Reese, Laughlin, Reynolds, with other tried and true officers whose names I do not now recall, and the old First Ohio went into the campaign with a dash and spirit equal to anything it had ever shown.

At Jasper, Company A, in advance of the regiment, struck a small body of the enemy and brushed them aside; but two of its men, Peter Getz and William Vincent, in some manner becoming separated from the command, were captured by a half dozen rebels of the command whom the company had just routed. They marched with them two or three days when finally, in the interior of Alabama, the rebels sat down to breakfast, and Getz, who had been upon the outlook, suddenly nudged Vincent; they jumped and seized the rebels arms, captured and paroled them, and then rejoined the regiment at Selma. It had always been said of Getz that a division like him turned loose in the Confederacy could have stolen it poor, and he seemed to have verified on this occasion in a small way what had been before universally said of him. The regiment and division had forded the Black Warrior without waiting for the pontoons on which Long's division afterwards crossed. This was the roughest ford that ever was crossed by a body of mounted men, and it was done with the loss of but two or three horses and one or two men. Indeed, the ford was almost as rapid where the division crossed, and the guide who led it across stripped himself before crossing. The river at this point was about three hundred yards wide. The ford was filled with immense rocks, many of them four and five feet in height, which projected above the water, while the greater part of the ford itself was filled with large slippery stones that tripped up many of the horses, and left the men standing in mid-stream by these large rocks, whence they were rescued by their comrades. At the lower edge of the ford there was a sudden descent into deep water, along which there was an occasional sandbar, but in most places so deep as to compel the horses to swim. The first of the column passed along the lower edge of the ford and one or two horses and men were swept over by the current and would have been drowned but for one of these sand-bars. The brigade then commenced crossing forty or fifty yards up stream through a roaring rapid that no man could have stemmed alone, and many a horse went down. It was the most terrible ford that the writer ever saw crossed by mounted men in four years experience in mounted warfare.

From here the division marched rapidly to the crossing of the Cahawba River. The First Ohio, being in the front, found the ford occupied with rebels. Two or three companies forded, drove them away, then cut out and removed as far as possible the trees which had been felled across the ford. The balance of the division planked the high railroad bridge and crossed in that way, the ford having become dangerous by reason of quick sands and the trees that had fallen therein. On the twenty-ninth two companies of the First Ohio, in the advance under the direct command of the Assistant Inspector-General of the brigade, charged down from the mountains into the little town of Elyton, just at dusk, brushed away the rebels, established pickets, and waited for the balance of the command. Elyton was then but a small town, and as these companies came into it, it was surrounded by a mist created by a drizzling rain, and the sharp crack of the rifles rang out in the early night in a country that had never before felt the touch of war. Elyton is now the city of Birmingham, the centre of the great iron trade of the South. Here Jones Valley opened before us, a vision of peace and beauty and plenty. And here were great manor houses; here were great barns; here were long lines of cabins, where the farm-hands sang their songs after the work was done at night-fall; here were great granaries filled with grain for our tired horses; here were great smoke-houses filled with the finest and sweetest hams that a Yankee soldier ever tasted. The First Ohio being fortunate enough to be in the advance, it was but a short time until a ham swung from every man's saddle, and the boys could be heard singing the old refrain, "Who wouldn't sell his farm and go for a soldier?" The writer thinks that in some period of his life he has eaten sweet hams, but he is willing to give the palm to those captured in Jones Valley.

Here Croxton's brigade of McCook's division was detailed to capture Tuscaloosa, Ala., which it did, flanking and evading Jackson's division of Forest's corps, and finally joining us after the campaign was over near Macon. On the thirtieth we reached Montavello, a little Southern hamlet, also now noted as being one of the centres of the southern iron trade. Here the men were given their first breathing spell. They were washing their clothes and taking care of their horses and equipments, and preparing for the movement in the afternoon, when about ten o'clock in the morning Roddy's brigade attached to Forest's command struck the pickets. The Fifth Iowa was ordered out and drove them headlong five miles to the crossing of a little creek, which they had barricaded with rails and covered guns. The First Ohio was getting ready for a flank movement, when the rebels reconsidered the matter and withdrew from the immediate creek-crossing. The Fifth Iowa pushed across the creek and dismounted, and a battalion was pushed up the hill in the advance. The writer of this was riding with General Upton immediately in the rear of this battalion; Frank Allen, a Quartermaster Sergeant of our regiment, who had received permission to turn the wagons over to another Sergeant, was riding with the advance, as he always did when the enemy was in front of us; and just as the battalion crowned the crest of a little hill, from the thick brush there rang out a sharp volley, cutting the leaves around the heads of the men, and involuntarily the whole battalion shrank back a step or two. But it was only for a moment. Frank Allen, the darling soldier of the regiment, mounted on a handsome gray horse, received the fire as if he had been a statue of stone, and rode forward through the ranks of the battalion as if he had never heard the volley fired. General Upton turned to the writer and said: "Splendid soldier! Splendid soldier! Who is he?" Upton was one of those men who never saw a gallant thing without admiring it, who never missed an opportunity to commend a gallant act; and it was he who, after the battle of Ebenezer Church, at the instance and request of the writer, recommended Frank Allen, then stricken with a mortal wound, to be brevetted. Here Alexander's dismounted brigade, having dislodged the enemy at this stand, was withdrawn to remount, Winslow's brigade came up and passed to the front and pushed the enemy through the woods far into the night. The next morning was April 1. From our encampment in the woods there lay between us and the little town of Randolph a field about a mile wide. On the other side lay the enemy. The First Ohio and General Alexander's brigade again took the lead. A battalion of the First Ohio was ordered out, and as the writer rode out with it the gallant little soldier, Upton, said, "Give them an April fool this morning." The battalion pushed across the field, rapidly developed the enemy at Randolph and drove him beyond the town. Here the roads fork, there being two roads that lead to Plantersville or Ebenezer Church. The upper or ridge road was the direct road. This battalion of the First Ohio moved out and engaged Forest's skirmishers and held the direct road until Upton's division had passed down on the lower Plantersville road, and Long's division entered upon the direct road. Upton's division was then halted and the battalion moved to the front along with the regiment Both divisions then advanced simultaneously along the upper and lower roads. The enemy were more directly concentrated on the upper road, but with the intention not to fight until they came near the junction of the two roads. Long's skirmishers were heavily engaged all the time and they carried barricade after barricade with conspicuous gallantry. In the meantime Forest had been planning a trap in front; instead of leaving a simple rear guard he massed an entire brigade and placed it so as to be practically concealed from view, and reared a barricade in front which seemed to be defended by but a small number of men. Colonel White of the Seventeenth Indiana, who was in front, as soon as he came in sight of the barricade charged with the battalion that was with him, but as he came up to it he perceived in some way the trap and ordered fours about. Captain Taylor, of Company A, a gallant little soldier, weighing a little over one hundred pounds, was in the advance with his company, and he either did not hear the order or was carried away with his own ardour, and he jumped the barricade, his company following him, when sixteen of them were shot from their saddles, and Taylor himself, seeing a group of men, charged them at once, realizing that it was Forest and his staff. Single-handed and alone he attacked Forest in the midst of his staff, and this with his sabre only; and it is said that if he had had a sharp sabre he would have killed that fearless but brutal cavalry officer. He disabled his right arm, cut his head and ear with his sabre, hacked his pistol barrel three or four times in the fight, until finally Forest shot him dead. He said afterwards to General Wilson, in an interview held under a flag of truce, that he never so much regretted shooting any man, as he was the bravest man he had ever seen.

In the meantime the First Ohio was moving forward rapidly, dismounted, but without any seeming opposition to it, being the lull which immediately precedes the storm. The roar of the conflict above alarmed General Alexander, who feared that Forest was making one of his famous coups and attempting to get a bulge on the flank, and he ordered the First Ohio to mount at once, and ordered a squadron of the Seventh Ohio to move forward rapidly and take the advance, and the whole column went plunging forward at a trot. The squadron under Lieutenant-Colonel Warmalsdorf, accompanied by the adjutant-general and the inspector-general of the brigade, moved forward, and in about six hundred yards, at a turn of the road, struck a rebel picket. They charged it immediately through a little skirt of woods in which it was stationed out in the open and down the road about four hundred yards, when an entire brigade from a fringe of woods opened upon it. There was some kind of a shed beside the road and the bullets rattled upon it like a hail-storm. The staff officers attempted to dismount the men and hold the position until the First Regiment could come through the thicket and deploy, fearing that if they fell back at once the enemy in front of them might charge the oncoming brigade in column and double them up. The men were all dismounted except the two staff officers and the orderly of the inspector-general and the lieutenant commanding the squadron, and made the best show of fighting they could. Notwithstanding their being dismounted, the first sergeant of one company was killed, the second sergeant was killed, the third sergeant had five balls shot into him, and every man in the squadron, with one exception, was either killed, wounded or had his clothes cut. The jacket of the mounted orderly, of the writer, Henry T. Resler, of Company A, was fairly ragged; and he said to him after the fight: "Lieutenant, you owe me a new jacket."

The answer was: "I will give you a whole suit for standing by me like you did today."

In less than five minutes the First Ohio had come on at a gallop through the thicket, deployed rapidly, dismounted, and were running forward with their Spencers on a charge; the Fifth Iowa came up on their left; and these two regiments formed under the crest of the hill, and as the cheery bugle rang out the "Forward" they charged the guns upon the crest. It was a short, sharp, quick fight, but it was all over in less than ten minutes; and in that time Taylor was avenged; the man who had killed him had met his first defeat as a cavalry officer in many years, and the guns that were planted to cover the converging roads were captured. The First Ohio Regiment captured these three guns in the most brilliant style. Leading the regiment was that soldier of soldiers, Frank Allen. He captured one of the guns himself, but did not stop even for a moment to secure the trophy, but plunged on after the flying enemy, and about twenty yards beyond the gun fell, shot through the abdomen. The writer was upon the left of the line and did not know it until the fight was over. Then General Alexander told him that his friend, Allen, was mortally wounded and in an ambulance. I went at once to see him; told him of all the kind things that General Upton and General Alexander had said of him, sought in every way to cheer him; but he lay there and said: "Lieutenant, I never thought of that, I never cared for that; all that I ever cared for was to do my duty." I told him that Alexander and Upton had both promised to brevet him. He put it aside in words as if it were nothing; and it was indeed little to him, as the future proved. We left him at Selma when we moved on, and he died of gangrene of the wound going up the river. I have never known a more brilliant soldier; I have never known a more lovable man. About twenty years of age, with curly brown hair, clear blue eyes, and well built, he was as handsome as a Greek god. The writer had only known him in the year since he joined the western army; but during that time, in all the campaigns and skirmishes, he had always seen Frank Allen in the front. It was his rifle that cracked first on the advance and rang out last on the retreat. Handsome, smiling, cool, self-contained, he rode into the fight like a young American St. George; and it is a matter of love to speak of him as he was. On the retreat he always stayed with the rear of the column. And as it moved from Jonesboro to go toward the fatal Lovejoy Station on the Kilpatrick raid, I remember him as I moved past him in the early morning, just as the day was breaking and you could not see more than two or three hundred yards away, how handsome, how fearless, and yet withal how careful, alert and soldierly he looked to be. I had passed with my company not more than five hundred yards away at that time, when I heard the crack of his rifle, and I knew that a part of Cleburne's division was pushing our rear guard and that Frank Allen was giving them his compliments. In skirmish, picket, foray, or in the closer clash of battle, you could always see him leading, with his carbine gleaming or his sabre flashing. Death seemed to avoid him, and this handsome and fearless boy never was touched by the enemy until this fatal day near the close of the war. Peace to his ashes. No man of the First Ohio was more tenderly and gently beloved. He and Captain Scott, who was mortally wounded at Lovejoy Station, deserve to be immortalized in these pages. To another pen has been assigned the duty and the pleasure of paying a tribute to Captain Scott. I bring this little garland to the memory of Frank Allen.

The next morning the advance was taken by Long's division, and to it belongs the principal honour of the capture of Selma, and one of the most remarkable feats ever achieved by mounted men. Selma lies about twenty miles from Plantersville, and it was late in the afternoon when Upton's division drew up to the left. The siege guns in position threw shells out toward the line that could be plainly seen hurtling through the air. The plan of the attack was to have Upton first reconnoitre and then assault the left where the works rested upon a swamp and where they were neither so strong in themselves nor so well defended. In the meantime Long had invested the works upon the right. Chalmer's division of Forest's army had not succeeded in entering Selma and it attacked vigorously Long's rear. Long became apprehensive of this attack upon the rear and without waiting for Upton, who was then reconnoitering the left, ordered a charge. Fifteen hundred men of his division, consisting largely of the Third and Fourth Ohio, First Pennsylvania, and Fourth Michigan, made this charge, rushing upon the works, delivering volley after volley from their Spencers as they charged. In front of the ditch was a stockade; this was one of the heaviest stockades ever placed in front of an earthwork; they tore down this stockade, scaled the works, carried them in a hand-to-hand conflict and repulsed, General Wilson reports, seven thousand men behind these works. In the meantime Upton, hearing the fight upon the left, ordered his division in and it went in in columns of fours on the lower Selma road, charged into the town and followed the rout and wreck of Forest's army several miles to Burnsville, capturing four pieces of artillery and a large number of wagons and prisoners. This was the battle of Selma; taken all in all it was the most remarkable feat of arms ever achieved by mounted men. Twenty-five per cent, of the assaulting columns were killed and wounded in this assault lasting not over twenty minutes.

Selma was a very important town of the Confederacy on account of its arsenal and its position upon the Alabama River, and although in the interior, it had been entrenched at the time Sherman made his raid to Meridian in the winter of '63-'64, under the belief that Sherman was about to attack it. The writer has seldom seen stronger entrenchments. There were mounted on these entrenchments twenty-six pieces of artillery, most of them thirty-two pounders, and many of them of still larger calibre. And it reads like a romance that fifteen hundred dismounted cavalry should have assaulted and carried these fortifications, with Forest's cavalry behind them and commanded by Forest himself, and that the line moved forward steadily from the time the order was given, without ever suffering even for an instant a check.

General Wilson reports that there were captured at this point two thousand prisoners and twenty-six guns in position, beside seventy siege-guns in arsenals, and other munitions of war. We remained here for seven days, thoroughly destroying the arsenals and everything that was advantageous for the future conduct of war.

In the meantime, General Wilson, with marvellous energy, prepared to bridge the Alabama, which was then at a flood. This was practically completed, when floating logs struck the pontoons and broke them near the centre. The farther end from Selma swung down the river with the leader of the corps upon it and floated in toward the bank. On the other end General Upton and a few officers and men of the First Ohio, holding on to the ropes, ran over the pontoon boats as the water came up to their knees, pulled them up and helped anchor that end in mid-stream. It was a dangerous movement and a thrilling moment.

The next day was spent in repairing the same; and as the logs came down upon the ropes, General Alexander was in front with some men, attempting to get the logs away, when his boat was upset and a log struck him and knocked him against the pontoon and almost crushed him. He was pulled in by his staff; and the two men in the boat went under the pontoon, but were picked up below. The bridge was broken three times, but on the ninth the entire corps was crossed, and on the morning of the tenth Upton's division took the advance toward Montgomery, Ala., the first capital of the Confederacy. We entered it on the afternoon of the twelfth day of April. There was cotton piled in the streets ready for burning, and but for the vigilance of our men in this place, where secession first held its capitol, where the Confederacy was first proclaimed and the Confederate government was inaugurated, would have shared the fate of Columbia. We remained at Montgomery until the morning of the fourteenth day of April, when our columns resumed the march towards

Columbus, Ga., eighty-four miles away. We moved rapidly at about thirty miles a day and on the evening of the fifteenth camped at the little hamlet of Crawford, consisting of but two or three houses and a jail. Columbus lay about fifteen to twenty miles away. One of the roads led directly forward into Columbus. Another turned to the right at the town of Crawford and by a longer road reached Columbus by another route. Both roads crossed a deep and sluggish stream through a swamp, and it was necessary to save the bridges in order that the column should not be delayed, as it would have taken some time in the swamp to have laid our pontoons. General Upton came out to the picket line, explained the situation to the writer, who at that time had the advance, and charged him with the duty of saving the bridges. He was given a squadron of the First Ohio Cavalry, and instructed that the division would follow at as rapid a rate as possible, but to press on and capture the bridges at all hazards if the force was not too great. The pickets were struck at the Crawford cross-roads, and immediately took the lower or longer road to Columbus. This reached the bridge and the swamp at about nine miles, instead of six miles as on the direct road. The direct road was guarded by a large body of men; the upper road by but a small body of men. As the pickets were on the upper road, they were followed by the squadron, charging on a dead run for nine miles. As the head of the column reached a turn in the road about three hundred yards from the bridge there were but three men of the squadron in sight; there were nearly a dozen upon the bridge attempting to fire it. These three men of the First Ohio took the bridge, put out the fire, the men retreating, evidently fearing that there was a larger column coming. They waited then for the balance of the squadron to come up, went on through the swamp, thinking that there might be another bridge, and then waited at the further end of the swamp for the division to appear.

BRIGADIER-GENERAL A. J. ALEXANDER.

It was more than an hour before General Upton arrived with his division, and complimented the squadron upon the notable feat it had performed.

After Upton's division came through it massed on the lower road, leaving Long to take the direct road to Columbus. No body then knew the exact situation as to the bridges, which will be explained hereafter; but General Upton's blood was up and he ordered out six companies of the First Ohio, Colonel Eggleston in command. While Colonel Eggleston was given command, the general supervision of it was given to the writer as a staff officer of Alexander's brigade, and as we rode out Upton said to us, "Can you give us the bridge across the Chattahoochee?" We saluted and said "we would try." This column immediately threw out skirmishers on each side of the road and went driving the enemy at a quick walk and sometimes at a sharp trot along the road to Columbus for nearly five miles, Then as we reached the hill that looked down on Columbus the skirmishers were drawn in, the column formed by fours, and a mile and a half, straight away down the hill, lay the bridge across the Chattahoochee. It was the prize we sought; could we win it? This was at the head of navigation and a gun-boat lay under the banks; but it was useless as a means of defence on account of the high banks. It was a smooth pike and it looked like a beautiful run down there. As we reached the crest of the hill and turned to go downward we could see the upper bridge across the Chattahoochee and the railroad bridge that was surrounded by a *tête-du-pont* and formidable earthworks, with from twenty-five to forty guns in position. The writer then could not understand why it was that these guns did not open on our column. The reason will be apparent in a moment. It looked as if the range was almost perfect and as if our column could have been destroyed from these guns in place. But not a gun was fired, and it looked as if the town was at our mercy. Colonel Eggleston and the staff officers placed themselves at the head of this column of six companies, the order was given to draw sabres, then the bugle rang out the trot, then the gallop, then the wild charge, and away we went, straight down for Columbus. We had nearly reached the bridge when Upton, standing on the hill, said, "Columbus is ours without firing a shot!" On this side the bridge lies the little town of Girard, a suburb of Columbus, composed of about three or four hundred people. It was a good place to shelter a column in who were attacking Columbus, because it could not be reached by guns or fired upon without firing into the houses of their friends. When within about six or seven hundred yards of the bridge the writer turned to Colonel Eggleston and said, "Colonel, I see that the bridge upon the other side has three guns planted at its mouth, covering it completely, and so planted as to sweep it from end to end. They are certainly loaded with grape and cannister, because they have not fired a shot If we go on the bridge mounted, the first discharge will cut down the head of the column and fill it up with dead horses, and it will be impossible to get the balance of the command over — the dead horses will choke up the bridge; and it is far better to dismount here, cross on foot, and then be prepared to hold the town until Upton throws his division in." Colonel Eggleston at once assented, ordered a left oblique on the impulse of the moment, and we rode in on the pavement, in shelter of the houses, while orders were at once given to dismount and fight on foot. While these preparations were going on, it was suggested to throw a few sharp shooters at this end of the bridge to cover the guns and shoot down the gunners while we were forming in front of it for the charge. This was immediately done, and while the column was forming in the road ready for the charge, one of the men on the bridge shot down one of the gunners; as he fell, he pulled the lanyard, the gun was discharged, and immediately the flame from the gun caught the bridge, which had already been saturated with turpentine and cotton, and in a moment it was in flames from end to end. So quickly did the flames spread that the men standing at this end of the bridge caught the breath of the fire in their very faces. This change in the method of attack saved the whole battalion; for whatever number of the battalion had attempted to cross the bridge, no man would have ever gotten out of it alive. The bridge itself was four or five hundred yards long. But more than this: on the further side of the bridge, just beyond the centre, the plank had been removed for about fifty feet; so it was intended to trap the column and have it precipitate itself into the Chattahoochee. The entire battalion would have gone down into the Chattahoochee, which is here navigable; horses and men would have plunged through this chasm, repeating on a smaller but more terrible scale the sunken road of Ohain. The fire was intended only for those who might have drawn up their horses and otherwise escaped this death trap.

While there were no immediate results from this charge, that it was made at all under the circumstances attested the courage and the morale of the regiment. In order to determine the character of this charge and of the men who made it, it must be remembered that this was a city of nearly twelve thousand people, that the column that made this charge knew that there were two thousand men defending the city, either across the bridge they were to carry, or in the earthworks that covered the upper bridge. They also knew that they were moving by the flank of earthworks containing more than twenty-five guns in position that could be seen, and otherwise equally as well manned and armed. It was as if you were to launch three hundred men alone into an entrenched camp of over two thousand. This was what the First Ohio Cavalry undertook to do. And when they went plunging down the road with their horses at full gallop and sabres drawn, every officer and man who went on that charge expected to charge squarely across the bridge and into that town. That they did not, and that they escaped the dire calamity and the terrible trap which was planned for them, was only a matter of good fortune, or rather one that came from an intelligent suggestion of a better method and line of attack. So that the regiment is entitled to have the credit of charging a fortified town defended by two thousand men with its nearest support a mile away. Captain Kirkendall, with his usual coolness and gallantry, rode at the head of the column of Company D.

While we were massed in the town, one Aden Harper, of Company D, rode out of the little town of Girard and across the bridge over the little creek which separated the earthworks from the town of Girard, and rode almost up to the works, and then rode back again. It was a gallant and an inspiring thing to do.

After the bridge was burned, this portion of the regiment received orders from General Alexander to retire gradually beyond the crest of the hill and rejoin the brigade there. This was done and the brigade proceeded to invest the works upon the right. In the meantime Upton had prepared to make an assault upon the left. He had moved Winslow's brigade of his division across the road and concealed it in the woods, expecting to make an attack before nightfall; but unexpected delays in making the movement so retarded it that the brigade was not in position till long after dark. There was a deep creek, called Mill Creek, almost impassable, that lay between the second brigade and the enemy's works. This was almost a dry creek, but had been cut down by storms and rains in a soil that washed easily, until the sides were very abrupt, and it was almost impossible for any man to get down one side and scale the other. Alexander waited till after nightfall for the charge to be made upon the left; the assault being given there, he had orders to throw our brigade in on the right. He had been down along the front and thought the attack had been abandoned, and had retired about six or seven hundred yards in the rear of his line, when suddenly, as if hell itself had broken loose, we heard the rattle and roar of the guns, musketry and cannon, and saw the flames from the guns leaping into the night. Upton had dismounted eleven hundred men, and himself at the head, assaulted the works. The order was immediately given for our brigade to advance, but we found it almost impossible to get across the ravine, and drifted down to a lower crossing. In the meantime the guns roared, the musketry crashed, the flames leaped out from the mouths of the guns, even while the gallant soldiers, of the First Brigade were storming over the enemy's works. In less than fifteen minutes from the beginning of the assault Upton himself rode over the works with the eleven hundred men who had carried it against twenty-seven hundred of the enemy. It was one of the most brilliant assaults in human history. Nothing but the night attack and the darkness saved the assaulting column from almost absolute destruction.

The result of this capture was twenty-four guns in position, west of the upper railroad bridge, and twelve hundred prisoners, by actual count, six seven-inch rifle guns on the iron-clad *Jackson*, and forty-four other guns in addition to those captured in the works, making, in all, seventy guns.

The Second Brigade, on account of the difficult ground in front of it, had but little share in its capture. After the capture of the works we found that the upper bridge had also been saturated with cotton and turpentine, the same as the lower bridge; but our men followed the retreating enemy so closely that they did not have time to fire it. Immediately General Upton placed an officer with men on the bridge, with orders to permit not even a match to be lighted or pipe to be smoked in crossing the bridge. One single spark of fire would not only have ignited the bridge, but would also have burned every one of the men upon it. The bridge was saved, and that night our column crossed into Columbus, for which we had gallantly fought, and fairly won.

In three days we had marched through Montgomery, Ga., to Columbus, a distance of eighty-four miles, fought a battle, and captured a fortified town. It is a record of celerity and courage unsurpassed in the annals of cavalry warfare. We found at Columbus the rebel iron-clad ram, *Jackson*, ready for sea. This was destroyed, together with the arsenal; some ten thousand bales of cotton were burned; and on the eighteenth day of April we started on the march to Macon, one hundred and four miles distant. Macon was a fortified town that Sherman, in his march to the sea, not caring to fight a battle without a base, avoided, sweeping to the left. It had been thoroughly fortified in view of the fact that it might be one of the points which Sherman might attack after the capture of Atlanta. There were in place some sixty to seventy field guns. This was our next point of attack.

On the march that day we heard for the first time of the assassination of Lincoln and the attempted assassination of Mr. Seward. The men were in an ugly mood; and if we had had any fighting to do, I doubt but that the bitterness in our hearts would have been reflected in less humane modes of warfare. It was a good thing for us that the end was come, for many a soldier might have done a deed that he might have regretted thereafter.

On April 20 Lieutenant-Colonel Frank White, of the Seventeenth Indiana, was in the advance, and when within about six or seven miles of Macon he met a large body of troops under General Robertson, stating that General Lee had surrendered to General Grant at Appomattox, and that there was an armistice between General Johnson and General Sherman and that armistice extended to the troops under command of General Wilson. Colonel White himself did not know whether it was true or not, or whether it might be a ruse of the enemy to delay the attacking column. He said, "I don't know anything about that. I am a soldier, and my orders are to go into Macon, and I am going in. I will give that flag of truce just five minutes to get out of the road, and if it doesn't keep out of my way I will run over it." Having given five minutes, White started the head of the column toward Macon, and passed the General who was in command of the party carrying the flag of truce so closely that they had to take to the woods.

The enemy not expecting an attack, and expecting that the truce would be observed on our part, did not prepare for an attack until White charged into the town. Wilson immediately followed with a portion of his troops. General Cobb insisted that this was a violation of the armistice and that he must withdraw to the position where he was at the time that he first heard of the truce between Johnson and Sherman. This Wilson refused to do, and at one time it seemed as if there would be a collision between the small body of troops that Wilson had in Macon and the troops under Cobb. But this was averted, and the next day, April 21, Wilson took possession of Macon with his entire cavalry corps, paroling Cobb and his officers; thus capturing Macon and ending the great Wilson raid, that was, without parallel, the greatest of all raids known to history. We captured at Macon sixty pieces of artillery, three hundred and fifty officers, and two thousand enlisted men.

If this mounted expedition had occurred at any other time it would have been the subject of more favourable comment than any other expedition of mounted soldiery in history. But it came after the great events that began at Petersburg, ending in the capture of Lee at Appomattox, the surrender of Johnston to Sherman, and the assassination of Lincoln, and the close of the great war, and was practically lost sight of by all except those who were engaged therein. This column left Chickasaw Landing on the twenty-third day of March and entered Macon on the twentieth day of April. It had marched during that time six hundred miles; had forded both branches of the Black Warrior, one of them at a place that the oldest inhabitants declared was not fordable; one portion had forded the Cahawba River; they had marched for three days over a sterile and mountainous country, devoid of forage for the horses; they had fought at Montevallo; routed the enemy at Ebenezer Church; stormed and captured the fortified town of Selma; bridged the Alabama at a flood, the pontoon bridges being three times broken in the attempt; captured Montgomery, the cradle of the Confederate government; stormed the fortified town of Columbus, and captured Macon.

This was a thirty days campaign; but we lay at Selma from the second until the tenth of April and spent two days at

Columbus, Ga., making the actual number of days engaged in the march twenty, instead of thirty; so that we averaged thirty miles a day for the actual time marching, including the time occupied in fighting, and assaulting these towns. The First Ohio in all its history has no more glorious page than the part it bore in this great expedition.

General Upton recommends as follows

First Lieutenant J. A. O. Yeoman, First Ohio Cavalry, and Acting Assistant Inspector-General, Second Brigade, Fourth Division, for his many and repeated acts of gallantry and indefatigable courage, energy and perseverance exhibited on all occasions during the campaign, to be Brevet Captain. (*Official Record of the Rebellion*, Series 1, Volume 49, Part 1, Page 477.)

Headquarters
Second Brigade
Fourth Division, M. D. M.
Macon, Ga.
May 3, 1865

Major J. W. Latta
Assistant Adjutant-General
Major: I have the honour to request that First Lieutenant J. A. O. Yeoman, First Ohio Veteran Volunteer Cavalry, may be brevetted for gallantry in the charge at Montevallo,, in the fight at Ebenezer Church, in the advance on Columbus, when he followed the enemy so closely with two men as to prevent their burning the bridges. He also behaved with his usual conspicuous gallantry in the charge into Girard. Lieutenant Yeoman is an officer of education, a good disciplinarian, and has been of great value as the Inspector-General of this brigade.
Very respectfully, your obedient servant,
A. J. Alexander, Brevet Brigadier-General
(Indorsement)

Headquarters
Cavalry Corps
Military Division of the Mississippi,
Macon, Ga.
June 27, 1865

Respectfully forwarded, approved and strongly recommended. There is no more gallant officer in service than Lieutenant Yeoman.

J H Wilson, Brevet Major General.

Headquarters
Cavalry Corps
Military Division of the Mississippi
Macon, Ga.
May 3, 1865

No. 68. 1. Under the provisions of the convention agreed upon between Major-General Sherman and General Johnson on the twenty-sixth of April, Colonel B. B. Eggleston, First Ohio Cavalry, is designated to receive the surrender of the Confederate troops at Atlanta. He will proceed to that point without delay for the purpose of carrying out the terms of the convention.

J. H. Wilson, Major-General

Headquarters
U. S. Forces
Atlanta, Ga.
May 5, 1865

General Judah
Commanding U. S. Forces
Kingston, Ga.

General: I have the honour to submit the following item of news, which I have just received from an intelligent U. S. soldier, who has been for some time a prisoner. His name is Michael Lightner, Fifty-fourth Pennsylvania Infantry. This soldier left Washington, Ga., day before yesterday at 4 p. m. and arrived here at 12 m. to-day. He states that Jefferson Davis was at Washington, Ga., on the third and that he

(Davis) left that point at 12 m. of the same day. Said soldier fell in with Davis and his cavalry at the Catawba River, N. C., at the railroad crossing, where Davis remained two days. Then he marched in company with them, for three days, passing through Chesterville, Abbeville, and thence to Washington. He represented Generals Bragg and Breckenridge in company; also Wheeler's cavalry fifteen hundred strong. The cavalry refused to go farther south unless paid, whereupon they were paid $30 each in gold, with the promise of $100 each when they had crossed the Mississippi River. He is supposed to have $15,000,000 in coin, and wagons, perhaps fifty. I have no mounted men here as yet, but will have my regiment tomorrow evening.

B. B. *Eggleston,* Colonel
First Ohio Cavalry, Commanding Post

Resaca
May 6, 1865

Major S. B. Moe
Assistant Adjutant-General

A Sergeant and three men have just arrived from Atlanta. They left there last night. Colonel Eggleston, First Ohio Cavalry, by order of General Wilson, reports to me that he occupies the place with two companies; rest coming on. He also sends me a very interesting communication, which I will forward by mail to-morrow, in which his informant, an intelligent C. S. soldier, states that he travelled with Jeff. Davis for three days, passing through Chesterville, Aberdeen, and thence to Washington, Ga., where he was on the third. Generals Bragg and Breckenridge are with him. Wheeler, with fifteen hundred cavalry, was with him. They refused to go farther unless paid. Davis gave them $30 each, with promise of $100 more when they crossed the Mississippi River. He is supposed to have had $15,000,000 with him, and about fifty wagons. My information was therefore correct. I think Davis must be overtaken unless he drops his *specie.*

H. M. *Judah,* Brigadier-General, Commanding

Macon, Ga.
May 6, 1865

Brevet Major-General E. Upton
Augusta, Ga.

Go. ahead, but put no price upon his head; offer simply for his apprehension and delivery and on the condition, that the reward shall be paid out of the treasure to be captured with the fugitive. Lieutenant Yeoman, of Alexander's staff, has sent in from Greensborough substantially the same information that you have obtained. Catch Jeff. Davis, if possible, and act as you think best.

J. H. Wilson, Brevet Major-General

Atlanta, Ga.
May 7, 1865

Major-General Wilson

I have sent Captain Siverd, with three strong companies, to Talladega; Lieutenant Reese, with two companies, to Columbus; Captain Krumdick, with one company, to General Judah; Lieutenant Brooks, with one company, to communicate with Stoneman's cavalry; one company patrolling between Sandtown and this point; two companies between this point and Pinckeyville, and one company on courier duty. No movement of Davis has been ascertained, later than your dispatches.

B. B. Eggleston, Colonel, Commanding Post

May 8, 1865

General Wilson

General: Lieutenant Yeoman says that Ferguson, with one division cavalry, is *en route* for Macon under flag of truce; that Dibrell's division is following, but he don't know that the latter is going to Macon. Davis and cabinet are following in rear, with one hundred picked men as escort. Yeoman is with one of the parties yet. lie says that all passed through Madison on the sixth inst, and he writes us from a point five miles from that place, under date of the sixth inst.

Winslow

Macon, Ga.
May 8, 1865

Colonel B. B. Eggleston
Atlanta

Have published and circulated the President's proclamation offering a reward for Jeff. Davis' arrest. Send me any news you may have, and forward the following telegram to General Steedman at Resaca.

Major-General J. B. Steedman

Everything is on the lookout for J. D. His cavalry escort is dissolved and he a fugitive, but in what direction is not known.

J. H. Wilson

Macon, Ga.
May 10, 1865

Major-General Sherman

Captain Abraham, of General Upton's division, yesterday received the surrender of two brigades of rebel cavalry, two thousand strong, at Washington, Ga., including Generals Vaughn, Dibrell, Elzey, Williams, Lewis, Gilmer and Lawton. General Croxton is now engaged in paroling Ferguson's brigade at Forsyth. The balance of the rebel cavalry which started as Davis escort has either been paroled or gone home. General Vaughn told Upton that he had received positive orders to escort Davis to the Mississippi, but on his arrival at Washington, determined to go no farther. The money that Davis had with him has been paid to his troops and scattered through the country about Washington. Lieutenant Yeoman, a very energetic and capable officer, reports that Davis on the night of the seventh tried to cross the Chattahoochee at Warsaw, but lost his trail. Yeoman himself crossed the river at Vining's late same night; since then he has not heard from him.

J. H. Wilson

GENERAL ORDERS No. 21

Headquarters
Fourth Division Cavalry Corps
Military Division of the Mississippi
Edgefield, Tenn.
June 10, 1865

Before severing his connection with the command, the Brevet Major-General commanding desires to express his high appreciations of the bravery, endurance and soldierly qualities displayed by the officers and men of his division in the late cavalry campaign. Leaving Chickasaw on the twenty-second of March as a new organization, and without status in the Cavalry Corps, you in one month traversed six hundred miles; crossed six rivers; met and defeated the enemy at Montevallo, capturing one hundred prisoners; routed Forest, Buford and Roddy in their chosen position at Ebenezer Church, capturing two guns and three hundred prisoners; carried the works in your front at Selma, capturing thirteen guns, eleven hundred prisoners and five battle-flags, and finally crowned your successes by a night assault upon the enemy's entrenchments at Columbus, where you captured fifteen hundred prisoners, twenty-four guns, eight battle-flags, and vast munitions of war. April 21 you arrived at Macon, having captured, on your march, three thousand prisoners, thirty-nine pieces of artillery and thirteen battle-flags. Whether mounted with sabre or dismounted with the carbine, the brave men of the Third, Fourth and Fifth Iowa, First and Seventh Ohio, and Tenth Missouri Cavalry triumphed over the enemy in every conflict. With regiments led by brave colonels, and brigades commanded with consummate skill and daring, the division in thirty days won a reputation unsurpassed in the service. Though many of you have not received the rewards your gallantry has entitled you to, you have won the admiration and gratitude of your countrymen. You will return to your homes with the proud consciousness of having defended the flag of your country in the hour of the greatest national peril, while through your instrumentality, liberty and civilization will have advanced the greatest stride recorded in history. The best wishes of your commanding General will ever attend you.

E. Upton

CHAPTER 21

Companies A & C First Ohio Cavalry

A brief history of Companies A and C becomes necessary to a complete history of the regiment by reason of the fact that their service up to the winter of 64-5 was entirely apart from that of the regiment. Company A was raised at Washington C. H., Ohio, and officered by Captain John H. Robinson, First Lieutenant Samuel L. Hooker, Second Lieutenant Noah Jones. Company C was raised in Cincinnati and was officered as follows: Captain, N. D. Menken; First Lieutenant, S. N. Stanford; Second Lieutenant, B. R. Kirby.

These were the first two companies organized at Camp Chase; and in September, 1861, when Lee was threatening the troops under General Reynolds at Elkwater, and the advanced posts of the Union army in the Tygart Valley and Cheat Mountain, this squadron was dispatched to West Virginia and learned its first lessons of warfare in the arduous scouting and picket duty that devolved upon the small cavalry command attached to this portion of the army of occupation of West Virginia. Captain Robinson, who commanded the squadron, was a man of dignified appearance, who had commanded an expedition across the plains in 49. He had the entire confidence of his command as well as of his superior officers, and made for the squadron an enviable reputation during the few months that he was in command. But he was already dying with consumption, and illy withstood the arduous campaigning that fell to the lot of these companies in West Virginia, and was compelled to leave us in the spring of '62, and soon afterwards died at his home in Washington C. H.

First Lieutenant Samuel L. Hooker resigned as early as he could, and Second Lieutenant Noah Jones, who afterwards became captain, commanded the company with signal ability until the fall of 64. Captain John W. McElwain commanded it until December, 1864, and Lieutenant and Captain J. A. O. Yeoman from that date until it was mustered out.

Captain Menken, a daring, handsome and brilliant officer, resigned in the early summer of 62, and thereafter Company C was under the command of Captain Coon.

The squadron, under Captain Robinson, first smelled fire at an armed reconnaissance against one of the Jacksons, not Stonewall, at Greenbrier, W. Va., under the command of General Reynolds, in October, 62. And soon thereafter Company A, with the gallant Thirteenth Indiana under Colonel Sullivan, made a two weeks scout through the almost impassable mountains and by-paths of West Virginia, under the lead of a local Union guide, capturing and breaking up bands of bushwhackers and guerillas.

The winter of 61-2 was spent at Springfield, near Romney, scouting almost daily to the north toward Big Cacapon and Bloomery Gap, endeavouring to advise the command of a raid by Ashby's cavalry or Stonewall Jackson's infantry that then lay near Winchester. In February, 1862, it fell back with the troops that had been occupying Romney to a station at Patterson Creek, W. Va., on the line of the Baltimore and Ohio Railway, and thence moved northward and eastward to Pawpaw Tunnel.

This portion of the army was at that time under the command of Brigadier-General F. W. Lander, a pioneer Californian, and a man of great courage and marked individuality. The squadron was attached to his headquarters and acted as his personal escort, doing messenger and other service in addition to the scouting duties that were imposed upon it.

Shortly after its arrival at Pawpaw Tunnel a considerable part of Lander's forces proceeded north to Bloomery Furnace, which was then occupied by an outlying post of Jackson's army. Lander marched to surprise it with the First Virginia Loyal Cavalry. Its Colonel, Anisansel, was one of the foreign adventurers who so largely officered our army at its beginning and were absolutely useless for any purpose except to draw their pay and to wear gold braid. The First Virginia Cavalry, although it afterwards proved itself a magnificent regiment, signally failed under the charge of this chattering Colonel, and Lander himself brushed them aside and with his escort of the Ohio squadron captured the post in the most brilliant and dashing manner. The squadron retired to camp highly elated and fully satisfied with its General and its own conduct, as the General was with it.

Some three days thereafter some twenty of the members of Company A were sent out as a scouting party to the scene of this action. They were under the direct command of Lieutenant Jones, who was under the command and direction of Captain Fitz-James O'Brien, of General Lander's staff. Few men now living, except those who are readers of magazines, ever have heard him mentioned; but he was one of those brilliant Irish exiles who cast their lot and their fortunes with the young republic, and who in the ranks of letters and on the field of war have done so much to elevate and adorn the history of the country of their adoption. He was a brilliant young Irish poet and the author of that pathetic poem, "The Shamrock"; and but for his untimely death would have made a great figure in American literature, if he had not become famous as an Irish hero, like Meagher and Corcoran. On that bright winter morning as he was advancing along the winding mountain road of West Virginia, at a turn of the road he came upon a cavalry column; at its head rode one of the most distinguished soldiers of the war, on either side, and who, but for an early death at the hands of Kone's able regiment in the early spring of 62, would undoubtedly have been a greater cavalry leader than the famous Stuart. This was the distinguished Colonel Ashby, a man of aristocratic breeding, singular courage, and a born cavalry soldier. As he and young O'Brien faced each other he called out, "What troops are you?" And young O'Brien answered, "Union troops, God damn you!" And their pistols cracked in the morning sunlight and O'Brien reeled backward in the saddle with a wound through the body. The little scouting party formed and received the first charge of the enemy, while O'Brien was sent to the rear. It was a running fight for some miles, and the jarring of the horses undoubtedly had its effect upon the latter, so that within forty-eight hours he was dead.

If one will turn to the pages of *Harper's Magazine* in the early part of 62, he will read some lines written by this young Irish poet that indicate that he had a premonition of his early death upon the field. And yet it was a pity that he did not fall upon some glorious field instead of a lonely scouting expedition. General Lander himself, while the army was on the march to Martinsburg to join General Banks in an attack upon Winchester, died of disease, and was succeeded by General James Shields, one of the heroes of the Mexican War and famous for the fact that he survived a grape-shot wound of such extent that a silk handkerchief was drawn through his body. It will be remembered of him in the early days when he and Lincoln were at the Illinois bar that he fell a victim to the verse of some witty and mischievous young lady and challenged the future President. That Lincoln bore him no malice and that this did not stand in his way, was proved by the fact that he was appointed to the command of the magnificent division left vacant by the death of General Lander.

Companies A and C were again assigned to duty at the headquarters of General Shields. But this duty by no means exempted them from their share of the dangers and hard fighting of that division. Jackson, at the advance of the armies under Banks and Shields, fell back beyond Cedar Creek; then Banks' division received orders to march across the Manassa Mountains to Folmouth, thence to reinforce a portion of the army under General McClellan. Taking advantage of his absence, Jackson returned to fight the division of Shields. This movement was covered by Ashby's cavalry. And on the twenty-second of March, while reconnoitering, General Shields, in front of Ashby's cavalry, was struck by a piece of a shell from one of his guns, and he retired and turned over the command to Colonel Nathan W. Kimball, of the Fourteenth Indiana, who assumed command and fought the battle of Kernstown, sometimes called the first battle of Winchester, and the only battle in which Stonewall Jackson was thoroughly beaten. Late in the afternoon the Ohio brigade, consisting of the Sixty-second, Sixty-sixth, Seventh and Fifth Ohio infantry, were thrown around to the right in a movement to turn Jackson's flank. The Ohio squadron was placed directly in the rear of it. The brigade struck the left of Jackson's army, stationed behind an ugly stone wall, and at the end of fifteen or twenty minutes sharp fighting carried it; and a part of the squadron, consisting of about seventy-five troopers, were then ordered to charge. Before them lay a routed army; to their rear was Ashby's cavalry drawn up to cover the retreat; a stone wall, impassable for cavalry, lay in front. The squadron was compelled to charge along the stone wall for half a mile before it found an opening through. Then it plunged into the midst of this routed army and followed Jackson's army until near nightfall, capturing over three hundred and twenty-five prisoners.

And here let me lay a little flower upon the grave of the bravest man I ever knew, a captain in some Virginia regiment, a mere boy, weighing not over one hundred and fifteen pounds, he turned alone to face our column. He seemed to be the only unbeaten man in that entire army. As the advance of the column came up he halted it and kept firing shot after shot until surrounded by nearly a dozen men, when he threw away his empty pistol and pulled his sword and lunged at the men on horseback with the fierceness of an ancient Viking. He fell before the shot of one into whose side he was plunging his sword. He raised himself half way up and threw his sword at him and then started to reload his pistol. One man hastened to disarm him and as he did so, the Confederate hero pulled a ring from his finger, giving an honoured Virginian name, and said: "Send this to my mother and tell her I died rather than surrender." He was tenderly cared for by his former foes, but died that night from four or five bullet wounds that he had received in the contest. The writer has seen many a fearless man in the midst of a heated charge who seemed to have no idea of the name of fear or death; but he never before or since has seen a man in the midst of panic and rout rise so entirely above it and be so absolutely fearless as this young Virginian soldier.

The squadron bivouacked late that night, and in the morning took up the pursuit of Jackson's broken army, which was covered by Ashby's cavalry, charging time and time again the squadron of the Virginia cavalier, and led the Union forces in pursuit of Jackson's army, skirmishing constantly up the valley with Jackson's rear guard, composed of Ashby's cavalry and other troops, driving them back beyond the now famous Cedar Creek and Fisher's Hill. Returning to camp at Strasburg, they were sent upon a scout with Colonel D. H. Strother, then on Banks' staff, and who was famous before the war as "Porte Crayon," delineating with pen and pencil those delightful papers in *Harper's Magazine* known as "Winter Scenes in the South"; we crossed the north branch of the Shenandoah by swimming, the bridges having been burned, and plunged down into the little town of Front Royal. Here Company A drew up beside the long, rambling Virginia hotel of the town; and as the writer of this sat in his saddle beside Wm. Price, who had formerly lived in Virginia, but then lived in Washington C. H., he was astonished to hear a rather remarkable looking young woman say from the second story, "Why, Billy Price, is that you here with these nasty Yankees? I'll tell M—— on you!" She having been Price's sweetheart in the days when as little children they trudged together to school. And as we rode away I asked him who it was, and he replied that it was Miss Belle Boyd; she was afterwards known as the famous spy who led Stonewall Jackson's troops in through Front Royal to the rear of Banks.

After a few days rest at Strasburg Shield's division was ordered to Falmouth, opposite Fredericksburg, where McDowell's corps then lay, which was then under orders to move toward and join McClellan upon the Peninsula. Banks was left to entrench himself at Strasburg and Front Royal and hold the Shenandoah and Luray Valleys. Our division had scarcely reached Falmouth before we heard that Jackson, receiving reinforcements, had crept stealthily up the Luray Valley, struck the First Maryland Loyal Infantry at Front Royal and sent Banks broken and defeated across the river to Hancock, Md. This relieved Richmond for the time being and diverted the column of McDowell and Shields from its flank attack, and they were ordered to the valley again, toward which Fremont was already marching from West Virginia for the capture of Jackson.

Fremont arrived at Strasburg about the first of June, just as Shield's division reached Front Royal, and Jackson slipped in between the two, Fremont following up the Main Valley, and the First Ohio squadron, with Shield's, following up the Luray Valley. Neither Shields nor Fremont were in communication one with the other and the Massanutten Mountains lay between them, and Company A was thrown out through the gap at New Market and opened up communications, unfortunately too late; for upon the eighth the battle of Cross Keys was fought, and upon the ninth the bridge was wrested from the First Virginia Cavalry of Shield's division, and two of his brigades under Colonel Carroll of the Eighth Ohio were badly beaten.

Thence Jackson marched through the mountains, struck McClellan and relieved Richmond. In the meantime the squadron, with the balance of the division, was ordered to join the army which Pope was then concentrating beyond the Manassas Mountains for the protection of Washington. The squadron was immediately attached to Pope's headquarters and took a very active part as messengers, couriers, staff and general orderlies in that most momentous and tragic campaign. They served at the battle of Cedar or Slaughter Mountain and were with Pope in his remarkable defence of the line of the Rappahannock, where the line was finally turned by Jackson's marching north and turning through the Manassas Mountains and striking the line of Pope's army and Pope's communications at Briston Station, near Centerville. They accompanied Pope as he abandoned the line of the Rappahannock and concentrated his forces on the old battle-field of Bull Run and accepted battle in the firm belief that he would be able to destroy Jackson before he was reinforced by Lee. This he would no doubt have done had it not been for the treachery of Fitz-John Porter and the inaction and jealousy of McClellan and the tardy march of Franklin's corps. This turned what would have been a brilliant victory and decisive victory into an almost fatal defeat. And the squadron that night was amongst the last to fall back from this ill-fated field, and marched with the defeated army back to the defences of Washington, where Pope was relieved. Thence it moved with the reorganized army into Maryland and participated in the battle of Antietam.

In the fall and winter of '62 it was attached to Stahl's cavalry and was stationed near Fairfax C. H. while Burnside was confronting Lee near Fredericksburg. In the latter part of May, 1862, Lee, who had been reorganizing his forces after the battle of Chancellorsville, took advantage of the mustering out of the two years troops and the depletion of the army at Falmouth to threaten Washington and make his ill-fated Pennsylvania campaign. Hooker then performed the best service that was ever done for the cavalry of the Army of the Potomac by giving it daring and efficient cavalry leaders. Stahl was replaced by the daring Kilpatrick; the gallant Captain Farnesworth was made Brigadier-General and sent to command one of the brigades; and the brilliant Custer, then but a boy of twenty-three, but a magnificent and knightly soldier, to the command of the other brigade. Then began the service upon which the Ohio squadron mostly prides itself. They were attached to Kilpatrick's headquarters, who always, upon the skirmish line, or in a sabre charge, never lost an opportunity of throwing his favourite squadron into the fight to carry some part of the line or dislodge some ugly knot of skirmishers. It was with him covering the front of Hooker's army while Hooker covered Washington on that remarkable campaign from Falmouth to Warrenton, from Warrenton to Aldie, from Aldie skirting the entire Blue Ridge to the upper Potomac, keeping always in front of Lee and foiling every endeavour of his to turn his flank or thrust his columns between him and Washington, until Lee finally gave up the endeavour and started on that wild raid into Maryland and through a part of Southern Pennsylvania, burning Chambersburg and threatening Harrisburg. The cavalry under Kilpatrick and Buford moved rapidly forward to Fredericksburg, Md., from Fredericksburg to Emmetsburg, Md., from there to Hanover and Abbotstown, Pa., covering the front of Meade's army and trying to definitely locate Lee. Here Hooker was relieved and Meade took command. At Hanover Kilpatrick struck Stuart, who was absent from Lee's army, and a brilliant cavalry fight occurred between a portion of Kilpatrick's division and a part of Stuart's army in its very streets, which ended in Stuart's repulse and the capture of a rebel flag. The second day there after Reynolds and Buford developed Lee's army in front of Gettysburg and opened the fight on that glorious and immortal field. Kilpatrick's division was sent to our extreme right at Hagerstown, where it attacked and had a fight with Stuart's cavalry on the night of the second, in which the squadron, as usual, participated.

On the morning of the third it was drawn up and placed on the extreme left beyond Big Round Top, where a brigade under the gallant but ill-fated Farnsworth, charging the rebel infantry behind stone walls, leaving its brilliant leader dead upon the field. After the charge of Picket's[1] division hostilities ceased between the armies, both looked after the dead and wounded on the fourth, and on the evening of that day Lee began to withdraw through the mountains toward the fords of the upper Potomac. A portion of the army was ordered in direct pursuit, and the balance marched toward Hagerstown with the intention of trying to intercept Lee. Near midnight on the night of the fourth Kilpatrick's division overtook one of the rear columns of Lee's army guarding a wagon-train and some of his wounded.

---

1. Private J. I. Thornton was an orderly for Gen. Hayes, commanding a division of the 2nd Corps, and during Pickett's charge behaved with such extreme gallantry as to be promoted to a lieutenancy on the recommendation of Gen. Hayes.

It was at the summit of a small mountain, near the Pennsylvania and Maryland lines, and at a point called Monterey; a two-gun battery and other rebel troops were covering the rear. Two different regiments of Custer's brigade had been ordered to the charge, but were repulsed. Kilpatrick then ordered the Ohio squadron to lead, supported by the First Virginia Union Cavalry. No greater test of men's courage could have been had than to have led in this night attack. It had been raining hard. The night was extremely dark; and the white turnpike and the tops of the white wagons were all that could be plainly seen. The squadron, under the lead of Captain Jones, charged down the turnpike, received the fire of the rear guard, plunged down the mountain road alongside the wagons and followed it for seven miles under a scattering fire from wagons and mountain side when they reached the head of the train. They were loyally supported by the First Virginia, and the balance of Kilpatrick's division followed at its leisure. This charge, taking into account the darkness, the unknown numbers and character of the foe, was as brilliant an attack as was ever made within the history of mounted warfare. Its net results were a large wagon-train and over a thousand prisoners, beside the wounded that were accompanying the train. That the squadron escaped with four or five killed and wounded and was not annihilated was due in part to the darkness and in part to the demoralized condition of the enemy.

The squadron was engaged daily in skirmishing with the enemy, and on the eleventh of July drove Stuart's cavalry back beyond Hagerstown toward the Potomac River. In the early part of this fight Kilpatrick had formed one of his brigades upon one crest, while a brigade of Stuart was upon the opposite crest; midway between the two some forty or fifty skirmishers behind a stone wall were making it very hot for the staff and the headquarters. Kilpatrick gave Captain Jones an order to drive them out, and about forty men of Company A, under his leadership, made a brilliant dash and drove them back so quickly that they had not time to remount, capturing twenty-six of them before they could rejoin the main body. On the thirteenth the squadron operated on the left of Lee's army, and Myron Judy, a most gallant and fearless young soldier, about eighteen years of age, who was then carrying the division flag, was mortally wounded, but refused to give up the colours until he had placed them again into the general's own hands.

On the morning of the fourteenth it was found that Lee, during the night time, had abandoned his entrenchments, and the cavalry were ordered rapidly to the front, picking up stragglers by the hundreds. Sam Gillespie, the bugler of Company A, a little in advance, came upon a single gun accompanied by a sergeant and his men, which in some way had been stalled or fallen behind. He rode up to the sergeant and ordered him to surrender and turn around the gun. The sergeant said, "What! six men surrender to one!" Gillespie said, "If you don't surrender I will blow your brains out!" And at the moment the head of the squadron appeared and the sergeant and his gunners surrendered to Gillespie.

The squadron took part in the brilliant cavalry fight at Falling Water, where a part of Kilpatrick's division in a mounted charge captured Pettigrew's brigade in earthworks that was covering the remnant of Lee's army, killing its commander and taking over a thousand prisoners, inflicting the last blow upon the broken and defeated army which, thirty days before, had marched with flaunting banners and gallant tread on its mission of insolent invasion.

Lee's army fell back and entrenched themselves along the line of the Rapidan, with Stuart's cavalry in front of his army on the line of the Rappahannock. Meade's army occupied the country extending from Warrenton to Bristow Station, down toward Falmouth, with his cavalry covering our left toward Harwood's Church.

On the morning of the thirteenth of September, 1863, Buford's cavalry division crossed at the Rappahannock Ford, on the line of the railway, and Kilpatrick's division at Kelly's Ford, seven miles below, and took a road converging toward the one taken by Buford near Brandy Station. As the division emerged on the old Brandy Station cavalry battle-ground, we found our old foe in front of us, and it was then a strife between these two rival divisions to see which could drive the enemy the fastest. Buford upon the right, and Kilpatrick upon the left, with cavalry pennons flying, batteries firing, and squadrons charging, kept the enemy moving rapidly toward Culpepper. Brandy Station is an ideal battle-ground, and was fought over time and again by the rebel and Union cavalry. Culpepper C. H. is nearly three miles from Brandy Station. Off to the left as you go toward Culpepper lies Stevensburg, and about a mile and a half beyond Culpepper. Culpepper and Brandy Station and Stevensburg form the three points of an irregular triangle. In the morning, before reaching Buford, Kilpatrick had ordered a couple of regiments of the Michigan brigade to occupy a point at or near Stevensburg. Believing that they were in possession of this point, and seeing how rapidly he was driving the enemy, he conceived the idea of having these two regiments barricade them selves across the road that leads from Culpepper to the Rapidan, and to hold it with their Spencer rifles while Buford and the balance of his division charged the enemy in front. It was a brilliant idea, and if successful, would have insured the capture of a large part of Stuart's command, or its complete rout.

As we drove the enemy from Brandy Station and prepared for the final attack near Culpepper C. H., he ordered Major Bacon to take an orderly with him and ride over to Stevensburg and order these two regiments to throw themselves across the road leading to Raccoon Ford on the Rapidan, barricade themselves and hold it to the last extremity. He took with him, as an orderly, Private Yeoman.

After riding directly toward Stevensburg a mile and a half from our flank, the Major noticed little squads of troops over in a field, between half and three-quarters of a mile away, that seemed to be facing in the opposite direction from that which the Michigan troops should face. He rode down to a house and asked a negro whether they were Johnnies. The negro laughed and said, "I dunno, boss." While the Major was reconnoitring at one point, his orderly asked permission to ride down the lane and examine from that point. The troops that they were first looking at were up to the right of the lane in a field, and the orderly had no idea that he was in any danger from them, as there was a considerable fence between them and a fair field behind him toward our left flank. As he rode down the lane for a couple of hundred yards, watching them, he suddenly noticed that there were a couple of soldiers riding in front of him, two or three hundred yards ahead, and he followed along behind, unable to ascertain from their uniform whether they were Union or rebel soldiers, as they had on blue pants, and a mixed blue and gray uniform of English cloth. He followed them for about one hundred and fifty yards, when he saw them dismount in a persimmon thicket; and, lying asleep around the smouldering embers of the morning's fire, were a half dozen or more soldiers in the well-known butternut. He had seen enough and turned to go back. But just as he turned he saw another knot of about fifteen or twenty of the same men up on the hill to the left, whom he had not noticed, and who were then a little nearer the gap where he came in than he was. Two soldiers were coming there-from directly toward him. It struck him at once that they had come to see who he was. Fortunately, that morning he had heard Kilpatrick questioning a prisoner and found that the two divisions in front of us were commanded by Hampton and Robertson. So he rode a little way toward them, determined to commence the cross-examination himself rather than await it; and he hallooed out, "Are you the pickets of Robertson's division?"

"No," said they.

"Then you belong to Hampton's?"

"Yes," said they.

"What in hell are you doing here?" said he.

"On picket," said they.

"On picket, the devil! Don t you know that our men are being driven back yonder and you will be cut off and nipped!"

By this time they and the orderly were within fifty feet of each other. One of them replied, as if still doubting and questioning, "Are those you'ns men yonder?"

"No," said the orderly, "they are God-damn Yankees, and I came over to order your company in. Tell the Lieutenant to take his company back immediately upon the Stevensburg road."

"We will," said they; and turned around and went toward the Lieutenant, while the orderly started leisurely over toward the gap where he had entered the lane, met the Major coming and said to him: "Major, they are Johnnies; I have been talking with them."

Said he, "Don't look back!"

"Oh, I have no business back there."

Then having reached a safe distance, both Major and orderly trotted along toward the gap; when they reached it they galloped off and the Major reported to General Kilpatrick that he had not gone into Stevensburg as he found the road occupied by a company of rebel pickets that he didn't feel able to capture with a single orderly, and he thought he would come back before they captured him.

In a few minutes thereafter Kilpatrick's division, with the squadron at its head, made a gallant charge that drove Stuart's cavalry from Culpepper and down toward the Rapidan.

It is needless to say that they were not stopped at Stevensburg, because the Michigan regiments were not there.

In the latter part of November, 1863, while Grant was fighting at Chattanooga, and Sherman was pounding the rebel right, and Hooker was fighting his battle above the clouds on old Lookout, and Sheridan and Woods were storming over and breaking Bragg's centre at Mission Ridge, Meade, who had been lying in front of Lee's entrenched lines at the Rapidan, threw his infantry corps across the river by one of its lower fords in the endeavour to force Lee out of his entrenchments and compel him to give battle. This was only partially successful; Lee temporarily abandoned the entrenched line directly in front of him, leaving only his cavalry in occupation thereof, but Meade found him thoroughly entrenched at Mine Run, and refusing battle except behind his works. The cavalry division of Kilpatrick, after some manoeuvring, crossed the Rapidan and occupied the entrenchments vacated by Lee. The squadron led in this operation, and while it all seemed easy at first, within two hours we got into a fight with Stuart's cavalry, such as an Irish enthusiast would have described as "perfectly beautiful." The fight and the trial of metal between these two bodies of cavalry soldiers was almost the sole result of this movement, for Meade found Lee's new line impregnable to assault, and it was deemed best by him and his corps commanders to withdraw to our old line across the Rapidan.

The following winter Kilpatrick conceived the idea that Richmond might be taken and burned by a sudden dash on it by a cavalry column. From spies it was ascertained that it was almost stripped of troops. The Confederate government relying upon Lee's army in front and a few Confederate brigades to the south and not thinking of any such operations as that proposed by Kilpatrick, had withdrawn and sent to the front nearly all the garrison. A part of Meade's cavalry, supported by infantry, made a strong demonstration on one flank, drawing away Stuart's cavalry, leaving the road open for Kilpatrick on the other flank, who cut loose and made one of the most rapid marches on record. When his cavalry appeared in front of the same a few troops had been recalled from the works south of Richmond; this disheartened Kilpatrick, but it is still believed by many who were with him that he might have been successful, if he had not lost heart and faith in the enterprise. Some of the squadron entered the suburbs of Richmond and Jake Miller, a private of Company A, who had always a keen eye for a piece of rebel horse-flesh, captured a fine horse in the outskirts.

Kilpatrick finally gave up the attempt, proceeded down the peninsula, pursued by rebel cavalry and infantry, which had been hastily drawn to Richmond. He found the bridges gone across some of the rivers, and was compelled to counter-march and fight the rebel columns, and was in an almost desperate situation when a division of negro troops from Butler came to his rescue.

It was on this expedition and in connection therewith that Colonel Ulric Dahlgren, in command of a small party of cavalry, was fired on by rebel bushwhackers and murdered. Dahlgren was a son of Admiral Dahlgren and one of the most chivalrous and knightly men that ever rode at the head of embattled squadrons. It was he who, with a small party of men, while Lee was at Gettysburg, captured and destroyed his pontoons at Williamsburg, Md., and forced him, on his return, to rebuild the same, causing him an almost fatal delay and one that would have been fatal had he been opposed by a more enterprising General than Meade. As it was, he crossed his army during the night before and the early morning of the day that Meade moved to assault his lines. In the performance of this brilliant service Dahlgren, who was then but a captain, lost a leg. When he was fired on and wounded on this last fatal expedition one of the rebels attempted to pull off his boots, when Dahlgren, with that indomitable courage of which he was possessed, resented the insult, took off the wooden leg and struck the rebel over the head with it, who then completed the murder. Here fell in this midnight foray a man by nature and a genius formed for cavalry operations, and who, if he had lived, would have been one of the great cavalry leaders of the war.

In the spring of 1864 General Wilson relieved General Kilpatrick of the command of his division, and the latter was sent West to Sherman, and the squadron which had been so long his body guard and the leaders in many of his most brilliant charges, was at the same time ordered West, and their history thereafter became merged in the history of the regiment.

This is but a brief and imperfect sketch of the services of this remarkable squadron. It is written without memoranda, and the writer has had no opportunity to consult with his comrades, who could undoubtedly refresh his memory as to many heroic events in which they were engaged. It is only the most notable of them that came to the memory of the writer more than thirty years thereafter that are here given. Company A was particularly distinguished for the high grade of intelligence pervading its ranks, and many of its privates had left colleges to carry sabres in the defence of their country; they served in all the important campaigns of the valley with Shields and Lander; with Pope on the Rappahannock; with McClellan at Antietam; with Hooker and Meade on the Gettysburg campaign, where the Confederate cause reached high water mark. Such confidence was reposed in them, their courage and intelligence by the Generals for whom they acted as escorts and bodyguards, that they were used almost constantly to do the duty of staff officers to carry orders both on the march and in battle. It is doubtful if any like body of men ever performed so varied and distinguished services.

LIST OF BATTLES OF COMPANIES A AND C
FIRST OHIO VOLUNTEER CAVALRY

Greenbrier Elver, Va	October 3, 1861
Bloomery Gap, Va	February 14, 1862
Kearnstown, Va	March 23, 1862
Port Republic, Va	June 9, 1862
Cedar Mountain, Va	August 9, 1862
Five days battle along the Rappahannock River	August 12, 13, 14, 15 and 16, 1862
Second Bull Run, Va	August 29 and 30, 1862
Chantilla, Va	September 1, 1862
Antietam, Md	September 16, 1862
Hanover, Pa	June 30, 1863
Shepherdstown, Pa	July 1, 1863
Gettsburg, Pa	July 1 to 4, 1863
Monterey Gap, Pa	July 4, 1863
Smithtown, Md	July 5, 1863
Boonesborough, Md	July 8 to 10, 1863
Hagerstown, Md	July 11, 1863
Williamsport, Md	July 14, 1863
Falling Waters, Md	July 14, 1863
King George Co, Va	August 24, 1863
Brandy Station, Va	September 6, 1863
Culpepper C H, Va	September 12, 1863

James City, Va	October 10, 1863
Raccoon Ford, Va	October 19, 1863
Robinson River, Va	October 10, 1863
White Sulphur Springs, Va	October 12 and 13, 1863
Brandy Station, Va	October 17, 1863
Briston Station, Va	October 19, 1863
Stevensburg, Va	November 7, 1863
Richmond Raid, Va	February 28 to March 4, 1864
Nashville, Tenn ,	December 16, 1864

Wilson Raid through Alabama and Georgia, and capture of Jeff Davis March and April, 1865

The enclosed is to the best of my knowledge and a truthful statement of the principal engagements of Companies A and C, First O.V. Cavalry.

Kindly yours,

Noah Jones, Late Captain Company A, First O.V. Cavalry

CHAPTER 22

The Capture of Jefferson Davis

by Lieutenant Joseph A. O. Yeoman

I have been frequently asked to write the history of the capture of Jefferson Davis, and especially that part pertaining to the men under my command. I have always refused on the ground, that while such a narrative ought to be made a part of the history of the times, if fully written by myself it would seem to be too personal; but in justice to the men who were under my command, and to complete the history of the operations resulting in the capture of Jefferson Davis, I have concluded to write it. It must in its nature be largely personal; more so than I would desire, but its complete details ought to be given, and my excuse for the narrative and especially the personal part that I took therein, are given above.

On the twenty-first of April, 1865, the great cavalry expedition commanded by General Wilson, having stormed and captured the fortified cities of Selma, Ala., and Columbus, Ga., occupied Macon, and there for the first time learned that we were playing but a minor part in the great tragedy of the Civil War, that great events had occurred in the East, that Lee had surrendered to Grant at Appomattox, and Johnson to Sherman in the Carolinas. This was news to us, and good news, too. There was only one thing left to mar the happiness of our command and the completeness of our victories, and that was that Davis himself, with his cabinet, had escaped from Richmond, evaded the armies both of Grant and Sherman, and were somewhere in the Carolinas with a cavalry column estimated at four or five thousand, determined on making another stand, if possible, in the Southwest, which Wilson had just rendered impossible, or on joining Kirby Smith in the trans-Mississippi department. General Wilson, ever active and alive to the interests of the Government, sought every source of information that he could concerning the probable location and destination of the rebel chief. He received various information from citizens and others who arrived at Macon, who had seen Davis at Charlotte, N. C., a few days before.

On the morning of the third of May, General Alexander came into my tent, where I was preparing the inspection rolls of the brigade for transmission to corps headquarters, and stated to me that Davis had been at Charlotte, N. C., some days before and was supposed to be at that time somewhere near the southern border of South Carolina, and that General Wilson had directed that six or seven of the best scouts of the brigade be sent out in rebel uniform to penetrate the rebel lines and send information to the General commanding, who would dispatch troops from the nearest and most accessible point to intercept his line of retreat and effect his capture. I presume that General Alexander came to me rather than to any other of his staff from the fact that during the campaign I had been with the advance of the brigade, which was, with one or two exceptions, at all times in the advance of the army, and had had charge of the scouts and was better personally acquainted with them than with any other. I took it as a mark of high personal regard that I should have been first consulted in the matter; and after listening to him I said, "General, I should like to make a suggestion, if you please."

He answered, "I will hear you, Mr. Yeoman."

I said, "As this is the last and most important service that can be rendered our Government by Union soldiers, it is a matter that ought not to be left entirely to enlisted men. I know that the enlisted men whom I would choose are men of great individuality, extreme courage, and loyal to every call of duty; and yet the very individuality of the men would make them but illy brook receiving orders one from the other; each man whom I would be likely to send would be very likely to have his own notions about the matter. Some officer should go who would have general charge of the expedition, whom the men had confidence in, and who they would implicitly obey; he should have enough men with him so that he would be able at any time to detach some of them as couriers to carry dispatches to the commanding general, and in case Davis should be found with an escort of not to exceed one hundred and fifty to two hundred men, to effect his capture. This command should mingle with the rebel commands, be under the command and eyes of this officer, be scattered and concentrated at his pleasure and act as he might at the time determine."

He said to me, "Who will go on an expedition of that kind?"

I said, "If you will relieve me from the duty of perfecting these rolls and assign another officer thereto, I myself will go."

He answered, "Ride over to General Wilson, explain your plan to him, tell him it meets my approval, and that I will vouch for you that the duty will be performed if it is in the power of any officer to do it."

In ten minutes I was in the saddle, rode over to General Wilson, and told him my plan. He smiled and said he liked the plan, but he said that he had never thought of an officer commanding an alien body within the enemy's ranks, and claiming to be a part of their army. "You will find it a very difficult feat to perform; and you understand that if taken in rebel uniform you will be tried by drum-head court martial and executed within twenty-four hours. So you see that it is a very dangerous service and that you must not be taken."

I told him that I had anticipated all that, and that I should, under no circumstances, be captured, and I was confident that the men whom I took with me would avoid capture by fighting to the last, if it came to a clash of arms. He directed me to make my detail, use my own judgement in making the same, to make it as large or as small as I pleased, to call on the quartermaster of the corps for captured clothing or any other thing that I could properly use, and called in the quartermaster and instructed him to honour any demands that I might make.

I had never at any time in all my life performed any service that in any manner required me to doff the Union blue and encase myself in the rebel gray. I knew that while spies were necessary to the success of every army, that the service performed by them, while extremely hazardous and dangerous, was never regarded as highly honourable. But this, it seemed to me, was an unusual service. To effect the capture of the man who for years had maintained armies in the field against the Government I loved, who had been responsible almost more than any other man for the original acts or secession, seemed to justify to my youthful mind at the time any ruse that promised success. I did not feel as if I were performing any ordinary scout or spy service, or that there was anything dishonourable in penetrating in this manner the rebel lines to make the capture of Davis certain. More than that, I felt that the extraordinary hazard and danger would, at least with my comrades, compensate for any feeling that they might have in this respect as to the character of the service. The expedition that I proposed was unique and stands single and alone of its kind. Individual scouts and spies have been common in all species of warfare; but never before to my knowledge had any person attempted in ancient or modern warfare to transform an entire company of men, penetrate the lines of the enemy, march with and mingle with their various commands as a part thereof. But the magnitude of the prize justified the attempt; the very danger itself, in requiring an alert intellect and cool action, made it fascinating. But much as such an expedition was desirable, it would have been impossible in any other stage of the war than that of which I am now writing. The rebel columns themselves were rapidly disintegrating and the few brigades that had remained loyal to the rebel chief were rapidly breaking up, discipline was but slightly maintained, and the usual precaution but slightly observed. The first matter of importance upon my return to brigade headquarters was the selection of the men. While the Congressional Report shows but twenty-seven men with me, there were actually thirty-three, as I now remember it. Three of these were chosen by me from the Fifth Iowa, men who had been constantly with me in the advance, whom I had noticed as cool, courageous men, ready to undertake any desperate enterprise. Their names were Thomas H. Wright, Company E, Fifth Iowa, and two others whose names were unknown to me at the time of making the report to Congress, but who afterwards proved their identity. The reason I do not know them all was that at the time of making the detail it was an oral one, with no expectation that their names would afterwards be required for any purpose what ever. There were chosen by me from the Seventh Ohio: John Gotts, Corporal, Company E; a private of Company L, name unknown; and Lee Wood, of Company E, now a resident of Ripley, O., and one of the coolest of all men of the command, and one who rendered an important and distinguished service, of which I shall hereafter speak. There were of my own regiment twenty seven men, the names of many of whom I did not remember, when called upon by the chairman of the committee on claims to make my report; nor can I now give them in full. Eight of them were from my own Company A, and were as follows:

Detachment First Ohio Volunteer Cavalry accompanying Captain Joseph A. O. Yeoman in pursuit and capture of Jefferson Davis.

George P Barnes	Sergeant, Company A
John H McElwaine	Q M Sergeant, Company A
Samuel Robertson	Corporal, Company A
Ripley L Walm	Corporal, Company A
Henry T Ressler	Private, Company A
Samuel J Rice	Private, Company A
Spencer C Phares	Private, Company A
George W Blair	Private, Company A
John Camm	Sergeant, Company A
William Hampden	Private, Company C
John W Newlove	Sergeant, Company D
William Power	Private, Company D
Bushrod W Click	Private, Company F
Thomas R Kennard	Private, Company I

William Place	Private, Company I
John F Young	Private, Company K
William Van Houten	Private, Company F
Robert Peters	Private, Company E
John Malone	Private, Company H
William Schwartz	Corporal, Company H

There were others of the First Ohio Cavalry, also, whom I cannot, for the reasons above given, now name.

At least three of these, *viz*.: Samuel J. Robertson, George W. Blair and Bushrod W. Click, were of the recruits that had entered the army in the spring of 1864, and were but seventeen years of age at most. It was a great compliment to them to be chosen; and I placed no greater reliance in any one, so far as mere courage and the standing by me in a desperate place was concerned, than in these three boys that were not beyond the age of school-children.

Lee Wood, Thomas W. Kennard, John W. Newlove, Ripley M. Walm, John W. McElwaine and Samuel J. Robertson and John Camm were among the most faithful and loyal of these men whom it was safe to say that better and more courageous soldiers never set foot in a stirrup or carried a sabre in a charge. But where all were so cool and courageous, it seems invidious to especially mention any one.

The service of next importance was to prepare the disguise in which we should march, and determine what arms and equipments we should carry. Unfortunately for us, General Upton, who was a very conscientious officer, acting in the interests of the Government, had, a few days before, had every captured horse in the command branded, so that our expedition was rendered more difficult and dangerous from the fact that every man had to ride a horse branded U. S. We had nothing but Spencer rifles, and as the rebels had no Spencer rifles, and no ammunition therefore, it was thought, in view of the fact that our disguise at best was not as good as it should be, that we discard rifles and carry only our revolvers, and do what fighting we might have to do, if any, at close quarters. There was another difficulty here because we could get no Confederate belts, and the U. S. was plainly to be seen upon the belts that carried our revolvers. As the rebels themselves had little to eat, and their haversacks were somewhat different from ours, and seldom contained hardtack or the food which we had, it was deemed best to march without haversacks, trusting to our genius for foraging to procure supplies.

We found plenty of rebel clothing amongst the stores that we had captured at Macon. These were taken and distributed amongst the men. I was at the time a first lieutenant, holding a captain's commission, however, but not yet mustered, and as I had been known simply as a lieutenant in the campaign, I chose a handsome gray lieutenant's uniform. In order that no word might escape from the camp and be borne ahead of us by spies or otherwise, there were but three persons who knew our purpose or our destination while we were preparing for the march; these were General Wilson, General Alexander, and myself.

At about four o'clock in the afternoon of May 3 we marched through the outposts of the Wilson cavalry corps on our hazardous expedition. We marched steadily and passed through the little town of Clinton sometime between midnight and morning. It then became daylight in that latitude at about five, and we halted at about three a. m. at a large manor house to get some forage for our horses. I knocked at the door of the house and inquired how far it was to Macon, stating that I commanded a company of the Eighth Kentucky Cavalry; asked if the Yankee raiders were there, and said that I wanted some forage for my horses. This was given me rather reluctantly; but I said I had to have it, and told them I would give them an order on the quartermaster-General of the Confederate army therefore; and so I did. And if the good gentleman who furnisged us the last feed our horses had for two or three days still preserves it, he has a beautiful order written by an ostensible Confederate lieutenant, receipting to him for so much forage as given to a company of the Eighth Kentucky Confederate Cavalry. It was not a very valuable voucher, but as good at that time as if it were genuine. We fed our horses in a grove near the house. As the men had nothing to eat, they lay down. Myself and a Sergeant or two sat up, and just as day was breaking I called them into line. Then for the first time I told them the object of our expedition; that it was given to us before any other troops in the army to effect this capture; and if we did it, we would achieve enough of honour for all the risks that we might take. I told them how I intended to march, what I intended to do; that I expected to penetrate the rebel columns, and that if I found Davis with two hundred men or less, I expected to break up his column by a sudden dash, capture and carry him off. And I said to them, that with the men that I have chosen here, and the attack coming seemingly from their own soldiers, I think it can be done. At least it will be tried. If there are more than this number, I shall detail some of you as messengers to carry what actual news we may obtain to the general commanding, so that he may act. I further instructed them that they were to be Company A of the Eighth Kentucky Cavalry. During the campaign, while we were operating against Forest, we had captured some officers from this regiment and I knew the roster of the regimental officers thoroughly. I cannot give them at this late date, but this knowledge served me well in an adventure that occurred during the expedition, of which I shall hereafter speak. I instructed them where the regiment had served; but said, as the regiment and the brigade (Roddy's) with which it served, are hundreds of miles from here, it will be necessary to say that we were detailed a year or two ago for special service upon the Coosa, guarding against deserters and runaway niggers, and that we had been down there since that time. I instructed them also that they must use the broad speech so common amongst the soldiers of the South, and never at any time forget or neglect its peculiarities. I myself was very proficient in it, for I had been born in a little town in Southern Ohio that belonged to the old Virginia military land district and that was settled largely by Virginians and Kentuckians, and was overrun with the Randolph and other negroes who had been fed by kind-hearted masters before the war. Being brought up amongst these people I had naturally a little of the brogue, so with my swarthy complexion and the long hair that I wore at that time, I made a fairly passable Confederate officer. General Wilson, in the *Century* for February, 1890, describes my personal appearance in the following manner:

> This party was placed under the command of Lieutenant Joseph A. O. Yeoman, of the First Ohio Cavalry, a brave and enterprising young officer, at that time serving on the staff of Alexander as Acting Assistant Inspector-General of Brigade. He was tall, slender, and of a somewhat swarthy complexion, which, with hair that for lack of a barber's services had grown long enough to brush back of his ears, and a Confederate major's (lieutenant's) brand-new uniform, gave him such a close resemblance to his erring but gallant countrymen of the South that his most intimate friend would not have suspected him of being a Yankee. His men were quite as successfully fitted out in captured clothing, and after receiving instructions at my own headquarters to report frequently by courier, he gaily set off on what afterwards proved to be a most successful expedition.

Having given this explanation to my men we resumed the march at daybreak and marched rapidly through Monticello and reached the Oconee River at Park's Ferry at sundown of the fourth. We marched over the same road that was taken by one of Sherman's columns in his march to the sea, and it is needless to say that we found neither forage for our horses nor food for ourselves; and only here and there was there a house left. In most places there were only chimneys standing that spoke most emphatically of the horrors of war. What few women and children we saw looked pale and wasted; and I would not have had the heart to have taken food from them if any could have been found, which I very much doubt. When we arrived at Park's Ferry we found it to consist of but a single ferry boat, capable of holding only two men and two horses at a time, and it required at least fifteen or twenty minutes to make the trip and return. There was a part of a Texas cavalry regiment that had been crossing during the day still crossing and lying in camp near the ferry. Jenkin's Mill, I think it was, was near this ferry. The officers were up there. But as we had to wait some time in order to cross, I avoided conversation as much as possible and remained with my men at the ferry. The Texas troops were a little ugly. For some reason or other they regarded us with suspicion; not a great deal, I think, but just enough to be a trifle ugly; then they were beaten and were going to war-wasted homes, and there was much talk amongst them about our men; they said something about coming over and taking our horses away from us, anyway, it made no difference who we were. While here, two of my men strayed away to a house, a short distance, where they found a little something to eat, and sat down at the table with four rebel soldiers. One of them was one of the best scouts in the army. The other was a little indiscreet of tongue and one of two men whom I did not personally choose, but were detailed from the regiment, and were the only men whom I could not absolutely trust. While at the table the conversation turned upon prison life. One of the rebels detailed the history of his life on Kelly's Island, and another had been in prison at Camp Douglas, Chicago; when my indiscreet fellow spoke up and said he had been in prison, too, and he had suffered a good deal and had a mighty hard time. One of the rebels asked what prison he had been in. He said Belle Island (a rebel prison). It was a stunner. The rebels looked up quickly and at each other significantly. My other scout delivered a vigorous kick under the table and looked across sternly and quickly at him; then he said, "O, I meant Johnson's Island." This answer, promptly given in response to the kick, while it did not wholly relieve the tension, was sufficient for the time being. The two men who had been very hungry before suddenly lost their appetites and, making some excuse, withdrew and came down to the bank of the river where I was waiting to cross the men, and one of them told me the story. This was not at all reassuring, but I was there and there I had to stay. About nine o'clock I got control of the ferry and began crossing my men.

In the meantime I had two or three men who mingled constantly with the rebels, and were lying around in the rebel camps, listening to what they were saying. About eleven o'clock I had about half my command across. There were still quite a number up in the rebel camps who were talking in anything but a pleasant strain about us, and my men came over and said that they thought we would be attacked pretty soon. By the first ferry that crossed over I sent to have all the men, but one or two who had crossed, return, leaving their horses there, as the ferry would carry fifteen or twenty men without horses. As our numbers were constantly diminishing and those behind were cumbered with their horses, I desired these men to guard the crossing of the balance. We lay down on the sand of the river bank in a little circle, with our pistols in our hands, expecting almost any moment to be attacked. I kept watching the ferry with the greatest anxiety until finally the last of the horses were transported across; then the ferry boat came back and I placed the dismounted men in, and as I stepped in the last myself and pushed it off, I felt a great relief, knowing that the first serious danger had been passed. Immediately upon arriving at the other side of the ferry I mounted my men and marched toward Greensboro, which we reached about three a. m. From conversation with the Texas troops, I expected at this point to meet some other commands, and not caring to strike them in the night time, I dismounted my men in a thicket by the roadside and waited two hours for the approach of dawn. As soon as it was daylight we moved through the little town of Greensboro and just on the other side met two rebel soldiers. I addressed them and asked them what division they belonged to, and they stated, to Dibrell's division of cavalry, and that the brigade to which they were attached was in camp a few miles out on the road and would be along in a short time. I then asked them if they knew where President Davis was. They said that he was in Washington, Ga., on yesterday. I asked them if they were certain of that, adding that I had a message that I desired to carry to him and desired to be absolutely sure of his present location. They stated that they had seen him themselves. Then further to verify the statement I asked if the *specie* wagons were there, which I had been informed were travelling with him; and they said yes, and that the troops had been given two months pay in coin, and they showed me $26 each which they had received.

I then felt absolutely sure of my ground. I placed my men, who had had no sleep for two nights, in the woods, so that they might not be interrupted by any passing column, rode back into Greensboro, knocked at a door, aroused a family and asked for paper and pencil; and was given a piece of paper that looked as if it might have served our ancestors of a hundred years ago for wall paper. Upon this I hurriedly wrote a dispatch, detailing all that I had been able to ascertain at that time, advising General Wilson of the exact location of Davis on the fourth, this being the morning of the fifth, and that I thought from what I had learned from these and other parties that he intended going south from there and would avoid our troops at Macon by a detour east thereof and, since he found this field occupied by Wilson's command and the road to the trans-Mississippi barred, would try and reach the Florida coast, if not intercepted. I returned immediately to my command and selected there-from John Camm and William Hampden, both of Company C, and who lived at Cincinnati, Ohio, when enlisted. I told them the contents of the dispatch, so that if for any purpose it became necessary to destroy it, it might be delivered orally. I directed them to push their horses to the utmost they could stand, and if opportunity offered, to exchange them and get the dispatch in the hands of Wilson before daylight next morning. They rode back through the town of Greensboro, down to the Oconee ferry, and were waiting there to cross with other troops, when for some reason or other they became convinced that they were objects of suspicion, and they started quietly down the river. They had gotten about a mile away when a dozen rebels started in pursuit of them, followed them down the river five or six miles, and, threatening to head them off in a bend, they jumped into and swam the Oconee under a shower of balls, but fortunately escaped and reached General

Alexander at Atlanta, who immediately telegraphed to General Wilson at Macon the contents of the dispatch. And acting upon this dispatch he sent out Lieutenant-Colonel Harnden, of the First Wisconsin Cavalry, who afterwards first struck the trail of Davis at Dublin, Georgia, on the eighth day of May. After dispatching these couriers, I left all the men of my command in the woods near Greensboro, with the exception of five, whom I chose to accompany me. One of these rode with me, two a couple of hundred yards behind, and two two or three hundred yards behind them. Our object was to meet the brigade, which I had been informed was two or three miles behind, and see if Davis might not have come with it. We passed, and I saluted the officer at the head of the column, had a few minutes guarded conversation with him, and immediately passed on, one of us taking one side of the column and the other the other until the entire brigade had passed. Davis was not with it, I determined, unless he might be in an ambulance; and while I had no considerable idea that he was there, still I did not want to pass this brigade and go on to Washington, Ga., until I was absolutely certain that he was not with it.

After passing the brigade, I went down to a point where the roads fork, one going toward South Carolina, and the other towards Washington, Ga. This was about six miles beyond Greensboro. I had met the brigade about three miles out. At the forks of the road was a toll-gate, and about twenty or thirty dismounted rebel soldiers. I stopped for a moment for the men who were in the rear to come up. As the two men in the rear came up, Lee Wood, who was one of them, said to me: "Lieutenant, there has been a man following us ever since, we left that brigade. He has kept about the same distance behind us, and now that we have halted, he has also halted under the tree up yonder," pointing to him. I looked and saw a man sitting on his horse under the tree about eight hundred yards away. I knew that Wood was one of the coolest men in the world, not likely to be rattled; but I saw he was greatly worried.

At the time I did not think it a matter of much importance

myself; I laughed and said, "I don't think it amounts to much," jumped off my horse and talked to the rebel soldiers five or ten minute? The six of us then turned back toward Greensboro together; the horseman still remained under the tree, and as we came near him I saw he was a man of very distinguished figure, finely mounted, and with a handsome gray uniform. There was nothing to indicate his rank, but I felt certain that he was a man of considerable rank and great intelligence. I saluted him and we passed on; he did not return the salute, but looked at us sternly; he closely scanned our equipments, looked at the U. S. on our belts, and the U. S. on our horses, and after we had passed him two or three hundred yards fell in our rear and followed us along the road, keeping about the same distance behind us. After a mile or two of this conduct on his part I myself became worried and consulted with the man who was riding beside me as to what best to do. We could not capture him because we were apparently rebels. To capture him was to declare ourselves Union soldiers, and we could not hold him where we were constantly meeting rebel troops. If we captured him, we must kill him. And so I marched back to the point where my command was in the woods, letting the matter drift without making up my mind what to do. I had determined upon sending a part of my men back through the town of Greensboro to the ferry across the Oconee to make certain after all that Davis might not be in any of the ambulances, and take the balance of them and push on to Washington. As we came to a point about two miles from Greensboro another road crossed the Greensboro road. I stopped there, it being within about half a mile of where my command was placed in the woods. But a couple of my men, yielding to the foraging instinct in them, were over in a potato patch and hallooed my name and said something which was indistinguishable to me, and the rebel drew up until he was not more than forty feet away from us and stopped and listened too. I was fearful lest something might be said that might give away the object and character of our expedition. I twisted nervously in my saddle and turned my face in the direction of the rebel to observe him. My face must have betrayed the perplexity I was in, for just then Geo. Blair, a boy of my company, only seventeen years of age and one of the coolest and bravest boys I ever knew, but what was strange for a boy of that character, absolutely cruel and hardened, rode up and whispered to me, "Lieutenant, you capture him and I'll take him out in the woods and kill him." And he would have killed him as he would a rat. I thought for a moment that I had never killed a man in cold blood. Then I thought, there are thirty-three men whose lives are in my charge; they may be all killed in a desperate conflict, and hanged or shot if captured; I owe them a duty that will not excuse scruples of this kind; then I thought further it was my first duty to my government to make certain of the capture of Davis, and no man's life should stand in the way; that this man surely suspected us and might betray us to some rebel column and thus prevent his capture: and as the mind and body unconsciously act together, the mind was yielding to these arguments of its own, and my hand was unconsciously travelling toward the holster for my revolver and had reached it, when he turned his horse and walked off toward Greensboro. In a moment more I should have drawn it and shot him. I drew a sigh of relief that I was not compelled to kill him in this manner. For the two minutes he was there neither of us spoke a word. He sat his horse as motionless as a statue, eyeing me critically, as I him. He was measuring me and determining me and the character of my troops; and I was weighing his life in the balance against the lives of my men and the capture of Davis. The nervous tension was intense, but I was revolving our chances more coolly than I a in writing this narrative. I then got my men out of the woods, and with the intention of flanking Greensboro and avoiding trouble, I marched northward about two miles, but found a swamp on that side and that I could not flank it without great delay. I was afraid of that, lest by some chance my quarry might escape me, and I determined to march directly through the town. I then returned to the main Greensboro road; I drew my men up in line and told them I was going through Greensboro; that I had intended to send only two or three through to the Oconee ferry, but after the events of the morning I did not like to send them through alone and thought I should share the danger with them; that from the brief conversation I had held in the morning with the officer in command it was almost certain that a large portion of the brigade would still be there waiting for the advance to cross the ferry; that I thought the chances were ninety-nine out of a hundred that we would not get through without a fight; but that I must take that chance. I further said to them, if we do get into a fight I want no man to surrender, but that I desire each man to fight his way out for himself, as the expedition would then be at an end, and surrender meant death in any event. And as we had before that been intentionally marching in groups of three and four so as to attract as little attention as possible, I ordered them to march in close column, to loosen their revolvers in their holsters and be ready to fight at a moment's notice. Thus instructed, with grim and determined faces we marched down into the town, feeling as if we were going to a funeral rather than anything else; and the quick wit and the coolness displayed in the story that I am about to tell can only be fully appreciated when it is understood that the man himself who was the hero of it expected in a few minutes to be in a desperate conflict for his life.

The town of Greensboro itself is, like many of those southern hamlets, a little town strung out along the road; it was not platted, and had but one road, not more than forty-five feet wide, through it. There were no cross streets, and it would have been a desperate place for a fight, had one occurred. A considerable portion of the rebel brigade, as I had supposed, was still in Greensboro. The men were lying down under the trees and beside the fences on both sides of the road, while many of the officers were sitting on the *piazzas*, talking to the ladies. We had passed about half way through the town when some officer to our left and about fifty feet away, whether it was the same man who had followed us in the morning or not, I could not at the time ascertain, sung out in that drawling Southern tone: "I'll bet a thousand dollahs those men are God damn Yankees!" I turned to say something, but quicker than a flash Lee Wood shook his long hair back, turned on his saddle, laughed quietly and with as much ease and quiet grace as if he had been born on the stage, and mimicking him to the echo, answered back: "I'll bet a thousand dollahs you're a God damn liar!'" Wood's manner was so careless and easy, but withal half way reckless; the mimicry was so perfect and so droll, so quickly done, that it was infectious, and the entire command, that a moment before had been expecting to have a desperate fight, broke into a hearty laugh.

I turned in my saddle and said: "You'd better let that boy alone; you've got more than you can carry away thar," using a colloquialism that I had learned from my Virginia friends when a lad. While I know it is not good form to use profane language in written narrative and I regret the necessity therefore, yet the spirit and wit of this remarkable story could not have been preserved without giving it just as it was.

We passed rapidly on and toward the other end of the town there was a large manor house, and the road widened out there, and a large block was placed, where in slavery days the guests were received who were coming to visit the master and lady of the house. As we passed by it a somewhat distinguished looking man ran down toward us, reached out his hand to me and said, "How are you, General," supposing, from the little knot of men behind me, that I was a general; or perhaps, on account of Southern courtesy, he did not want to call me anything less than a general anyway. I reached down, grasped his hand cordially and said: "How do you do, sir? How do you do?"

Then he went on to say: "We have just heard that the Yankees are in Macon, suh, and that they will soon be here, and we thought it would be a good deal better to give the quartermaster stores to our own troops than to let the Yankees have them, and we have broken up the quartermaster department and are distributing the clothing." He said: "Won't you stop your men and get some?"

I said: "No, I believe not. My men are very well dressed now and do not need any more clothing; and the weather is getting very hot, and I believe I will move on to the river." I thought it was a good deal hotter than he knew anything about, and that I should just then like to get rid of what we had of that kind of clothing, if possible. I passed through the balance of the town, and about three-quarters of a mile beyond it I saw a wooded ravine that wound first away from the town and then around it toward the right and in the direction of Washington, Ga. As soon as I saw it I thought, this is the place to take care of my men; we have averted the danger, but for the moment only; the man who called us Yankees will not be content with the answer and the laugh he got; as soon as he can consult with other officers and mount a column, they will be in hot pursuit of us to satisfy themselves whether we are Yankees or not. We had marched in an ordinary walk, but when we struck that ravine we turned off on a gallop, went down the ravine, swung around it, and after we had gone about a mile I halted my men, went up to the top of a slight hill that over looked the road, and saw a rebel column of about a hundred men go by on a thundering gallop, evidently in hot pursuit of the bogus rebels who had just passed through their midst. I thought, my gentlemen, you are just a little bit too late; the Yankee has been just a trifle too smart for you this time. This incident and the precautions that were thereafter necessary lost us much valuable time and had much to do with giving the actual capture of Davis to the Fourth Michigan and First Wisconsin, instead of to my command, to whom it fairly belonged, as it delayed our march toward Washington and necessitated more caution, lest intelligence might have been transmitted to the troops still with Davis of a suspicious body of men, for whom they should be on the lookout. That this was done I have every reason to believe from circumstances occurring thereafter. After the entire rebel command had moved out of Greensboro, having given up of course my trip to the Oconee ferry, I flanked the town again on the south and passed again eastward toward Washington, Ga. We marched a considerable part of that night, but as we had lost two entire nights of sleep, we camped in the woods toward daylight, but took the road at daylight again. As we approached Washington I formed a plan to seize Davis' person at night-fall in the midst of what troops were left, which were not then guarding him closely, the usual pickets and outposts being almost, if not entirely, abandoned. It would have been a desperate undertaking, and it is better as it turned out that its execution was not attempted. I had fully determined to kidnap and carry Davis off bodily, but the suspicions of the Confederate Cavalry with whom we mingled for several days had been aroused and their renewed vigilance prevented it. I scattered my men, as it would have been useless and criminally reckless of their lives to make the attempt or to keep them together just then.

But during the day I sent two more couriers with dispatches to General Wilson confirming my previous dispatch and especially that Davis was certain of going southward from Washington. Upon the receipt of this second dispatch a part of the Fourth Michigan Cavalry, under the command of Lieutenant-Colonel Pritchard, was sent out, which met Harnden near Abbeville, Georgia, on the afternoon of the ninth, and on the morning of the tenth, moving by a different route, effected his capture. I spent the entire day of the seventh mingling with rebel troops and scattering my men amongst the various bands and endeavouring to find ourselves the actual route taken by Davis, so that we might be first in at the death instead of sending the information upon which he might be captured, but without avail until it was too late.

In our attempt to be absolutely certain that Davis was not with any of the commands through which we passed, we had given him too far a start to the South and had given to Harnden and Pritchard the honour of the actual capture, which fairly belonged to us. But when Pritchard and Harnden overtook Davis at Erwinsville, Ga., on the morning of the tenth of May, his followers had dwindled to a mere handful. There was honour in it, but no great danger and no hazardous service. We were upon the strain all the time. The lack of sufficient disguise made that which was a perilous and hazardous duty before doubly perilous and hazardous thereby. But we had some good luck withal; indeed, we had much good luck withal, or many a man who went upon the expedition would never have returned. On one occasion we had passed through a rebel regiment and were passing by the wagon train connected therewith; I had dropped about half way back of the company, and as I passed a rebel sitting by a tree I heard him count: "One, two, three, four, five, by George, Harry," he said, "these fellows have captured a whole company of Yanks horses." It was lucky for us that he thought that we had captured a company of Yanks' horses, rather than that we were Yanks ourselves in rebel uniform.

It may not be out of place, I think, if in this connection I relate an adventure that was purely personal to myself. It illustrates almost as much as the incident related of Wood the necessity for coolness, readiness, quick invention and invincible nerve; it also illustrates the character of the service my men and myself were almost hourly rendering. On the forenoon of the eighth my men had gone ahead and I had remained behind entirely alone, trying to get some information from a few rebel soldiers whom we had met. I then started on to join the command. As I turned the corner of a road I saw in front of me, about six or seven hundred yards away, a wagon with six or seven officers behind it. Over to the right was what had been once a regiment of infantry, but now carrying but about two hundred muskets only. As I neared the wagon I saw these officers engaged in earnest conversation and knew instinctively that I was the object thereof. To know this was to know that I was suspected, because there was no other reason in the world for directing so much attention to me. I was alone, my men by that time over a mile ahead, and I felt I was in for it. As I rode up I thought I did not care for the men lying down with their muskets stacked; a sudden dash would carry me out of all danger from them. But I was interested in the fellows who were in the road with their revolvers at their sides and to whom I must talk and whom I must fight if necessary at close quarters, not more than three or four feet away. As I rode up I planned in my own mind exactly what I would do. I was mounted on a powerful horse, and I determined to ride as close as I could get to the little knot of officers, leaving my left foot close to my horse, ready to put a spur in him at the first sign of hostilities on their part. Acting on this, I crowded my horse right up against them, and I felt perfectly sure that should one of them attempt to draw on me, the spur on the opposite heel, driven into my horse, would make him jump against and knock them all down or so deflect their aim that I should be in no danger. As I drew near it was certain that they had been talking with my men somewhat, for one of them, a red headed, inquisitive little hornet, said: "Lieutenant, your men say that you belong to the Eighth Kentucky."

I said: "Yes, suh, I do."

Then he said: "Where has the Eighth Kentucky been serving?"

I said it has been serving under General Roddy, but "my company has been detached down on the Coosa, guarding against desertahs and niggars, suh; and I haven't been with the regiment for more than a year."

He said: "Who is the Colonel of the Eighth Kentucky?"

(I cannot give it now, but I knew the roster of the field officers then.) I smiled and said: "Why, Colonel Shackleford, suh." (Which will answer for the present just as well as any other name.) "Who's the Lieutenant-Colonel?"

"Colonel Jones, suh."

"Who's the major?"

"Major Wheeler, suh." (These are not the names. I have forgotten them. But I give them in place of the real names, which I then knew.) I do not know if he knew the roster of the regimental officers, but I did; so much did the hospitality given to a rebel officer one evening in our tent serve me in my hour of need.

He then said to me: "Where are you going, suh?"

"I'm going back here."

"Why are you going back there?"

"Because," I said, "it is my business, suh. I don't know that I need answer to you. I have business back here."

He said: "It doesn't look right, suh."

"I can't help how it looks to you; it is simply my business to perform the duty that is imposed upon me as a Confederate officer, suh."

He then said to me: "I have a brother" (calling him by name, which I have now forgotten) "on General Roddy's staff; do you know him?"

It flashed through my mind that possibly he might have a brother on the staff and possibly he might not. At the same time I knew that while the staff did not know all the line, that every line officer ought to know the staff, and it would not do for me to say that I did not know the brother of this fellow, if there really was such a man on Roddy's staff. And so I thought I would take the poet Horace's advice and go *in medias res* or, as Tom Watson more vigorously puts it, take "the middle of the road," and answer in such a non-committal manner as to let me out in case I was wrong. I said: "Yes, suh, I think I have heard of such a man as that being on General Roddy's staff; but as I told you before, suh, I have been down on the Coosa and would not be certain; but I think I have heard of his name being on the staff, suh." Well, I must have gotten it right; he must have been on the staff. He then asked one question of me that called for an abrupt ending of the conversation, and as I could not answer it, I simply had to bluff it out.

He said: "Does he look like me, suh?"

This was further than I could go; this was a little red-headed wasp that put this question to me: the other might have been a black-haired Southern giant, and so, as the only thing to do, I called him with a bluff, and said: "Does he look like you, suh? Do you set yourselves up as models of Southern beauty that a Confederate officer should have nothing else to do except to see which one of you looks the most like the other? Good day, suh; your questions are getting d——d impertinent." And I turned my horse and walked away. I am not unduly nervous, and I certainly was not then, a boy of twenty-two, vigorous and healthy; but I can say that for every step that I took it seemed as if I felt a bullet in my back. When I had gotten about forty feet distant, I determined I could run the gauntlet if necessary, and take the chances. I turned in my saddle; they were talking vigorously together and they were still suspicious, but uncertain. I called out "Good day, gentlemen; I hope you are satisfied," and rode off on a gallop.

It did not seem much to me then; but relating the story now, it seems as if every nerve was on edge while I am telling it. On the eighth two of my men, Thos. R. Kennard, of Company I, First Ohio, and John Gotts, Corporal of Company E, Seventh Ohio, rode up to a house where there was a knot of rebels, made some inquiries, and started to go away. They had to go to some bars to get out on the road again; as they nearly reached these bars, some six or seven of the rebels dashed in front of them, and they had to fight their way out. This they did with the utmost gallantry and courage, both of them escaping with out surrendering, although Kennard was shot through the breast and Gotts through the face.

I have endeavoured to relate briefly a few of the circumstances attending our expedition. I have only given a few of the most prominent of these. It is more than thirty years since, and without memoranda of any sort only those occurrences which were most dramatic and striking can be remembered and told. For the men under my command there was a constant and continuous strain; there was the hazard of detection as spies; there was necessary the keen wit ever alert to have a ready answer when interrogated; there was the consciousness that we must keep in mind the character of speech of these men with whom we were mingling and be ready at all times to imitate it, and if all else failed our hands must be ready to reach our revolvers and fight to the death. Not alone was the strain mental, but our physical endurance was tested to the utmost. Marching without rations through a country impoverished by war, it was almost impossible to secure anything to eat, even if we had taken the time to do so. I did not eat a mouthful from noon of the third until the afternoon of the sixth and not more than four or five of my men were more fortunate. Our situation was constantly so perilous that I never thought of food or of hunger until that time. Some of my men got a couple of hours sleep the first night out and a couple of hours the next night while we were waiting for daybreak to enter Greensboro, but personally I did not close my eyes the first two nights nor until after midnight of the third, when I slept about two hours before commencing the fourth day's operations. While the men under my command did not actually effect the capture of Davis, the Congress of the United States thought that their services were more meritorious on account of the information furnished, as well as more dangerous and hazardous than that of the column that did actually effect the capture of Davis. There was at the time a reward offered of $100,000 for his capture. Of this neither myself nor the men under me had any knowledge at the time, and we had no mercenary motive in attempting the hazards of this expedition.

After the war the Fourth Michigan and the First Wisconsin became involved before the Congress in a contest over this reward; and then for the first time the evidence of General Wilson and General Alexander, which I append hereto as a part of the records of that time, showing the part that myself and my men had performed in that important service ; and the chairman of the committee on claims wrote me for a detail of my men, which it was almost impossible for me to give fully, but which I gave in part; and without ever presenting any claim on our part, the Fortieth Congress, at its second session, reporting upon the capture of Davis, placed the service of myself and men in importance before that of either Pritchard or Harnden, It placed General Wilson first, myself and men second, and Colonel Pritchard and Colonel Harnden equally third, and awarded to each of the four officers, Wilson, Yeoman, Harnden and Pritchard, $3,000 apiece. I append herewith extracts from the report of the committee, which is No. 60 of the second session of the Fortieth Congress. The same facts, with the exception of the recommendation of Congress, appear in the dispatches of General Wilson and General Alexander, and in the Forty-ninth Volume, Part 1 of the official record of the war of the rebellion.

I have thought it best to submit these official reports in connection with this brief history of the part my men bore in the capture of Jefferson Davis, together with a portion of an article by General Wilson in the February number of the Century for 1890, from which I have already quoted, and they are annexed as part of this article.

General Wilson reports as follows

Brevet Brigadier-General A. J. Alexander, with the second brigade of Upton's division, having reached Atlanta in advance of the division, was directed by General Winslow to scout the country to the northward as far as Dalton, or until he should meet the troops under General Steedman in that region. On beginning his march from Macon, General Alexander was authorized to detach an officer and twenty picked men, disguised as rebel soldiers, for the purpose of trying to obtain definite information of Davis' movements. This party was placed under the command of Lieutenant Joseph A. O. Yeoman, First Ohio Cavalry, and at the time acting as Inspector-General of the brigade. After a rapid march toward the upper crossings of the Savannah River in North-eastern Georgia, Lieutenant Yeoman's detachment met and joined Davis' party, escorted by Dibrell's and Ferguson's divisions of cavalry, probably under Wheeler in person, and continued with them for several days, watching for an opportunity to seize and carry off the rebel chief. He was frustrated by the vigilance of the rebel escort. At Washington, Georgia, the rebel authorities must have heard that Atlanta was occupied by our troops, and that they could not pass that point without a fight. They halted and for some time acted with irresolution in regard to their future course. The cavalry force which had remained true to Davis, estimated at five brigades and probably numbering two thousand men, now became mutinous and declined to go any farther. They were disbanded and partially paid off in coin, which had been brought to that point in wagons. Lieutenant Yeoman lost sight of Davis at this time, but dividing his party into three or four detachments, sought again to obtain definite information of his movements, but for twenty-four hours was unsuccessful. Persevering in his efforts, he became convinced that Davis had relinquished his idea of going into Alabama, and would probably try to reach the Gulf or South Atlantic Coast and escape by sea. Couriers were sent with this information to General Alexander, and by him duly transmitted to me at Macon. With the view of intercepting him in this attempt, I directed the crossings of the Ocmulgee river to be watched with renewed vigilance all the way from the neighbourhood of Atlanta to Hawkinsville, and on the evening of May 6, I directed Brigadier-General Croxton to select the best regiment in his division and to send it under its best officer, with orders to march eastward *via* Jeffersonville to Dublin on the Oconee river. General Croxton selected for this purpose the First Wisconsin Cavalry, commanded by Lieutenant-Colonel Henry Harnden, an officer of spirit, experience, and resolution. From the foregoing narrative it will be seen that the first perfectly reliable information in regard to the movements of Davis was that sent in by Lieutenant Joseph A. O. Yeoman, of General Alexander's staff. (*Official Record of the Rebellion*, Series 1, Volume 49, Pages 372-3-4-9.)

General Alexander reports as follows

Shortly after the armistice between Generals Sherman and Johnson I was ordered to send one regiment of my brigade to Atlanta, rapidly to apprehend Davis, who was reported moving in that direction with an escort of cavalry. I accordingly sent the First Ohio Cavalry, Colonel B. B. Eggleston commanding. A few days after I was ordered to move to the same point with the remainder of my brigade. Previous to this movement I obtained permission from the Major-General commanding the corps to send an officer and twenty men, disguised in rebel clothing to meet Davis, watch and if possible capture him. This delicate operation I intrusted to Lieutenant Joseph A. O. Yeoman, a dashing young officer of the First Ohio Cavalry, of great intelligence and coolness, and who was at that time acting as Inspector General for my brigade. Lieutenant Yeoman moved rapidly to North-eastern Georgia, where he met and joined Davis' escort, consisting of Dibrell's division of cavalry. He marched with them two or three days, but could not get an opportunity of seizing on the person of Davis on account of the close watch on every one who approached his person. At Washington, Georgia (I think), the forces under Dibrell heard that Atlanta was occupied by our troops, and that they could not pass that point without a fight, accordingly disbanded during the night, and sought their homes in small parties. Lieutenant Yeoman scattered his men among the various bands to try and get some trace of Davis, but for twenty-four hours was unsuccessful. He finally found that he had abandoned the idea of going into Alabama, and was making south to leave the country. Lieutenant Yeoman kept the command at Atlanta advised of all of his movements and the commanding officer advised the Major-General commanding the troops by telegraph. I trust Lieutenant Yeoman will receive some recognition of his services, as he was the only officer who really risked his life; and I believe the information furnished by him caused the Major-General commanding to send out the party that made the arrest. (*Official Records of the Rebellion*, Series 1, Volume 49, Pages 382-3.)

General Wilson, in February Century, 1890

Yeoman and his followers marched rapidly towards the upper crossings of the Savannah River, entered South Carolina, and by diligent but cautious inquiry and much hard riding found and joined the party they were looking for, without attracting unusual attention themselves. The country was full of disbanded Confederate soldiers all more or less demoralized and going home. Discipline was at an end, and every man of them was looking out for himself. The condition of affairs facilitated the operations of Yeoman, and encouraged him to believe that he might find an opportunity to seize and carry off the rebel chief; but the vigilance and devotion of the escort rendered it impossible to put his daring plan into effect, though it did not prevent his sending couriers into the nearest Federal picket post to report the movements of the party he was with. The information thus obtained was promptly transmitted to Generals Alexander and Upton, and by them to me. At Washington, Georgia, there was much confusion, growing out of the further disbanding which was rendered necessary by the proximity of our forces, and Yeoman lost sight of Davis for about twenty-four hours, during which time he divided his party into three or four squads, and sought again to obtain definite information of the Confederate chieftain's movements and plans. Persevering in his efforts he learned enough to convince him that Davis had relinquished all hopes of getting through the country to the westward, and would most probably try to reach the South Atlantic or Gulf Coast and escape by sea. This it will be remembered was the plan which Pollard, the historian of the *Lost Cause*, says was deliberately adopted many weeks before Lee's catastrophe. Relying upon this information Yeoman sent in couriers to make it known, and as soon as it reached him Alexander repeated it to me by telegraph, which was now completely in our possession. On the afternoon of May 6, immediately after receiving the intelligence from Yeoman, I sent for General Croxton, commanding the First (McCook's) Division, and directed him to select his best regiment in his division, and send it forthwith, under its best officer, eastward by the little town of Jeffersonville to Dublin on the Oconee River, with orders to march with the greatest possible speed, scouting the country well to the northward of his route, leaving detachments at all important cross-roads and keeping a sharp lookout for all rebel parties, whether large or small, that might be passing through this region. It was hoped by this means that the route pursued by Davis might be intercepted and his movements discovered, in which event the commanding officer was instructed to follow wherever it might lead, until the fugitive should be overtaken and captured.

Report No. 60, Second Session Fortieth Congress, is as follows:

In review it appears that the first and most important service was that of planning the capture, disposition of troops, and the special instruction to subordinate officers which resulted in the success of the enterprise. That this duty was performed in a skilful manner by Major-General Wilson is not doubted. That he made no claim for a share of the reward does not, in the opinion of the committee, lessen his merits or the value of his services as a man and an officer. The service of next importance is regarded as that of Captain Yeoman, of the First Ohio Cavalry, and his detachment of scouts and spies, who made the first discovery and gave the first information which led to the capture. The march of this officer was almost unexampled for celerity and self-denial, even for mounted soldiers. No application was made in his behalf, and the narrative of his march is in reply to the inquiry addressed him by the chairman of this committee.

As to the remaining question between the two cavalry regiments, the committee unanimously agree that they be regarded alike and that the commanding officers be awarded equal shares with General Wilson and Captain Yeoman for equally meritorious services, and that the amount of each be fixed at the sum of $3,000. In thus arbitrarily recommending this sum for the four principal officers, it is admitted that all rules but that of equity and justice are set aside, but it is regarded as not too small, and it is insisted that the officers share should not be large. In this respect the naval rule would do injustice between the officers mentioned while their services are regarded as so nearly equal.

To all the officers and men present of both cavalry regiments and the detachment of Captain Yeoman, it is recommended that the remainder, $88,000, be distributed according to the grade of each in the military service at the time of the capture.

Chapter 23
Reminiscences & Incidents
by Comrades of the Regiment

CHARGE OF THE FIRST OHIO VOLUNTEER CAVALRY AT THE
BATTLE OF STONE'S RIVER, TENNESSEE, DECEMBER 31, 1862
Drawn by N. Finegan, Company D

The ground will be recognized by every member of the regiment who participated in the charge or who may have examined the ground afterwards.

The house used as a Confederate hospital is on the left, with the infantry battle line and battery in the distance, and is very realistic and life-like.

The charging columns have just met in the shock, and are shown in the noise, confusion and struggle of the *mêlée* that follows, and in which the revolver and sabre play a prominent part.

The artist has avoided that great error, so usual in pictures, representing cavalry charges of straight lines, horses heads all erect and troopers all in the same position in their saddles, which looks well on paper, but is far from being true to life.

What adds so much to the value of the picture is the fact that it was drawn on the ground only a few days after the battle under the direction of some of the officers of the regiment

It represents the true cavalry *mêlée* in which horse and rider are in all kinds of positions in the supreme moment of the cavalryman's highest ambition.

Charge of the First Ohio Volunteer Cavalry at the Battle of Stone's River, Tennessee, December 31, 1862

Cavalry Raids

Capt. A. E. Wood, 4th U. S. Cavalry, defines a cavalry raid, in a military sense, "to be an incursion or irruption of mounted troops into the theatre of war, occupied by or under control of the enemy."

One of the main duties of cavalry in time of war is to make raids in the rear of the enemy's main army. These raids, when successful, always add to the efficiency and raises the morale of the cavalry arm of the service, and gives the forces engaged confidence for any expedition, however hazardous it may seem. In fact, the cavalryman is always in his element when on reconnaissance or raid, teeming with dash and adventure. While cavalry raids have been in vogue more or less from the earliest times of which we have any history of the cavalry service, yet in no prior war was it practised to the extent that it was during the war of the rebellion.

There is no kind of service that so develops the skill of the officers and the endurance and intelligence of the soldier, as the cavalry raid. From the time he cuts loose from the main army until the object of the raid is accomplished, the commander must depend on his own resources, as he has nothing to draw from, and his command is being constantly weakened by contact with the enemy. His men are being killed and wounded, his horses are exhausted or killed by hard marching or by the bullets of the enemy, his ammunition is being rapidly consumed, his rations eaten up, and there is a continuous destruction of his force.

The object of the raid is to destroy the enemy's communication by burning bridges, filling up tunnels and railroad cuts with rocks and timber, cutting telegraph wires, burning ties, heating and destroying rails, burning and destroying army supplies, capturing railroad and bridge guards, and creating general consternation and havoc in rear of the enemy's lines. As a raiding expedition must carry all of their ammunition from the start, they have no resources from which to draw, should their ammunition become exhausted. Therefore they usually endeavoured to avoid all large bodies of the enemy, excepting those in their immediate front who are endeavouring to repel the expedition from striking some point on a railroad or depot of supplies. They capture all prisoners that come in their line of march, but they are usually all paroled, as the command moves so rapidly, often marching fifty and sixty miles a day, that prisoners cannot be guarded, mounted, and if on foot, could not march the distance required; besides, all the good mounts captured are needed for the dismounted troopers of the command, as many horses become exhausted, while others are killed or wounded by the enemy.

When prisoners are taken on such raids, they are taken to the commanding officer and questioned very persistently as to their commands, strength, name of commanding officer, and any other information that may be of interest or benefit to the commander.

But the good soldier, when taken prisoner, is either such a "knownothing" or liar, that the officer interrogating gets but little satisfaction regarding the command to which he belongs. The writer has a very distinct recollection of having been captured by General Armstrong's division of rebel cavalry, and was volunteering some information to a squad of rebel soldiers about the strength of our army. A surgeon, who was one of the listeners and who no doubt thought the information as to the resources of the North would be somewhat discouraging to the rank and file, very promptly called me a liar, to shut my d——d Yankee mouth, to all of which I most gracefully complied.

No rule can be adopted for the time and place for raids, but the commander must be governed by the development of the campaign. If he sees an opportunity that he may think desirable to draw the enemy's cavalry away from his front, before making an attack in force, if he has the cavalry to spare from his own army, a raid may be made in the enemy's rear, or if he fears the enemy will receive reinforcements, he may attempt to cut his communication. All these matters must be governed by circumstances, and the commander always considers carefully all the surroundings and whether or not the sacrifice will justify sending out the expedition.

General Wheeler, "Little Joe," the great cavalry leader of the

Confederate army of Tennessee, started on his raid in the rear of Rosecrans' army in Chattanooga, ten days after the battle of Chickamauga. He crossed the Tennessee River at Cotton Port, fifty miles above Chattanooga, on the first day of October, 1863, with two divisions of cavalry. His object was to destroy the railroad in the rear of the Army of the Cumberland, thus compelling Rosecrans' army, then living on very short rations, to evacuate Chattanooga and retreat back to Nashville, as he had but one line of railroad to supply his army from Louisville, Ky. The rebel army had possession of the railroad from Chattanooga to Bridgeport, south of the Tennessee River, and at that date all supplies were hauled by wagon trains from Stevenson and Bridgeport over the mountains and through the Sequatchie Valley to Chattanooga. It was a slender thread, and the Confederate commander was quick to see his opportunity.

The Second Cavalry Division, under General George Crook, was guarding the river from Chattanooga to Cotton Port, on the alert for the anticipated cavalry raid. Crooks' division was stretched out in a thin line, and Wheeler, with his whole command concentrated, met with feeble opposition from the battalion of the First Ohio Cavalry stationed at the ford. Wheeler marched rapidly down the valley and by the time Crook had his command concentrated, Wheeler was about a day in advance. He swept down the valley with his bold riders, and in the Sequatchie Valley, near Anderson's cross-roads, he attacked one of our wagon trains, loaded with ammunition and rations, headed for Chattanooga, burned three hundred wagons, destroyed everything-, shot the mules down in the harness, and captured the drivers and train-men.

He then marched rapidly toward McMinnville, and at the foot of the mountain Crook's division attacked his rear guard and pushed him rapidly through McMinnville, Murfreesboro, Shelbyville, Farmington, Pulaski and forced him on the run across the Tennessee River at Lamb's Ferry, October 9.

Nine days after Wheeler crossed the river with such confidence and audacity he was driven across the river with a loss of fully two thousand men, six pieces of artillery, hundreds of horses, and small arms. His men were very badly demoralized and the raid was a complete failure, excepting the destruction of the wagon train in the valley, a few supplies, and taking a few prisoners at McMinnville. He did not have time to destroy either railroads or supplies after Crook's gallant division of dashing troopers struck him near McMinnville.

Had Crook not been on the watch for Wheeler and pushed him from the start, as he did, the Confederate cavalry might have struck the railroad at Murfreesboro and destroyed it to Nashville and well down to Stenvenson, thus compelling Rosecrans to retreat for lack of transportation. As it was, the raid was barren of results to the Confederate commander, besides placing several thousand of his cavalrymen *hors de combat*.

General Kilpatrick started on his raid around Hood's army in Atlanta with forty-seven hundred men, including two batteries of horse artillery and eight guns, on the evening of August 18, 1864. He moved very rapidly, destroying the Atlanta and Montgomery railroad for a considerable distance near Red Bank.

He then struck the Atlanta and Macon railroad at Jonesboro, tearing up two miles of railroad track, destroying the rails and ties, also burning and destroying a large amount of army supplies stored at Jonesboro. Drawing off to the east, after making a circuit of several miles, he again struck and tore up the railroad track at Lovejoy. Here he was surrounded by cavalry and infantry, but cut his way out, inflicting great damage on the enemy, capturing many prisoners and five pieces of artillery. *The Memphis Appeal,* in an article published a few days after this fight, which occurred August 20, stated that the "Yankee cavalry run over two brigades of cavalry and three brigades of infantry and two batteries."

Kilpatrick and his command made the complete circuit of Hood's army, starting at Sandtown, the extreme right of Sherman's army, and came into the lines again at Decatur, the extreme left of the Union army. They were out five days and nights, and did not unsaddle but once. This was a very successful raid, and was no doubt the four hardest days and nights continuous service in which the First Ohio Cavalry participated during the war.

Many of the raids made by the Confederate cavalry under Forrest, Wheeler and John Morgan carried havoc in the rear of the Army of the Cumberland, as well as in other departments, and were very destructive to railroads and army supplies.

One of the most daring raids undertaken by either the Union or Confederate cavalry during the war was that of General John Morgan and his bold riders in the summer of 1863, but it resulted very disastrously for the forces engaged, as Morgan and almost his entire command were captured.

He crossed the Ohio River at Brandenburg, July 8, 1863, with about four thousand as dashing and dare-devil riders as ever mounted a thoroughbred from the blue grass regions of old Kentucky. He dashed through the villages of Indiana and Ohio, marauding and destroying property with a speed and audacity worthy of a better cause.

But when these reckless raiders swept through the suburbs of Cincinnati the whole country was awakened and there was a general uprising of the loyal citizens of the southern part of the state to repel this invasion.

Morgan and his men were chased back and forth like a hunted fox by cavalry, infantry and hundreds of citizens, armed with shot-guns and squirrel rifles. Finally he was surrounded and surrendered at Buffington Island on the nineteenth day of July, 1863, only a remnant of his command escaping across the Ohio River. The raid was a complete failure and was very disheartening to the Confederate leaders, as it convinced them that there was a loyal army yet in reserve in the northern states, amply able to repel any forces that might invade the north.

Raids were of almost daily occurrence by either the Union or Confederate cavalry along some parts of the battle line, extending from the Atlantic coast to Missouri, during the last two years of the war, but the most destructive and successful raid made during the Civil War, and it may well be doubted if any has equalled it in the annals of that service, was the raid made by the cavalry corps of General James H. Wilson of the Army of the Cumberland after the battle of Nashville.

Wilson Raid

With twelve thousand five hundred cavalry, consisting of the divisions of Long, Upton and E. M. McCook, splendidly mounted and equipped, Wilson crossed the Tennessee River, March 22, 1865, with Selma, Ala., his objective, one hundred and eighty miles distant. But it proved that each division, all marching on different roads, had to travel about two hundred and fifty miles before reaching Selma.

The whole country was covered with water, the banks of the streams were overflowing, and the conditions could not have been more unfavourable for undertaking such an expedition, but all of these obstacles were overcome, and the swollen streams were crossed by swimming the horses or bridging the streams.

General Forrest, the great cavalry leader of the Confederates, crossed Wilson's front and made a desperate attempt to check him, but after a brisk fight he was brushed away.

Wilson's bold riders dashed rapidly forward, sweeping everything before them, although Forrest made a stubborn resistance. Selma was strongly fortified with ditches and more than twenty bastions and redans, with several strong forts in the inside lines. The works were mounted by thirty field guns and two thirty-pounder siege guns.

The works were stormed by eight thousand of Wilson's veterans and the city was captured with nearly three thousand prisoners, thirty-two field guns and twenty-six field pieces, fully mounted, in the arsenal and gun foundry located there, with forty-six siege guns, sixty-six thousand rounds of artillery ammunition, two thousand horses and one hundred thousand small arms.

The arsenal, with more than forty buildings, were destroyed, with powder works, three gun foundries, three rolling mills, machine shops, with quartermaster and commissary stores, with all kinds of war material. Wilson then moved on to Montgomery, bridging the Alabama River, one thousand feet wide, at high tide. Montgomery was captured, with many steamers loaded with supplies. The column then moved rapidly toward Columbus, Ga., saving the bridges across the Chattahoochee at both

Columbus and West Point. The works at West Point were strong, and were attacked by dire assault, the Union forces capturing two hundred and sixty men, three heavy guns, five hundred small arms, twenty locomotives, and about two hundred and fifty cars loaded with supplies. Moving on to Columbus, Wilson found the three bridges across the Chattahoochee protected by strong breast-works, which he attacked in the night. The Confederates made a vigorous defence, but were driven from the works and across the bridge, closely followed by our forces, and the city was soon in possession of General Wilson's command.

The capture here was upward of sixty guns, the ram *Jackson* with six guns, one hundred thousand bales of cotton, fifteen locomotives, two hundred and fifty cars, a navy yard and arsenal, powder mill, ten factories, a large amount of artillery, ammunition and war material.

Wilson then made a rapid march to Macon, capturing the city, with a large amount of army supplies, and wound up the campaign by the capturing of Jeff. Davis.

General Boynton, one of the most reliable and careful historians of the war, thus writes of the Wilson raid:

"It is a chapter in our war history, than which no other is more replete with thrilling and brilliant incident, with skilful and bold, successful execution.

"No purely cavalry campaign during the war approached it in these features, and it is doubtful whether its parallel can be found in the cavalry annals of any modern nation."

The First Ohio Cavalry was prominent in the Wilson raid and also in the Wheeler raid through Tennessee and Kilpatrick's raid around Atlanta.

CAMP LIFE
by C. M. Riggs, Sergeant-Major, First O. V. C.

A distinguished writer once said:

No truer history will ever be written than that which records the daily life of the soldier, as witnessed by himself. The outlines have been sketched by master hands; but the living panorama, the rugged reality is yet unwritten. Occasionally one who shared in the trials of that time lets memory colour up again the deeds in which he was an actor, and through the delicate tracery of his tongue or pen we gather the true story of the real and stirring scenes of the bivouac, the march and the struggle.

This, then, comrades, is my aim, to carry you with me through the varied scenes of our camp-life, including the almost daily routine of picket duty, skirmishes and scouting and the hardships and privations of a cavalryman at a time when the infantry and artillery are enjoying the rest, recreation and comforts of an undisturbed camp-fire, feeling secure from the enemy, as all outposts and approaches are carefully guarded by the cavalry. Then go with me in your duties as a soldier from the memorable thirty-first of December, 1862, when General Bragg with his forces greeted us quite early on that eventful morn, and from which, as the extreme right, we were compelled to fall back. On a rising piece of ground and near the Bole Jack Pike, our regiment made a stand, where a shell from a battery of the enemy took the life of our brave Major Moore. Just before crossing this pike we came near being flanked by a brigade of rebel infantry, who, on ascending a ridge, came plainly in view, being then about two hundred yards in front of us, and immediately opened fire. I remember that at this time I was riding before a two-story frame house, and from the crashing of the panes of glass in the upper story of the dwelling, that could be plainly heard, I was very glad to realize that they were shooting over our heads.

Shortly after, while passing through a strip of woods a short distance from where Colonel Millikin issued his last command of "Fours right about; forward, gallop, charge!" I heard him say, in speaking of the death of Major Moore: "How sad, but none of us know how soon some of us will meet the same fate." All who were with us on that day will ever remember the scenes and incidents of that grand charge in which Colonel Millikin and Lieutenant Condit were killed, and many others of our brave comrades killed, wounded and taken prisoners. Some of our regiment became sadly demoralized, and after the charge retreated as fast as their horses could carry them. Adjutant "Scotty" was wounded and taken by the Confederates to a house within sight of the place where he fell.

Surgeon Wirth and Hospital Steward Doty were captured and taken to Murfreesboro, where they did noble duty in administering and caring for the wounded in the temporary hospital at this place. Several of the boys who were captured were afterwards paroled.

Sergeant Newton, of Company G, tells the following of his escape. While being taken within the enemy's lines he thought of making a certain sign of a secret order. He did so, and the guard, without replying, looked away from him, as much as to say, "Now go, and go quickly." The sergeant acted on the hint, turned his horse, and spurred away to our lines without a shot being fired at him.

On January 1 Major Laughlin took command of the regiment, with Major Pugh, of the Fourth O. V. C., commanding the brigade. Colonel Zahm at this time was at Nashville. For three days the regiment did picket duty near Wilson Creek, and on the night of the fourth guarded the railway bridge which crosses Stone's River, the enemy having retreated. Lieutenant Fordyce and I slept in a deserted rebel camp, and it was here that I first formed the unpleasant acquaintance of the "grayback," which did not forget to make me several visits afterward. On the fifth our brigade passed through Murfreesboro and out some three or four miles on the Shelbyville Pike, but being ordered to return, we came back through town and went about three miles to Wilson Creek, where we went into camp. On the eighth our regiment went out Wilson Pike to the Bole Jack Pike and then north on said pike to Stuart's Creek, near which we camped for the night.

The next day we went to where Stuart's Creek is crossed by the Murfreesborough and Nashville Pike, in which vicinity we remained until the fourteenth of April.

To relate the almost daily scouting, skirmishes, night patrols and other duties of our regiment during this time would take more space than could be given me. I will give only a few of the most important.

My messmates were Quartermaster-Sergeant Lieb, Commissary-Sergeant Parsons and Bugler Bush. Sergeant Lieb left us about the fifth of February, he being commissioned Second Lieutenant and assigned to Company I, and our chief Bugler, Henry Bush, about the twenty-fifth of March was detailed in the Topographical Department under General Rosecrans at Murfreesboro.

The weather of January and February and up to near the middle of March was often very cold and blustering, with the thermometer once or twice marking zero; but part of the time we were camped in a cedar thicket, which was a good protection from the winds.

We had the experience of a second Camp Frankenberger on the night of January 14. During the night the waters of the creek had flooded the valley where a part of our boys were camped. In the morning many of the tents were swimming in the angry waters, the occupants having escaped, although many of them barely saving their lives, by wading or swimming to higher ground. To add to these discomforts it rained, snowed and sleeted all day of the fifteenth, causing some of our horses to die from exposure. Many of the comrades will remember the good fire the writer had in his tent during all this day, where the unfortunate ones were made warm, dry and happy. While here the regiment had very little rest, as we all remember the heavy and tiresome scouts by day and night to the Nolinsville hills, Triune, Jeffersonville, and across Stone's River at different points, and even to Nashville to act as escort to wagon trains for Murfreesboro, as the railway was not completed until the middle of February.

These duties, especially that of picket duty and patrolling at the fords of the river and other points, were unusually severe until the sixth of February, when they were somewhat lightened by our force attacking Wheeler and Forrest's cavalry at Franklin, where they defeated the enemy and took possession of the town, and also about this time a Union force was stationed at Nolinsville.

Lieutenant Fordyce was Adjutant up to the fifth of March, when he was promoted to Captain, and Lieutenant Woodlief was detailed to act instead.

About this time an order was issued by General Stanley, Chief of Cavalry, to send a body of men to act as couriers between Triune and the line of couriers of the Murfreesboro Pike. Captains Pattin and Conn, Lieutenant Shultz, eight non-commissioned officers and fifty men were detailed for this duty.

One pleasant feature of our stay here was when Major Whitehead, the paymaster, gave us our monthly allowance from Uncle Sam; our visits to the Sutler of the Tenth Indiana Infantry for Hostetter's Bitters, etc.; letters and newspapers from home; games of "seven up," and especially after pay-day making a raid against "chuck-a-luck," going into the fray with a full purse and shortly after retreating with empty pockets. The boys will also remember the barbecue given by the Third O.V.C., in which many of us participated.

Many of our officers took advantage of our camp-life to pay a visit to friends in Ohio, among them being Majors Cupp, Eggleston and Laughlin, and Captains Waddle, Pattin and others.

Among the many scouts and hard rides, I distinctly recall the one of the twenty-fifth of March, when we crossed Stone's Elver at Atkinson's Ford, burnt the Buchanan Mills and took the old gent prisoner. We had crossed Falls Creek about one mile beyond the river, when we gave chase to some rebels. The old gent living near said they were his sons and only skedaddled for fear we would take their horses. An old lady and a girl made Rome howl when we took the old gent prisoner. Their antics were quite laughable. On returning, we found the river very high on account of the heavy rains, but into it we went. My horse had to swim for several rods, and as it was now dark, the horse became entangled in some brush and fell, throw-

CO. B

Capt. Samuel W. Fordyce

CO. D

Capt. Wm. H. Scott
Assistant Inspector General on the Staff of General E. L. Long.
Mortally wounded at Lovejoy, Ga., Aug. 20, 1864.

ing me into the water, but by clinging to the mane finally reached the bank, wet and cold. Luckily, on reaching camp at 9 p. m., found a good fire to warm and dry.

About the first of April Lieutenant-Colonel Laughlin left us and many of the boys will remember some of the stirring incidents which occurred around the keg of beer in the cedar thicket at the time of his departure. Major Eggleston, who soon afterward was promoted to colonel, now assumed command.

On the evening of the tenth of April the First Texas and Second Georgia Cavalry, under Colonel Ferrel, captured a train at Antioch Church, and captured several officers and got quite a sum of money. Major Cupp, Captains Fordyce and Pattin, Lieutenants Pierce and Lieb, and Sergeant Gordon were among the number. Captain Pattin, however, escaped.

On the fourteenth of April the field and staff, with Companies B and D, left the pleasant and unpleasant memories of Stuart's Creek to join the rest of the regiment at Lavergne, which was a burnt village, where the railway crosses the pike and being midway between Nashville and Murfreesboro.

On the seventeenth Lieutenant Woodlief and four men went to Nashville to escort his brothers, John and Tom, who were coming with sutler's supplies for our camp. On their way to Lavergne they were attacked by a squad of fifteen rebels, but after a sharp skirmish were repulsed by our small force. Lieutenant Woodlief had his horse shot, and one of the rebels was wounded.

The enemy retreated across the river. Stone's River seemed to be the dividing line of the enemy and our troops, as scarcely a day passed but shots were exchanged across the river.

On the twenty-second of April the detail from our regiment, who were escorts to General Thomas, returned and Captain Barker, of Company L, with his company took their places as escort. On the twenty-sixth Captains Cutler and Hamilton left us, their resignations being accepted.

If you want to know of the horseback rides where pleasure and good times were combined, you must consult Lieutenants Curry, Roush, Siverd, Lutz, Woodlief, Erwin and many others of my friends as to the hospitality of the Southern ladies, such as were found in the families of the brothers Luck, Len Davis, Peoples, Waldrens and Burnetts, who so often entertained us, singing with them the Southern songs and they joining with us in our patriotic songs. The boys will especially remember one of the daughters of Mr. Burnett, whose husband was in the Southern army, by showing her love for the South by wearing a C. S. Belt.

During our stay at Lavergne many of the officers had their wives with them. I believe that "Aunt Mag" was one of the number, who was then the wife of Captain Pickering.

From May 7 to 30 I was with a detail at Louisville after horses. There I met father, mother and wife, and other of my comrades met their friends, and we all had a most enjoyable visit. On June 18 our camp life was over, as orders had been received to report to Colonel Long, commanding Second Brigade, at Murfreesboro.

Of the advance southward, where we were placed on the extreme left, the incessant rains, the muddy roads, the tiresome march, and the battles, I will leave for history to record, and now, although one-third of a century has passed, my memory often reverts to the scenes and incidents at and around Stuart's Creek and Lavergne, and I often think of the associations which clustered within those times, the songs, the games and the drinks around the sutler's tent or from the same canteen, the visits to the homes of the Southern belles, the patrols on Stone's River, at Charlton, Dobson, Atkinson and other fords, the hard rides and scouts on the Jeffersonville, Nolinsville, Bole Jack and Murfreesboro Pikes, and to Antioch Church, Scroggsville, Smyrna and other points. And now, my dear comrades, wherever you may be, I can only say, "Good cheer and happiness to you and yours."

Captain William H. Scott
by Captain John P. Rea

One, who by the unaided force of his own personality unconsciously commands the respect, confidence and admiration of his associates, and while rapidly rising in rank and authority over them awakens no jealousies, but fastens them to him with constantly strengthening bonds of friendship, shows the possession of the best elements of true nobility. Such a man was Captain William H. Scott, of Company D.

He fell in youth, but his short life grew a manhood as strong, rugged, gentle, symmetrical and complete as ever awakened the hope of country, inspired the confidence of friend, or warmed the heart of home. No words can paint him here as he rides ever in the old picture painted by himself on the canvas of his comrades memory.

Not only among the men of his own regiment is he remembered, but by all who ever met or knew him. Twenty years after the war I was addressing a soldiers gathering in Minnesota, when a voice called to me from the rear of the hall, saying: "Tell us about Scotty, the ideal soldier of the old brigade."

The voice, as I afterwards learned, came from a member of the Third O.V.C.

In July, 1897, I spent a day in Calhoun, East Tennessee, where our regiment was stationed for some weeks in the winter of 1863-4. I found the old residents full of reminiscence and praise of Lieutenant Scott. They only knew him for a few weeks, a third of a century before, as an officer in war time, enforcing military rule in their midst. Their fresh and kindly remembrance is a better monument than stone or bronze.

His soldier record is told in the regimental history. It may be epitomized thus: An unknown, friendless Irish boy; a private soldier; Sergeant-Major; Lieutenant; Adjutant; Captain; Staff Officer; the trusted friend and subaltern of Millikin, Cupp and Long; every rank attained and every confidence secured by demonstrated merit. To say that he was brave in battle is to accord him only the just tribute due every manly man who goes into battle. Gentle by nature, tender of heart, with out the slightest suggestion of braggadocio; careful of his men; alert to every contingency of danger of which personally he never seemed conscious, he revelled in the storm when it broke and rode the fiery front of battle, a veritable prince of war. He rose with so little friction from the ranks, and breasted every duty and occasion with such ease, that those who knew him best felt that they had never fathomed his full capacity of daring and doing. He had decision without arrogance, and in places of peril seemed instinctively to know what to do and where to strike. He had all the enthusiasm of a knight of old combined with the reckless daring of the typical American cavalryman.

Those who saw him ride like a centaur upon the enemy's lines at Stone's River, and saw him in his last fight, on foot, with his shattered right arm dangling by his side, waiving his sabre in his left hand as he charged through Wheeler's lines at Lovejoy Station, know that ever and always he was the same dashing, undaunted, unconquerable soldier. He was a strict disciplinarian, but not a martinet. His men always spoke affectionately of him as "Scotty," but there was a quiet, unpretentious air about him that forbade familiarity. His dignity was not of the kind that had to assert itself, it was "native and to the manor born"; it commanded instinctive respect; his men loved him and never feared to follow where he led, and he always led if the enemy were in front. He belonged to the fated ones, who while eagerly seeking, not infrequently emerged from, glorious battle covered with wounds.

In that heroic charge of the regiment at Stone's River, riding by the side of the chivalric Millikin, he received a terrible wound in the groin; a moment after, as he lay in his blood, he saw his Colonel and best friend fall a few feet away, while at the same time he knew that his old Captain, who first of all had recognized his worth, was dead on the same field.

It was months before he was fit for duty, but he was in his saddle when the order came to advance in the summer of 1863, and though saddened by the loss of his friends, he was buoyant and brilliant as ever. He rode heroically through the campaigns of that and the succeeding year, making a record full of dash and enterprise, dazzling with valour and ending with out a stain. Shot through the right shoulder and knocked from his horse in Kilpatrick's charge at Lovejoy Station in August, 1864, he rose to his feet and, waving his sword in his left hand, followed the charging column through the enemy's lines. For seventy-five miles he rode uncomplainingly over rough roads under a broiling August sun in an ambulance: all the weary way, though in intense pain, cheering his wounded companions.

The morning after reaching our camp within the lines, I was awakened by Surgeon Canaan and asked to go with him to see "Scotty." On the way he told me that Scott's life could only be saved by amputating his right arm, which he refused to permit. When I reached his ambulance he welcomed me with a smile and cheerful words. I sat by his side in the ambulance and talked for an hour. He then told me the story of his short but eventful life. I urged him to let the surgeon have his way. He answered, "No". To amputate my arm it must be dislocated at the shoulder. That will leave me maimed and disfigured. I can die, but I can not fight the battle of life alone without my good right arm. I have no mother, no wife, no relative in America; except my comrades there are none to mourn my death; I want to live, but will not purchase life at such a cost. No persuasion could induce him to consent to the operation, and after lingering some weeks, he died.

An incident occurred while I was talking with him that morning that lies a precious pearl on the beaten shore of memory. A noble boy of my own company was lying mortally wounded in the next ambulance. He was moaning in great pain. The surgeon came up and was getting ready to dress his wound, when Scott heard the moans from the next ambulance. He raised his head, and with an air of command and an unselfish heroism, equalling that which made the dying Sidney immortal, said: "Doctor, don t you hear poor Steve Barton? Never mind me, let me alone and go and relieve the suffering of that brave, dying boy."

In the centre of one of the circles of dead in the National Cemetery at Chattanooga, on a slope looking out toward the East and catching the first rays of the morning sun as it rises above the hallowed heights of Missionary Ridge, there is a little mound with a little head-stone marked "Captain William H. Scott, First Ohio Cavalry."

No kindred have ever visited it, no woman's tears have ever moistened it: but under that mound lies one whose life was as clean, whose brain was as clear, whose heart was as true and loyal, whose soul was as chivalric and unselfish as the story of any land or age can furnish.

At Chickamauga
by Sergeant John W. Chapin
Company K, First-Ohio Volunteer Cavalry

On a pleasant morning in September, 1863, just as breakfast was over, the bugles called the First Ohio Cavalry to "boots and saddles." There was nothing remarkable in that to old troopers who had completed two years of campaigning with the Army of the Cumberland, but it was the summons to a day's duty long to be remembered, the last day of the Battle of Chickamauga.

The First Ohio Cavalry at that time belonged to the Second Ohio Brigade, Second Division of the Corps of Cavalry. The division was commanded by General George Crook and the brigade by Colonel Eli Long. To our brigade was attached two guns of the Chicago Board of Trade Battery. The brigade was composed of the First, Third and Fourth Ohio Volunteer Cavalry and the Second Kentucky Cavalry.

The regiments of the brigade took turns, a day at a time, in supporting the artillery, and this day it was supported by the First Ohio. We soon mounted, moved into the road, followed the battery over a small stream, through a thin wood, and took our position in line of battle, near the edge of an open field, on the extreme right of McCook's corps. Some days before this, in our marching over ridges and through valleys, I had got a piece of Sand Mountain in my eye. It had caused me not a little trouble, and I had tied a handkerchief over it. As we came into line I heard a comrade remark, "Sergeant Chapin is going one eye on it!" But I saw enough that day with one eye to satisfy me fully. Company K, to which I belonged, was on the left of the regiment, with our battery immediately to the left of this company and about thirty feet away.

Before we were in line that morning we heard the roar of big guns and the clatter of the small ones off to the left, giving us distinctly to understand that the battle was on once more. We sat on our horses with the open field before us. The enemy was too far away to be reached by our carbines. The battery immediately opened fire, and it was not long before it was answered by the enemy's artillery. For more than three hours we sat there mounted beside our big guns, listening to the music of shot and shell as they cavorted past us and over our heads. As I now remember, not a man of the regiment was that day hit by shot or shell of the artillery; their firing was too high and went over our heads. Damage was done to the troops immediately in our rear by falling branches cut from the trees by these shots.

Colonel Eggleston being in Ohio on recruiting service, the command of the regiment devolved on Lieutenant-Colonel Valentine Cupp. It was about half past twelve o'clock when the rebel infantry came out of the woods into the open field in front of us. We had been in line under fire of the artillery at least three hours, but it hardly seemed fifteen minutes, so interesting was the occasion.

They were Longstreet's men, and they advanced in three perfect lines of battle with no attempt at flanking, but apparently with a determination to take by main force all that was before them. On they came, and when within about three hundred yards a Lieutenant of General Crook's staff rode to us, met Adjutant Scott near the left of the regiment and called out, "The orders from the General are 'Prepare to charge!'". The adjutant immediately reported to Colonel Cupp, and the commands were given to sling carbines and draw sabres, and in this position we waited, every moment expecting to hear the command that would move us into the jaws of death at a gallop. I remember as distinctly as if it were but yesterday how I felt, and what I thought during the few moments we thus held ourselves, and I took in the situation before us. Three lines of rebel infantry with loaded guns and bayonets fixed, were before us and coming our way, and we were to charge into those bristling walls of steel. I said to Sergeant Irwin, on my left: "If the charge is made not a man can come out alive."

The suspense was not long continued, for General Crook, seeing that all was not right, came to our line and said: "The order was, prepare to resist the charge!" That was quite different, and I, for one, felt much easier.

During the preparation for a charge the left of the regiment had been moved forward some three or four rods, so that we were that distance in advance of our battery. As it was thought best that we should be on a line with it, we were moved by fours left about, and to the rear, until we were even with the guns, and then by fours left about again to the front and in line. Thus it will be seen that we turned twice by fours left about in the very face of the infantry, while volley after volley from the small arms was poured into us.

All this time our artillery had kept up a continuous firing. Great gaps were made in their lines, but only those who were mowed down halted; the living came on. Then came the struggle; all that could be done with carbine and revolver to keep back lines of infantry was done; we were simply overpowered by numbers. The killed and wounded stopped not, nor even checked the forward movement of the living. A desperate effort was made to capture our battery, and its last shot was fired when the advance rebel line was fifty yards away. When it was useless to remain longer it limbered up and went to the rear with little less speed than its last shot had gone to the front. When the guns which it was our duty to support were gone, Colonel Cupp gave the command, "Fours, left about, march!" That was his last command. Ere the movement was completed, a minnie ball struck him in the bowels and he fell from his horse mortally wounded. For a while he was left where he fell, but late in the evening he was picked up by some of the members of his old company (F), who had been captured, but permitted to return to look for him, and placed in one of the hospital tents near Crawfish Springs, where he died before morning.

Just as we had nearly completed the "fours left about" in the face of the charging infantry, a rebel officer had the impudence to shoot me with his revolver. The ball struck me just back of the right shoulder, passing through the right lung and lodging against a rib, where it still remains. I have had the pleasure of carrying it there for more than twenty-six years. I can't say that the shot hurt; it was only a sting, but served to cut my breathing short and bring me off my horse. However, I held him, and in a moment remounted hoping to be able to ride away from the fellows in gray, who were making themselves very disagreeable.

I had not the power to guide my horse; he ran my knee against a sapling, a knot in which tore a hole in my pants and skinned my knee and shin about six inches, which made me lame for two or three months. I concluded that my only salvation was to leave my horse, or rather, to allow my horse to leave me, and to try walking. I therefore rolled to the ground while the horse was on the run, with as much ease and grace as a drunken man might roll off a log.

Once more on *terra firma*, I cleared myself of carbine, sabre, belt, cartridge box and revolver, expecting to be able without these traps to walk away. I soon found that I had not enough breath to do so, and therefore secured myself as best I could, from flying balls and running horses, behind a tree. Just as I sat down, a company passed me, and one or two comrades offered to take me along with them. I could not talk, and knew I could not ride a horse, so only waved my hand for them to go on, and they left me. On the advice of these comrades the next morning's report said that I had been killed in battle. The Fourth Michigan Cavalry, which belonged to another division, had been stationed in our rear. A number of that organization advancing, came near me. I was thirsty. My canteen, with haversack, blanket and overcoat, had gone with my horse. Seeing a Michigan man's canteen, I asked him for a drink of water. He dropped his canteen to me as though in a great hurry, levelling his carbine as he did so. "There goes another Reb!!" he cried. I turned my head in the direction he had indicated just in time to see a very large soldier in a gray uniform fall forward on his face. He was dead. I saw him next morning lying as he had fallen.

The racket of war went merrily on around me. The Union forces gradually fell back, leaving the battle ground in possession of the enemy. I remained right there all night without dinner or supper. I don t think I thought about eating. After an hour or so the noise of the battle had entirely died away and quiet reigned. I sat by that tree I could not lie down. and reflected upon my situation. With neither overcoat nor blanket I was uncomfortably cool, wounded, maybe mortally (although I did not think so), five hundred miles from home, not a friend near, in an enemy's country and surrounded by rebels. Then, too, to cap the climax, in the deep hours of the night, when darkness had settled around us, there came to my ears the terrible groans of the wounded and dying. That was the longest night of my life. I cannot say that I was blue, but I certainly did not enjoy my surroundings.

Dawn was hailed with gladness. As soon as it was light I looked around me, and at a little distance saw a blue smoke curling up through the brush. It was a welcome sight, for I was cold. I immediately started in its direction as rapidly as possible. I was still quite short of breath. On my way I passed several dead bodies, but one in particular attracted my attention. It was that of a Union soldier, lying on his back, his face toward heaven, his features in no way disfigured or discoloured.

He was a medium sized man, with a rather dark complexion, black hair and beard. As I stopped and looked at him, I thought how would his wife feel if she could see him lying there, cold, stiff, dead. Doubtless she was at that time anxiously waiting for the tidings from him that never came. I was in a good condition to be impressed by such scenes and such thoughts. I went on my way and soon reached the fire. An old pine stump was burning. I placed myself close to it and so as to get the benefit of the fire and at the same time avoid the smoke. I had been there probably half an hour and was becoming quite comfortable, when I heard a crackling in the brush off to the south a little. Looking in the direction of the noise, I saw a rebel lieutenant on a horse and a private on a mule coming single file leisurely toward me. They were ducking their heads and craning their necks, as though looking for something particular. I watched them closely, wondering if there would be more shooting when they saw me. I had no gun. They soon discovered me, came to a halt and asked me if I was wounded. They came up and the first demand the officer made was: "I want those spurs!"

I had a first class pair, for which I had paid my own good money; however, I made neither objection nor reply, but simply stretched out my legs, as much as to say, "If you want them, take them." The lieutenant dismounted, took them off, and with the composure of a soldier who is willing to do his whole duty, adjusted them to his own boots.

The next demand was for my canteen, but that I asked to keep until I got where I could get water. The request was granted, with the injunction not to let any one else have it. I was then directed to walk right straight up to the vidette on picket post, and remain there until my captor returned, and should anyone attempt to take that canteen away from me I was instructed to say that it belonged to the lieutenant. I did as directed, and when at a proper distance from the picket was halted, questioned and ordered to advance. The first friendly remark the guard made was, "I want that air canteen." When I told him the order I had received from the lieutenant, he muttered an oath, adding, "That is always the way, the d——d officers get everything that is worth having." He already had a canteen; it was not made of tin, but of wood, and looked like the end of a small barrel.

I learned this was an outpost of the enemy, and that the party which had made a prisoner of war belonged to the Fourth Georgia Cavalry. They were right clever fellows, and I had no reason to complain of their treatment. In a few minutes the lieutenant and private returned. The officer rode up beside a log and ordered me to mount behind him, saying he would take me to a house near by, where were other captured "Yanks." With the assistance of the soldier I mounted. He undertook to trot his horse, but on my objecting, he walked his horse the rest of the way. On our way up we passed the reserve guard, composed of an officer and a few men. The officer asked me to what regiment I belonged, and when I told him the First Ohio Cavalry he said he had heard of that regiment before, and added that when he saw me he thought I belonged to that "d— East Tennessee gang." I did not take this remark as a compliment. He also asked me what we meant, anyway, by coming down there to fight them, and what we expected to do. I replied that I was too short winded to talk much, but if he would wait till I got my breath, I would argue the case with him. He did not seem to be in a very good humour; I do not think he had been to breakfast, or perhaps he had been disturbed in his last night's rest. I was somewhat uneasy in his presence, and was relieved when the officer who had me in charge moved on towards the house.

We soon reached the place, a log house with a "lean to," and there, sure enough, were about forty Union prisoners, and one of our surgeons who had been captured and retained to dress wounds. A guard was around the house and yard. When I had been put inside the enclosure, the lieutenant took my canteen, or rather the one belonging to the Michigan cavalryman, bade me good-bye, and that was the last I saw of him. I have often wished I could have that canteen back. About eleven o'clock that day I ate for the first time since breakfast the morning before. The entire meal consisted of mush made with a great deal of water and a very little corn meal. There was no salt in it. Nor did we get anything more while we remained at this house. Sometime during the forenoon of the next day the surgeon got around to me. After learning the location of my wound, he assisted me in taking off my jacket, slit my shirt, and when I told him that the ball had not come out he began talking about probing for it. That made me tremble. I felt sure that I could not endure the process of probing through my lung, so I said quietly, "I am not much hurt, there are many others here who need your attention more than I do." That seemed to call his attention to the work before him. He looked at the wound, took a piece of muslin about an inch and a quarter square, covered one side with simple cerate, put something sticky around the edges, and slapped it over the wound. That was all the dressing it ever had, although it was over two months before I could lie on my left side.

On Wednesday afternoon it was thought best to move the patients to the great hospital tents which had been captured and put up near Crawfish Spring. There was no ambulance in sight; a farm wagon of ancient pattern was found, the reach lengthened so that the longest slabs and poles on the premises would fit as bottom boards, a mule and an old horse were harnessed with "gears" peculiar to that country at that time, the wounded men were piled on and the load started for the hospital tents. That vehicle and its load were a picture. Thanks to the driver for his care and judgement, the wagon reached its destination without an accident or a scare. We went into the tents with other wounded captives. There was not too much room for comfort, but we were not expecting comfort, and were satisfied if only allowed to live. I could walk by taking my time to it, so each day during our stay here I visited the big spring several times and partook of the water freely; it seemed to do me about as much good as the mush.

Many poor fellows died every day. Some were shockingly hurt. I remember a case where the ball had passed in at the corner of the mouth on the right side, hardly cutting the skin, through the tongue, and out back of the jaw, at the lobe of the left ear. That man could not talk when I saw him on account of his tongue being too big. I saw another man with both eyes shot out; the ball had gone just far enough to destroy his sight. There were many peculiar wounds and many terribly distressing ones.

While here General Bragg sent word to General Rosecrans, who was at Chattanooga, that if he would load his ambulance with the badly wounded Confederate prisoners at Chattanooga, parole them, and send them through the lines as far as Crawfish Springs, he (Bragg) would immediately return the ambulances filled with badly wounded Union soldiers. This Rosecrans agreed to, and on the twenty-ninth of September, nine days after the battle, the ambulance train made its appearance. The wounded "Johnnies" were taken out, the ambulances turned by driving around a loop, our men were put in and the procession moved slowly toward the North. I was one of the number of more than two thousand wounded men who were thus saved. At that time I did not appreciate what I missed, for those who were only slightly wounded and therefore not permitted to join us were sent to the fearful Andersonville Prison. The trains moved back over the road along which General Thomas did his desperate fighting on the twentieth. The dead bodies had been taken out of the track and piled up at the sides of the road to allow the wagons to pass and not run over them. There they were on either side, so close I could have touched them with my hand as the ambulance passed along. Some were in blue and others in gray, but all so black and swollen one could not have recognized the features of his nearest friend. No tongue, no pen can describe the scene; its horrors cannot even be imagined. It was the most horrible sight I have ever witnessed.

A white flag had been placed about half way between the Union and Confederate lines; at that point officers of each army were stationed. As each vehicle came to the flag the rebel driver got off, and the Union driver got on. Ere we reached the line it was dark, and ten o'clock by the time we were safe in Chattanooga.

The most of us put up at the Critchfield House, apparently the most popular house in the city. I bothered neither clerk for a room nor porter with my baggage, but without waiting for supper, hung myself up on the floor, took a lean on the wall and thought myself lucky. There was not an inch of space on the floor that night not occupied by a wounded soldier.

At that time I did not appreciate my good fortune in being sent through the lines, but now, when I reflect upon the damnable treatment of Union soldiers in rebel prisons, I am doubly thankful that I was sent north, for those of us who were left on the battlefield of Chickamauga, and who, by reason of the slightness of their wounds, were not sent with us to Chattanooga, went the other way, and stopped at the first station this side of Hades, Andersonville!

Extracts from the *Cavalier*
A Paper Published by the Members of the Regiment at Fayetteville, Tenn., in the Summer of 1863

Fayetteville, Tenn.
July 31, 1863

Messrs. Editors: Some of your readers will be interested with the detail of the cavalry fight which took place on Elk River on the second day of July.

Our cavalry left Hillsboro, Tenn., at break of day, and marched rapidly in the direction of Winchester, where we came within a short distance of the river. Our advance came up to a party of rebel cavalry and drove them back. Dismounted skirmishers were thrown out, who soon succeeded in driving them across the river.

With the river between us, and a forest on either side, the contest could not be decided, so one piece of artillery from the Board of Trade Battery, commanded by Captain Stokes, and supported by Colonel Eggleston, of the First Ohio Cavalry, with Company F of his command, was put into position. A few rounds of shell put them to flight, and their musketry was not again heard from.

For quite a while all was quiet, and our officers were consulting as to the propriety of crossing the river, when the rebel artillery opened upon us from an elevated position on the other side. At once we moved our guns to a more commanding position, and at once dismounted one of the rebel guns, and so demoralized their forces that they gave up the position.

After resting a short time and receiving reinforcements, we proceeded to cross the river, which we did without any opposition whatever.

We had proceeded but a short distance on the other side, when we found their cavalry in line. But this did not stop our progress, for on we went, charge after charge was made with the sabre, laying open the heads and piercing the hearts of those in arms against us. Thus the battle went on until night had thrown her sable curtain over the battle-field and put an end to the fight.

The following day our infantry buried twenty-two rebels who were killed in this fight. Colonel Webb, of the Fourth Georgia Cavalry, was mortally wounded. He died next day. This is the officer who received Vallandigham at the rebel pickets. One other colonel was wounded, whose name cannot be given.

This, Messrs. Editors, is a very short account of one day's work during our advance from Murfreesboro.

J. W. L.

Fayetteville, Tenn.
July 31, 1863

Messrs. Editors: In compliance with several requests, I herewith furnish you with the details of the part taken in the pursuit of Bragg's army from Tullahoma by Company B, First Ohio Cavalry. The company marched with the regiment from Murfreesboro the twenty-fourth of June; remained with the regiment from Murfreesboro at Manchester, at which place we, with three other companies of our regiment, were detached and ordered to report to General Branan, in advance on the road leading to Tullahoma. On the morning of the first of July information was received of the evacuation of Tullahoma by the rebel forces. We were then ordered to report to General Negley, whose division was in the advance on the road leading to the bridge on the direct Tullahoma and Winchester road. We were deployed on the right of Negley's division, and moved forward in the direction of Elk River bridge. Skirmishing commenced early, and continued at intervals until late in the afternoon, when we struck a column of rebel infantry and cavalry marching on the Tullahoma road in the direction of Elk River bridge. A sharp fight ensued, which lasted about twenty minutes. We, Companies B, H and D, First Ohio, and Companies A and L of Second Kentucky Cavalry, holding our ground against more than four times our number until our ammunition exhausted, and we were ordered back to make room for our infantry. Prisoners of the Seventh Alabama Cavalry, subsequently taken, report the enemy's loss in this fight to have been seven killed and twenty-three wounded. We marched from that place to Winchester, at which place we arrived on the third day of July. On the seventh we were sent back to Estel Springs, seven miles from Tullahoma, to bring rations forward for the regiment. We crossed Elk River and procured the rations, but on returning found the river past fording and that we would be compelled to swim our horses, which we did without any accident or loss. After the horses were all over, Sergeant Bumgardner, of Company B, in company with seven others, attempted to cross in a canoe. When they reached the middle of the stream the canoe capsized, and despite the efforts of a dozen of the best swimmers present, Sergeant Bumgardner was drowned. The other six came safely to shore.

Sergeant Bumgardner was a gentleman and a soldier the full sense of the term. It was only necessary that every one should know, to love and admire him. We all share and mourn with his friends and relatives his untimely loss.

Company B is now in fine condition for service, except clothing, which is well worn, and the supply at this time happens to be short; but we think it will not be long until we have an ample supply.

C

A PERILOUS NIGHT RIDE DURING THE ADVANCE UPON CORINTH, MISS.
by John S. Dollinger Late Sergeant-Major formerly Member of Company I, First Regiment O. V. C.

Early in the War of the Rebellion it was my fortune to be detailed for duty at the headquarters of that noble Virginian, grand "Old Pap Thomas" under whom I served for over a year. During the advance of the Union forces, under command of

General Halleck, upon Corinth, Miss., after the bloody battle of Shiloh, or Pittsburg Landing, we passed through and beyond the little hamlet of Monterey and were nearing the enemy's lines. The general, staff, and escort being in advance, a mounted skirmish line of the escort was formed under command of Lieutenant Barker, and was ordered to advance. We moved forward in column of fours into a heavy belt of timber, in the midst of which we were halted and ordered to see that every carbine was loaded, and the necessary instructions were given in case the enemy's position was uncovered. The command "Forward" was given, and upon reaching the edge of the timber the column was deployed and moved out into the open field and within a short distance of another densely wooded and more extensive tract, where we were halted. Of course we, or I, at least, imagined a rebel behind every tree, and expected every moment to see the flash of the guns and hear the whistle of the balls; but, fortunately for the, then, inexperienced line of skirmishers, the enemy had urgent business a little nearer Corinth and we were not molested. The recall was sounded and we withdrew and went into camp at the outskirts of the little hamlet. This movement was made by the general for the reason that the infantry columns were still to the rear struggling through the sea of mud, he intending to establish his headquarters for the night at this place, and in order to satisfy himself of the proximity of the enemy, he sent out this skirmish line of his escort, as no other troops were near. After having made the necessary preparations for some sort of shelter, we being without tents for the night, and had just about completed a "couch" without the "down" in the shape of a section of bark stripped from a large tree. I carefully placed pieces of timber and bark in as dry a spot as I could find, and then the bark previously provided was laid on top of this superstructure to keep out of the mud. which was almost deep enough to sink one "out of sight" with out these precautions. My saddle was placed for a pillow, the blanket spread and the "poncho" for cover, and was about to turn in, when the lieutenant rudely disturbed my anticipated "snooze" by ordering me to saddle my horse, take carbine and revolver and report at once to Captain Flint, who was the Assistant Adjutant-General on the staff of General Thomas. It being the duty of a soldier to obey orders without question, I rather reluctantly left my quarters, saddled my horse and reported. The captain handed me a dispatch, gave me the "countersign," and instructed me to proceed to the headquarters of General Lanman, on the right of our army, deliver the dispatch, take a receipt for the same and return in the shortest possible time. He also gave me the information that our lines and those of the enemy's were only a short distance apart, and that I should exercise the greatest caution to keep within our own lines. After receiving these instructions, it being then already dark, I started and soon entered a piece of woods where the darkness grew intense. Numerous camp-fires were seen ahead, and towards them I rode and was soon halted by a camp guard. I satisfied him that my business to be outside of the line was all right, and he permitted me to proceed. I managed to get through these woods all right and had an open space for quite a distance, and then again into the woods. I did not ride very far when a sharp and determined "Halt, who comes there?" startled me, in fact, scared me so that I imagined my cap was slowly moving in the direction of the tree-tops.

However, I managed to reply, in time, "Friend, with the countersign." The cheeky infantryman compelled me to dismount and at the point of the bayonet received the magic word. He was, however, not satisfied until he had called the sergeant, who permitted me to pass and also gave additional instructions. I got along all right for some time, but got into trouble once more in the inky darkness. My horse stumbled on a fallen log, and down he went, but I managed to hang on until he regained his footing, and before I had time to think about my mishap I was still worse scared by one of those unseen pickets, who, no doubt, was as badly demoralized as I was by the manner in which I approached his post. This soldier was easily satisfied that I was "all right" and entitled to pass. I was glad to find I had not struck a rebel picket and still without the enemy's lines, as I was outside of our lines several times. After receiving the welcome information that I was near the end of my ride Lanman's division was next to their right I rode on and finally reached his headquarters without further mishap. I delivered the dispatch to the general in person, who receipted for it, noting hour and minute when received. He also instructed me as to the proper directions to take and the different bodies of troops through whose camps I must pass. I thanked him, bid him good night, and started upon my return. I had almost a similar experience, only I managed to keep in line of the camps, and had only the guards of these camps halt me, instead of the pickets. I finally reached headquarters about two o'clock a. m., reported to Captain Flint, and then attended to the wants of my horse, after which I took possession of the bark trough, and it was some time before I got over the excitement of the night ride and fell asleep. I was a boy then, and I sometimes want to make believe I am a boy yet, but the gray beard gives that away. I am very much inclined to think that such, and still many vastly more dangerous experiences during a term of four years' active service at the front, had much to do with the change to gray. I notice nearly all of the "old boys" are stuck on the same colour, but whether it was caused by similar experiences or not, it is not for me to say; but this I do say, it is a great wonder indeed that the entire crop was not lost before it had time to turn gray.

Flags of Truce

The first flag of truce that came into our lines after we went into the service was in front of Corinth, Miss., about the middle of May, 1862. A general forward movement of the Army of Ohio had been made on the left across swamps, and through dense woods and thickets, and we had some sharp skirmishing. When the line halted, the pickets were thrown well forward and the reserve was located at the "Driver House," where there were cross-roads. The Driver House was a very important point in our lines for some time, and was well known to all soldiers of the Army of Ohio on the left. Company K was detailed for picket and the videttes were in easy hearing distance of the drums beating the calls in the rebel fortifications in Corinth. We were on duty all night and the next day about noon the attention of the picket was attracted by the shrill notes of a bugle in the direction of the rebel camps, and it seemed to be slowly approaching our lines. In a few minutes a cavalry command was seen advancing with a bugle at the head of the column sounding the calls, and we were at first of the opinion that the enemy contemplated an attack on the outposts.

They moved steadily forward and the white flag soon appeared, which was quite a relief, and the reserve galloped for ward and halted the cavalcade at the picket line. My recollection is that General Pegram was in command, and they had in charge a number of prisoners. The escort and prisoners were detained at the outpost until a communication from General Bragg was sent to General Halleck's headquarters. The escort was a cavalry company from New Orleans, and they were of the elite of the city, elegantly equipped and splendidly mounted. They were detained about two hours and we had a very pleasant visit, as they dismounted and Yank and Reb were soon engaged in a game of "Poker" or "Seven up."

During the truce there was no firing on the picket line, but as soon as they left our picket line and had sufficient time to get back to the main line, the pickets commenced banging away as usual, and the seeming friends of a few minutes before were again deadly enemies seeking each other's lives. Such are some of the episodes of war and, as was truly said by General Sherman, "War is cruelty and you cannot refine it." When the prisoners brought in under the flag of truce were halted at the outpost they were ragged, tired, and hungry, and we at once commenced dividing up our rations with them. I rode up to a fine-looking young cavalryman, to whom I was attracted by his unusual appearance, as his hair was very black, excepting the eyebrow and eyelashes on one side and a streak of hair on the same side of his head about an inch wide was white as snow. I divided up my rations with him and learned that his name was Eb. Cook, that he was a sergeant in the Fifth Ohio Cavalry and had been captured about the time of the battle of Shiloh. He had neither jacket or blouse, was in his shirt sleeves, and was very much rejoiced to get back to our lines again. These prisoners were paroled by the rebels and were sent North to parole camp by order of General Halleck. And now the sequel to this incident, which perhaps had almost passed out of my mind when I was taken prisoner a few months later.

I was paroled and sent to Camp Jackson, near Columbus, in the fall of 1862, and one of the first men I met was Sergeant Cook, and he and I became warm friends, and this friendship continued until his death a few years after the war. We often talked of our first meeting on the picket line near Corinth, when he was foot sore, tired, ragged and hungry on that warm May day in 1862, when I divided my rations with him and "we drank from the same canteen."

Another flag of truce came into our lines when our regiment was on outpost duty near Bardstown, Ky., in the fall of 1862. The escort of the flag was commanded by Major Prentice, of Kentucky, a son of Geo. D. Prentice, editor of the *Louisville Courier-Journal*. Among the escort were some Texas Rangers who prided themselves as being very fine horsemen, and they entertained our boys by giving some exhibition of their feats by picking up hats and handkerchiefs from the ground while their horses were at full speed. Some of the boys got into a game of poker with the rebs, which resulted in a general quarrel between Geo. Pearl, of Company K, and a Texan, arms were drawn, and the two proposed to fight it out, but the officers on both sides interfered and ordered the men to their horses, and it seemed for a little while as if we were going to have a general skirmish. As soon as the conference had been finished, they mounted and galloped back to their own lines and the truce was ended.

Geo. Pearl was afterwards killed in a fight at Lovejoy, Ga., August 20, 1864, when we were making a raid around Hood's army in Atlanta under General Kilpatrick, and at the time of his death his term of service was within about two weeks of being completed. Pearl was well known throughout the regiment as a brave soldier and belonged to a "mess" all of whom were canal boatmen, and the mess was known as the "hornet's nest" for the reason if you stirred one of them the whole nest would pounce on you. Their names were Lucas, Hants, Brant, Longly, Hassen, Buell, Newland, Orr and Pearl, of whom all are dead, unless it is Buell, and he was living a few years ago.

Letter from General Thomas

In 1868, before the death of General Thomas, he was invited to attend the reunion of the regiment. The following reply, written in his own hand, showing his high regard for the soldiers of the First, will be read with interest by every survivor.

Louisville, Ky.
September 25, 1868

Captain W. L. Curry
Corresponding Secretary
First Ohio Volunteer Cavalry
Dear Sir: I acknowledge with pleasure the receipt of your letter of the seventeenth inst., inviting me to meet the surviving members of the First Ohio Volunteer Cavalry at their proposed reunion, to be held at Columbus, Ohio, on the eighth of October next.
From long association with the First Ohio Cavalry, and from a daily observation of the soldierly bearing of the officers and men, I learned to esteem them as among the best troops under my command. I learn with pleasure that the recollections of the dangers, hardships and pleasure of your service have been a sufficient inducement to you to desire to have a reunion of comrades in arms. I shall have to decline your invitation to be present with you on the sixth *proximo*, because it is absolutely necessary that I be in Washington City on that day in discharge of official duties. Hoping that you may have a most cordial reunion, I remain yours very truly,
Geo. H. Thomas, Major-General, U. S. A.

War Reminiscences
by M. T. Vanpelt, Company H

The spring of 1862, if it had not given a new aspect to the progress of the war, had at least brought to the people north and south, as well as to the rank and file of both armies, a clearer realization of the magnitude of the struggle in which they were engaged. The North, at last aroused by the disasters of Bull Run, Ball's Bluff and others, but now hopeful from the victories of Mill Springs, Forts Henry and Donelson, were giving united support to war measures of gigantic compass, while the South, heretofore boastful in their expectation of an easy conquest of a soldier and people, toward whom they had manifested the utmost contempt, now seen by the steady front maintained both upon the open field and in front of defences, were to be feared if not respected; and by the wide sweep of the Union armies far into the South, transferring the scenes of actual war to their very doors, now began to realize that the independence of the Confederacy was not so certain after all. So the First O.V. C., belonging at that time to General Thomas' division, or the "Army of the Ohio," as it was called, and a part of Buell's army, with Grant's army concentrated on the west bank of the Tennessee River at Pittsburg Landing, and with Buell's army marching through Tennessee from Nashville to join him, we were at last in the enemy's country, where at any moment in our marching and scouting we were liable to become engaged in conflict with the enemy. It was two Sergeants from our regiment that as scouts successfully passed across the state of Tennessee and through the enemy's lines, carrying a dispatch from Buell to Grant announcing our march to his support.

Our regiment, divided up into companies and battalions, scouted upon the flanks of the marching army and guarded and protected the moving wagon train and the line of march, the army marching in brigades and divisions, General Nelson taking the lead, with baggage and supply trains between. Just before leaving Columbia it was reported that a Confederate force of cavalry at Pulaski threatened our line of march and perhaps the supply depot at Columbia, and a battalion of our regiment, under command of Major Scott, was ordered on a secret march to that point, with the view of surprising and capturing or dispersing the same. On a rainy evening we received orders to provide ourselves with three days rations and fifty rounds of ammunition. None knew of the purpose of the scout other than perhaps the commanding officer. The writer being with the company at the time was permitted to go. We assembled after dark on the pike just outside of Columbia, and after a short inspection as to the character of our mounts, counting off by fours and throwing a strong guard to the front, we faced toward Pulaski and commenced an all night's march of fifty miles. It had been raining at intervals for several days, and commenced with the march and rained without intermission all night long. We reached Duck Creek I think it is a tributary of Duck River within one mile of Pulaski just as day began to break, to find the bridge torn up and the creek so swollen by the rains as to seem dangerous to attempt to cross it. Here was a "fix." The town nearly in sight, or would be when light enough, and the rebels supposed to be there in considerable force. After an examination up and down the stream for some way of getting across, finally some of the officers selected a place where it was easy to get down and up the banks, plunged in, calling on all who could swim to follow. The current carried them down the stream some distance, but they landed safely. The most of us commenced undressing ourselves to follow, taking off our heavier outer clothing, wrapping them around our carbines and the sabres and revolver belts around that, so that we could hold them up and out of the water. We plunged into the swift, muddy current, and about seventy-five or one hundred of us got over. Many of the men refused to take the plunge. While taking such care of my clothes, my gun and revolver, I forgot all about my haversack that contained all my rations, which was tied at the cantel of my saddle, among which I had provided myself with some ginger snaps, cheese, etc., and by the time that haversack had washed through and under that muddy current for a hundred and fifty yards it was so mixed with clay and mud and horse-hairs that I could not tell any part from the others. But we had no time to mourn the loss of grub. Hastily dressing our selves, we formed on the pike and some eight or ten of us took the advance and with carbines at an advance we charged down the pike and entered the village about the time it was broad daylight. We of course expected every moment of our advance to receive the fire of the pickets of the enemy, if not the whole force somewhere in ambush. But not a living person was to be seen at first, which looked and was suspicious, and we feared some trap. But just as we reached what appeared to be the centre of the town and had drawn up, we of the advance saw some four or five mounted men skulking along the back street toward a bridge that crossed a small stream on the other side of town. We immediately opened out upon them, but they put spurs to their horses and galloped across the bridge and over the hills out of sight. Finding the rebels had left, after a few hours rest we started back to Columbia, reaching there just before daylight next morning. The distance marched, I believe, in the two nights and one day was one hundred miles. It was a hard march and I remember that night on our way back we were all very tired and naturally sleepy. I had gone to sleep in the saddle during the night's march and was finally awakened by my horse rubbing up against some bushes in the fence corner. When I awoke I found myself all alone and with out my hat, which had dropped off somewhere. As soon as I realized where I was I began to think I was in a fix or in a fair way to get in one. I could not hear or see anything of the column, and from the way my horse stood I could not tell which way we had been marching. My horse, probably growing tired, had fallen behind and finally stopped in the fence corner. Knowing I was in an enemy's country and likely to be picked up by the guerillas or rebel scouts, I was anxious to get with my comrades again. I was afraid to ride out on the road, for fear of taking the wrong direction, but finally, getting down, I examined the tracks of the horses and found which way they had gone. I jumped back into the saddle and after a gallop of two miles or more I came upon some stragglers who, like myself, had fallen asleep and were strung out for some distance.

This beautiful historical poem, dedicated to the First Ohio Cavalry, was written by T. C. Harbaugh, of Casstown, Ohio, and was first recited by him at the reunion of the regiment held at Covington, Ohio, October 8, 1888:

> The Trooper's Wreath by T. C. Harbaugh
> Dedicated to the First Ohio Cavalry
>
> *O gallant men who rode to fame*
> *With spur and blade through battle's flame—*
> *Who mounted fast with courage true*
> *When loud Kilpatrick's bugles blew—*
> *And sabred hard beneath the sun*
> *Where Chickamauga's waters run,*
> *I would entwine a wreath I've made*
> *With love around each trusty blade;*
>
>> *And o'er the graves of comrades dead*
>> *Earth's sweetest blossoms I would spread.*
>> *All are not here who rode afar*
>> *To duty 'neath the southern star;*
>> *Some hands have left for er the rein,*
>> *They will not clasp the spur again;*
>> *Your bugles sounding far away*
>> *Would never break their sleep today;*
>
> *And all your war steed's thund'ring tramp*
> *Would not disturb their silent camp.*
> *With shattered health and many a wound*
> *You meet once more the camp-fire round;*
> *I see the marks of time today,*
> *In feeble steps and locks of gray;*
> *The spring has left the warrior's heel,*
> *The hand doth shake that drew the steel.*

> *I ask myself: "Are these the men*
> *Who galloped once through battle's glen?*
> *Are these the boys who thundered down,*
> *With shout and yell through alien town?*
> *Then they were young, but now behold!*
> *A lot of troopers growing old!"*
> *No more their brightly burnished blades*
> *The sunlight kiss in Southern glades;*

No more their golden pennons fly
Against the far off Georgian sky.
Their gallant steeds no longer neigh
To meet the enemy in gray;
The crimson spur and warrior's plume
Lie mingled on Kilpatrick's tomb!
There lingers in your memory still
The close, hot fight at Perryville;

> *This is the day that marks it well,*
> *With all its rain of shot and shell,*
> *And you have met, as oft before,*
> *To fight that glorious battle o'er.*
> *But other fields which I could name*
> *Re-crown your well-won wreath of fame.*
> *There is a stream neath spreading pines*
> *Where once you closed your battle lines;*

Upon its banks at close of day;
In death's embrace your comrades lay;
Yes, near its little crystal bed
The North's one Millikin fell dead;
And there in Murfreesboro town,
The gallant Moore his life laid down,
To you who all your dead revere,
Stone River's name is doubly dear.

> *Another leader, brave and true*
> *At Chickamauga fell in blue:*
> *A wreath that ne'er shall fade away*
> *Upon the breast of Cupp I'd lay,*

  And one for Emery, nobly brave,
  Who fills a loyal soldier's grave.
  Let Mission Ridge, renowned in war
  Tell how you won another star;
Let Kenesaw and Love joy, too,
Retouch with pride your coats of blue.
Remember how the noble Scott
Went down amidst the carnage hot;
Recall how Allen, in his youth,
The flag of Freedom, Right and Truth,
Heroic bore amid the strife,
And sealed its triumph with his life.
  The names of all your dead are dear,
  Their deeds on honour's roll appear;
  The wreath that decks the private brave
  Adds lustre to the colonel's grave;
  Where Glory guards the soldier's sod,
  Rank is unknown, or lost, thank God!
  There all are equal, in their blue—
  The Private and the Colonel, too.
The raid is o'er; no more you ride
With clanking sabre far and wide;
No more doth Wheeler fiercely low'r
Around your flanks at midnight's hour;
You knew his tricks; you followed fast,
And beat the sly old fox at last.
No more for you the fevered cot,
The ebbing pulse, the forehead hot;
  But when the hour of death came nigh—
  Aye, when some comrades had to die,
  A loving hand was near, and true,
  As gentle as a woman's too.
  He lives who cooled the burning brow,
  You loved him then, you love him now;
  And mid the richest bloom of earth,
  I'd twine that love for Doctor Wirth.

Oh, heroes of the spur and blade,
I envy you the name you've made!
The great Napoleon never saw
Your betters ride behind Murat;
And braver troopers never bled
Than those whom once Kilpatrick led.
A few more years and one and all
Will answer to Death's bugle call;

> *For evermore your flags are furled—*
> *Such flags! the envy of the world!*
> *The shadows of your brave videttes*
> *No longer touch War's grim lunettes,*
> *And larger grows the Silent Camp,*
> *Which Honour guards with ceaseless tramp,*
> *Think not that you have ceased to ride,*
> *As once you thundered side by side;*

Though frosted by the touch of age,
You gallop still o'er history's page,
And down the corridors of Time,
Forever in our beauteous clime,
Imagination oft will see
The First Ohio Cavalry!

RECOLLECTIONS OF THE BATTLE AT STONE'S RIVER, TENN.
by John S. Dollinger,
Late Sergeant-Major First Ohio Veteran Volunteer Cavalry
formerly on Escort Duty at
Major-General Geo. H. Thomas' Headquarters.

The forward movement of the Fourteenth Army Corps (or Army of the Cumberland) from Nashville, Tenn., under the command of Major-General W. S. Rosecrans, commenced on Friday, December 26, 1862. Shortly after daylight the writer carried the order to Major-General L. H. Rousseau to advance his division. General Thomas moved his column of over thirteen thousand men on the Franklin Pike. The country over which the army was marching afforded great advantages to the enemy; a small force could retard the advance of superior numbers considerable tracts of cultivated lands occurred at intervals on either side of the pike between Nashville and Murfreesboro, the intervening spaces were heavily wooded and interspersed with dense cedar thickets, which formed formidable barriers to the march of an aggressive army. Negley's division of Thomas' command bivouacked near Nolensville, to which point he had pushed in support of General Davis, who had uncovered the enemy. The following day the column moved to the east, over rugged roads, to connect General Crittenden's right near Stewartsboro, on the Murfreesboro Pike. The heavy rains made the by-roads almost impassable, and in consequence the movements were necessarily slow and fatiguing. Headquarters were pitched near the pike for the night, and on the following day, Sunday, Rousseau's division was struggling through the mud from Nolensville toward the Murfreesboro Pike, to take the proper position in the column. The army laid quietly in bivouac during Sunday.

On Monday morning, before daylight, the general and staff and part of the escort moved out on the pike, leaving the writer and the rest of the escort to bring forward headquarters, which were established that night on the north side of Overalls Creek near the pike and a short distance in rear of the lines. Tuesday, the thirtieth, dawned drearily; it had rained heavily during the night and many of the troops had lain all night in the mud without shelter or fires. We joined the general on the field in the immediate rear of the centre. He was standing by a small fire, surrounded by part of his staff and escort, intently listening to the heavy skirmishing in the cedars to his right. A drizzling rain was falling and the air was cold and crisp. The fire of the skirmishers, constantly increasing, interspersed with the booming of cannon at short intervals, formed an almost perfect imitation of thousands of axe-men engaged in felling the trees in the forest. The general mounted, rode forward and into the cedars, where Negley had fought his way into position, Rousseau being held in reserve. The centre was posted slightly in advance, Crittenden to the left and McCook on the right. The enemy was strongly posted in the timber in our front and entrenched to the left. The general (Pap Thomas) commanding the centre established temporary headquarters for the night in a small cabin in the woods near the pike, and a short distance in rear the second line of battle. On the following and never-to-be- forgotten morning, December 31, long before daylight, the army was awake and alert, waiting for the opening of the battle. We did not have long to wait until the disastrous attack of Hardee on the right of our line commenced. Everything being in readiness the general, with part of the escort and staff, rode to the front. McCook failed to hold Hardee, and his shattered columns were rapidly driven back upon the centre. The general halted at the edge of a belt of timber, on the right and left of the pike, took his field glass and eagerly scanned the lines. While in this position, in column of fours, the general, with staff and escort in plain view, made a conspicuous mark for the enemy, and in very short order a battery in our front sent in their compliments in the shape of a twelve-pound solid shot, which struck the hard pike just in front of the general, ricochetted and passed over our heads and again struck the ground and bounded to the rear, smashing a stump in its way before it stopped. The next moment a battery on the left front of us sent a shell which passed over our heads and fell among a body of infantrymen, who were lying down in the woods to our right; the shell exploded as it struck and quite a number of men were killed and wounded. The General ordered Lieutenant Barker to move the escort off the pike and out of range of the cross-fire of the batteries. I happened to be in the first fours and as the shell had passed uncomfortably close I was quick to obey the command "Fours left!" I had just uncovered the man in rear of me, when the second shot came from the left— it proved to be a six-pound solid shot— and struck Fulton Gitteau full in the left breast and tore a hole through him almost large enough to run an arm through. The poor fellow fell out of his saddle on the hard pike, gave a convulsive shudder, and was dead. We were formed in rear of a battery to the left and the body of our comrade was picked up and tenderly carried to the rear. We now moved forward to the right and into the cedars, where Negley and Sheridan were heavily engaged. They made heroic efforts to stem the tide and were steadily pressed back. Sheridan's division being out of ammunition was forced out of the cedars by the rebels on the double quick, firing as they ran. The general and part of the staff and escort were just to the left and partly in range of the fire of this rushing body of the enemy with their fierce yells of triumph. General Rosseau, who was at this time, with his staff and escort, close by General Thomas, was ordered by him to move his division into the cedars to aid Sheridan and Negley. His division was in reserve just at the edge of the cedars and it took only a few moments time for the leading regiments to enter the woods. I will always remember this as one of the most inspiring sights I witnessed during my term of service. After a lapse of over thirty years I have forgotten the name and number of the regiment in advance, of that magnificent body of "boys" who came rushing on, in column, with arms at "right shoulder shift," on the double quick, as calmly as if on parade, never halting or wavering. Like an enormous (living) wedge they forced themselves between our struggling and sorely pressed columns and the exultant foe; came to a front and delivered a murderous fire at short range, which for a short time checked them, but were finally forced to slowly recede, and a new line was formed. I remember the Ninety-fourth Ohio Volunteer Infantry was a part of that splendid division, and the survivors no doubt recollect the frantic wild turkeys that were so paralysed with fright, that some of them were easily caught. While this disaster occurred in the cedars, the rebel cavalry was busy in our rear. An orderly rode up to General Thomas and informed him that their cavalry was then capturing and burning our trains. Sergeant Woodall, myself and four men were ordered by the general to go to the rear and remove headquarters, which were still beyond Overalls Creek. The detail was quickly made and we rode at a gallop out of that uncomfortably "hot place." We soon reached the open fields about one-half mile to the rear, where we were hailed by a Second Kentucky cavalryman, a mere boy in fact, and badly demoralized, who informed us that the rebel cavalry had possession of our wagon train on the pike only a short distance ahead of us and were in plain view. As they were between us and where we intended to go, we thought it policy to await further developments. We could see them taking our ambulances, prisoners, etc., across the field to their left rear. Whilst watching them, a number of rebel cavalry prisoners were brought up to where we halted. They were captured with our blue over coats on their backs, a fact that Sergeant Woodall soon noticed and ordered one of them, in no very polite terms, to take off the coat and hand it to him. The Johnnie complied without a word. While this was going on I noticed the Fourth U. S. Cavalry emerging from the woods to our left rear; they marched in column and when within a short distance from the rebel line came to a front and made a magnificent charge and recaptured our ambulances and prisoners. I noticed also one of the regulars overhauling a Johnnie and when within a few paces from him he killed him with a shot from his revolver. I saw when he tumbled off his horse that a large bundle of "Uncle Sam's" blankets also dropped to the ground. Being in need of a blanket, I rode over and selected a nice, clean and new one, which he evidently took from one of our poor boys a few moments before. The way being cleared we rapidly rode to the rear and soon came upon the scene of murder and pillage. The poor negro teamsters were shot in their tracks like dogs; the mules were killed while yet hitched to the wagons, and the finest artillery horses I ever saw shared a like fate, while all along the pike to Overalls Creek the stiff and blue coated forms of our comrades were stretched, still in death. Further on to the rear our train of over two hundred wagons, with contents, were burned, nothing being left but the irons. We crossed the creek and just beyond found a line of infantry, the Tenth Ohio, stopping stragglers from going to the rear. We found headquarters safe, removed them, and rejoined the general and staff at the front.

The day's fighting closed leaving us masters of at least part of our original ground, and new lines were advantageously formed. A night conference was held at the headquarters of General Rosecrans, at which it was determined, in the language of the general, "to fight or die right here." The troops lay down upon their arms that night, many of them where they fought. It was a cold and dreary night, no fires being permitted at the front, and many of the troops had no rations, while others were more fortunate. The desperation of hunger compelled some to carve the steaks from Colonel Starkweather's black horse, who had been killed in battle. This I saw while riding along the pike. During the night it rained, and when daylight came everywhere were masses of mud. The day following, the desperate attempt of Breckenridge to turn our left took place; but the fifty-eight pieces of artillery massed hurling shot, shell, grape, case and cannister, together with the heroic efforts of our infantry, proved too much for even veteran troops to with stand, and in a very short time were completely repulsed.

More or less fighting took place on the second and third of January, and on the fourth General Thomas advanced into Murfreesboro. As none of the rebel dead had been buried, in the fallow field to the right and in front of Hell's Half Acre, where Hazen fought, I saw the fearful effect of the iron and leaden hail from our side, together with the sad scenes witnessed during the battle, will never be effaced from memory as long as life lasts.

Horses and Horse Racing

In the cavalry service horse racing was the great sport. and the First Ohio was no exception to the rule. When we were in camp for any length of time, and the service was not too hard, the lovers of that sport would improvise a track on some straight stretch of road, or across some old fields or pastures, and the "sprinters" would be put in training under the care of some experienced horsemen and jockeys, of which there were a number in the regiment. In a cavalry regiment of nearly a thousand horses there were, as would be expected, some pretty good flyers, and the horse fanciers were always looking out to pick up a fast one, now and then, through the country, and frequently got a Kentucky or Tennessee thoroughbred from the far-famed blue grass region.

Very often races were made with horses of other regiments and the betting would be heavy and the excitement run high. In the spring of 1863 the regiment was in camp at Lavergne, Tennessee, for some time, and a very good track was made near the camp, where scrub races were of daily occurrence, with now and then a race by the fast ones. A part of the regiment was in camp at Stewart's Creek, and an Indiana infantry regiment was also in camp there. The quartermaster of that regiment was quite a sport and a race was arranged between his best horse and Captain Conn's sorrel horse, named "Billy Button." A half mile track was made across a big clover field at quite a considerable expense and all the preliminaries were arranged by Sergeant Frank Allen, of Company K, who was the acknowledged authority on all such matters, and the best jockey in the regiment. He gave a great deal of attention to the preparation of the track, saw that Button had the best of care, gave him daily canters, and when the time for the race arrived Button was in the "pink of condition." It was a beautiful May day and the whole garrison turned out to see the race, including Chaplain and Sutler. The stake, I think, was two hundred and fifty dollars, and there were many side bets from five dollars up to fifty. Sergeant Allen rode Button and won the race, but it was a close one. The Indiana boys were not satisfied and another race was soon arranged, but before the day arrived, we were ordered to the front at Murfreesboro, and the race was declared off and never was run. This was perhaps the most exciting race ever had in the regiment and is well remembered by every soldier who was in the regiment at that time.

The boys would work all kinds of schemes to learn the speed

of each others horses without testing them together, and one instance of this kind comes to mind in Company K. The Orderly Sergeant, Sergeant Lucas, and Sergeant Kilgore, each had a pretty fast horse, but they had never been tested together, and as Lucas was anxious to make a match with one of the others, Kilgore and the orderly decided that without giving Lucas the "tip" they would try the speed of their two horses, and then get up a race with the winner. So one Sunday morning after inspection they mounted their horses and rode out of camp leisurely and innocently for a little exercise, and were soon followed by a few of their friends who had been given the "tip." Going out on the Somerset road from Lebanon, Ky., a couple of miles, they came to a long, pretty stretch of sandy road in the best of condition, four hundred yards were soon measured off, the horses were stripped and went over the track under the whip. The orderly's horse came in a few necks ahead, and the boys all mounted and rode back to camp, looking as innocent as if they had been out in the country to church, and in a few days a match was made between Lucas' horse "Dandy" and "Billy." Lucas lost the race and his money as well, and he never understood just how it was.

Among the boys that "talked horse" and were always ready to make a match and keep a fast horse or two was Captain Conn, Kirkendall, Curry, Erwin, Frank Allen, Adjutant Neil, Sergeant Lucas, Sergeant Kilgore, Lieutenant High, Lee Tway, Lieutenant Roush, Geo. Geiger, of Company M, and many others. After 1863 there was but little racing, as the regiment was on the campaign all the time, and were never in camp more than a day or two in succession.

There were a great many superb horsemen in the regiment who could pick up a hat or sabre from the ground without dismounting, and being every day in the saddle and a great deal of the time in a rough country, jumping logs, fences and ditches, it was very seldom a cavalryman was unhorsed, especially after two years in the saddle, as they were more at home there than dismounted. Horse and rider would become very much attached to each other and were inseparable. Although thousands of horses of different regiments would be tied to their picket ropes in adjoining camps, and many of them would break their halters or they would become unloosed, yet but few horses would wander away from their own company, they were so attached to each other; and it was a rare thing to hear of a horse being lost. Many of the horses knew a number of the bugle calls, and when the "Stable" or "Water call" was sounded they would whinny and would respond to the "Forward" or "Halt" without being urged or spoken to by the rider. Horses seemed to know when we were getting ready for a fight, even before the firing commenced, and especially when we were advancing slowly and carefully through the woods or fields. When the skirmishers were throwing down the fences, the ears of the horses would be erect and rolling nervously about and looking cautiously on either side, as if they "snuffed the battle afar off." At the first crack of a carbine on the skirmish line, although it might be far to the front, every horse was nerved up, sniffing the air. They would soon become accustomed to the firing, but the singing or whizzing of the balls would make them snort and jump.

No doubt, many of the boys can remember just what colour and just what kind of a horse the officers and each man of his company rode, as well as he can remember the men themselves, for the horses and men were companions and we always identify them together. The writer, and no doubt many other members of the regiment, can remember the horses of almost every officer in the regiment, but I will only give those of some of the field and staff, as it may bring back some pleasant recollections to all of the boys as they go back in memory to our early campaigns. Colonel Ransom rode a dark dun or clay bank with white tail; Colonel Smith a fine black and roan; Colonel Millikin an elegant high-stepping bay, named Archer; Colonel Laughlin a bay; Colonel Cupp an iron gray; Colonel Writer a bay; Colonel Eggleston a large dark bay and iron gray; Major Scott a large brown; Major Dennison a fine black; Major Frankenberger a sorrel; Surgeon Canaan a black; Major Moore a black. Many horses were killed and wounded in action, and taking one company as a criterion, in which the losses in horses have been carefully verified, it is safe to say that the losses in killed and wounded were equal to that of the men in the First Ohio.

Coloured Men in the Regiment

There were a great many coloured men in the regiment, officers' servants, who were very faithful, and no doubt some of them are well remembered by the boys. Colonel T. C. H. Smith took into the service a coloured man by the name of Harry, and it must be borne in mind that a coloured man in the service never had but one name. An old coloured fellow by the name of "Uncle Dick," interrogated regarding this matter, said: "There was so many darkies before de wah dat de could not afford to gib dem but one name"; and as he was good authority, his statement was never questioned. Harry was a firm believer in the rabbit's foot and all kinds of hoodoo business, and anything that might transpire out of the ordinary, Harry would say, "Dat was a mighty bad sign," and Scotty and the other wags around headquarters kept him up at a high tension all the time. Harry always swore by "de Kunnel," and when Colonel Smith left the regiment Harry went with him. Uncle Dick, of Company M; was another well-known character.

He lived in Tennessee and was not a farm hand, but had always worked about his master's house and was a very tidy old darkey and an excellent cook. He could make excellent biscuit, and when we could get any flour, Uncle Dick would hustle around and get an oven from some Old Dinah and the biscuit or pig pot-pie would be forth coming. He could neither read nor write, but he was an unusually smart old man, and when on the march in the night, if the stars were shining, he could tell the hour of the night and never failed. He could always tell the points of the compass which was very important at times when the advance would be uncertain about the roads. Pies, of Company D, Captain Kirkendall's boy, was another faithful coloured fellow and well remembered. He served through to the end of the war, and Captain Kirkendall brought him home to Ohio, and he now lives near Columbus and is doing well.

A soldier of the First who was with the regiment during the last two years of the war that did not know "Brick," of Company K, did not know much about the coloured men of the regiment. "Brick," like "Topsy," "jest growed up in Old Tennessee," and Lieutenant Curry picked him up in 1863. Brick was a great character, about sixteen or seventeen years of age, black as the ace of spades, and a typical plantation darky. He had been raised on the back of a mule, and was a good rider, and sat in the saddle as if he had grown there. He knew nothing about cooking and his chief value was as a forager for both man and beast, and when he started out for forage, if there was any in the country, Brick came in loaded. When the regiment went around Atlanta on the Kilpatrick Raid, Brick was along as usual, and when we were ordered to cut our way out, Brick was impressed by the company officers with the importance of bringing the company pack mules out, as all of the company officers rations for the expedition was carried by the mule.

Brick and another coloured boy had the mule in charge, and while one led the other was to apply a long hickory stick to the mule vigorously. Before the start was made both darkies were admonished that in the event they did not bring the mule out safely, two darkies would dangle from a limb of the nearest tree.

The distance from the start to the rebel lines was eight or ten hundred yards, and when we had covered about half the distance, Brick dashed up to and through the centre of Company K under the spur, with his eyes bulged out as large as two saucers, and that was the last of the mule and rations. No doubt the mule was abandoned soon after the start, and when it was learned by the officers that the rations were all gone, they were very much out of humour and their wrath was poured out on the heads of Brick and Henry in language more forcible than elegant. Brick served until the end of the war and came to Ohio with Lieutenant Reece. He only remained for a year or two and then returned to the old plantation in Tennessee.

Captain Woodlief had a coloured boy by the name of Henry who was quite a musical genius. He was a beautiful whistler and would entertain the boys often in the summer evenings with not only the old plantation melodies, but mocking bird imitations and all kinds of bird songs. He would make a couple of reeds out of cane stalks and these he would place between his lips and play beautifully, something like a piccolo.

Lieutenant Roush, of Company H, got a coloured man at Cleveland, Tenn., at the time of the battle of Missionary Ridge, by the name of Billy Barber. Before the close of the war he enlisted in a coloured regiment and served until the end of the war. Billy was a faithful fellow and swore by the First Ohio at all times and thought they were the wildest riders in the service. He now lives in Columbus, Ohio, and if any fellow is spoiling for a tight, he can be accommodated by hunting Billy up and commence saying something derogatory of the service of the First Ohio. There were many other good and faithful coloured men who saw long service in the regiment, whose names cannot be recalled. coloured men became very much attached to soldiers and officers of the commands to which they belonged and would take all kinds of chances of being killed by the rebels in foraging for both officers and horses. They were a part of the army and were always true to the Union soldiers in giving information that was of benefit to our army. They looked upon the Yankees as their saviours, and the first soldier they would see wearing the blue uniform they would leave their old masters, home and family, although the surroundings would be of the most pleasant, and follow the boys in blue if they were permitted to do so. It was a common occurrence for these old gray headed men to come into camp during the night, travelling perhaps many miles through the pine woods, to give information as to the movements of the rebels, when they knew full well if they were detected their lives would be in jeopardy. But they took the chances, and often their information would be of the most vital importance to our army. They were always true to the Union soldiers, and how many of them were fed and cared for by these faithful coloured people when they had made their escape from rebel prisons and were trying to make their way through to our lines! Many a soldier's life was saved by their good work, and every good soldier has a warm place in his heart for the faithful old slaves of the South.

Old Shady—A Contraband Song

When Companies E and K were stationed at Courtland, Ala., in July, 1862, and before President Lincoln's Emancipation Proclamation had been issued, I remember of hearing for the first time, sung by the plantation negroes, the song "Old Shady." The following rare lyric was the favourite freedom-song of the Mississippi and Alabama contrabands. Its character and enthusiasm are great and, among songs of its kind, it has no superior.

Oh! Ya, ya! Darkies, laugh with me;
For de white folk say old Shady's free!
Don't you see dat de jubilee
Is comin', comin'! Hail mighty day!

> Chorus:
> *Den away, Den away, for I can't stay any longer;*
> *Hurrah, hurrah For I am going home.*

Massa got scared, and so did his lady!
Dis chile broke for ole Uncle Aby;
Open de gate out! here's ole Shady
Comin', comin'! Hail, mighty day.

Good-bye, Massa Jeff! Good-bye, Missus Stevens!
'Scuse dis nigger for taking his leavens
'Spec, pretty soon, you ll see Uncle Abram's
Comin', comin'! Hail, mighty day.

Good-bye, hard work, and never any pay—
I m going up North, where de white folks stay;
White wheat bread, and a dollar a day!
Comin', comin'! Hail mighty day.

I've got a wife, and she's got a baby,
Way up North in Lower Canada—
Won't dey shout, when dey see ole shady
Comin', comin'! Hail, mighty day.

At this time they were firmly impressed with the belief that they would soon be set free, and believed that President Lincoln was their saviour. Wherever our army appeared, they flocked to our camps in great numbers, and the joy of the old gray-haired negroes men and women was wonderful to behold. They would shout, dance, sing and make all kinds of demonstrations to show their joy, and at the first sight of a Yankee in his blue uniform they would go almost wild. Here is where we first saw "patting Juba" by the plantation negroes for the little darkies to dance, and I remember one little darky that Sergeant John Lucas, of Company K, took a great fancy to — he was a bright boy, about ten years of age, a good rider and fine dancer. Lucas kept him in camp for some time, but finally his old master came to our camp and found him, and Lucas offered him a very fine horse for the boy. This horse "Dandy," as he was called, Lucas traded or sold to Lieutenant Cutler, and he was mounted on him the day our camp was attacked at Courtland, and horse and rider were taken prisoner and poor "Dandy" fell into the hands of the rebels. I saw a rebel riding him the next day after we were taken prisoners, galloping proudly through the streets of Moulton, Ala., amid the shouts of admiring girls and women, waving one of our guidons, which he had captured the day we were captured. No doubt the old planter, after Lincoln's Emancipation Proclamation was issued September 17, 1862, wished he had traded the little darky for Dandy, but it was too late.

When we were in camp at Courtland, Lieutenant Cutler had a negro servant named "Sam," whom he had picked up somewhere in Kentucky or Tennessee. Sam was an ignorant slave boy, but was anxious to learn to read and put in all his spare time, from grooming horses and cooking, in learning the alphabet from an old primer he had picked up somewhere, and several of us had become very much interested in the boy. On the day of the fight at Courtland, July 25, 1862, Sam was taken prisoner, as he was wearing a pair of old blue cavalry pants and was in company with a soldier along the creek bank in rear of our camp. During the fight a squad of rebel cavalry rode up to the creek on the opposite bank and ordered them to surrender. The soldier and Sam started to wade across the creek, and when in the middle of the stream, the rebels ordered the soldier to return and get his carbine; and being frightened and fearing that the rebels would fire on him, he ordered Sam to go back and get his carbine. When Sam handed the gun to the squad, they took it as a pretext to claim that he was armed and in the ranks, and as Sam had on a pair of blue pants the case looked bad for him. When at Moulton the next day after the capture, Sam was arrested by the provost guard and put in jail. When he was arrested he appealed to us to save him, but we were utterly powerless, as we were prisoners ourselves; and I will never forget his appealing look as he was hurried off to jail. As the negroes were still slaves, of course, the feeling of the rebel soldiers was very bitter against them, if they had the least suspicion that they were carrying arms or were in any manner aiding or abetting the Union army. This incident made a deep impression on Lieutenant Cutler and myself at the time, as we had no doubt, from the manner in which he was arrested and treated and the bitter feeling exhibited among the rebels, that he would either be hung or shot, and we have often talked about poor Sam and wondered what his fate was.

Well Known Characters in the First Ohio Cavalry

While the First Ohio did not have any "Si Kleggs," at least by name, yet there was not a company but what had some members that were known for their peculiar characteristics of some kind, so that they were known all over the regiment as well as the colonel. Some were clowns, some were sports, some were ready to fight at the "drop of a hat" at all times and on all occasions, but it was a well-known fact among good soldiers that the fellow that was always walking around camp with a "chip on his shoulder spoiling for a fight," was not at all times in the front rank when a real fight was on where bullets and cold steel were no respecter of persons, even if he "tipped the beam" at two hundred pounds and was a veritable John Sullivan. This of course did not always hold true, but there were many cases of that kind in every regiment. After a lapse of thirty years since the close of the war no one man can remember all of the funny fellows, the sports, fighters, etc., but I now recall a few of them well remembered by every soldier of the regiment. Sergeant Billy Scott, of Company D, who was promoted to a captain and was killed at Lovejoy, Ga., September 20, 1864, was one of the bravest soldiers in the regiment, and was an Irish boy brim full of "Mother wit." He nicknamed many of the officers of the regiment, and some of these names clung to them all through the war. He did not do this out of any disrespect, but just from some incident or peculiarity of the man, as for instance, Colonel Eggleston he named "Bolivar Bob," Colonel Writer "Lady Writer," Colonel Pattin "Bough and Beady," Captain O'Harra "Shell Bark," Major Frankenberger "Old Hail Columbia," and many others that I do not recall; but those named will be well remembered by the boys, and they have had many a good joke and laugh at the expense of the officers so dubbed.

"Scotty," as he was familiarly called, never tired of a good joke, and when Colonel Smith was in command of the regiment on the Shiloh and Corinth campaign, he was continuously playing some practical joke around headquarters, as he was the Sergeant-Major of the regiment Colonel Smith was a good man, an earnest and zealous officer, and very matter-of-fact in all things and unsuspicious. Scotty took advantage of these things, and there was no end of his "grape vine" stories around headquarters.

The chief bugler was a Frenchman and his name was Paul Petard, but we always called him "Vic," and Scotty was continuously at some trick and kept "Vic" very much irritated at times. "Vic" was an excellent soldier, was always prompt in all his duties and was very neat and precise about his dress and equipments. When he came out of his tent to blow a call he would step out with jacket buttoned tight, give his bugle a few flourishes over his head, with the long yellow cord and tassel dangling gracefully below, and would then place the bugle to his lips and give a blow, and very often it would give a harsh, unearthly squall, and on examination he would find straws in his bugle. He would be fighting mad and report to the colonel, and no one around headquarters would be more indignant than Scotty, and he would demand that the offenders be arrested and punished severely, when it was well known that he was the instigator of all this mischief himself.

Colonel Smith had a coloured servant named Harry, who was a little scary and superstitious, and Scotty took great delight in teasing him. At one time Harry was pitching the colonel's tent among the leaves and brush, and all at once Scotty became very much excited, picked up a long club and commenced pounding the leaves and brush and shouting "snakes" at the top of his voice, at which Harry pulled the tent down and hauled it off to another spot, very nervous over the imaginary snake, and said he was "mighty glad Mr. Scott found dat snake before de Kunnel got in dat tent, for it was mighty bad sign."

A week or two after the battle of Shiloh, when our wagon train came up and we were pitching our tents for the first time on the battle-field, Harry was busy putting up the colonel's tent and Scotty was looking on innocently and commenced sniffing the air as if there was something very offensive in the vicinity. He stepped inside the tent as if following the trail, and stamping around with his feet pretended that he had found a soft spot in the ground, and went out and got a stick and began to prod around with it, and Harry asked him what he was doing. Scott replied very quietly and indifferently that "there was a dead rebel buried there, but he supposed it would not smell very bad as he was a good foot under the ground." To say that the tent was hustled to another place in a hurry is drawing it very mildly, and, as usual, Harry was very thankful to "Maser" Scott for "findin' dat dead rebel fore de Kunnel got in." And so from day to day Scott was inventing some new fish story to keep headquarters stirred up.

He was brave and very reckless and was just in his element when in a fight, and he had no use for a coward or a shirk. When talking with a soldier that was a little nervous or weak-kneed, he was sure to tell him some canard about an expected attack or that the "enemy was advancing in force," just to try his nerve. When the army was making the advance from Pittsburg Landing to Corinth in the spring of 1862, the regiment had a great deal of picket and outpost duty to do, and often in very close proximity to the enemy's lines, and the orders were very strict, instructions given the videttes at all times not to let any one outside of the lines. But by his smooth talk Scotty would find a sentry on some part of the line that would turn his back while Scott rode outside the picket and he would make a reconnaissance on his own hook and was never satisfied until he located the enemy's pickets and often drew their fire, and he would then come riding leisurely back and report the exact location of the rebel pickets. At one time, just before the evacuation of Corinth, he created quite an excitement in our camp and the whole regiment was drawn up in line of battle on account of one of his innocent (?) reports. He had been at the front and came galloping into camp on his little dun horse and some soldier asked him what the news was out at the front, and Scott, in his usual serious and earnest manner, shouted; "The rebels are coming," and rode on quietly through the camp and a short distance beyond to water his horse. The news soon flew to headquarters and the colonel ordered "Vic" to sound "Boots and Saddles" and "To horse" in quick succession, and in a few minutes the regiment was drawn up in line of battle, with drawn sabres, in a field adjoining the camp. It was a very hot day; the sun boiled down on our heads, and to still add to our discomfort a ration of whisky was issued to nerve the boys up for the trying ordeal. After standing in line for an hour or two, it seemed to dawn on some one that it was a "false alarm," and we were ordered back to our quarters. The true inwardness of this false alarm did not leak out until Colonel Smith had been promoted to a brigadier-general and left the regiment. Had he known it while still in command of the regiment, he would no doubt have made it lively for Sergeant Scott.

On the Atlanta Campaign in the summer of 1864 we were fighting almost every day, and one day he and another young officer of the regiment were sitting on a line of breast-works watching the firing of a rebel battery from the top of Kenesaw Mountain and calculating the distance by measuring the time from the moment of seeing the puff of white smoke until they heard the report of the gun. As it was a long distance and the guns had to be depressed, the shells were going wild and falling far wide of the mark. After a long silence Scott referred to some trouble a few young officers and himself had had in the regiment, and, continuing, said: "The next fight we get into, which may be today or tomorrow, we must rush in and get some of these old officers killed, so we will be promoted." This was said in half jest and half earnest, and little did he think that he would be the first officer to fall. In a short time after that the regiment joined General Kilpatrick in his famous raid around Hood's army in Atlanta, and the brave and gallant Captain Scott, "booted and spurred," rode into the "jaws of death". He died the death of his choice, and as he was mortally wounded while with sabre in hand with his regiment charging a battery, shouting, "Take the guns!"

The Whacker Boys

A soldier of the First Ohio that did not know the Whackers, did not know much about the regiment. Joe and Alf Deerwester were twins and members of Company G, and just why they were called the "Whacker Boys" was never, to my knowledge, explained; but it was supposed to be on account of their combative proclivities, for they never let an opportunity slip to get into a little "Kari" just for the "fun of the thing." If there was any kind of devilment going on in camp or out of camp that Alf and Joe were not in it, it was not their fault. When the regiment was at Camp Buell, near Louisville, Ky., there was a hotel near at hand, called the Oakland House, where liquids were dispensed at all hours, day and night, and of that kind that would make a fellow feel like fighting a whole regiment single handed, if he imbibed enough of it. It was a convenient place for a "first chance" when going to the city and a "last chance" on returning. One evening Bill Legg, of Company M, and one or two friends had been in the city and after the theatre was out were returning, and dropped into the Oakland to take a last nip, and found the Whackers running the house and everybody in it. They insisted that Bill should "sing, dance a jig or fight," or do something to entertain the crowd. Bill begged off and said he "was out of voice" and was opposed to dancing, and being a Quaker, had religious scruples about fighting, and asked to be excused. But that would not go with the Whacker boys, and they said that while they could not make Bill dance or sing, they could make him fight or run, and proposed to mop up the floor with him in the most approved style, just to entertain the crowd, as it had been a little dull that evening and the audience was not satisfied. They commenced crowding Bill into a corner, and as he saw he was in for it, he went at them hammer and tongs fashion and knocked them both out in the first round and the floor mopping was on the other side. It is said that he satisfied the audience to the "queen's taste," at least such was the story circulated in camp the next day. Joe and Alf usually had things their own way, but they did run up against a stump now and then. They were strapping big fellows, and when they got on a spree they ran Company G in great style, but when Scotty took command of the company, he called time on the boys, and as he was a boxer, the boys had great respect for him.

Joe is dead and Alf is now a sober, steady-going citizen of Illinois, and during the war they were only "sowing their wild oats."

Lem Dewey, of Company E, was a "shoulder striker" and when he got a "jag" on by drinking a canteen of commissary with a mixture of apple-jack, he was a regular cyclone. He would amuse the crowd by knocking down everybody in reach, and then form a ring and get a few other boys at it while he kept every soldier that attempted to interfere with his menagerie at a safe distance, and gave the officers of the company no end of trouble.

Jim Stratton, of Company H, was also a "holy terror" when he took on a good load of old Kentucky corn juice. A company was too small for Jim to display his generalship in, and at times he undertook the arduous task of running the whole regiment. When the regiment returned to Nashville, Tenn., in the spring of 1864, after we had been home on veteran furlough, we were camped near that city, being mounted and equipped for the Atlanta Campaign. The boys made frequent visits to the city, and the fellows that indulged in the ardent often came into camp in a hilarious condition. One day Stratton came out to camp loaded to the guards and surrounded the regiment and demanded unconditional surrender. The patrol guard objected to this proceeding and put him under arrest, and as we had no guard-house, and it took two of the guards to hold him, the next question was what to do with him. Lieutenant Curry, who was officer of the day, ordered him tied to the fence and directed the corporal of the guard to perform that duty. The corporal was a new recruit by the name of Erwin, and had only had his stripes on a few days, and he declined to tie Jim up as directed, as he claimed it was "cruel, barbarous and dangerous." The officer of the day did not see it in that light and told the corporal that if he did not do his duty he would take his stripes off, and Erwin said "let 'em go," and they did go, and the officer of the day proceeded to tie Jim up himself. Corporal Erwin often expressed his gratitude for having got rid of his corporal stripes so easy and said it was "too high a rank for him, as he was a small man and just the right size for a high private in the rear rank."

Bony, of Company I, was one of the great wags of the regiment. He was a great talker, and a loud talker, and his voice was heard on all occasions day and night. He called Captain Writer "Old twos right," as he claimed that was all the command he ever gave the company.

Several members of Company I were wounded in the foot and two or three of them had a toe shot off and among them "Bony," and he named them the "Nine Toed Company." The writer remembers about Bony's toe being shot off and thinks it was the day of the evacuation of Corinth, and it is safe to say he did not get off any of his jokes that day.

As betting was so common in the army, it was not considered gambling, as the term is generally used, for nearly everybody bet, not so much for the gain that was in it, but for the excitement and fun of the thing. Sergeant John Lucas, of Company K, was the boss sport of the regiment, and he would bet on anything from pulling at "square toe" by two little darkies to a hundred dollars or two on a big horse race. John's favourite game was "draw poker," and he also carried a Faro Kit, with silver deal box, and many an officer, as well as men of the ranks, contributed their sheckles to his exchequer. As soon as the soldiers were paid off, all the little dealers would get out their "chuck a luck 7 boards with the mysterious white figures on a black oil-cloth and the games would commence all along the line-in tents, on cracker boxes, on forage sacks and wherever seats could be improvised. In fact, at some points where the troops were paid off there was nothing to buy and nothing to spend money for, and the boys that did not send their money home must spend it in some manner, and in some instances a devotee of the alluring game of "draw poker" or "old sledge" would sit down after being paid off and at one sitting put every dime he had in the "Jack pot." But the players were all very liberal, good-hearted fellows, and when a comrade got "broke" they would always "put up a stake" for him until next pay day, if he was "a square fellow."

Some soldiers always had money, and would loan it to the comrades that were always broke, and usually never had a scratch of a pen for it. It was a debt of honour, and if the soldier lived and was with his command the next pay day, he would pay it, and if he died the account was settled and the lender was perfectly satisfied and charged it up to "profit and loss."

If the small dealers gave Sergeant Lucas a chance to play "without limit" he would break their banks every time, for he always had plenty of money and carried a big roll of greenbacks in his inside vest pocket, on the right side, and when the players saw John go down into that pocket with his left hand and take out his big roll it made them turn pale. Sometimes the dealer would buy him off not to play for a day and perhaps give him fifty dollars. But the temptation was so great that he could not keep away from the game, and he would come around and look on a while and become so interested that he would say to the dealer: "Just let me play once," and would give him ten dollars for the privilege, and if the dealer consented, John would go down after that big roll and likely take out a fifty dollar bill and put it down. If he won, he would quietly put it in his pocket, and if he lost he would walk off as unconcerned as if he had been playing pin. If there were hundreds of dollars on the board all depending on the turn of a card you never could detect the least change in his countenance, but he would get very much wrought up, if it was not noticeable, for at times he would place a faro or poker chip between his front teeth and bite it in two pieces.

In the spring of 1864 the regiment was stationed at Columbia, Tenn., for a short time after we had returned from veteran furlough, and Lucas got into a game with some citizens and his winnings were very heavy, and at one time he sent home five thousand five hundred dollars.

Sheeley Long, of Company F, was another well-known character and a great forager. He was into mischief continuously, but was usually smart enough to get out of it without getting caught or punished, but if he was punished he always came up smiling and ready for some new adventure. He was a little light-haired fellow and could stand up and look you in the eye, the very personification of innocence, if he was accused of any misdemeanour, and at the same time be stealing your watch or pocket-book. When the regiment was at Lebanon, Ky., in the winter of 1862, Captain Cupp had bracelets put on his ankles, with a chain about a foot long, and he hobbled around camp in that plight for some time. At another time the captain had him tied to the rear end of a wagon, when we were on the march, and compelled him to walk, and gave strict orders to the mule driver to not, under any circumstances, allow him to ride. But before the end of the day Sheeley, by his smooth tongue, got on the good side of the mule whacker and was driving the mules, and the driver was riding in the wagon.

He was always on the good side of the sutler and in a busy time after pay-day would offer his good services to the sutler and help him out as clerk, all for nothing, of course; but Sheeley paid himself well, all the same, and the old shark of a Jew was none the wiser. He was a very liberal clerk and the boys all wanted to buy of him, and often there would be a great jam in front of the counter in front of the sutler's tent, and frequently, when some soldier would purchase a dime's worth of cheese, Sheeley would hand out the cheese with one hand and with the other hand out a bottle of wine under the counter, worth two or three dollars, and would keep this up for some time and perhaps hand out a dozen bottles in a few minutes, if the boys would keep up the rush.

Sutlers usually were regular sharks, and their methods of doing business was by sutler's checks from one pay-day to another. These checks were either tickets or metal representing from ten cents to one dollar, and any soldier could go and get a limited amount of checks and the sutler would charge him up on his books with the full amount of them, and then when the soldier made his purchases the sutler would charge him up so as to get at least one hundred per cent, profit for instance, fifty cents a pound for cheese, one dollar for a plug of Navy tobacco, and three dollars for a canteen full of commissary whisky, warranted to kill at a hundred yards. When pay-day arrived, the sutler was on hand at the table beside the paymaster to collect, and he always got his full share of the greenbacks paid out, and would not miss the amount of a few bottles of wine, if the boys did confiscate one now and then. We had a Jew sutler, and a few days after the evacuation of Corinth our wagon train was parked out on the road toward Booneville, and as there were a great many troops passing, the sutler erected his tent by the roadside and did a thriving business. Some of our trainmen gave the passing troops a hint one day that if they would give the thing a start, there would be no serious opposition from anyone in the regiment to confiscating the sutler's stock, as it was getting pretty well run down anyway. No sooner said than done, for two or three fellows gave a few yanks at the guy-ropes and down came the tent and the goods were confiscated in a jiffy, and the Jew sutler in the First Ohio was a thing of the past.

Up went the Jew
And the mourners were few.
Requiscat in pace.

An Interesting Relic

J. W. Johnston, First Sergeant of Company C, accidentally shot himself about thirty miles from Charleston, S. C., near the Cooper River, and died July 7, 1865. He was buried near the village called "The Barrons," and one of his comrades carved very skillfully, out of yellow pine, a neat headboard, and placed it at the head of his grave.

In 1866 an ex-Confederate soldier by the name of Ernest H. Rowell, of Oakley, S. C., wrote a letter to the *National Tribune* regarding the grave of Johnston. Sergeant John W. Chapin, who was then a clerk in the Adjutant-General's office, had his attention called to the letter published in the *Tribune*, and wrote a letter to the department at Washington, asking that the remains be removed to one of the National Cemeteries, and at his request the Quartermaster-General of the U. S. Army had the remains moved to the Florence National Cemetery, Grave No. 3998, Section A, and the headboard was forwarded to Chapin by the superintendent of the cemetery at Florence, S. C., and it is now in the Relic Room at the State House, Columbus, O., in a good state of preservation.

The letters in the *National Tribune*, giving account of this matter, discovered two brothers of Johnston, and they were much pleased to learn of the disposition of his body, as it seems they had never learned the particulars regarding his death and burial. No doubt, surviving members of Company C will recall the circumstance connected with the accident and Johnston's death.

Reunions of the Regiment

Soon after the close of the war two or three informal reunions of the regiment were held in Columbus, O. But few members of the regiment were in attendance, and no record was kept of these meetings. The first minutes kept was at the reunion held at Columbus, O., August 10, 1880, and below is given the date and place of all reunions since 1880, with names of the President and Secretary elected each year.

Columbus, Ohio, August 10, 1880
J W Chapin, Secretary,   W L Curry, President

Columbus, Ohio, September 2, 1881
J W Chapin, Secretary,   W L Curry, President

Columbus, Ohio, September 20, 1882
J W Chapin, Secretary,   George R Carr, President

Columbus, Ohio, July 25, 1883
W L Curry, Secretary,   J W Kirkendall, President

Marysville, Ohio, September 17, 1884
W L Curry, Secretary,   J W Kirkendall, President

Washington C H, Ohio, August 10, 1885
T D McElwaine, Secretary,   C M Riggs, President

Dayton, Ohio, September 23, 1886
William Rhoads, Secretary,   J W Chapin, President

Columbus, Ohio, August 17, 1887
William Rhoads, Secretary,   L F Knoderer, President

Columbus, Ohio, September 11, 1888
William Rhoads, Secretary,   R Wirth, President

Covington, Ohio, October 8, 1889
W L Curry, Secretary,   N B Teeter, President

Columbus, Ohio, September 16, 1890
W L Curry, Secretary,   M T Vanpelt, President

Newark, Ohio, September 15, 1891

W L Curry, Secretary,   J W Kirkendall, President

Galloway, Ohio, September 13, 1892

W L Curry, Secretary,   D B Peters, President

Columbus, Ohio, August 29, 1893

W L Curry, Secretary,   J W Chapin, President

Basil, Ohio, September 4, 1894

W L Curry, Secretary,   Adam Roley, President

National Military Park, Chickamauga, Ga, September 19, 1895

L F Knoderer, Secretary,   D B Peters, President

Millersport, Ohio, September 16, 1896

W L Curry, Secretary,   C W Click, President

Columbus, Ohio, September 22, 1897

W L Curry, Secretary,   Matthew Williams, President

THE ARMY MULE

You may sing of your beans and hardtack
Of bad water you drank from the pool;
Of tincup, canteen and haversack;
But you must not forget the old mule.

Chorus:
Good old mule, army mule,
Both your ears were so graceful and long.
You were true to our flag,
So we'll praise you in story and song.

The much-abused, patient and long-enduring mule was a very important factor during the war and he deserves the sincere thanks of every boy who wore the blue for his long, faithful and loyal service. The old saying, that a mule will live quietly and peaceably with his owner for twenty years just to get to kick him once when opportunity offers, is a base slander, and if it were true, the owner has no good reason for making a kick, if the mule did kick, for a service of so many years a part of the time, no doubt, feeding on weeds and wagon-tongues, should entitle him to some privileges and a little pleasure as he is about to wind up his useful career.

The mule is a generous animal, which is abundantly demonstrated by his acts of kindness and charity, of which we have many examples, where he divided up his rations with the boys.

When General Thomas army was in and about Chattanooga in the fall of 1863 and the cracker line was cut off down as far as Bridgeport, Ala., and all supplies had to be wagoned over the mountains, rations were pretty short Many animals starved, and during a part of the time the soldiers lived on parched corn, and that was issued out very sparingly. One morning a good-looking, waggish soldier went up to General Thomas' head quarters, and finding "Pap Thomas" out in front of his tent, saluted and then requested the general to give him an order on the quartermaster for a quart of shelled corn. The general, who always looked very carefully after his soldiers, enquired if he had not received his ration of corn from the quartermaster the day before. "Yes," said the wag, "I did; but last night I was on guard, and, getting very hungry, I borrowed a quart of corn of a mule and promised to pay him back this morning. I went down to the quartermaster this morning and asked him about it, but he said he had just enough corn to go around and not an extra grain. You see, general, I am up a stump, and the whole mule brigade will be kicking, if I don t pay up, and I won't be able to borrow any more corn." The general smiled, took in the situation, and the soldier got his order for the extra quart of corn.

Another good story is told about General Wilson and some cavalrymen down at Gravelly Springs, Ala. After the battle of Nashville, in December, 18G4, General Wilson with his cavalry corps followed up Hood's retreating army to the Tennessee River and went into camp at Gravelly Springs. For some reason rations were very short and corn was issued and parched by the soldiers. Many of the soldiers were very indignant and the commanding officer came In for his share of abuse. When General Wilson and staff would ride through the camp, the soldiers would shout: "Hard tack! Hard tack!" One day a clown of a fellow got a piece of picket rope and pressed four of his comrades into the service and made pretence of hitching them up like mules. He then got a long whip and commenced driving his team up toward General Wilson's headquarters, swearing and urging his refractory team along in the most approved mule-whackers' style. A staff officer out in front of Wilson's headquarters yelled at the driver rather gruffly and wished to know what he was doing. "Doing?" said the trooper. "Can't you see? Why, I have just fed my mules and now I am driving 'em down to water. Get up there, Jack!" and on they went, the mules giving the familiar Ah, he! as they started off.

The mule was just as much a part of the necessary equipments of an army as the musket or sabre. An army cannot march or fight unless they are fed, and in a mountainous and rough country, in which the theatre of war was largely located during the rebellion, rations, ammunition and supplies could only be transported by mules either in wagons or by the pack saddle.

The mule is a headstrong, independent and stubborn creature and requires a certain amount of drill and discipline before he is ready for army service. It is a mistaken idea generally that people have about mules being hard to break. While he will kick and has an inclination to either pull back or lie down when his education is commenced, still in a few days he is subdued, and his driver has but little trouble with him there after, excepting now and then he will kick or balk. He does not scare like a horse, but when there is anything like a general stampede, which would happen sometimes when a wagon train was attacked, then look out; for when a mule starts, he never knows when to stop, but goes on until he is compelled to halt by reason of running up against a fence, a tree or something stronger than a mule team, or stops from sheer exhaustion. Then, as if to show his utter contempt for the stampede, and to convince his driver that he was not scared half as bad as the driver himself, he will go to nibbling grass as serene and composed as if he had just been turned out to graze.

The morning after the battle of Perryville, a mule was found eating grass upon the field with a hole through his neck, made by a four or six-pound cannon ball. By examination it was found that the ball had passed entirely through the neck, leaving a gaping wound through which you could see; still the mule was enjoying his morning meal.

The mules, delivered by the boat-load and train-load at Louisville, Kentucky, and Nashville, Tennessee the main depots of supplies for the Army of the Cumberland were young and unbroken, and the large majority of them had never been haltered. They were run into dirty and unusually muddy corrals, hundreds of them together, and in a few days were issued out to the quartermasters, and in a short time were doing duty for Uncle Sam, either hauling rations or ammunition to the front.

The mule did not submit gracefully and without protest. No, indeed; he had to be "broken in" just like the tenderfoot soldier who joined a veteran regiment at the front, as both mule and recruit generally made a vigorous kick.

All around these corrals were funnel-shaped shoots, with wide end running toward the centre of the corral and getting narrower until it was just wide enough for one mule to squeeze in, and this narrow part was sufficiently long to take in perhaps twenty-five mules. When a quartermaster required a certain number of mules, he would make his requisition, and when all was in readiness he would report at the corral with just twice the number of men as the mules he was to draw. The fun would then begin, as the soldiers would drive a large number of mules into the shoot, and keep crowding and urging them forward until the narrow part of the shoot was full, and then strong bars were run across in rear of the last mule and the whole twenty-five were safely corralled, as they could neither move forward, backward or sideways. When a sufficient number were run into the shoots, the men mounted the platforms, erected along the outside, and commenced the work of haltering or bridling. When this was finished the front bars were taken out and the front mule would make a lunge for liberty, but find himself checked somewhat by a pull on the strong halter by two earnest, reckless, swearing mule drivers, who would curb his vigorous spirit for a moment. But after a brief pause he eyes his captors with a tired, disdainful look, and then commences operations earnestly by another rapid run and jump, carrying the two trainers off their feet and dragging them through the mud, which is a perfect lake, half boot-top deep, several rods and then comes another halt, which the boys improve by wrapping the rope halter around a friendly tree. By this time there are perhaps fifty mules out, with mules and men all cutting about the same kind of gymnastics, but varied a little according to the size and activity of the mule and the grit of the soldiers. After duly considering the situation, mule No. 1 will likely open up the play again by making an attempt to pull down the tree around which his cruel captors have tightly wrapped the strong rope halter. He gives a hard pull, then a vigorous lunge and proceeds to settle down to a long, hard pull, but the tree is too strong and he is choked down, but not conquered, as he commences kicking and pawing the mud as he lies down with a rapidity that would shame a drummer beating the "long roll." The boys are now splattered from head to foot and look like they had taken an up-to-date mud bath. The mule now lays quietly in his soft mud bed, but a few sharp kicks in the back and jerking of the rope brings him to his feet, ready for a grand-stand play. The boys chuckle and say "he is broke," and one of them proceeds in a moment of thoughtlessness or absent-mindedness to venture up and pat him on the head, but a moment afterwards, as he picked himself up out of the mud, having run against the mule's hind foot, he took it all back and declared he was honestly mistaken. The halters were long, and at times the mules and men would be mixed up in a general *mêlée* as they jumped, kicked and ran around each other; and the mule, heeding the admonition of the Irishman in the fight, when he said, "Whenever you see a head, hit it," would let loose with both heels, and was not particular whether he hit a mule or a man.

Finally the mules would all be worked out through the gates and to the camp after many pulls, licks and kicks, and after getting out on the pike it was absolutely necessary to take a little stimulant to keep off the malaria, and the quartermaster usually "set em up" by producing a few canteens full of bourbon or Robinson County.

But the trouble was not all over when the mules were all safely landed at the camp, for they must be harnessed, hitched up to a big government wagon and made to pull a load, for that is what they entered the service for. The wagons were new, the harness was new and strong, some of the collars were large enough to go around the mule's body, and now the picnic begins. A mule would be jammed back into fence-corner perhaps by four or five men to be bridled and harnessed, and before the harnessing was completed he would likely be lying down, and when after a long, hard fight all was ready, the wagon wheels were locked with six mad, stubborn mules in front of it and a resolute young soldier at the head of each mule, and when the word "go" was given, perhaps the first move would be into the ditch or against the fence. This would be kept up all day, and perhaps there would be a runaway or two, but the boys did not care for that, for it was all in the business. With the first day the hard work was over, and while the driver would have a man or two to help him for a few days, yet within a week he would be riding the wheel mule and driving the leader of a six-mule team with a single line.

Every quartermaster, wagonmaster and mule driver knows that this account of breaking mule-teams is not overdrawn in the least. It was most ridiculous and amusing to witness the antics of the mules in the process of breaking-in.

This kind of work could only be done by a lot of reckless, resolute young soldiers, who seemed to enjoy the whole business, although at times some of them would get pretty badly banged up; but he would laugh it off by consoling himself that some other fellow got used as bad as he did.

The mule, unlike the horse, is subdued in a few days and goes to work as faithfully as if he were drawling a good salary from the government. But he would kick now and then, balk and lie down for a rest, and was more liable to halt in the mud than on dry ground. When a mule makes up his mind to lie down, no amount of persuasion can convince him that he is wrong, and down he goes. The mule driver's "black snake" often only seemed to amuse him as the driver applied it with the regulation cussing.

Lieutenant Cole, of the Third O.V. C., Quartermaster of the Second Brigade, was the champion convincer and never failed, but his methods were rather severe. When a mule laid down in the mud, Cole would have the balance of the team unhitched and would then fasten a picket rope around the mule's body, just behind the fore legs; to this picket rope he would hitch a mule team and drag the recalcitrant animal out of the mud and over the dry ground until he began to scramble to his feet. And it was a sure cure, as the mule would resume work with great earnestness and solemn promise that he would never lie down in the mud again as long as Cole was in command of the wagon train.

Mules make the best teams for army service, and in fact they are the only animal that can be depended upon for transportation of army supplies in a mountainous country as Virginia, Kentucky, Tennessee, Georgia, Alabama and the Carolinas, the great theatre of the war of the rebellion. They can live and travel much longer without water than the horse; they can subsist on much less grain, but they must have coarse forage, as the mule would often leave grain untasted in the feed trough for dead weeds.

Thousands of wagon-tongues and wagon-beds were literally eaten up by mules, when they were short of hay, straw or other coarse forage. With great loads of ammunition or army supplies they would ascend or descend steep and dangerous mountain passes, where a cavalryman was compelled to dismount and lead his horse, picking his steps carefully, momentarily in danger of making a misstep and toppling over some precipice.

In addition to the mule-teams the pack-mule was indispensable in the cavalry service. In raids where the movements were very rapid, the pack-teams were the only means of transportation for rations and ammunition. The pack-saddle consists of a wooden tree with cantel and pommel running up high, and on either side of the saddle are great pockets, made of tarpaulin or wicker baskets, holding from two to three bushels each. In these panniers were packed rations, ammunition, picks, shovels and cooking utensils. Little mules would carry enormous loads, and if the load was not packed equally on either side, in ascending steep mountain roads, the pack-mule would often fall, and then the load had to be unpacked, or three or four soldiers, by dint of hard lifting, would raise him to his feet, then off he would go as nimble as ever. In the night, pack-mules would frequently fall over the ledges and down the mountain side; and wagons with a six-mule team attached would often topple over, taking mules and drivers down among the brush and trees, In many places the mountain passes would be so steep that the wagon had to be let down by ropes and manned by perhaps twenty-five stalwart soldiers to keep the loads from running over and crushing the teams. During the last two years of the war the soldiers carried everything, including their "dog tents," with perhaps one wall tent to the regiment for the colonel's headquarters, one quartermaster's tent and one or two hospital tents. Where we had ten wagons the first two years of the war, we had one the last two years. Each company had about six pack-mules, and on the march, if we were not anticipating a fight, the pack-train of each company marched in the rear of the company to which they belonged; but if we struck the enemy, all pack-trains soon dropped back to the rear and were put in charge of the quartermaster-sergeant or commissary. A long train of pack-mules winding up a mountain road was a grotesque and interesting picture that is indelibly impressed on the memory of every soldier of the regiment.

The Cavalier

While stationed at Fayetteville the First Ohio published a newspaper called the *Cavalier*, which was edited by William Davis, of Company M, and A. Thompson, of Company D, with

T. C. Stevenson and Joe Devreux, of Company D, publishers. The motto at the heading read: "We Go Where Rebs Await Us." As will be remembered, it was a spicy sheet, and some poetic cavalryman wrote a parody on Morgan's mule, which ran thus:

Turchin's Got Your Mule

A planter came to camp one day,
His niggers for to find,
His Mules had also gone astray,
And stock of every kind.
The planter tried to get them back,
And thus was made a fool,
For every one he met in camp
Cried "Mister here's your Mule."

    Chorus:— *Go back, go back, go back, old scamp,*
    And don t be made a fool,
    Your niggers they are all in camp
    And Turchin's got your Mule.

His corn and horses all were gone
Within a day or two,
Again he went to Col. Long,
To see what he could do.
I cannot change what I have done,
I won't be made a fool,
Was all the answer he could get,
The owner of the mule.

And thus from place to place we go,
The song is e'er the same,
'Tis not as once it used to be,
For Morgan's lost his name.
He went up North and there he stays,
With stricken face, the fool;
In Cincinnati now he cries,
    "My Kingdom for a Mule."

An Incident of the Tullahoma Campaign
An Unwritten Chapter in the History of the War

On the morning of the first of July, 1863, the Second Cavalry Division, having passed through Manchester, closed up with the army and took position directly east and some three miles distant from Tullahoma.

The First Ohio Cavalry having the advance, Company K was immediately detailed for picket duty and was posted on the direct road to Tullahoma. The position chosen for the reserve picket was closely flanked on either side of the road by a thick growth of low, scrubby timber and thickets of brushwood, while the videttes were thrown well forward to a turn in the road, in such position that they could observe any advance by the enemy two or three hundred yards to the front. We were sup ported by a grand guard of a regiment of infantry. Scarcely was there time to make a disposition of the guard, when a sharp picket fire began in our front, and was kept up with but little cessation for an hour or two. Just about sunset the enemy's cavalry made a dash on our picket post and were warmly received by the videttes, the ever vigilant Tom Gregg and Ned Garner, who emptied their carbines and fell back to the reserve in good order. This little skirmish was followed by a comparatively quiet night.

The videttes were relieved on the morning of the second and fell back to the reserve, tired and sleepy, and reported "all quiet in front." By eight o'clock the sun was coming down hot, with 100 Fahrenheit in the shade, and the reserves were glad to seek the inviting shade of the thick woods which skirted the road.

Everything seemed unusually still; not a sound was heard save now and then a stray picket shot at the front. About ten o'clock a shot was heard near the road, on the advance line, and in a few moments a shout came from the thick woods, as if from some one in distress. Riding out to the videttes to learn if any of our men were wounded, it was found that the shot had been fired by one of our pickets, and it was thought that one of the enemy's pickets had been wounded, or that it was a ruse, often practised by both armies, to induce the pickets to make a reconnaissance in front in order to get a fair shot. The shouting still continuing, we became satisfied that it was no ruse, and, riding back to the grand guard, asked the officer in command to send a company forward and reconnoitre the front, as the men of our company were all on duty, but he declined to do so. Two troopers of our company were then dismounted and moved down into the thick woods and soon reached a wounded man, who was stretched out on his back and seemed to be suffering intense pain. The boys raised him up and, forming a stretcher by locking their hands together, carried him hastily back to the reserve and laid him down beside the road.

He was an old man, dressed in the usual Confederate gray, but was not armed, and had nothing about his person to indicate that he was a soldier, except that an old haversack hung over his shoulders. He was shot through the body near the lungs, and was pale and weak from loss of blood.

We immediately began interrogating him in regard to the Confederate army at Tullahoma, and he declared emphatically that the place had been evacuated at daybreak that morning, and that there was not a soldier within the works. We doubted his word and so told him, as we knew it was usual for a good soldier, when taken prisoner by the enemy, to evade giving any information in regard to the army to which he belonged. But I shall never forget the pale face of that old man, as he looked up, trembling with fear and pain, and said, in low and measured tones: "There is no reason why I should tell you a falsehood now. I am not long for this world." His voice was so earnest, his pale face so impressive, that we could not doubt his statement. Questioned as to his name, command and residence, he said that he was not a soldier, but had been at Tullahoma, and in trying to make his way through our lines to his home at Manchester, twelve miles to the east, had been taken for a rebel soldier and shot by one of our pickets, and that his name was Duncan.

Immediately on receiving the information that Bragg had evacuated Tullahoma, which, if true, I knew to be very important to the commanding general, I mounted my horse and galloped rapidly back to the lines and encampments. The first headquarters reached were General George Crook's, who, with one of his staff, sat in front of his tent playing chess, to whom I rapidly related Duncan's story. "Why in the d—l," said he, "didn't you take your company, make a dash and capture the works and put a big feather in your cap?" But I replied that as "discretion" was considered "the better part of valour," I had not been anxious to distinguish myself and company by making a dash against Bragg's fortifications. He then directed me to ride rapidly to General Thomas' headquarters and deliver the information, a command I lost no time in obeying.

I was only too glad to be the bearer of such important information to the grand old hero.

Reaching headquarters on the gallop and covered with mud, I was of course known to be from the front, and at once relieved by the orderlies of my horse and directed to the general's tent. As I approached, I saw him rise from a cot, on which he had been lying in his shirt sleeves, and advance to the door of the tent to receive me. Saluting, I at once related in detail the news as given by Duncan of the evacuation of Tullahoma, to which he gave earnest attention. He inquired particularly of Duncan, of his story of himself, his manner, the gravity of his wound, if I believed the wound fatal, and if I put faith in his statement. I had myself not a moment's doubt of the wounded man, and so stated, and my confidence seemed to decide the general, who at once called to his Adjutant, Flint, to order an immediate forward movement of the army.

The first order was for Brannan's division to move out carefully, and in five minutes the bugles were blowing "boots and saddles," drums beating the "long roll," and the quiet camp was all astir with the bustle and preparation for the forward move. My mission ended and about to take my horse, I said to the General that ours was the only cavalry command immediately on the Tullahoma road, and that the "boys" were anxious to lead the advance when the army moved, and asked that they be permitted to do so. The permission was readily given, and I was ordered to join my company and particularly directed to feed our horses from a little field of wheat, just ripened near the reserve, and be ready to move as soon as the advance of the infantry and artillery reached the outposts.

This little wheat field had possibly escaped my notice, but here was a commanding General, burdened with the care and responsibility of a great army, whose notice it had not escaped, and who in that hasty moment thoughtfully turned it over to the horses of our command. The circumstance impressed me at the time as a striking exhibit of one of the qualities of mind which made a great general of George H. Thomas.

Reaching the outpost, our horses were soon profiting by the good general's kindly order, and in less than thirty minutes there was scarcely a straw of that little field of wheat left standing.

Very soon after, the advance of the infantry, General Reynold's division, reached the outposts, marching at a "right shoulder shift," with artillery well closed up. Halting a few moments, the general in command questioned particularly in regard to the enemy in front, and as to the story of the evacuation as told by Duncan. He then directed that our company should form a skirmish line and move rapidly forward toward Tullahoma, and not halt until we should strike the enemy.

We did move forward, as directed, and marched straightway, without firing a shot, into the abandoned works of the rebels, who, as Duncan truthfully stated, were gone, "horse, foot and rider."

I had suggested to General Thomas that an ambulance should be sent out to the picket post for the wounded man, and on inquiry a few days after found that he had been removed to the hospital. Supposing his wound a fatal one, I had no doubt he would soon die, and I had so stated to General Thomas. Still I had never been certain of his death, and in relating the incidents of the campaign, had wondered if he were really dead or living. And as he had given us the news which caused the army to move, I could never get the man out of my mind as connected with the evacuation of Tullahoma.

A few years ago I received a Washington newspaper, in which

was a letter by General Rosecrans giving a history of the Tullahoma campaign. Again I thought of the man Duncan, and resolved to try and learn if he had really died of his wounds, or was still living. I accordingly wrote to the postmaster at Manchester, Tenn., inquiring for the man and narrating the circumstance of his being shot. I asked to be informed particularly of him if alive, and, if dead, for the address of some of his family or friends to whom I might communicate the particulars of the shooting.

In a few days a reply came from the postmaster, saying that Duncan was still living, and that he had often heard him tell the perilous story of his being wounded. He said that Duncan still suffered from the wound, and further that he had always been a loyal man, never borne arms against the government, and when wounded was simply making his way home from a visit to a son who was in the rebel army at Tullahoma.

He at the same time gave me Duncan's address, to whom I wrote and from whom I very soon received a thankful reply. He was rejoiced to find some of the soldiers who knew of his being wounded; he had been for many years seeking the officer who was at the time in command of the outpost. He said he was now, as he had always been, a loyal man, and that although he had been suspected and his property confiscated, he had never lost faith that the "god of battle" would some day set him right; and that since hearing so kindly from the Union soldiers who had been the unwitting cause of his sufferings, he could see the dawn of better days. He was over seventy-six years of age, and had all these years been in constant pain from the wound. He sent me his photograph, which shows a tall, gray-haired old man, with an honest, sympathetic face; and it seems to me that after all these years I can detect in the features the same pale-faced and suffering man who lay by the roadside that memorable second day of July, 1863, and truthfully told the story of the evacuation of Tullahoma by the Confederates.

The incident of the wounding and the importance of the news communicated by Duncan made such an impression on my mind that the man's face has been ever since before me like a vision. Although I saw him but a few moments, and that in the excitement of a hurried interrogation as to the movements of the enemy, the impression was so vivid that time has served only to strengthen the memory of it. And an unseen hand seems to have directed me to write, for when I saw him lying wounded, I firmly believed that in a few hours time he would surely die.

He referred very feelingly in his letter to the fact of his having had considerable Confederate money at the time, which had been taken from him by some of the grand guard, not of our command, and which we had ordered returned. Among other things taken from him and returned he mentioned an old tobacco box, carried by his grandfather in the Revolutionary War, and which he still had in his possession. He also said that he has always believed that his life was saved by the use of the "square and compass," signs of the Masonic order, of which he seems to have been a member. What I myself did for him, however, was through common humanity, as I too had once been a prisoner and knew how to sympathize with him. It seems that he was some two weeks in our hospital, where he had received, at General Rosecrans' special order, the best possible attention.

It seems strange that, after so many, many years, I should so easily reach the man and find myself in friendly correspondence with him. I carried on a friendly correspondence with him for some time, and at his suggestion wrote to two or three ex-Confederate officers and made inquiry as to his loyalty, and several of these officers made affidavit that he was a strong Union man through all the years of the war.

I then wrote Congressman Houk, of Tennessee, and General J. S. Robinson, member of Congress from the district where I resided, and enlisted them in his behalf. I then procured a large number of affidavits from both Union and Confederate soldiers as to his loyalty and the value of his property confiscated by our army. Everything was in readiness to have a bill introduced in Congress to pay him for the property confiscated, but just as his papers had been completed and before the bill was introduced, he died, on the eighth day of December, 1883.

A Visit to Chickamauga
Thirty Years After the Battle of September 20, 1863

On the evening of September 13, 1892, with Captain Kirkendall and my daughter, I took the Big Four train for Cincinnati *en route* for Chattanooga to attend the reunion of the Army of the Cumberland, to be held on the Chickamauga battle field, September 15 and 16. From Cincinnati we took the Queen and Crescent route at eight o'clock on the morning of September 14 for Chattanooga, and had a delightful ride across the States of Kentucky and Tennessee, passing through the famous blue-grass region and Lexington noted for its fine cattle, fast horses and handsome women.

The road runs through a very rough and mountainous region from Danville, Ky., there being upward of twenty tunnels cut through the mountains and many of them quite long. On this line is the highest trestle in America at "High Bridge" across the Kentucky River, being two hundred and eighty-four feet in height, and next to the highest in the world; one bridge in Switzerland being six inches higher.

The road passes through Somerset, Ky., near the battle field of Wild Cat, where General Thomas defeated Zollicoffer on the twentieth day of January, 1802, and the latter officer lost his life. As will be remembered by all comrades who were in the regiment in 1861, the First Ohio was ordered from Camp Buell, at Louisville, to join General Thomas, but when we reached Lebanon, Ky., the battle had been fought and we halted here and went into camp for several weeks. The mention of the name of the famous Camp Frankenberger, I think, will refresh the memory of every comrade as to the history of this march and the camp on the side of the mountain, and the torrent that rushed through the valley below and swept oft the saddles and equipments of the companies that camped near the stream.

The next morning after arriving at Chattanooga we were up bright and early and took the train for Crawfish Springs, distant thirteen miles. The railroad runs along the line of the Dry Valley road and about two hundred yards west from the Widow Glenn's house, where General Rosecrans had his headquarters September 20, 1863, during the battle.

Arriving at Crawfish Springs, or Chickamauga, as the station is called, we were just in time to attend the business meeting of the Society of the Army of the Cumberland, held at the Park Hotel, a very large summer hotel and resort erected near the Spring. Generals Rosecrans, Morgan, Reynolds, Tom Wood, Boynton, Baird, Beatty, Barnett and other brigade and division commanders were present at the meeting, all with hair white as snow, but all happy and seemingly renewing their youth again, as they meet and greet each other after a lapse of twenty- nine years since the great battle of Chickamauga.

The stream formed by the spring has been dammed up about a hundred yards below where the spring bursts from the bank, thus forming a lake, but destroying the old spring completely. The old water-wheel is gone and not a vestige of anything remains by which the Crawfish Springs of September 20, 1863, can be recognized.

We visited the Lee House just up the hill from the spring about two hundred yards, where our division hospital was established Sunday afternoon, and where Colonel Cupp died in the south-east parlour about 4 p. m., September 20, and found but little change in the grand old brick plantation house with its wide halls and beautiful lawn dotted with flowers and stately forest trees. This house has just passed out of the hands of the Lees, and is owned by the land syndicate that platted the village of Chickamauga adjoining. We went back to the rear of the house about one hundred yards to the edge of the woods and facing east looked south-west across the old fields, where the second line was formed after we fell back from our first line near Glass Mills. There was no change in the old fields, and as we gazed again and again it seemed that we could see the line of tramping horses and bright, gleaming sabres as we formed the long lines on that bright Sabbath day and waited anxiously and watched intently for the attack of the enemy from the woods;

but, as will be remembered, no attack was made, and we formed a skirmish line and moved into the woods and brought Colonel Cupp and many other wounded back to the hospital. We then fell back into the woods and stood to horse until about 5 o'clock p. m., and during the time we held this line and listened to the thundering of Thomas guns on Snodgrass Hill to the left. I have always thought that this was the heaviest cannonading we ever heard during our four years' service. The old road running north-west from the rear of the Lee House to Chattanooga Valley and over which we fell back and lighted our fires Sunday evening, does not seem to have changed, and is yet unfenced, running through the woods.

General Beatty, Colonel Kellogg—who was an aid on General Thomas staff,—Captain Barker and Captain Kirkendall, of the First Ohio Cavalry, Captain James Thomson, of the Fourth Ohio Cavalry, and myself were in the group that examined our lines, and it was an intensely interesting meeting, as all took part in the battle on some part of the field.

In the afternoon we hired a rig consisting of a pair of historic army mules, a big wagon and a native Georgia boy, with a complexion as red as the Georgian sand, and who could give us the Southern brogue and spit tobacco juice in true Southern style. Our party consisted of Captain Thomson, Captain Kirkendall, my daughter Ivaloo and self.

We had also secured the services of a citizen by the name of K. S. Shaw, who was in the Fourth Georgia Confederate Cavalry and under command of General Wheeler in the fight of Sunday, and was with the dismounted cavalry that attacked us in the morning.

The distance from Crawfish Springs to our first line near Glass Mills, where Colonel Cupp was wounded, is about one and a half miles, and over one of the stoniest and roughest roads in Georgia; but after about an hour's bouncing over the rocks we arrived on the grounds all safe and with no broken bones. We had no difficulty in locating the grounds and satisfied our selves beyond a doubt as to almost the exact location of the Chicago Board of Trade Battery, as I had in company with comrade A. A. Hill, of Company K, examined the grounds three years ago, as had also Sergeant C. S. Irwin, of Company K, who was wounded on the spot.

Shaw, who had lived in the vicinity before, and ever since the war, was very positive that we had our first line, where Colonel Cupp was wounded, correctly located, and we spent the afternoon examining the surroundings. The next day we hired another mule team from Frank Osborn, who was also a Confederate soldier and served under John Morgan, and perhaps they were some of Morgan's mules, made famous in story and song. We devoted the day to visiting other points on the battle-field, and, as may not be known to all, the government has purchased about seven thousand acres of land, comprising the greater part of the battle-field, for a military park, and are now constructing some very fine drives and boulevards of gravel and crushed stone, also cutting out the underbrush, and this will be for all future time a grand military park, protected and cared for by the government. We started from Battle Station, situated on the railroad and about three miles from Crawfish Springs, and first visited Snodgrass Hill, where the "Rock of Chickamauga," General Thomas, held the whole rebel army at bay during that long and bloody battle Sunday afternoon.

The old Snodgrass house stands there yet and the oak tree in the yard, where the brave old hero made his headquarters during the great struggle, and the cotton-field in front, where balls may yet be found, shot from thousands of hot musket-barrels. From noon until night the five divisions of "Thomas' line" successfully resisted and held in check the entire Confederate army.

As the principal object of this reunion was to mark the lines of battle, everywhere we would see groups of officers and soldiers earnestly discussing the situation and marking the lines of regiments and brigades. The Second Brigade, Second Cavalry Division, to which our regiment belonged, consisted of the First, Third and Fourth Ohio Cavalry, Second Kentucky Cavalry and the Chicago Board of Trade Battery, the brigade being commanded by Colonel Eli Long and the division by General Geo. Crook. The delegates appointed to fix the line of battle and select the position for erecting the monuments for the brigade consisted of Captain James W. Kirkendall and Captain W. L. Curry, First O.V. C,; Hon. G. W. Salsgaber, Third O.V. C., and Captain Jas. Thomson, Fourth O.V. C.

We had a consultation with members of the National Commission and also with the Ohio Commission, and as the line of battle of our brigade was some distance to the right of the centre of the battle-field and on a country road but little travelled and outside of the park, it was decided to erect our monuments on the grounds of the military park, the position selected being on the Dry Valley Road, about two and a half miles north from Crawfish Springs and two hundred yards south-west from the Widow Glenn's house, where General Rosecrans' headquarters were on Sunday, the twentieth, and where Wilder's brigade is now erecting a monument one hundred feet high. The point selected is a prominent place and will be visited by all persons who visit the battle-field, as it is only a half mile from Battle Station.

After completing our work on the battle-field we spent one day visiting the objects of interest in Chattanooga, Lookout Mountain, Missionary Ridge and the National Cemetery. The objects of interest about Chattanooga are numerous. For a good view of the city you should visit Cameron Hill, in the heart of the city, which is reached by an inclined plane, and also Orchard Knob and Missionary Ridge and the National Cemetery. It contains the graves of 13,060 Union soldiers; 8,092 known, and 4,968 unknown. It is beautifully laid out and well kept, and contains seventy-five and one-half acres of land and is enclosed by a heavy limestone wall four and one-half feet high. I was informed by the superintendent that the site for this cemetery was selected by General Thomas, while he stood on Orchard Knob, during the progress of the battle of Mission Ridge in November, 1863, and shortly after that battle active steps were taken to prepare it for interments, so that its establishment dates from

1863. The number of unknown Ohio troops interred is 1,792. It is located just on the eastern boundary of the city, and its eastern slopes were the camping ground of Sheridan's division, just prior to the assault on Missionary Ridge.

The following description of the scene from Lookout Mountain is copied from a Chattanooga newspaper.

"Lookout Mountain is reached by a standard-gauge rail road, ascending to the summit and depositing visitors close to Lookout Inn. An inclined cable railway also runs from the base of the mountain, at the village of St. Elmo to the foot, of the cliff at the nose of the mountain, and connects with a narrow-gauge railroad running along the west side to Sunset Rock and on to the National Bridge Hotel. From Sunset Rock a fine view of the Valley of Lookout Creek is had, and objects can be distinctly seen in three states, Tennessee, Alabama and Georgia. The battle-ground of Wauhatchie is seen below, just beyond Wauhatchie railroad station."

Arriving on top of the mountain, and going forward to the point and standing on the cliff, a magnificent panorama is spread out five states are visible. Beginning at the left, the Wauhatchie battle-ground in the valley; Raccoon Mountain, the high mountain on the left, and Walden's Ridge across the Tennessee River on the right. The Tennessee is visible for a length of twenty miles. The very sharp bend under Lookout Mountain forms Moccasin Point. At the left hand side of the neck of the bend is Brown's Ferry, the scene of an exploit previous to the battle of Chickamauga. A picked force of the Union army proceeded in boats down the river during the night, and scaling the deep hill on the left bank of the river, seized it from the rebels. To the north-east Chattanooga is spread out. When the war broke out, its population was three thousand, nestled close to the river, between Cameron Hill and the high ground to the right of it, The creek between the mountain and the city is Chattanooga Creek. Further to the right, in the plain below, is the National Cemetery, three and a half miles distant; and in line with it and one mile farther away is Orchard Knob, the scene of the second day of the battle of Chattanooga. Missionary Ridge is in full view for many miles. Looking a little north of east, to the summit of Missionary Ridge, is the site of the headquarters of the Confederate commander, General Braxton Bragg. South-east is Rossville Gap, which is in Georgia, just south of the state line, often alluded to in the history of the battle of Chickamauga, which was fought a few miles beyond. The high range of mountains in the distant background, to the north-east, are the Unaka and Great Smoky Mountains, bounding the states of Tennessee and North Carolina.

The entrenchments of our army previous to the three-days' battle enclosed Chattanooga in an arc of a circle of a mile radius, extending from the river at the small towhead in Moccasin Bend, below, to about where Citico Furnace now stands above the town, making a line of fortifications two and a half miles long. The Confederate line extended along the crest of Missionary Ridge five miles, from East Chattanooga station on the north to a point about east of the point of Lookout Mountain, and then four miles farther across the valley toward the observer, and up the mountain to below the nose. The Confederate Fort Bragg still stands on the mountain a few hundred yards back from the point. During the siege a battery on top of the point of the mountain threw shells into the Union army entrenchments for several weeks. In the battle of Lookout Mountain the Union forces under Hooker approached from Wauhatchie, on the west side, and attacked the Confederates stationed under the point. The latter finally retreated to the summit of the mountain and held the Federals at bay until, under cover of the obscurity, they found a place to scale the cliffs on the west side, a short distance back from the point.

About a mile and a half back from Point Lookout is the Natural Bridge; and farther south Rocky City, a great mass of conglomerate rocks, several acres in extent, split up at intervals into crevasses, or streets, as they are called.

Each visit to Lookout Mountain increases the wonder that everybody who can does not go to see it. Aside from the intense interest with which the events of the war clothes its steeps, and the country about it, by the testimony of those who have visited the most natural scenes of the globe, it has a charm and grandeur that gives it high rank even with those who have been the most industrious travellers.

We exchanged our tickets and returned to Cincinnati *via* the L. & N. R. R., passing through many of the old towns so well known to the First Ohio during the war, and where many of the "boys" saw the girl they "left behind" in a few days.

The principal towns being White Sides, Bellfont, Bridgeport, Stevenson, Tantallon, Bell Buckle, Decherd, Murfreesboro the battle-field of Stone River, Lavergne and Nashville. The Stone's River Cemetery contains twenty acres inside of enclosing walls and the interments are as follows:

Known Union soldiers	3,811
Unknown Union soldiers	2,325
Known civilians	5
Unknown civilians	5
Total	6,146

The monument in the cemetery is a shaft of very handsome scrolled sandstone fifteen feet high, surmounted with a large bronze eagle, the feet resting on a large, round, solid cannon ball. The inscription on one side is as follows:

In memory of the officers an enlisted men of the Fifteenth, Sixteenth, Eighteenth and Nineteenth U. S. I. and Battery H, Fifth U. S. Artillery, who were killed or died of wounds received in the battle of Stone River, Tenn., December 31, 1862, to January 3, 1863.

On the other side:

Erected by their comrades of the Regular Brigade, Army of the Cumberland. Erected in 1882." (Also the badge of the Fourteenth Army Corps cut in raised letters.) "The blood of one-third of its soldiers, twice spilled in Tennessee, crimsons the battle-flag of the Brigade, and inspires to greater deeds. The Veterans of Shiloh have left their deathless heritage of fame on the field of Stone River.

Then from Nashville to Louisville over the old route we travelled so often during the war.

We were gone just one week, and had a most enjoyable time, and only wish that every member of the First Ohio living could have been with us.

Prisoners of War

A regiment that was in more than fifty fights, and at least as many more skirmishes was necessarily in contact with the enemy a great many times. As a result many soldiers of both armies would be taken prisoner, and the First Ohio was no exception to that rule. A great many of the First Ohio were taken prisoner, and a short account of their experiences will be of interest to every member of the regiment. While it is not possible to give the total number of soldiers of the regiment, captured, still I have the names of quite a number, and herewith devote a short chapter to some incidents connected with their capture and imprisonment.

When General Wheeler crossed the Tennessee River at Cotton Port, September 30, 1863, one battalion of the First Ohio was guarding a ford and a number of men of Companies K and B were taken prisoners. Of Company K the names were Sergeant Elliott Young, Sergeant Cornelius Byers, Pressley E. Goff, Edward Garner, James Henry, James Stanton, David Nedrow and Frederick Wedo. Of this number, Garner, Wedo, and Goff died in Andersonville, and all of the others had an experience that is well worth relating. They were all sent to Libby Prison, via Atlanta, and in November of the same year were transferred from Libby to Danville, Va. The names of the prisoners taken from Company B I have not been able to find. They were sent from Richmond to Danville in box-cars, and were very closely packed in, with two Confederate guards in each car. In one of these cars it was arranged that they should cut a hole in the end of the car large enough for a soldier to crawl through, and when it became dark, a soldier was to slip through the end of the car, and uncouple the train. They were then to make an attempt to escape. At the front end of the car the large number of prisoners crowded around to cover the operations of two comrades who were cutting a hole through the end of the car with pocket-knives. The next important matter was to look after the guards, and two of the best talkers, including Sergeant Young, were detailed to uncap the muskets of the guards, and they became very familiar with the guards and handled their guns, and finally succeeded in uncapping both of them. The hole in the end of the car was completed, and every thing was arranged to uncouple the train as soon as it was dark, but some of the prisoners became nervous and thought that they were nearing Danville, and uncoupled the train before dark. The front of the train moved forward after the engine, and all of the cars in rear of the one in which the prisoners were making an attempt to escape were of course stopped on the track. As the hole in the end of the car was quite small, it took some time for the prisoners to get through, and there was a great commotion as to who should go out first. Eight of the boys of the First Ohio succeeded in getting out, and of course immediately ran across the fields and woods as rapidly as possible, and the guards began firing and pursuing them. All of the eight who made their escape were recaptured, excepting David Alt, of Company F, who had been left as nurse with Colonel Cupp when he was left at the Lee House at the battle of Chickamauga, and when Colonel Cupp died, he was taken prisoner. Dave Laporte, of Company F, was also one who attempted to escape. Sergeant Young gives a very interesting and graphic description of this escape, as the boys were all intensely excited and were willing to take any kind of chances of being killed in hopes of escape from the rebel prison at Danville, which they well knew was awaiting them. These prisoners remained at Danville until about May, 1864, and were sent from there to Andersonville. They remained at Andersonville until October, 1864, and during this time Garner, Wedo and Goff had all died. From there they went to Charleston, S. C., where they remained about a month, and in November, 1864, were transferred to Florence, where they remained until March, 1865. While at Florence, the prisoners were transferred to another camp, and having some notice of this fact, many of them tried to escape by digging holes under their tents, then covering them over with boards or sticks, and when the order came to move, they crawled down in these holes, and the boards were covered over with sand. Young and another soldier of a different regiment made this attempt, and Jim Stanton, of Company K, covered them over carefully, and when the prisoners had marched out and it was thought that all was safe, some soldier who had been making the same attempt crawled out from his hiding-place, and the guard noticing him, a company of guards was called and made a thorough search of the whole camp by going over the camp and running their bayonets down into the ground to see if they could strike any boards where men were concealed. Young and his comrade were thus routed out, and were taken back to prison in a hurry. In March, 1865, Young and Stanton were sent to Wilmington, S. C., to our lines, and then to Annapolis, Md., where they were exchanged March 14, 1865. Nedrow was exchanged from Andersonville in the fall of 1864, and Henry was exchanged from Libby Prison in the spring of 1864. Byers was separated from the other members of the First Ohio, and was sent back from Andersonville to Richmond, to hospital and then to Annapolis, Md., where he was paroled in the spring of 1864. During the time they were in prison they met many other members of the First Ohio, but I can learn the names of but few of them.

Sergeant Young relates a story about William Miller, of Company F, and himself making an attempt to escape while at Charleston. It seems that Miller had succeeded in getting a detail to assist in a bake-shop, and he and Young laid a plan of escape. In order to have some rations to eat on their long journey from Charleston to our line, Young bought a barrel of flour, for which he paid $1300 in Confederate money, and Miller was to have it baked up, and they were then to make the attempt. After the matter was all arranged, it was learned that Sherman's army was nearing the coast, and the attempt was abandoned and the thirteen hundred dollar barrel of flour was baked up and sold to the other prisoners. It will be under stood by this statement that flour was very high in the Southern Confederacy or that Confederate money was very cheap.

Another story is related about a Confederate soldier who had a horse that he wished to sell, and being offered three thousand dollars for the horse, he spurned the offer indignantly, stating that he had just that morning paid a fellow a thousand dollars to curry his horse.

Thomas A. Morrison, of Company B, was also taken prisoner at the battle of Chickamauga, September 20, 1863. He was then taken to Belle Isle, then to Richmond, Va., and remained there two months, and was then removed to Danville, where he made an escape from prison No. 5 by tunnelling out of the prison, January 28, 1864, in company with A. G. Laughlin, of Company B, Thaddeus McVay, of Company B, David Laporte, of Company F, and Charles Vaughn, of the Second Kentucky Cavalry. After untold hardships during the winter of 1864, laying out in all kinds of weather and almost starved for thirty-six days, they reached our lines at Fayetteville, W. Va., where they were entertained for a few days by the Eleventh and Twelfth O. V. I. They were sent to Charleston, W. Va., and from there to Cincinnati, where they were furloughed home for twenty days, and then joined the regiment at Nashville, Tenn., in the spring of 1864.

Captured
by George W. Spielman, late Saddler Sergeant Company I, First Regiment Ohio Veteran Volunteer Cavalry

During the advance of Buell's army east of Corinth, Miss., along the line of the Memphis and Charleston Railroad, detachments of the regiment were guarding the different bridges and trestles on this road. A part of my company, I, was stationed near Decatur, Alabama, guarding a small bridge. While at this place, on or about the sixteenth day of July, 1862, a regiment of infantry and a squad of about twelve men of the company were sent out to within a short distance of Summerville for the purpose of protecting a large number of refugees who desired to come within our lines and enlist in our army. Our cavalry squad, under, command of Captain S. C. Writer, were sent forward as an advance guard. A reliable guide, who lived in the part of the country where the force was going, accompanied our cavalry. About eight miles out from Decatur the guide informed Captain Writer that we were nearing the residence of a noted "bushwhacker" and would probably find him at home. When we came within sight of the house he was observed sitting on the porch in company of two ladies and an old man. When he saw the Yankee cavalry coming, he jumped up, ran into the house, picked up his shot-gun, and fled out the back way. Some delay was caused in getting through the gate and we were just in time to see his fleeing form going across a field. A number of shots were fired, but without effect. I dismounted, took a careful aim and brought him to the ground. He was seen to scramble to his feet and start on. I quickly placed another cartridge in my carbine and gave him a parting shot just as he climbed over a fence to make his escape into the woods. I saw the same "old chap" after I was captured a few days later, and he told me one of the Yankees, the one that fired the second last shot, broke his right arm above the elbow. Of course, I did not claim the honour of being the "best shot"

A few miles further on, the guide cautioned the captain that the country was infested with guerillas and it would be advisable to halt until the infantry column came up. The captain replied that he was in command and ordered him to lead on to his destination. We then proceeded about four miles further and were nearing a house, the owner of which, the guide informed us, was a "Union man." Two men were left in the road as a picket, and the rest of the squad rode into the barn yard, were ordered to dismount and feed the horses. The captain proceeded to the house and ordered supper. Being some what suspicious, I and Sergeant Sullenberger kept near our horses, while the rest went to the house. A part of them had eaten and came out, when the picket in the rear was fired on and driven in, a force of about two hundred of Paterson's rebel cavalry following up. Having my horse bridled, I led him to the fence and commenced to throw it down, the cavalry mean while firing into us at short range, and when I attempted to mount I found my stirrup had been shot away. I started to go to the opposite side, and the next volley killed my horse and I received three shots in my right leg, but which did not quite disable me. I ran on as best I could into a cornfield near by and succeeded in eluding the cavalry. That night I wandered through woods and fields until about four o'clock a. m. I was so weak and tired that I concluded to lay down and rest myself. I soon fell asleep, and when I woke up the sun was high in the heavens. I arose and started in what I thought was the right direction for Decatur, keeping within the shelter of the woods as much as possible. Becoming very thirsty, I endeavoured to find water without going near any house and finally came to the bed of a creek, but no signs of water anywhere. I followed the dry bed and much to my joy I found a "muskrat hole," at the bottom of which I saw water. Having nothing to dip it up, I tried to find a hollow weed. Failing in this, I took off my boot, sank it in the hole and drew out an abundance of the precious fluid. After satisfying my thirst, I slowly moved on, and when night came I laid down by a tree and slept until morning. Not having a mouthful to eat during this time, I was very weak and my pace was necessarily slow and painful. I travelled all day and some time after dark I came to a barn and crept into the yard to a pump and drank my fill out of the watering-trough. Dogs at the house near by commenced to bark furiously. I turned quickly back into the woods again and shortly afterwards I wandered into a dense prickly ash thicket, and after lengthy effort succeeded in working my way through. My wounds, not having any care, began to get very painful and my limb greatly swollen, making it almost impossible to proceed, but I toiled slowly along. In the afternoon of this day I met a coloured man going to mill with a sack of corn on his back. Upon questioning him, I was informed that I was then about ten miles from Decatur. He directed me the way I should go and cautioned me to keep away from the public roads, as the country was full of rebel cavalry and I was liable to be picked up any moment I followed in the direction given me until night, when I again sought the shelter of the forest and rested as best I could until morning, when I again resumed my painful march. I had not proceeded very far until I came to an open space on my side of the road, which I dared not cross in daylight. I attempted to go across the road and into the woods on the opposite side and had almost succeeded in gaining its shelter, when I chanced to look to my left and saw a "bushwhacker" within about forty paces from me. He was in the act of taking deliberate aim, but before he could fire I succeeded in gaining shelter. I was almost exhausted and unable to get away. I prepared to defend myself, as I still retained my carbine and revolver. He kept cautiously advancing and watching for me, and when he came within a short distance from where I stood I raised my carbine and, taking a quick aim, I fired and he fell. I was afterwards told by my captors I had shot him squarely through the breast, killing him instantly. I got away from there as fast as I possibly could in my weak condition. I finally became so thoroughly exhausted and, coming to a cane-brake, I slowly made my way into it and dropped down, overcome with fatigue. I did not lay long until I heard the voices of someone at the edge of the brake, and by the conversation I overheard I found I was the object of their search. At times they were very close to where I lay, but fortunately they left without discovering my hiding-place. In their tramp on the outskirts of the brake they disturbed an immense rattlesnake, which came gliding along a little gully in which I lay. It came slowly towards me and I dared not move. It crawled across my wounded limb, and to my great relief it disappeared beyond. Late in the night I made my way out of my hiding-place and started on, and in the morning, just as daylight appeared, I attempted to cross the road again, when a squad of twelve rebel cavalrymen came onto me and demanded my surrender in the usual terms, which all old veterans know. Before complying, I managed to let my carbine drop by a log where I stood and pushed it under with my foot, and they failed to get it. I was taken by them to Summerville, where I received the first treatment after being wounded. During my wanderings through the woods I often lost my bearings and made very slow progress, in fact going at times in an almost opposite direction. An old citizen doctor dressed my wounds, after which the question arose what to do with me. After a lengthy parley, they finally decided to take me to General Paterson's headquarters. They pressed the old doctor's horse into service, and searching around, they found an old side-saddle, which was placed on the horse and I was helped to mount, and another painful march began. We travelled about twenty miles, stopping that night on top of a mountain at an old cabin, where I received the best attention, being put into a good bed, the first I had enjoyed for many months. After a good night's rest we resumed our march and arrived at Paterson's camp that evening. My wound was very painful by this time, being irritated from the long ride. The general treated me very nicely and told me, after I had something to eat, to lay down and get a good rest, and he would parole me the next morning. But on account of the proposed raid on our camp at Courtland, Ala., by his command, he refused the next morning to give the parole, but notified me that I would be sent to Tupello, Miss., a distance of probably one hundred and twenty-five miles. You may rest assured this was very unwelcome news to me, but I had to undergo the ordeal. Here I met an old comrade of my company, Casper Miller, who had also been captured at the time I was, but I was not aware of it until I met him. We started after breakfast, the four guards and myself being mounted, but Comrade Miller had to march on foot.

    An amusing incident occurred on this trip. Miller cut a good, stout stick for a cane to aid him in walking, and one evening, as we were about to encamp for the night, Miller, who was an expert in the use of the sabre, having served seven years in the Prussian Cavalry, made a few cuts and parries with his stick. One of the guards noticing it, requested him to give him a lesson in sabre exercise. The old veteran gleefully consented, the rebel using his sabre and he the stick. After playing with him a short time, he brought his cane down with a mighty sweep and across the rear of Mr. Johnnie reb and fairly raised him off his feet. He was inclined to get angry, but finally put up his sabre and said he thought that would do.

The next morning we resumed our march and after a few days travel reached our destination completely tired out. We were placed in an old frame building, used as a guard-house. The next morning, looking out of the window, I saw Captain Eggleston, of Company E of the First Ohio Cavalry, walking across the camp. Of course I could not talk to him, but during the day, having learned of our presence, he came to our prison and told us how they had been surprised and captured at Courtland, Ala.

We remained at this place about two weeks, and while here I saw General Bragg's entire army on review, preparatory to his invasion of Kentucky. This was a very inspiring sight and I will always remember it.

After the rebel army left Tupello, we were put on cars and taken to Columbus, Miss., and the next day to Mobile, Ala. We remained here one day and one night, and were then taken back to Jackson, Miss. Here we remained about six weeks, encamped on the common below the town. Here I witnessed the horrible treatment of one of our prisoners who was sick with typhoid fever. We were required to answer the roll-call three times a day, and on this morning, when we were ordered out for roll-call this comrade was too sick to respond, and when his name was called one of his comrades answered that he was sick and unable to come out. He was then lying in the little shelter his comrades had constructed for him. The rebel officer in charge became very angry and ordered a Sergeant and two guards to go and bring that ——, you can readily guess the meaning, out; he would show him whether or not he was too sick to attend roll-call. The guard pulled him out by the legs and pushed and kicked him into line, and when they let go of him he sank to the ground. They then took him outside of the guard line and sat him in the burning hot sun from seven o'clock in the morning until sundown, without any food or water. He died that night about ten o'clock.

While at this place we were very poorly fed, our rations consisting of one pint of cornmeal, with cob ground in, and about two ounces of spoiled meat. No salt was issued to us. One morning General Tiglman, of Fort Henry fame, came and took command of the Federal prisoners in the state of Mississippi. He came to our camp and talked very nice to us and sent us much better rations, but we stayed here only a few days after that. One morning we were ordered to get ready to march. We got ready in short order and were marched to the railroad station and placed on board of a freight train and informed we were going to Vicksburg for exchange, where we arrived that evening and placed in charge of a rebel guard. About two o'clock p. m. next day we were marched to the river and onto a small steamer and taken up the river to the mouth of the Yazoo, where two of our gunboats lay. We were put aboard of them and the little steamer returned. We remained at this place during the night and next morning steamed up the stream, We soon met a fleet of boats with sixteen thousand rebel prisoners from Camp Chase and other Northern prisons. We were ordered back and accompanied them to Vicksburg, where the rebel prisoners were disembarked, and we took another start for the North. After several days we arrived at Cairo, Ill., where I secured transportation to Louisville, Ky., where I found my regiment in camp greatly reduced in numbers. My wounds not being healed, I was unfit for duty, but went with the regiment as far as Bardstown, Ky., where I was sent to the hospital for treatment and to aid in caring for the wounded until able for duty.

Taken Prisoner at Courtland, Ala.

I was taken prisoner July 25, 1862, at Courtland, Alabama, and I always celebrate this anniversary as the day of deliverance, as I had a hair-breadth escape from instant death. In fact my hair did not escape, as a minnie ball went through my hat, cutting the cross sabres on the front of the hat in two, and making a hole through the hat crown six inches long, and cutting the hair from my head down to the scalp, so that I pulled out a handful of hair from my head.

After the evacuation of Corinth, Miss., on the night of May 28, 1862, General Buell's army was scattered along the Memphis and Charleston Railroad from Corinth east to Huntsville, Ala. My company, K, and Company E of the same regiment, First Ohio Cavalry, and two companies of the Tenth Kentucky Infantry, were stationed at Courtland, Ala., guarding a railroad bridge.

Courtland was a beautiful town, situated about midway between Tuscumbia and Decatur, Ala., about twenty-five miles from each, on the Memphis and Charleston Railroad. It was a lazy little town of fifteen hundred to two thousand inhabitants, noted for the beautiful shade trees that lined the streets, and pretty Southern girls, who would insist on making mashes on the dashing cavalry boys, in defiance of their protests that they must continue true and loyal to the "Girl they left behind them" among the hills and valleys of the bonnie Buckeye state. We had been stationed here from about the first of July. Our camp being in a beautiful grove, along a creek and distant about half a mile from town, and the camp was supplied with water from several fine springs, within a stone's throw of headquarters. The duty of the detachment was guarding the railroad bridges and pickets were thrown out on all of the roads, about a mile from camp, to guard against a surprise from the enemy's cavalry, who were making frequent dashes against these small detachments.

Compared with the campaign of the siege of Corinth, during the months of April and May, this was considered a soft snap, as rations were of the best and duty light. Our camp was on the plantation of an old fellow by the name of Bynam, who professed to be intensely loyal to the old flag, and his cornfield along one side of our camp, just in good roasting ears, was carefully guarded, and a soldier that even plucked one ear had the guard-house staring him in the face and visions of extra duty policing the quarters with a pine-brush broom. This was in the early days of the war, before the emancipation proclamation, and before any property had been confiscated; but we got bravely over such fastidious ideas before another year rolled around, and learned, as Sherman said, "that war was cruelty and we could not refine it," and required as well the destruction of the sinews of war as the destruction of life.

A detachment of cavalry and infantry was stationed at Town Creek, about ten miles from Courtland, Ala., and drew their supplies from our garrison, and couriers passed over the line every day carrying dispatches.

On the morning of July 24 a wagon train was loaded with rations and forage and, under a mounted escort, started for the camp at Town Creek, and when about five miles from camp, hearing firing in advance, the train was halted and the guard made a reconnaissance to the front and found a dead cavalry man in the road, who proved to be B. F. Lucas, of Company K, First O.V.C., a courier. Lucas and another soldier were together, and in passing through a dense wood, a regiment of rebel cavalry was lying in ambush, waiting for the wagon train, which they intended capturing. When the couriers had passed through the lines, they were halted and ordered to surrender; but Lucas stuck the spurs into his horse and undertook to run the gauntlet lined on either side of the road with hundreds of armed rebels, and fell from his horse, pierced with a half dozen balls. His comrade surrendered and was paroled and returned to camp next day, and gave the particulars of the capture and death of Lucas.

The rebels, knowing that the firing would arouse the camp and that we would be after them in hot haste, mounted their horses and were off on the gallop, as it was not their intention to fight, but only to make a raid and capture the wagon train.

The soldier that had been captured and paroled reported that a force of rebel cavalry was concentrating on the Tupelo road, a few miles south toward Bragg's headquarters, for the purpose of making raids on the railroads, and on the strength of this report the pickets were doubled and ordered to be on the lookout and report at once if any reconnoitering parties of the enemy were observed.

On the morning of July 25, after guard mount, the weather being very warm, the men were scattered over the camp, taking it quiet and easy and many of them sitting in the shade in front of their tents, or on the piles of forage sacks, having a game of old sledge or poker with a ten cent ante, while others were writing letters to the clear ones at home, or to their best girls, which was more often the case, little dreaming that the enemy in large force was rapidly marching and preparing to pounce down upon our little handful of men like a hurricane.

Lieutenant James Cutler, being a physician, had charge of the sick of the post and had established a temporary hospital over in the town in a brick church, and he was making his usual morning visit to the sick, and I, being next in rank, had command of the company. Just as I had settled down on my cot for a little rest, as I was sick with malaria and camp fever, Captain Eggleston, commanding Company E, came running to my tent in his shirt sleeves and bare head and shouted to me that the rebels were advancing upon our camp. I called to the bugler to sound "boots and saddles" and ran down through the quarters, directing the men to saddle their horses and mount as rapidly as possible.

Looking across the camp and toward old Bynam's house, I saw a cloud of dust raising and in five minutes time the advance of the rebel column came down the road, within three hundred yards of our camp, and gave the rebel yell that would have raised the hair on the head of a Comanche Indian.

I had loaned my horse Billy that morning to Sergeant Chapin to go out on picket, and I made up my mind with but little deliberation and in a moment's time that I was in for it and would be taken prisoner right in the camp; but after the company had all saddled and were in line, I saw one horse still at the picket rope, that I knew belonged to William Johnson, who had gone into town to shoe horses, and I ran down to the line, saddled and bridled this horse, and by this time the rebels were in camp, banging away in a very careless manner.

Just as I had buckled on my sabre and revolver, Lieutenant Cutler came dashing into camp from town, and I ran into his tent, got his belt and sabre and handed it to him and mounted. By this time the rebels were right upon us and we were the only two left, and the enemy had cut us off from our command, which was forming with the infantry behind the railroad embankment.

"Halt! halt! you d——d Yankees," they shouted; but we halted not and "stood not upon the manner of our going," but stuck the spurs into our horses and dashed across the creek, intending to join the command near the railroad bridge.

A high railroad embankment lay between the camp and town, and two other soldiers who had been cut off from the command, having joined us at the ford, I suggested that we reconnoitre toward town to see if we were surrounded and then report to the commanding officer. Spurring our horses over the embankment we run right into a regiment of rebels galloping along the street close to the embankments and hidden from view, and we were prisoners in less time than it takes to tell the story.

We were run off to the side of the street on the pavement and surrendered our horses and arms as gracefully as could be expected under the excitement and confusion, as the advance had fired a volley when they first hailed us and the balls whizzed uncomfortably near our heads. After we had surrendered, a guard was put over us and we were watching the rebel cavalry as they charged down the street in platoons. It was a very pretty sight from the pavement. Just at this moment a rebel soldier wheeled his horse out of the ranks not more than three rods from us, raised his carbine and banged away at us three prisoners and fired three shots in quick succession as we stood quietly looking him in the face, expecting each shot to kill one of us.

As before stated, the third shot went through my hat and stunned and blinded me for a moment, and I reeled and grasped the fence for support. I was so dazed that I was confident that I was shot, and putting my head down toward one of the boys, I asked him where I was wounded, and taking off my hat and seeing that there was a bullet hole in front and that there was a hole in the crown at least six inches long, I became more and more impressed with the belief that the ball had gone through my head. Of course it was preposterous to even imagine that a ball could go through the head without causing instant death; but in my dazed condition my reasoning faculties were rather "knocked out of working order."

I put my hand upon the top of my head and pulled out a handful of hair and wool from my hat ground as fine as powder, and kept on pulling out the loose hair and feeling the top of my head and looking at my fingers to see if I could discover any blood, and continued this for a moment or two until I recovered from the shock, before I was convinced that I was not wounded.

It was a hair-breadth escape, and had the ball struck an eighth of an inch lower it would have blown the whole top of my head off and I would have been killed so suddenly that I would not have known what hurt me. I have often been asked the question, when persons would examine this hat, if I was not badly frightened and what my sensations were.

I was not frightened during the time the rebel was firing the shots and did not attempt to dodge down or run, but stood still and looked at him very intently as he pulled the trigger of his carbine, but fully convinced that he would kill all three of us. I thought very fast and wished that we had our navy revolvers again that we had surrendered a few minutes before, and we would have fought it out as long as we had a load in our revolvers.

After it was over I felt weak and nervous, but at the time I was as cool as I ever was under fire, and I think I can safely say that I was under fire a hundred times during my service, but this was the "closest call" I ever had.

The fellow made such an impression on me as he sat on his sorrel Texas pony in his shirt sleeves, with brown beard and long yellow hair, and a broad-brimmed, brown-coloured slouch hat on his head, that I have never forgotten his face, and think I would know him to-day if I should meet him, if he looked as he did then, although our meeting thirty-six years ago was very brief and rather abrupt. He was so near to me and the heavy report of his carbine, the flash and the ball all combined, knocked me blind and I was bewildered for a moment and there was a stinging sensation, but different from a blow, and my hand seemed to fly out from my body in a kind of tremor, and after I had recovered there was a prickling sensation all over my head for some minutes.

Until this day, if I hear the report of a musket near at hand, I imagine that I can feel that ball passing through my hat and hair in exactly the same direction that that ball plowed a track so near my skull the day I was captured.

I have heard the balls "zip" rather near for comfort many times, and I remember one instance particularly when we made a dash on a reserve picket at night and had a pretty sharp skirmish, and a ball seemed to come so near the side of my head that it brushed my hair and made my ear sing, but it did not come with such force and such a jar.

I have only attempted to describe the sensations minutely for the reason that many persons have asked me what my sensations were and whether I was frightened, etc., at the time, and I have simply related the facts so indelibly impressed at the time. No doubt there are thousands of other similar incidents that happened during the war, and only relate this as one in which it was my fortune to play a part as principal actor.

The rebel cavalry was still charging along the street, and there sat that long, yellow-haired cuss on his sorrel pony, with murder in his eye and his carbine thrown across the pommel of his saddle, as if taking a rest before commencing another fusillade on three dangerous, unarmed Yankee prisoners. Just at this moment a rebel officer was galloping slowly along near the pavement, reining his horse in, as if to close up his company. I appealed to him, stating that we were prisoners, that we had surrendered our arms and that we were entitled to protection, and, pointing to the long-haired sinner still sitting on his sorrel pony, informed the officer that he had been practising on us at short range and in my opinion was getting ready for another engagement. This officer ordered the fellow to join his command, much to our relief, and then ordered the guard to start us to the rear on double-quick. At this time the pavements were lined with women and children and the few men that were left at home, and they had been seized with the general enthusiasm of the occasion, and while the soldiers were giving the genuine rebel yell as they swept up the street at a long gallop, the women and children cheered them on with "Hurrah for Jeff. Davis!" "Give it to the Yanks" and such like patriotic exclamations. Now the "fight was on" and the balls from our own command, stationed behind the railroad embankment, began to come over, rattling against the houses and fences and knocking up the dust in the streets like big drops of rain. While it was not a very comfortable situation for us to be placed in-between two fires still it was amusing to see how quickly the citizens scattered and vanished into their houses, and in a few minutes we had the streets all to ourselves.

The guards hurried us along on the double-quick, for they seemed as anxious to get out of the range of the flying bullets as we were. When we reached the eastern outskirts of the town along the railroad, a brief halt was made to allow us to catch our breath. By this time I was about "laid out," as I was sick and very weak, not having been on my horse for duty for three or four weeks. I said to the guard, that if he wished to take me very far, he would have to furnish me a way to ride, as he could see that I was sick and could not march at such a gait as they were rushing us along at, and in fact I was not in good light marching order, as I had on a pair of high cavalry boots that came above my knees, with a pair of spurs, and being a cavalryman, we had been drilled to believe that it was very humiliating for a trooper to be compelled to march on foot.

The guard that was looking after my welfare was of the same opinion, and as there were several riderless horses running loose on the common, the riders having been killed or wounded, or in some manner thrown from their horses, the guard caught a fine gray, which he directed me to mount in "one time and two motions." Not waiting for a second invitation, I mounted in hot haste. He proved to be an officer's horse, well equipped, with two revolvers in the holsters fully loaded, and my first thoughts were that if we had found those revolvers a few minutes sooner, we would have made it lively for our long-haired friend on the sorrel pony.

By this time many stragglers were galloping to the rear to get out of danger, which is a very usual occurrence during a fight, and a person to be in the rear of a battle line and see the cowards retreating and the confusion and demoralization would imagine that the whole army was retreating; but when you arrive at the front you find that the line is steady and everything well in hand, and the fighting soldiers are under as complete control as if on battalion drill.

The guard took the rein of my horse and we started back with the general rabble, across cornfields and meadows, off to the south toward a range of steep and rugged hills and into the forest. After going pell-mell for perhaps a distance of two miles, we halted on a by-road and we could still hear a few scattering shots off toward our camp. As we sat on our horses, there now being five of us prisoners, with perhaps a hundred guards, a big rebel sergeant rode up to our group and, taking a look at the horse I was riding, he then asked me where I got that horse, and I informed him that the guard had caught him for me. He then took out a big navy revolver, and riding up close to my side, said: "That is my brother's horse, and if he is killed, that is what you will get," and he placed the muzzle of the revolver against my head just back of my ear. I then thought we were in for it, as he was a long-haired, devilish-looking fellow; but I think if he had made the attempt the guard that had me in charge would have interfered, as he was a fine, manly-looking young soldier and was very kind to me afterwards and during the few days he was with us, and when he could get anything to eat he divided it with me, if I could eat anything. The rebel cavalry depended almost entirely in foraging off the country as they passed along, and we passed through several small towns and the citizens turned out *en masse* to see the "Yanks" and fed the rebels on the best they had, which usually consisted of corn-bread and fat pork.

The women were abusive to us and used the vilest epithets, the more mild terms being "nigger soldiers" and "thieving Yanks," and never would give us anything to eat, and the Johnnies told them some great war stories, how they had "licked you'uns" and our boys would laugh it off and try to enjoy the situation.

After our little episode with the big sergeant, who was anxious to distinguish himself by blowing the heads off of a few unarmed prisoners, instead of being up at the front of his command, we started on a by-road through the woods and hills, and after travelling two or three miles came out on the Tupelo road leading to Bragg's headquarters. After waiting here a short time, the balance of the prisoners were brought up, and there were now one hundred and thirty-four of us. We were then put under a regular guard, commanded by Major Smith, of Missouri, who proved to be a gentleman and a good soldier, and the prisoners were then protected from insult. We learned that the big sergeant's brother, who was a lieutenant, had been killed in the early part of the fight, and had the sergeant known this at the time he found me on his brother's horse, I have no doubt but he would have executed his threat and have killed all of us on the spot, but it was too late when we were put under a regular guard.

The command that had attacked us was General Armstrong's brigade of cavalry, consisting of about seventeen hundred men, and including Colonel Roddy's regiment that had been recruited in Northern Alabama, in and around Courtland, Tuscumbia and Decatur. General Armstrong was an officer of the old army and a fine-looking soldier, and became quite a noted cavalry leader during the war.

The rebel commander attacked our camp on three sides simultaneously, and he had been piloted through woods and mountains on by-roads by citizens of the vicinity, who knew every cow-path in the country, and knew the position of every picket, as they passed in and out of camp at will. They had reached a position near our camp before daybreak, and when the picket guard was relieved in the morning they were in plain view of the rebel advance, concealed in the woods, and the rebels then advanced through the woods and ravines and passed two or three of the picket posts unobserved and cut the pickets off from camp; but I think all of these pickets made their escape after the camp was attacked and they found themselves cut off from the command.

The total number of men in our command in the two companies of infantry and the two companies of cavalry was about one hundred and sixty men, and when they took position behind the railroad embankment, they made it lively for the rebel brigade for a short time, and in the fight the rebels lost seventeen killed and twenty-seven wounded; but the rebels closed in on three sides and it seemed useless and hopeless to prolong the fight, and Captain Davidson, of the Tenth Kentucky Infantry, the senior officer, raised the white flag and surrendered, and when this was done our cavalry charged out through the lines and all escaped but twenty-five. Captain B. B. Eggleston and Lieutenant Alkire, of Company E, and Lieutenant Cutler, of Company K, First O.V.C., were taken prisoners.

The following-named soldiers of Company K were taken prisoners: A. L. Sessler, Lewis Latham, Sergeant A. S. Chears, John Patterson, John Winters, S. P. Clark, John Johnson, William Johnson and myself.

The first day we marched to Moulton, Ala., the county seat of Lawrence County, a distance of about fifteen or twenty miles, and were quartered in the court-house, sleeping on the soft side of a bench in this magnificent temple of justice. We lingered here the next day until late in the evening, when all at once there was a great commotion among the rebels, the guards rushed from the court-house, the bugles sounded "boots and saddles," drivers commenced harnessing their mules and orderlies were galloping through the streets. We surmised that something unusual had occurred on the outposts, and it was soon learned that a scouting party of our cavalry had attacked their pickets and we were in high glee, hoping that we would soon be within our own lines again; but the rebel commander did not propose to be so easily cheated out of his prize and he directed that the prisoners be started south on the Tupalo road toward General Bragg's headquarters on "double-quick."

We were soon formed in line, fronting toward the courthouse, and General Armstrong came down the walk toward us, and I remember what a fine-looking soldier he was, tall and erect, and fine figure, with a neat-fitting gray uniform, and as he reached the steps at the side-walk, he buttoned up his coat and adjusted a red sash around his waist. Lew Latham, who was known as the most inquisitive soldier in the First Ohio, stepped out in front of our ranks and, saluting the general, said: "What are you going to do with us now, General?"

And the general, looking at him savagely, answered: "I will shoot every d——d one of you if you don't keep your mouths shut." It is useless to say that Lew did not pursue his inquiries any further, but subsided, although he said on the quiet "that he would give fifteen hundred dollars to know what we were going to do next."

General Armstrong mounted his magnificent horse, that had just been brought up to him by his coloured servant, and galloped off in the direction of the firing. Our officers were directed to get into the wagons and a mounted guard was placed around the balance of us and we were hurried off South on double-quick. When we started, about sundown, I did not think that I would be able to march more than a mile or two, as I was so weak from long-continued camp fever. I crowded up to the front of the column, as it is much easier to march in front than in rear of a column, for the reason that you are not interested by any of the halts which may occur in all marching bodies of soldiers, and the front regulates the march at will.

With several other sick soldiers I strained every nerve to keep up at the front, and when darkness came on, a file of guards were placed on either side of our column, in addition to the platoons in front and rear, and the guards were ordered by the captain commanding to "draw sabre and cut down any prisoner who fell out under any pretence whatever."

The horses of the mounted guard were kept on a brisk walk all the time and this kept us on about a half run, and after marching in this manner from about 5 p. m. until 10 p. m. without a moment's halt and without a drop of water on a hot July night in Alabama was enough to prostrate the strongest soldier. About this time we sick boys began to fall back, and nothing but the cold steel of the guard kept us from falling in our tracks, but we felt that it was a march for life. As I staggered on over the stones, for it was a very rough road, feeling that I must soon give up, I was fortunate enough to fall in with Lew Latham and John Winters, two comrades of my own company, and they supported me under either arm and fairly dragged me along for two hours more.

About midnight a courier came dashing up from the rear with a message, and the officer in command called a halt. We were then just in front of a plantation residence, and I remember that there was a wagon just at the side of the road, loaded with long wood, and the captain commanding mounted this wagon and made a speech to the guard and stated that he had the pleasure of announcing that they had gained a great victory at Spangler's Mills. At this the guard cheered, but it was not a very cheerful message for us prisoners. We afterwards learned that it was a little skirmish between a scouting party of our soldiers and the rebel pickets, in which two or three men were wounded.

We were then ordered to lay down on the chip pile, on which we were standing, and we did not need a second invitation, as we were completely exhausted and ready to fall in our tracks. Sergeant Chears and myself had about half of a rubber blanket that one of us had picked up, and finding a stick of wood for a pillow, we tumbled down on the ground and covered our breasts with this piece of rubber blanket. Our clothing was dripping wet with perspiration and as soon as we halted we began to feel the chill of the cold mountain night air, but from sheer exhaustion we slept from midnight until daybreak.

When I attempted to get upon my feet I could not do so, as my limbs were so cramped and chilled. It seemed to me that there was not a joint in my body, and I had to rub my limbs for some time before I succeeded in standing upon my feet. Under ordinary circumstances this kind of treatment and being compelled to lie on the ground with our clothing dripping with perspiration and in the chilly night air, without clothing or shelter of any kind, it now seems would have caused the death of every one of us sick men at least. We had been living on very short rations of hard tack and a little fat pork since we were captured, and on this Sunday morning we had green corn boiled, and eaten without either salt or pepper, bread, crackers or meat, and in fact all we had for three or four days was boiled green corn, without anything else. We would halt at a plantation and a guard would direct the slaves to bring out some big iron washkettles and fill them with water, and then pull off some green corn and throw it over to us, husk and all. The boys would husk the corn, tramp around on the husks and squeal like a lot of pigs, laugh and joke, and try to make the best of it; but after three or four days boiled corn, without anything else and without any seasoning, became a little monotonous. Like the fellow with the codfish, we relished it three times a day, but did not care to have it for a regular diet.

This being Sunday, the citizens were out to see us in force as we marched through the country, and as our coming had been heralded by the rebel cavalry scouting through the country, at every cross-road we would find carriages filled with ladies and gentlemen, waiting to get their first look at a live Yankee prisoner. Some of the boys would ask a great many silly questions of these citizens and furnished amusement, not only to our boys, but to our guard.

A little fat pork was issued to us during the day, and as we had no haversacks we had to carry the meat in our hands or run a little stick through it, and as the weather was very hot, the grease dropped out as we marched along. We were a motley looking crowd, some being bare-headed, while others were in their shirt sleeves and bare feet. We did not present a very soldierly appearance, and no doubt the citizens thought us a genuine lot of mudsills and "five to one" was only a breakfast spell for the chivalry.

After marching a few days and before we reached General Bragg's headquarters at Tupalo, we were paroled and permitted to return to our lines, and before being paroled we were searched and all papers, diaries, etc., in our possession were carefully examined to see if there were any spies among us, or to see if we had any written information of importance. We then signed a written parole not to take up arms again against any of the Confederate states until regularly exchanged, and I have my parole now, as I have it framed to preserve it.

Our paroles were signed by a Colonel Frank Breckenridge, and after we were paroled Colonel Breckenridge made us a speech in which he said "we had fought them well, and if we were exchanged and returned to our commands, they would fight us again like gentlemen; but if we joined our commands again before being exchanged, if we were taken prisoners they would hang every d——d one of us." He then advised us to get a white cloth and carry it on a pole, so as to keep any scouting parties from firing on us.

A short distance after taking up our line of march for our own lines, we came to a little town, named Mt. Hope, and here we bought a yard of thin, narrow muslin, which would now sell for about four cents a yard, and for which we paid a dollar and a half. We put this on a pole and gave it to a wild Irishman, who belonged to some infantry regiment, to carry, and he ran away from us the first day and reached our lines about a day ahead of the cavalrymen. He confiscated our flags of truce and we never saw nor heard of him afterward, and we still mourn the loss of that dollar and a half yard of muslin. The last day of our march, before reaching our lines at Tuscumbia, Ala., we sick boys hired a citizen to hitch up a dilapidated pair of mules to an old wagon and haul us to our outposts, paying him fifty cents each, and when we reached the pickets he stopped and refused to go any further; but as it was two or three miles to Tuscumbia, we pressed the old planter in and compelled him to go on, much to his disgust, as he was afraid his team and wagon would be confiscated.

On reaching the command we found that our old friend Bynum at Courtland, who professed to be so loyal to the Union, had piloted General Armstrong's cavalry through the mountain paths into our camp, notwithstanding the fact that we were guarding his cornfields at the time. We were only prisoners a short time in the hands of the enemy, as this was before the days of establishing those horrible prison pens, such as Andersonville, Saulsbury and Florence. We were sent to Camp Chase, Ohio, and were exchanged and returned to our regiment stationed at Lavergne, Term., about March 1, 1863.

But I would not go through the same experience again as I did the day I was captured and take my chances of being shot and then of being murdered by the big rebel sergeant who threatened to take our lives in cold blood, for the whole Southern Confederacy.

Reminiscence of the Battle of Chickamauga
from a newspaper article

In answer to a question regarding the battle, Colonel Curry said:

Yes, I was in that battle and commanded a company in the First Ohio Cavalry. I do not know that I could describe the fight better than to quote the words of General George Crook, who commanded our division. In a conversation a few years after the war he said: We got into a hot place at Chickamauga. We were under fire perhaps a hundred times, including battles and skirmishes, but this was the only fight I was in during my service in which I threw up the sponge and thought I was going to be killed. I do not know why it was, as I had been in some pretty hot places before, but I had a premonition that I would be killed. Our division reached the battle-field on Sunday morning, September 20, 1863, about nine o'clock, We marched up through McLamore's Cove with McCook's division on Saturday, the nineteenth. I was on picket all night The weather was clear and cold. Next morning we all felt tired, sleepy and worn out. We were in the saddle at sunrise, Marching a few miles, we were ordered to deploy and move forward toward Glass Mills, on Chickamauga Creek, about a mile and a half south-east from Crawfish Springs.

It was a beautiful Sabbath morning. The sun was shining brightly. Not a leaf stirred. It was ominously quiet. Not a sound was heard excepting the sharp, quick command of the officers forming the lines. Staff officers dashed here and there carrying orders. I tell you, boys, the stillness that often precedes a battle is awful. It tries the nerves of the bravest soldier. It seemed especially oppressive that calm Sabbath morning.

Before our lines were formed and ready to move forward a rebel battery posted on a hill across Chickamauga Creek, about a thousand yards distant, opened up on our lines and the shells were crashing through the pine trees above our heads. You could hear the command, "Steady! Steady!" down the line as men and horses became a little nervous. I commanded next to the right flanking company of the regiment, a company to which I had been assigned only a few weeks previous, and the men were comparative strangers to me. I rode out in front of the company and looked down the line of officers toward the left of the regiment and saw my old company, in which I had served two years, forming on the left flank; and as it seemed evident we were going to get into a hot fight, I made up my mind that I would be killed and wished myself with my old company. I felt that should I be wounded or killed, my old boys would see to it that I did not fall into the hands of the enemy; whereas the soldiers in the company I was commanding had known me for so brief a time, that I felt they would have no particular interest in my welfare other than they would in any officer or soldier of the regiment. But I did not have very long to reflect on the subject. The skirmishers were moving out and my company and Company G of he same squadron were ordered to the right to protect the ford. We were soon in the fight. At every lull in the firing I would think of my first impressions in the morning, that I would be killed. As the battle raged and we were driven back and Colonel Cupp, commanding the regiment, was mortally wounded and my own horse was shot, I still felt confident that I would be wounded or killed. One man of my company had been killed and five others wounded. I was dismounted, and as we fell back slowly, stubbornly contesting the ground, I saw our regimental butcher riding to the rear, leading the horse of a trooper which I recognized as the horse of Sergeant Irwin of my old company. Bodkins, the butcher, informed me that Irwin was severely wounded and was in an ambulance. I then mounted Irwin's horse, and found the saddle and horse covered with blood, which had run down over both fore legs and hoofs of the animal. The balls were still cutting the brush and trees on every side. A strong line of dismounted cavalry of the enemy was sweeping up through a cornfield in our front. Our squadron was soon in imminent danger of being cut off and captured. We moved to the left and rear and formed on the second line, near Crawfish Springs, where we stood in line of battle for two hours awaiting the attack of the enemy. But they had got enough of it and, instead of attacking, they fell back and marched up on the east side of Chickamauga Creek to Lee and Gordon's Mills and then marched to Crawfish Springs, arriving and taking possession of our hospitals at the Lee House about 5 o'clock p. m.

After the battle had ended and I realized that I had escaped without a scratch, while I felt very thankful, still it seemed to me that things had gone wrong at least not as I expected. The thought of the early morning, that I would be shot, had been before me like a spectre all day. No, I was not frightened or any more nervous than I had been in any other fight.

While I was cool and self-possessed all day, yet I never was in a fight before or after that affected me as I was affected in that battle.

Yes, you will find it the experience of every soldier that in many instances in a skirmish or picket fight he lost his head more than in a hard battle. Many men and officers who were brave to a fault would get rattled at times, and at other times would be as cool as a cucumber. I know that was my own experience. No, you cannot tell what any soldier will do until he is tried under fire. Often some little pale-faced sprig of a boy would go into the hottest fight without showing any signs of fright, and the bully or street fighter would cower with fear. It is a soldier's honour and high sense of duty, as he touches elbows with his comrades, that keeps him in the fight. The soldier who is spoiling for a fight at all times is usually, when the test comes, like a case of milk sickness, in the next township.

Field Service in the Hospitals in Camp and on the Battlefield
by R. Wirth late Surgeon First O. V. C.

Columbus, Ohio
July 21, 1898

My dear Curry: I am in receipt of your kind note requesting me to write an article for your history of the First Ohio Volunteer Cavalry regarding the medical service in the army as it was then, my experience on the march, in camp, on the battlefield, in the hospital, and especially in the field at Stone River and Chickamauga, believing that it would be interesting to the "boys"— meaning of course the surviving members of the regiment.

While I feel very willing to oblige you, and through you, "the old boys," I am at the same time very diffident about attempting the task before me, for various reasons. Unfortunately all notes and records of what befell me (chiefly in letters to my family) have been lost, and my memory has become dimmed by age, so that it is impossible for me to give anything like a connected and complete history of the medical department of our regiment. Further, while I have gone through many thrilling scenes during my three and one half years of service in camp and hospital, I have not the gift of relating them in a manner that would make them appear interesting and lifelike to others. This I regret ; but I shall nevertheless attempt something, and if it should be found by you and the boys too dull and heavy and uninteresting, you and they are entirely at liberty to "skip" it. So here we go:

I was mustered in as Surgeon of the First O.V. C. on the 10th of October, 1861. The regiment was then in Camp Chase. All companies were full, but without horses and arms, which were, however, furnished a few days later, when military life began in earnest. It was drill, drill with the men all day and theoretical instruction all evening. I had been in West Virginia Assistant Surgeon of the Ninth Ohio Infantry all summer, had been active in two battles— Rich Mountain and Carnefax Ferry— and was therefore not unacquainted with military life and my duties as a medical officer.

A regiment was then entitled to a surgeon, an assistant surgeon, and a hospital steward—the latter to be appointed by the surgeon. My first duty was to appoint a steward, make requisitions for medicines and instruments, and organize my department; select nurses, ambulance driver, cook, etc., with the approval of the colonel. All officers and men will know what it means to organize a thousand men coming from all walks of life, some well educated and many scarcely at all, but all wholly unacquainted with military life and duties, into battalions, companies, squads, and platoons, and teach them the various duties of a soldier. No doubt many mistakes and blunders were made, sometimes laughable and sometimes more serious, as for instance when the gallant soldier, standing guard, put the commander-in-chief of the camp into the guard-house because he had for gotten the countersign (given out by himself). Now I do not mean to say that the recruit made a blunder, but certainly the commander of the camp did by forgetting his own countersign.

However that may be, it was not all smooth sailing in my own department. I had selected for my Steward a trooper who represented himself to be a member of my own profession, and whom, consequently, I felt inclined to favor. He was a pleasant, jolly fellow, and we got along capitally as long as we both had nothing to do, but when our medical supplies came my trouble began. Among these medicines were a dozen or two bottles Spirit *Frumenti*, Spirit *Vini Gallici* and also several gallons of alcohol,— very important medicines in the different diseases and injuries which are apt to befall a soldier, but rather injurious when taken indiscriminately. I very soon found that my steward became more jolly, more boisterous, and sometimes— especially toward evening even quarrelsome and inclined to insubordination. I also found by a casual inspection of my supplies that a frightful large number of my Spirit *Frumenti* bottles were empty. Putting this and that together, I asked him for an explanation, intimating that he drank and got drunk on the whisky and brandy furnished by the government for medical purposes only. "You wrong me," said he, putting his hand to his cap and standing in proper position; "indeed you do. The whisky has been used strictly for the purposes for which it was issued."

"How do you make that out? I certainly have not prescribed more than half a pint since it is here, and here are six empty quart bottles!"

"You see it is this way. At surgeon's call you have repeatedly ordered castor oil for a soldier having bowel complaint, with a little whisky after it to take the nasty taste away. Now being a physician myself, the boys of my company frequently come to me when their bowels trouble them and I give them the same dose. It is excellent treatment, but of course takes considerable whisky. There are so many of them and their number increases. It must be in the water."

The situation and the impudence of the man were so comical, that I could not help laughing and forgiving him, taking the precaution, however, of putting the balance of the spirits under lock and key. To my sorrow, as I discovered later, I neglected to put the alcohol also out of his reach.

The next day I was compelled to go to Columbus and was

detained until after dark. On nearing my quarters I heard a howling and yelling and laughing, as if a parcel of Indians had been let loose, and entering the room I found my Steward with two or three companions performing a war-dance and singing, "We won't go home till morning," and on the table the alcohol bottle, a pitcher of water and a sugar bowl, which furnished all the ingredients for a very strong punch. I was so taken partly by surprise and partly with indignation that I was speechless. So were the visitors, who sneaked away before I could find words to express my sentiments, while my Steward put himself, as well as he could, to attention, and saluting, addressed me as follows: "Sir, I have to report that everything in my department is in excellent condition! I take this opportunity to resign my position, believing from your looks that it is not healthy for me to remain."

His successor was a civilian, a real druggist, who came highly recommended, and who certainly was accomplished and competent. He condemned the conduct of his predecessor very strongly and gave me to understand that he was as much opposed to the use of intoxicating liquors as Neal Dow himself. However I was soon to learn to my sorrow that this was not strictly true, unless that venerable gentleman was himself subject to occasional relapses. The regiment was ordered to the front. It was transported, men, horses, and baggage, to Cincinnati by rail, and from there by steamer to Louisville, where we went in camp. Several transports being used for the embarkation of men, horses, and baggage, and the steward being left in charge of the hospital stores, I was astonished on my arrival to find the goods but no steward, and ascertained subsequently that he had stayed in Cincinnati in such a condition as would have made it utterly futile for him to walk in a straight line, or any line whatever. "He was d— drunk" said my informant, and I never saw him again. By this time the government allowing two stewards to a cavalry regiment, I selected two privates, E. M. Doty and J. C. Caldwell, who proved to be intelligent, industrious, and willing to perform their duties, and from their entrance I had no more trouble in this department.

Shortly after my arrival at Camp Chase Dr. John Canaan was appointed Assistant Surgeon of the regiment. He was of English birth, but educated in this country. He remained with the regiment during the war and became its Surgeon after my resignation. He is so well known to all the surviving members, that it is unnecessary to enter into his history. He died many years ago at his home in Lorain County.

The First O.V.C. was on the whole perhaps as healthy as any regiment in the service, the men and officers with a few exceptions being perfect specimens of vigorous manhood, mostly farmers' boys and strong mechanics. Only twice during my service were there any large number really sick, and this in the first winter of our field service at Camp Buell, near Louisville, where an epidemic of measles broke out, which was severe, and was followed in many cases by pneumonia, which proved fatal in one case; while several cases had to be discharged subsequently on account of chronic lung trouble. Then in front of Corinth, on the battlefield of Shiloh, many were attacked with camp fever and diarrhoea, among them myself, so that I had to leave for home. Ordinarily the attendance at surgeon's call was not large.

Every morning the orderly sergeant of each company brought those that claimed to be sick and unfit for duty to the surgeon for examination and treatment. Now the complaints were often of a very trifling or obscure and contradictory character, so that I could not help suspecting that the soldier was more after an excuse from an unpleasant duty, than relief from actual suffering. In such cases I invariably gave the invalid the benefit of the doubt, but made him swallow in my presence a harmless but disagreeable dose, such as castor oil or quinine, and usually had the satisfaction of seeing him next morning ready for duty. However, when the order for breaking camp came or a fight, was in prospect, these men invariably reported themselves well and I frequently had to use my authority to send men, really sick, to the hospital, who would insist on marching or going into battle, when they were physically unable to do so. There is no discount on the bravery of American soldiers.

While it is the soldier's duty in battle to kill and wound as many of the enemy as possible, it is the surgeon's duty to save as many lives and to relieve as much suffering as possible, and this irrespective of friend or foe. Nor does the soldier himself show other than mercy to the wounded enemy when the battle is over. This is civilized warfare as contra-distinguished from savage warfare, where the wounded enemy is as mercilessly butchered as if he were encountered with arms in his hand. It is a noble duty that the surgeon has to perform, and a hard one I assure you. Where a general battle is to be fought, certain preparations are made. The medical officers do not remain with their commands. They are under the immediate direction of the medical director of the army, generally an experienced surgeon of the regular army, who designates each surgeon and assistant Surgeon his place and duty. Temporary hospitals are established in houses, churches, or where they are needed; in some secluded place near the line of battle, but protected as much as possible from the stray bullets of the enemy. These places are invariably marked with the hospital flag, as much for the purpose of directing the wounded to them, as for informing the enemy of the nature of the place and the character of its occupants. Some surgeons are sent into or near the battle line with attendants and stretchers and ambulance to pick up the severely wounded and bring them to the hospital, where some surgeons apply bandages, others select the cases requiring immediate amputation, and others still are continually engaged in cutting off arms and legs. It is a gruesome place, such a temporary hospital during and shortly after a battle. The ground is drenched with blood, and heaps of shattered legs and arms lie around promiscuously. Some of the poor fellows die under the knife, some shortly after, and some even before an effort can be made to save their life or relieve their sufferings. And there they lie, for there is no time to bury them.

It is clear that when our line gives way, such a hospital is first to fall into the hands of the enemy, and surgeons, attend ants and wounded become prisoners of war; for it is a sacred duty with a surgeon never to leave the wounded to save himself though he may be able, under the circumstances, to run as fast as anybody. This happened to my friend Doty and me in the memorable battle of Stone River.

The surviving members of the First O. V. C. will never forget Stone River, for here it lost some of its most distinguished members, of which I need only mention Colonel Millikin and Major Moore, although many more equally brave, if not as distinguished, laid down their life for their country and the restoration of the Union.

On the advance from Nashville toward Murfreesboro I was mostly in the company of Colonel Millikin. We had frequent conversation about the impending battle. He knew more of our own strength and position and of the enemy's than I did, and seemed altogether in a more serious mood than I had ever seen him before. In light of subsequent events I am almost inclined to believe that he had a premonition of his fate. The night before the battle we spread our blankets in an abandoned negro cabin, slept in our uniforms, ready and expecting to be alarmed at any moment, and in the morning we joined our little stores and had breakfast together. At daybreak the regiment formed and before we mounted he said to me, "Let us shake hands, Doctor. This will be a hot day for all of us and we may never have a chance to do it again." Silently I grasped his hand, alas! for the last time. Shortly afterward we were separated.

Captain Cupp, who was on picket duty with his company, sent an orderly to me to come and assist one of his men who was seriously wounded. Doty and I went with the messenger and soon met the Captain with his company and the wounded man on a horse, held up by a trooper on each side. In the far distance the enemy was plainly visible in force and the intervening cotton-fields covered by our infantry rapidly retreating toward us. Seeing a hospital flag on a cluster of farm buildings not far in the rear and to the left, I directed the man there and followed immediately. The house was already filled with wounded, but we found a place where we (Doty and I) could strip the man and dress his wound. While thus employed I heard the terrible rebel yell that nobody, who has once heard it, forgets in fifty years, and immediately our hospital was surrounded by a regiment of Texas Hangers and we all were prisoners of war. Almost before we had time to realize our position we were surgeons and attendants hustled into the yard, questioned as to our name, rank, regiment, etc., and then paroled on condition that we should strictly attend to our work; and while we were given the freedom of the grounds, we were warned that any attempt to reach the Union lines would be made at the risk of our lives. It is needless to say that we lived up to the condition of our parole. We had no other indignity offered us than the jeers of some of the men about the "cowardly Yankees," how they had run, how the army was in full retreat to Nashville. Having no means to ascertain the truth or untruth of these assertions, we were in our then state of mind only too ready to believe them, and felt accordingly depressed and unhappy. The fact the sound of the cannonading was retreating more and more gave indeed some colour of truth to their statements.

Our horses and whatever in our possession that struck the fancy of our captors was unceremoniously confiscated. We employed the day in picking up more wounded and making them as comfortable as possible. A rumbling farm wagon served as ambulance and did valiant service until late at night, when the driver declared that neither lie nor the horses could stand it any longer. In fact, we were all utterly exhausted; but there was no rest to be thought of. Word came that a house a mile or two distant was full of wounded and not a single person with them able to take care of them. Doty and I and a Kentucky surgeon volunteered to at once to go to their relief.

Weary almost to exhaustion we dragged ourselves along until we arrived at last at the house, and, I believe, not a minute too soon. The house was a new one, as yet unfinished, for in front of the fire-place were deep holes, probably designed to be covered by hearth-stones. The whole ground floor was covered with wounded men, whose moans and cries for water could be heard from a distance. The night was bitter cold, but a bright fire, made of cedar fence rails and posts, burned in the fire-places. There were no guards, no nurses. By whom the fires were made and kept up, I do not know; possibly the only one who could have done it was our informant, who stayed behind, believing himself entitled to a rest, as undoubtedly he was. However, we came just in time to extinguish flames in a number of blankets with which the poor fellows were covered too severely wounded to do it themselves. From this time we had our hands full keeping up the fires, quenching the feverish thirst of the men and guarding against a conflagration, for the sparks from the dry cedar posts frequently flew a distance of several yards. All night we were engaged in walking from place to place with a tin cup and water bucket, which we used as much to extinguish incipient conflagration as to quench the thirst of the sufferers. I honestly believe that if we had relapsed one half hour in our vigilance or fallen asleep, house and all in it would have been consumed. That was a terrible night, that New Year's eve! It was the longest and most dreary night I ever lived, but it came to an end at last. A rebel officer appeared in the morning requesting us to report to the provost marshal in Murfreesboro. When asked what was to become of the men whose wounds needed dressing, and above all, who were starving, he assured us they would soon be taken care of and urged us to be prompt, as we were needed in Murfreesboro. So ended the first and commenced the second day of the battle of Stone River for us.

On our way to Murfreesboro we saw evidences of the terrible destruction of war everywhere dead horses, burned houses, broken wagons, ammunition boxes, but very few soldiers. The wounded seemed to have been picked up and the dead buried in that part of the battle-field. On the porch of one house we saw the body of General Sims, shot square in the forehead. He certainly died with his face to the enemy.

We heard only occasional cannon shots in the far distance,

and from what we saw and heard could only conclude that our army was thoroughly defeated, and if not completely disorganized, at least in full retreat to Nashville. We had seen the defeat of our right wing (McCook's corps), but we were utterly in the dark as to the centre (Thomas) and the left (Crittenden); nor did the rebels enlighten us, but insisted that our whole army was whipped.

Upon arrival in Murfreesboro we were shown a large store room full of wounded Union soldiers — or as a Louisiana officer would have it, — Yankee soldiers with orders to attend to them. We found one hundred and eighteen, mostly severely wounded men, with a few paroled prisoners as nurses, but no surgeon. Nearly all belonged to Missouri and Illinois regiments. Their wounds had not been dressed and were in a dreadful condition. Some of the cases required immediate amputation. But amputation cannot be performed without assistants, instruments, anaesthetics and bandages, and I had none of these. I therefore went immediately to the medical director and stated my desperate situation and urgent wants. I found him to be a true physician and a thorough gentleman. He pointed to the room opposite and said, "Doctor, there is our store. It is all we have. Go in and take anything you can make use of; but I am sorry to say it will not be much. As to an assistant, I will send one as soon as possible with an amputating case." I repaired to the room, expecting to find it full of medical and surgical stores, but to my disgust found only empty shelves, with here and there a bottle, mostly quinine, salts, castor oil and morphine. I took one of each and a few bandages and returned to my charge with a heavy heart and almost in despair.

On my return I found an officer of the provost guard, who informed me that the body of an officer of my own regiment was in the cellar, who had fallen in a terrible charge of the regiment on the previous day, in which the colonel, several officers and many soldiers had also been killed. I went with him to the cellar and found a body decently covered with a cloth, on the removal of which I saw that it was Major Moore. Part of his forehead was torn away by a piece of shell. He also had died like a hero, with his face to the enemy. The day was passed in attending to the wants of the wounded as well as could be under the circumstances. The promised assistant did not arrive until late at night, when the work of amputating commenced and did not cease until the rebel surgeon, Doctor Pendleton, Steward Doty and I were utterly exhausted and nature compelled us toward morning to seek some rest. So passed the second day of our captivity, Thursday, January 1, 1863.

The third did not materially differ as far as our occupation was concerned. We did not hear as much noise and cheering as on the day before, but that did not especially attract our attention. We were also not so often reminded that the Yankees were on their way to Nashville. In the morning an officer appeared whose serious face indicated that his mind was not at ease and requested me to point out among the wounded all that were able to bear transportation, as they were to be sent to Vicksburg.

Poor fellows, they were so anxious to go, hoping, when in Vicksburg, that they would soon be exchanged; but unfortunately most of them were too seriously wounded to admit of removal. Those fit to travel were conveyed to the depot and left for Vicksburg within an hour.

During the night we were awakened by the cries of the wounded, that they could not wake the nurses, that they wanted water, etc. We got up to investigate and found, to our consternation, that every one of the nurses had sneaked away, probably in the hopes of getting on the train and so to Vicksburg. Nothing was left for us to do but to get up and take their places for the balance of the night In the morning another difficulty arose. These poor fellows were hungry and cried for their breakfast; but the cook had left with the rest. So we had to go to cooking. We settled on biscuit and coffee for breakfast; this more from necessity than choice. Our cooking utensils consisted of a camp-kettle and a small Dutch oven, and our provisions of some flour and coffee. Doty made the dough, mixing flour and water together, while I tended to the baking. The baking was rather a slow process, as our oven would bake only five biscuits at a time. Nevertheless, by eleven o'clock we had served each man with a bun (which would have served better as a cannon ball than digestible food) and a cup of coffee, and had one left to divide between ourselves. The biscuits were so hard that it took the men an hour to masticate them, so they could dispense with dinner, which was very fortunate for the cooks. As soon as breakfast was over I went to the provost marshal and requested him to furnish me new nurses and a cook, which he cheerfully did.

This was Saturday morning. By this time a mysterious change had taken place at Murfreesboro, which Doty noticed sooner than I. We heard no more cheers. Soldiers hastened about the streets silently and with serious faces. There was a constant rumbling of railroad trains leaving in a southern direction. Most of the prisoners of war had disappeared.

"I believe they are retreating" said Doty.

"Retreating? Yes, toward Nashville!"

"No, sir! Come and see!"

I slipped to the window, where we could look upon the road coming from Nashville towards the south. There we saw first irregular masses of men marching without order, some without arms or hats, then single cannon, then whole batteries, then cavalry, then infantry, all mixed up, but still with a certain degree of order. This lasted the whole night, but at daybreak the town was as still as a graveyard, with only a few cavalry pickets, who soon disappeared also. The rebels had made an orderly retreat, and left nothing but their own wounded and some wounded prisoners.

What a change! The city was as quiet and deserted as a churchyard at midnight. Not a soldier nor a citizen to be seen. We were free again! There was no doubt now that the rebels had been defeated. We expected every moment to see our men appear in hot pursuit, but in this we were bitterly mistaken. The whole Sunday passed and not a soldier appeared. What did it mean? Didn't General Rosecrans know that the enemy had retreated? Was he so crippled that he was unable to pursue? Is the retreat only a feint? Will the rebels return? The questions were asked a hundred times during that lonely day, but no satisfactory answer was found. Nor did the night bring any solution. If we could only communicate with our army. But there was no messenger, and we did not know where to send. The night passed in the same painful suspense. Seven o'clock passed, eight o'clock. Are we left to our fate entirely? Are the poor men to perish for want of food and medicine and proper care?

"There! Didn't you hear that bugle-blast? Cavalry is coming! It sounds so familiar, it must be our regiment."

We hastened to the street and in a few minutes we were surrounded by our friends and our captivity was at an end a thing of the past.

The army marched through Murfreesboro and went into camp a few miles distant. The medical director took charge of the wounded, regular hospitals were established, and we at last were relieved and returned to our commands.

I might still relate many stirring incidents of the war in which I myself took part, but I am reminded that my time and space are limited, and will refer to only one the tragic end of Colonel Cupp at Chickamauga. I was then acting Brigade Surgeon on the staff of General Long, commanding the brigade to which the First O. V. C. was attached. We had been in Broomtown valley on the extreme right, observing and also skirmishing with the enemy. The country is extremely rough and broken, full of deep valleys and high mountain ranges covered with forests and unfavourable for the evolutions of cavalry. One morning we were suddenly withdrawn from our position and entered upon a forced march. The conformation of the country alluded to made it impossible to form a distinct idea of where we were going to. I remember even a dispute between some soldiers whether there would be a battle or not, and this while the battle had already been raging two days and, as it turned out, already lost. Suddenly we came to a halt. The brigade was deployed in front of a clearing partly concealed by underbrush. Whether anyone saw the enemy I do not know; but I am sure I did not, though I was close to General Long.

Suddenly we heard a horrible volley in our immediate front, as if a whole brigade had fired, and many a saddle was emptied in an instant and many a horse bit the dust. A rapid retreat was necessary to get out of range. We had run into Hindman's division of infantry and Wheeler's cavalry.

I was soon overtaken by a member of the First O.V. C., who informed me that Colonel Cupp was severely wounded and requested my immediate attendance. Seeing an ambulance near, I ordered the driver to follow me, and turned again toward the place which we had so suddenly left. I soon found the Colonel, lying on his back, holding his abdomen with both hands and moaning dreadfully. A hasty examination convinced me that his case was hopeless— he was shot through the stomach. While engaged in lifting him tenderly into the ambulance we were suddenly surrounded by a company of rebels, apparently irregulars, for they were in homespun clothes. And so it appeared I was a prisoner for the second time. However, I got off better than the first. I was accosted by the leader with the question: "What are you'uns doin' thar?"

I gave the driver a sign to move on and, turning to the captain, said in an authoritative tone: "Don't you see what we are doing? We are taking the wounded off the field." He seemed to reflect for some time on this information, and then said, pointing in the direction of the woods: "Wall, there are some more of you'ns laying over thar."

"I know it," said I, "and as soon as the ambulance returns I shall take care of them." This gave him again something to reflect on. Whether he took me for a confederate surgeon or a sacred person exempt from the ordinary usages of war, I do not know; at any rate, without another word he marched his men off in a different direction from that the ambulance had taken and left me at liberty to follow. This I attempted to do; but being entirely unacquainted with the roads, I missed it in the confusion and excitement and never saw Colonel Cupp again. He died in the Lee House, Crawfish Springs, about 4 p. m. the same evening. After many hair-breadth escapes from capture I found my way to Chattanooga (where the regiment had preceded me) one of the last to enter the city.

Here I must close, fearing that my reminiscences of two memorable battles have already tired your readers, our old comrades. If so, I hope they will pardon me, remembering that old age makes men garrulous. On the other hand, should they derive any pleasure from the perusal, I shall be more than gratified, and as I am not unmindful that the last grand call may soon be sounded for me, I take this opportunity to bid them each and every one an affectionate farewell on this my seventieth birthday anniversary.

The Courier Line

Courier duty in the cavalry service is very exciting and at times quite dangerous. Courier lines are established in the army for the purpose of carrying dispatches between the different headquarters, and it is usually important that they be carried very rapidly, and for that purpose the best mounts are selected. From four to six men are on duty at each station, and the stations are three or four miles apart, according to the number of men on duty and the distance to be covered by the whole line.

To do good service on a line of twenty miles, it would take from thirty-six to forty men. The men are often stationed in abandoned houses, barns or sheds, if they can be found at about the proper distances apart; and if such shelter cannot be found along the road, if the weather is bad shelter tents are put up at the stations. The couriers at the stations must always be on the lookout on both ends of the line, and at least two horses must be kept saddled and bridled at all times, ready to mount, and when a courier is seen coming, a trooper of the proper relief mounts and as the incoming courier dashes up, he receives from him the dispatch, wheels his horse and is off under the spur like a flash for the next station. The courier is in light marching orders, carrying usually only his rubber poncho mailed to the cantel of his saddle with belt and revolver, leaving his sabre, carbine, blanket and haversack at the station. On

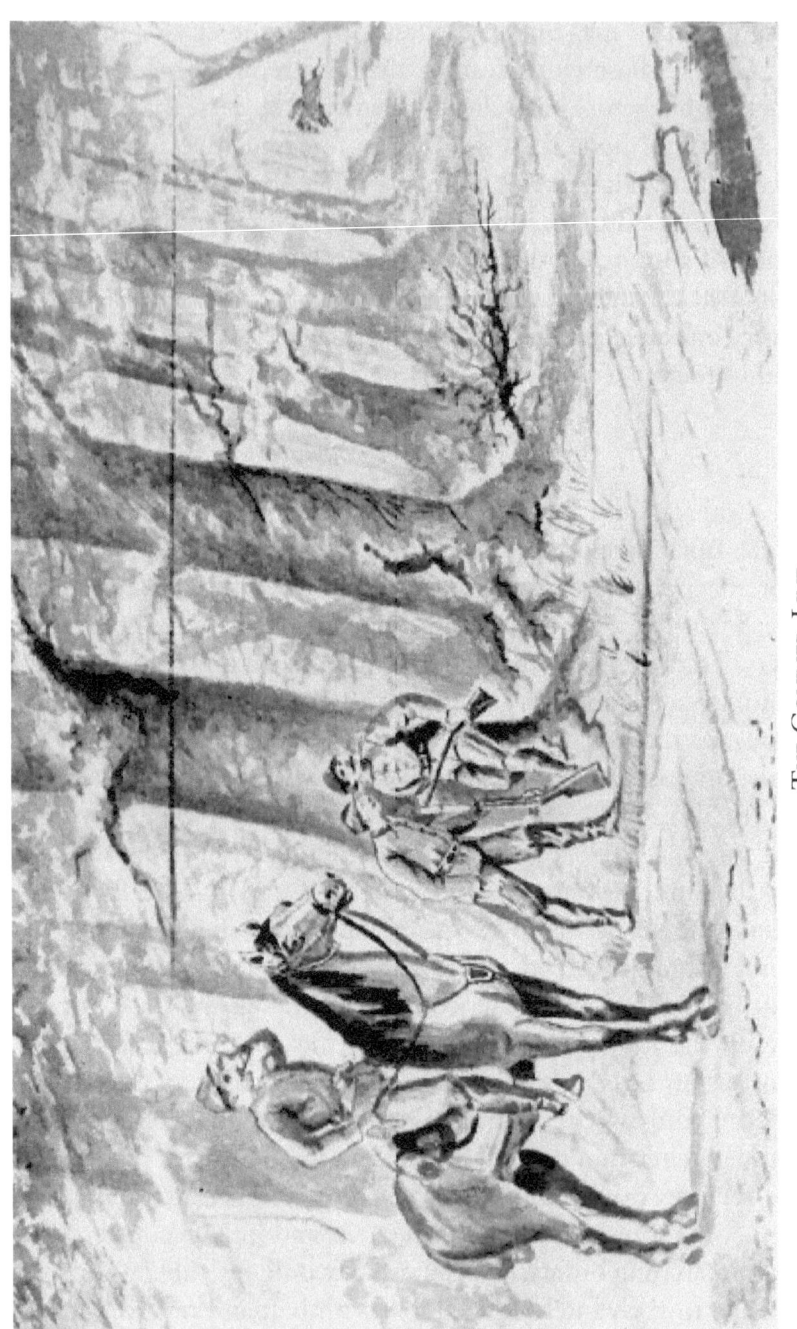

The Courier Line

delivering a dispatch, the courier gives his horse time to blow and then returns slowly to his station.

During the war of the rebellion, very often the courier line run over mountains and through thickly wooded and uninhabited parts of the country, invested by bushwhackers and scouting parties of the rebel cavalry, and it was a dangerous service. The carrier of dispatches always had orders not to allow the dispatches under any circumstances to fall into the hands of the enemy, and if he was attacked or pursued, he must act on his better judgement to either keep the road or take to the woods, and if too hard pressed to destroy the dispatch in some way. A courier was not expected to do much fighting, but if he was cornered and was in danger of being captured and there was not to exceed half a dozen of the enemy, he did not hesitate to use his revolver and often emptied some saddles and made his escape. Where the stations were not more than three miles apart, a run of twenty miles was usually made in less than two hours.

Altogether this was at times a very hazardous service, as the couriers at isolated stations were frequently attacked and captured; yet it was a very attractive and exciting service, and the ideal trooper enjoyed it. The illustration is true to life, showing the courier post, in the thick forest, with the troopers on duty, waiting and watching intently for the horseman just coming in sight around the turn in the road. This cut was made by the direction of the author especially for the history of the First O.V.C. and will recall vividly to the minds of many comrades courier duty in the mountains of Tennessee and Georgia.

Biographies

Colonel Minor Millikin

The biography of Colonel Millikin was copied from the biography written by Whitelaw Reid and published in his history *Ohio in the War*.

Colonel Millikin was the eldest son of Major John M. Millikin, formerly a lawyer of Hamilton and long known as the President of the State Board of Agriculture, and one of the foremost among that body of retired professional men of wealth and culture who adorn the vocation of Ohio farmers. Minor was born on the ninth of July, 1834. His early education was acquired in the high schools of Hamilton, and under the watchful eye of his parents. In 1850 he was sent to Hanover College, Ind., where he passed through the course of study of the Fresh man and Sophomore classes. In 1852 he went to Miami University and there completed his collegiate education. He ranked foremost among all the students then in that honoured old institution. He was not known as a remarkable scholar, nor was he ever popular. But there was about him an individuality so intense and so striking, that wherever he was placed he was the centre of attraction. He was the most nervous and original writer and altogether the most striking debater in his society.

He was graduated with high, though not distinguished standing in 1854. He went immediately to the Harvard Law School. The next year he returned to Cincinnati and entered the law office of his father's friend, Thomas Corwin. A year later he married Miss Mollyneaux, of Oxford, to whom he had been engaged while at college, and started to Europe on a bridal tour, which was prolonged for a twelve-month.

On his return he purchased the *Hamilton Intelligencer,* the Republican organ of his native county, and for the next two years edited it. He had never intended to practice his profession, but he improved the opportunities of leisure now afforded him, to review and extend his studies. Then disposing of his newspaper, he retired to his farm, near that of his father, in the vicinity of Hamilton, and was engaged in improving it and building, when the war broke out.

His tastes and his superb horsemanship naturally inclined him to the cavalry service. There was a great difficulty at first in getting cavalry companies accepted, and recruiting was consequently discouraged. But he enlisted himself as a private, and soon had the nucleus of a company. The Government could not be induced to furnish horses in time, and to get the company off for the West Virginia campaign he advanced the funds to purchase twenty-four out of his own pocket. His recruits were united to Captain Burdsall's Cincinnati Company, and Millikin presently became Sergeant, and then Lieutenant. He returned from the three months campaign in West Virginia, with the confidence of his men and the indorsement of his commanders as the best of the cavalry officers on duty in that department. Thus recommended, he was appointed a major in the First Regiment of Ohio Cavalry, raised for the three years service.

Colonel Ransom, the first Colonel of the regiment, resigned in January, 1862, and Minor Millikin, the junior Major of the regiment, was promoted to the vacant colonelcy. The promotion was based on his acknowledged merits, but it wrought him great harm. One of the officers over whose heads he was thus lifted, was brother to the Governor of the state, another had such influential friends as presently to secure a brigadier-general's commission. All were older than himself. Dissatisfaction of course arose, all manner of complaints were made, officers threatened to resign by wholesale, and finally the charge was made that Colonel Millikin was too young and too ignorant of cavalry tactics to lead Ohio's first cavalry regiment.

The result was that he was ordered before a board of regular officers for examination. Some delays ensued, but when at last the examination was held he passed it triumphantly, and received the warmest compliments of his examiners.

While the matter was pending, Colonel Millikin served on the staff of General George H. Thomas. But he was not long to lead the disciplined organization he had created. In the battle of Stone's River he was sent to repel attacks of rebel cavalry on the rear of the army. Seeking to protect a valuable train he ordered a charge, and himself led it. The force of the enemy at that point was superior, and he presently found himself with a small part of his regiment cut off. He refused to surrender, and encouraged his men to cut their way out. A hand-to-hand encounter followed. Colonel Millikin's fine swordsmanship enabled him to protect himself with his sabre. After a contest for some minutes with several assailants, one of them, enraged at his obstinate resistance, shot him with a revolver while he was engaged in parrying the strokes of another. The regiment charged again a few minutes later and recovered the body, but not before it had been stripped of sword, watch and purse.

After Colonel Millikin's death, General Thomas addressed a letter to the bereaved father, in which are these words:

> It affords me the sincerest pleasure to express to you and to Mrs. Millikin my utmost confidence in him, both as a friend and as a brave, accomplished, loyal officer one on whose judgement and discretion I placed the greatest reliance. By his judicious, forbearing, and yet firm course of conduct, he was enabled to overcome all prejudices against him in his regiment, and his death was sincerely regretted by all. While mourning his loss, you have the consolation of knowing that he fell a Christian and patriot gallantly defending the honour of his country.

Brigadier-General Beroth B. Eggleston

Beroth Ballard Eggleston was born in Corinth, Saratoga County, New York, July 14, 1818. He attended the district school in winter until fifteen years old, then his father moved to New Plymouth, Ohio, where Beroth clerked in a store for a short time, when he went to Chillicothe, Ohio, and apprenticed himself for four years to D. Adams & Co. He afterwards embarked in the dry goods business, but this proved unsatisfactory. He studied law three years and then travelled through the country, doing a large collecting and pettifogging business. From that he turned his attention to the lumber business with Mr. Massie, of Massieville. While here he received from President Fillmore the appointment of Postmaster and retained the office three years. After Mr. Massie's death he entered into partnership with Job Stevenson and engaged in farming, which he gave up in June, 1861, to begin the career of a soldier. He married, in 1844, Martha M. Phillips, of Chillicothe. Five children were born of this union Arthur, Edward, Clara, Mary and Laura. Mrs. Eggleston died in Mississippi in 1867. General Eggleston died in Wichita, Kansas, May 27, 1890.

After leaving the army General Eggleston became a citizen of Mississippi. He settled on a plantation and soon became engaged in politics. At the Constitutional Convention he was elected its President, and remained so until its close. He was the first Governor elected in Mississippi after the war, but as Congress would not then re-admit the state, he did not take his seat. He was then appointed Collector of Internal Revenue. Then he bought the gas-works in Columbus, Miss., and in 1878 he sold out all interest in Mississippi and moved to Wichita, Kansas, where he lived until his death.

He enlisted in Company E, First O.V. C., August 8, 1861, and was promoted to Captain, August 29, 1861; promoted to Major, June 20, 1862; to Colonel, April 1, 1863; Brevet Brigadier-General, March 13, 18G5, and was mustered out with his regiment at Hilton Head, S. C., September 13, 1865. Colonel Eggleston was with the regiment almost continuously from the time of its organization until the regiment was mustered out; and on the Atlanta Campaign, when Colonel Long, who commanded the brigade, was wounded, August 20, 1864, he was assigned to the command of the brigade, which he commanded until the close of that campaign. In the cavalry campaign under General Wilson, in the spring of 1865, he commanded the regiment and received the surrender of Atlanta at the end of that campaign. The fact that he served more than four years is sufficient evidence of his patriotism, and his promotion from a private to the rank of Brigadier-General shows without comment that he was an officer of ability and that he had the confidence of the distinguished soldiers under whom he served. After the surrender of Atlanta he proceeded with his regiment to Orangeburg, S. C., and was appointed by General Gilmore Chief of Staff for the department, which position he held until mustered out.

Lieutenant-Colonel Valentine Cupp

Valentine Cupp was born June 30, 1830, at Pleasantville, Fairfield County, Ohio, and was married March 12, 1850, to Hannah Winter of same county. Four children survive him. He was a farmer and stock dealer up to the time of entering the service. Died September 20 at battle of Chickamauga, was buried there, and was afterwards removed to Greenlawn, Columbus, Ohio.

He was commissioned Captain of Company F, First O. V. C., September 5, 1861; promoted to Major, December 31, 1862, and to Lieutenant-Colonel, April 1, 1863. Killed at battle of Chickamauga, Ga., September 20, 1863.

Colonel Cupp, as a Captain and in all the grades through which he served, was one of the most popular officers in the regiment. He was at all times and under all circumstances the same genial, high-toned gentleman and true soldier. Kind-hearted to a fault, and if he had occasion to discipline or punish a soldier, he was sure to pay him back tenfold by some act of kindness the first opportunity that offered. He served in the regiment two years and fifteen days, at the front at all times, and commanded the regiment through the Tullahoma and Chickamauga Campaign with distinction. It is sufficient to say of his service that he never shirked any duty and was held in high esteem by General Thomas and General Long.

On the beautiful Sabbath day, September 20, 1863, with drawn sabre, amid the carnage among the pines of bloody Chickamauga, he fell mortally wounded at the head of the regiment he loved so well. He was removed from the field by Surgeon Wirth back to Crawfish Springs and died the same evening in the south-east parlour of the Lee House about 4 p. m.

Brigadier-General Thomas C. H. Smith

Colonel Smith was born at Acushnet, Mass., in 1819 and died at Nordhoff, Cal., April 8, 1897. He graduated at Harvard in 1841 with distinguished reputation for force of character. On leaving college he went to Ohio and took up his residence at Marietta, and began the study of law. He completed his course and practised in Cincinnati until 1848. In 1847 he married Lucy Woodbridge, of Marietta, Ohio. In 1848 he completed a telegraph line from Pittsburg to Cincinnati, and another line from Sandusky, Ohio, to New Orleans, and in 1851 again resumed the practice of law in Cincinnati.

August 23, 1861, he was commissioned Lieutenant-Colonel of the First Ohio Cavalry. He served with the First Ohio Cavalry in the fall of 1861 and through the winter of 1862 in Kentucky, and participated with his regiment in the siege of Corinth after the battle of Pittsburg Landing and until June, 1862. He was then promoted to Brigadier-General, to date from November 29, 1862, and was transferred to the staff of General Pope, and served with General Pope during his campaign, while in command of the Army of the Potomac in the summer of 1862, afterwards accompanying General Pope to Minnesota. In 1863 he commanded the District of Wisconsin, performing important service in subduing the resistance to the draft.

His last war service was as commander of the Department of Missouri. During Hayes administration he served in the Treasury Department in 1878 and was appointed Paymaster and Major in the regular army. He was retired from the army in 1883, at the age of sixty-four, and resided in California until he died.

Colonel Smith was a gentleman of high character and fine executive ability. He served with the First Ohio about ten months and was a brave and very efficient officer, full of zeal and patriotic ardour. During his service with the regiment he was highly respected by both officers and soldiers, and he was mentioned in special orders by General Buell for bravery and military ability while in command of a detachment of the First Ohio in a fight at Booneville, Miss., in June, 1862.

Lieutenant-Colonel Thomas J. Pattin

Thomas Jefferson Pattin was born on a farm on the Ohio River about six miles below Marietta, Ohio, October 11, 1823. His father's name was Thomas Pattin, and his mother's maiden name was Nancy Cole.

He learned the mechanic's trade after receiving a district school education, and in 1850 went to California by the Nicarauga route, but not meeting the success hoped for in the land of gold, returned in 1851 to Marietta, Ohio, where he married Ann Eliza Locker, and shortly afterwards became a member of the firm of Putnam, Poole & Co., manufacturers of wooden ware, hardware and machinery. He continued in this business until the breaking out of the war. After the war he became connected with a firm in Cincinnati, Ohio, in the manufacture of sugar mills and bells, and while returning from a trip to Louisville was killed in a railroad accident on the Louisville & Nashville E. R., January 7, 1870. He left three sons and one daughter W. S. and D. P. Pattin, manufacturers of Marietta, Ohio, Dr. Thomas Pattin, who died in 1896, and Miss Louanna Pattin, now living with her mother at Marietta, Ohio.

He was commissioned Captain of Company L, First O.V. C., September 16, 1861; promoted to Major, December 31, 1862; to Lieutenant-Colonel, September 20, 1863, and mustered out November 25, 1864, at Louisville, Ky. Colonel Pattin was with the regiment continuously for more than three years, and the history of the regiment during that period is the history of his service. He was a gallant officer, brave and full of that reckless dash necessary for a good cavalry soldier. He was always at the front, and no officer in the regiment had the confidence of the men in a greater degree than Colonel Pattin.

Major D. A. B. Moore

Major D. A. B. Moore yielded up his life in the service of his country, having been mortally wounded in the battle of Stone River. He was born October 9, 1821, at Newark, Ohio, and was the son of Moses Moore, one of Newark's first pioneers and a soldier in the war of 1812.

Major Moore, being an only son, received the full name of his grandfathers, David Moore and Alexander Blackburn. He subscribed himself as D. A. B. Moore, but was familiarly known to his friends as "Blackburn," or as "Black Moore."

In May, 1847, he entered the service of our government, in the war with Mexico, as First Lieutenant of the Licking Rangers, a mounted company which served throughout the war.

In 1856 Governor Salmon P. Chase commissioned him Captain of the Newark Guards, which office he retained until the disbandment of the Guards in 1860.

When the Civil War broke out he raised a company in Newark and Licking County, and on the fifth of August received his commission as Captain of Company D in the first regiment of cavalry that volunteered from the state of Ohio. Captain Moore served as Major some months previous to his appointment, which was made by Governor Todd in September, 1862.

He fell in the battle of Stone River, December 31, 1862, wounded by a piece of shell, and died in hospital at Murfreesborough, Tennessee, on the third of January, 1863. During that period the tide of battle turned and hospital and field had been taken by the enemy, but through the kindness and courtesy of a Confederate Colonel, into whose hands Major Moore's personal effects fell, his official documents, private papers and personal effects were forwarded to his widow, and upon the back of his commission as Major was written: "Major Moore died in Confederate hospital, January 3, 1863, at Murfreesborough, Tenn. He was wounded in the head, the ball entering the centre of the forehead. E. C. Tyler, Colonel and Pro. General."

After nearly six weeks had elapsed, during which time the Federal army had regained its lost position, the remains of Major Moore were disinterred and brought by loving friends to Newark, where they are now resting in the peaceful shade of Cedar Hill Cemetery.

He was deeply imbued with the military spirit and early developed those soldierly qualifications which distinguished him in life and brought him a soldier's death. He died at the age of forty-one years, having enjoyed a brief but an active career.

Major John C. Frankenberger

John Corwan Frankenberger grew to manhood at Sidney, Ohio, where he was born September 13, 1829. He was attacked with the gold fever of 1849 and went in search of riches by way of New York, the Atlantic Ocean, Mexico, the Pacific Ocean and the Golden Gate to California. He could not become acclimated, and returned as penniless as he went. At the breaking out of the war he was handling the agency for the Wheeler & Wilson Sewing Machine, at Dayton, Ohio, and at its close entered the same business again. He died at Toledo, Ohio, May 22, 1879, at which time he was connected with the *Daily Bee*. He was laid away beside the remains of his wife and only son at Sidney, May 24, 1879, leaving two daughters.

He was appointed Quartermaster of the First O. V. C., September 11, 1861, and was promoted to Captain of Company G June 6, 1862, and to Major, September 20, 1863. Mustered out January 11, 1865. Major Frankenberger, as Quartermaster of the regiment, was a very industrious and efficient officer, and commanded Company G from June 6, 1862, until after the battle of Chickamauga. He was a brave and gallant officer, and he never was more at home than when riding at the head of his command, not waiting for the enemy to find him, but looking for the enemy. On the Chickamauga Campaign, Companies G and M were in the same squadron and held the ford on Chickamauga Creek at the extreme right of our line. Major Frankenberger was very highly complimented for bravery in this action and was immediately promoted to Major. At the beginning of the Atlanta Campaign he met with an accident by falling and injuring his ankle so that he was prevented from taking part in the Atlanta Campaign, much to his regret, and he never fully recovered from this injury. During the summer of 1864 he had command of the dismounted cavalry at Columbia, Tenn.

Major Martin Buck

Major Martin Buck was born at Northfield, Vermont, February 4, 1822. He was the son of Chester and Dina Buck. Early in life he went to Montreal, Canada, and engaged with his uncle in the milling business. At the breaking out of the Canadian insurrection he commenced his military career as a volunteer in the Queen's service. Returning to the United States on July 20, 1848, he became Adjutant of the Sixty-fifth Regiment New York Infantry and went to the Mexican War. For meritorious conduct he was promoted to a Captaincy. After the close of the Mexican War he lived in Aspinwall and also in Cuba. He came to Hillsboro, Ohio, and was engaged in milling at the breaking out of the war in 1861. He organized Company H, First O. V. C., August 14, 1861, was promoted to Major, December 31, 1862, and resigned February 1, 1863. Major Buck, having served in the British army in Canada during the insurrection, and also having served as an officer during the Mexican War, was well versed in military matters at the breaking out of the war of the rebellion. He was an excellent officer, and served with the regiment through the campaign in Kentucky in the winter of 1861, the campaign of Pittsburg Landing, and the retreat of Buell's army up through Kentucky and Tennessee in the fall of 1862. When the regiment left Nashville a few days before the battle of Stone's River, Major Buck, being sick, was compelled to remain in the camp at Nashville; but on the thirty-first day of December, the day that Colonel Millikin was killed, he left Nashville and went to the front, and after the death of Colonel Millikin, Major Buck commanded the regiment until the next day, when he was relieved by Major Laughlin. He was a thorough military man, had the respect of every officer of the regiment, and was compelled, by reason of his ill health, to resign.

Major James Nicholas Scott

James Nicholas Scott, son of Dr. Joseph Scott, an eminent physician of Lexington, Ky., was born in Lexington, Ky., March 17, 1828.

He came to Ohio in 1848, engaged in farming and stock raising in Ohio and afterwards in Texas. He returned to Ohio the year before the war. In 1853 he married Sarah, daughter of Mr. John Woodbridge, of Chillicothe, Ohio.

He never entirely recovered his health after the war, and through his rapid failing health he was unable to engage in any business, and died April 5, 1867, while on a visit to his sisters in Lexington, Ky.

Major Scott enlisted in Company M, First O.V.C., August 30, 1861, and was promoted to Captain October 1, 1861, and Major April 1, 1863. Mustered out September 13, 1865. Major Scott was very active in all the campaigns of the regiment, excepting when he was sick, up to and including the campaign of Chickamauga. After that date, by reason of ill health, he was absent from the regiment for some time. He was an officer of intense bravery, and was always with the regiment at the front when there was any prospect of a fight.

He commanded a battalion of the First Ohio Cavalry at Cotton Port on the thirtieth clay of September, 1863, where General Wheeler forced a crossing at the ford when starting on his great raid through Tennessee. In this fight he defended his position for some time against the large force of General Wheeler, and several of his command were wounded and taken prisoner.

Captain Lafayette Pickering

Captain Lafayette Pickering, son of James Pickering, was born near Pickerington, Fairfield County, Ohio, April 30, 1828, and died December 14, 1866, near the spot where he was born.

In the year 1848 he was united in marriage to Miss Margaret Winter, near Pleasantville, Fairfield County, Ohio. During the late war, when his country called for help, he promptly responded and enlisted September 5, 1861, for three years in Company F, First Regiment Ohio Cavalry. On the organization of his company he was elected First Lieutenant, and soon after the regiment was ordered into service he was promoted to Captain, December 31, 1862, in which office he served faithfully until December 20, 1864, and was mustered out by reason of the expiration of his term of service.

He participated with the regiment in all of the battles of the Army of the Cumberland, and was severely wounded at the battle of Noonday Creek, Ga., June 16, 1864. His death was caused by camp fever, contracted in the service. He was one of the best officers of the regiment, and was highly respected by every officer and soldier. At the time of his death he was a member of the M. E. Church, and said to his wife a few days before his death, when he felt that the end was near, "The harder the battle, the brighter the victory." He left a widow and two boys at the time of his death.

Captain George F. Conn

George F. Conn was born in Coshocton County, Ohio, October 30, 1836, and was a teacher before the war. Studied dentistry after leaving the army. Died at Soldiers Home (National) at Milwaukee, Wis., October 13, 1886.

Captain Conn was appointed First Lieutenant of Company B, First O.V. C., August 17, 1861, and was promoted to Captain, June 10, 1862, and resigned September 20, 1864. Company B left Camp Chase about October 1, 1861, and about two months before the balance of the regiment left for the front. It was sent on an expedition against Humphrey Marshall and had a sharp fight at Liberty, Ky., before the balance of the regiment arrived. Captain Conn was with his command almost continuously during his three years service, and commanded his company after Captain Laughlin was promoted to Major. While in command of his company at Washington, East Tennessee, defending a ford against the crossing of General Wheeler's forces, September 30, 1863, he was wounded in the hand. He was then sent home on leave of absence and did not see much further active service on account of his health.

Captain Hugh Hicks Siverd

Hugh Hicks Siverd was born December 28, 1839, near Harrisburg, Pennsylvania. He was a spinner in a woollen mill when the war broke out. He died at Winfield, Kansas, October 25, 1895. He was shot and killed while in the performance of official duty.

Captain Siverd had arrested a desperado from the Indian Territory for some crime, and as he was taking his prisoner to jail one of the desperado's pals met them on the street and shot Captain Siverd, killing him instantly. He was held in high esteem by the citizens of Winfield, and his untimely death was mourned by hundreds of the best citizens. As a testimonial to his memory, the citizens of Winfield erected a beautiful monument over his grave.

Captain Siverd enlisted in Company B, First O.V. C., August 21, 1861, and was promoted to Sergeant-Major; promoted to Second Lieutenant, October 1, 1862; First Lieutenant, April 1, 1863; to Captain. December 14, 1864, and was mustered out with his regiment at Hilton Head, S. C., September 13, 1865, having served almost one month more than four years. Captain Siverd was an ideal cavalry soldier, full of dash, with an utter disregard of danger, and at all times full of enthusiasm. He was for a long time Provost Officer of the brigade, and many of the surviving members of the brigade will no doubt have a very distinct recollection that at some time during their service they were put under arrest by Captain Siverd for straggling. He was one of the best known young officers in the regiment, as he was always at the front, and where there was a fight or any prospect of a fight, Captain Siverd was always found in line.

Lieutenant Frank P. Allen

Franklin Putnam Allen was born at Darby Creek, Madison County, Ohio, August 31, 1841. His father, William Allen, was of the Ethan Allen family, and his mother Harriet was a daughter of Joshua Ewing, also of revolutionary stock, and the first white settler of Darby Creek.

He enlisted in Company K, First O. V. C., September 22, 1861, and was an efficient Corporal and Sergeant, re-enlisted as a veteran, was on non-commissioned staff as Quartermaster-Sergeant, and later was commissioned as First Lieutenant, but died without learning of it. He was a much loved man and officer, trusty and intelligent, and was a fighting soldier. At Ebenezer Church, Ala., April 1, 1865, as he laid his hand on the gun of a rebel battery, hot and smoking, claiming it as his capture, he fell, shot through the groin. He lived to be taken from Selma on a hospital boat, on which he died near Cairo, Ill., May 25. A month later his body was removed to the home burial ground at Plain City, Ohio. His parents lie beside him now; but in their grief they rejoiced in the message he left the day he was shot: "If you get home, tell pa and ma it is all right with me; it all came right after I was hit."

Lieutenant Amos D. Leib

Amos David Leib was born near Bremen, Fairfield County, Ohio, on January 12, 1827, and died at his Island Home in the same county December 14, 1892. He spent his childhood days and early youth under his parents guiding care, receiving a good country school education and taking a course of study at the Ohio Wesleyan University.

At the breaking out of the war was a salesman at Keokuk,

Iowa. After the war he filled many responsible positions in his county and was unswerving in his connections of duty as a citizen. The deprivations and exposures of army service shortened his life by many years. In 1866 he married Elizabeth Ann Pope, of Marysville, Ohio, who still survives him with two children, a son and a daughter.

He was a member of the Masonic fraternity, and in politics a zealous Republican.

He enlisted in Company F, First O.V. C., September 5, 1861, and at the organization of the company was appointed Quartermaster-Sergeant, and soon afterward was promoted to Battalion Quartermaster-Sergeant and to Second Lieutenant, Company I, November 20, 1862; to First Lieutenant and Regimental Commissary, April 18, 1863, and mustered out January 10, 1865. Lieutenant Leib served as staff officer almost continuously during his term of service and was a prompt, energetic, efficient officer and had the confidence of his superior at all times. In addition to his duties as Commissary, he rendered important service during active campaigns in carrying orders on the field, and was always ready for any duty required of him. He was twice a prisoner of war. Once he was taken a prisoner on a train, captured by Dick McCann near Lavergne, Tenn., in, April, 1863, but was soon paroled. He was also captured by General Wheeler's cavalry while carrying dispatches near Cotton Port, Tenn., September 30, 1863. Johnnie Clem was a prisoner at the same time, and when they were paroled, Clem accompanied Lieutenant Leib to his home in Ohio. When Colonel Cupp was killed at the battle of Chickamauga, Lieutenant Leib had his body taken up and accompanied the remains home, and they were interred in Fairfield County, Ohio.

Lieutenant Harvey Ferguson

Harvey Ferguson was born April 26, 1829, in Ross County, Ohio, and came with his parents to Newark, Licking County, Ohio, when about six years old, where he ever afterwards resided. His education was obtained in the public schools of Newark. After leaving school he learned the carpenter trade with his father, but engaged in different occupations at different times. Was Sergeant-at-arms two terms and Postmaster one term in the House of Representatives, Columbus, Ohio. In the years 1851-2-3 was Deputy Clerk in Newark Post-office under Postmaster William Bell in 1855. In 1856 and 1857 was engaged in the grocery business with Enoch Wilson, Newark, Ohio. Was married to Mary C. Frey, September 22, 1852. Died June 12, 1876, in Newark, Ohio.

He enlisted in Company D, First O.V.C., as private, August 5, 1861. He was appointed Sergeant and then promoted to Second Lieutenant of Company H, April 18, 1863; promoted to First Lieutenant and Adjutant, to date from May 25, 1864, and was mustered out November 25, 1864, on expiration of term of service. Lieutenant Ferguson served continuously with the regiment from the time of his enlistment until he was discharged, and had special qualifications for the duties of a staff officer, as he was quite active, a good clerk and a fine-appearing officer. Both as a company and staff officer he rendered excellent service throughout the war, and during the Atlanta Campaign, as Adjutant of the regiment, and was especially active in all of his arduous duties, and was regarded as a very excellent officer by Colonel Eggleston.

LIEUTENANT CHARLES H. GOODRICH

Charles H. Goodrich was born at Sharon, Ohio, on January 20, 1844. Received his education at Sharon College, and afterwards learned the printing trade in the Noble County Republican office at Caldwell, Ohio.

At the close of the war he followed the occupation of a newspaper publisher until November of 1889, he having received the appointment of door-keeper of the National House of Representatives at Washington, D. C.; but later he was transferred to a more lucrative position in the U. S. Treasury Department. He died August 31, 1892, at Washington, D. C. He published during his newspaper career *The Noble County Republican*, Caldwell, Ohio; *The Miller County Monitor*, California, Mo.;

The Newcomerstown Argus, Newcomerstown, Ohio; *The Caldwell Press*, Caldwell, Ohio; *The Monroe Gazette*, Woodsfield, Ohio; *The Troy Chronicle* and *Daily Trojan*, Troy, Ohio.

He enlisted in Company D, First O. V. C., August 5, 1861; appointed Corporal, and October 2, 1862, appointed Sergeant; appointed First Sergeant and commissioned as First Lieutenant, Company M, June 28, 1865; mustered out at Cincinnati, Ohio, July 12, 1865, having served within twenty-three days of four years. He was a good soldier and won his bars by hard service in the field.

Lieutenant John M. Renick

John M. Renick, son of Mr. and Mrs. George Renick, was born near Chillicothe, Ross County, Ohio, October 1, 1831. His occupation before entering the service was that of a farmer. Died at Corinth, Miss., May 28, 1862.

He was appointed Second Lieutenant of Company M, August 30, 1861, and served with the regiment through the campaign in Kentucky in the winter of 1861 and 1862; he was also through the campaign of the siege of Corinth in April and May, 1862, and on that campaign he contracted the disease from which he died. Lieutenant Renick was a gentleman of high character, and had his life been spared, would no doubt have made his mark in the regiment, as he was very much attached to the service. He was buried with military honours, this being the first military funeral of any officer in the regiment.

Brevet Major-General Eli Long

Graduated at Military School near Frankfort, Kentucky (in charge of Colonel E. W. Morgan, a distinguished graduate of the Military Academy at West Point in the class of General Benham), in the month of June, 1855. At the instance of Hon. James Guthrie, of Kentucky, he was appointed Second Lieutenant in the First U. S. Cavalry. Joined his regiment at Lecompton, Kansas, on recruiting service, and stationed at New-Albany, Indiana, during the winter of 1856- 57. Rejoined his regiment in April, 1857, was with it on the Cheyenne Expedition, in the summer of 1857. He served on the frontier at Fort Leavenworth, Fort Riley, Fort Lyon, and other points, participating in a number of hard and dangerous expeditions against the Indians, and when the war of the rebellion commenced he was stationed at Fort Lyon.

In August, 1861, he prevented serious loss and damage to the Government by surprising and capturing near Fort Lyon, without firing a shot, a well armed and equipped company of thirty-eight men and fifty or sixty animals, *en route* from Denver City to join Price in Missouri. General Long was promoted in his regiment to First Lieutenant, March 21, and to Captain, May 24, 1861. With one squadron of his regiment he went from Fort Lyon to Fort Leavenworth, in December, 1861. In February, 1862, reported with the same squadron for duty to General Buell at Louisville, Ky. Participated in the battle of Chaplain Hills, near Perryville, Ky. Remained on duty with his regiment as General Rosecrans' escort until the battle of Stone River, where he was wounded by a ball in the left shoulder while leading his company in the charge made by his regiment on the thirty-first of December, 1862. Through the recommendations of General Rosecrans and General D. S. Stanley he was appointed Colonel of the Fourth Ohio Volunteer Cavalry. He participated in the operations of the cavalry from that time until the battle of Chickamauga, where his brigade was used very roughly, losing one hundred and thirty-four officers and men out of nine hundred, killed, wounded and missing (most of them of the first two classes), in very short time. He commanded his brigade in the pursuit of the rebel General Wheeler from the Tennessee River, at Washington, East Tennessee, to the Tennessee River at Lamb's Ferry. There is no doubt about the fact that the division of which Colonel Long's brigade formed a part was the means of keeping Chattanooga in our possession by its rapid pursuit and successful engagements with General Wheeler's command, thus preventing him from destroying the communications of our army.

Colonel Long commanded and led his brigade in a charge at

McMinnville and at Farmington, Tenn., at both of which places the enemy was badly defeated, losing at the last named place three or four hundred prisoners and three pieces of artillery, and losing on the trip over one thousand prisoners. Colonel Long's horse was shot at McMinnville, and both horse and rider were shot at Farmington. During the battle of Missionary Ridge, Colonel Long, in command of fifteen hundred cavalry, marched to Cleveland, East Tennessee, destroying thirty miles of the Knoxville and Chattanooga Railroad, burning a valuable cap factory and rolling mill at Cleveland, capturing and destroying a wagon train of eighty-two wagons, and capturing three hundred and twenty-two prisoners, with which he returned to Chattanooga within three days after leaving there. Shortly after this, with the same command, he reported to General Sherman and marched two days in advance of his infantry column into Knoxville, thence through the western part of North Carolina into Northern Georgia, having marched four hundred and sixty-three miles in seventeen marching days, with little food for the stock and less for the men. Soon after returning to Calhoun he administered a severe castigation to General Wheeler, completely routing his command and capturing nearly five hundred stands of small arms and one hundred and twenty-seven prisoners, including five officers, he having less than one hundred and fifty men in his column when he made the charge.

In February, 1864, he participated with his command in the reconnaissance on Dalton with the Fourteenth Army Corps, having several sharp skirmishes. From thence, in March, he had a leave of absence for a month. Rejoined his brigade in Columbia, Tenn., where it had been ordered to refit. Superintended its remount and refitting, and marched in the month of May south, joining the Seventeenth Army Corps, under General Blair, at Decatur, Alabama, and marching thence with him to Kingston, Georgia (*en route* badly defeating the rebel General Roddy and his command at Moulton, Alabama, capturing a number of prisoners from him), where he joined the main army under General Sherman and participated from that time in all or nearly all of the operations of the army up to the twenty-first of August, 1864, when he was wounded in the right leg and arm, his horse being shot in the head at the same time, on the raid of General Kilpatrick, near Lovejoy Station, south of Atlanta. He was appointed Brigade General of Volunteers, August 18, 1864.

Returning from a leave of absence, owing to his wounds, he rejoined his command at Nashville, Tenn., in November, 1864, when he was assigned to the command of the Second Division of Cavalry Corps, M. D. M. Returning to his command at Louisville, Ky., in a very disorganized condition, partially unavoidably so, and partially owing to Circular 75, War Department, 1864, having deprived the command of over half its officers. The division was remounted, armed and equipped, and left the place on the twenty-eighth of December, 1864, in better condition than it had ever been. He started, in command of his division, on the late expedition of Brevet Major-General Wilson, through Alabama and Georgia; his division, twelve hundred and fifty men in line, dismounted, attacked and captured Selma, Alabama, on the second of April, 1865, which was defended by earthworks intended to resist infantry. Thirty pieces of artillery in position, with three or four thousand of General Forrest's best cavalry, also from three to four thousand militia, twenty-seven hundred prisoners, two hundred pieces of artillery in the works and arsenals, and a vast amount of materials of war were captured at this place. Many persons think this the handsomest thing done by cavalry during the war. The works were taken within twenty-five minutes after the advance was sounded. But three hundred and twenty officers and men of the twelve hundred and fifty engaged were killed and wounded.

In this engagement General Long was wounded by a bullet on the top and right side of his head, indenting the skull, producing a severe concussion of the brain, and paralysing the tongue, right side of the face and right arm. He still suffers from the effects of this wound, and the recovery of the use of his hand is extremely doubtful.

Throughout the war he never, in a single instance, received

aught but the commendations of his superior officers, and the War Department has shown its appreciation of his services by making him a Brevet Major-General of Volunteers, and Brevet Colonel, U. S. A., from the thirteenth of March, 1865.

General Long commanded the brigade in which the First Ohio served from the battle of Stone's River, December 31, 1862, until November, 1864, when he was assigned to the command of the Second Cavalry Division, Wilson's Cavalry Corps. General Long was held in high esteem by the officers and soldiers of the brigade which he commanded so long, and it may be safely said that no officer could have had the confidence of his command in a greater degree than he had.

Major-General David S. Stanley

Born in Ohio June 1, 1828; retiring year 1892; appointed from Ohio. Graduated M. A., class of 1852; Brevet Second Lieutenant, Second Dragoons, July 1, 1852; Second Lieutenant, September 6, 1853; Second Lieutenant, First Cavalry, March 3, 1855; Captain, Fourth Cavalry, March 16, 1861; Brigadier-General of Volunteers, September 28, 1861; Major-General of Volunteers, November 29, 1862; accepted April 10, 1863; honourably mustered out February 1, 1866; Major, Fifth U. S. Cavalry, December 1, 1863; Colonel Twenty-second Infantry, July 28, 1866; Brigadier-General, U. S. Army, March 24, 1884. Brevet Lieutenant-Colonel, U. S. Army, December 31, 1862, for gallant and meritorious service in the battle of Stone River, Tenn; Colonel, May 15, 1864, for gallant and meritorious services in the battle of Resaca, Ga.; Brigadier-General, March 13, 1865, for gallant and meritorious service in the battle of Buff's Station, Ga.; Major-General, March 13, 1865, for gallant and meritorious services in the battle of Franklin, Tenn.

On frontier duty, 1852-1861, serving with distinction against Indians, especially the Comanches. He commanded a division in the army of General Rosecrans at the battle of Corinth, October 4, 1862, and distinguished himself as commander of all the cavalry at the battle of Stone River, which ended January

2, 1863; Chickamauga Campaign, September, 1863; Missionary Ridge, November, 1863; Atlanta Campaign, 1864. About August 1, 1864, he obtained command of the Fourth Corps in Sherman's army. Took part in the battle of Franklin, November 30, 1864, where he was severely wounded; led the brigade which restored the break in the main line, which had just been penetrated by the Confederate forces. In 1872- 73 he commanded expeditions in Dakota and Montana. Commissioned to locate Brule Indians under Spotted Tail, and Ogallalla Indians under Red Cloud, summer of 1878. Fort Clark, Texas, from 1879 to 1882; 1883, headquarters removed to Fort Lewis, Col; engaged during the year in pacifying semi-hostile Navajo Indians; 1884, headquarters at Santa Fe; commanding Department of Texas from 1884 to April 21, 1890.

He was appointed Chief of Cavalry, Army of the Cumberland, in November, 1862, and commanded the cavalry of that army with distinction throughout the Stone Elver, Tullahoma and Chickamauga campaigns.

Among the many letters of recommendation now on file in the War Department regarding the service of General Stanley, we only have room to quote from one written by General Thomas regarding the battle of Franklin, Tenn.

"It was here that his personal bravery was more decidedly brought out, perhaps, than on any other field, and the terrible destruction and defeat, which disheartened and checked the fierce assaults of the enemy is due more to his heroism and gallantry than to any other officer on the field."

Major-General James Harrison Wilson

Major-General James Harrison Wilson was born in Shawneetown, Ill., September 2, 1837, and was educated in the common schools and McKendree College, and graduated from West Point in 1860. Appointed Second Lieutenant of Topographical Engineers, July 1, 1860; First Lieutenant, September 9, 1861; Captain, May 7, 1863; Lieutenant-Colonel, Thirty-fifth Infantry, July 28, 1866; discharged December 31, 1870.

He was also brevetted in the regular army; Major, April 11, 1862; Brevet Lieutenant-Colonel, November 24, 1864; Brevet Colonel, May 5, 1864; Brevet Brigadier-General, March 13, 1865, and Brevet Major-General, March 13, 1865. All of these promotions were made "for gallant and meritorious service on the battle-field" during the war of the rebellion.

General Wilson was Chief of the Topographical Engineers on the Port Royal Expedition, including bombardment of Fort Pulaski, and he was aid on the staff of General McClellan at the battle of South Mountain, and was Inspector-General of the Army of the Tennessee during the Vicksburg Campaign in 1863. He was with General Grant's army at the battle of Missionary Ridge and relief of Knoxville in the fall of 1863. For a short time after that he had charge of the Cavalry Bureau at Washington, D. C., and was then appointed to the command of the Third Cavalry Division under General Sheridan and served in that capacity in the Shenandoah Valley from May to August, 1864. In October, 1864, he was assigned to command the cavalry corps of the Military Division of the Mississippi under General Thomas at Nashville, Tenn. lie organized the cavalry of that department very rapidly and contributed very largely to the success of General Thomas at the battle of Nashville. After the battle of Nashville he organized the greatest cavalry expedition of the Civil War, and through the months of March and April, 1865, made a raid through Alabama and Georgia, and in twenty-eight days captured the fortified cities of Selma, Montgomery, Columbus, Ga., and Macon, Ga., capturing twenty-three stands of colours, two hundred and eighty-eight pieces of artillery and six thousand eight hundred and twenty prisoners, including Jeff. Davis.

General Wilson has recently been appointed Major-General of Volunteers in the war with Spain.

Major-General George Crook

George Crook was born in Montgomery County, near Dayton, Ohio, September 8, 1828. Entered West Point in 1848 and graduated July 1, 1852. He was appointed Brevet Second Lieutenant of the Fourth U. S. Infantry. Promoted to Second Lieutenant in 1853; to First Lieutenant, March 11, 1853; and to Captain, May 4, 1861. Appointed Colonel of the Thirty-sixth O.V. I., September 12, 1861, and was promoted to Brigadier-General, September 7, 1862, and served in the Army of West Virginia and in the Army of the Potomac until January, 1863. In that month he was transferred to the Army of the Cumberland and commanded the Second Cavalry Division under General Rosecrans with great distinction through the Chickamauga and Chattanooga campaign. In February, 1864, he was again detached from the Army of the Cumberland and assigned to the command of the Third Division in West Virginia. During the summer of 1864 his command was engaged in continuous fighting in Western Virginia. July 20, 1864, he was brevetted Major General for distinguished gallantry. During July and August his army operated with that of General Sheridan, and in September he was assigned to the command of the Department of West Virginia. In all of the campaigns in West Virginia, and in the Shenandoah Valley, General Crook commanded with distinguished ability, and in January, 1865, he was promoted to a full Major General.

He participated in all the movements of Sheridan's Cavalry until the close of the war, and in the eleven days preceding General Lee's surrender, his division lost one-third of its number, killed and wounded. After the close of the war he was assigned to the command of the District of Wilmington, N. C., which he commanded until mustered out of the volunteer service on the 15th of January, 1866. After the close of the war, he served on the frontier fighting the Indians for a number of years, and was promoted to Brigadier-General, October 29, 1873, and to Major-General, April G, 1888. He died on the twenty-first day of March, 1890. General Crook was one of the most distinguished Cavalry Commanders of the war, and no officer of the Army of the Cumberland had the confidence of the Cavalry in a greater degree than had General Crook.

Whitelaw Ried, in his *Ohio in the War*, speaks of General Crook in the great Cavalry Raid of Wheeler after the battle of Chickamauga as follows:

With two thousand five hundred men he drove General Wheeler before him, and in three battles routed and defeated him, capturing all his artillery. In these battles the use of the sabre was first introduced in the Cavalry of that army, and General Crook was thanked in orders and privately both by General Rosecrans and General Thomas.

General Emory Upton

General Emory Upton commanded the Fourth Division of General Wilson's Cavalry Corps, in which the First Ohio was brigaded in the Cavalry expedition through Alabama and Georgia in March and April, 1865.

He was a brave, dashing young officer and commanded his division with great skill throughout Wilson's great raid. He died in California a number of years ago.

He graduated from West Point and was appointed Second Lieutenant Fourth U. S. Artillery, May 6, 1861, and Colonel of the One Hundred and Twenty-first New York Volunteers October 23, 1862. For meritorious service on the field during the war, he was brevetted in the regular army as Major and Lieutenant-Colonel and Colonel. He was promoted to Brigadier-General of Volunteers May 12, 1864, for a distinguished service at the battle of the Wilderness and brevetted Major-General of Volunteers October 19, 1864. Brevetted Brigadier-General U. S. A. and brevetted Major-General U. S. A., March 13, 1865, for gallant and meritorious services on the field during the war. After the war he served as Lieutenant-Colonel of the Twenty-fifth U. S. Infantry, Eighteenth Infantry, First Artillery, Fourth Artillery, and was made Colonel of the Fourth Artillery, July 1, 1880.

General Andrew J. Alexander

General Andrew J. Alexander was born in Woodford County, Kentucky, November 21, 1833. He married Avelina Throop Martin, of Auburn, New York. He was educated at St. Louis, Mo., in the common schools and afterward attended college at Danville, Ky.

When the war of the rebellion broke out, he entered the army as a Second Lieutenant of the Third Regular Cavalry. Early in the war he was ordered to Washington for duty on the staff of General McClellan, and in March, 1862, he was designated to act as A. A. G. of the Cavalry forces under General Stoneman, and was with McClellan through the Peninsula Campaign, and also served as Staff Officer with General Banks at Washington in October, 1862. He was assigned as A. A. G. of the Third Army Corps under General Stoneman and at the Battle of Gettysburg, he was A . A. G. to General Pleasanton and was distinguished for services on that field. In the spring of 1864 he was ordered west, and assigned as A. A. G. of the Seventeenth Corps, commanded by General Frank P. Blair, and served through the Atlanta Campaign with distinction.

At the Battle of Nashville he was General Wilson's Chief of Staff, was promoted to Brigadier-General in January, 1865, and was assigned to the command of the Second Brigade, Fourth Division in Wilson's Cavalry Corps. Soon after the close of the war, he was brevetted by General Grant, "Colonel" in the Regular Army and "Brigadier-General" for distinguished gallantry in the Cavalry engagements at Ebenezer Church, Ga., and Columbus, Ga. After the war he joined his regiment, the Third U. S. Cavalry, under his proper rank as Captain and served with distinction on the frontier, fighting the Indians, and was promoted to Lieutenant-Colonel of the Second U. S. Cavalry in 1879. While in command at Fort Custer, in 1881, his health failed and in 1885 he was placed on the retired list. He died on a railroad train between New York and Utica on the 4th day of May, 1887.

He was an ideal Cavalry officer and General Upton after the great Wilson Raid, declared him to be "equal to any command the fortunes of war might bring him." General Wilson, in his biography of Alexander says:

> He was gentle and considerate in social life, faithful and devoted in friendship, calm and deliberate in council, vigilant and industrious in camp and on the march, bold and resolute in action ; he was a model husband and father, a noble citizen and model soldier.

The First Ohio Cavalry served in his brigade from January, 1865, until the close of the war, and Captain Yeoman was Inspector General on his staff.

Major John H. Robinson

Major John H. Robinson was born in New York City about the year 1818, but removed to Martinsburg, Va., early in his childhood, and moved from that place to Decatur, Brown County, Ohio, in 1838, where he engaged in the merchant tailoring business. In the year 1845, he moved to Washington, C. H., where he was engaged in the same business, and in 1850 he went across the plains to California with emigrants and stock and returned in 1851. Returned to California again in 1852, but soon returned and engaged in the dry goods business in Illinois until the breaking out of the war. From his early youth he was very much interested in military matters and during all of his life made a study of military tactics. In August, 1862, he was appointed Captain of Company A, First O. V. C. This was the first commission issued to any officer in that regiment. The men in his company furnished their own horses, and about the middle of August went into Camp Chase, O. His company soon became very efficient in drilling and were equipped some time before the other companies of the regiment. As Cavalry was very much in demand in Virginia, Companies A and C, First O. V. C., were sent to Virginia before the other companies of the regiment were equipped. They did good service in Virginia up to the fall of 1864, when they were again united with the regiment at Nashville, Tenn.

Captain Robinson was a very efficient officer, very fond of military service, but as he was in delicate health when he enlisted he was not able to stand the rigours of the hard campaigns. June 1, 1862, he was promoted to Major and died at his home in Washington, C. H., October 29, 1862. Had his life been spared, he would no doubt have gained distinction during the war.

Major-General Judson Kilpatrick

General Judson Kilpatrick was born in New Jersey and was appointed to West Point from that state. He was appointed Second Lieutenant of Artillery May 6, 1861, and First Lieutenant May 14, 1861; Captain, November 30, 1864, for gallant and meritorious service during the war, and was brevetted Lieutenant-Colonel and Colonel in the regular army, and for gallantry at the battle of Resaca, Ga., brevetted Brigadier-General March 13, 1865, and for gallant service during the campaign in the Carolinas was promoted to Brevet Major-General. He resigned December 1, 1865.

General Kilpatrick was a brave and gallant cavalry officer during the war, serving in the Army of the Potomac through all of the campaigns of that army up to the spring of 1864, and was a division commander. In the spring of 1864 he was ordered to report to General Sherman, who was then organizing his great campaign from Chattanooga to Atlanta. At the beginning of this campaign in May, 1864, General Kilpatrick was assigned to command a division of cavalry, and at the battle of Resaca he was severely wounded. He was disabled from duty until about the middle of August, when he again returned to the front and commanded two divisions of cavalry in his raid around Hood's army in Atlanta in the latter part of August, 1864. On "Sherman's march to the sea" he was in command of the cavalry forces, and did excellent service. It is sufficient to say of his military career that on the campaign from Chattanooga to Atlanta, and from Atlanta to the sea, he had the full confidence of General Sherman and was highly complimented by that officer for his many successful cavalry expeditions. After the war he served two terms as minister to Chile, and died many years ago while in discharge of his duties as minister in that country. He was an ideal cavalry officer, and the members of the First O.V.C. have good reason to remember him, as they were in his command on some of the hardest and most dangerous charges in which they participated during the war.

The End

After the surrender of the rebel forces in Central Georgia to Colonel Eggleston, who was in command at Atlanta, and the capture of Jeff. Davis, in which a detachment of the regiment played so important a part, there was but little service to perform in closing up the great drama of war that had been deluging the country with the blood of the flower of our armies North and South for four years. The regiment was broken up into detachments, and did garrison duty in Georgia and South Carolina during the summer of 1865 until it was mustered out, and any incidents of the last four months service of the regiment would seem very tame and barren of danger and adventure compared with the four years of continuous, active and dangerous service of the war just closed.

When Sherman started on his march to the sea, he had thoroughly destroyed the railroad from Atlanta north and south toward Macon, and when our cavalry occupied these two last-named cities, the matter of getting supplies at once was very important. As both the Union and Confederate armies had swept back and forth over this country in the summer of 1864, it had been stripped of everything in the way of forage and provisions. But with Wilson's bold riders no obstacle seemed insurmountable, and the following account of an expedition planned and successfully executed, shows how the soldier in the field adapts himself to the surroundings and is ready for any exigency.

When the regiment was stationed at Macon it was learned that there was a little steamer on the Ocmulgee River, at Hawkinsville, that the rebels had been using for transporting supplies from toward Savannah to Macon. Captain Kirkendall was given a detail of about thirty men from the regiment and was ordered to press the boat into service and go down to Savannah after supplies. He marched his command to Hawkinsville on foot about thirty miles, pressed the steamer into the U. S. service, secured the service of an old coloured man, who had run on the river, as pilot, and started for Savannah. The river was narrow, water shallow, and he was compelled to. tie up at night, so the progress was slow. Finally the boat arrived at Savannah, was loaded with supplies, and as the regiment had left Macon, the boat was run up the Savannah River to Augusta, and the supplies were delivered to the command at that point. It was quite an experience for these bold troopers, after a service of nearly four years in the saddle, to assume the role of "roustabouts" on a steamer; but no doubt they could do the swearing necessary to be ranked as a first class "Jack Tar," and it is said that Captain Kirkendall was not slow in picking up the lingo and was as much at home in giving his commands as he was in giving orders to "draw sabre" or "advance carbine".

The regiment marched via Augusta, Ga., leaving Atlanta June 19, 1865, to Orangeburg, S. C., where Colonel Eggleston was appointed Inspector of Cavalry on General Gillmore's staff. During the summer the regiment did garrison duty at Orangeburg, Summerville, Charleston and Hilton Head, and found that duty rather monotonous after their incessant active service.

Marches

It is hardly possible to name every point struck by the regiment during the war, or the number of miles marched; but after careful examination of all the records bearing on the service of the regiment and consultation with many officers and soldiers, the following points named will be found as near correct as it can be made.

The regiment left Columbus, Ohio, December 9, 1861, and the route over which it marched will be followed with great interest by every survivor.

Columbus to Cincinnati, Ohio, and by boat to Louisville, Ky. Louisville via Bardstown and Springfield to Lebanon, Ky. Lebanon to Louisville. Louisville by river to Smithland and up the Cumberland Elver to Nashville, Tenn. Nashville to Pittsburg Landing, Tenn., *via* Columbia, Waynesboro and Savannah. Pittsburg Landing to Corinth, Miss. Corinth to Booneville, and back to Corinth. Corinth to Huntsville, Ala. Huntsville *via* Athens, Decherd, Altamont, McMinnville to Nashville. Nashville to Louisville, Ky. Louisville *via* Perryville and Bardstown to Nashville. Nashville to Murfreesboro, Manchester, Tullahoma, Decherd, Winchester, Athens, Ala., Huntsville, Ala., Fayetteville, Tenn., Pulaski, Winchester, Stevenson, Ala. Down the Tennessee River fifty miles and across Lookout Mountain to Alpine, Ga., Lafayette, Ga., and back to Alpine. Over the mountain to McLamore's Cove and to Crawfish Springs, Ga. Crawfish Springs, Ga., to Chattanooga; up the Tennessee River to Washington; back to Smith's Cross-roads; over the mountains to McMinnville, Murfreesboro, Shelbyville, Farmington, Pulaski and Muscle Shoals on the Tennessee River, Ala.; back to Fayetteville, Tenn., Winchester, Stevenson, Ala., Paint Rock, Ala., Bridgeport, Chattanooga, Cleveland, Tenn.; back to Chattanooga and up the Tennessee River and over the Tellico Mountains into North Carolina to Murphy; back to Calhoun, Tenn., four hundred and fifty miles. Calhoun to Knoxville, and back to Chattanooga, Paint Rock, Ala., Huntsville, Athens, Pulaski, Tenn., Columbia, Nashville, Louisville, Ky., Cincinnati and Columbus, Ohio, on veteran furlough. Columbus to Nashville, Tenn., Columbia, Tenn., Decatur, Ala., west to Courtland, Moulton, and east to Rome, Ga., Kingston, Big Shanty, Marietta, Roswell, Decatur, Ga. Then in rear of our army from Decatur west to Sandtown, Kilpatrick raid around Hood's army in Atlanta, via Jonesboro, Lovejoy, McDonough, Stone Mountain to Decatur. With Sherman's army to right of Atlanta, to Jonesboro. Then back to Atlanta. From Atlanta to Resaca, and then to Gaylesville, Ala., and Rome, Ga. Then to Chattanooga, to Nashville, and Louisville, Ky., and back to Nashville *via* Columbia and Pulaski to Muscle Shoals and

Gravelly Springs on the Tennessee River, Ala. Wilson's raid *via* Montevallo and Plantersville to Selma, Ala., and then to Montgomery and Columbus, Ga., Macon and back to Atlanta and to Augusta, Ga. To Hilton Head, S. C.; by ocean steamer to New York City; then to Camp Chase, Ohio. Total, 7,660 miles.

In the table above only the regular marches of the regiment are mentioned. Adding to this one-half, which is a very conservative estimate, for scouting, reconnoitering and outpost duty, and we have a grand total of 11,490 miles.

The following table shows the total enlistment in the regiment during the war, by companies:

Number of Men in the Regiment

A	171
B	141
C	117
D	139
E	126
F	132
G	161
H	168
I	156
K	140
L	158
M	162
Total	1771
Field and staff	50
Unassigned recruits	56
Total	1877
	32
	1845

Thirty-two of the field and staff were promoted from the ranks and from officers of the line, which leaves a total enlistment of 1845 men. The strength of the regiment when mustered out was 733.

Losses

In the record of losses in the regiment as they appear in the "Roll of Honour" published by the Adjutant-Generals, Department of Ohio, and herewith attached, there are many errors.

The roster of each company has been submitted to some of the officers and soldiers of the company for inspection, and many corrections in casualties have been made, but cannot be noted on the roster, as the rosters were printed by the state some years ago. We could only add the casualties found by the inspection made, as noted above, to the total in each company and to the grand total of the regiment, and no doubt there are many others that should have been reported. The muster-out-roll of many of the companies in cavalry regiments are very imperfect, and the First Ohio is no exception in this regard. This can be accounted for by reason of the fact that cavalry regiments, when off on raids or other expeditions, would often not see their wagon trains for weeks and would have neither books nor paper to make reports, and when they did reach the wagons, some casualties would be overlooked and would not be reported. In some instances troopers would be dismounted by their horses either being wounded, killed or giving out, and the soldier was left to look out for himself, and was perhaps wounded or captured, or both, and would be sent back to the dismounted cavalry rendezvous, from which he would be discharged, and the "muster out" would only have him marked "missing in action."

In compiling casualties, all these matters have been to contend with by the author, and every possible effort has been made by writing letters and making inquiry of comrades at reunions and all occasions to obtain reliable information on all these points.

Field and Staff

Killed and died of wounds and disease	5
Wounded	4
Captured	3
	12

Company A
Killed and died of wounds and disease	11
Wounded	11
Captured	11
	33

Company B
Killed and died of wounds and disease	19
Wounded	12
Captured	8
	39

Company C
Killed and died of wounds and disease	13
Wounded	7
Captured	6
	26

Company D
Killed and died of wounds and disease	14
Wounded	11
Captured	14
	39

Company E
Killed and died of wounds and disease	17
Wounded	9
Captured	12
	38

Company F
Killed and died of wounds and disease	16
Wounded	9
Captured	10
	35

Company G
Killed and died of wounds and disease	17
Wounded	9
Captured	14
	40

Company H
Killed and died of wounds and disease	24
Wounded	12
Captured	9
	45

Company I
Killed and died of wounds and disease	13
Wounded	17
Captured	12
	42

Company K
Killed and died of wounds and disease	21
Wounded	12
Captured	13
	46

Company L
Killed and died of wounds and disease	16
Wounded	7
Captured	6
	29

Company M
Killed and died of wounds and disease	17
Wounded	10
Captured	14
	41

Three unassigned recruits died before reaching the regiment. In some cases the rolls are marked "wounded in action" and then "died in hospital" and there may be a doubt whether the soldier died of wounds or disease; but of those who were killed on the field, in addition to those who died of wounds, the record shows as follows and of this number six were commissioned officers.

Killed on the Field
Field and staff	4
Company A	5

Company B	4
Company C	3
Company D	5
Company E	4
Company F	5
Company G	4
Company H	5
Company I	5
Company K	7
Company L	4
Company M	5

The losses as given in the above tables make an aggregate of 461 casualties or almost 25 per cent, of the total number of enlistments in the regiment. The number wounded, as shown, is 134, which no doubt is too small, as the record of many of the slightly wounded does not appear on the muster-out rolls. A very conservative average is four wounded to one killed, and taking this as a basis, it would add upward of eighty to the list of wounded, which would bring the casualties up to 535 or almost thirty per cent; and after a careful examination of the records and all official data, the losses as above stated can be relied on as almost absolutely correct. The number taken prisoner was 130, and the average in each company is almost the same. No large number of prisoners were taken at any one time, but they were captured all along through the years of the war in small squads, usually when on outpost duty or scouting. Many who were captured and were only in the hands of the enemy a few days were never reported, and the number captured was remarkably small for a regiment that was in contact with the enemy as many times as the First. At the battle of Stone River, when the regiment charged clear through the lines of the enemy, and the lines were closed up both in rear and on the flanks, about one hundred men of the regiment were captured, but all excepting a few cut their way out soon afterwards. About twenty were captured at Courtland, Alabama, July 25, 1862, and fifteen at Cotton Port, Tenn., September 30, 1863, this being the largest numbers captured at any one time. The regiment was engaged in fifty-one battles and skirmishes, as shown by the official record on the first page of this history, and many picket fights and skirmishes are not named; but it is known positively that the regiment was under fire upward of one hundred times. The regiment fought on many of the great and decisive battle-fields of the war, and has written in characters of blood on its battle-flag Corinth, Perryville, Stone River, Chickamauga, Mission Ridge, "one hundred days under fire from Chattanooga to Atlanta" the great cavalry raid under General Kilpatrick around Atlanta, the Wheeler raid through Tennessee, and the Wilson raid through Alabama and Georgia in the spring of 1865, and were in the saddle when the last gun of the war of the great rebellion was fired. The best evidence of the hard and dangerous service of a regiment are the casualties, and the graves of the heroic dead of the First Ohio dot every mountain and valley that marks the battle-fields of the Army of the Ohio and Army of the Cumberland. It was no braver nor better than many other regiments, its roll of honoured dead is not as long as some others, but it never failed to respond to any and every call to duty. The record is made and the story is told. Every member of the grand old regiment is justly proud of the history of our service, and of which he was a part; and when the last survivor has answered "Here!" and "Taps" is sounded over his grave will our descendants remember well that the goodly heritage left them of a "country one and undivided" was bought by the blood of their fathers.

The regiment was mustered out at Hilton Head, South Carolina, September 13, 1865, and discharged at Camp Chase, Ohio, September 28, 1865.

Roster of Troops

FIRST OHIO VOLUNTEER CAVALRY.

THREE YEARS' SERVICE.

This Regiment was organized at Camp Chase, Ohio, from August 17th to October 5th, 1861, to serve three years. On the expiration of their terms of service, the original members (except veterans) were mustered out, and the organization, composed of veterans and recruits, continued in service until it was mustered out by companies, as follows: A to K, inclusive, and M September 13, 1865, at Hilton Head, S. C., and Company L September 26, 1865, at Nashville, Tenn., in accordance with orders from the War Department.

Companies A and C were ordered to West Virginia in September, 1861, and were attached to the commands of Gens. Shields and Banks, in the Shenandoah Valley; and with the Army of Virginia under Gen. Pope and the Army of the Potomac, and as Headquarters Guard of the Cavalry Divisions of Gens. Gregg and Kilpatrick, they bore an honorable part in the campaigns and engagements in Virginia, Maryland and Pennsylvania, until the spring of 1864, when they were ordered to join the regiment.

The official list of battles in which this Regiment was engaged is not yet published by the War Department, but the following list has been compiled after careful research during the compilation of this work. It does not include numerous battles and skirmishes in which single companies and small detachments of the regiment were engaged:

BOONEVILLE, MISS.,	May 30, 1862.
RUSSELLVILLE, ALA.,	July 1, 1862.
COURTLAND, ALA.,	July 25, 1862.
BARDSTOWN, KY.,	October 4, 1862.
PERRYVILLE, KY.,	October 8, 1862.
STONE RIVER, TENN.,	December 31, 1862, to January 2, 1863.
ELK RIVER, TENN.,	July 2, 1863
ALPINE, GA.,	September 10, 1863.
CHICKAMAUGA, GA.,	September 19-20, 1863.
WASHINGTON, TENN.,	October 1, 1863.
PAINT ROCK, ALA.,	October 30, 1863.
CLEVELAND, TENN.,	November 27, 1863.
CALHOUN, TENN.,	December 16, 1863.
DECATUR, ALA.,	May 26, 1864.
MOULTON, ALA.,	May 29, 1864.
NOONDAY CREEK, GA.,	June 15, 1864.
LOVEJOY STATION, GA.,	August 20, 1864.
ATLANTA CAMPAIGN.	
EBENEZER CHURCH, GA.,	April 1, 1865.
SELMA, ALA.,	April 2, 1865.
COLUMBUS, GA.,	April 16, 1865.

1st REGIMENT OHIO VOLUNTEER CAVALRY.

FIELD AND STAFF.

Mustered in Oct. 5, 1861, at Camp Chase, O., by John R. Edie, Major 15th Infantry, U. S. A. Mustered out Sept. 13, 1865, at Hilton Head, S. C., by Leslie Smith, Brevet Major and Captain 1st Infantry, U. S. A., and Commissary Musters, District of South Carolina.

Names.	Rank.	Age.	Date of Entering the Service.	Period of Service.	Remarks.
Owen P. Ransom	Colonel	46	Aug. 17, 1861	3 yrs.	Resigned Dec. 10, 1861.
Minor Milliken	do	27	Aug. 24, 1861	3 yrs.	Promoted from Major Jan. 11, 1862; discharged March 15, 1862; re-instated June 6, 1862; killed Dec. 31, 1862, in battle of Stone River, Tenn.
Beroth B. Eggleston	do	45	Aug. 8, 1861	3 yrs.	Promoted to Major from Captain Co. E June 20, 1862; to Colonel April 1, 1863; Brevet Brig. General March 13, 1865; mustered out with regiment Sept. 13, 1865.
Thomas C. H. Smith	Lt. Col.	42	Aug. 23, 1861	3 yrs.	Promoted to Colonel Dec. 31, 1862, but not mustered; to Brig. General to date, Nov. 29, 1862.
James Laughlin	do	40	Aug. 17, 1861	3 yrs.	Promoted to Major from Captain Co. B June 10, 1862; to Lieut. Colonel Dec. 31, 1862; resigned April 1, 1863.
Valentine Cupp	do	30	Sept. 5, 1861	3 yrs.	Promoted to Major from Captain Co. F Dec. 31, 1862; to Lieut. Colonel April 1, 1863; died Sept. 20, 1863, of wounds received Sept. 20, 1863, in battle of Chickamauga, Ga.
Thomas J. Pattin	do	37	Sept. 16, 1861	3 yrs.	Promoted to Major from Captain Co. L Dec. 31, 1862; to Lieut. Colonel Sept. 20, 1863; mustered out Nov. 25, 1864, at Louisville, Ky., on expiration of term of service.
Stephen C. Writer	do	33	Aug. 17, 1861	3 yrs.	Promoted to Major from Captain Co. I April 1, 1863; to Lieut. Colonel Dec. 9, 1864; mustered out with regiment Sept. 13, 1865.
Michael W. Smith	Major		Oct. 31, 1861	3 yrs.	Resigned June 13, 1862.
Erasmus B. Denniston	do		Nov. 27, 1861	3 yrs.	Resigned June 21, 1862.
David A. B. Moore	do	40	Aug. 5, 1861	3 yrs.	Promoted from Captain Co. D Sept. 7, 1862; killed Dec. 31, 1862, in battle of Stone River, Tenn.
James N. Scott	do	34	Aug. 30, 1861	3 yrs.	Promoted from Captain Co. M April 1, 1863; mustered out with regiment Sept. 13, 1865.
John C. Frankeberger	do	32	Sept. 11, 1861	3 yrs.	Promoted to Captain Co. G from 1st Lieutenant and Regt. Quartermaster June 6, 1862; to Major Sept. 20, 1863; mustered out Jan. 11, 1865, on expiration of term of service.
William McBurney	do	25	Aug. 17, 1861	3 yrs.	Promoted to 1st Lieutenant and Regt. Quartermaster from Sergeant Co. B Feb. 19, 1862; to Major from Captain Co. L Feb. 28, 1865; to Brevet Major U. S. Army, May 19, 1865; mustered out with regiment Sept. 13, 1865.
Rudolph Wirth	Surgeon	33	Sept. 7, 1861	3 yrs.	Resigned May 29, 1862; re-commissioned Sept. 3, 1862, to date, Feb. 1, 1862; discharged Nov. 20, 1863.
Wilson V. Cowan	do	45	Dec. 16, 1863	3 yrs.	Resigned Oct. 4, 1864.
John Cannan	do	29	Oct. 10, 1861	3 yrs.	Appointed Asst. Surgeon Oct. 10, 1861; mustered out Nov. 22, 1864, on expiration of term of service; commissioned as Surgeon Dec. 14, 1864, at Louisville, Ky.; mustered out with regiment Sept. 13, 1865.
John B. McDill	Asst. Sur		Aug. 21, 1861	3 yrs.	Discharged Feb. 5, 1863.
Stephen S. L'Hommedieu	Adjutant	30	Aug. 22, 1861	3 yrs.	Discharged June 11, 1862.
William H. Scott	do	24	Aug. 5, 1861	3 yrs.	Promoted from 2d Lieutenant of Co. K Oct. 1, 1862; wounded Dec. 31, 1862, in battle of Stone River, Tenn.; promoted to Captain Co. G, March 16, 1864.
Carter M. Riggs	2d Lt. & Act. Adj	23	Aug. 6, 1861	3 yrs.	Promoted to Regt. Q. M. Sergeant from Sergeant Co. G ——; to Sergt. Major Oct. 1, 1862; to 2nd Lieutenant Co. G to date, Jan. 1, 1863; appointed Act. Adjutant July 9, 1863; resigned June 18, 1864.
Harvey Ferguson	Adjutant	22	Aug. 5, 1861	3 yrs.	Promoted from 2d Lieutenant Co. D June 23, 1864, to date, May 23, 1864; mustered out Nov. 25, 1864, on expiration of term of service.

ROSTER OF OHIO TROOPS.

Names.	Rank.	Age.	Date of Entering the Service.	Period of Service.	Remarks.
John W. Laughlin	Adjutant	24	Jan. 20, 1862	3 yrs.	Promoted to Sergt. Major from Private Co. B April 7, 1864; to 2d Lieutenant Co. I July 20, 1864; to 1st Lieutenant Co. B Dec. 14, 1864; appointed Adjutant Dec. 18, 1864; promoted to Captain Co. K March 18, 1865, veteran.
James C. Caldwell	do	21	Jan. 20, 1862	3 yrs.	Promoted to Hospital Steward from private of Co. B Sept. 1, 1862; to 1st Lieutenant and Adjutant March 18, 1865; mustered out with regiment Sept. 13, 1865; veteran.
Carter B. Harrison	Batt. Adj	21	Oct. 12, 1861	3 yrs.	Transferred to 51st O. V. I. Oct. 28, 1861.
John H. Piatt	do		Oct. 10, 1861	3 yrs.	Discharged June 13, 1862; appointed Captain Add'l A. D. C. Vols. July 11, 1862.
George P. Ladd	do	24	Aug. 13, 1861	3 yrs.	Promoted to 1st Lieutenant and Batt. Adjutant from private of Co. G Oct. 25, 1861; discharged June 13, 1862.
Henry Topping	do		Oct. 30, 1861	3 yrs	Discharged June 14, 1862.
Llewellyn Gwynne	do		Oct. 30, 1861	3 yrs.	Missing since June —, 1862; commissioned Major 4th Kentucky Volunteer Cavalry June 13, 1862; resigned as Lieut. Colonel same regiment Sept. 15, 1864.
Moses H. Neil	do		Dec. 19, 1861	3 yrs.	Resigned June 18, 1862.
Peter B. Cool	R. Q. M.	35	Sept. 5, 1861	3 yrs.	Promoted from 2d Lieutenant of Co. F June 16, 1862; discharged Dec. 8, 1862.
David W. Hart	do	23	Sept. 16, 1861	3 yrs.	Promoted to Regt. Q. M. Sergeant from Sergeant of Co. K Jan. 4, 1864; to 1st Lieutenant and Regt Quartermaster Dec. 14, 1864; to Captain March 18, 1865, but not mustered; mustered out with regiment Sept. 13, 1865; veteran.
James M. Allan	Batt. Q. M		Oct. 10, 1861	3 yrs.	Resigned Jan. 28, 1862.
John D. Moxley	Reg.Com of Subs't	46	Aug. 30, 1861	3 yrs.	Appointed from 1st Lieutenant Co. M Nov. 1, 1862; transferred to Co. B —
Amos D. Leib	do	24	Sept. 5, 1861	3 yrs.	Promoted to Batt. Q. M. Sergeant from Q. M. Sergeant Co. F —; promoted to 1st Lieutenant and Regt. Commissary of Subsistence from 2d Lieutenant Co. I April 18, 1863; mustered out Jan. 10, 1865, on expiration of term of service.
Andrew M. Bard	do	29	Sept. 29, 1861	3 yrs.	Promoted from Com. Sergeant Co. M March 18, 1865; mustered out with regiment September 13, 1865; veteran.
Jeremiah M. Drake	Chaplain		Dec. 13, 1861	3 yrs.	Resigned May 29, 1862.
Hugh H. Sivord	Ser. Maj.	21	Aug. 21, 1861	3 yrs.	Promoted from private Co. B —; to 2d Lieutenant Co. B Oct. 1, 1862.
John S. Dollenger	do	22	Oct. 11, 1861	3 yrs.	Promoted from private of Co. I Sept. 8, 1864; discharged May 25, 1865, at Camp Dennison, O., on Surgeon's certificate of disability; veteran.
Emanuel Deeter	do	17	June 15, 1862	3 yrs.	Promoted from private Co. I July 9, 1865; mustered out with regiment Sept. 13, 1865; veteran.
Joseph T. Reynolds	Q.M.Ser.		Sept. 25, 1861	3 yrs.	Promoted from Sergeant Co. F Dec. 24, 1862; reduced at his own request and returned to company Aug. 1, 1863.
Franklin P. Allen	do	20	Sept. 22, 1861	3 yrs.	Promoted from Sergeant Co. K Dec. 21, 1864, to 1st Lieutenant March 18, 1865, but not mustered; died May 25, 1865, at Cairo, Ill., of wounds received April 1, 1865, in battle of Ebenezer Church, Ala.; veteran.
John R. Lindsey	Com. Ser	21	Aug. 17, 1861	3 yrs.	Promoted from private Co. B April 7, 1864; mustered out with regiment Sept. 13, 1865; veteran.
Charles Welch	Sad. Ser.	26	Sept. 22, 1861	3 yrs.	Also borne on rolls as "Charles W.;" promoted from private Co. K January 4, 1864; mustered out with regiment Sept. 13, 1865; veteran.
Alexander C. Davis	Chf. Bug.	26	Aug. 17, 1861	3 yrs.	Promoted from Corporal Co. B —; mustered out Oct. 6, 1864, at Columbia, Tenn., on expiration of term of service.
John Rocket	do	22	Aug. 14, 1861	3 yrs.	Promoted from Corporal Co. H Nov. 1, 1864; mustered out with regiment Sept. 13, 1865; veteran.
Emanuel Doty	Hos. Std.	23	Sept. 5, 1861	3 yrs.	Promoted from Corporal Co. M June 23, 1862; mustered out Oct. 6, 1864, at Columbia, Tenn., on expiration of term of service.
John W. H. Noble	do	19	Aug. 17, 1861	3 yrs.	Promoted from Sergeant Co. B March 1, 1865; mustered out with regiment Sept. 13, 1865; veteran.
James H. Miller	Chf. Vet. Surgeon	42	Sept. 8, 1861	3 yrs.	Promoted from Farrier Co. M Jan. 1, 1862; discharged March 25, 1864, by order of War Department.
George W. Smitley	do	30	Aug. 17, 1861	3 yrs.	Promoted from private Co. B June 26, 1864; mustered out with regiment Sept. 13, 1865; veteran.

FIRST REGIMENT OHIO VOLUNTEER CAVALRY.

COMPANY A.

Mustered in August 21, 1861, at Camp Chase, Ohio, by Howard Stansbury, Captain Topographical Engineers U. S. A., Mustering Officer. Mustered out September 13, 1865, at Hilton Head, S. C., by Leslie Smith, Brevet Major and Captain 1st U. S. Infantry, Commissary of Musters, District of South Carolina.

Names.	Rank.	Age.	Date of Entering the Service.	Period of Service.	Remarks.
John H. Robinson	Captain	43	Aug. 6, 1861	3 yrs.	Appointed Aug. 16, 1861; promoted to Major June 1, 1862, but not mustered; died Oct. 31, 1862, at his home at Washington C. H., O.
Noah Jones	do	22	Aug. 6, 1861	3 yrs.	Promoted to 1st Lieutenant from 2d Lieutenant April 16, 1862; to Captain Oct. 31, 1862; mustered out Nov. 15, 1864, on expiration of term of service.
Joseph A. O. Yeoman	do	18	Aug. 6, 1861	3 yrs.	Mustered as private; promoted to 2d Lieutenant Co. H Jan. 29, 1864; to Captain from 1st Lieutenant of Co. H March 18, 1865; mustered out with company Sept. 13, 1865; veteran.
Samuel L. Hooker	1st Lieut.	32	Aug. 6, 1861	3 yrs.	Appointed Aug. 16, 1861; resigned April 16, 1862.
Albert E. Chester	do	23	Aug. 6, 1861	3 yrs.	Mustered as Corporal; promoted to 2d Lieutenant April 16, 1862; to 1st Lieutenant Oct. 31, 1862.
John N. McElwain	do	20	Aug. 6, 1861	3 yrs.	Mustered as Corporal; promoted to 2d Lieutenant Oct. 31, 1862; to 1st Lieutenant March 1, 1864; discharged Jan. 28, 1865.
Martin V. Little	do	22	Aug. 12, 1861	3 yrs.	Promoted from 1st Sergeant of Co. G March 18, 1865; mustered out with company Sept. 13, 1865; veteran.
Marcus T. C. Williams	2d Lieut.	21	Aug. 6, 1861	3 yrs.	Mustered as Corporal; promoted to 2d Lieutenant March 1, 1864; to 1st Lieutenant Dec. 14, 1864, but not mustered; mustered out Jan. 13, 1865, at Nashville, Tenn., on expiration of term of service.
George P. Barnes, Sen.	do	30	Aug. 6, 1861	3 yrs.	Mustered as a Corporal; appointed Sergeant Feb. 22, 1863; 1st Sergeant Sept. 18, 1864; promoted to 2d Lieutenant March 18, 1865; mustered out with company Sept. 13, 1865; veteran.
Joseph W. Quamley	1st Sergt.	31	Aug. 6, 1861	3 yrs.	Mustered out Sept. 17, 1864, on expiration of term of service.
Robert W. Vincent	do	21	Aug. 6, 1861	3 yrs.	Appointed Corporal ——; Sergeant. Sept. 18, 1864; 1st Sergeant, May 15, 1865; mustered out with company Sept. 13, 1865; veteran.
John Backenstoe	Q.M.Ser.	44	Aug. 6, 1861	3 yrs.	Mustered out Sept. 17, 1864, on expiration of term of service.
John W. McElwaine	do	20	Feb. 12, 1864	3 yrs.	Mustered as private; appointed May 15, 1865; mustered out with company Sept. 13, 1865.
James Squire	Com. Ser.	34	Aug. 9, 1862	3 yrs.	Mustered as private; appointed April 1, 1864; mustered out June 13, 1865, at Nashville, Tenn., by order of War Department.
Henry C. Denions	do	18	Aug. 6, 1861	3 yrs.	Appointed Corporal Sept. 9, 1864; Sergeant, March 1, 1865; Com. Sergeant June 11, 1865; mustered out with company Sept. 13, 1865; veteran.
Abraham Thomas	Sergeant	25	Aug. 6, 1861	3 yrs.	Mustered out Sept. 17, 1864, on expiration of term of service.
Henry J. Harrison	do	21	Aug. 6, 1861	3 yrs.	Discharged June 23, 1862, on Surgeon's certificate of disability.
William McMasters	do	23	Aug. 6, 1861	3 yrs.	Mustered out Sept. 6, 1864, on expiration of term of service.
Henry E. Kingman	do	26	Aug. 6, 1861	3 yrs.	Mustered out Sept. 17, 1864, on expiration of term of service.
Abner R. Riggins	do	21	Aug. 6, 1861	3 yrs.	Appointed Corporal April 14, 1864; Sergeant Sept. 18, 1864; mustered out with company Sept. 13, 1865; veteran.
John C. Ball	do	31	Aug. 9, 1862	3 yrs.	Mustered as private; appointed Sergeant Sept. 18, 1864; mustered out June 13, 1865, at Nashville, Tenn., by order of War Department.
Henry Keifer	do	22	Aug. 6, 1861	3 yrs.	Mustered as private; appointed Sergeant Sept. 19, 1864; mustered out with company Sept. 13, 1865; veteran.
George P. Barnes, Jr.	do	18	Aug. 6, 1861	3 yrs.	Appointed Corporal March 1, 1865; Sergeant April 1, 1865; mustered out with company Sept. 13, 1865; veteran.
John Hay	do	21	Aug. 6, 1861	3 yrs.	Appointed Corporal Sept. 19, 1864; Sergeant June 14, 1865; mustered out with company Sept. 13, 1865; veteran.

ROSTER OF OHIO TROOPS.

Names.	Rank.	Age.	Date of Entering the Service.	Period of Service.	Remarks.
George W. Freman	Sergeant	18	Mch. 26, 1863	3 yrs.	Appointed Corporal Sept. 10, 1864; Sergeant June 14, 1865; mustered out with company Sept. 13, 1865.
Thomas J. Hoover	Corporal	22	Aug. 6, 1861	3 yrs.	Died June 9, 1862.
Stephen Ransom	do	41	Aug. 6, 1861	3 yrs.	Discharged May 10, 1862, on Surgeon's certificate of disability.
Frank Foulk	do	29	Aug. 6, 1861	3 yrs.	Discharged June 28, 1863, to re-enlist as a Hospital Steward in U. S. Army.
Madison Squire	do	21	Aug. 9, 1862	3 yrs.	Appointed ——; mustered out June 13, 1865, at Nashville, Tenn., by order of War Department.
Peter Gets	do	20	Aug. 22, 1861	3 yrs.	Appointed Dec. 1, 1864; mustered out with company Sept. 13, 1865; veteran.
Reuben D. Bhatt	do	25	Aug. 9, 1862	3 yrs.	Appointed ——; mustered out June 13, 1865, at Nashville, Tenn., by order of War Department.
John Bentz	do	18	Jan. 8, 1864	3 yrs.	Appointed Dec. 18, 1864; mustered out with company Sept. 13, 1865.
Samuel Robertson	do	18	Mar. 31, 1864	3 yrs.	Appointed March 1, 1865; mustered out with company Sept. 13, 1865.
William J. Hesler	do	19	Feb. 13, 1864	3 yrs.	Appointed June 25, 1865; mustered out with company Sept. 13, 1865.
Ripley M. Waln	do	20	Feb. 7, 1864	3 yrs.	Appointed June 14, 1865; mustered out with company Sept. 13, 1865.
William Tudor	do	23	Feb. 15, 1864	3 yrs.	Appointed June 14, 1865; mustered out with company Sept. 13, 1865.
Hiram B. Ferguson	do	27	Feb. 3, 1864	3 yrs.	Appointed Farrier Jan. 20, 1865; Corporal June 14, 1865; mustered out with company Sept. 12, 1865.
Henry T. Resler	do	18	Feb. 13, 1864	3 yrs.	Appointed June 14, 1865; mustered out with company Sept. 13, 1865.
Thomas D. McElwain	Bugler	18	Aug. 6, 1861	5 yrs.	Mustered out Aug. 29, 1864, on expiration of term of service.
Samuel L. Gillespie	do	22	Aug. 6, 1861	3 yrs.	Mustered out Sept. 17, 1864, on expiration of term of service.
P. J. Johnson	Farrier	42	Aug. 6, 1861	3 yrs.	Discharged July 25, 1862, on Surgeon's certificate of disability.
Ernest Denner	do	27	Aug. 15, 1861	3 yrs.	Transferred from Co. C, ——; mustered out Sept. 17, 1864, on expiration of term of service.
Thomas J. Mooney	do	32	Aug. 22, 1861	3 yrs.	Appointed June 14, 1865; mustered out with company Sept. 13, 1865; veteran.
Lenox Campbell	Saddler	30	Aug. 6, 1861	3 yrs.	Discharged Dec. 11, 1862, on Surgeon's certificate of disability.
William H. Bayley	do	28	Aug. 6, 1861	3 yrs.	Appointed July 1, 1865; mustered out Sept. 14, 1865, at Columbus, O., by order of War Department; veteran.
Adams, Nathaniel	Private	18	Feb. 3, 1864	3 yrs.	Mustered out with company Sept. 13, 1865.
Aldrich, Abram	do	37	Aug. 6, 1861	3 yrs.	Mustered out Sept. 17, 1864, on expiration of term of service.
Allen, John	do	18	Feb. 13, 1864	3 yrs.	Mustered out with company Sept. 13, 1865.
Backenstoe, Frederick W.	do	18	Aug. 9, 1862	3 yrs.	Mustered out June 13, 1865, at Nashville, Tenn., by order of War Department.
Baldwin, Frank J.	do	26	Aug. 24, 1864	1 yr.	Mustered out June 13, 1865, at Nashville, Tenn., by order of War Department.
Bates, Joseph	do	21	Jan. 19, 1864	3 yrs.	Mustered out with company Sept. 13, 1865.
Bates, Richard	do	18	Feb. 25, 1864	3 yrs.	Mustered out with company Sept. 13, 1865.
Blair, George W.	do	18	Feb. 7, 1864	3 yrs.	Mustered out with company Sept. 13, 1865.
Blackemore, Charles C.	do	22	Aug. 6, 1861	3 yrs.	Discharged Sept. 5, 1861, on Surgeon's certificate of disability.
Blackemore, Francis L.	do	20	Oct. 23, 1863	3 yrs.	Discharged June 26, 1865, on Surgeon's certificate of disability.
Blackemore, Wyatt D.	do	18	Feb. 6, 1863	3 yrs.	Mustered out May 17, 1865, at Nashville, Tenn., by order of War Department.
Bloomer, Jesse M.	do	23	Aug. 6, 1861	3 yrs.	Mustered out Sept. 17, 1864, on expiration of term of service.
Boga, Leroy	do	18	Aug. 6, 1861	3 yrs.	Died March 9, 1863.
Bonn, Nathan C.	do	31	Mar. 3, 1865	1 yr.	Discharged Sept. 12, 1865, on Surgeon's certificate of disability.
Brindley, Samuel	do	44	Aug. 6, 1861	2 yrs.	Mustered out Sept. 17, 1864, on expiration of term of service.
Britton, Harvey	do	19	Feb. 25, 1864	3 yrs.	Mustered out with company Sept. 13, 1865.
Burns, William	do	18	Feb. 11, 1864	3 yrs.	Mustered out with company Sept. 13, 1865.
Butts, Anthony	do	24	Feb. 20, 1864	3 yrs.	Mustered out with company Sept. 13, 1865.
Bybee, John C.	do	21	Oct. 23, 1863	3 yrs.	Promoted to 1st Lieutenant Co. D, 187th Regiment, O. V. I., March 8, 1865.
Clark, Daniel B.	do	33	Aug. 6, 1861	3 yrs.	Mustered out Sept. 17, 1864, on expiration of term of service.
Cleaveland, Wm. P.	do	22	Aug. 6, 1861	3 yrs.	Mustered out Sept. 17, 1864, on expiration of term of service.
Coleman, Edward N.	do	22	Aug. 10, 1861	4 yrs.	Mustered out with company Sept. 13, 1865; veteran.
Collins, John	do	24	Aug. 6, 1861	3 yrs.	Mustered out Sept. 17, 1864, on expiration of term of service.
Cox, Isaac H.	do	21	Feb. 13, 1864	3 yrs.	Mustered out with company Sept. 13, 1865.

FIRST REGIMENT OHIO VOLUNTEER CAVALRY.

Names.	Rank.	Age	Date of Entering the Service.	Period of Service.	Remarks.
Creary, John B	Private	23	Aug. 22, 1861	3 yrs.	Mustered out Sept. 17, 1864, on expiration of term of service.
Cummings, George W	do	18	Feb. 22, 1864	3 yrs.	Mustered out with company Sept. 13, 1865.
Demon, John	do	24	Aug. 6, 1861	3 yrs.	Mustered out with company Sept. 13, 1865; veteran.
Devore, Joseph	do	20	Feb. 26, 1864	3 yrs.	Mustered out with company Sept. 13, 1865.
Devore, William	do	23	Aug. 6, 1861	3 yrs.	Mustered out with company Sept. 13, 1865; veteran.
Dickey, John	do	18	Aug. 6, 1861	3 yrs.	Mustered out Sept. 17, 1864, on expiration of term of service.
Draise, Lawson	do	20	Aug. 6, 1861	3 yrs.	Discharged Sept. 22, 1862, on Surgeon's certificate of disability.
Draper, William	do	21	Feb. 9, 1864	3 yrs.	Mustered out with company Sept. 13, 1865.
Duffee, Charles	do	40	Aug. 6, 1861	3 yrs.	Discharged Nov. 22, 1862, on Surgeon's certificate of disability.
Duffee, George W	do	21	Feb. 18, 1863	3 yrs.	Mustered out with company Sept. 13, 1865.
Dyer, Achelous	do	19	Aug. 6, 1861	3 yrs.	Mustered out Sept. 17, 1864, on expiration of term of service.
Edwards, Elisha	do	19	Jan. 10, 1864	3 yrs.	Mustered out with company Sept. 13, 1865.
Elster, Jesse V	do	25	Aug. 6, 1861	3 yrs.	Mustered out Sept. 17, 1864, on expiration of term of service.
Evans, Richard D	do	19	Aug. 6, 1861	3 yrs.	Mustered out Sept. 17, 1864, on expiration of term of service.
Foley, John	do	23	Aug. 22, 1861	3 yrs.	Discharged Feb. 21, 1863, on Surgeon's certificate of disability.
Fout, Thomas	do	23	Aug. 6, 1861	2 yrs.	
Gaittan, James	do	41	Oct. 23, 1863	3 yrs.	
Gardner, Thomas F	do	29	Aug. 6, 1861	3 yrs.	Discharged Sept. 20, 1862, on Surgeon's certificate of disability.
Gaskill, Thomas J	do	19	Aug. 6, 1861	3 yrs.	Mustered out with company Sept. 13, 1865; veteran.
Gatlin, Wm. J	do	29	Feb. 24, 1864	3 yrs.	Mustered out with company Sept. 13, 1865.
Givens, Michael	do	19	Aug. 6, 1861	3 yrs.	Mustered out with company Sept. 13, 1865; veteran.
Goldsberry, Monroe	do	39	Feb. 25, 1864	3 yrs.	Mustered out with company Sept. 13, 1865.
Gordon, Lorenzo J	do	20	Feb. 13, 1864	3 yrs.	Mustered out with company Sept. 13, 1865.
Gordon, William S	do	20	Aug. 6, 1861	3 yrs.	Mustered out Sept. 17, 1864, on expiration of term of service.
Gunkel, George	do	30	Feb. 13, 1864	3 yrs.	Died Sept. 13, 1865.
Gunning, James A	do	38	Aug. 6, 1861	3 yrs.	Discharged July 18, 1864, on Surgeon's certificate of disability.
Harley, John G	do	26	Aug. 6, 1861	3 yrs.	Discharged July 30, 1862, on Surgeon's certificate of disability.
Harper, Jacob A	do	21	Aug. 9, 1862	3 yrs.	Mustered out June 12, 1865, at Nashville, Tenn., by order of War Department.
Hawk, Josiah G	do	21	Feb. 27, 1864	3 yrs.	Mustered out with company Sept. 13, 1865.
Haymer, Joseph	do	41	Feb. 13, 1864	3 yrs.	Mustered out with company Sept. 13, 1865.
Hendson, Simeon	do	21	Feb. 8, 1864	3 yrs.	Mustered out with company Sept. 13, 1865.
Herald, Amos J	do	22	Feb. 16, 1864	3 yrs.	Also borne on the rolls as "Herrold;" mustered out with company Sept. 13, 1865.
Hill, John N	do	20	Aug. 6, 1861	2 yrs.	
Howe, Thomas J	do	31	Aug. 9, 1862	3 yrs.	Mustered out June 12, 1865, at Louisville, Ky., by order of War Department.
Hughs, George W	do	24	Aug. 6, 1861	3 yrs.	Mustered out Sept. 17, 1864, on expiration of term of service.
Jenkins, Nelson B	do	20	Aug. 6, 1861	3 yrs.	Mustered out Sept. 17, 1864, on expiration of term of service.
Jennings, Joseph O	do	18	Feb. 11, 1864	3 yrs.	Mustered out with company Sept. 13, 1865.
Johnson, James H	do	19	Feb. 5, 1864	3 yrs.	Mustered out with company Sept. 13, 1865.
Judy, Elihu	do	19	Aug. 22, 1861	3 yrs.	Mustered out Sept. 17, 1864, on expiration of term of service.
Judy, Henry	do	21	Aug. 22, 1861	3 yrs.	Discharged Oct. 13, 1863, on Surgeon's certificate of disability.
Judy, Marion	do	18	Aug. 22, 1861	3 yrs.	Died July 20, 1863.
Kenelty, Daniel	do	21	Aug. 6, 1861	3 yrs.	
Knotts, John R	do	18	Aug. 6, 1861	3 yrs.	Discharged Sept. 5, 1861, on Surgeon's certificate of disability.
Leake, Walter S	do	31	Feb. 11, 1864	3 yrs.	Mustered out with company Sept. 13, 1865.
Lee, Samuel G	do	24	Aug. 6, 1861	3 yrs.	
Lewis, Andrew F	do	31	Aug. 9, 1862	3 yrs.	Mustered out May 31, 1865, at Nashville, Tenn., by order of War Department.
Limes, Henry S	do	19	Aug. 6, 1861	3 yrs.	Mustered out Sept. 17, 1864, on expiration of term of service.
Lively, John C	do	36	Aug. 9, 1862	3 yrs.	Mustered out May 31, 1865, at Nashville, Tenn., by order of War Department.
Long, William	do	19	Aug. 6, 1861	3 yrs.	
McCandless, George H	do	19	Jan. 19, 1864	3 yrs.	Mustered out with company Sept. 13, 1865.
McClelland, William	do	24	Aug. 9, 1862	3 yrs.	Mustered out June 12, 1865, at Nashville, Tenn., by order of War Department.
McGinnis, Andrew J	do	30	Aug. 6, 1861	3 yrs.	Killed Aug. 2, 1862, in action, while carrying dispatches.
McLaughlin, Jonathan	do	28	Aug. 6, 1861	3 yrs.	Mustered out Sept. 17, 1864, on expiration of term of service.
Manuel, Thomas	do	25	Aug. 6, 1861	3 yrs.	Died Nov. 9, 1861.

Names.	Rank.	Age.	Date of Entering the Service.	Period of Service.	Remarks.
Martindale, Thomas	Private	36	Feb. 12, 1864	3 yrs.	Mustered out with company Sept. 13, 1865.
Miller, Jacob D	do	23	Aug. 6, 1861	3 yrs.	Mustered out Sept. 17, 1864, at Nashville, Tenn., on expiration of term of service.
Millikan, William	do	34	Aug. 6, 1861	3 yrs.	Mustered out Sept. 17, 1864, on expiration of term of service.
Mitchel, William	do	19	Nov. 4, 1863	3 yrs.	Also borne on rolls as "William L.;" mustered out Sept. 15, 1865, at New York City, by order of War Department.
Nidy, Robert	do	43	Aug. 6, 1861	3 yrs.	Mustered out Sept. 17, 1864, on expiration of term of service.
Painter, Henry C	do	26	Aug. 6, 1861	3 yrs.	Mustered out Sept. 17, 1864, on expiration of term of service.
Parrett, Willis	do	24	Aug. 6, 1861	3 yrs.	Discharged May 27, 1862, on Surgeon's certificate of disability.
Pharis, George	do	21	Aug. 6, 1861	3 yrs.	Mustered out Sept. 17, 1864, on expiration of term of service.
Pharis, Spencer C	do	22	Aug. 22, 1861	3 yrs.	Mustered out with company Sept. 13, 1865; veteran.
Pharis, William O	do	20	Aug. 6, 1861	3 yrs.	Discharged Sept. 24, 1862, on Surgeon's certificate of disability.
Plumley, Granville	do	22	Aug. 22, 1861	3 yrs.	Mustered out Sept. 17, 1864, on expiration of term of service.
Price, William H	do	21	Aug. 6, 1861	3 yrs.	Mustered out Sept. 17, 1864, on expiration of term of service.
Priddy, James	do	22	Aug. 6, 1861	3 yrs.	Mustered out Sept. 17, 1864, on expiration of term of service.
Reed, Hiram	do	33	Aug. 6, 1861	3 yrs.	Discharged Feb. 23, 1863, on Surgeon's certificate of disability.
Reese, John L	do	20	Aug. 6, 1861	3 yrs.	Mustered out March 3, 1865, at Columbus, O., on expiration of term of service.
Rice, Samuel J	do	19	Feb. 16, 1864	3 yrs.	Mustered out with company Sept. 13, 1865.
Rodgers, John	do	23	Aug. 6, 1861	3 yrs.	Died March 28, 1862.
Rodgers, Samuel	do	21	Aug. 9, 1862	3 yrs.	Mustered out June 13, 1865, at Nashville, Tenn., by order of War Department.
Roselle, Charles D	do	22	Aug. 6, 1861	3 yrs.	Discharged Jan. 27, 1863, on Surgeon's certificate of disability.
Ross, Seth	do	34	Aug. 6, 1861	3 yrs.	Discharged Jan. 8, 1862, on Surgeon's certificate of disability.
Sanders, John A	do	20	Aug. 9, 1862	3 yrs.	Mustered out May 31, 1865, at Nashville, Tenn., by order of War Department.
Saxton, Lycurgus	do	18	Mch. 25, 1863	3 yrs.	Discharged May 18, 1863, on Surgeon's certificate of disability.
Sears, Ransom	do	19	Feb. 6, 1864	3 yrs.	Mustered out with company Sept. 13, 1865.
Seymour, Abel R	do	19	Oct. 5, 1863	3 yrs.	Discharged May 27, 1865, on Surgeon's certificate of disability.
Shoemaker, Curtis M	do	22	Oct. 19, 1863	3 yrs.	Discharged Dec. 9, 1863, on Surgeon's certificate of disability.
Shreekengaust, Anthony	do	22	Aug. 6, 1861	3 yrs.	Mustered out Sept. 17, 1864, on expiration of term of service.
Silcott, Francis M	do	18	Feb. 25, 1864	3 yrs.	Mustered out with company Sept. 13, 1865.
Silcott, Landon	do	41	Aug. 6, 1861	3 yrs.	Discharged Aug. 8, 1862, at Columbus, O., on Surgeon's certificate of disability.
Smith, Jacob	do	23	Aug. 22, 1861	3 yrs.	Mustered out with company Sept. 13, 1865; veteran.
Smith, Morgan T	do	19	Feb. 11, 1864	3 yrs.	Mustered out with company Sept. 13, 1865.
Stover, Benjamin T	do	27	Aug. 6, 1861	3 yrs.	Mustered out with company Sept. 13, 1865; veteran.
Straley, John H	do	23	Aug. 6, 1861	3 yrs.	Also borne on rolls as "Strayley;" mustered out with company Sept. 13, 1865; veteran.
Terry, Anthony T. B	do	24	Aug. 9, 1862	3 yrs.	Discharged May 24, 1865, on Surgeon's certificate of disability.
Thomas, Lewis C	do	39	Aug. 9, 1862	3 yrs.	Mustered out May 31, 1865, at Nashville, Tenn., by order of War Department.
Thornton, Amos	do	32	Aug. 9, 1862	3 yrs.	Mustered out May 31, 1865, at Nashville, Tenn., by order of War Department.
Thornton, Jonas L	do	20	Aug. 19, 1861	3 yrs.	Promoted to 2d Lieutenant Aug. 1, 1863, but not mustered; mustered out Sept. 17, 1864, at Nashville, Tenn., on expiration of term of service.
Thurston, George W	do	25	Aug. 9, 1862	3 yrs.	Mustered out June 13, 1865, at Nashville, Tenn., by order of War Department.
Tidy, Henry	do	28	Aug. 9, 1862	3 yrs.	Mustered out June 13, 1865, at Nashville, Tenn., by order of War Department.
Tweedale, Robert	do	19	Aug. 6, 1861	3 yrs.	Also borne on rolls as "Tweeder;" died April 24, 1864, at Andersonville, Ga., while a prisoner of war.
Ustick, George McJ	do	19	Aug. 9, 1862	3 yrs.	Mustered out May 31, 1865, at Nashville, Tenn., by order of War Department.
Vincent, Albert C	do	18	Feb. 25, 1864	3 yrs.	Mustered out with company Sept. 13, 1865.
Vincent, Collins	do	23	Aug. 6, 1861	3 yrs.	
Vincent, William	do	19	Aug. 9, 1862	3 yrs.	Mustered out June 13, 1865, at Nashville, Tenn., by order of War Department.
Welch, William	do	31	Aug. 19, 1861	3 yrs.	Killed March 21, 1865, at Cherokee Station, Ala., by accidental gun shot; veteran.
Wells, Henton	do	18	Feb. 18, 1863	3 yrs.	Discharged June 24, 1865, on Surgeon's certificate of disability.

First Regiment Ohio Volunteer Cavalry.

Names.	Rank.	Age.	Date of Entering the Service.	Period of Service.	Remarks.
West, John W.	Private	26	Aug. 6, 1861	3 yrs.	Discharged Sept. 5, 1861, on Surgeon's certificate of disability.
Williams, Daniel F.	do	29	Feb. 15, 1864	3 yrs.	Mustered out with company Sept. 13, 1865.
Worrell, Henry W.	do	18	Feb. 11, 1864	3 yrs.	Mustered out with company Sept. 13, 1865.

COMPANY B.

Mustered in Aug. 17, 1861, at Camp Chase, Ohio, by Howard Stansbury, Captain Topographical Engineers, U. S. A., Mustering Officer. Mustered out Sept. 13, 1865, at Hilton Head, S. C., by Leslie Smith, Brevet Major and Captain 1st Infantry, U. S. A., and C. M., D. S. C.

James Laughlin	Captain	40	Aug. 16, 1861	3 yrs.	Promoted to Major June 10, 1862.
George F. Conn	do	23	Aug. 17, 1861	3 yrs.	Promoted from 1st Lieutenant, June 10, 1862; resigned Sept. 29, 1864.
Hugh H. Siverd	do	21	Aug. 21, 1861	3 yrs.	Promoted to Sergt. Major from private ——; 2d Lieutenant Oct. 1, 1862; to 1st Lieutenant April 1, 1863; to Captain Dec. 14, 1864; mustered out with company Sept. 13, 1865.
Samuel W. Fordyce	1st Lieut.	21	Aug. 17, 1861	3 yrs.	Wounded Oct. 23, 1861, in action at West Liberty, Ky.; promoted from 2d Lieutenant June 10, 1862; to Captain Co. H. to date Dec. 31, 1862.
John D. Moxley	do	46	Aug. 30, 1861	3 yrs.	Transferred —— from Field and Staff; promoted to Captain Co. M April 1, 1863.
John W. Laughlin	do	24	Jan. 29, 1862	3 yrs.	Mustered as private; promoted to Sergt. Major April 7, 1864; transferred as 2d Lieutenant from Co. I Aug. 28, 1864; promoted to 1st Lieutenant Dec. 14, 1864; appointed Adjutant Dec. 18, 1864; veteran.
William Brooks	do	24	Aug. 6, 1861	3 yrs.	Promoted from 1st Sergeant, Co. G Jan. 6, 1865; commanded Co. F from March 1, 1865, to June 1, 1865; mustered out with company Sept. 13, 1865; veteran.
Edwin L. Hall	2d Lieut.	22	Aug. 17, 1861	3 yrs.	Appointed 1st Sergeant from Q. M. Sergeant July 16, 1862; promoted to 2d Lieutenant Jan. 1, 1863; to 1st Lieutenant Sept. 8, 1864, but not mustered; resigned Sept. 15, 1864.
Norvell W. Taylor	1st Sergt.	21	Aug. 17, 1861	3 yrs.	Discharged June 22, 1862, on Surgeon's certificate of disability.
Ezekiel Braden	do	23	Aug. 17, 1861	3 yrs.	Mustered as a private; appointed Sergeant June 6, 1863; appointed 1st Sergeant Oct. 7, 1864; mustered out with company Sept. 13, 1865; veteran.
Robert H. Barton	Q. M. S.	21	Aug. 17, 1861	3 yrs.	Appointed Corporal March 1, 1864; Q. M. Sergeant Oct. 7, 1864; mustered out with company Sept. 13, 1865; veteran.
Solomon Redd	Com. Ser.	19	Aug. 17, 1861	3 yrs.	Appointed Corporal March 1, 1864; Com. Sergeant Oct. 7, 1864; mustered out with company Sept. 13, 1865; veteran.
William McBurney	Sergeant	25	Aug. 17, 1861	3 yrs.	Promoted to 1st Lieutenant and Regt. Quartermaster Feb. 19, 1862.
Justus C. Taylor	do	19	Aug. 17, 1861	3 yrs.	Mustered out Oct. 6, 1864, on expiration of term of service.
William Rosemond	do	21	Aug. 17, 1861	3 yrs.	Promoted to 1st Lieutenant, Co. A, 97th O. V. I., July 11, 1862.
William Hannum	do	27	Aug. 17, 1861	3 yrs.	Mustered out Oct. 6, 1864, on expiration of term of service.
John M Brown	do	19	Aug. 17, 1861	3 yrs.	Mustered as private; appointed ——; captured Sept. 30, 1864, at Cotton Port, Tenn.; no further record found.
Martin T. Lindsey	do	25	Aug. 17, 1861	3 yrs.	Appointed from Corporal ——; mustered out Feb. 3, 1865 at Columbus, O., on expiration of term of service.
John W. H. Noble	do	19	Aug. 17, 1861	3 yrs.	Appointed Corporal May 22, 1864; Sergeant Oct. 7, 1864; promoted to Hospital Steward, March 1, 1865; veteran.
Charles W. Hayes	do	19	Aug. 17, 1861	3 yrs.	Mustered as private; appointed Oct. 7, 1864; mustered out with company Sept. 13, 1865; veteran.
Jason S. Crossen	do	19	Aug. 17, 1861	3 yrs.	Also borne on the rolls as "John C.;" appointed Corporal Oct. 7, 1864; Sergeant, March 3, 1865; mustered out with company Sept. 13, 1865; veteran.
William H. C. Hanna	do	19	Aug. 17, 1861	3 yrs.	Appointed Corporal Oct. 7, 1864; Sergeant April 23, 1865; mustered out with company Sept. 13, 1865; veteran.

ROSTER OF OHIO TROOPS.

Names.	Rank.	Age	Date of Entering the Service.	Period of Service.	Remarks.
Stout P. Wallace........	Sergeant	22	Aug. 17, 1861	3 yrs.	Appointed Corporal Oct. 7, 1864; Sergeant May 1, 1865; mustered out with company Sept. 13, 1865; veteran.
Henry E. Bumgardner...	Corporal	21	Aug. 17, 1861	3 yrs.	Drowned July 6, 1863.
George W. Gibbs........	do....	29	Aug. 17, 1861	3 yrs.	Discharged Dec. 11, 1861, at Louisville, Ky., on Surgeon's certificate of disability.
George W. Burwell......	do....	20	Aug. 17, 1861	3 yrs.	Discharged Dec. 29, 1861, on Surgeon's certificate of disability.
Alexander C. Davis.....	do....	29	Aug. 17, 1861	3 yrs.	Promoted the Chief Bugler ——.
Moses B. Kennedy......	do....	25	Aug. 17, 1861	3 yrs.	Discharged Oct. 4, 1864, at Columbia, Tenn., on expiration of term of service.
George Frazier.........	do....	30	Aug. 17, 1861	3 yrs.	Mustered out Oct. 6, 1864, on expiration of term of service.
Warren D. Whitely......	do....	21	Aug. 17, 1861	3 yrs.	Also borne on the rolls as Sibley; appointed March 1, 1864; died Oct. 5, 1864, at Atlanta, Ga.; veteran.
George C. Shuback......	do....	19	Aug. 17, 1861	3 yrs.	Appointed Oct. 7, 1864; killed April 1, 1865, in action near Selma, Ala; veteran.
George W. Shaw........	do....	29	Aug. 17, 1861	3 yrs.	Appointed Oct. 7, 1864; mustered out with company Sept. 13, 1865; veteran.
John H. Smith.........	do....	26	Aug. 17, 1861	3 yrs.	Appointed Oct. 7, 1864; mustered out with company Sept. 13, 1865; veteran.
Henry H. Garrett.......	do....	23	Feb. 27, 1864	3 yrs.	Appointed Oct. 7, 1864; mustered out with company Sept. 13, 1865.
James Sills.............	do....	18	Aug. 17, 1861	3 yrs.	Appointed Dec. 1, 1864; mustered out with company Sept. 13, 1865; veteran.
William A. Booher......	do....	24	Jan. 20, 1862	3 yrs.	Appointed March 1, 1865; mustered out with company Sept 13, 1865; veteran.
John T. Bell...........	do....	21	Aug. 17, 1861	3 yrs.	Appointed April 2, 1865; mustered out with company Sept. 13, 1865; veteran.
Seldon Banker..........	do....	24	Feb. 24, 1864	3 yrs.	Appointed April 23, 1865; mustered out with company Sept. 13, 1865.
Louis E. Holland.......	do....	18	Aug. 17, 1861	3 yrs.	Appointed May 1, 1865; mustered out with company Sept. 13, 1865; veteran.
Moses A. Bell..........	do....	20	Aug. 17, 1861	3 yrs.	Appointed ——; killed July 1, 1862, in action at Russellville, Ala.
John Barkley...........	Farrier	...	Dec. 10, 1861	3 yrs.	Mustered out Jan. 10, 1865, at Nashville, Tenn., on expiration of term of service.
Ador, Andrew M........	Private	21	Aug. 17, 1861	3 yrs.	Veteran.
Ader, Benjamin........	do....	19	Aug. 17, 1861	3 yrs.	Also borne on the rolls as Arburthnot; mustered out June 9, 1865, from hospital at Camp Dennison, O. by order of War Department
Arbothnot, Samuel B....	do....	42	Feb. 29, 1864	3 yrs.	
Baker, Calvin..........	do....	30	Feb. 29, 1864	3 yrs.	Mustered out with company Sept. 13, 1865.
Baker, George W.......	do....	18	Feb. 29, 1864	3 yrs.	Mustered out April 12, 1866, at Columbus, O., to date Sept. 13, 1865, by order of War Department.
Bates, Alexander.......	do....	18	Feb. 24, 1864	3 yrs.	Mustered out with company Sept. 13, 1865
Bates, James..........	do....	42	Feb. 24, 1864	3 yrs.	Mustered out Sept. 26, 1865, by order of War Department.
Beard, Robert.........	do....	21	March 5, 1864	3 yrs.	Mustered out with company Sept. 13, 1865
Beymer, William.......	do....	22	Feb. 29, 1864	3 yrs.	Mustered out with company Sept. 13, 1865.
Bowers, George W.....	do....	25	Aug. 17, 1861	3 yrs.	Discharged Dec. 9, 1861, on Surgeon's certificate of disability.
Brooks, William........	do....	43	Feb. 23, 1864	3 yrs.	Mustered out June 3, 1865, at Louisville, Ky., by order of War Department.
Brown, Albert M.......	do....	19	July 16, 1862	3 yrs.	Mustered out June 17, 1865, at Nashville, Tenn., by order of War Department.
Brumley, William D....	do....	22	Feb. 24, 1864	3 yrs.	Mustered out with company Sept. 13, 1865.
Barnes, Thomas H......	do....	19	Dec. 18, 1863	3 yrs.	Captured Sept. 5, 1864; escaped from prison at Millen, Ga., and joined Sherman's army Dec. 24, 1864; captured again March 30, 1865, while with Wilson's forces near Monte Valley, Ala.; mustered out June 12, 1865, at Columbus, O., by order of War Department.
Caldwell, James C.....	do....	21	Jan. 20, 1862	3 yrs.	Promoted to Hospital Steward Sept. 1, 1862; to 1st Lieutenant and Adjutant March 18, 1863; veteran.
Calvert, Francis C.....	do....	20	Aug. 17, 1861	3 yrs.	Discharged Dec. 9, 1861, on Surgeon's certificate of disability.
Carey, Isaac R........	do....	31	Aug. 17, 1861	3 yrs.	Discharged Aug. 6, 1862, on Surgeon's certificate of disability.
Caskey, Samuel.......	do....	21	Dec. 16, 1863	3 yrs.	Mustered out with company Sept. 13, 1865.
Clayton, Joseph........	do....	18	Aug. 17, 1861	3 yrs.	Transferred to Co. C., 1st Mississippi Marine Brigade ——; mustered out Jan. 25, 1865, with Co. D, 1st Mississippi Marine Brigade, by order of War Department, to which transferred from Co. C.
Cox, John W..........	do....	21	Aug. 17, 1861	3 yrs.	Discharged Nov. 22, 1861, on Surgeon's certificate of disability.
Cromer, William K.....	do....	45	Feb. 11, 1864	3 yrs.	Mustered out with company Sept. 13, 1865.
Crupper, Elisha.......	do....	34	Feb. 17, 1864	3 yrs.	Mustered out with company Sept. 13, 1865
Cunningham, James L..	do....	21	Aug. 17, 1861	3 yrs.	Died March 17, 1864.
Davis, William........	do....	18	Feb. 17, 1864	3 yrs.	
Deter, William L......	do....	22	Feb. 24, 1864	3 yrs.	Mustered out with company Sept 13, 1865
Decker, Theodore A...	do....	22	Feb. 29, 1864	3 yrs.	Mustered out with company Sept. 13, 1865

First Regiment Ohio Volunteer Cavalry.

Names.	Rank.	Age.	Date of Entering the Service.	Period of Service.	Remarks.
Dugan, Thomas	Private	23	Jan. 20, 1862	3 yrs.	Died May 21, 1864, in prison at Andersonville, Georgia.
Eaton, Joel H	do	20	Aug. 17, 1861	3 yrs.	Mustered out Oct. 6, 1864, on expiration of term of service.
Errington, Thomas	do	30	Aug. 17, 1861	3 yrs.	Mustered out Oct. 6, 1864, on expiration of term of service.
Fife, Jacob L	do	27	Feb. 26, 1864	3 yrs.	Mustered out with company Sept. 13, 1865.
Finley, Milton	do	19	Feb. 24, 1864	3 yrs.	Mustered out with company Sept. 13, 1865.
Frame, James M	do	18	Feb. 29, 1864	3 yrs.	Discharged May 13, 1864, on Surgeon's certificate of disability.
Fulton, Marcus	do	42	Feb. 29, 1864	3 yrs.	Mustered out with company Sept. 13, 1865.
Garrett, John W	do	28	Feb. 27, 1864	3 yrs.	Discharged May 19, 1865, at Columbus, O., on Surgeon's certificate of disability; leg amputated.
Gaston, Alexander J	do	43	Feb. 22, 1864	3 yrs.	Mustered out with company Sept. 15, 1865.
George, Simpson	do	35	Aug. 17, 1861	3 yrs.	Discharged July 18, 1862, on Surgeon's certificate of disability.
Gibson, Samuel B	do	18	Feb. 24, 1864	3 yrs.	Mustered out with company Sept. 13, 1865.
Gleason, Charles	do	32	Aug. 17, 1861	3 yrs.	Discharged June 3, 1862, on Surgeon's certificate of disability.
Grier, Wilson S	do	21	Aug. 17, 1861	3 yrs.	Discharged June 12, 1862, on Surgeon's certificate of disability.
Hall, Edward H	do	21	Aug. 17, 1861	3 yrs.	Mustered out Oct. 6, 1864, on expiration of term of service.
Hall, John W	do	18	Aug. 17, 1861	3 yrs.	
Hareholizer, John C	do	22	Feb. 8, 1864	3 yrs.	Died Sept. 5, 1864, at Jonesboro, Ga.
Heald, William	do	21	Aug. 17, 1861	3 yrs.	Mustered out Oct. 6, 1864, on expiration of term of service.
Hood, Charles F	do	30	Aug. 17, 1861	3 yrs.	Discharged Aug. —, 1862, at Camp Dennison, O., on Surgeon's certificate of disability.
Hoxer, Henry	do	36	Aug. 17, 1861	3 yrs.	
Humphrey, Allen	do	25	Aug. 17, 1861	3 yrs.	Discharged Jan. 29, 1862, on Surgeon's certificate of disability.
Jeffries, David T	do	18	Feb. 29, 1864	3 yrs.	Mustered out Sept. 14, 1865, at New York City, by order of War Department.
Jeffries, Joseph R	do	29	Feb. 26, 1864	3 yrs.	Died March 19, 1864.
Johnson, Ferdinand S	do	23	Feb. 27, 1864	3 yrs.	Mustered out with company Sept 13, 1865.
Johnston, Robert V	do	19	Aug. 17, 1861	3 yrs.	Mustered out Oct. 6, 1864, on expiration of term of service.
Johnston, Samuel	do	24	Aug. 17, 1861	3 yrs.	Mustered out Oct. 6, 1864, on expiration of term of service.
Kennedy, Joseph R	do	23	Aug. 17, 1861	3 yrs.	Mustered out Oct. 6, 1864, on expiration of term of service.
Kimble, James V	do	21	Aug. 17, 1861	3 yrs.	Died Dec. 18, 1861.
Kimble, Nathan	do	19	Aug. 17, 1861	3 yrs.	Discharged Jan. 14, 1862, on Surgeon's certificate of disability.
Leeper, John A	do	18	Aug. 17, 1861	3 yrs.	Discharged Dec. 9, 1861, on Surgeon's certificate of disability.
Lindsey, John R	do	24	Aug. 17, 1861	3 yrs.	Promoted to Regt. Com. Sergeant Jan. 4, 1864; veteran.
Lister, James	do	21	Aug. 17, 1861	3 yrs.	Mustered out Oct. 6, 1864, on expiration of term of service.
Lowry, Alexander L	do	20	Jan. 20, 1862	3 yrs.	Discharged Aug. 30, 1864, at Columbus, O., on Surgeon's certificate of disability.
McCluskey, Joseph	do	19	Aug. 17, 1861	3 yrs.	Discharged April 23, 1863, on Surgeon's certificate of disability.
McCraery, John L	do	20	Aug. 17, 1861	3 yrs.	Drowned April 24, 1862.
McCune, John B	do	18	Feb. 22, 1864	3 yrs.	Mustered out with company Sept. 13, 1865.
McMullin, Alexander	do	24	Aug. 17, 1861	3 yrs.	Killed July 1, 1862, in action at Russellville, Ala.
McVicker, Alexander	do	21	Aug. 17, 1861	3 yrs.	Mustered out with company Sept. 13, 1865; veteran.
Mackey, James T	do	16	Mch. 6, 1865	1 yr.	Mustered out with company Sept. 13, 1865.
Miles, David	do	21	Aug. 17, 1861	3 yrs.	Died Oct. 16, 1863.
Miller, Lewis	do	21	Feb. 23, 1864	3 yrs.	Mustered out with company Sept. 13, 1865.
Morris, Samuel	do	21	Aug. 17, 1861	3 yrs.	Mustered out Oct. 6, 1864, on expiration of term of service.
Moore, Hiram	do	35	Aug. 28, 1861	3 yrs.	Discharged March 1, 1862, on Surgeon's certificate of disability.
Nicholson, Erastus H	do	22	Aug. 17, 1861	3 yrs.	Discharged Aug. 9, 1862, on Surgeon's certificate of disability.
Parker, George W	do	19	Feb. 25, 1864	3 yrs.	Mustered out with company Sept. 13, 1865.
Robinson, John M	do	18	Feb. 25, 1864	3 yrs.	Mustered out with company Sept. 13, 1865.
Rose, Vincent F	do	19	Aug. 17, 1861	3 yrs.	Mustered out with company Sept. 13, 1865; veteran.
Ryan, Thomas C	do	43	Aug. 17, 1861	3 yrs.	Mustered out Sept. 8, 1865, at Columbus, O., by order of War Department; veteran.
Schmidt, John A	do	30	Aug. 17, 1861	3 yrs.	Died Dec. 29, 1861.
Shear, Joseph	do	34	Feb. 22, 1864	3 yrs.	Mustered out with company Sept. 13, 1865.
Shipman, George M	do	20	Aug. 17, 1861	3 yrs.	Died Aug. 15, 1864.
Sills, Jonathan	do	18	Sept. 29, 1864	1 yr.	Also borne on the rolls as "Sellx;" mustered out July 27, 1865, at Camp Dennison, O., by order of War Department.
Skinner, Harrison	do	23	Feb. 27, 1864	3 yrs.	Mustered out with company Sept. 13, 1865.
Smith, Walter C	do	26	Aug. 17, 1861	3 yrs.	Mustered out Oct. 6, 1864, on expiration of term of service.

Names.	Rank.	Age	Date of Entering the Service.	Period of Service	Remarks.
Smitley, George W	Private	30	Aug. 17, 1861	3 yrs.	Promoted to Regt. Veterinary Surgeon June 20, 1864; veteran.
Spence, David P	do	24	Aug. 17, 1861	3 yrs.	Mustered out Oct. 6, 1864, on expiration of term of service.
Steel, William	do	28	Aug. 17, 1861	3 yrs.	Mustered out Oct. 6, 1864, on expiration of term of service.
Stewart, John B	do	23	Aug. 17, 1861	3 yrs.	Mustered out Oct. 6, 1864, on expiration of term of service.
Swingle, George I	do	29	Aug. 17, 1861	3 yrs.	Discharged Nov. 26, 1862, on Surgeon's certificate of disability.
Taylor, Daniel	do	30	Sept. 20, 1864	1 yr.	Mustered out Aug. 17, 1865, at Cincinnati, O., by order of War Department.
Taylor, George	do	17	Aug 17 1861	3 yrs.	Died Jan. 1, 1862.
Terrell, David F	do	22	Jan. 20, 1862	3 yrs.	Captured Sept. 30, 1863, at Cotton Port, Tenn.; died June 3, 1864, in prison at Danville, Va.
Thompson, John K	do	24	Aug. 17, 1861	3 yrs.	Mustered out Oct. 6, 1864, on expiration of term of service.
Todd, George M	do	19	Feb. 23, 1864	3 yrs.	Mustered out with company Sept. 13, 1865.
Valentine, James	do	18	Aug. 17, 1861	3 yrs.	Mustered out with company Sept. 13, 1865; veteran.
Vandyke, Arthur	do	35	Feb. 22, 1864	3 yrs.	Died Aug. 25, 1864, at Vining Station, Ga.
Vanhorn, George F	do	19	Aug. 17, 1861	3 yrs.	
Vatusckie, Augustus H	do	24	Aug. 17, 1861	3 yrs.	Mustered out Oct. 6, 1864, on expiration of term of service.
Ward, Mark E	do	20	Aug. 17, 1861	3 yrs.	Discharged Dec. 9, 1861, on Surgeon's certificate of disability.
Watt, Joseph W	do	27	Aug. 17, 1861	3 yrs.	
Webster, Herchel	do	18	Jan. 20, 1862	3 yrs.	Died Dec. 26, 1862, in prison at Danville, Va
Webster, Stocton	do	18	Feb. 22, 1864	3 yrs.	Mustered out with company Sept. 13, 1865.
Wharton, William	do	21	Aug. 17, 1861	3 yrs.	Mustered out Oct. 6, 1864, on expiration of term of service.
Williams, Austin P	do	23	Feb. 8, 1864	3 yrs.	Mustered out with company Sept. 13, 1865.
Wilson, Samuel	do		Sept. 3, 1861	3 yrs.	Discharged May 22, 1862, at Louisville, Ky.

COMPANY C.

Mustered in Sept. 12, 1861, at Camp Chase, Ohio, by Howard Stansbury, Captain Topographical Engineers, and John R. Edie, Major 15th Infantry, U. S. A., Mustering Officers. Mustered out Sept. 13, 1865, at Hilton Head, South Carolina, by Leslie Smith, Brevet Major and Captain 1st U. S. Infantry, Mustering Officer and Commissary of Musters, District of South Carolina.

Names.	Rank.	Age	Date of Entering the Service.	Period of Service	Remarks.
Nathan D. Menken	Captain	24	Aug. 7, 1861	3 yrs.	Appointed Aug. 21, 1861; resigned Dec. 2, 1862.
Samuel N. Stanford	do	23	Aug. 15, 1861	3 yrs.	Appointed 2d Lieutenant Aug. 21, 1861; promoted 1st Lieutenant Nov. 7, 1862; Captain Dec. 2, 1862.
Jacob K. Kuhn	do	25	Aug. 7, 1861	3 yrs.	Promoted to 2d Lieutenant from Sergeant Nov. 7, 1862, to 1st Lieutenant Dec. 2, 1862; Captain May 9, 1864; mustered out Jan. 13, 1865, at Nashville, Tenn, on expiration of term of service.
Henry Krumdick	do	22	Aug. 25, 1861	3 yrs.	Appointed Corporal ——; 1st. Sergeant Oct. 1, 1861; promoted to 1st Lieutenant May 9, 1864; to Captain to date Jan. 6, 1865; mustered out with company Sept. 13, 1865; veteran.
Bestcome R. Kirby	1st Lieut.	30	Aug. 7, 1861	3 yrs.	Appointed Aug. 21, 1861, resigned Nov. 7, 1862.
James Moore, Jr	do	21	Aug. 7, 1861	3 yrs.	Appointed Corporal ——; Sergeant Jan. 1, 1862; 1st Sergeant May 9, 1864; promoted to 1st Lieutenant March 18, 1865; mustered out to date Sept. 13, 1865; veteran.
Charles W. Florence	2d Lieut.	24	Aug. 15, 1861	3 yrs.	Appointed 1st Sergeant from Q. M. Sergeant ——; promoted to 2d Lieutenant Dec. 2, 1863; resigned April 8, 1864.
John A. Drexel	1st Sergt.	58	Aug. 15, 1861	3 yrs.	Discharged Jan. 8, 1865, at Gallipolis, O., on Surgeon's certificate of disability.
John W Johnson	do	19	Aug. 7, 1861	3 yrs.	Appointed Corporal ——; Sergeant Sept. 18, 1864; 1st Sergeant May 15, 1865; died July 7, 1865, at Oakley Station, S. C., of wounds received in line of duty; veteran.
Daniel Donovan	do	22	Aug. 15, 1861	3 yrs.	Mustered as private; appointed Sergeant Dec. 20, 1863; 1st Sergeant July 8, 1865; mustered out with company Sept. 13, 1865; veteran.
Samuel C. Bixey	Q. M. S.	28	Aug. 7, 1861	3 yrs.	Appointed Corporal ——; Q. M. Sergeant ——; discharged Feb. 17, 1863, at Annapolis, Md., on Surgeon's certificate of disability.

FIRST REGIMENT OHIO VOLUNTEER CAVALRY.

Names.	Rank.	Age	Date of Entering the Service.	Period of Service	Remarks.
John Camm	Q. M. S.	21	Oct. 1, 1862	3 yrs.	Appointed Corporal Oct. 1, 1863; Sergeant Feb. 1, 1865; Q. M. Sergeant July 9, 1865; mustered out with company Sept. 13, 1865.
Henry Bertram	Sergeant	26	Aug. 15, 1861	3 yrs.	
Hays Clark	do	42	Aug. 25, 1861	3 yrs.	Discharged Nov. 29, 1862, on Surgeon's certificate of disability.
Curtis Snyder	do	22	Aug. 17, 1861	3 yrs.	
John J. Johnson	do	23	Sept. 30, 1862	3 yrs.	Appointed Corporal Nov. 1, 1862; Sergeant Sept. 18, 1864; mustered out with company Sept. 13, 1865.
James Weiland	do	23	Aug. 15, 1861	3 yrs.	Appointed Corporal Dec. 29, 1863; Sergeant Feb. 1, 1865; mustered out with company Sept. 13, 1865; veteran.
Philip Kleiber	do	24	Aug. 15, 1861	3 yrs.	Appointed Corporal Dec. 29, 1863; Sergeant Feb. 1, 1865; mustered out with company Sept. 13, 1865; veteran.
Gustavus A. Springer	do	28	Aug. 7, 1861	3 yrs.	Mustered as private; appointed ——; captured Nov. 5, 1863, at Dartwood, Va.; mustered out Jan. 28, 1865, at Columbus, O., on expiration of term of service.
Lewis Noser	Corporal	30	Aug. 15, 1861	3 yrs.	Discharged July 12, 1862, near Alexandria, Va., on Surgeon's certificate of disability.
Joseph M. Gaddis	do	20	Aug. 7, 1861	3 yrs.	Killed Aug. 9, 1862, in the battle of Cedar Mountain, Va.
Benjamin F. Maynard	do	38	Aug. 15, 1861	3 yrs.	Died July 28, 1863.
John Peterman	do	22	Aug. 25, 1861	3 yrs.	Mustered out Sept. 17, 1864, on expiration of term of service.
Matthias Dann	do	25	Aug. 15, 1861	3 yrs.	Discharged Sept. 28, 1863, on Surgeon's certificate of disability.
Jacob Bayha	do	24	Aug. 7, 1861	3 yrs.	Also borne on the rolls as "Bahaw;" appointed June 1, 1864; mustered out with company Sept. 13, 1865; veteran.
Francis H. Gilker	do	23	Sept. 30, 1862	3 yrs.	Appointed Feb. 1, 1865; mustered out with company Sept. 13, 1865.
Marcus Hummel	do	25	Aug. 27, 1861	3 yrs.	Appointed Feb. 1, 1865; mustered out with company Sept. 13, 1865; veteran.
Albert Hirst	do	19	Oct. 2, 1862	3 yrs.	Appointed Feb. 1, 1865; mustered out with company Sept. 13, 1865.
David P. Fouts	do	27	Sept. 29, 1862	3 yrs.	Appointed Feb. 1, 1865; mustered out June 19, 1865 at Nashville, Tenn., by order of War Department.
William Auth	do	21	Aug. 15, 1861	3 yrs.	Also borne on the rolls as "Adam Authr;" appointed ——; mustered out Sept. 17, 1864, at Nashville, Tenn., on expiration of term of service.
Henry G. Buff	Bugler	19	Aug. 15, 1861	3 yrs.	Discharged Jan. 3, 1863, on Surgeon's certificate of disability.
David H. Cummings	do	20	Aug. 7, 1861	3 yrs.	Mustered out Sept. 17, 1864, on expiration of term of service.
Paul During	do	19		3 yrs.	Appointed Sept. 18, 1864; died Sept. 21, 1865; veteran.
James Kirk	B. Smith	36	Aug. 25, 1861	3 yrs.	Mustered out with company Sept. 13, 1865; veteran.
Ernest Benner	Farrier	27	Aug. 15, 1861	3 yrs.	Transferred to Co. A ——.
Henry Hertz	do	28	Sept. 28, 1862	3 yrs.	Appointed ——; mustered out June 17, 1865, at Nashville, Tenn., by order of War Department.
Alexander J. Proctor	Saddler	39	Sept. 4, 1861	3 yrs.	Appointed Dec. 20, 1863; mustered out with company Sept. 13, 1865; veteran.
Ed Freeman	Wagoner	43	Aug. 25, 1861	3 yrs.	Discharged July 18, 1862, on Surgeon's certificate of disability.
Acres, Thomas	Private	27	Aug. 29, 1861	3 yrs.	
Atherton, Washington C.	do	18	Aug. 30, 1861	3 yrs.	
Binge, Stephen D.	do	23	Sept. 30, 1862	3 yrs.	Discharged Dec. 29, 1862, on Surgeon's certificate of disability.
Biggs, James L.	do	22	Sept. 30, 1862	3 yrs.	
Bird, Benjamin P.	do	19	Aug. 7, 1861	3 yrs.	Mustered out with company Sept. 13, 1865; veteran.
Bohl, John	do	36	Aug. 21, 1861	3 yrs.	
Bowes, James	do	25	Jan. 14, 1864	3 yrs.	Also borne on the rolls as "Bowes;" mustered out with company Sept. 13, 1865.
Bowers, George	do	25	Aug. 7, 1861	3 yrs.	Mustered out Sept. 17, 1864, on expiration of term of service.
Bowmann, Jacob	do	23	Aug. 15, 1861	3 yrs.	Mustered out Sept. 17, 1864, on expiration of term of service.
Bridel, Stephen	do	29	Sept. 8, 1861	3 yrs.	
Bryan, Robert	do	35	Aug. 25, 1861	3 yrs.	Died June 4, 1864.
Collins, Alfred	do	24	Aug. 25, 1861	3 yrs.	Mustered out Sept. 17, 1864, at Nashville, Tenn., on expiration of term of service.
Davis, William	do	18	Aug. 15, 1861	3 yrs.	Died March 3, 1864.
Deaupo, James	do	27	Aug. 15, 1861	3 yrs.	Mustered out with company Sept. 13, 1865; veteran.
Erstine, George	do	40	Jan. 28, 1864	3 yrs.	Mustered out with company Sept. 13, 1865.

ROSTER OF OHIO TROOPS.

Names.	Rank.	Age	Date of Entering the Service.	Period of Service	Remarks.
Flattich, Christian	Private	33	Aug. 21, 1861	3 yrs.	Mustered out Sept. 17, 1864, on expiration of term of service.
Fernshill, Thomas W	do	24	Aug. 7, 1861	3 yrs.	
Forsyth, William E	do	20	Dec. 26, 1863	3 yrs.	Discharged Aug. 2, 1865, on Surgeon's certificate of disability.
Gadills, Jonathan J	do	18	Sept. 14, 1861	3 yrs.	Mustered out with company Sept. 13, 1865; veteran.
Garbeson, T. G	4e	22	Aug. 15, 1861	3 yrs.	Transferred to 2nd United States Cavalry Oct. 31, 1862.
Grottendick, Henry	do	35	Sept. 30, 1862	3 yrs.	Mustered out with company Sept. 13, 1865.
Gnarberson, John J	do	23	Dec. 26, 1863	3 yrs.	
Haley, Patrick	do	19	Sept. 1, 1861	3 yrs.	Mustered out Sept. 17, 1864 on expiration of term of service.
Hampton, William	do	18	Oct. 2, 1862	3 yrs.	Mustered out with company Sept. 13, 1865.
Harkkins, John	do	19	Sept. 1, 1861	3 yrs.	Discharged Dec. 2, 1863, on Surgeon's certificate of disability.
Harrod, John Wesley	do	19	Aug. 25, 1861	3 yrs.	Mustered out Sept. 19, 1864, on expiration of term of service.
Hill, Charles	do	20	Aug. 7, 1861	3 yrs.	
Holloway, G. W	do	18	Aug. 15, 1861	3 yrs.	Died May 26, 1864.
Hull, Joel D	do	18	Aug. 15, 1861	3 yrs.	Mustered out Dec. 23, 1864, on expiration of term of service.
Hunt, Enoch	do	24	Aug. 15, 1861	3 yrs.	Mustered out Sept. 17, 1864, on expiration of term of service.
Jeffries, Ambrose	do	19	Sept. 30, 1862	3 yrs.	
Kecsceker, George H	do	20	Dec. 26, 1863	3 yrs.	Mustered out with company Sept. 13, 1865.
Kennedy, Moses	do	21	Oct. 1, 1862	3 yrs.	
Kohler, Lewis	do	28	Aug. 15, 1861	3 yrs.	Died Oct. 28, 1863.
Latchford Richard	do	23	Sept. 29, 1862	3 yrs.	
Lawson, W. W	do	28	Aug. 15, 1861	3 yrs.	Mustered out Sept. 17, 1864, on expiration of term of service.
Leroy, Francis C	do	22	Sept. 5, 1861	3 yrs.	Discharged Jan. 13, 1863, on Surgeon's certificate of disability.
Lewis, William H	do	19	Aug. 15, 1861	3 yrs.	
Malden, William I	do	17	Oct. 1, 1862	3 yrs.	Mustered out with company Sept. 13, 1865.
Meat, Lafayette	do	19	Sept. 4, 1861	3 yrs.	
Miller, Henry	do	28	Aug. 25, 1861	3 yrs.	
Miller, John	do	24	Aug. 15, 1861	3 yrs.	Mustered out with company Sept. 13, 1865; veteran.
Mooney, Patrick	do	29	Aug. 7, 1861	3 yrs.	Transferred to Company I Dec. 16, 1861.
Neargarter, Henry	do	19	Aug. 15, 1861	3 yrs.	Mustered out with company Sept. 13, 1865; veteran.
Niles, Henry P	do	27	Sept. 29, 1862	3 yrs.	
Ormston, William	do	20	Sept. 30, 1862	3 yrs.	Mustered out with company Sept. 13, 1865.
Pote, Augustus	do	19	Sept. 5, 1861	3 yrs.	Mustered out with company Sept. 13, 1865; veteran.
Price, James L	do	34	Oct. 1, 1862	3 yrs.	Transferred to Navy May 19, 1865, by order of War Department.
Puntler, Henry	do	21	Aug. 15, 1861	3 yrs.	Also borne on rolls as "Henry Ponzer;" discharged Oct. 13, 1861, on Surgeon's certificate of disability.
Randolph, Edward L	do	32	Aug. 7, 1861	3 yrs.	Died Aug. 3, 1863.
Relly, John	do	20	Aug. 20, 1861	3 yrs.	
Schulttker, Henry	do	23	Aug. 25, 1861	3 yrs.	Mustered out Sept. 17, 1864, on expiration of term of service.
Schmittker, Lewis	do	27	Aug. 25, 1861	3 yrs.	Mustered out Sept. 17, 1864, on expiration of term of service.
Schmittker, William	do	25	Aug. 25, 1861	3 yrs.	Died Nov. 22, 1861.
Seddions, Albert	do	18	Sept. 29, 1862	3 yrs.	
Shields, John H	do	26	Sept. 28, 1862	3 yrs.	Mustered out June 17, 1865, at Nashville, Tenn., by order of War Department.
Sifred, John	do	18	Sept. 30, 1862	3 yrs.	Mustered out with company Sept. 13, 1865.
Sinsclair, John	do	43	Aug. 7, 1861	3 yrs.	Also borne on rolls as "Sinclair;" discharged March 15, 1862, on Surgeon's certificate of disability.
Smith, John H	do	24	Oct. 1, 1862	3 yrs.	
Smith, Thomas	do	30	Jun. 14, 1864	3 yrs.	Mustered out with company Sept. 13, 1865.
Steinbrick, Francis	do	42	Aug. 15, 1861	3 yrs.	Discharged Jan. 24, 1862, on Surgeon's certificate of disability.
Stevens, Henry	do	24	Oct. 1, 1862	3 yrs.	Discharged May 29, 1865, on Surgeon's certificate of disability.
Stone, Daniel L	do	24	Sept. 1, 1861	3 yrs.	Died June 9, 1862.
Stringham, William	do	30	Aug. 9, 1863	3 yrs.	Also borne on rolls as "William H."
Sweeney, Thomas	do	44	Jan. 18, 1864	3 yrs.	Mustered out with company Sept. 13, 1865.
Teneyk, Daniel	do	31	Aug. 15, 1861	3 yrs.	Mustered out Sept. 17, 1864, on expiration of term of service.
Tirolf, Joseph	do	28	Aug. 24, 1861	3 yrs.	
Thompson, Hiram	do	18	Aug. 25, 1861	3 yrs.	
Trimp, Martin	do	22	Oct. 2, 1862	3 yrs.	Also borne on rolls as "Martin A."
Updum, Firman	do	23	Aug. 15, 1861	3 yrs.	Mustered out Sept. 17, 1864, on expiration of term of service.
Vinten, Pierce	do	22	Aug. 29, 1861	3 yrs.	
Volodine, Davy	do	39	Aug. 15, 1861	3 yrs.	Mustered out Sept. 17, 1864, on expiration of term of service.

FIRST REGIMENT OHIO VOLUNTEER CAVALRY.

Names.	Rank.	Age.	Date of Entering the Service.	Period of Service.	Remarks.
Webb, Albert............	Private	21	Sept. 29, 1862	3 yrs.	Discharged Feb. 10, 1864, on Surgeon's certificate of disability.
White, James M........	...do...	23	Sept. 30, 1862	3 yrs.	Mustered out with company Sept. 13, 1865.
Willhouse, Anthony.....	...do...	21	Aug. 15, 1861	3 yrs.	Mustered out Sept. 17, 1864, on expiration of term of service.
Willhouse, Henry.......	...do...	19	Aug. 15, 1861	3 yrs.	Mustered out Sept. 17, 1864, on expiration of term of service.
Williams, George A. F...	...do...	18	Aug. 15, 1861	3 yrs.	Died Feb. 19, 1862.
Wilson, William R......	...do...	18	Jan. 4, 1864	3 yrs.	Mustered out with company Sept. 13, 1865.
Yockee, Frederick......	...do...	25	Sept. 12, 1861	3 yrs.	Mustered out Sept. 17, 1864, at Nashville, Tenn., on expiration of term of service.

COMPANY D.

Mustered in Aug. 31, 1861, at Camp Chase, Ohio, by Howard Stansbury, Captain Topographical Engineers, U. S. A., Mustering Officer. Mustered out Sept. 13, 1865, at Hilton Head, S. C., by Leslie Smith, Brevet Major and Captain 1st Infantry, U. S. A., Commissary of Musters, District of South Carolina.

Names.	Rank.	Age.	Date of Entering the Service.	Period of Service.	Remarks.
David A. B. Moore......	Captain	40	Aug. 5, 1861	3 yrs.	Appointed Aug. 30, 1861; promoted to Major Sept. 7, 1862.
Samuel G. Hamilton....	...do...	32	Aug. 5, 1861	3 yrs.	Appointed 1st Lieutenant Aug. 30, 1861; promoted to Captain Sept. 7, 1862; resigned April 22, 1863.
Leonard Erwin.........	...do...	25	Aug. 6, 1861	3 yrs.	Transferred from Co. G June 6, 1863; transferred to Co. G Aug. 8, 1864.
William H. Scott.......	...do...	24	Aug. 5, 1861	3 yrs.	Promoted to 2d Lieutenant Co. K from Q. M. Sergeant June 10, 1862; transferred from Co. G Aug. 8, 1864; died Sept. 23, 1864, of wounds received Aug. 20, 1864, in the battle of Lovejoy Station, Ga.
James W. Kirkendall...	...do...	23	Aug. 5, 1861	3 yrs.	Wounded Oct. 8, 1862, in the battle of Perryville, Ky.; promoted to 2nd Lieutenant from 1st Sergeant Jan. 1, 1863; to 1st Lieutenant March 31, 1864; to Captain Jan. 6, 1865; mustered out with company Sept. 13, 1865.
Lewis M. Thayer.......	1st Lieut.	21	Aug. 14, 1861	3 yrs.	Promoted from Sergeant Co. H Jan. 6, 1865; mustered out to date Sept. 13, 1865; veteran.
Ira Stevens...........	2d Lieut.	34	Aug. 5, 1861	3 yrs.	Appointed Aug. 30, 1861; died Oct. 31, 1862, at Danville, Ky.
Samuel H. Putnam.....	...do...	25	Sept. 16, 1861	3 yrs.	Promoted from Q. M. Sergeant Co. L Nov. 29, 1862; to 1st Lieutenant Co. L Feb 11, 1863, to date Sept. 7, 1862.
Harvey Ferguson......	...do...	32	Aug. 5, 1861	3 yrs.	Mustered as private; appointed Sergeant ——; promoted to 2d Lieutenant Co. H April 18, 1863; transferred from Co. H ——; promoted to 1st Lieutenant and Adjutant to date May 25, 1864.
Charles H. Goodrich...	1st Sergt.	18	Aug. 5, 1861	3 yrs.	Appointed Sergeant from Corporal Oct. 2, 1862; 1st Sergeant ——; promoted to 1st Lieutenant Co. M June 28, 1865, to date, March 18, 1865.
John Newlove.........	Com. Ser.	20	Aug. 26, 1861	3 yrs.	Mustered as private; appointed Sergeant Jan. 31, 1863; Com. Sergeant March 1, 1864; participated in the capture of Jefferson Davis; mustered out with company Sept. 13, 1865; veteran.
James Linton.........	Sergeant	21	Aug. 5, 1861	3 yrs.	
E. A. Trowbridge......	...do...	28	Aug. 5, 1861	3 yrs.	Mustered out Oct. 6, 1864, on expiration of term of service.
Frank McKinney......	...do...	20	Aug. 7, 1861	3 yrs.	Discharged Jan. 21, 1863, at Columbus, O., on Surgeon's certificate of disability.
Frank Bills..........	...do...	24	Aug. 5, 1861	3 yrs.	Discharged Jan. 14, 1862, on Surgeon's certificate of disability.
Daniel Shobbell......	...do...	40	Aug. 5, 1861	3 yrs.	Appointed from Corporal Jan. 4, 1864; missing Aug. 19, 1864, in the battle of Lovejoy Station, Ga.; no further record; veteran.
Adin Harper.........	...do...	18	Aug. 5, 1861	4 yrs.	Wounded Dec. 31, 1862, in the battle of Stone River, Tenn.; appointed Corporal March 1, 1864; Sergeant Nov. 1, 1864; mustered out with company Sept. 13, 1865; veteran.
Henry Wheeler.......	...do...	29	Aug. 5, 1861	3 yr.	Appointed Corporal March 1, 1864; Sergeant Nov. 1, 1864; wounded April 15, 1865, in action at Columbus, Ga.; mustered out with company Sept. 13, 1865; veteran.

ROSTER OF OHIO TROOPS.

Names.	Rank.	Age	Date of Entering the Service.	Period of Service.	Remarks.
Theodore Stevenson	Sergeant	21	Aug. 5, 1861	3 yrs.	Also borne on rolls as "Thaddeus Stevenson;" appointed Corporal March 1, 1864; Sergeant Nov. 1, 1864; mustered out with company Sept. 13, 1865; veteran.
Thomas Amarine	do	18	Aug. 26, 1861	3 yrs.	Also borne on the rolls as "Thomas H.;" appointed Corporal March 1, 1864; Sergeant Nov. 1, 1864; mustered out with company Sept. 13, 1865; veteran.
Nathan Finegan	do	25	Aug. 5, 1861	3 yrs.	Appointed Corporal ——; Sergeant Oct. 28, 1862; detached as draughtsman in Topographical Engineer Department from March 11, 1863, to Sept. 20, 1864; mustered out Oct. 6, 1864 at Columbia, Tenn., on expiration of term of service.
Alvin Thompson	do	24	Aug. 26, 1861	3 yrs.	Mustered as private; appointed ——; mustered out Oct. 6, 1864, at Columbia, Tenn., on expiration of term of service.
Moses S. Lahue	Corporal	22	Aug. 5, 1861	3 yrs.	Mustered out Oct. 6, 1864, on expiration of term of service.
James Z. Milligan	do	24	Aug. 5, 1861	3 yrs.	Captured April 19, 1863, at Stone River, Tenn.; mustered out Oct. 6, 1864, on expiration of term of service.
Henry C. Ellis	do	30	Aug. 5, 1861	3 yrs.	Transferred to 60th Company, 2nd Battalion Veteran Reserve Corps ——, from which discharged March 28, 1864, on Surgeon's certificate of disability.
Wesley Realhorn	do	24	Aug. 5, 1861	3 yrs.	Mustered out Oct. 6, 1864, on expiration of term of service.
Charles J. Scott	do	22	Aug. 26, 1861	3 yrs.	Died May 8, 1862.
Charles Wells	do	22	Aug. 5, 1861	3 yrs.	Discharged Oct. 7, 1862, on Surgeon's certificate of disability.
Andrew Casteel	do	18	Aug. 5, 1861	3 yrs.	Appointed Aug. 1, 1864; mustered out with company Sept. 13, 1865; veteran.
Joseph Cross	do	25	Aug. 5, 1861	3 yrs.	Appointed Aug. 1, 1864; mustered out with company Sept. 13, 1865; veteran.
William Shepard	do	24	Oct. 6, 1863	3 yrs.	Appointed Nov. 1, 1864; mustered out with company Sept. 13, 1865.
Mason H. Palmer	do	18	Sept. 5, 1861	3 yrs.	Appointed Nov. 1, 1864; mustered out Sept. 15, 1865, at New York City, by order of War Department; veteran.
William Benjamin	do	37	Aug. 22, 1861	3 yrs.	Appointed Nov. 1, 1864; mustered out with company Sept. 13, 1865; veteran.
Marcenus Cole	do	18	Aug. 26, 1861	3 yrs.	Appointed Nov. 1, 1864; mustered out with company Sept. 13, 1865; veteran.
Samuel D. Palmer	do	41	Jan. 14, 1864	3 yrs.	Appointed Nov. 1, 1864; mustered out with company Sept. 13, 1865.
David E. Sandles	do	20	Aug. 22, 1861	3 yrs.	Appointed Nov. 1, 1864; mustered out with company Sept. 13, 1865; veteran.
James S. Hastings	do	28	Aug. 5, 1861	3 yrs.	Appointed ——; transferred to 137th Co., 2nd Battalion Veteran Reserve Corps ——, from which mustered out Aug. 31, 1864, on expiration of term of service.
Henry Bush	Bugler	19	Aug. 5, 1861	3 yrs.	Detached at Headquarters Topographical Department from April —, 1863, to Sept. 20, 1864; mustered out Oct. 6, 1864, at Columbia, Tenn., on expiration of term of service.
Russell B. Montgomery	do	18	Mch. 11, 1864	3 yrs.	Appointed Nov. 1, 1864; mustered out with company Sept. 13, 1865.
Joseph Devereaux	B. smith	19	Aug. 5, 1861	3 yrs.	Appointed Nov. 1, 1864; mustered out with company Sept. 13, 1865; veteran.
Isaac Strickler	Saddler	27	Jan. 5, 1861	3 yrs.	Appointed Nov. 1, 1864; mustered out Sept. 15, 1865, from hospital, New York City, by order of War Department.
Peter McFarland	do	39	Sept. 3, 1861	5 yrs.	Appointed ——; mustered out Aug. 22, 1865, from hospital, Camp Dennison, O., by order of War Department; veteran.
Daniel L. Bellair	Wagoner	44	Aug. 5, 1861	3 yrs.	Discharged Nov. 15, 1862, at Louisville, Ky., on Surgeon's certificate of disability.
Alward, George	Private	23	Jan. 14, 1864	3 yrs.	Also borne on rolls as "Alvard;" died May 12, 1864.
Anderson, James	do	22	Aug. 5, 1861	3 yrs.	Wounded May 30, 1862, in action at Boonville, Miss.; injured April 27, 1866, by the explosion of the steamer Sultana, on the Mississippi River, near Memphis, Tenn.; mustered out May 25, 1866, by order of War Department; veteran.
Baker, Samuel B	do	37	Aug. 15, 1864	3 yrs.	Mustered out with company Sept. 13, 1865.
Barber, John	do	40	Aug. 26, 1861	3 yrs.	Discharged July 22, 1862, on Surgeon's certificate of disability.
Barron, John	do	39	Aug. 22, 1861	3 yrs.	Mustered out with company Sept. 13, 1865; veteran.
Beverly, Edward A	do	18	Mch. 24, 1865	1 yr.	Mustered out with company Sept. 13, 1865.
Beverly, John W	do	19	Mch. 24, 1865	1 yr.	Mustered out with company Sept. 13, 1865.
Brooking, Abraham	do	18	Mch. 7, 1865	1 yr.	Mustered out with company Sept. 13, 1865.
Buckland, Charles B	do	18	Feb. 15, 1864	3 yrs.	Mustered out with company Sept. 13, 1865.

First Regiment Ohio Volunteer Cavalry.

Names.	Rank.	Age	Date of Entering the Service.	Period of Service.	Remarks.
Buckland, Edwin R.	Private	29	Jan. 5, 1864	3 yrs.	Mustered out with company Sept. 13, 1865.
Barney, Ezkiel	do	22	Mch. 4, 1865	1 yr.	Mustered out with company Sept. 13, 1865.
Barrows, Enoch	do	41	Aug. 26, 1861	3 yrs.	Discharged Jan. 14, 1862, on Surgeon's certificate of disability.
Bush, Charles	do	23	Dec. 27, 1861	3 yrs.	Mustered out Dec. 8, 1864, on expiration of term of service.
Cain, Lewis	do	19	Mch. 7, 1865	1 yr.	Mustered out with company Sept. 13, 1865.
Chapman, George W	do		Nov. 6, 1861	3 yrs.	Mustered out Nov. 5, 1864, at Columbia, Tenn., on expiration of term of service.
Cole, Joshua	do	27	Aug. 26, 1861	3 yrs.	Discharged Jan 14, 1862, on Surgeon's certificate of disability.
Coulter, George W	do	38	Aug. 5, 1861	3 yrs.	Mustered out with company Sept. 13, 1865; veteran.
Cox, Frank	do	18	Feb. 22, 1864	3 yrs.	Transferred from Co. G March —, 1864; mustered out with company Sept. 13, 1865.
Cross, Robert	do	24	Aug. 5, 1861	3 yrs.	
Denman, Allen	do	19	Aug. 5, 1861	3 yrs.	Mustered out with company Sept. 13, 1865; veteran.
Denman, William	do	23	Aug. 5, 1861	3 yrs.	Also borne on rolls as "William L;" mustered out with company Sept. 13, 1865; veteran.
Drumm, Daniel	do	38	Aug. 5, 1861	3 yrs.	Mustered out Oct. 6, 1864, on expiration of term of service.
Ellsworth, John P	do	23	Feb. 23, 1865	1 yr.	Mustered out Sept. 20, 1865, at New York City, by order of War Department.
Evans, Edward W	do	18	Aug. 5, 1861	3 yrs.	Captured April 1, 1865, in the battle of Plantersville, Ala.; mustered out Sept. 20, 1865, by order of War Department; veteran.
Foot, Horace	do	21	Aug. 26, 1861	3 yrs.	Mustered out Oct. 9, 1864, on expiration of term of service.
Gamble, James	do	18	Jan. 14, 1864	3 yrs.	Mustered out Oct. 11, 1865, at New York City, by order of War Department.
Gloyd, Lewis A	do	22	Aug. 5, 1861	3 yrs.	Mustered out with company Sept. 13, 1865; veteran.
Harris, William T	do	22	Mch. 2, 1865	1 yr.	Mustered out with company Sept. 13, 1865.
Hildredth, Harrison	do	18	Aug. 5, 1861	3 yrs.	Discharged Feb. 3, 1864, on Surgeon's certificate of disability.
Hinton, George W	do	21	Aug. 5, 1861	3 yrs.	Mustered out with company Sept. 13, 1865; veteran.
Holliday, Thomas	do	45	Aug. 26, 1861	3 yrs.	Discharged Jan. 14, 1862, on Surgeon's certificate of disability.
Houck, James	do	18	Aug. 5, 1861	3 yrs.	Mustered out with company Sept. 13, 1865; veteran.
Humbarger, Adam	do	21	Jan. 14, 1864	3 yrs.	Mustered out with company Sept. 13, 1865.
Imhoff, Jacob	do	20	Jan. 14, 1864	3 yrs.	Mustered out with company Sept. 13, 1865.
Imhoff, Sebastian	do	21	Aug. 5, 1861	3 yrs.	Mustered out with company Sept. 13, 1865; veteran.
Ingman, George	do	24	Aug. 5, 1861	3 yrs.	Mustered out Oct. 6, 1864, on expiration of term of service.
Irwin, Robert W	do	25	Aug. 26, 1861	3 yrs.	Wounded May 30, 1862, at Boonville, Miss.; captured May 28, 1864, at New Hope Church, Ga.; paroled Feb. 24, 1865, at Aiken's Landing, Va.; mustered out June 22, 1865, at Camp Dennison, O., by order of War Department.
Jackson, Harry	do	20	Aug. 15, 1864	3 yrs.	Mustered out with company Sept. 13, 1865.
Jones, David	do	31	Nov. 17, 1864	1 yr.	Mustered out with company Sept. 13, 1865.
Kelly, Sherman D	do	23	Sept. 5, 1861	3 yrs.	Discharged July 24, 1862, at Tuscumbia, Ala., on Surgeon's certificate of disability.
Kipp, William H	do	19	Aug. 5, 1861	3 yrs.	Mustered out Oct. 6, 1864, at Columbia, Tenn., on expiration of term of service.
Landsdown, Marion	do	21	Aug. 26, 1861	3 yrs.	Discharged June 22, 1862, on Surgeon's certificate of disability.
Lenhart, Jacob	do	24	Aug. 31, 1861	3 yrs.	
Leslie, James	do	20	Aug. 5, 1861	3 yrs.	Discharged Jan. 14, 1862, on Surgeon's certificate of disability.
McVay, Thaddeus	do	17	Aug. 5, 1861	3 yrs.	Wounded Dec. 31, 1862, in the battle of Stone River, Tenn.; mustered out Oct. 6, 1864, on expiration of term of service.
Mann, Robert	do	17	Mch. 27, 1865	1 yr.	Mustered out with company Sept. 13, 1865.
Marler, Isaiah	do	19	Aug. 22, 1861	3 yrs.	Mustered out with company Sept. 13, 1865; veteran.
Martin, John	do	22	Aug. 5, 1861	3 yrs.	Mustered out with company Sept. 13, 1865; veteran.
Miller, John	do	17	Aug. 5, 1861	3 yrs.	Captured Dec. 31, 1862, in the battle of Stone River, Tenn.; mustered out with company Sept. 13, 1865; veteran.
Montgomery, Henry D	do	20	Sept. 5, 1861	3 yrs.	Mustered out with company Sept. 13, 1865; veteran.
Moorehead, George A	do	29	Aug. 5, 1861	3 yrs.	Mustered out Oct. 6, 1864, on expiration of term of service.
Morrison, George	do	20	Aug. 5, 1861	3 yrs.	Discharged July 24, 1862, on Surgeon's certificate of disability.
Mulet, Lemuel	do	18	Mch. 17, 1865	1 yr.	Mustered out with company Sept. 13, 1865.
Myers, James	do	22	Aug. 5, 1861	3 yrs.	Mustered out Oct. 6, 1864, on expiration of term of service.

Roster of Ohio Troops.

Names.	Rank.	Age	Date of Entering the Service.	Period of Service.	Remarks.
Myers, George	Private	21	Jan. 11, 1864	3 yrs.	Mustered out with company, Sept. 13, 1865.
Myers, William H.	do	26	Aug. 5, 1861	3 yrs.	Mustered out with company Sept. 13, 1865; veteran.
Newman, James	do	27	Aug. 5, 1861	3 yrs.	Died June 11, 1862, at Boonville, Miss.
Nugent, William	do	47	Aug. 26, 1861	3 yrs.	Discharged June 26, 1862, on Surgeon's certificate of disability.
O'Grady, Thomas	do	19	Nov. 12, 1864	1 yr.	Mustered out with company Sept. 13, 1865.
Parish, Nathan	do	27	Aug. 5, 1861	3 yrs.	Also borne on the rolls as "Nahan Parish;" mustered out with company Sept. 13, 1865; veteran.
Pierce, Absalom	do	20	Mch. 23, 1865	1 yr.	Mustered out with company Sept. 13, 1865.
Poland, Wesley	do	19	Aug. 5, 1861	3 yrs.	Killed Dec. 31, 1862, in the battle of Stone River, Tenn.
Poulton, Charles	do	10	Jan. 3, 1864	3 yrs.	Also borne on the rolls as "Charles W.;" mustered out with company Sept. 13, 1865
Powers, Joseph W.	do	19	Mch. 9, 1864	3 yrs.	Mustered out with company Sept. 13, 1865.
Powers, William M.	do	22	Feb. 27, 1865	1 yr.	Mustered out Sept. 13, 1865, at New York City, N. Y., by order of War Department.
Price, Davis	do	28	Aug. 5, 1861	3 yrs.	Mustered out Oct. 6, 1864, on expiration of term of service. Mustered out with company Sept. 13, 1865.
Puffer, George	do	19	Mch. 23, 1865	1 yr.	Mustered out Oct. 6, 1864, on expiration of term of service.
Reese, David	do	18	Aug. 5, 1861	3 yrs.	Mustered out with company Sept. 13, 1865.
Ricketts, John	do	18	Mch. 24, 1865	1 yr.	Died April 11, 1862.
Robertson, John	do	27	Aug. 5, 1861	3 yrs.	Also borne on rolls as "Elvin J.;" mustered out with company Sept. 13, 1865.
Sanborn, Elvin	do	18	Feb. 15, 1864	3 yrs.	Mustered out with company Sept. 13, 1865.
Sawyer, James B.	do	25	Mch. 24, 1865	1 yr.	Borne on Detached Muster in roll as "Harmon Crithman;" mustered out with company Sept. 13, 1865.
Scratchman, Harmon	do	19	Feb. 22, 1864	3 yrs.	
Simfer, Samuel	do	18	Feb. 29, 1864	3 yrs.	Mustered out with company Sept. 13, 1865.
Smith, John J.	do	23	Aug. 5, 1861	3 yrs.	Discharged June 23, 1862, on Surgeon's certificate of disability.
Snider, George	do	20	Aug. 5, 1861	3 yrs.	
Snider, Henry	do	19	Aug. 5, 1861	3 yrs.	Mustered out with company Sept. 13, 1865; veteran.
Staley, Frederick	do	26	Feb. 23, 1864	3 yrs.	Mustered out June 14, 1865, at Louisville, Ky., by order of War Department.
Stevenson, John	do	18	Aug. 5, 1861	3 yrs.	Transferred to Co. A, 17th Regiment Veteran Reserve Corps ——, from which mustered out Sept. 16, 1864, on expiration of term of service.
Stevenson, John R.	do	21	March 8, 1865	1 yr.	Mustered out with company Sept. 13, 1865.
Taylor, Wright B.	do	24	Aug. 8, 1861	3 yrs.	Mustered out with company Sept. 13, 1865; veteran.
Thorn, William N.	do	26	Aug 21, 1862	3 yrs.	Mustered out June 17, 1865, at Nashville, Tenn., by order of War Department.
Tracy, Daniel J.	do	19	Aug. 26, 1861	3 yrs.	Discharged Jan. 14, 1862, at Camp Buell, Ky., on Surgeon's certificate of disability.
Turner, Sylvester T.	do	19	Mch. 7, 1864	3 yrs.	Mustered out with company Sept. 13, 1865.
Vermillion, Henry	do	20	Feb. 15, 1864	3 yrs.	Also borne on rolls as "Henry A.;" discharged Aug. 14, 1865, on Surgeon's certificate of disability.
Vermillion, Richard R.	do	18	Feb. 15, 1864	3 yrs.	Died Sept. 15, 1864, at Atlanta, Ga.
Wagy, John H.	do	28	Jan. 5, 1864	3 yrs.	Mustered out with company Sept. 13, 1865.
Welle, Wesley	do	19	Aug. 5, 1861	3 yrs.	
Warner, George	do	30	Aug. 5, 1861	3 yrs.	
Wheelan, Thomas J.	do	21	Mch. 8, 1865	1 yr.	Mustered out with company Sept. 13, 1865.
Williams, Leroy S.	do	26	Aug. 5, 1861	3 yrs.	Reported Dec. 31, 1861; died in hospital at Camp Chase, O., date unknown; medical records; Furloughed from hospital Dec. 29, 1861, to Jan. 26, 1862; no further record.
Willison, David	do	18	Feb. 29, 1864	3 yrs.	Also borne on roll as "David I.;" mustered out with company Sept. 13, 1865.
Young, David	do	20	Aug. 5, 1861	3 yrs.	Discharged March 17, 1864, on Surgeon's certificate of disability.

COMPANY E.

Mustered in Aug. 30, 1861, at Camp Chase, Ohio, by Howard Stansbury, Captain Topographical Engineers, U. S. A., and John B. Edie, Major 15th Infantry, U. S. A. Mustering Officers. Mustered out Sept. 13, 1865, at Hilton Head, S. C., by Leslie Smith, Brevet Major and Captain 1st U. S. Infantry, Commissary of Musters, District of South Carolina.

Names.	Rank.	Age	Date of Entering the Service	Period of Service	Remarks.
Beroth B. Eggleston	Captain	43	Aug. 8, 1861	3 yrs.	Appointed Aug. 29, 1861; promoted to Major June 20, 1862.
John C. O'Hara	...do....	26	Aug. 8, 1861	3 yrs.	Promoted to 2d Lieutenant from 1st Sergeant Jan. 9, 1862; to 1st Lieutenant June 20, 1862; to Captain to date June 20, 1862; mustered out Nov. 27, 1864, at Louisville, Ky., on expiration of term of service.
Jacob M. Sullenberger	...do....	28	Aug. 28, 1861	3 yrs.	Promoted to 1st Lieutenant from Com. Sergeant of Co. I Dec. 14, 1864; Captain March 18, 1865; mustered out with company Sept. 13, 1865; veteran.
Michael J. Alkire	1st Lieut.	34	Aug. 8, 1861	3 yrs.	Appointed Aug. 29, 1861; promoted to Captain June 20, 1862, but not mustered; resigned Nov. 22, 1862.
Robert C. Manley	..do....	18	Aug. 8, 1861	3 yrs.	Mustered as private; appointed Sergeant ——; promoted to 2d Lieutenant June 20, 1862; to 1st Lieutenant to date June 20, 1862; resigned Jan. 28, 1863.
Alfred D. Lutz	..do....	20	Aug. 8, 1861	3 yrs.	Mustered as private; appointed Sergeant ——; promoted to 2d Lieutenant June 20, 1862; to 1st Lieutenant Feb. 1, 1863; to Captain of Co. M May 25, 1864.
Erastus R. McNeal	2d Lieut.	26	Aug. 8, 1861	3 yrs.	Appointed Aug. 29, 1861; resigned Dec 12, 1861.
William G. Lawder	...do....	19	Aug. 25, 1861	3 yrs.	Promoted from 1st Sergeant of Co. I April 22, 1863; transferred to Co. I ——.
George W. Keys	1st Sergt.	33	Aug. 8, 1861	3 yrs.	Mustered as private; appointed Sergeant ——; 1st Sergeant ——; promoted to 2d Lieutenant of Co. F, April 1, 1863.
Henry E. Rector	...do....	19	Aug. 8, 1861	3 yrs.	Appointed Corporal ——; Sergeant Feb. 1, 1863; 1st Sergeant ——; promoted to 2d Lieutenant of Co. I, March 1st, 1865; veteran.
William H. Nich......	...do....	24	Sept. 5, 1861	3 yrs.	Mustered as private; appointed Sergeant Feb. 1, 1863; 1st Sergeant May 15, 1865; mustered out with company Sept. 13, 1865; veteran.
Tarlton C. Collins	Q. M. S.	42	Aug. 8, 1861	3 yrs.	Mustered out Oct. 16, 1864, on expiration of term of service.
Robert Johns	Com. Ser	27	Aug. 26, 1861	3 yrs.	Mustered as private; appointed Com. Sergeant ——; promoted to 1st Lieutenant Co. I, Jan. 6, 1865; veteran.
Jonas M. Sees	Sergeant	25	Aug. 8, 1861	3 yrs.	Mustered as private; appointed Sergeant Feb. 1, 1863; mustered out with company Sept. 13, 1865; veteran.
John T. C. McKitrick	..do....	24	Aug. 26, 1861	3 yrs.	Mustered as private; appointed Sergeant Feb. 1, 1863; mustered out with company Sept. 13, 1865; veteran.
Thomas V. Harper	...do....	19	Aug. 24, 1861	3 yrs.	Mustered as private; appointed Sergeant Jan. 6, 1864; mustered out with company Sept. 13, 1865; veteran.
Hugh O'Harra	..do....	26	Mch. 21, 1864	3 yrs.	Mustered as private; appointed Sergeant April 1, 1864; mustered out June 5, 1865 at Camp Dennison, O., by order of War Department. Also borne on rolls as "Crastro;" appointed Corporal ——; Sergeant Feb. 10, 1865; mustered out with company Sept. 13, 1865; veteran.
Jonathan H. Casto	..do....	24	Sept. 3, 1861	3 yrs.	
Patrick Sichan	..do....	27	Aug. 8, 1861	3 yrs.	Appointed Sergeant from Corporal Feb. 10, 1865; mustered out with company Sept. 13, 1865; veteran.
Frederick Walter	Corporal	42	Aug. 8, 1861	3 yrs.	Died Feb. 2, 1863.
Jonas Smith	..do....	23	Aug. 8, 1861	3 yrs.	Died Aug. 9, 1862.
Thomas Splak	..do....	26	Aug. 8, 1861	3 yrs.	Discharged Dec. 10, 1862, on Surgeon's certificate of disability.
Daniel M. Koffman	..do....	18	Sept. 3, 1861	3 yrs.	
William B. Beaty	..do....	21	Sept. 3, 1861	3 yrs.	Appointed ——; mustered out with company Sept. 13, 1865; veteran.
John McKim	..do....	19	Oct. 2, 1861	3 yrs.	Appointed ——; mustered out with company Sept. 13, 1865; veteran.
George W. Vaughn	..do....	21	Aug. 8, 1861	3 yrs.	Appointed ——; discharged May 23, 1865, on Surgeon's certificate of disability; veteran.

ROSTER OF OHIO TROOPS.

Names.	Rank.	Age.	Date of Entering the Service.	Period of Service.	Remarks.
William E. Hayden	Corporal	18	Sept. 3, 1861	3 yrs.	Appointed ——; mustered out with company Sept. 13, 1865; veteran.
Ephraim Hanlin	do	28	Sept. 3, 1861	3 yrs.	Appointed ——; mustered out with company Sept. 13, 1865; veteran.
William A. Hewitt	do	22	Sept. 3, 1861	3 yrs.	Appointed Feb. 10, 1865; mustered out Sept. 29, 1865, at New York City, by order of War Department; veteran.
Edward Clark	Bugler	22	Aug. 8, 1861	5 yrs.	Discharged Feb. 14, 1863, to enlist in Co. F, 4th U. S. Cavalry, from which mustered out Aug. 1, 1864, near Atlanta, Ga., on expiration of time of service.
Charles Kornien	do	26	Aug. 8, 1861	3 yrs.	Discharged Dec. 18, 1861, at Camp Chase, Ohio, on Surgeon's certificate of disability.
Andrew F. Kingsbury	Farrier	38	Aug. 8, 1861	3 yrs.	Discharged Dec. 9, 1861 on Surgeon's certificate of disability.
John Leach	do	22	Sept. 24, 1861	3 yrs.	Transferred from Co. K, April 13, 1864; mustered out with company Sept. 13, 1865; veteran.
James Anderson	Wagoner	29	Aug. 8, 1861	3 yrs.	
Alkire, Alexander	Private	28	Sept. 5, 1861	3 yrs.	Mustered out with company Sept. 13, 1865; veteran.
Alvis, George	do	32	July 27, 1864	3 yrs.	Mustered out with company Sept. 13, 1865.
Anderson, LeGrand	do	37	Aug. 8, 1861	3 yrs.	Mustered out Oct. 16, 1864, on expiration of term of service.
Ater, Milton	do	20	Aug. 8, 1861	3 yrs.	Discharged Jan. 28, 1864, on Surgeon's certificate of disability.
Baker, William A	do	20	Feb. 15, 1864	3 yrs.	Mustered out with company, Sept. 13, 1865.
Barrett, Elisha H	do	22	Sept. 3, 1861	3 yrs.	Transferred to 2nd U. S. Cavalry Feb. 10, 1863.
Barton, Jeremiah	do	18	Aug. 8, 1861	3 yrs.	Mustered out Oct. 16, 1864, on expiration of term of service.
Bland, John	do	42	Aug. 26, 1861	3 yrs.	Discharged April 9, 1864, at Louisville, Ky.
Boucher, George	do	25	Feb. 15, 1864	3 yrs.	Mustered out with company Sept. 13, 1865.
Boyd, James M	do	19	Aug. 19, 1863	3 yrs.	
Bradfield, Hiram L	do	30	Feb. 25, 1864	3 yrs.	Mustered out with company Sept. 13, 1865.
Brown, William	do	23	Aug. 8, 1861	3 yrs.	
Burton, John	do	18	Aug. 8, 1861	3 yrs.	
Childester, James	do	18	Oct. 1, 1861	3 yrs.	Transferred from Co. M ——; mustered out Sept. 16, 1864, on expiration of term of service.
Cochran, Hugh	do	24	Aug. 8, 1861	3 yrs.	Mustered out Oct. 16, 1864, on expiration of term of service.
Coverston, Wilson	do	18	Sept. 3, 1861	3 yrs.	Mustered out Oct. 16, 1864, on expiration of term of service.
Dail, Daniel	do	18	Sept. 3, 1861	3 yrs.	Borne on muster-in roll only.
Dail, Thomas	do	17	Sept. 3, 1861	3 yrs.	Mustered out with company Sept. 13, 1865; veteran.
Dewey, Lemuel	do	20	Aug. 8, 1861	3 yrs.	Mustered out with company Sept. 13, 1865; veteran.
Dugan, Thomas	do	22	Aug. 8, 1861	3 yrs.	Mustered out Oct. 16, 1864, on expiration of term of service.
Ellis, Ezra F	do	20	Aug. 8, 1861	3 yrs.	Transferred to Co. F, 1st Mississippi Marine Brigade ——; mustered out Jan. 17, 1865, with Co. G, 1st Mississippi Marine Brigade, to which transferred from Co. F.
Evans, William T	do	34	Sept. 3, 1861	3 yrs.	Mustered out Oct. 16, 1864, on expiration of term of service.
Fairman, Harvey W	do	44	Aug. 17, 1861	3 yrs.	Discharged Nov. 13, 1862, at Nashville, Tenn., on Surgeon's certificate of disability.
Finn, John	do	18	Aug. 19, 1863	3 yrs.	Mustered out with company Sept. 13, 1865.
Foley, Barney	do	23	Aug. 17, 1861	3 yrs.	In hospital at Columbia, Tenn., May 1, 1864; no further record.
Gardner, John	do	37	Feb. 23, 1864	3 yrs.	Mustered out with company Sept. 13, 1865.
Gardner, Wilson	do	23	Feb. 24, 1864	3 yrs.	Mustered out with company Sept. 13, 1865.
Geiger, George	do	18	Sept. 25, 1861	3 yrs.	Transferred from Co. M ——; mustered out Oct. 16, 1864, on expiration of term of service.
Gilmore, Marcus	do	21	Sept. 3, 1861	3 yrs.	Mustered out Oct. 16, 1864, on expiration of term of service.
Greene, Charles	do	18	Aug. 8, 1861	3 yrs.	Sent to hospital, Louisville, Ky., April 27, 1862; no further record.
Greene, William	do	18	Sept. 3, 1861	3 yrs.	Mustered out with company Sept. 13, 1865; veteran.
Hall, Henry	do	23	Oct. 10, 1861	3 yrs.	At Huntsville, Ala., hospital, Jan. 20, 1864; no further record.
Hanlin, Ephraim L	do	44	Sept. 3, 1861	3 yrs.	Discharged Feb. 1, 1865, on Surgeon's certificate of disability.
Hanson, Charles M	do	22	Aug. 29, 1861	3 yrs.	
Hendricks, Charles W	do	18	Sept. 8, 1863	3 yrs.	Died Oct. 16, 1863.
Heddin, John	do	19	Mch. 5, 1864	3 yrs.	Mustered out with company Sept. 13, 1865.
Heffin, Thomas	do	23	Mch. 5, 1864	3 yrs.	Mustered out with company Sept. 13, 1865.
Henry, Thomas	do	18	Aug. 15, 1863	3 yrs.	Captured Aug. 15, 1864, while on foraging and scouting duty; mustered out with company Sept. 14, 1865.
Hogle, James	do	19	Aug. 8, 1861	3 yrs.	

FIRST REGIMENT OHIO VOLUNTEER CAVALRY.

Names.	Rank.	Age.	Date of Entering the Service.	Period of Service.	Remarks.
High, Elias	Private	27	Aug. 8, 1861	3 yrs.	Mustered out with company Sept. 13, 1865; veteran.
Hovermale, Nathan	do	23	Mch. 29, 1865	1 yr.	Mustered out Sept. 20, 1865, at New York City, by order of War Department.
Huddleson, Stephen L.	do	19	Feb. 28, 1864	3 yrs.	Mustered out with company Sept. 13, 1865.
Iman, Hiram	do	24	Sept. 3, 1861	3 yrs.	Also borne on the rolls as "Hiram G.:" discharged ——, on expiration of term of service.
Irvin, Washington	do	18	Aug. 8, 1861	3 yrs.	Mustered out Oct. 16, 1864, on expiration of term of service.
Karos, John	do	20	Sept. 25, 1861	3 yrs.	Temporarily transferred to 6th O. V. C. ——; rejoined 1st O. V. C. July 26, 1864; mustered out Oct. 16, 1864, at Columbia, Tenn., on expiration of term of service.
Kiser, John	do	19	Sept. 15, 1861	3 yrs.	Transferred from Co. M ——; mustered out Oct. 16, 1864, on expiration of term of service.
Konkle, Jacob	do	18	Aug. 8, 1861	3 yrs.	Died Aug. 13, 1862.
LaBue, William T.	do	18	Feb. 15, 1864	3 yrs.	Mustered out with company Sept. 13, 1865.
Lomasney, William	do	35	Aug. 8, 1861	3 yrs.	Discharged Dec. 6, 1861, on Surgeon's certificate of disability.
McClintick, Joshua	do	24	Aug. 26, 1861	3 yrs.	Mustered out June 17, 1865, at Nashville, Tenn., by order of War Department.
McGath, Willis	do	30	Aug. 8, 1861	3 yrs.	Mustered out Nov. 11, 1864, at Columbus, O., on expiration of term of service.
McMillen, Alfred	do	24	Aug. 8, 1861	3 yrs.	Mustered out Oct. 16, 1864, on expiration of term of service.
Maloon, Samuel	do	19	Sept. 3, 1861	3 yrs.	
Martin, William	do	18	Sept. 3, 1861	3 yrs.	
Medzger, David	do	20	Aug. 8, 1864	3 yrs.	Died Jan. 31, 1862.
Merriam, Charles P.	do	20	Sept. 25, 1861	3 yrs.	Transferred from Co. M ——; mustered out Oct. 16, 1864, on expiration of term of service.
Mitchel, Louis T.	do	25	Feb. 5, 1864	3 yrs.	Mustered out with company Sept. 13, 1865.
Myers, James	do	19	Aug. 17, 1861	3 yrs.	Discharged July 25, 1862, on Surgeon's certificate of disability.
Nihizer, Joseph	do	19	Aug. 8, 1861	3 yrs.	Died March 2, 1864.
Peel, Lewis	do	18	Aug. 26, 1861	3 yrs.	Mustered out Oct. 16, 1864, on expiration of term of service.
Pendergrass, E. D.	do	21	Sept. 7, 1861	3 yrs.	Transferred from Co. M ——; mustered out Oct. 16, 1864, on expiration of term of service.
Peters, David B.	do	18	Feb. 24, 1864	3 yrs.	Mustered out with company Sept. 13, 1865.
Peters, Edwin	do	20	Aug. 27, 1864	1 yr.	Died Sept. 12, 1864.
Peters, Robert W.	do	18	Feb. 29, 1864	3 yrs.	Mustered out with company Sept. 13, 1865.
Powers, Michael	do	24	Aug. 8, 1861	3 yrs.	Mustered out Oct. 16, 1864, on expiration of term of service.
Quinn, James	do	43	Aug. 22, 1861	3 yrs.	Discharged Sept. 6, 1862, on Surgeon's certificate of disability.
Roach, William	do	29	Sept. 2, 1861	3 yrs.	Transferred from Co. M ——; mustered out Oct. 16, 1864, on expiration of term of service.
Sanderson, James	do	26	Aug. 17, 1861	3 yrs.	Discharged Sept. 3, 1862, on Surgeon's certificate of disability.
Sands, Thomas	do	27	Aug. 8, 1861	3 yrs.	Died May 28, 1862.
Seeds, William	do	45	Feb. 29, 1864	3 yrs.	Mustered out with company Sept. 13, 1865.
Shugart, Reuben	do	24	Aug. 8, 1861	3 yrs.	Died Aug. 17, 1864.
Shulenberger, Frederick	do	23	Aug. 26, 1861	3 yrs.	Mustered out June 3, 1865, at Indianapolis, Ind., by order of War Department; veteran.
Sikes, Henry	do	30	Sept. 9, 1861	3 yrs.	Discharged Aug. 9, 1862, on Surgeon's certificate of disability.
Smith, Michael C.	do	22	Oct. 1, 1861	3 yrs.	Transferred from Co. M ——; mustered out Oct. 16, 1864, on expiration of term of service.
Spangler, Henry	do	18	Sept. 25, 1861	3 yrs.	Transferred from Co. M ——; mustered out Oct. 16, 1864, on expiration of term of service.
Sponsler, Oliver	do	25	Aug. 26, 1861	3 yrs.	Killed June 15, 1863, in action.
Standou, William	do	20	Aug. 8, 1861	3 yrs.	Mustered out Oct. 16, 1864, on expiration of term of service.
Stewart, William	do	26	Aug. 8, 1861	3 yrs.	Died July 14, 1862.
Story, John B.	do	28	Feb. 25, 1864	3 yrs.	Mustered out with company Sept. 13, 1865.
Swanke, John A.	do	29	April 2, 1864	3 yrs.	Mustered out with company Sept. 13, 1865.
Sweky, Frederick	do	22	Aug. 26, 1861	3 yrs.	Mustered out Oct. 16, 1864, on expiration of term of service.
Tallifaro, Isaac N.	do	19	Sept. 3, 1861	3 yrs.	Mustered out Aug. 31, 1865, at Louisville, Ky., by order of War Department; veteran.
Thompson, Edward	do	19	Sept. 3, 1861	3 yrs.	Died May 28, 1862.
Thompson, John	do	28	Sept. 3, 1861	3 yrs.	
Tootle, Jerome B.	do		Sept. 25, 1861	3 yrs.	Died April 10, 1862, at Nashville, Tenn.
Van Wey, William	do	27	Oct. 2, 1861	3 yrs.	Mustered out with company Sept. 13, 1865; veteran.
Walterhouse, Chas. W.	do	22	Aug. 8, 1861	1 yr.	
Warner, Anthony	do	29	Dec. 1, 1861	3 yrs.	Discharged Dec. 23, 1863, on Surgeon's certificate of disability.
Wells, George	do	19	Aug. 8, 1861	3 yrs.	Died Oct. 2, 1861.

Names.	Rank.	Age.	Date of Entering the Service.	Period of Service.	Remarks.
Wells, James	Private		Aug. 8, 1861	3 yrs.	Discharged Oct. 1, 1862, on Surgeon's certificate of disability.
Whitney, McClure	...do...	31	Sept. 6, 1861	3 yrs.	Transferred from Co. M ——; mustered out Oct. 16, 1864, on expiration of term of service.
Yarhouse, Jacob	...do...	42	Aug. 8, 1861	3 yrs.	Died Dec. 13, 1862.

COMPANY F.

Mustered in Sept. 17, 1861, at Camp Chase, Ohio, by Howard Stansbury, Captain Topographical Engineers, and John R. Edie, Major 15th Infantry, U. S. A. Mustering Officers. Mustered out Sept. 13, 1865, at Hilton Head, S. C., by Leslie Smith, Brevet Major and Captain 1st U. S. Infantry, Commissary of Musters, District of South Carolina.

Names.	Rank.	Age.	Date of Entering the Service.	Period of Service.	Remarks.
Valentine Cupp	Captain	30	Sept. 5, 1861	3 yrs.	Appointed Sept. 17, 1861; promoted to Major Dec. 31, 1862.
Lafayette Pickering	...do...	32	Sept. 5, 1861	3 yrs.	Appointed 1st Lieutenant Sept. 17, 1861; promoted to Captain Dec. 31, 1862; mustered out Dec. 29, 1864, on expiration of term of service.
Joseph H. Pearse	1st Lieut.	24	Sept. 5, 1861	3 yrs.	Promoted to 2d Lieutenant from Sergeant June 16, 1862; to 1st Lieutenant Dec. 31,1862; resigned Aug. 9, 1863.
Allen T. Overly	...do...	23	Sept. 5, 1861	3 yrs.	Promoted from 2d Lieutenant Co. M March 31, 1864; transferred to Co. M ——
William G. Lawder	...do...	19	Aug. 22, 1861	3 yrs.	Transferred from Co. M ——; promoted to Captain Co. I, Dec 14, 1864.
George V. Ward	...do...	21	Sept. 5, 1861	3 yrs.	Mustered as private; appointed Sergeant Nov. 4, 1862; 1st Sergeant Nov. 1, 1864; promoted to 1st Lieutenant March 18, 1865; mustered out with company Sept. 13, 1865; veteran.
Henry G. Ward	2d Lieut.	36	Sept. 5, 1861	3 yrs.	Appointed Sept. 17, 1861; resigned Feb. 9, 1862.
Peter B. Cool	...do...	25	Sept. 5, 1861	3 yrs.	Appointed Corporal ——; promoted to 2d Lieutenant Feb. 9, 1862; to 1st Lieutenant and Regt. Quartermaster June 16, 1862.
William T. Brison	...do...	34	Sept. 5, 1861	3 yrs.	Promoted to Sergt. Major of 3rd Battalion from 1st Sergeant Sept. 6, 1861; to 2d Lieutenant Sept. 1, 1862; to 1st Lieutenant Co. G April 1, 1863.
George W. Keys	...do...	33	Aug. 8, 1861	3 yrs.	Promoted from 1st Sergeant of Co. E April 1, 1863, to 1st Lieutenant May 20, 1864, but not mustered; resigned July 1, 1864.
John H. Roley	1st Sergt.	22	Sept. 5, 1861	3 yrs.	Mustered as private; appointed Sergeant Oct. 7, 1864; 1st Sergeant May 15, 1865; mustered out with company Sept. 13, 1865; veteran.
Amos D. Leib	Q. M. S.	24	Sept. 6, 1861	3 yrs.	Promoted to Batt. Q. M. Sergeant ——; to 2d Lieutenant Co. I Nov. 20, 1862.
John H. Neff	...do...	35	Sept. 5, 1861	3 yrs.	Mustered as private; appointed Sergeant Jan. 1, 1862; Q. M. Sergeant Jan. 4, 1864; mustered out with company Sept. 13, 1865; veteran.
John Wells	Com. Ser.	40	Sept. 17, 1861	3 yrs.	Mustered as private; appointed Jan. 4, 1864; mustered out with company Sept. 13, 1865; veteran.
Jacob Kuhns	Sergeant	26	Sept. 5, 1861	3 yrs.	Mustered out Oct. 6, 1864, on expiration of term of service.
John W. Hill	...do...	20	Sept. 5, 1861	3 yrs.	Mustered as private; appointed Sergeant ——; mustered out Oct. 6, 1864, on expiration of term of service.
Sylvester P. Stevenson	...do...	30	Sept. 5, 1861	3 yrs.	Also borne on the rolls as "Sylvester S;" discharged May 31, 1863, at Laverne, Tenn., on Surgeon's certificate of disability.
William H. Broyles	...do...	22	Sept. 5, 1861	3 yrs.	Appointed Corporal Jan. 4, 1864; Sergeant Nov. 1, 1864; mustered out with company Sept. 13, 1865; veteran.
Peter B. Cool	...do...	37	Feb. 22, 1864	3 yrs.	Mustered as private; appointed Sergeant, Nov. 1, 1864; promoted to 2d Lieutenant Aug. 15, 1865, but not mustered; mustered out with company Sept. 13, 1865.
William P. Miller	...do...	19	Sept. 5, 1861	3 yrs.	Appointed Corporal Feb. 1, 1865; Sergeant June 1, 1865; mustered out with company Sept. 13, 1865; veteran.

First Regiment Ohio Volunteer Cavalry.

Names.	Rank.	Age.	Date of Entering the Service.	Period of Service.	Remarks.
John B. Ensor............	Sergeant	20	Feb. 11, 1864	3 yrs.	Appointed Corporal Nov. 1, 1864; Sergeant June 18, 1865; mustered out with company Sept. 13, 1865.
Benjamin F. Harner......	do	21	Sept. 5, 1861	3 yrs.	Mustered as private; appointed Sergeant Nov. 1, 1864; mustered out March 23, 1866, at Columbus, O., to date Sept. 13, 1865, by order of War Department; veteran.
Samuel Stiff.............	do	21	Sept. 5, 1861	3 yrs.	Appointed from Corporal ——; mustered out Oct. 6, 1864, on expiration of term of service.
George W. Nesley.........	do	25	Sept. 5, 1861	3 yrs.	Appointed from Corporal ——; mustered out Oct. 6, 1864, on expiration of term of service.
Francis H. Littlejohn....	do	40	Sept. 5, 1861	3 yrs.	Appointed from Corporal ——; mustered out Oct. 6, 1864, on expiration of term of service.
James Pumphrey..........	do	24	Sept. 5, 1861	3 yrs.	Appointed from Corporal ——; discharged Aug. 28, 1862, at Columbus, O., on Surgeon's certificate of disability.
Peter R. Egolph.........	Corporal	24	Sept. 5, 1861	3 yrs.	Appointed ——; mustered out Oct. 6, 1864, on expiration of term of service.
William M. Miller........	do	18	Sept. 24, 1861	3 yrs.	Appointed June 10, 1862; mustered out May 25, 1865, at Columbus O., on expiration of term of service.
James Sutphin............	do	22	Sept. 5, 1861	3 yrs.	Died April 10, 1862, in hospital at Columbia, Tenn.
David Ault...............	do	22	Sept. 5, 1861	3 yrs.	Appointed ——; mustered out Oct. 6, 1864, on expiration of term of service.
John C. Boyle............	do	21	Oct. 1, 1861	3 yrs.	Appointed ——; mustered out Oct. 6, 1864, at Columbia, Tenn., on expiration of term of service.
D. H. Watson.............	do	44	Sept. 5, 1861	3 yrs.	Appointed from Bugler ——; mustered out Oct. 6, 1864, on expiration of term of service.
David Laport.............	do	24	Sept. 5, 1861	3 yrs.	Appointed June 1, 1865; died Sept. 9, 1865, in hospital at Hilton Head, S. C.; veteran.
Wallace Graham...........	do	28	Feb. 17, 1864	3 yrs.	Appointed Nov. 1, 1864; wounded April 1, 1865, in battle of Plaatersville, Ala; mustered out June 16, 1865, from Tripler Hospital, Columbus, O., by order of War Department.
Joseph F. Leib...........	do	18	Feb. 15, 1864	3 yrs.	Appointed Nov. 1, 1864; mustered out with company Sept. 13, 1865.
Daniel I. Petty..........	do	22	Sept. 6, 1861	3 yrs.	Appointed Feb. 1, 1865; mustered out with company Sept. 13, 1865; veteran.
Samuel Sharp.............	do	27	Feb. 22, 1864	3 yrs.	Appointed Nov. 1, 1864; mustered out with company Sept. 13, 1865.
Wendle Emering...........	do	25	Sept. 5, 1861	3 yrs.	Appointed June 1, 1865; mustered out with company Sept. 13, 1865; veteran.
Elijah Fishbaugh.........	do	24	Feb. 19, 1864	3 yrs.	Appointed June 1, 1865; mustered out with company Sept. 13, 1865.
John Fogle...............	do	22	Feb. 17, 1864	3 yrs.	Appointed June 1, 1865, mustered out with company Sept. 13, 1865.
George Foskett...........	Bugler	41	Sept. 5, 1861	3 yrs.	Discharged March 17, 1863, by order of War Department.
William H. Turley........	Farrier	23	Sept. 5, 1861	3 yrs.	Mustered out Oct. 6, 1864, on expiration of term of service.
Abraham L. Fritz.........	B. Smith	21	Sept. 5, 1861	3 yrs.	Appointed ——; mustered out Oct. 6, 1864, on expiration of term of service.
Edward Vaughn............	Farrier	28	Sept. 5, 1861	3 yrs.	Appointed Nov. 1, 1864; mustered out with company Sept. 13, 1865; veteran.
George Golloher..........	do	23	Feb. 13, 1864	3 yrs.	Appointed April 10, 1864.
Stephen E. Hager.........	Artificer	21	Feb. 18, 1864	3 yrs.	Appointed Nov. 1, 1864; mustered out with company Sept. 13, 1865.
John D. Leady............	Wagoner	21	Sept. 24, 1861	3 yrs.	Mustered out with company Sept. 13, 1865; veteran.
Elias Miller.............	do	33	Sept. 5, 1861	3 yrs.	Died May 16, 1862, at Columbia, Tenn.
John W. Snider...........	do	29	Sept. 5, 1861	3 yrs.	Appointed Jan. 4, 1864; mustered out with company Sept. 13, 1865; veteran.
Ball, William............	Private	21	Sept. 5, 1861	3 yrs.	Killed July 2, 1863, in action at Elk River, Tenn.
Beard, Edward L..........	do	26	Sept. 5, 1861	3 yrs.	Discharged Nov. 10, 1862, at Nashville, Tenn., on Surgeon's certificate of disability.
Berry, William...........	do	21	Sept. 5, 1861	3 yrs.	
Boyer, George W..........	do	18	Feb. 6, 1864	3 yrs.	Mustered out with company Sept. 13, 1865.
Bryant, John.............	do	22	Sept. 5, 1861	3 yrs.	Mustered out Oct. 6, 1864, on expiration of term of service.
Click, Bushrod...........	do	19	Feb. 19, 1864	3 yrs.	Mustered out with company Sept. 13, 1865.
Click, John..............	do	18	Feb. 19, 1864	3 yrs.	Killed May 29, 1864, in action at Moulton, Ala.
Cokenhour, Moses.........	do	20	Feb. 18, 1864	3 yrs.	Mustered out with company Sept. 13, 1865.
Compton, William H.......	do	18	Feb. 27, 1864	3 yrs.	Mustered out with company Sept. 13, 1865.
Conkle, Henry............	do	18	Sept. 5, 1861	3 yrs.	Discharged June 19, 1862, at Camp Chase, O., on Surgeon's certificate of disability.
Conklin, John............	do	18	Mch. 7, 1864	3 yrs.	Discharged March 25, 1865, by order of War Department.

ROSTER OF OHIO TROOPS.

Names.	Rank.	Age.	Date of Entering the Service.	Period of Service.	Remarks.
Cullers, Henry B......	Private	21	Sept. 5, 1861	3 yrs.	Mustered out Oct. 6, 1864, on expiration of term of service.
Curfis, William D......	do...	18	Sept. 5, 1861	3 yrs.	Also borne on rolls as "Curfus;" veteran.
Dellinger, John........	do...	44	Sept. 5, 1861	3 yrs.	Mustered out with company Sept. 13, 1865; veteran.
Dunaway, Thomas......	do...	21	Sept. 5, 1861	3 yrs.	Mustered out Sept. 5, 1864, on expiration of term of service.
Emch, John............	do...	20	Mch. 17, 1864	3 yrs.	Also borne on rolls as "John W.;" mustered out with company Sept. 13, 1865.
Felch, Allen S.........	do...	44	Feb. 29, 1864	3 yrs.	Transferred to 139th Co. 2d Battalion Veteran Reserve Corps Apr. 16, 1864, at Nashville, Tenn., on detached service at hospital at Nashville, Tenn. and Louisville, Ky.; mustered out Nov. 15, 1865, at Louisville, Ky., by order of War Department.
Ferry, Samuel.........	do...	22	Feb. 18, 1864	3 yrs.	Mustered out May 24, 1866, at Columbus, O., to date Sept. 13, 1865, by order of War Department.
Fishbaugh, Samuel....	do...	21	Sept. 5, 1861	3 yrs.	Mustered out Oct. 6, 1864, on expiration of term of service.
Flick, Isaac T. P	do...	21	Sept. 5, 1861	3 yrs.	Mustered out Oct. 6, 1864, on expiration of term of service.
Frazier, George W....	do...	19	Sept. 5, 1861	3 yrs.	Mustered out with company Sept. 13, 1865; veteran.
Fry, Ambrose B	do...	18	Sept. 5, 1861	3 yr.	Discharged Aug. 9, 1862, at Decherd, Tenn., on Surgeon's certificate of disability.
Funk, Joseph..........	do...	26	Mch. 3, 1865	1 yr.	Mustered out with company Sept. 13, 1865.
Gates, Calvin.........	do...	29	Sept. 5, 1861	3 yrs.	Discharged July 24, 1862, on Surgeon's certificate of disability.
Gates, Calvin	do...	32	Feb. 18, 1864	3 yrs.	Mustered out with company Sept. 13, 1865.
Gierhart, Henry A ...	do...	22	Sept. 5, 1861	3 yrs.	Also borne on the rolls as "Abraham Gearhart;" detached as teamster at Headquarters, 4th Cavalry Division; mustered out Sept. 18, 1865, at Columbus, O., by order of War Department; veteran.
Gierhart, George R ...	do...	18	Feb. 12, 1864	3 yrs.	Mustered out with company Sept. 13, 1865.
Ginnville, John.......	do...	21	Sept. 10, 1861	3 yrs.	Discharged Nov. 22, 1861, at Camp Chase, O., on Surgeon's certificate of disability.
Goss, George W......	do...	21	Sept. 5, 1861	3 yrs.	Died Nov. 22, 1862, in Regimental Hospital, near Nashville, Tenn.
Hall, Jeremiah........	do...	27	Sept. 5, 1861	3 yrs.	Died April 16, 1862, at Indian Creek, fifteen miles north of Savannah, Tenn.
Hedden, Jonathan.....	do...	19	Sept. 5, 1861	3 yrs.	Discharged June 12, 1862, at Corinth, Miss., on Surgeon's certificate of disability.
Hedden, Jonathan.....	do...	22	Jan. 5, 1864	3 yrs.	Also borne on the rolls as "Jonathan J.;" died Dec. 4, 1864, in hospital at New Albany, Ind.
Hedden, Reason.......	do...	18	Sept. 5, 1861	3 yrs.	Died Feb. 16, 1862, in hospital at Lebanon, Ky.
Hixey, Tagwell.......	do...	35	Sept. 26, 1864	1 yr.	Mustered out June 17, 1865, at Nashville, Tenn., by order of War Department.
Howard, Abram S.....	do...	28	Sept. 5, 1861	3 yrs.	Prisoner of war; mustered out April 13, 1865, at Columbus, O., on the expiration of term of service.
Hoy, William L.......	do...	21	Sept. 10, 1861	3 yrs.	Mustered out Oct. 6, 1864, at Columbia, Tenn., on expiration of term of service.
Johnson, William A...	do...	18	Feb. 16, 1864	3 yrs.	Mustered out with company Sept. 13, 1865.
Kodenbarger, Jacob B.	do...	21	Feb. 19, 1864	3 yrs.	Appointed Corporal Nov. 1, 1864; reduced at his own request March 10, 1865; mustered out with company Sept. 13, 1865.
Kendall, Jacob N.....	do...	19	Sept. 5, 1861	3 yrs.	Died Dec. 1, 1861, at his home, Etna, O.
King, Henry G.......	do...	28	Nov. 11, 1863	3 yrs.	
Laney, Franklin	do...	19	Sept. 5, 1861	3 yrs.	Mustered out Oct. 6, 1864, on expiration of term of service.
Lape, John W........	do...	18	Feb. 11, 1864	3 yrs.	Mustered out with company Sept. 13, 1865.
Lawyer, Alexander...	do...	20	Sept. 5, 1861	3 yrs.	Mustered out with company Sept. 13, 1865; veteran.
Lawyer, Peter C......	do...	18	Feb. 18, 1864	3 yrs.	
Lawyer, Robert H....	do...	20	Feb. 22, 1864	3 yrs.	Mustered out with company Sept. 13, 1865.
Lawyer, Samuel H....	do...	21	Feb. 11, 1864	3 yrs.	Mustered out with company Sept. 13, 1865.
Leady, George D.....	do...	20	Feb. 20, 1864	3 yrs.	Mustered out with company Sept. 13, 1865.
Leef, John W........	do...	18	Sept. 5, 1861	3 yrs.	Also borne on rolls as "John L." and "John J. Leet;" mustered out Oct. 6, 1864, on expiration of term of service.
Lones, Andrew J.....	do...	22	Feb. 18, 1864	3 yrs.	Also borne on rolls as "Lions."
Long, Amos..........	do...	19	Sept. 5, 1861	3 yr.	
Lovebury, Jonathan..	do...	28	Sept. 19, 1861	3 yrs.	Discharged Aug. 9, 1862, at Decherd, Tenn., on Surgeon's certificate of disability.
McCollum, William H.	do...	18	Feb. 27, 1864	3 yrs.	Mustered out with company, Sept. 13, 1865.
McCue, John.........	do...	25	Sept. 12, 1861	3 yrs.	Mustered out Oct. 6, 1864, at Columbia, Tenn., on expiration of term of service.
McGlaughlin, Philip..	do...	19	Sept. 10, 1861	3 yrs.	Discharged Sept. 15, 1861, by civil authority.
McGuowan, Allen.....	do...	21	Sept. 5, 1861	3 yrs.	Died April 8, 1862, at Columbia, Tenn.
Miller, Ed...........	do...	22	Sept. 28, 1864	1 yr.	Mustered out June 17, 1865, at Nashville, Tenn., by order of War Department.

FIRST REGIMENT OHIO VOLUNTEER CAVALRY.

Names.	Rank.	Age.	Date of Entering the Service.	Period of Service.	Remarks.
Milner, John W..........	Private	21	Sept. 5, 1861	3 yrs.	Transferred to 1554 Co. 2d Battalion Veteran Reserve Corps ——; from which mustered out Sept. 5, 1864, on expiration of term of service.
Morton, Thomas...........	...do...	22	Sept. 5, 1861	3 yrs.	Reduced from Corporal at his own request Jan. 29, 1862; discharged June 12, 1862, on Surgeon's certificate of disability.
Mosier, Darius	...do....	18	Feb. 18, 1864	3 yrs.	Mustered out with company Sept. 13, 1865.
Nicely, Albert............	...do....	18	Sept. 5, 1861	3 yrs.	Died Oct. 18, 1862, in hospital, at Nashville, Tenn.
Peterman, Jacob S........	...do...	19	Feb. 20, 1864	3 yrs.	Mustered out with company Sept. 13, 1865.
Peters, Joseph A.........	...do....	18	Feb. 18, 1864	3 yrs.	Mustered out Sept. 12, 1865, at Columbus, O., by order of War Department.
Powell, Brice............	...do...	18	Feb. 18, 1864	3 yrs.	Mustered out with company Sept. 13, 1865.
Reynolds, Joseph T.......	...do....		Sept. 25, 1861	3 yrs.	Appointed Sergeant from private Jan. 1, 1862; promoted to Regt. Q. M. Sergeant Dec. 24, 1862; reduced at his own request Aug. 1, 1863; promoted to 2d Lieutenant Co. M March 25, 1864.
Rhodes, William..........	...do ...	22	Sept. 12, 1861	3 yrs.	Mustered out Oct. 6, 1864, at Columbia, Tenn., on expiration of term of service.
Robertson, Albert........	...do	22	Sept. 5, 1861	3 yrs.	Died Jan. 23, 1863.
Roley, Adam.............	...do...	20	Mch. 17, 1864	3 yrs.	Mustered out with company Sept. 13, 1865.
Ross, John..............	...do....	18	Feb. 6, 1864	3 yrs.	Mustered out with company, Sept. 13, 1865.
Schofield, Daniel A......	...do....	18	Oct. 24, 1861	3 yrs.	Wounded June 25, 1864, in action at Noonday Creek, Ga.; veteran.
Seitz, David A..........	...do....	22	Sept. 5, 1861	3 yrs.	Mustered out with company Sept. 13, 1865; veteran.
Smith, John Q...........	...do....	21	Sept. 5, 1861	3 yrs.	Discharged June 22, 1862, at Corinth, Miss., on Surgeon's certificate of disability.
Snider, Adam............	...do ...	19	Sept. 5, 1861	3 yrs.	Discharged July 24, 1862, on Surgeon's certificate of disability.
Sperry, Samuel..........	...do.....	22	Sept. 5, 1861	3 yrs.	Discharged June 12, 1862, on Surgeon's certificate of disability.
Swanger, Henry M........	...do....	20	Feb. 17, 1864	3 yrs.	Mustered out with company Sept. 13, 1865.
Taylor, Emery W.........	...do....	20	Sept. 5, 1861	3 yrs.	Died Dec. 19, 1862.
Thompson, Isaac.........	...do....	20	Sept. 5, 1861	3 yrs.	Veteran.
Undrick, John...........	...do....	35	Sept. 5, 1861	3 yrs.	Also borne on rolls as "Underoch;" mustered out with company Sept. 13, 1865; veteran.
Vanhouten, William O....	...do....	18	Feb. 20, 1864	3 yrs.	Mustered out with company Sept. 13, 1865.
Watson, Eli T...........	...do....	19	Sept. 5, 1861	3 yrs.	Mustered out Oct. 6, 1864, on expiration of term of service.
Welch, George...........	...do....	18	Sept. 5, 1861	3 yrs.	Veteran.
Welch, Jacob............	...do....	26	Sept. 12, 1861	3 yrs.	Captured at Stone Mountain, Georgia, Aug. 16, 1864; mustered out Feb. 28, 1865, at Columbus, O., on expiration of term of service.
Willison, Elisha C	...do....	18	Feb. 20, 1864	3 yrs.	Mustered out with company Sept. 13, 1865.
Wright, Thomas..........	...do....	19	Sept. 5, 1861	3 yrs.	Mustered out Aug. 24, 1865, at Camp Dennison, O., by order of the War Department; veteran.

COMPANY G.

Mustered in Sept. 30, 1861, at Camp Chase, Ohio, by John R. Edie, Major 15th Infantry, U. S. A. Mustered out Sept. 13, 1865, at Hilton Head, S. C., by Leslie Smith, Brevet Major and Captain 1st Infantry, U. S. A., and Commissary of Musters, District of South Carolina.

Andrew B. Emery......	Captain	42	Aug. 6, 1861	3 yrs.	Appointed Aug. 21, 1861; died July 15, 1862, of wounds received July 1, 1862, in battle of Russellville, Ala.
John C. Frankeberger...	...do ...	22	Sept. 11, 1861	3 yrs.	Promoted from 1st Lieutenant and Regt. Quartermaster to date June 6, 1862; to Major Sept. 24, 1864.
Leonard Erwin.........	...do....	25	Aug. 6, 1861	3 yrs.	Appointed 2d Lieutenant Aug. 21, 1861; promoted to 1st Lieutenant April 18, 1862; to Captain April 18, 1863; transferred to Co. D June 6, 1864; transferred from Co. D Aug. 8, 1864; resigned Sept. 24, 1864.
William H. Scott.......	...do	24	Aug. 5, 1861	3 yrs.	Promoted from 1st Lieutenant and Adjutant to date March 16, 1864; transferred to Co. D Aug. 8, 1864.
Alfred D. Lutz	...do....	20	Aug. 8, 1861	3 yrs.	Transferred from Co. M Oct. 1, 1864; mustered out with company Sept. 13, 1865.

ROSTER OF OHIO TROOPS.

Names.	Rank.	Age.	Date of Entering the Service.	Period of Service.	Remarks.
Philip Sinizer	1st Lieut.	42	Aug. 6, 1861	3 yrs.	Appointed Aug. 21, 1861; resigned Dec. 26, 1861.
William T. Brison	do	34	Sept. 5, 1861	3 yrs.	Promoted from 2d Lieutenant of Co. F April 1, 1863; mustered out Nov. 26, 1864, at Louisville, Ky., on expiration of term of service.
Thaddeus Scott	do	31	Sept. 4, 1861	3 yrs.	Promoted from Q. M. Sergeant of Co. M Dec. 14, 1864; commanded Co. H from Feb. 1, 1865, to June 1, 1865; mustered out with company Sept. 13, 1865.
William H. Woodlief	2d Lieut.	23	Aug. 6, 1861	3 yrs.	Promoted from 1st Sergeant April 11, 1862; to Captain Co. K April 22, 1863.
Carter M. Rigg	do	25	Aug. 6, 1861	3 yrs.	Promoted to Regt. Q. M. Sergeant from Co. Q. M. Sergeant ——; to 2d Lieutenant from Sergt. Major to date Jan. 1, 1863; appointed Act. Adjutant July 9, 1863, and served as such to date of resignation, June 18, 1864
William Brooks	1st Sergt	24	Aug. 6, 1861	3 yrs.	Appointed Corporal ——; Sergeant ——; 1st Sergeant March 16, 1864; promoted to 1st Lieutenant of Co. B Jan. 6, 1865; veteran.
Martin V. Little	do	22	Aug. 12, 1861	3 yrs.	Mustered as private; appointed Sergeant Aug. 17, 1862; 1st Sergeant Jan. 16, 1865; promoted to 1st Lieutenant of Co. A March 18, 1865; veteran.
Jeremiah D. Ferne	do	19	Feb. 21, 1864	3 yrs.	Appointed Corporal Nov. 1, 1864; Sergeant Jan. 10, 1865; 1st Sergeant July 1, 1865; mustered out with company Sept. 13, 1865.
Samuel Jackson	Q. M. S.	26	Aug. 6, 1861	3 yrs.	Mustered as private; appointed Sergeant Nov. 8, 1862; Q M. Sergeant ——; mustered out Sept. 14, 1865, at New York City, by order of War Department; veteran.
Robert Hodge	Com. Ser	22	Aug. 17, 1861	3 yrs.	Mustered as private; appointed Sergeant March 6, 1864; Q. M Sergeant ——; mustered out with company Sept. 13, 1865; veteran.
Arthur Lyon	Sergeant	30	Aug. 12, 1861	3 yrs.	Discharged June 22, 1862, on Surgeon's certificate of disability.
John O. Quent	do	26	Aug. 20, 1861	3 yrs.	Mustered out Nov. 5, 1864, on expiration of term of service.
Jasper Newton	do	22	Aug. 19, 1861	3 yrs.	Appointed from Corporal ——; mustered out Oct. 16, 1864, on expiration of term of service.
Absalom J. Ford	do	27	Aug. 13, 1861	3 yrs.	
Daniel K. Gordan	do	18	Aug. 6, 1861	3 yrs.	Discharged March 5, 1864, on Surgeon's certificate of disability.
Benjamin L. Ready	do	21	Aug. 18, 1861	3 yrs.	Appointed Corporal Jan. 4, 1864; Sergeant Nov. 1, 1864; mustered out Sept. 15, 1865, at New York City, by order of War Department; veteran.
Joseph Deerwester	do	21	Sept. 14, 1861	3 yrs.	Mustered as private; appointed Sergeant Nov. 1, 1864; mustered out with company Sept. 13, 1865; veteran.
Barney Keefer	do	08	Sept. 14, 1861	3 yrs.	Mustered as private; appointed Sergeant Nov. 1, 1864; mustered out with company Sept. 13, 1865; veteran.
George Ampert	do	24	Sept. 23, 1861	3 yrs.	Mustered as private; appointed Sergeant Nov. 1, 1864; mustered out with company Sept. 13, 1865; veteran.
Isaac C. Mefford	do	18	Aug. 19, 1861	3 yrs.	Also borne on rolls as "Clinton Mefford," appointed Corporal Nov. 1, 1864; Sergeant July 1, 1865; mustered out with company Sept. 13, 1865; veteran.
George Pierce	Corporal	31	Sept. 9, 1861	3 yrs.	Mustered out Oct. 16, 1864, on expiration of term of service.
James Sweeney	do	27	Aug. 6, 1861	3 yrs.	Transferred to Co. K, 11th Regiment Veteran Reserve Corps, Jan. 30, 1864, from which mustered out Aug. 25, 1864, at Washington, D. C., on expiration of term of service.
Lewis Windsor	do	37	Aug. 15, 1861	3 yrs.	Discharged June 22, 1862, on Surgeon's certificate of disability.
Theodore Lyon	do	24	Sept. 9, 1861	3 yrs.	Discharged March 7, 1862, on Surgeon's certificate of disability.
Oliver Pinkham	do	20	Oct. 22, 1861	3 yrs.	Appointed ——; mustered out Oct. 25, 1864, at Columbus, O., on expiration of term of service
Shadrack C. Burton	do	20	Feb. 16, 1864	3 yrs.	Appointed Nov. 1, 1864; mustered out with company Sept. 13, 1865.
Mahlon Nay	do	19	Feb. 27, 1864	3 yrs.	Appointed Nov. 1, 1864; mustered out with company Sept. 13, 1865.
Joseph Belston	do	24	Feb. 14, 1864	3 yrs.	Also borne on the rolls as "Beltson," appointed Nov. 1, 1864; mustered out with company Sept. 13, 1865.
William L. Ready	do	21	Feb. 29, 1864	5 yrs.	Appointed Nov. 1, 1864; mustered out with company Sept. 13, 1865.

First Regiment Ohio Volunteer Cavalry.

Names.	Rank.	Age	Date of Entering the Service.	Period of Service.	Remarks.
William H. Hopkins	Corporal	23	Feb. 21, 1864	3 yrs.	Appointed Jan. 16, 1865; mustered out with company Sept. 13, 1865.
Alfred Deerwester	do	21	Sept. 14, 1861	3 yrs.	Appointed Feb. 1, 1865; mustered out with company Sept. 13, 1865; veteran.
Thomas J. Buchanan	do	17	Aug. 10, 1861	3 yrs.	Appointed Feb. 1, 1865; mustered out with company Sept. 13, 1865; veteran.
William Miller	do	18	Aug. 19, 1861	3 yrs.	Appointed July 1, 1865; mustered out with company Sept. 13, 1865; veteran.
Paul V. Petard	Bugler	26	Aug. 6, 1861	3 yrs.	Honorably discharged Dec. 2, 1862.
Albert H. Williams	do	25	Aug. 6, 1861	3 yrs.	Discharged Nov. 16, 1861, on Surgeon's certificate of disability.
James F. Skillen	do	17	Dec. 31, 1863	3 yrs.	Appointed ——; mustered out June 5, 1865, from hospital at Camp Dennison, O., by order of War Department.
Oliver Gregg	do	16	Dec. 11, 1863	3 yrs.	Appointed ——; mustered out with company, Sept. 13, 1865.
Lewis Bisher	Farrier	26	Aug. 11, 1861	3 yrs.	Appointed Oct. 1, 1864; mustered out with company Sept. 14, 1865; veteran.
Silas M. Jordan	Wagoner	22	Aug. 12, 1861	3 yrs.	Appointed Jan. 4, 1861; mustered out with company, Sept. 13, 1865; veteran.
Alexander, Noah S.	Private	18	Mch. 6, 1865	1 yr.	Mustered out with company Sept. 13, 1865.
Allen, Edward	do	32	Aug. 14, 1861	3 yrs.	Discharged June 1, 1863, on Surgeon's certificate of disability.
Anderson, James	do	18	Aug. 6, 1861	3 yrs.	Discharged to date July 20, 1865, by order of War Department; veteran.
Argar, Joseph	do	18	Mch. 1, 1865	1 yr.	Mustered out with company Sept. 13, 1865.
Ashby, Samuel	do	24	Mch. 6, 1865	1 yr.	Accidentally drowned July 12, 1865, at Atlanta, Ga.
Beaver, Henry	do	24	Sept. 17, 1861	3 yrs.	Mustered out Oct. 6, 1864, on expiration of term of service.
Beck, Henry A.	do	20	Feb. 17, 1864	3 yrs.	Mustered out with company Sept. 13, 1865.
Boorom, Frederick	do	25	Sept. 14, 1861	3 yrs.	Transferred to Co. F. 8th Regiment Veteran Reserve Corps ——; from which mustered out Sept. 29, 1864, on expiration of term of service.
Boyer, William	do	19	Mch. 13, 1864	3 yrs.	Died June 5, 1864.
Breeding, James W.	do	19	Aug. 6, 1861	3 yrs.	Mustered out Sept. 14, 1865, at New York City, by order of War Department; veteran.
Caldwell, Richard	do	20	Aug. 6, 1861	3 yrs.	Mustered out with company Sept. 13, 1865; veteran.
Carmean, Mathew	do	21	Mch. 18, 1865	1 yr.	Mustered out with company Sept. 13, 1865.
Chamberlain, Oliver P.	do	21	Oct. 9, 1861	3 yrs.	Admitted to Marine U. S. Gen. Hospital May 12, 1864; discharged Jan. 7, 1865, on Surgeon's certificate of disability.
Clayton, Starkey	do	18	Sept. 9, 1861	3 yrs.	Died April 14, 1862.
Cloud, Samuel	do	24	Aug. 6, 1861	3 yrs.	Discharged Mar. 10, 1862, on Surgeon's certificate of disability.
Coon, David F.	do	18	Feb. 16, 1864	3 yrs.	Mustered out with company Sept. 13, 1865.
Day, Andrew J.	do	18	Mch. 30, 1864	3 yrs.	Died May 16, 1864.
Day, Gabriel	do	19	Aug. 6, 1861	3 yrs.	Mustered out Oct. 16, 1864, on expiration of term of service.
Divine, John W.	do	38	Mch. 8, 1865	1 yr.	Mustered out with company Sept. 13, 1865.
Dolan, Jerome	do	25	Mch. 4, 1865	1 yr.	Mustered out with company Sept. 13, 1865.
Downs, Henry	do	45	Jan. 1, 1864	3 yrs.	Mustered out June 12, 1865, at Louisville, Ky., by order of War Department.
Eggleston, George B.	do	21	Sept. 16, 1864	1 yr.	Mustered out June 17, 1865, at Nashville, Tenn., by order of War Department.
Elliott, Harvey	do	23	Aug. 6, 1861	3 yrs.	Mustered out Oct. 6, 1864, on expiration of term of service.
Falway, Dennis	do	31	Aug. 29, 1861	3 yrs.	Mustered out Oct. 6, 1864, on expiration of term of service.
Feeny, George	do	18	Feb. 1, 1864	3 yrs.	Mustered out with company Sept. 13, 1865.
Feeny, Michael	do	19	Aug. 6, 1861	3 yrs.	Mustered out with company Sept. 13, 1865; veteran.
Ferguson, Thomas	do	21	Sept. 17, 1861	3 yrs.	Mustered out Oct. 6, 1864, on expiration of term of service.
Fiscus, Clinton	do	28	Sept. 30, 1861	3 yrs.	Mustered out Oct. 6, 1864, on expiration of term of service.
Flatley, Thomas	do	23	Mch. 5, 1864	3 yrs.	Mustered out with company Sept. 13, 1865.
Gerhart, Charles	do	22	Aug. 29, 1861	3 yrs.	Mustered out Oct. 16, 1864, on expiration of term of service.
Golden, John	do	33	Aug. 24, 1861	3 yrs.	Transferred to 187th Co. 1st Battalion Veteran Reserve Corps ——; from which mustered out Aug. 24, 1864, on expiration of term of service.
Graham, John W.	do	21	Aug. 12, 1861	3 yrs.	Discharged Feb. 8, 1863, on Surgeon's certificate of disability.
Graham, Martin V.	do	19	Aug. 6, 1861	3 yrs.	Died July 22, 1862.
Harris, Henry	do	19	Sept. 9, 1861	3 yrs.	Mustered out with company Sept. 13, 1865; veteran.
Hart, Andrew	do	31	Dec. 27, 1864	1 yr.	Mustered out with company Sept. 13, 1865.
Harp, John	do	21	Aug. 6, 1861	3 yrs.	Mustered out Oct. 6, 1864, on expiration of term of service.
Hayes, Alexander	do	31	Aug. 15, 1861	3 yrs.	Discharged Feb. 19, 1862, on Surgeon's certificate of disability.

ROSTER OF OHIO TROOPS.

Names.	Rank.	Age.	Date of Entering the Service.	Period of Service.	Remarks.
Haywood, John	Private	28	Aug. 6, 1861	3 yrs.	Missing and probably killed Aug. 20, 1864, in battle of Lovejoy Station, Ga.; veteran.
Hodges, John	do	26	Sept. 9, 1861	3 yrs.	Mustered out Oct. 16, 1864, on expiration of term of service.
Helm, Edward	do	21	Aug. 6, 1861	3 yrs.	Died Oct. 4, 1862.
Hogan, John	do	20	Mch. 14, 1865	1 yr.	Mustered out with company Sept. 13, 1865.
Holley, Hezekiah	do	19	Mch. 12, 1864	3 yrs.	Discharged May 5, 1865, at Camp Dennison, on Surgeon's certificate of disability.
Holley, Lewis	do	18	Mch. 13, 1864	3 yrs.	Mustered out with company Sept. 13, 1865.
Hnidleson, Philip	do	23	Aug. 15, 1861	3 yrs.	Mustered out Oct. 16, 1864, on expiration of term of service.
Hussey, Frank M	do	21	Sept. 27, 1864	1 yr.	Mustered out June 17, 1865, at Nashville, Tenn., by order of War Department.
Ichtt, Christian	do	40	Aug. 14, 1861	3 yrs.	Discharged Dec. 17, 1861, on Surgeon's certificate of disability.
Jeffries, James H	do	22	Jan. 16, 1864	3 yrs.	Mustered out with company Sept. 13, 1865.
Kearns, Thomas	do	20	Mch. 7, 1865	1 yr.	Mustered out Sept. 15, 1865, at New York City, by order of War Department.
Kingsley, James	do	23	Mch. 4, 1865	1 yr.	Mustered out with company Sept. 13, 1865.
Ladd, George P	do	21	Aug. 13, 1861	3 yrs.	Promoted to 1st Lieutenant and Batt. Adjutant Oct. 25, 1864.
Leever, Wesley	do	21	Aug. 6, 1861	3 yrs.	Mustered out Oct. 16, 1864, on expiration of term of service.
Lewis, William	do	19	Aug. 14, 1861	3 yrs.	Mustered out Oct. 16, 1864, on expiration of term of service.
Long, Alonzo	do	22	Aug. 19, 1861	3 yrs.	Mustered out with company Sept. 13, 1865; veteran.
Long, Henry	do	34	Aug. 12, 1861	3 yrs.	Mustered out Oct. 6, 1864, on expiration of term of service.
Long, Jacob	do	27	Mch. 1, 1865	1 yr.	Mustered out with company Sept. 13, 1865.
Long, James	do	24	Mch. 1, 1865	1 yr.	Mustered out with company Sept. 13, 1865.
Long, Orlando	do	17	Mch. 6, 1865	1 yr.	Mustered out with company Sept. 13, 1865.
Lucky, William	do	21	Sept. 14, 1861	3 yrs.	Died June 14, 1862.
Lyons, John	do	25	Mch. 6, 1865	1 yr.	Mustered out with company Sept. 13, 1865.
Lyon, John K	do	31	Feb. 29, 1864	3 yrs.	Mustered out with company Sept. 13, 1865.
McGarey, Thomas	do	35	Aug. 9, 1861	3 yrs.	Transferred to 45th Co. 2d Battalion Veteran Reserve Corps ——; from which mustered out Sept. 5, 1864, on expiration of term of service.
McKinzie, Marcus A. D. L	do	21	Sept. 30, 1861	3 yrs.	Died June 12, 1862.
McLaughlin, Edward	do	27	Mch. 1, 1865	1 yr.	Mustered out with company Sept. 13, 1865.
McLaughlin, William	do	30	Mch. 6, 1865	1 yr.	Mustered out with company Sept. 13, 1865.
McMullen, David	do	24	Sept. 17, 1861	3 yrs.	Discharged May 20, 1862, on Surgeon's certificate of disability.
McMullen, Levi	do	18	Aug. 14, 1861	3 yrs.	Mustered out Oct. 16, 1864, on expiration of term of service.
McVey, Russell B	do	18	Feb. 17, 1864	3 yrs.	Mustered out with company Sept. 13, 1865.
Martels, Charles	do	19	Feb. 29, 1864	3 yrs.	Mustered out Sept. 15, 1865, at New York City, by order of War Department.
Moore, William	do	20	Aug. 20, 1861	3 yrs.	Mustered out Oct. 16, 1864, on expiration of term of service.
Morgan, James A	do	28	Aug. 6, 1861	3 yrs.	Mustered out Oct. 16, 1864, on expiration of term of service.
Morton, James	do	22	Mch. 6, 1865	1 yr.	Mustered out with company Sept. 13, 1865.
Moser, Christopher	do	21	Mch. 18, 1865	1 yr.	Mustered out with company Sept. 13, 1865.
Myers, Henry H	do	21	Mch. 28, 1864	3 yrs.	Killed June 15, 1864, in action at Noonday Creek, Ga.
Newton, Clinton A	do	18	Mch. 14, 1865	1 yr.	Mustered out with company Sept. 13, 1865.
Nixon, William	do	22	Mch. 1, 1865	1 yr.	Mustered out with company Sept. 13, 1865.
Null, John	do	27	Aug. 15, 1861	3 yrs.	Mustered out with company Sept. 13, 1865; veteran.
O'Mara, John	do	17	Aug. 6, 1861	3 yrs.	Died May 6, 1863.
O'Neal, Thomas	do	19	Feb. 4, 1864	3 yrs.	Died March 15, 1865, at Jeffersonville, Ind.
Orahood, Andrew J	do	27	Nov. 23, 1863	3 yrs.	Mustered out with company Sept. 13, 1865.
Orr, Alfred W	do	26	Aug. 26, 1861	3 yrs.	Mustered out Oct. 16, 1864, on expiration of time of service.
Pace, Francis	do	23	May 19, 1864	3 yrs.	Substitute; mustered out with company Sept. 13, 1865.
Patterson, William	do		Aug. 28, 1861	3 yrs.	
Patterson, William W. D	do	21	Mch. 9, 1865	1 yr.	Mustered out with company Sept. 13, 1865.
Payton, Daniel	do	18	Aug. 10, 1861	3 yrs.	Discharged Aug. 9, 1862, on Surgeon's certificate of disability.
Pierce, James A	do	20	Sept. 9, 1861	3 yrs.	Mustered out Oct. 16, 1864, on expiration of term of service.
Porter, George	do	22	Sept. 20, 1861	3 yrs.	
Quigley, Sylvester	do	35	Mch. 10, 1865	1 yr.	Mustered out with company Sept. 13, 1865.
Ragan, Jeremiah	do	18	Aug. 6, 1861	3 yrs.	Mustered out Oct. 16, 1864, on expiration of term of service.
Ramsey, John	do	34	Aug. 6, 1861	3 yrs.	Mustered out Oct. 16, 1864, on expiration of term of service.
Ray, William H	do	27	Aug. 14, 1861	3 yrs.	Discharged April 7, 1862, at Nashville, Tenn., on Surgeon's certificate of disability.
Read, Leroy	do	22	Aug. 6, 1861	3 yrs.	Mustered out Oct. 6, 1864, on expiration of term of service.
Ready, Daniel	do	18	Feb. 29, 1864	3 yrs.	Mustered out with company Sept. 13, 1865.

FIRST REGIMENT OHIO VOLUNTEER CAVALRY.

Names.	Rank.	Age	Date of Entering the Service.	Period of Service.	Remarks.
Ready, Lain	Private	23	Aug. 10, 1861	3 yrs.	Transferred to Co. K, 11th Regiment Veteran Reserve Corps ——; mustered out Aug. 29, 1864, at Washington, D. C., on expiration of term of service.
Reddick, William	...do...	25	May 21, 1864	3 yrs.	Also borne on rolls as "William M;" mustered out with company Sept. 13, 1865.
Riley, Patrick	...do...	36	Jan. 26, 1864	3 yrs.	
Roney, Andrew J	...do...	20	Sept. 30, 1861	3 yrs.	Transferred to Co. H, April 15, 1864.
Roosu, Sylvester	...do...	18	Feb. 29, 1864	3 yrs.	Also borne on rolls as "Rose;" mustered out with company Sept. 13, 1865.
Sharp, Isaac W	...do...	18	Feb. 23, 1864	3 yrs.	Mustered out with company Sept. 13, 1865.
Shields, James	...do...	20	Aug. 6, 1861	3 yrs.	Discharged Dec. 5, 1861, on Surgeon's certificate of disability.
Shrade, Dittmer	...do...	28	Feb. 26, 1864	3 yrs.	Mustered out with company Sept. 13, 1865.
Simeoe, William	...do...	19	Aug. 26, 1861	3 yrs.	Mustered out Oct. 16, 1864, on expiration of term of service.
Slagle, John W	...do...	23	Feb. 29, 1864	3 yrs.	Died May 6, 1865, at Macon, Ga.
Slagle, Joseph J	...do...	20	Feb. 29, 1864	3 yrs.	Mustered out to date Sept. 13, 1865, by order of War Department.
Sly, Benjamin F	...do...	25	Sept. 24, 1861	3 yrs.	
Smith, James J	...do...	42	Aug. 18, 1861	3 yrs.	Mustered out Oct. 6, 1864, on expiration of term of service.
Steele, James A	...do...	21	Feb. 19, 1864	3 yrs.	Died Nov. 14, 1864, at Sidney, O.
Stovall, Philip S	...do...	28	Mch. 3, 1865	1 yr.	Mustered out with company Sept. 14, 1865.
Thompson, Emery	...do...	21	Aug. 19, 1861	3 yrs.	Transferred to 149th Co. 2d Battalion Veteran Reserve Corps ——; from which mustered out Aug. 23, 1864, on expiration of term of service.
Thompson, Gilbert W	...do...	27	Mch. 7, 1865	1 yr.	Mustered out Sept. 15, 1865, at New York City, by order of War Department.
Thompson, Samuel	...do...	18	Mch. 18, 1865	1 yr.	Mustered out with company Sept. 13, 1865.
Trovillo, James M	...do...	23	Aug. 6, 1861	5 yrs.	Mustered out March 1, 1865, at Gravelly Springs Ala., on expiration of term of service.
Walston, Andrew J	...do...	34	Feb. 28, 1865	1 yr.	Mustered out with company Sept. 13, 1865.
Wicking, Christian	...do...	18	Aug. 18, 1861	3 yrs.	Mustered out Oct. 16, 1864, on expiration of term of service.
Williams, Nathaniel W.S	...do...	18	Feb. 25, 1865	1 yr.	Mustered out with company Sept. 13, 1865.
Windsor, James K	...do...	22	Aug. 18, 1861	3 yrs.	Mustered out Oct. 16, 1864, on expiration of term of service.
Wray, Joseph	...do...	21	Aug. 20, 1861	3 yrs.	Discharged June 30, 1864, by order of War Department; veteran.
Young, Benjamin F	...do...	40	Sept. 30, 1861	3 yrs.	Mustered out Sept. 13, 1865, by order of War Department; veteran.

COMPANY H.

Mustered in Sept. 18, 1861, at Camp Chase, Ohio, by Howard Stansbury, Captain Topographical Engineers and John R. Edie, Major 15th Infantry, U. S. A., Mustering Officers. Mustered out Sept. 13, 1865, at Hilton Head, South Carolina, by Leslie Smith, Brevet Major and Captain 1st U. S. Infantry, Commissary of Musters, District of South Carolina.

Martin Buck	Captain	30	Aug. 14, 1861	3 yrs.	Appointed Aug. 29, 1861; promoted to Major Dec. 31, 1862, but not mustered; resigned Feb. 1, 1863.
Samuel W. Fordyce	do	21	Aug. 17, 1861	4 yrs.	Promoted from 1st Lieutenant Co. B to date Dec. 31, 1862; resigned Jan. 28, 1864.
William McBurney	do	25	Aug. 17, 1861	3 yrs.	Promoted from 1st Lieutenant and Regt. Quartermaster Jan. 23, 1864; transferred to Co. L April 21, 1864.
Charles H. Shultz	do	21	Sept. 29, 1861	3 yrs.	Promoted from 1st Lieutenant Co. M May 25, 1864; resigned Sept. 12, 1864.
John D. Moxley	do	46	Aug. 30, 1861	4 yrs.	Transferred from Co. M ——; promoted to Major Feb. 25, 1865, but not mustered; on detached duty as Act. Asst. Inspector General at Camp Webster, Nashville, Tenn.; released from duty at Edgefield, Tenn., by order dated Oct. 3, 1865, and mustered out as Captain of Co. H at Columbus, O., June 17, 1866, to date Sept. 13, 1865.
Cary A. Doggett	1st Lieut.	38	Aug. 14, 1861	3 yrs.	Appointed Aug. 29, 1861; resigned June 29, 1862.
Robert R. Waddle	do	29	Aug. 14, 1861	4 yrs.	Appointed 2d Lieutenant Aug. 29, 1861; promoted to 1st Lieutenant Jan. 29, 1862.

ROSTER OF OHIO TROOPS.

Names.	Rank.	Age	Date of Entering the Service.	Period of Service.	Remarks.
David A. Roush	1st Lieut.	23	Aug. 14, 1861	3 yrs.	Appointed 1st Sergeant from Sergeant ——; promoted to 2d Lieutenant Dec. 31, 1862; to 1st Lieutenant to date Jan. 1, 1863; mustered out Nov. 2, 1864, on expiration of term of service.
Andrew L. Small	do	36	Aug. 27, 1861	3 yrs.	Promoted from Sergeant Co. I March 18, 1865; commanded company since June 9, 1865; mustered out with company Sept. 13, 1865; veteran.
Harvey Ferguson	2d Lieut.	32	Aug. 5, 1861	3 yrs.	Promoted from Sergeant Co. D April 18, 1863; transferred to Co. D ——.
Joseph A. O. Yeoman	do	18	Aug. 6, 1861	3 yrs.	Promoted from private Co. A to date Jan. 29, 1864; to Captain of Co. A March 18, 1865; veteran.
Isaac W. Tucker	1st Sergt.	31	Aug. 14, 1861	3 yrs.	Discharged Jan. 13, 1862, on Surgeon's certificate of disability.
George H. Cooper	do	27	Aug. 14, 1861	3 yrs.	Mustered as private; appointed Sergeant Oct. 6, 1864; 1st Sergeant Jan. 1, 1865; mustered out with company Sept. 13, 1865; veteran.
William Grady	Q. M. S.	24	Sept. 7, 1861	3 yrs.	Mustered as private; appointed Oct. 6, 1864; died Aug. 18, 1865, in hospital at Charleston, S. C.; veteran.
Henry W. B. Vance	Com. Ser.	26	Aug. 14, 1861	3 yrs.	Appointed Corporal Jan. 4, 1864; Sergeant Oct. 6, 1864; Com. Sergeant ——; mustered out with company Sept. 13, 1865; veteran.
Samuel Millikin	Sergeant	18	Aug. 14, 1861	3 yrs.	Mustered out Oct. 6, 1864, on expiration of term of service.
Daniel W. Evans	do	20	Aug. 14, 1861	3 yrs.	
David Stafford	do	20	Aug. 14, 1861	3 yrs.	Died Feb. 14, 1863.
Lewis M. Thayer	do	21	Aug. 14, 1861	3 yrs.	Appointed from Corporal Jan. 1, 1862; promoted to 1st Lieutenant of Co. D Jan. 6, 1865; veteran.
Benjamin F. Young	do	25	Sept. 3, 1861	3 yrs.	Mustered as a private; appointed Sergeant May 1, 1863; 1st Sergeant Oct. 6, 1864; reduced Jan. 1, 1865, and appointed Sergeant same date; mustered out with company Sept. 13, 1865; veteran.
John H. Strange	do	25	Aug. 14, 1861	3 yrs.	Appointed Corporal Jan. 4, 1864; Sergeant Oct. 6, 1864; mustered out Sept. 25, 1865, at New York City, by order of War Department; veteran.
Jacob Groves	do	18	Aug. 14, 1861	3 yrs.	Appointed Corporal Jan. 4, 1864; Sergeant Oct. 6, 1864; mustered out with company Sept. 13, 1865; veteran.
Jacob Hulse	do	19	Aug. 14, 1861	3 yrs.	Mustered as a private; appointed Oct. 6, 1864; absent sick in hospital at Conwayboro, S. C., since Aug. 13, 1865; no further record; veteran.
Lewis Vance	do	21	Aug. 14, 1861	3 yrs.	Appointed Corporal Jan. 1, 1865; Sergeant Feb. 1, 1865; mustered out with company Sept. 13, 1865; veteran.
Charles L. Shermer	Corporal	35	Sept. 2, 1861	3 yrs.	Transferred from Co. I ——; mustered out Oct. 6, 1864, on expiration of term of service.
Charles S. Drake	do	22	Sept. 2, 1861	3 yrs.	Transferred from Co. I ——; mustered out Oct. 6, 1864, on expiration of term of service.
John W. Grady	do	20	Aug. 14, 1861	3 yrs.	Mustered out Oct. 6, 1864, on expiration of term of service.
Henry F. Smith	do	37	Aug. 14, 1861	3 yrs.	Discharged Oct. 9, 1862, at Nashville, Tenn., on Surgeon's certificate of disability.
William Fulton	do	26	Aug. 14, 1861	3 yrs.	
Beebe Barrett	do	19	Aug. 14, 1861	3 yrs.	Died Oct. 24, 1862.
David Coleman	do	28	Aug. 14, 1861	3 yrs.	Discharged July 10, 1862, on Surgeon's certificate of disability.
John Rockel	do	22	Aug. 14, 1861	3 yrs.	Appointed Corporal ——; promoted to Regt. Bugler Nov. 1, 1864; veteran.
Calvin A. Webber	do	19	Sept. 7, 1861	3 yrs.	Appointed Oct. 6, 1864; mustered out with company Sept. 13, 1865; veteran.
William Schwartz	do	18	Aug. 14, 1861	3 yrs.	Appointed Oct. 6, 1864; mustered out with company Sept. 13, 1865; veteran.
Martin T. Vandelt	do	18	Aug. 14, 1861	3 yrs.	Appointed Oct. 6, 1864; mustered out with company Sept. 13, 1865; veteran.
David L. Kellis	do	18	Aug. 14, 1861	3 yrs.	Appointed Oct. 6, 1864; mustered out with company Sept. 13, 1865; veteran.
George O. Young	do	20	Aug. 14, 1861	3 yrs.	Appointed Jan. 1, 1865; mustered out with company Sept. 13, 1865; veteran.
John Shotts	do	27	Aug. 14, 1861	3 yrs.	Appointed March 1, 1865; mustered out with company Sept. 13, 1865; veteran.
Jacob Gates	do	24	Feb. 27, 1864	3 yrs.	Appointed March 1, 1865; mustered out with company Sept. 13, 1865.
James H. Hall	do	23	Feb. 27, 1864	3 yrs.	Appointed March 1, 1865; mustered out with company Sept. 13, 1865.
Henry H. Maddox	Bugler	24	Aug. 14, 1861	3 yrs.	Mustered out Oct. 6, 1864, on expiration of term of service.

First Regiment Ohio Volunteer Cavalry.

Names.	Rank.	Age.	Date of Entering the Service.	Period of Service.	Remarks.
David Sauter	Bugler	24	Aug. 14, 1861	3 yrs.	Discharged May 27, 1862, at Nashville, Tenn., on Surgeon's certificate of disability.
Walter C. Cromer	do	38	Feb. 6, 1864	3 yrs.	Enrolled as Bugler; mustered out with company Sept. 13, 1865.
Charles C. Taylor	Farrier	24	Aug. 14, 1861	3 yrs.	Appointed Jan. 4, 1864; absent sick in hospital at Conwayboro, S. C., since Aug. 15, 1865; no further record; veteran.
William Leuman	B. Smith.	23	Aug. 14, 1861	3 yrs.	Mustered out Oct. 6, 1864, on expiration of term of service.
Thomas Brown	do	45	Sept. 14, 1861	3 yrs.	Discharged Jan. 11, 1862, on Surgeon's certificate of disability.
Thompson B. Smith	do	26	Mch. 28, 1864	3 yrs.	Appointed Oct. 6, 1864; mustered out with company Sept. 13, 1865.
Carey A. Smith	Saddler	24	Aug. 14, 1861	3 yrs.	Discharged July 10, 1862, on Surgeon's certificate of disability.
John Stewart	Wagoner	40	Aug. 14, 1861	3 yrs.	Discharged June 18, 1862, on Surgeon's certificate of disability.
Barey, James	Private	18	Sept. 2, 1861	3 yrs.	Transferred from Co. I ——; mustered out Oct. 6, 1864, at Columbia, Tenn., on expiration of term of service.
Barrere, Hazard	do	18	Aug. 14, 1861	3 yrs.	Killed Nov. 27, 1863, in action at Cleveland, Tenn.
Barrere, Milton	do	19	Aug. 14, 1861	3 yrs.	Mustered out Oct. 6, 1864, on expiration of term of service.
Barrett, Jonathan	do	24	Feb. 11, 1864	3 yrs.	Mustered out with company Sept. 13, 1865.
Beaty, Pearson	do	33	Aug. 14, 1861	3 yrs.	Discharged Aug. 6, 1862, on Surgeon's certificate of disability.
Beckwith, Barnes	do	32	Aug. 18, 1864	1 yr.	Mustered out June 17, 1865, at Nashville Tenn., by order of War Department.
Bingamon, Cornelius	do	19	Aug. 14, 1861	3 yrs.	
Brabham, John W	do	26	Oct. 1, 1864	1 yr.	Discharged June 25, 1865, at Nashville, Tenn., on Surgeon's certificate of disability.
Brabham, Wellington	do	19	Oct. 1, 1864	1 yr.	Discharged June 25, 1865, at Nashville, Tenn., on Surgeon's certificate of disability.
Bracken, Craig	do	18	Jan. 5, 1864	3 yrs.	Died June 25, 1865, in hospital at Atlanta, Ga.
Bragg, John W	do	19	Aug. 14, 1861	3 yrs.	Mustered out Oct. 6, 1864, on expiration of term of service.
Britt, James	do	32	Sept. 12, 1861	3 yrs.	Mustered out Oct. 6, 1864, on expiration of term of service.
Brown, Charles	do	40	Aug. 14, 1861	3 yrs.	Discharged June 22, 1862, on Surgeon's certificate of disability.
Brown, John	do	23	Aug. 14, 1861	3 yrs.	Mustered out Oct. 6, 1864, on expiration of term of service.
Campbell, Isaac E	do	20	Aug. 14, 1861	3 y's.	Died April 12, 1864.
Campbell, James S	do	19	Sept. 30, 1861	3 yrs.	Died Jan. 19, 1865, in hospital at Edgefield, Tenn.; veteran.
Caniff, Andrew	do	35	Aug. 14, 1861	3 yrs.	Transferred to 187th Co. 1st Battalion Veteran Reserve Corps ——; to 203rd Co. 1st Battalion Veteran Reserve Corps ——; to Co. A, 9th Regiment Veteran Reserve Corps ——; from which mustered out with company Nov. 16, 1865.
Carr, George R	do	20	Aug. 14, 1861	3 yrs.	Mustered out Oct. 6, 1864, on expiration of term of service.
Chaffin, James	do	23	Sept. 14, 1861	3 yrs.	Died Sept. 28, 1862.
Charles, Philip	do	38	Feb. 11, 1864	3 yrs.	Mustered out with company Sept. 13, 1865.
Clark, William	do	28	Sept. 14, 1861	3 yrs.	
Claybaugh, William	do	29	Aug. 27, 1861	3 yrs.	Transferred from Co. I ——; mustered out Oct. 6, 1864, on expiration of term of service.
Colligan, John B	do	37	Sept. 14, 1861	3 yrs.	Discharged March 1, 1865, on Surgeon's certificate of disability.
Conover, George W	do	19	Aug. 29, 1861	3 yrs.	Transferred from Co. I ——; mustered out Oct. 6, 1864, on expiration of term of service.
Daugherty, James	do	22	Feb. 11, 1864	3 yrs.	Also borne on rolls as "James W."; mustered out with company Sept. 13, 1865.
Davis, William T	do	17	Aug. 19, 1864	1 yr.	Died Dec. 19, 1864.
Deckhoff, Antonio	do	40	Mch. 21, 1864	3 yrs.	Died Aug. 14, 1865, in hospital at Charleston, S. C.
Deitrich, Benjamin	do	24	Aug. 24, 1861	3 yrs.	Transferred from Co. I ——; mustered out Oct. 6, 1864, at Columbia, Tenn., on expiration of term of service.
Dongan, Calvin	do	21	Feb. 10, 1864	3 yrs.	Mustered out June 5, 1865, from hospital at Camp Dennison, O., by order of War Department.
Dye, Ross N	do	18	Sept. 28, 1864	1 yr.	Mustered out June 17, 1865, at Nashville, Tenn., by order of War Department.
Dye, Thomas M	do	18	Sept. 28, 1864	1 yr.	Mustered out June 17, 1865, at Nashville, Tenn., by order of War Department.
Easter, Elias	do	34	Feb. 15, 1864	3 yrs.	Mustered out with company Sept. 13, 1865.
Erbs, John	do	18	Sept. 28, 1861	1 yr.	Also borne on rolls as "Arbs;" mustered out June 17, 1865, at Nashville, Tenn., by order of War Department.

ROSTER OF OHIO TROOPS.

Names.	Rank.	Age	Date of Entering the Service.	Period of Service.	Remarks.
Engelken, Barthold	Private	25	Aug. 25, 1861	3 yrs.	Transferred from Co. I ——; mustered out Oct. 6, 1864, on expiration of term of service.
Fairlee, John W	do	18	Jan. 16, 1864	3 yrs.	Also borne on the rolls as "Farley;" transferred from Co. I April 1, 1864; mustered out Sept. 14, 1865, at New York City, by order of War Department.
Feely, George W	do	20	Aug. 14, 1861	3 yrs.	Died April 18, 1865, in hospital at Camp Chase, O.; veteran.
Fenner, Jacob R	do	20	Feb. 27, 1864	3 yrs.	Died Nov. 4, 1864, while at home on furlough.
Frost, William	do	23	Sept. 7, 1861	3 yrs.	Discharged Nov. 26, 1862, on Surgeon's certificate of disability.
Galbreath, Alexander	do	39	Aug. 10, 1863	3 yrs.	Transferred from Co. I April 21, 1864; mustered out with company Sept. 13, 1865.
Gates, Charles L	do	27	Jan. 5, 1864	3 yrs.	Transferred from Co. L April 1, 1864; mustered out with company Sept. 13, 1865.
Harper, William	do	43	Oct. 4, 1864	1 yr.	Died Aug. 29, 1865, in hospital at Darlington, S. C.
Harris, Eli	do	20	Feb. 11, 1864	3 yrs.	Mustered out with company Sept. 13, 1865.
Harris, Joel	do	25	Aug. 14, 1861	3 yrs.	Seriously wounded Dec. 31, 1862, in the battle of Stone River, Tenn.; no further record.
Headershot, Jacob	do	32	Feb. 13, 1864	3 yrs.	Killed June 15, 1864, in action at Noonday Creek, Ga.
Hickman, Jackson	do	19	Aug. 14, 1861	3 yrs.	Died July 1, 1863.
Horr, C. B	do	20	Aug. 14, 1861	3 yrs.	Discharged Nov. 22, 1861, on Surgeon's certificate of disability.
Hulse, George	do	21	Aug. 14, 1861	3 yrs.	Mustered out Oct. 6, 1864, on expiration of term of service.
Jenny, Charles	do	31	Sept. 14, 1861	3 yrs.	Mustered out Oct. 6, 1864, on expiration of term of service.
Johnson, Jarrett	do	23	Aug. 14, 1861	3 yrs.	Wounded June 16, 1864, at Kenesaw Mountain, Ga.; discharged May 30, 1865, at Camp Dennison, O., on Surgeon's certificate of disability; veteran.
Keesbery, John W	do	18	Feb. 15, 1864	3 yrs.	Also borne on rolls as "Keysbury;" mustered out with company Sept. 13, 1865.
Kelso, John M	do	18	Sept. 7, 1861	3 yrs.	Mustered out with company Sept. 13, 1865; veteran.
Keplinger, Elias	do	23	Sept. 19, 1861	3 yrs.	Transferred from Co. I ——; mustered out Oct. 6, 1864, on expiration of term of service.
King, William	do	23	Aug. 20, 1864	1 yr.	Mustered out Sept. 19, 1865, at Columbus, O., by order of War Department.
Knight, Jasper	do	20	July 12, 1862	3 yrs.	Transferred from Co. I April 21, 1864; sick in hospital at Stevenson, Ala., since Sept. 2, 1864; no further record.
Lambert, John	do	29	Sept. 7, 1861	3 yrs.	Mustered out Oct. 6, 1864, at Columbia, Tenn., on expiration of term of service.
Lemons, Samuel B	do	20	Feb. 12, 1864	3 yrs.	Mustered out with company Sept. 13, 1865.
Lynch, James	do	42	Sept. 29, 1864	1 yr.	Captured April 17, 1865, at Columbus, Ga.; no further record.
McKenzie, John	do	26	Feb. 17, 1864	3 yrs.	Mustered out with company Sept, 13, 1865.
McMasters, George T. W	do	22	Sept. 2, 1861	3 yrs.	Transferred from Co. I ——; mustered out Oct. 6, 1864, on expiration of term of service.
McMullen, Joseph	do	25	Mch. 15, 1864	3 yrs.	Mustered out with company Sept. 13, 1865.
Malone, John W	do	19	Dec. 16, 1864	1 yr.	Mustered out with company Sept. 13, 1865.
Mathers, Henry	do	20	Sept. 28, 1864	1 yr.	Mustered out June 17, 1865, at Nashville, Tenn., by order of War Department.
Mercer, George W	do	22	Sept. 7, 1861	3 yrs.	Captured April 12, 1865, at Columbus, Ga.; no further record.
Miller, Casper	do	34	Sept. 3, 1861	3 yrs.	Transferred from Co. I ——; mustered out Oct. 6, 1864, on expiration of term of service.
Miller, James G	do	23	Aug. 14, 1861	3 yrs.	Mustered out Oct. 6, 1864, on expiration of term of service.
Morrow, James	do	31	Sept. 3, 1861	3 yrs.	Mustered out Oct. 6, 1864, on expiration of term of service.
Mulford, John W	do	30	Aug. 28, 1861	3 yrs.	Transferred from Co. I Feb. 29, 1864; mustered out Oct. 6, 1864, at Columbus, O., on expiration of term of service.
Muncy, Isaac N	do	16	Aug. 13, 1864	1 yr.	Mustered out June 17, 1865, at Nashville, Tenn., by order of War Department.
Onetto, Charles	do	23	Sept. 28, 1864	1 yr.	On detached duty at Cavalry Depot, Edgefield, Tenn., since June 1, 1865; no further record.
Overman, Elijah	do	19	Aug. 14, 1861	3 yrs.	Died Jan. 10, 1864.
Overman, William	do	21	Sept. 30, 1861	3 yrs.	Mustered out May 4, 1865, on expiration of term of service.
Petribone, John H	do	31	Dec. 31, 1863	3 yrs.	Transferred from Co. L April 1, 1864; mustered out with company Sept. 13, 1865.
Pitts, Monroe	do	18	Oct. 4, 1864	1 yr.	Mustered out with company Sept. 13, 1865.
Purdum, Jeremiah	do		Sept. 22, 1861	3 yrs.	Captured and paroled Oct. 13, 1862, near Harrodsburg, Ky.; returned to company March 28, 1863; captured Nov. 27, 1863, at Cleveland, Tenn.; paroled March 7, 1864, at City Point, Va.; mustered out Oct. 6, 1864, at Columbia, Tenn., on expiration of time of service.

FIRST REGIMENT OHIO VOLUNTEER CAVALRY.

Names.	Rank.	Age	Date of Entering the Service.	Period of Service.	Remarks.
Pyers, Martin E	Private	18	Aug. 14, 1861	3 yrs.	Also borne on rolls as "Emmett Pyers;" mustered out with company Sept. 13, 1865; veteran.
Reed, William H	do	24	Sept. 5, 1861	3 yrs.	Transferred from Co. I ——; mustered out Oct. 6, 1864, on expiration of time of service.
Robinson, Lines	do	22	Feb. 19, 1864	3 yrs.	Mustered out with company Sept. 13, 1865.
Roney, Andrew J	do	20	Sept. 30, 1861	3 yrs.	Transferred from Co. G April 15, 1864; mustered out with company Sept. 13, 1865; veteran.
Ross, David C	do	19	Aug. 31, 1861	3 yrs.	
Roush, Absalom	do	18	Sept. 28, 1864	1 yr.	Mustered out June 17, 1865, at Nashville, Tenn., by order of War Department.
Roush, James	do	28	Sept. 30, 1864	1 yr.	Mustered out June 17, 1865, at Nashville, Tenn., by order of War Department.
Roush, William	do	24	Sept. 30, 1864	1 yr.	Mustered out June 17, 1865, at Nashville, Tenn., by order of War Department.
Rumbold, Joseph	do	20	Sept. 30, 1864	1 yr.	Died Feb. 13, 1865, in hospital at Camp Dennison, O.
Schwartz, Jacob	do	19	Aug. 31, 1861	3 yrs.	Transferred to 3d U. S. Cavalry Feb. 14, 1863.
Scott, Alexander H	do	19	Aug. 14, 1861	3 yrs.	Mustered out with company Sept. 13, 1865; veteran.
Scott, John W	do	27	Aug. 14, 1861	3 yrs.	On detached duty as forage master at Headquarters Cavalry Corps, Middle Military Division, since Feb. 28, 1865; mustered out Aug. 11, 1865, at Columbus, O., by order of War Department; veteran.
Shoemaker, Abram	do	44	Feb. 20, 1864	3 yrs.	Died Feb. 18, 1865, in hospital at New York City.
Shoemaker, William	do	18	Feb. 20, 1864	3 yrs.	Also borne on rolls as "William H.;" discharged June 7, 1865, on Surgeon's certificate of disability.
Smith, James	do	45	Sept. 12, 1861	3 yrs.	Discharged June 18, 1862, on Surgeon's certificate of disability.
Smith, Jeremiah	do	32	Sept. 14, 1861	3 yrs.	Discharged May 19, 1862, on Surgeon's certificate of disability.
Smith, John B	do	38	Sept. 2, 1861	3 yrs.	Discharged June 22, 1862, on Surgeon's certificate of disability.
Smith, Van Buren V	do	18	Aug. 14, 1861	3 yrs.	Mustered out Oct. 6, 1864, on expiration of term of service.
Smith, William	do	19	Feb. 16, 1864	3 yrs.	Mustered out with company Sept. 13, 1865.
Stafford, A. R	do	26	Aug. 14, 1861	3 yrs.	Mustered out Oct. 6, 1864, on expiration of term of service.
Stage, William	do	35	Oct. 4, 1864	1 yr.	Absent sick since Jan. 26, 1865, in No. 8 General Hospital, Nashville, Tenn.; no further record.
Still, Smith	do	18	Aug. 14, 1861	3 yrs.	Mustered out Oct. 6, 1864, on expiration of term of service.
Stoker, Joseph W	do	18	Sept. 2, 1861	3 yrs.	Transferred from Co. I April 20, 1864; prisoner of war; mustered out Jan. 28, 1866, at Columbus, O., on expiration of term of service.
Stratton, Gilmer	do	18	Aug. 14, 1861	3 yrs.	Discharged July 5, 1865, from Tripler Hospital, Columbus, O., on Surgeon's certificate of disability; veteran.
Stratton, Thomas B	do	20	Feb. 8, 1864	3 yrs.	Mustered out with company Sept. 13, 1865.
Strickler, Charles	do	26	Sept. 26, 1864	1 yr.	Mustered out June 17, 1865, at Nashville, Tenn., by order of War Department.
Stults, George	do	23	Feb. 13, 1864	3 yrs.	Mustered out with company Sept. 13, 1865.
Stuart, Charles	do	24	Dec. 12, 1861	1 yr.	Absent sick in hospitals since April 30, 1865; returned to duty Oct. 5, 1865, from Cumberland hospital, Nashville, Tenn., where he was admitted Sept. 30, 1865; no further record.
Taylor, Carey	do	41	Feb. 29, 1864	3 yrs.	Mustered out with company Sept. 13, 1865.
Timmons, Warren	do	19	Sept. 14, 1861	3 yrs.	Discharged April 16, 1863, to date Jan. 4, 1863, on Surgeon's certificate of disability.
Troutrine, Andrew	do	43	Sept. 14, 1861	3 yrs.	Discharged Feb. 19, 1862, on Surgeon's certificate of disability.
Turner, William	do	16	Sept. 26, 1861	1 yr.	Also borne on rolls as "William P.;" mustered out June 17, 1865, at Nashville, Tenn., by order of War Department.
Upp, James M	do	22	Aug. 14, 1861	3 yrs.	Died May 12, 1862.
Vaney, Henry A	do	44	Aug. 14, 1861	3 yrs.	Drowned March 1, 1862, in the Ohio River by falling from steamer "Sunny South," while en route to Nashville, Tenn.
Vanpelt, John B	do	19	Aug. 14, 1861	3 yrs.	Mustered out Oct. 6, 1864, on expiration of term of service.
Vinson, Charles O	do	24	Aug. 14, 1861	3 yrs.	Also borne on rolls as "Charles Vincent;" on detached service at Edgefield, Tenn., since May 16, 1865; mustered out Sept. 13, 1865, at Columbus, O., on expiration of term of service.
Welch, Edward	do	21	Sept. 17, 1861	3 yrs.	Transferred from Co. I ——; mustered out Oct. 6, 1864, on expiration of term of service.

Names.	Rank.	Age.	Date of Entering the Service.	Period of Service.	Remarks.
Wells, Thenton	Private				Mustered out Aug. 28, 1865, by order of War Department, per special order No. 463, Adjt. General's Office.
Whalen, Nimrod	..do..	20	Sept. 16, 1861	3 yrs.	Mustered out Oct. 6, 1864, on expiration of term of service.
Whitney, Charles L	..do..	30	Dec. 6, 1862	3 yrs.	Transferred from Co. I April 21, 1864; sent to Government Hospital for the Insane March 31, 1864.
Williams, Andrew J	..do..	41	Aug. 14, 1861	3 yrs.	Mustered out with company Sept. 13, 1865; veteran.
Wilkins, Philip	..do..	18	Feb. 11, 1864	3 yrs.	Died Aug. 12, 1864, in hospital at Columbia, Tenn.
Yoerine, Emanuel	do	18	Oct. 1, 1861	1 yr.	Discharged June 25, 1865, at Nashville, Tenn., on Surgeon's certificate of disability.
Young, Francis	..do	25	Aug. 14, 1861	3 yrs.	Died April 2, 1864, in hospital at Nashville, Tenn.; veteran.
Young, Thomas B	..do..	19	Feb. 29, 1864	3 yrs.	Mustered out with company Sept. 13, 1865.
Zurck, Clark M	..do..	19	Aug. 14, 1861	3 yrs.	Died Dec. 28, 1862.

COMPANY I.

Mustered in Sept. 23, 1861, at Camp Chase, Ohio, by John R. Edie, Major 15th Infantry, U. S. A., Mustering Officer. Mustered out Sept. 13, 1865, at Hilton Head, S. C., by Leslie Smith, Brevet Major and Captain 1st U. S. Infantry, Commissary of Musters, District of South Carolina.

Names	Rank	Age	Date of Entering the Service	Period of Service	Remarks
Stephen C. Writer	Captain	33	Aug. 17, 1861	3 yrs.	Appointed Sept. 23, 1861; wounded July 15, 1862, near Cortland, Ala.; promoted to Major April 1, 1863.
John P. Rea	..do..	21	Aug. 20, 1861	3 yrs.	Appointed 2d Lieutenant Sept. 23, 1861; promoted to 1st Lieutenant March 12, 1862; to Captain April 1, 1863; mustered out Nov. 25, 1864, at Louisville, Ky., on expiration of term of service.
William G. Lawder	..do..	19	Aug. 25, 1861	3 yrs.	Appointed 1st Sergeant from Sergeant ——; promoted to 2d Lieutenant Co. E April 22, 1863; transferred from Co. E ——; promoted to 1st Lieutenant Co. M to date March 31, 1864; to Captain from 1st Lieutenant Co. F Dec. 14, 1864; mustered out with company Sept. 13, 1865.
Ralph M. Horton	1st Lieut.	32	Aug. 25, 1861	3 yrs.	Appointed Sept. 23, 1861; resigned March 12, 1862.
Jonathan Carr	..do..	31	Aug. 28, 1861	3 yrs.	Promoted to 2d Lieutenant from 1st Sergeant to date April 1, 1863; to 1st Lieutenant March 31, 1864; to Captain Dec. 14, 1864, but not mustered; mustered out Dec. 29, 1864, at Nashville, Tenn., on expiration of term of service.
Robert Johns	..do..	27	Aug. 26, 1861	3 yrs.	Promoted from Com. Sergeant of Co. E Jan. 6, 1865; mustered out with company Sept. 13, 1865; veteran.
Amos D. Leib	2d Lieut.	21	Sept. 5, 1861	3 yrs.	Promoted from Q. M. Sergeant of Co. F Nov. 29, 1862; to 1st Lieutenant and Regt. Commissary April 18, 1863.
John W. Laughlin	..do..	24	Jan. 29, 1862	3 yrs.	Promoted from Sergt. Major July 30, 1864; transferred to Co. B Aug. 28, 1864.
Henry E. Rector	..do..	19	Aug. 8, 1861	3 yrs.	Promoted from 1st Sergeant Co. F March 18, 1865; to 1st Lieutenant Aug. 15, 1865, but not mustered; mustered out with company Sept. 13, 1865; veteran.
Nathan B. Teeter	1st Sergt.	19	Sept. 2, 1861	3 yrs.	Appointed Corporal Jan. 4, 1864; 1st Sergeant May 10, 1864; mustered out with company Sept. 13, 1865; veteran.
Frank A. T. Rupel	Q. M. S.	27	Aug. 29, 1861	3 yrs.	Discharged Feb. 9, 1863, on Surgeon's certificate of disability.
George W. Day	..do..	31	Aug. 25, 1861	3 yrs.	Mustered as private; appointed Sergeant Dec. 1, 1862; Q. M. Sergeant Jan. 4, 1864; mustered out with company Sept. 13, 1865; veteran.
Jacob M. Sollenberger	Com. Ser.	28	Aug. 28, 1861	3 yrs.	Appointed from Sergeant ——; wounded —— in action at Decatur, Ala.; promoted to 1st Lieutenant Co. L Dec. 14, 1864.
Cyrus W. Stickle	..do..	22	Sept. 17, 1861	3 yrs.	Appointed Corporal Jan. 4, 1864; Sergeant Nov. 1, 1864; Com. Sergeant ——; mustered out with company Sept. 13, 1865; veteran.

FIRST REGIMENT OHIO VOLUNTEER CAVALRY.

Names.	Rank.	Age.	Date of Entering the Service.	Period of Service.	Remarks.
Benjamin F. Steelman..	Sergeant	21	Aug. 27, 1861	3 yrs.	Wounded Oct. 4, 1862, in action at Bardstown, Ky.; mustered out Oct. 6, 1864, on expiration of term of service.
Richard M. Martin......	...do...	32	Aug. 27, 1861	3 yrs.	Mustered out Oct. 6, 1864, on expiration of term of service.
Andrew L. Small........	...do...	36	Aug. 27, 1861	3 yrs.	Appointed from Corporal Dec. 1, 1862; promoted to 1st Lieutenant Co. H March 18, 1865.
Nathaniel Tucker	...do...	22	Sept. 17, 1861	3 yrs.	Appointed Corporal Jan. 4, 1864; Sergeant July 4, 1864; mustered out Sept. 19, 1865, at Columbus, O., to date Sept. 13, 1865, by order of War Department; veteran.
William H. Acton......	...do...	22	Sept. 3, 1861	3 yrs.	Appointed Corporal Jan. 4, 1864; Sergeant Nov. 1, 1864; mustered out with company Sept. 13, 1865; veteran.
James Furnas..........	...do...	24	Oct. 11, 1861	3 yrs.	Appointed Corporal May 10, 1864; Sergeant Nov. 1, 1864; wounded Aug. 20, 1864, in action at Lovejoy Station, Ga.; mustered out with company Sept. 13, 1865; veteran.
John B. Small.........	...do...	20	Aug. 26, 1861	3 yrs.	Appointed Corporal May 10, 1864; Sergeant Jan. 1, 1865; wounded April 1, 1865, in action at Ebenezer Church, Ga.; mustered out with company Sept. 13, 1865; veteran.
John W. Martin........	...do...	21	Aug. 27, 1861	3 yrs.	Appointed Corporal July 16, 1864; Sergeant June 16, 1865; mustered out with company Sept. 13, 1865; veteran.
John C. Sawyer........	Corporal	19	Aug. 20, 1861	3 yrs.	Mustered out Oct. 6, 1864, on expiration of term of service.
William C. Allen......	...do...	22	Sept. 2, 1861	3 yrs.	Mustered out Oct. 6, 1864, on expiration of term of service.
Charles S. Drake......	...do...	22	Sept. 2, 1861	3 yrs.	Wounded in action ——; transferred to Co. H —.
Charles L. Shermer....	...do...	33	Sept. 2, 1861	3 yrs.	Transferred to Co. H —.
William A. Simpson....	...do...	19	Aug. 28, 1861	3 yrs.	Mustered out Oct. 6, 1864, on expiration of term of service.
John R. Swan..........	...do...	27	July 12, 1862	3 yrs.	Appointed ——; mustered out June 17, 1865, at Nashville, Tenn., by order of War Department.
George W. Morrin.....	...do...	18	Aug. 25, 1861	3 yrs.	Wounded July 15, 1862, in action near Courtland, Ala.; appointed Corporal Nov. 1, 1864; mustered out with company Sept. 13, 1865; veteran.
Jasper N. Jones.......	...do...	20	Sept. 5, 1861	3 yrs.	Appointed Nov. 1, 1864; mustered out with company Sept. 13, 1865; veteran.
William E. Place......	...do...	32	Feb. 25, 1864	3 yrs.	Appointed Nov. 1, 1864; mustered out with company Sept. 13, 1865.
William Wilson........	...do...	25	Sept. 27, 1861	3 yrs.	Appointed Nov. 1, 1864; mustered out with company Sept. 13, 1865; veteran.
Charles E. Barlow.....	...do...	18	Sept. 3, 1861	3 yrs.	Appointed Jan. 1, 1865; mustered out with company Sept. 13, 1865; veteran.
Milton Edgell.........	...do...	20	Aug. 31, 1861	3 yrs.	Appointed June 15, 1865; mustered out with company Sept. 13, 1865; veteran.
William F. Long.......	...do...		1861	3 yrs.	Appointed June 15, 1865; mustered out with company Sept. 13, 1865; veteran.
Lewis D. Doty.........	Bugler	36	Sept. 3, 1861	3 yrs.	Discharged Nov. 16, 1861, on Surgeon's certificate of disability.
Jedediah H. Darwin....	...do...	38	Aug. 30, 1861	3 yrs.	Discharged Dec. 12, 1862, on Surgeon's certificate of disability.
Theodore Brotherton...	...do...	18	Feb. 13, 1864	3 yrs.	Mustered out with company Sept. 13, 1865.
Burnett Brotherton....	...do...	17	Feb. 13, 1864	3 yrs.	Mustered out with company Sept. 13, 1865.
Oliver Birely.........	Farrier	25	Sept. 4, 1861	3 yrs.	Mustered out Oct. 6, 1864, on expiration of term of service.
Matthew Sioms.........	...do...	36	Sept. 19, 1861	3 yrs.	Appointed Jan. 4, 1864; mustered out with company Sept. 13, 1865; veteran.
John W. Powell........	...do...	22	Sept. 5, 1861	3 yrs.	Appointed Jan. 4, 1864; wounded in action ——; mustered out with company Sept. 13, 1865; veteran.
George W. Steelman....	Saddler	20	Aug. 27, 1861	3 yrs.	Appointed Jan. 4, 1864; wounded in action ——; mustered out Sept. 19, 1865, at Columbus, O., to date Sept. 13, 1865, by order of War Department; veteran.
Acton, Sidney.........	Private	20	Feb. 23, 1864	3 yrs.	Died July 17, 1864, in hospital at Nashville, Tenn.
Alexander, Charles W..	...do...	28	Aug. 31, 1861	3 yrs.	Mustered out with company Sept. 13, 1865; veteran.
Anderson, Francis M...	...do...	22	Feb. 19, 1864	3 yrs.	Mustered out with company Sept. 13, 1865.
Anderson, John W.....	...do...	18	Feb. 19, 1864	3 yrs.	Mustered out with company Sept. 13, 1865.
Barer, James.........	...do...	18	Sept. 2, 1861	3 yrs.	Wounded Jan. 1, 1863, in battle of Stone River, Tenn.; transferred to Co. H ——.
Barlow, George W.....	...do...	19	Aug. 28, 1861	3 yrs.	Died March 31, 1862.
Barton, Stephen......	...do...	20	Sept. 3, 1861	3 yrs.	Died Aug. 20, 1864, of wounds received in action Aug. 20, 1864, at Lovejoy Station, Ga.; veteran.
Behm, Frederick......	...do...	18	April 5, 1865	1 yr.	Mustered out with company Sept. 13, 1865.

ROSTER OF OHIO TROOPS.

Names.	Rank.	Age.	Date of Entering the Service.	Period of Service.	Remarks.
Bennett, John	Private	18	Sept. 2, 1861	3 yrs.	Mustered out Oct. 6, 1864, on expiration of term of service.
Bively, Sample C.	do	20	Sept. 10, 1861	3 yrs.	Mustered out with company Sept. 13, 1865; veteran.
Black, Thomas J.	do	23	Sept. 18, 1861	3 yrs.	Discharged Jan. 24, 1863, on Surgeon's certificate of disability.
Blevins, Nathan	do	27	Feb. 22, 1864	3 yrs.	Mustered out with company Sept. 13, 1865.
Blond, William F.	do	18	Feb. 10, 1864	3 yrs.	Mustered out with company Sept. 13, 1865.
Bodkin, Robert	do	27	Sept. 2, 1861	3 yrs.	Mustered out with company Sept. 13, 1865; veteran.
Brady, Peter	do	21	Sept. 2, 1861	3 yrs.	Mustered out with company Sept. 13, 1865; veteran.
Bray, Redding	do	20	Sept. 2, 1861	3 yrs.	Transferred to Co. C, 8th Regiment Veteran Reserve Corps ——; from which mustered out Sept. 8, 1864, on expiration of term of service.
Cass, William H.	do	18	Feb. 23, 1864	3 yrs.	Died Aug. 15, 1864, in hospital at Columbus, O.
Casteel, Francis	do	21	Feb. 24, 1864	3 yrs.	Mustered out June 7, 1865, at Louisville, Ky., by order of War Department.
Chroneberry, Frank	do	19	Sept. 18, 1861	3 yrs.	
Claybaugh, William	do	20	Aug. 27, 1861	3 yrs.	Transferred to Co. H ——.
Clement, Francis	do	20	Mch. 9, 1865	1 yr.	Mustered out with company Sept. 13, 1865.
Clumb, Francis A.	do	37	Aug. 30, 1861	3 yrs.	Mustered out with company Sept. 13, 1865; veteran.
Coate, James	do	24	Feb. 18, 1864	3 yrs.	Mustered out with company Sept. 13, 1865.
Conover, Alonzo	do	18	Mch. 19, 1864	3 yrs.	Killed Aug. 20, 1864, in action at Lovejoy Station, Ga.
Conover, George W.	do	19	Aug. 29, 1861	3 yrs.	Transferred to Co. H ——.
Coppock, Henry H.	do	22	Feb. 22, 1864	3 yrs.	Mustered out with company Sept. 13, 1865.
Crall, Richard	do	23	Sept. 20, 1861	3 yrs.	
Crowley, Andrew	do	18	Feb. 20, 1864	3 yrs.	Mustered out with company Sept. 13, 1865.
Crowley, Patrick	do	18	Dec. 7, 1861	1 yr.	Mustered out with company Sept. 13, 1865.
Dabns, Leonard	do	20	Sept. 16, 1861	3 yrs.	Wounded Aug. 20, 1864, in action near Lovejoy Station, Ga.; mustered out Oct. 6, 1864, on expiration of term of service.
Dabns, Lewis	do	20	Sept. 16, 1861	3 yrs.	Mustered out with company Sept. 13, 1865; veteran.
Deeter, Daniel E.	do	18	Feb. 17, 1864	3 yrs.	Mustered out with company Sept. 13, 1865.
Deeter, Emanuel	do	17	June 15, 1862	3 yrs.	Promoted to Sergt. Major July 9, 1865; veteran.
Deeter, Ephraim	do	18	Feb. 22, 1864	3 yrs.	Mustered out May 19, 1865, from hospital at Jeffersonville, Ind., by order of War Department.
Deitrich, Benjamin	do	24	Aug. 24, 1861	3 yrs.	Transferred to Co. H ——.
Devinney, John	do	28	Dec. 13, 1864	1 yr.	Mustered out with company Sept. 13, 1865.
Dollenger, John S.	do	22	Oct. 11, 1861	3 yrs.	Wounded Aug. 20, 1864, in the battle of Lovejoy Station, Ga.; promoted to Sergt. Major Sept. 8, 1864; veteran.
Donoghue, Daniel	do	18	Dec. 7, 1864	1 yr.	Mustered out with company Sept. 13, 1865.
Dorman, Augustus	do	25	Feb. 27, 1864	3 yrs.	Mustered out with company Sept. 13, 1865.
Dungan, Sylvanus	do	18	Feb. 25, 1864	3 yrs.	Also borne on rolls as "Sylvanus M.;" mustered out with company Sept. 13, 1865.
Enbody, George W.	do	19	Feb. 20, 1864	3 yrs.	Mustered out with company Sept. 13, 1865.
Encelken, Barthold	do	25	Aug. 25, 1861	3 yrs.	Transferred to Co. H ——.
Fenner, Rufus C.	do	24	Feb. 20, 1864	3 yrs.	Mustered out with company Sept. 13, 1865.
Foster, Franklin	do	18	Mch. 8, 1864	3 yrs.	Mustered out with company Sept. 13, 1865.
Gulbreath, Alexander	do	22	Aug. 18, 1863	3 yrs.	Transferred to Co. H April 21, 1864.
Green, William W.	do	19	Feb. 22, 1864	3 yrs.	Mustered out with company Sept. 13, 1865.
Grunert, Frederick	do	28	Sept. 4, 1861	3 yrs.	Transferred to 133d Co., 2d Battalion Veteran Reserve Corps ——, from which mustered out Sept. 6, 1864, on expiration of term of service.
Gurton, Theodore	do	21	Feb. 22, 1864	3 yrs.	Mustered out with company Sept. 13, 1865.
Hamel, James H.	do	18	Feb. 20, 1864	3 yrs.	Mustered out with company Sept. 13, 1865.
Hertle, Christian	do	25	Sept. 3, 1861	2 yrs.	Transferred to 56th Co. 2d Battalion Veteran Reserve Corps ——; then to Co. I, 12th Regiment Veteran Reserve Corps ——; from which mustered out Sept. 24, 1864, on expiration of term of service.
Hickson, Matthew	do	18	Feb. 27, 1864	3 yrs.	Mustered out with company Sept. 13, 1865.
Hilliard, Wm. H. B.	do	22	Aug. 30, 1861	3 yrs.	Mustered out with company Sept. 13, 1865; vet., rans.
Jones, Charles	do	19	Feb. 25, 1864	3 yrs.	Mustered out May 25, 1865, at Madison, Ind., by order of War Department.
Kennard, Thomas B.	do	24	Sept. 2, 1861	3 yrs.	Wounded in action ——; mustered out with company Sept. 13, 1865; veteran.
Kendinger, Elias	do	23	Sept. 19, 1861	3 yrs.	Transferred to Co. H ——.
King, Daniel E.	do	18	Mch. 9, 1864	3 yrs.	Mustered out with company Sept. 13, 1865.
Kiser, Nicholas	do	26	Sept. 2, 1861	3 yrs.	Died Jan. 22, 1864.
Knight, Jasper	do	23	July 12, 1863	3 yrs.	Transferred to Co. H April 21, 1864.
Lawder, Charles H.	do	18	Mar. 11, 1864	3 yrs.	Mustered out with company Sept. 13, 1865.
McGinnis, James	do	41	Sept. 2, 1861	3 yrs.	Discharged Feb. 19, 1862, at Bardstown, Ky., on surgeon's certificate of disability.
McGowan, Charles S.	do	19	Sept. 4, 1861	3 yrs.	Mustered out Oct. 6, 1864, on expiration of term of service.

First Regiment Ohio Volunteer Cavalry.

Names.	Rank.	Age.	Date of Entering the Service.	Period of Service.	Remarks.
McMaly, George W.	Private	18	Feb. 23, 1864	3 yrs.	Mustered out with company Sept 13, 1865.
McMasters, Geo. T. W.	do	22	Sept. 2, 1864	3 yrs.	Transferred to Co. H —.
Malosh, John D.	do	35	Feb. 19, 1864	3 yrs.	On detached service from Nov. 18, 1864, to June 4, 1865; mustered out with company Sept. 13, 1865.
Marshall, William F.	do	18	Feb. 23, 1864	3 yrs.	Mustered out with company Sept. 13, 1865.
Martin, Joseph H.	do	22	Feb. 25, 1864	3 yrs.	Mustered out with company Sept. 13, 1865.
Miles, Alexander C.	do	19	Feb. 23, 1864	3 yrs.	Mustered out with company Sept. 13, 1865.
Miller, Casper.	do	31	Sept. 5, 1861	3 yrs.	Transferred to Co. H —.
Miller, John.	do	25	April 11, 1865	1 yr.	Mustered out with company Sept. 13, 1865.
Minto, Robert H.	do	24	Sept. 3, 1861	3 yrs.	Mustered out Oct. 6, 1864, on expiration of term of service.
Mohler, Samuel.	do	35	Aug. 28, 1861	3 yrs.	Mustered out Oct. 6, 1864, on expiration of term of service.
Mooney, Patrick.	do	29	Aug. 7, 1861	3 yrs.	Transferred from Co. C Dec. 10, 1861.
Mulford, John W.	do	30	Aug. 28, 1861	3 yrs.	Transferred to Co. H Feb. 20, 1864.
Murray, John K.	do	18	Oct. 3, 1861	3 yrs.	Mustered out with company Sept. 13, 1865; veteran.
Neaves, Elihu.	do	18	Feb. 22, 1864	3 yrs.	Mustered out with company Sept. 13, 1865.
O'Harra, Thomas.	do	23	Sept. 5, 1861	4 yrs.	Died March 28, 1864, at Pleasant Hill, O.; veteran.
Patterson, Samuel H.	do	32	Aug. 29, 1861	3 yrs.	Mustered out with company Sept. 13, 1865; veteran.
Patty, Wilk F.	do	19	Feb. 25, 1864	3 yrs.	Mustered out with company Sept. 13, 1865.
Peifer, John.	do	21	Sept. 19, 1861	3 yrs.	Also borne on rolls as "Pifer;" mustered out with company Sept. 13, 1865; veteran.
Place, Benjamin.	do	25	Feb. 22, 1864	3 yrs.	Killed Aug. 21, 1864, in action near Lovejoy Station, Ga.
Price, James.	do	22	Sept. 19, 1861	3 yrs.	Mustered out with company Sept. 13, 1865; veteran.
Quick, Moses.	do	22	Feb. 9, 1864	3 yrs.	Mustered out with company Sept. 13, 1865.
Reed, Joseph.	do	18	Feb. 22, 1864	3 yrs.	Mustered out with company Sept. 13, 1865.
Reed, William H.	do	24	Sept. 5, 1861	3 yrs.	Transferred to Co. H —.
Richmond, John.	do	31	Aug. 29, 1861	3 yrs.	Wounded in action —; mustered out Oct. 6, 1864, on expiration of term of service.
Risk, David.	do	18	Mch. 9, 1864	3 yrs.	On detached service at Post Headquarters, Cincinnati, O.; mustered out July 31, 1865, from Harper's Hospital, Detroit, Mich., by order of War Department.
Robinson, William T.	do	29	Sept. 4, 1861	3 yrs.	Died March 29, 1862.
Rodgers, George.	do	36	Feb. 24, 1864	3 yrs.	Mustered out with company Sept. 13, 1865.
Rutter, George P.	do	18	Mch. 9, 1864	3 yrs.	Mustered out June 5, 1865, at Camp Dennison, O., by order of War Department.
Sanders, Peter F.	do	22	Aug. 28, 1861	3 yrs.	Wounded in action —; mustered out with company Sept. 13, 1865; veteran.
Savage, Jackson.	do	35	Sept. 16, 1861	3 yrs.	Died Jan. 4, 1863; suicide by pistol shot.
Shubert, John.	do	19	Sept. 25, 1861	3 yrs.	
Sinclair, Hiram R.	do	22	Sept. 4, 1861	3 yrs.	Mustered out Oct. 6, 1864, on expiration of term of service.
Sloan, William.	do	34	Sept. 19, 1861	3 yrs.	Discharged March 7, 1862, on Surgeon's certificate of disability.
Smith, Jacob.	do	25	Sept. 4, 1861	3 yrs.	Mustered out Oct. 6, 1864, on expiration of term of service.
Snyder, Joseph.	do	29	Sept. 2, 1861	3 yrs.	Mustered out Oct. 6, 1864, on expiration of term of service.
Speelman, William.	do	19	Feb. 25, 1864	3 yrs.	Mustered out with company, Sept. 13, 1865.
Stickle, Benjamin.	do	25	Sept. 17, 1861	3 yrs.	Mustered out with company Sept. 13, 1865; veteran.
Stoker, Joseph W.	do	18	Sept. 2, 1864	3 yrs.	Transferred to Co. H April 21, 1864.
Strachberry, Wm. P.	do	22	Oct. 2, 1861	3 yrs.	Wounded Sept. 20, 1863, in battle of Chickamauga, Ga.; mustered out with company Sept. 13, 1865; veteran.
Thra, DeWitt C.	do	18	Feb. 29, 1864	3 yrs.	Mustered out with company Sept. 13, 1865.
Vallery, Daniel.	do	29	Sept. 17, 1861	3 yrs.	Mustered out with company Sept. 13, 1865; veteran.
Van Tassel, Samuel.	do	27	Feb. 29, 1864	3 yrs.	Also borne on rolls as "Samuel M.;" mustered out with company Sept. 13, 1865.
Wabuhoof, Samuel.	do	18	Sept. 3, 1861	3 yrs.	Mustered out with company Sept. 13, 1865; veteran.
Ward, David.	do	18	Feb. 24, 1864	3 yrs.	Mustered out with company Sept. 13, 1865.
Weaver, Samuel.	do	31	Mch. 2, 1864	3 yrs.	Mustered out with company Sept. 13, 1865.
Webber, Martin.	do	31	Sept. 2, 1865	1 yr.	Mustered out with company Sept. 13, 1865.
Welsh, Edward.	do	21	Sept. 17, 1861	3 yrs.	Transferred to Co. H —.
Whitney, Charles L.	do	39	Dec. 6, 1862	3 yrs.	Transferred to Co. H April 21, 1864.
Wiley, William.	do	19	Aug. 27, 1861	3 yrs.	Mustered out Oct. 6, 1864, on expiration of term of service.
Wise, Henry.	do	18	Mch. 9, 1864	3 yrs.	Mustered out with company Sept. 13, 1865.
Wolfram, Charles.	do	35	Aug. 26, 1861	3 yrs.	Discharged July 24, 1862, on Surgeon's certificate of disability.
Wolfram, Charles.	do	36	Feb. 10, 1864	3 yrs.	

COMPANY K.

Mustered in Oct. 1, 1861, at Camp Chase, Ohio, by John R. Edie, Major 15th Infantry, U. S. A., Mustering Officer. Mustered out Sept. 13, 1865, at Hilton Head, S. C., by Leslie Smith, Brevet Major and Captain 1st Infantry, U. S. A., and Commissary of Musters, District of South Carolina.

Names.	Rank.	Age	Date of Entering the Service.	Period of Service.	Remarks.
Thomas W. Forshee	Captain	36	July 24, 1861	3 yrs.	Appointed Oct. 1, 1861; resigned June 6, 1862.
James Cutler	do	29	Sept. 1, 1861	3 yrs.	Appointed 1st Lieutenant Oct. 1, 1861; promoted to Captain July 14, 1862; captured July 25, 1862, at Courtland, Ala.; resigned April 29, 1863.
William H. Woodlief	do	21	Aug. 6, 1861	3 yrs.	Promoted from 2d Lieutenant Co. G April 22, 1863; resigned Sept. 18, 1864.
John W. Laughlin	do	24	Jan. 30, 1862	3 yrs.	Promoted from 1st Lieutenant and Adjutant to date March 18, 1868; mustered out with company Sept. 13, 1865; veteran.
William L. Curry	1st Lieut	22	Sept. 1, 1861	4 yrs.	Promoted from 1st Sergeant June 16, 1862; captured July 25, 1862, at Courtland, Ala.; promoted to 1st Lieutenant Dec. 31, 1862; to Captain Dec. 15, 1864, but not mustered; mustered out Dec. 30, 1864, on expiration of term of service, and on account of injuries received by being thrown from a horse Dec. —, 1864, at Louisville, Ky.
Robert K. Reese	do	26	Sept. 1, 1861	3 yrs.	Appointed Q. M. Sergeant from Sergeant ——; promoted to 1st Lieutenant to date Dec. 14, 1864; mustered out with company Sept. 13, 1865; veteran.
Abram F. McCurdy	2d Lieut.	33	Sept. 27, 1861	3 yrs.	Appointed Oct. 1, 1861; resigned June 16, 1862.
William H. Scott	do	24	Aug. 6, 1861	3 yrs.	Promoted from Q. M. Sergeant Co. D to date June 16, 1862; assigned to duty as Regt. Adjutant Oct. 31, 1862; promoted to 1st Lieutenant and Adjutant to date Oct. 1, 1862.
Martin V. High	do	23	Sept. 1, 1861	3 yrs.	Promoted from Sergeant Dec. 31, 1862; to 1st Lieutenant March 31, 1864, but not mustered; resigned Oct. 4, 1864.
Corydon S. Irwin	1st Sergt.	21	Sept. 27, 1861	3 yrs.	Appointed Sergeant from Corporal May 3, 1863; wounded Sept. 20, 1863, in the battle of Chickamauga, Ga.; appointed 1st Sergeant Nov. 1, 1864; mustered out with company Sept. 13, 1865; veteran.
Abijah S. Cheers	Q. M. S.	20	Sept. 24, 1861	3 yrs.	Captured July 25, 1862, in action at Courtland, Ala.; mustered out Oct. 6, 1864, at Columbus, O., on expiration of term of service.
Daniel Longnecker	do	36	Sept. 22, 1861	3 yrs.	Appointed Corporal Jan. 4, 1864; Q. M. Sergeant Nov. 1, 1864; mustered out with company Sept. 13, 1865; veteran.
Alanson L. Sesler	Com. Ser.	23	Oct. 26, 1861	3 yrs.	Mustered as private; captured July 25, 1862, in action at Courtland, Ala.; appointed Com. Sergeant Nov. 1, 1864; mustered out with company Sept. 13, 1865; veteran.
John Lucas	Sergeant	25	Sept. 27, 1861	3 yrs.	Mustered out Oct. 6, 1864, on expiration of term of service.
Asa L. Reese	do	21	Sept. 24, 1861	3 yrs.	Mustered out Oct. 6, 1864, on expiration of term of service.
John W. Chapin	do	24	Sept. 24, 1861	3 yrs.	Appointed from Corporal March 21, 1863; severely wounded Sept. 20, 1863, in the battle of Chickamauga, Ga.; captured and paroled Sept. 21, 1863; exchanged May 1, 1864; mustered out Oct. 6, 1864, at Columbia, Tenn., on expiration of term of service.
Franklin P. Allen	do	30	Sept. 22, 1861	3 yrs.	Appointed from Corporal Dec. 12, 1863; wounded Aug. 28, 1864, in action near Atlanta, Ga.; promoted to Regt. Q. M. Sergeant Dec. 21, 1864; veteran.
James W. Robbins	do	22	Oct. 1, 1861	3 yrs.	Wounded Aug. 28, 1864, in action near Atlanta, Ga.; appointed from private Nov. 1, 1864; mustered out with company Sept. 13, 1865; veteran.
Elliott Young	do	20	Sept. 27, 1861	3 yrs.	Appointed from Corporal March 12, 1862; captured Oct. 1, 1863, in action at Washington, Tenn.; mustered out March 14, 1865, at Columbus, O., on expiration of term of service.
David W. Hart	do	23	Sept. 10, 1861	3 yrs.	Transferred from Co. L ——; appointed Sergeant ——; promoted to Regt. Q. M. Sergeant Jan. 4, 1864; veteran.

FIRST REGIMENT OHIO VOLUNTEER CAVALRY. 39

Names.	Rank.	Age	Date of Entering the Service.	Period of Service.	Remarks.
Cornelius Byers	Sergeant	25	Sept. 1, 1861	3 yrs.	Appointed from Corporal ——; wounded and captured Oct. 1, 1863, in action at Washington, Tenn.; mustered out Oct. 5, 1864, on expiration of term of service.
Moses Roberts	do	22	Feb. 26, 1864	3 yrs.	Mustered as private, appointed Sergeant Nov. 1, 1864; mustered out with company Sept. 13, 1865.
Thomas B. Ward	do	26	Oct. 16, 1861	3 yrs.	Appointed Corporal Nov. 1, 1864; Sergeant Feb. 10, 1865; mustered out with company Sept. 13, 1865; veteran.
Elias Acton	do	19	Aug. 17, 1861	3 yrs.	Appointed Corporal Nov. 1, 1864; Sergeant Feb. 10, 1865; mustered out with company Sept. 13, 1865; veteran.
Edward Evans	do	27	Feb. 17, 1864	3 yrs.	Appointed Corporal Nov. 1, 1864; Sergeant July 1, 1865; mustered out with company Sept. 13, 1865.
Erastus D. Hartwell	Corporal	39	Sept. 1, 1861	3 yrs.	Mustered out Oct. 6, 1864, on expiration of term of service.
Thomas W. Andrews	do	22	Sept. 28, 1861	3 yrs.	Discharged July 5, 1862, on Surgeon's certificate of disability.
Thomas Kilgrove	do	24	Sept. 1, 1861	3 yrs.	Mustered out Oct. 6, 1864, on expiration of term of service.
William Griffith	do	19	Sept. 24, 1861	3 yrs.	Wounded Dec. 16, 1863, in action at Calhoun, Tenn.; appointed Nov. 1, 1864; wounded March 28, 1865, in action; discharged Aug. 10, 1865, on Surgeon's certificate of disability.
John F. Young	do	18	Sept. 28, 1861	3 yrs.	Wounded Sept. 20, 1863, in the battle of Chickamauga, Ga.; appointed Nov. 1, 1864; mustered out with company Sept. 13, 1865; veteran.
Augustus Hill	do	18	Feb. 18, 1864	3 yrs.	Appointed Nov. 1, 1864; mustered out with company Sept. 13, 1865.
William B. Herriott	do	25	Feb. 26, 1864	3 yrs.	Appointed Feb. 10, 1865; mustered out Sept. 14, 1865, at New York City, by order of War Department.
John M. Schultz	do	36	Sept. 22, 1861	3 yrs.	Wounded June 15, 1864, in action at Kennesaw Mountain, Ga.; wounded April 1, 1865, in the battle of Ebenezer Church, Ala.; appointed July 1, 1865; mustered out with company Sept. 13, 1865; veteran.
William Richards	do	23	Feb. 26, 1864	3 yrs.	Appointed July 1, 1865; mustered out with company Sept. 13, 1865.
Abel W. Lock	do	18	Sept. 22, 1861	3 yrs.	Wounded Oct. 8, 1862, in battle of Perryville, Ky.; appointed July 1, 1865; mustered out with company Sept. 13, 1865; veteran.
Frederick Ruff	do	22	Sept. 22, 1861	3 yrs.	Appointed July 1, 1865; mustered out with company Sept. 13, 1865; veteran.
Balers J. Aurand	Bugler	22	Sept. 29, 1861	3 yrs.	Discharged Jan. 15, 1862, on Surgeon's certificate of disability.
Lewis Latham	do	24	Sept. 1, 1861	3 yrs.	Captured July 25, 1862, at Courtland, Ala.; mustered out Oct. 6, 1864, on expiration of term of service.
Patterson Bradley	Farrier	26	Sept. 23, 1861	3 yrs.	Discharged Aug. 7, 1862, on Surgeon's certificate of disability.
Acton, Cyrus	Private	18	Feb. 26, 1864	3 yrs.	Mustered out with company Sept. 13, 1865.
Anderson, David	do	21	Sept. 23, 1861	3 yrs.	Died May 26, 1862, near Corinth, Miss.
Armstrong, Abraham	do	31	Aug. 13, 1861	3 yrs.	Discharged June 12, 1862, on Surgeon's certificate of disability.
Armstrong, Joseph B	do	30	Aug. 13, 1861	3 yrs.	Also borne on the rolls as "John B;" discharged March 19, 1863, on Surgeon's certificate of disability.
Armstrong, Thomas J	do	18	Aug. 13, 1861	3 yrs.	Discharged June 12, 1862, on Surgeon's certificate of disability.
Armstrong, Thomas W	do	28	Aug. 13, 1861	3 yrs.	Died Sept. 17, 1864, of wounds received in action near Atlanta, Ga.; veteran.
Beirsdorfer, John W	do	19	Mch. 7, 1865	1 yr.	Also borne on rolls as "Beyersdorfer;" mustered out July 18, 1865, at Camp Dennison, O., by order of War Department.
Bidwell, Mahlon	do	19	Feb. 17, 1864	3 yrs.	Mustered out Sept. 14, 1865, at New York City, by order of War Department.
Brant, Martin	do	35	Sept. 25, 1861	3 yrs.	Died Dec. 19, 1861, at Louisville, Ky.
Buel, Eckford	do	20	Oct. 10, 1861	3 yrs.	Mustered out Oct. 11, 1864, at Columbia, Tenn., on expiration of term of service.
Bull, Eugene M	do	26	Feb. 26, 1864	3 yrs.	Mustered out with company Sept. 13, 1865.
Calvert, Jarvis J	do	19	Sept. 24, 1861	3 yrs.	Discharged Dec. 5, 1861, on Surgeon's certificate of disability.
Campbell, William F	do	28	Sept. 24, 1861	3 yrs.	Discharged to date Oct. 3, 1862, by order of War Department.
Chapman, Silas W	do	18	Sept. 25, 1861	3 yrs.	Mustered out Oct. 6, 1864, on expiration of term of service.
Clark, Sanford P	do	23	Dec. 5, 1861	3 yrs.	Discharged Feb 11, 1865, on Surgeon's certificate of disability.
Clemens, James C	do	29	Sept. 2, 1861	3 yrs.	Discharged Feb. 9, 1863, at Stewart's Post, Tenn., on Surgeon's certificate of disability.

Names.	Rank.	Age.	Date of Entering the Service.	Period of Service.	Remarks.
Clemens, Jeremiah C.	Private	21	Sept. 22, 1861	3 yrs.	Mustered out Oct. 6, 1864, on expiration of term of service.
Columber, Thomas	do	44	Aug. 27, 1861	3 yrs.	Mustered out Oct. 6, 1864, on expiration of term of service.
Condiff, Laton	do	23	Aug. 25, 1861	3 yrs.	Discharged May 9, 1862, at Louisville, Ky., on Surgeon's certificate of disability.
Cooper, Salathiel	do	18	Feb. 17, 1864	3 yrs.	Wounded May 29, 1864, in action at Moulton, Ala.; mustered out with company Sept. 13, 1865.
Corry, Jacob	do	19	Feb. 11, 1864	3 yrs.	Also borne on rolls as "Carey;" mustered out with company Sept. 13, 1865.
Cythers, William	do	18	Sept. 27, 1861	3 yrs.	Discharged June 12, 1862, by order of War Department.
Darrah, Samuel	do	24	Sept. 24, 1861	3 yrs.	Captured flag of 7th Alabama Cavalry in action at Decatur, Ala., May 26, 1864; mustered out Oct. 6, 1864, on expiration of term of service.
Demchey, Jeremiah	do	20	Sept. 20, 1861	3 yrs.	Discharged Jan. 27, 1863, on Surgeon's certificate of disability.
Dorsey, Tyler	do	21	Sept. 10, 1861	3 yrs.	Discharged July 3, 1862, at Nashville, Tenn., on Surgeon's certificate of disability.
Erwin, William	do	25	Feb. 19, 1864	3 yrs.	Mustered out July 7, 1865, from hospital at Camp Dennison, O., by order of War Department.
Evans, Edward D.	do	24	Feb. 26, 1864	3 yrs.	Mustered out with company Sept. 13, 1865.
Fisher, Isaac	do	32	Feb. 17, 1864	3 yrs.	Mustered out with company Sept. 13, 1865.
Foyd, Isaiah	do	19	Feb. 17, 1861	3 yrs.	Mustered out with company Sept. 13, 1865.
Fox, Henry C.	do	18	Sept. 3, 1861	3 yrs.	Discharged June 12, 1862, on Surgeon's certificate of disability.
Garner, Alonzo M.	do	18	Feb. 26, 1864	2 yrs.	Mustered out with company Sept. 13, 1865.
Garner, Edward C.	do	19	Aug. 28, 1861	3 yrs.	Wounded and captured Oct. 1, 1863, in action at Washington, Tenn.; died July 5, 1864, in rebel prison at Andersonville, Ga.
George, Hannibal	do	28	Feb. 26, 1864	3 yrs.	Died May 29, 1864, of wounds received same day in action at Moulton, Ala.
Gill, James	do	23	Aug. 20, 1861	3 yrs.	Died June 26, 1862, at Corinth, Miss.
Goff, Presley E.	do	21	Oct. 18, 1861	3 yrs.	Wounded and captured Sept. 30, 1863, in action near Washington, Tenn.; died July 10, 1864, in rebel prison at Andersonville, Ga.
Gosnell, John	do	18	Feb. 29, 1864	3 yrs.	Discharged to date Nov. 28, 1864, by order of War Department.
Gregg, Thomas	do	43	Sept. 28, 1861	3 yrs.	Mustered out Oct. 6, 1864, on expiration of term of service.
Griffith, Jeremiah	do	28	Sept. 16, 1864	3 yrs.	Killed June 15, 1864, in action at Noonday Creek, Ga.
Hahn, Daniel G.	do	19	Mch. 29, 1865	1 yr.	Mustered out with company Sept. 13, 1865.
Hantz, Martin	do	24	Oct. 10, 1861	3 yrs.	Transferred to Co. E, 8th Regiment Veteran Reserve Corps ——, from which mustered out Oct. 10, 1864, on expiration of term of service.
Hancock, Harrison	do	31	Oct. 1, 1861	3 yrs.	
Hassan, John	do	22	Sept. 27, 1861	3 yrs.	
Heath, Daniel	do	28	Aug. 15, 1861	3 yrs.	Discharged Dec. 5, 1861, on Surgeon's certificate of disability.
Henry, James	do	23	Sept. 24, 1861	3 yrs.	Mustered out Oct. 6, 1864, on expiration of term of service.
Hersh, Henry H.	do	22	Sept. 18, 1861	3 yrs.	Mustered out Oct. 6, 1864, on expiration of term of service.
Hertzell, Joshua	do	23	Sept. 28, 1861	3 yrs.	Discharged June 17, 1862, on Surgeon's certificate of disability.
Hill, Edward A.	do	35	Aug. 15, 1861	3 yrs.	Killed Oct. 20, 1863, at Paint Rock, Ala.
Hizer, William	do	18	Aug. 15, 1861	3 yrs.	Wounded Sept. 20, 1863, in the battle of Chickamauga, Ga.; wounded Aug. 20, 1864, in the battle of Lovejoy Station, Ga.; discharged April 17, 1865, on Surgeon's certificate of disability, on account of wounds received; vet eran.
Haggert, Emanuel	do	19	Feb. 25, 1864	3 yrs.	Mustered out with company Sept. 13, 1865.
Johnson, John, Sr.	do	37	Aug. 24, 1861	3 yrs.	Discharged Sept. 4, 1862, on Surgeon's certificate of disability.
Johnson, John, Jr.	do	18	Nov. 24, 1861	3 yrs.	Captured July 25, 1862, at Courtland, Ala.; mustered out Nov. 26, 1864, at Louisville, Ky., on expiration of term of service.
Johnson, William	do		Oct. 1, 1861	3 yrs.	Captured July 25, 1862, at Courtland, Ala.; died Dec. 3, 1863, at Chattanooga, Tenn., of wounds received Nov. 27, 1863, in action at Cleveland, Tenn.
Jones, Francis	do	22	Feb. 26, 1864	3 yrs.	Drowned Aug. 21, 1864, in Cotton Indian River, Ga.
Jones, James	do	19	Mch. 17, 1865	1 yr.	Mustered out with company Sept. 13, 1865.
Klein, Ferdinand	do	33	Feb. 8, 1864	3 yrs.	
Lucas, Benjamin F.	do	19	Oct. 15, 1861	3 yrs.	Killed July 23, 1862, in action at Courtland, Ala.
Latham, Nelson	do	18	Aug. 20, 1861	3 yrs.	Discharged Aug. 27, 1862, on Surgeon's certificate of disability.

FIRST REGIMENT OHIO VOLUNTEER CAVALRY.

Names.	Rank.	Age.	Date of Entering the Service.	Period of Service.	Remarks.
Leach, John	Private	22	Sept. 21, 1861	3 yrs.	Transferred to Co. E April 13, 1864.
Likins, Isaac	do	22	Feb. 25, 1864	3 yrs.	Mustered out with company Sept. 13, 1865.
Longly, Monroe	do	31	Oct. 10, 1861	3 yr.	Discharged April 11, 1863, on Surgeon's certificate of disability.
McCormick, Francis M.	do	18	Feb. 19, 1864	3 yrs.	Mustered out with company Sept. 13, 1865.
McMahon, Jacob	do	38	Sept. 29, 1861	3 yrs.	Mustered out with company Sept. 13, 1865; veteran.
McPeak, Courtlin	do	24	Aug. 24, 1861	3 yrs.	Mustered out Oct. 6, 1864, on expiration of term of service.
Marshal, James A.	do	19	April 13, 1864	3 yrs.	Mustered out with company Sept. 13, 1865.
Medley, Elias	do	30	Sept. 25, 1861	3 yrs.	Mustered out with company Sept. 13, 1865; veteran.
Miller, William	do	29	Sept. 18, 1861	3 yrs.	Mustered out Oct. 6, 1864, on expiration of term of service.
Morris, Albert	do	21	Feb. 26, 1864	3 yrs.	Mustered out with company Sept. 13, 1865.
Newland, William	do	24	Oct. 22, 1861	3 yrs.	Drowned March 5, 1862, in the Cumberland River, near Clarksville, Tenn.
Nedrow, David	do	22	Sept. 10, 1861	3 yrs.	Captured Oct. 1, 1863, at Washington, Tenn.; mustered out Jan. 26, 1865, at Columbus, O., on expiration of term of service.
Orr, Abraham S.	do	23	Sept. 18, 1861	3 yrs.	Died Nov. 9, 1863, of wounds received Sept. 20, 1863, in the battle of Chickamauga, Ga.
Patterson, John E.	do	23	Sept. 1, 1861	3 yrs.	Captured July 28, 1862, in action at Courtland, Ala.; mustered out with company Sept. 13, 1865; veteran.
Pearl, George	do	21	Sept. 22, 1861	3 yrs.	Killed Aug. 19, 1864, in action near Lovejoy Station, Ga.
Pendlum, Charles	do	31	Aug. 28, 1861	3 yrs.	Died May 18, 1862.
Reece, David	do	30	Feb. 17, 1864	3 yrs.	Mustered out with company Sept. 13, 1865.
Reece, Samuel K.	do	29	Feb. 17, 1864	3 yrs.	Mustered out with company Sept. 13, 1865.
Reed, Samuel H.	do	21	Sept. 28, 1861	3 yrs.	Discharged Jan. 30, 1863, on Surgeon's certificate of disability.
Reuhlan, Samuel H.	do	29	Dec. 1, 1861	3 yrs.	Mustered out Dec. 6, 1864, on expiration of term of service.
Reuhlan, William	do	19	Sept. 28, 1861	3 yrs.	Mustered out Oct. 6, 1864, on expiration of term of service.
Robbins, David M.	do	18	Feb. 26, 1864	3 yrs.	Mustered out with company Sept. 13, 1865.
Robbins, Zenas S.	do	20	Feb. 23, 1864	3 yrs.	Discharged June 12, 1865, on Surgeon's certificate of disability.
Scribner, Orson	do	29	Sept. 10, 1861	3 yrs.	Discharged July 24, 1862, on Surgeon's certificate of disability.
Shirk, John W.	do	29	Oct. 1, 1861	3 yrs.	Discharged June 16, 1863, on Surgeon's certificate of disability.
Spicer, Orin L.	do	23	Oct. 1, 1861	3 yrs.	Mustered out Oct. 6, 1864, at Columbia, Tenn., on expiration of term of service.
Stamate, Matthew K.	do	25	Oct. 1, 1861	3 yrs.	Mustered out Oct. 6, 1864, on expiration of term of service.
Stanton, James	do	29	Sept. 30, 1861	3 yrs.	Captured Oct. 1, 1863, in action at Washington, Tenn.; mustered out March 23, 1865, at Columbus, O., on expiration of term of service.
Strickler, William	do	17	Feb. 22, 1864	3 yrs.	Mustered out May 29, 1865, from hospital, Columbus, O., by order of War Department.
Thompson, George W.	do	23	Feb. 15, 1864	3 yrs.	Mustered out with company Sept. 13, 1865.
Thompson, Milton L.	do	31	Feb. 23, 1864	3 yrs.	Mustered out June 5, 1865, from hospital, Camp Dennison, O., by order of War Department.
Timmons, Robert	do	22	Oct. 11, 1861	3 yrs.	Mustered out June 22, 1865, at Camp Dennison, O., by order of War Department; veteran.
Tobin, William H.	do	19	Feb. 15, 1864	3 yrs.	Mustered out with company Sept. 13, 1865.
Tway, Leander B.	do	21	Oct. 26, 1861	3 yrs.	Mustered out with company Sept. 13, 1865; veteran.
Warner, Henry D.	do	33	Feb. 17, 1864	3 yrs.	Died April 3, 1864, at Nashville, Tenn.
Wede, Frederick	do	20	Sept. 24, 1861	3 yrs.	Captured Sept. 30, 1863, near Washington, Tenn.; died Aug. 7, 1864, in rebel prison at Andersonville, Ga.
Welch, Charles	do	26	Sept. 22, 1861	3 yrs.	Also borne on rolls as "Charles W.;" promoted to Regt. Saddler Sergeant Jan. 4, 1864; veteran.
Welling, William C.	do	21	Feb. 27, 1864	3 yrs.	Discharged Feb. 10, 1865, for disability caused by accidental gun-shot wound.
West, George	do	21	Feb. 16, 1864	3 yrs.	Mustered out with company Sept. 13, 1865.
Williams, Francis W.	do	23	Sept. 22, 1861	3 yrs.	Mustered out Oct. 6, 1864, on expiration of term of service.
Williams, Matthew	do	23	Sept. 24, 1861	3 yrs.	Mustered out Oct. 6, 1864, on expiration of term of service.
Winters, John F.	do	31	Sept. 25, 1861	3 yrs.	Captured July 25, 1862, at Courtland, Ala.; mustered out Oct. 6, 1864, on expiration of term of service.
Yockey, Theodore	do	23	Feb. 29, 1864	3 yrs.	Mustered out with company Sept. 13, 1865.
Zebold, Christian	do	27	Sept. 28, 1861	3 yrs.	Mustered out Oct. 6, 1864, on expiration of term of service.

COMPANY L.

Mustered in Sept. 18, 1861, at Camp Chase, Ohio, by John R. Edie, Major 15th Infantry, U. S. A., Mustering Officer. Mustered out Sept. 26, 1865, at Nashville, Tenn., by J. W. Chickering, Captain and Acting Commissary of Musters, 2d Division, 4th Army Corps.

Names.	Rank.	Age	Date of Entering the Service.	Period of Service.	Remarks.
Thomas J. Pattin	Captain	32	Sept. 16, 1861	3 yrs.	Appointed Sept. 18, 1861; promoted to Major Dec. 31, 1862.
John D. Barker	do	29	Sept. 16, 1861	3 yrs.	Appointed 1st Lieutenant Sept. 18, 1861; promoted to Captain Dec. 31, 1862; resigned Jan. 11, 1864.
William McBurney	do	25	Aug. 17, 1861	3 yrs.	Transferred from Co. H April 21, 1864; promoted to Major Feb. 28, 1865.
Henry C. Reppert	do	26	Sept. 16, 1861	3 yrs.	Promoted to 2d Lieutenant from Sergeant Dec. 31, 1862; to 1st Lieutenant March 31, 1864; Captain to date Dec. 14, 1864; mustered out with company Sept. 26, 1865.
Samuel H. Putnam	1st Lieut.	25	Sept. 16, 1861	3 yrs.	Promoted to 2d Lieutenant of Co. D from Q. M. Sergeant Nov. 20, 1862; to 1st Lieutenant from 2d Lieutenant of Co. D to date Sept. 7, 1862; resigned Oct. 26, 1863.
Daniel W. Dye	do	21	Sept. 16, 1861	3 yrs.	Appointed Sergeant from Corporal Feb. 1, 1863; 1st Sergeant April 8, 1863; promoted to 1st Lieutenant July 24, 1865; mustered out with company Sept. 26, 1865; veteran.
Oscar H. Underwood	2d Lieut.	27	Sept. 16, 1861	3 yrs.	Appointed Sept. 18, 1861; resigned May 31, 1862.
Timothy L. Conditt	do	24	Sept. 16, 1861	3 yrs.	Promoted to 2d Lieutenant from Sergeant May 29, 1862; killed Dec. 31, 1862, in the battle of Stone River, Tenn.
Robert B. Rhodes	do	24	Sept. 16, 1861	3 yrs.	Promoted from 1st Sergeant April 8, 1864, to date Dec. 9, 1863; to 1st Lieutenant Jan. 6, 1865, but not mustered; discharged May 18, 1865.
Edward P. Burlingame	1st Sergt.	21	Sept. 16, 1861	3 yrs.	Appointed Corporal ——; Sergeant Sept. 1, 1864; 1st Sergeant Aug. 27, 1865; mustered out with company Sept. 26, 1865; veteran.
John Huff	Q. M. S.	20	Sept. 16, 1861	3 yrs.	Mustered as private; appointed Q. M. Sergeant Jan. 1, 1862; mustered out with company Sept. 26, 1865; veteran.
George Dye	Com. Ser.	21	Sept. 16, 1861	3 yrs.	Mustered as private; appointed Com. Sergeant ——; mustered out Sept. 17, 1864, on expiration of term of service.
Henry Duden	do	24	Feb. 1, 1862	3 yrs.	Mustered as private; appointed Com. Sergeant Sept. 19, 1864; mustered out with company Sept. 26, 1865; veteran.
David W. Hart	Sergeant	23	Sept. 16, 1861	3 yrs.	Transferred to Co. K ——.
William H. Wilson	do	20	Sept. 16, 1861	3 yrs.	Died April 19, 1862.
Arthur B. Chapin	do	20	Sept. 16, 1861	3 yrs.	Appointed from Corporal ——; mustered out Sept. 17, 1864, on expiration of term of service.
Charles Reese	do	24	Sept. 16, 1861	3 yrs.	Appointed from Corporal ——; mustered out Sept. 17, 1864, on expiration of term of service.
Jacob Gano	do	21	Sept. 16, 1861	3 yrs.	Appointed from Corporal ——; mustered out Sept. 17, 1864, on expiration of term of service.
Franklin W. Pranty	do	25	Sept. 16, 1861	3 yrs.	Mustered as private; appointed Sergeant Sept. 19, 1864; mustered out with company Sept. 26, 1865; veteran.
John W. Price	do	22	Sept. 16, 1861	3 yrs.	Appointed Corporal ——; Sergeant Sept. 19, 1864; mustered out with company Sept. 26, 1865; veteran.
Darius A. Fluck	do	21	Sept. 16, 1861	3 yrs.	Appointed Corporal ——; Sergeant Sept. 19, 1864; mustered out with company Sept. 26, 1865; veteran.
Benjamin S. Turner	do	18	Sept. 16, 1861	3 yrs.	Mustered as private; appointed Sergeant Sept. 19, 1864; mustered out with company Sept. 26, 1865; veteran.
William Harsha	do	20	Sept. 16, 1861	3 yrs.	Appointed Corporal Sept. 19, 1864; Sergeant Aug. 27, 1865; mustered out with company Sept. 26, 1865; veteran.
William M. Robinson	Corporal	19	Sept. 16, 1861	3 yrs.	Missing in action May 13, 1862; no further record.
Henry M. Harris	do	24	Sept. 16, 1861	3 yrs.	Appointed ——; mustered out Sept. 17, 1864, on expiration of term of service.
John C. Stewart	do	28	Sept. 16, 1861	3 yrs.	Mustered out Sept. 17, 1864, on expiration of term of service.

FIRST REGIMENT OHIO VOLUNTEER CAVALRY.

Names.	Rank.	Age	Date of Entering the Service.	Period of Service.	Remarks.
Charles Betts	Corporal	33	Sept. 16, 1861	3 yrs.	Appointed ——; mustered out Sept. 17, 1864, on expiration of term of service.
Darwin A. Scott	do	19	Sept. 16, 1861	3 yrs.	Appointed Sept. 19, 1864; mustered out with company Sept. 26, 1865; veteran.
Milton Gillingham	do	24	Sept. 16, 1861	3 yrs.	Appointed Sept. 19, 1864; mustered out with company Sept. 26, 1865; veteran.
Warren Riley	do	19	Sept. 16, 1861	3 yrs.	Discharged June 22, 1862, at Corinth, Miss., on Surgeon's certificate of disability; re-enlisted Jan. 4, 1864; appointed Corporal ——; mustered out with company Sept. 26, 1865.
Walter R. Reppert	do	20	Feb. 1, 1803	3 yrs.	Appointed Sept. 19, 1864; mustered out with company Sept. 26, 1865.
Charles Sanford	do	25	Sept. 16, 1861	3 yrs.	Appointed Sept. 19, 1864; mustered out Aug. 22, 1865, from hospital at Camp Dennison, O., by order of War Department; veteran.
Douglas P. Scott	do	18	Feb. 24, 1864	3 yrs.	Appointed July 19, 1865; mustered out with company Sept. 26, 1865.
Robert Harsha	do	19	Jan. 1, 1864	3 yrs.	Appointed July 29, 1865; mustered out with company Sept. 26, 1865.
Whitney R. Corner	do	21	Feb. 29, 1864	3 yrs.	Appointed Aug. 27, 1865; mustered out with company Sept. 26, 1865.
Rector R. Wilson	Farrier	24	Jan. 4, 1864	3 yrs.	Appointed ——; mustered out with company Sept. 26, 1865.
Milton G. Cook	B. Smith	43	Sept. 16, 1861	3 yrs.	Discharged March 23, 1863.
Peter Cline	do	22	Sept. 16, 1861	3 yrs.	Mustered out Sept. 17, 1864, on expiration of term of service.
Salmon M. Chambers	Saddler	21	Sept. 16, 1861	3 yrs.	Appointed ——; mustered out with company Sept. 26, 1865; veteran.
Owen Pattin	Wagoner	50	Sept. 16, 1861	3 yrs.	Discharged Jan. 19, 1862, on Surgeon's certificate of disability.
Joseph Rhodes	do	23	Sept. 16, 1861	3 yrs.	Also borne on rolls as "Joseph B;" appointed ——; mustered out Sept. 17, 1864, on expiration of term of service.
Adams, Joline J	Private	26	Sept. 16, 1861	3 yrs.	Mustered out Sept. 17, 1864, on expiration of term of service.
Ballobhe, Ives L	do	34	July 31, 1862	3 yrs.	Transferred to Co. C 9th Regiment Veteran Reserve Corps Aug. —, 1864, from which mustered out June 26, 1865, at Washington, D. C., by order of War Department.
Beagle, Jeremiah	do	19	Sept. 16, 1861	3 yrs.	Mustered out Sept. 17, 1864, on expiration of term of service.
Bigelow, Edward P	do	18	Sept. 16, 1861	3 yrs.	Mustered out with company Sept. 26, 1865; veteran.
Bishop, William	do	31	Jan. 5, 1864	3 yrs.	Mustered out with company Sept. 26, 1865.
Boring, Absalom	do	44	Jan. 5, 1864	3 yrs.	Also borne on rolls as "Bowing;" mustered out with company Sept. 26, 1865.
Bowers, Jacob	do	22	Jan. 5, 1864	3 yrs.	Sent to hospital at Nashville, Tenn., Sept. 18, 1865; returned to duty, Oct. 3, 1865, to I. G. office; no further record.
Broughton, Calvin C	do	20	Sept. 16, 1861	3 yrs.	Mustered out Sept. 17, 1864, on expiration of term of service.
Brown, Daniel	do	23	Sept. 16, 1861	3 yrs.	Discharged Feb. 28, 1803, on Surgeon's certificate of disability.
Brown, William H	do	22	Sept. 16, 1861	3 yrs.	Mustered out Sept. 17, 1864, on expiration of term of service.
Burchett, William	do	21	Aug. 16, 1864	1 yr.	Mustered out May 29, 1865, by order of War Department.
Carbin, Jerome	do	16	Sept. 16, 1861	3 yrs.	Discharged Oct. 9, 1861, by civil authority. on writ of habeas corpus.
Chambers, Otis J	do	23	Sept. 16, 1861	3 yrs.	Mustered out Sept. 17, 1864, on expiration of term of service.
Childers, Lewis	do	19	Sept. 16, 1861	3 yrs.	Mustered out with company Sept. 26, 1865; veteran.
Clogston, Luther E	do	35	Sept. 16, 1861	3 yrs.	Mustered out Sept. 17, 1864, on expiration of term of service.
Cole, John W	do	18	Jan. 16, 1864	3 yrs.	Died Sept. 10, 1864, in hospital at Atlanta, Ga.
Criswell, Isaac	do	33	Jan. 4, 1864	3 yrs.	Mustered out with company Sept. 26, 1865.
Dailey, William H	do	19	Sept. 16, 1861	3 yrs.	Discharged March 7, 1863, on Surgeon's certificate of disability.
Dailey, William H	do	21	Jan. 4, 1864	3 yrs.	Mustered out with company Sept. 26, 1865.
Danley, John W	do	31	Jan. 1, 1864	3 yrs.	Mustered out Sept. 10, 1865, at Camp Dennison, O., by order of War Department.
Davis, Freeman L	do	28	Sept. 16, 1861	3 yrs.	Mustered out Sept. 17, 1864, on expiration of term of service.
Doe, Frederick	do	33	Jan. 5, 1864	3 yrs.	Discharged Jan. 7, 1865, on Surgeon's certificate of disability.
Dotson, Samuel S	do	24	Sept. 16, 1861	3 yrs.	Appointed Corporal Sept. 19, 1864; reduced July 26, 1865, at his own request; mustered out with company Sept. 26, 1865; veteran.
Duden, John	do	21	Sept. 16, 1861	3 yrs.	Mustered out Sept. 17, 1864, on expiration of term of service.
Dulty, John	do	39	Sept. 16, 1861	3 yrs.	Mustered out Sept. 17, 1864, on expiration of term of service.
Dyer, Samuel	do	18	Jan. 25, 1864	3 yrs.	Mustered out with company Sept. 26, 1865.

Names.	Rank.	Age.	Date of Entering the Service.	Period of Service.	Remarks.
Eddleston, Hugh	Private	19	Sept. 16, 1861	3 yrs.	Mustered out Sept. 17, 1864, on expiration of term of service.
Edgerton, Luther, Jr	do	18	Sept. 16, 1861	3 yrs.	Died May —, 1862.
Farley, Kins	do	17	Aug. 10, 1864	1 yr.	Died April 9, 1865, in hospital at Chattanooga, Tenn.
Fish, James	do	24	Dec. 22, 1863	3 yrs.	Mustered out with company Sept. 26, 1865.
Fish, William	do	19	Jan. 18, 1864	3 yrs.	Died Feb. 28, 1864.
Gates, Charles L	do	37	Jan. 5, 1864	3 yrs.	Transferred to Co. H April 1, 1864.
Gilpin, Jackson	do	18	Oct. 6, 1864	1 yr.	Mustered out with company Sept. 26, 1865.
Greene, George L	do	18	Jan. 15, 1864	3 yrs.	Discharged Feb. 15, 1865, on Surgeon's certificate of disability.
Grimes, David M	do	20	Sept. 16, 1861	3 yrs.	Mustered out Sept. 17, 1864, on expiration of term of service.
Guin, Abraham	do	18	Jan. 22, 1864	3 yrs.	Also borne on rolls as "Gwin;" mustered out Aug. 30, 1865, from hospital at Camp Dennison, O., by order of War Department.
Guiteau, Fulton	do	20	Sept. 16, 1861	3 yrs.	Detailed for detached duty March 24, 1862; no further record.
Guyton, John	do	35	Sept. 16, 1861	3 yrs.	Mustered out Sept. 17, 1864, on expiration of term of service.
Hall, George W	do	19	Sept. 16, 1861	3 yrs.	Mustered out July 10, 1865, at Columbus, O., by order of War Department; veteran.
Hall, Lyman W	do	27	Jan. 18, 1864	3 yrs.	Mustered out with company Sept. 26, 1865.
Hazel, Frederick	do	18	Jan. 18, 1864	3 yrs.	Mustered out May 31, 1865, from hospital, at Chattanooga, Tenn., by order of War Department.
Hoff, Ford P	do	16	Oct. 3, 1864	1 yr.	Mustered out June 13, 1865, at Chattanooga, Tenn., by order of War Department.
Hoffman, John H	do	19	Jan. 5, 1864	3 yrs.	Mustered out with company Sept. 26, 1865.
Hoskisson, John	do	25	Sept. 16, 1861	3 yrs.	Mustered out Sept. 17, 1864, on expiration of term of service.
Jones, Wilders D	do	20	Jan. 5, 1864	3 yrs.	Mustered out with company Sept. 26, 1865.
Larkins, Elias	do	24	Sept. 16, 1861	3 yrs.	Also borne on rolls as "Elisha;" mustered out with company Sept. 26, 1865; veteran.
Lightfritz, John	do	19	Feb. 1, 1864	3 yrs.	Mustered out with company Sept. 26, 1865.
Little, Thomas O	do	24	Sept. 16, 1861	3 yrs.	Mustered out with company Sept. 26, 1865; veteran.
McAllister, James A	do	23	Sept. 16, 1861	3 yrs.	Appointed Sergeant ——; reduced Aug. 31, 1864, at his own request; mustered out with company Sept. 26, 1865; veteran.
McBeth, John	do	26	Sept. 16, 1861	3 yrs.	Mustered out with company Sept. 26, 1865; veteran.
McCullick, Anthony	do	18	Mch. 5, 1864	3 yrs.	Also borne on rolls as "McGurlick;" mustered out company Sept. 26, 1865.
McCulloch, John	do	42	Sept. 16, 1861	3 yrs.	Discharged Feb. 19, 1862, on Surgeon's certificate of disability
McGlade, John	do	26	Oct. 12, 1864	1 yr.	Mustered out with company Sept. 26, 1865.
McNamara, Thomas S	do	20	Sept. 16, 1861	3 yrs.	Discharged Dec. 17, 1861, on Surgeon's certificate of disability.
McNamara, William	do	21	Mch. 9, 1865	1 yr.	Discharged Aug. 21, 1865, on Surgeon's certificate of disability.
Magee, Ancil W	do	18	Jan. 4, 1864	3 yrs.	Mustered out with company Sept. 26, 1865.
Magee, George	do	20	Sept. 16, 1861	3 yrs.	Mustered out Sept. 17, 1864, on expiration of term of service.
Marsh, Brigham A	do	32	Jan. 5, 1864	3 yrs.	Mustered out with company Sept. 26, 1865.
Marvin, Lewis	do	19	Jan. —, 1864	3 yrs.	Mustered out with company Sept. 26, 1865.
Mathers, Joseph	do	18	Jan. 18, 1864	3 yrs.	Mustered out with company Sept. 26, 1865.
Mathers, Matthews	do	19	Jan. 19, 1864	3 yrs.	Mustered out with company Sept. 26, 1865.
Maxon, Edwin	do	18	Sept. 16, 1864	1 yr.	Mustered out May 29, 1865, by order of War Department.
Maxon, Henry C	do	18	Aug. 12, 1864	1 yr.	Mustered out May 29, 1865, by order of War Department.
Maxon, Russell W	do	18	Jan. 12, 1864	3 yrs.	Died Sept. 20, 1864, in hospital at Atlanta, Ga.
Milligan, William W	do	22	Jan. 5, 1864	3 yrs.	Transferred Jan. 31, 1865, to 9th U. S. Colored Heavy Artillery.
Morton, Andrew J	do	23	Sept. 16, 1861	3 yrs.	Mustered out Sept. 17, 1864, on expiration of term of service.
Muncey, John D	do	24	Jan. 5, 1864	3 yrs.	Transferred Jan. 31, 1865, to 9th U. S. Colored Heavy Artillery.
Muncey, Montgomery	do	19	Jan. 16, 1864	3 yrs.	Transferred Jan. 31, 1865, to 9th U. S. Colored Heavy Artillery.
Muncey, William H. H	do	17	Aug. 22, 1864	1 yr.	Transferred June 28, 1865, to 9th U. S. Colored Heavy Artillery.
Myers, James	do	20	Jan. 25, 1864	3 yrs.	Mustered out with company Sept. 26, 1865.
Naylor, Harrison	do	18	Sept. 16, 1861	3 yrs.	Discharged June 24, 1865, on Surgeon's certificate of disability; veteran.
Nelson, Philip	do	18	Jan. 16, 1861	3 yrs.	Mustered out with company Sept. 26, 1865.
Newberry, William	do	18	Jan. 16, 1864	3 yrs.	Also borne on rolls as "Newburgh;" mustered out with company Sept. 26, 1865.
Oliver, Benson	do	38	Aug. 8, 1864	1 yr.	Mustered out May 29, 1865, by order of War Department.
O'Neal, Gilbert	do	25	Sept. 16, 1861	3 yrs.	Discharged April 14, 1863, on Surgeon's certificate of disability.
Owen, Alexander D	do	18	Jan. 12, 1864	3 yrs.	Mustered out with company Sept. 26, 1865.

www.ingramcontent.com/pod-product-compliance
Lightning Source LLC
Chambersburg PA
CBHW021756220426
43662CB00006B/74

ROSTER OF OHIO TROOPS.

Names.	Rank.	Age.	Date of Entering the Service.	Period of Service.	Remarks.
Yager, Frederick	Private	30	Sept. 5, 1861	3 yrs.	Discharged July 26, 1862, on Surgeon's certificate of disability.
Yates, Amos T.	do	19	Feb. 3, 1864	3 yrs.	Mustered out with company Sept. 13, 1865.

UNASSIGNED RECRUITS.

Names.	Rank.	Age.	Date of Entering the Service.	Period of Service.	Remarks.
Anderson, George	Private	20	Sept. 29, 1862	3 yrs.	No final record found.
Angle, James	do	23	Dec. 21, 1863	3 yrs.	Died April 24, 1864.
Bower, George W	do	25	Feb. 8, 1864	3 yrs.	No final record found.
Brainsted, Hezekiah	do	24	April 28, 1864	3 yrs.	No further record.
Brown, Allen	do	20	Feb. 12, 1864	3 yrs.	No final record found.
Broyles, Yancy	do	20	Oct. 1, 1864	1 yr.	No final record found.
Bucker, Samuel	do	21	Oct. 27, 1862	3 yrs.	No further record.
Burson, Thomas O.	do	18	Mch. 30, 1865	1 yr.	Mustered out Sept. 19, 1865, at Columbus, O., by order of War Department.
Carson, Andrew	do	21	Feb. 1, 1864	3 yrs.	No further record.
Caustin, Patrick	do		Oct. 1, 1861	3 yrs.	No further record.
Clark, Darius A	do	18	Dec. 31, 1863	3 yrs.	No final record found.
Collins, John	do	26	Mch. 15, 1864	3 yrs.	No final record found.
Cox, Joseph F	do	17	Feb. 20, 1864	3 yrs.	No final record found.
Davis, John	do	27	Jan. 5, 1864	3 yrs.	No final record found.
Dickason, Gamaliel	do	21	Dec. 21, 1863	3 yrs.	No final record found.
Dillingham, Elwood	do	21	Oct. 8, 1862	3 yrs.	Enlisted in Regular Army—no date given.
Evans, Evan	do	21	Jan. 9, 1864	3 yrs.	No final record found.
Peters, Marcellus	do	18	Jan. 11, 1864	3 yrs.	No final record found.
Ford, Joseph F	do	23	Sept. 3, 1864	1 yr.	No final record found.
Francis, John	do	27	May 26, 1864	3 yrs.	Substitute; no final record found.
Gannon, John	do	22	Mch. 18, 1865	1 yr.	Also borne on rolls as "Garmon;" mustered out Sept. 19, 1865, at Columbus, O., by order of War Department.
Gibson, William H	do	21	Mch. 19, 1864	3 yrs.	No final record found.
Halliday, John	do	30	Mch. 12, 1864	3 yrs.	No final record found.
Harrison, James F	do	39	Sept. 21, 1864	1 yr.	No final record found.
Hanson, John	do	24	Sept. 30, 1862	3 yrs.	
Hughes, James	do	20	Feb. 11, 1864	3 yrs.	No final record found.
Jercunowski, Herman	do	45	Sept. 29, 1862	3 yrs.	No final record found.
Jewell, Zachariah	do	21	Sept. 24, 1864	1 yr.	Died Oct. 21, 1864.
Johnson, Edwent	do		Oct. 10, 1861	3 yrs.	No final record found.
Johnson, George	do	29	Feb. 2, 1864	3 yrs.	No final record found.
Logan, Thomas	do	19	Sept. 29, 1862	3 yrs.	No final record found.
McCollum, James	do	27	Mch. 7, 1865	1 yr.	No final record found.
McConoky, James	do		Oct. 11, 1861	3 yrs.	No final record found.
McGary, John	do	25	Sept. 29, 1862	3 yrs.	No final record found.
McManus, James S.	do	25	Sept. 28, 1864	1 yr.	No final record found.
Mikel, Adam	do	17	Feb. 3, 1864	3 yrs.	Discharged April 27, 1864, on Surgeon's certificate of disability.
Murphy, Michael	do	27	Feb. 17, 1864	3 yrs.	No final record found.
Obershaw, Francis	do	30	Feb. 24, 1864	3 yrs.	
Pennock, Francis	do	21	Oct. 7, 1864	1 yr.	No final record found.
Pickering, Daniel W	do	19	Feb. 29, 1864	3 yrs.	No final record found.
Pierce, Taylor	do	18	April 6, 1865	1 yr.	Mustered out May 6, 1865, at Columbus, O., by order of War Department.
Richardson, Howard	do	18	Feb. 29, 1864	3 yrs.	Discharged June 1, 1864, on Surgeon's certificate of disability.
Riley, John	do	18	Feb. 27, 1864	3 yrs.	No final record found.
Rogerson, Joseph	do	18	Aug. 19, 1863	3 yrs.	No final record found.
Scott, John A	do	18	Feb. 23, 1864	3 yrs.	No final record found.
Seyfried, Henry	do	33	Dec. 31, 1863	3 yrs.	No final record found.
Sims, Henry S	do		Aug. 6, 1861	3 yrs.	No final record found.
Sprinkle, Joshua	do	23	Feb. 5, 1864	3 yrs.	Died April 26, 1864.
Taylor, John T	do	23	Sept. 30, 1864	1 yr.	Mustered out Sept. 15, 1865, at Columbus, O., by order of War Department.
Tarman, John	do	20	Aug. 22, 1864	3 yrs.	No final record found.
Van Epp, Nicholas	do		Oct. 15, 1862	3 yrs.	No final record found.
Van Tasel, Daniel	do	25	Feb. 29, 1864	3 yrs.	No final record found.
Waites, George	do	25	Oct. 1, 1862	3 yrs.	
Will, John	do	23	Feb. 1, 1864	3 yrs.	No final record found.
Wintrode, Justus	do	18	April 6, 1865	1 yr.	Mustered out May 6, 1865, at Columbus, O., by order of War Department.
Wood, George	do	24	Mch. 2, 1864	3 yrs.	No final record found.

First Regiment Ohio Volunteer Cavalry.

Names.	Rank.	Age.	Date of Entering the Service.	Period of Service.	Remarks.
Moody, Andrew	Private	23	Sept. 10, 1861	3 yrs.	Drowned Dec. 10, 1861.
Moody, Joseph	do	27	Sept. 8, 1861	3 yrs.	Mustered out Sept. 14, 1865, at Columbus, O., by order of War Department; veteran.
Moor, John	do	22	Sept. 25, 1861	3 yrs.	Discharged Jan. 7, 1863, on Surgeon's certificate of disability.
Moore, Martin L	do	18	Feb. 20, 1864	3 yrs.	Died April 3, 1864, in hospital at Nashville, Tenn.
Morris, Samuel, Sr	do	26	Feb. 20, 1864	3 yrs.	Mustered out Aug. 5, 1864, by order of War Department.
Morris, Samuel, Jr	do	20	Feb. 29, 1864	3 yrs.	Mustered out with company Sept. 13, 1865.
Moxley, Kendrick P	do	19	May 10, 1862	3 yrs.	Discharged Oct. 16, 1862, on Surgeon's certificate of disability.
Myers, Hanson N	do	41	Feb. 20, 1864	3 yrs.	Mustered out with company Sept. 13, 1865.
Ninffer, Henry	do	18	Feb. 15, 1864	3 yrs.	Mustered out with company Sept. 13, 1865.
Newdorffer, John	do	38	Mch. 3, 1864	3 yrs.	Drowned March 12, 1864, in the Ohio River.
Pendergrass, E. D	do	21	Sept. 7, 1861	3 yrs.	Transferred to Co. E ——
Poe, Benjamin	do	26	Sept. 5, 1861	3 yrs.	Transferred to Co. G, 8th Regiment Veteran Reserve Corps ——; from which mustered out Oct. 10, 1864, on expiration of term of service.
Poe, James	do	21	Sept. 5, 1861	3 yrs.	Transferred to Veteran Reserve Corps ——; from which mustered out Jan. 24, 1865, at Columbus, O., on expiration of term of service.
Ranck, Israel	do	24	Sept. 26, 1861	3 yrs.	Captured Oct. 4, 1862, in action at Bard-town, Ky., and released on parole; appointed Corporal Feb. 15, 1865; reduced June 15, 1865, at his own request; mustered out with company Sept. 13, 1865; veteran.
Ranck, Jonas	do	19	Feb. 5, 1864	3 yrs.	Mustered out with company Sept. 13, 1865.
Renick, Werter W	do	18	Sept. 3, 1861	3 yrs.	Mustered out to date Aug. 5, 1864, by order of War Department; veteran.
Reynolds, Calvin H	do	21	Sept. 27, 1861	3 yrs.	Mustered out Oct. 6, 1864, on expiration of term of service.
Reynolds, Corrodon	do	34	Feb. 20, 1864	3 yrs.	Mustered out June 16, 1865, at Louisville, Ky., by order of War Department.
Ridgeway, William	do	18	Feb. 20, 1864	3 yrs.	Mustered out with company Sept. 13, 1865.
Roach, William	do	24	Sept. 2, 1861	3 yrs.	Transferred to Co. E ——
Rodgers, Levi	do	22	Sept. 9, 1861	3 yrs.	Discharged Sept. 9, 1862, at Camp Chase, O., on Surgeon's certificate of disability.
Romaine, A. J	do	22	Sept. 7, 1861	3 yrs.	Captured Aug. 6, 1862; paroled Aug. 10, 1862; mustered out Oct. 6, 1864, on expiration of term of service.
Rouse, Resen	do	26	Feb. 24, 1864	3 yrs.	Mustered out with company Sept. 13, 1865.
Rouse, Simeon	do	21	Feb. 12, 1864	3 yrs.	Mustered out June 23, 1865, at Louisville, Ky., by order of War Department.
Routt, Perry	do	22	Sept. 22, 1861	3 yrs.	Discharged June 12, 1862, on Surgeon's certificate of disability.
Schaffer, Charles A	do	19	Sept. 4, 1861	3 yrs.	On detached service, as teamster, at Cav. Corps Headquarters since March ——, 1865; mustered out Aug. 18, 1865, at Columbus, O., by order of War Department; veteran.
Sherrick, Henry	do	21	Sept. 25, 1861	3 yrs.	Mustered out Nov. 2, 1864, at Columbus, O., on expiration of term of service.
Smith, Michael C	do	21	Oct. 1, 1861	3 yrs.	Transferred to Co. E ——.
Smith, William H	do	25	Sept. 10, 1861	3 yrs.	Mustered out Oct. 6, 1864, on expiration of term of service.
Snider, Jacob	do	22	Feb. 13, 1864	3 yrs.	Mustered out June 5, 1865, from hospital at Camp Dennison, O., by order of War Department.
Spangler, Henry	do	18	Sept. 25, 1861	3 yrs.	Wounded Sept. 10, 1863, in action at Alpine, Ga.; transferred to Co. E ——
Sterrett, John R	do	33	Sept. 20, 1861	3 yrs.	Died Dec. 18, 1863, at Cincinnati, O.
Stiles, George	do	23	Sept. 4, 1861	3 yrs.	Mustered out Oct. 6, 1864, on expiration of term of service.
Tharp, George	do	20	Feb. 13, 1864	3 yrs.	Mustered out with company Sept. 13, 1865.
Toben, Edward	do	38	Mch. 23, 1864	3 yrs.	Mustered out with company Sept. 13, 1865.
Tuttle, Edward P	do	27	Feb. 18, 1864	3 yrs.	Mustered out with company Sept. 13, 1865.
Watterman, Aaron S	do	32	Sept. 10, 1861	3 yrs.	Mustered out Oct. 1, 1864, at Columbus, O., on expiration of term of service.
Welger, Conrad	do	22	Oct. 1, 1861	3 yrs.	Discharged June 12, 1862, on Surgeon's certificate of disability.
Wells, Ephraim C	do	36	Sept. 25, 1861	3 yrs.	Discharged Sept. 5, 1863, on Surgeon's certificate of disability.
White, Jerry	do	21	Sept. 12, 1861	3 yrs.	Captured June 5, 1863; returned to duty June 9, 1863; veteran.
Whitney, McClure	do	31	Sept. 6, 1861	3 yrs.	Transferred to Co. E ——
Wilkins, John W	do	27	Feb. 29, 1864	3 yrs.	Died April 3, 1864, in hospital at Nashville, Tenn.
Wilson, Morris	do	34	Sept. 29, 1861	3 yrs.	Discharged Jan. 15, 1862, on Surgeon's certificate of disability.
Wiltshire, Benjamin F	do	18	Feb. 22, 1864	3 yrs.	Mustered out Sept. 14, 1865, at Columbus, O., by order of War Department.
Winter, Charles	do	29	Sept. 8, 1861	3 yrs.	Discharged Jan. 6, 1863, at Cincinnati, O., on Surgeon's certificate of disability.

ROSTER OF OHIO TROOPS.

Names.	Rank.	Age	Date of Entering the Service.	Period of Service.	Remarks.
Carmean, Charles D	Private	39	Feb. 27, 1864	3 yrs.	Mustered out with company Sept. 13, 1865.
Cave, Isaac N	do	26	Feb. 22, 1864	3 yrs.	Transferred to Co. D, 4th Regiment Veteran Reserve Corps April 21, 1865; from which mustered out Nov. 11, 1865, at Springfield, Ill., by order of War Department.
Chambers, Hezekiah	do	40	Sept. 5, 1861	3 yrs.	Died Sept. 13, 1864, of wounds received Aug. 20, 1864, in action at Lovejoy Station, Ga.; veteran.
Chidister, James	do	18	Oct. 1, 1861	3 yrs.	Transferred to Co. E ——.
Christel, Michael	do	19	Sept. 6, 1864	3 yrs.	Mustered out Oct. 6, 1864, on expiration of term of service.
Clymer, Wesley T	do	25	Feb. 18, 1864	3 yrs.	Mustered out with company Sept. 13, 1865.
Cockrell, Abraham	do	18	Feb. 23, 1864	3 yrs.	Died April 4, 1864, at Cincinnati, O.
Cooper, Thomas	do	28	Sept. 25, 1861	3 yrs.	Died Jan. 26, 1862, at his home.
Creager, Otis W	do	21	Feb. 23, 1864	3 yrs.	Mustered out with company Sept. 13, 1865.
Davis, James P	do	18	Mch. 14, 1864	3 yrs.	Sent to hospital at Nashville, Tenn., March 20, 1864; sent to Camp Dennison, O., Sept. 12, 1864; no further record.
Delong, Christopher	do	26	Feb. 27, 1864	3 yrs.	Mustered out with company Sept. 13, 1865.
Dimity, Englehart	do	21	Feb. 18, 1864	3 yrs.	Mustered out with company Sept. 13, 1865.
Dishler, Philip J	do	22	Feb. 23, 1864	3 yrs.	Mustered out with company Sept. 13, 1865.
Dixon, John	do	38	Feb. 15, 1864	3 yrs.	Also borne on rolls as "Dickson;" discharged April 13, 1865, on Surgeon's certificate of disability.
Donaldson, Addison	do	28	Sept. 6, 1861	3 yrs.	Mustered out Aug. 1, 1865, at Camp Dennison, O., by order of War Department; veteran.
Donaldson, Theodore W	do	30	Sept. 15, 1861	3 yrs.	Mustered out with company Sept. 13, 1865; veteran.
England, William H	do	28	Feb. 15, 1864	3 yrs.	Mustered out with company Sept. 13, 1865.
Fay, John	do	31	Sept. 20, 1861	3 yrs.	Died Feb. 17, 1864, at Chillicothe, O., while at home on furlough; veteran.
Fry, Octavius T	do	26	Mch. 13, 1865	1 yr.	Mustered out with company Sept. 13, 1865.
Geiger, George	do	19	Sept. 25, 1861	3 yrs.	Transferred to Co. E ——.
Hanson, Thomas J	do	18	Feb. 26, 1864	3 yrs.	Mustered out May 23, 1865, at Covington, Ky., by order of War Department.
Harpster, Charles L	do	18	Feb. 15, 1864	3 yrs.	Mustered out with company Sept. 13, 1865.
Harris, John W	do	18	Feb. 14, 1864	3 yrs.	Mustered out with company Sept. 13, 1865.
Harwood, John	do	18	Sept. 5, 1861	3 yrs.	Discharged March 28, 1863, on Surgeon's certificate of disability.
Herman, Alexander F	do	18	Feb. 27, 1864	3 yrs.	Mustered out with company Sept. 13, 1865.
Herman, William W	do	25	Feb. 24, 1864	3 yrs.	Mustered out with company Sept. 13, 1865.
Herwick, Valentine	do	18	Feb. 20, 1864	3 yrs.	Mustered out with company Sept. 13, 1865.
Hickle, Amos	do	20	Feb. 20, 1864	3 yrs.	Mustered out Sept. 20, 1865, at New York City, by order of War Department.
Howell, James W	do	24	Feb. 6, 1864	3 yrs.	Mustered out Aug. 25, 1864, by order of War Department.
Hughes, Bale	do	22	Sept. 15, 1861	3 yrs.	Wounded Oct. 4, 1862, in action at Hardstown, Ky.; discharged Feb. 9, 1863, at Louisville, Ky., on Surgeon's certificate of disability.
Hulby, Jacob	do	30	Feb. 24, 1864	3 yrs.	Mustered out June 5, 1865, at Camp Dennison, O., by order of War Department.
Hutchinson, William	do	30	Feb. 23, 1864	3 yrs.	Mustered out with company Sept. 13, 1865.
Hyer, Jacob	do	18	Feb. 18, 1864	3 yrs.	Mustered out Sept. 26, 1865, to date Sept. 13, 1865, by order of War Department.
Iseman, William H	do	21	Feb. 27, 1864	3 yrs.	Mustered out with company Sept. 13, 1865.
Johnson, Lewis	do	28	Feb. 22, 1864	3 yrs.	Mustered out with company Sept. 13, 1865.
Keene, John M	do	18	Sept. 22, 1861	3 yrs.	Discharged Jan. 14, 1862, on Surgeon's certificate of disability.
Keene, H. C	do	21	Sept. 16, 1861	3 yrs.	Wounded Sept. 10, 1863, in action at Alpine, Ga.; mustered out Oct. 6, 1864, on expiration of term of service.
Keen, Henry C	do	23	Mch. 29, 1865	1 yr.	Mustered out with company Sept. 13, 1865.
Keller, Joseph	do	29	Feb. 29, 1864	3 yrs.	Mustered out with company Sept. 13, 1865.
Keltner, Isaiah	do	41	Oct. 1, 1861	3 yrs.	Also borne on rolls as "Izukah;" mustered out with company Sept. 13, 1865; veteran.
Kinney, James	do	28	Feb. 22, 1864	3 yrs.	Mustered out with company Sept. 13, 1865.
Kiser, John	do	19	Sept. 15, 1861	3 yrs.	Transferred to Co. E ——.
Kneadler, James W	do	27	Feb. 19, 1864	3 yrs.	Mustered out with company Sept. 13, 1865.
Lavcock, Charles	do	18	Feb. 15, 1864	3 yrs.	Mustered out with company Sept. 13, 1865.
Leffingwell, Samuel L	do	34	Feb. 25, 1864	3 yrs.	Mustered out May 12, 1865, at Nashville, Tenn., by order of War Department.
Legg, William	do	26	Sept. 4, 1861	3 yrs.	Mustered out Oct. 6, 1864, on expiration of term of service.
Lemile, Augustus	do	20	Sept. 28, 1861	3 yrs.	
Lowry, George W	do	28	Feb. 20, 1864	3 yrs.	Mustered out with company Sept. 13, 1865.
McArthur, A. J	do	23	Sept. 1, 1861	3 yrs.	Died Mar. 2, 1862, at Nashville, Tenn.
McGibbens, George	do	29	Feb. 20, 1864	3 yrs.	Mustered out with company Sept. 13, 1865.
McGowen, James	do	23	Sept. 2, 1861	3 yrs.	Also borne on rolls as "McGowan;" died May 10, 1862, at Columbia, Tenn.
McManaway, Thomas	do	25	Feb. 22, 1864	3 yrs.	Mustered out with company Sept. 13, 1865.
Mathews, John	do	21	Mch. 4, 1865	1 yr.	Mustered out with company Sept. 13, 1865.
Menser, William H	do	19	Feb. 23, 1864	3 yrs.	Mustered out with company Sept. 13, 1865.
Merrian, Charles P	do	20	Sept. 25, 1861	3 yrs.	Transferred to Co. E ——.
Messner, Joseph	do	18	Feb. 28, 1864	3 yrs.	Mustered out Sept. 23, 1865, at New York City, by order of War Department.

FIRST REGIMENT OHIO VOLUNTEER CAVALRY.

Names.	Rank.	Age	Date of Entering the Service.	Period of Service.	Remarks.
Patrick Crowley	Sergeant	20	Sept. 12, 1861	3 yrs.	Appointed Corporal March 18, 1864; Sergeant May 15, 1865; mustered out with company Sept. 13, 1865; veteran.
Henry C. Higgins	do	18	Dec. 9, 1861	3 yrs.	Appointed Corporal Nov. 1, 1864; Sergeant May 15, 1865; mustered out with company Sept. 13, 1865; veteran.
George A. Hickox	do	23	Sept. 19, 1861	3 yrs.	Appointed Corporal May 1, 1862; Sergeant July 9, 1863; mustered out Oct. 6, 1864, on expiration of term of service.
Emanuel Doty	Corporal	23	Sept. 5, 1861	3 yrs.	Promoted to hospital steward June 23, 1862.
Robert McMan	do	21	Sept. 4, 1861	3 yrs.	Mustered out Oct. 6, 1864, on expiration of term of service.
Bartholomew Ault	do	30	Sept. 2, 1861	3 yrs.	Appointed March 10, 1862; died July 4, 1862, of wounds received July 3, 1862.
John A. Fireling	do	22	Sept. 25, 1861	3 yrs.	Appointed Nov. 1, 1864; mustered out with company Sept. 13, 1865; veteran.
Richard Morris	do	27	Sept. 20, 1861	3 yrs.	Appointed Nov. 1, 1864; mustered out with company Sept. 13, 1865; veteran.
John W. Smith	do	20	Feb. 23, 1864	3 yrs.	Appointed Nov. 1, 1864; mustered out Sept. 14, 1865, at Columbus, O., by order of War Department.
Benjamin Smith	do	30	Feb. 23, 1864	3 yrs.	Appointed Dec. 2, 1864; mustered out with company Sept. 13, 1865.
Jacob B. Hayes	do	23	Feb. 24, 1864	3 yrs.	Appointed Nov. 1, 1864; mustered out Oct. 4, 1865, at New York City, by order of War Department.
James G. Hayes	do	24	Feb. 29, 1864	3 yrs.	Appointed May 15, 1865; mustered out with company Sept. 13, 1865.
Joseph Lewis	do	38	Sept. 25, 1861	3 yrs.	Appointed Oct. 1, 1862; mustered out Oct. 6, 1864, on expiration of term of service.
Thomas Shepler	do	31	Feb. 12, 1864	3 yrs.	Appointed May 15, 1865; mustered out with company Sept. 13, 1865.
William H. Sturgeon	do	20	Sept. 10, 1861	3 yrs.	Captured Oct. 4, 1862, in action at Hardstown, Ky., and released on parole; appointed Corporal June 15, 1864; mustered out with company Sept. 13, 1865; veteran.
Albert Ellis	do	25	Sept. 22, 1861	3 yrs.	Appointed April 24, 1862; transferred to 120th Co. 2d Battalion Veteran Reserve Corps Jan. 23, 1864; from which mustered out Sept. 26, 1864, on expiration of term of service.
Alvin Routt	do	19	Sept. 3, 1861	3 yrs.	Appointed Oct. 1, 1862; mustered out Oct. 6, 1864, on expiration of term of service.
Henry C. Davis	do	21	Sept. 8, 1861	3 yrs.	Appointed ——; died March 23, 1864, at Pottstown, Pa. while on furlough.
James H. Miller	Farrier	42	Sept. 8, 1861	3 yrs.	Promoted to Chief Veterinary Surgeon Jan. 1, 1862.
William Scharf	do	38	Sept. 8, 1861	3 yrs.	Mustered out Oct. 6, 1864, on expiration of term of service.
Hugh H. Miller	do	18	Sept. 8, 1861	3 yrs.	Appointed Jan. 2, 1862; mustered out Oct. 6, 1864, on expiration of term of service.
Charles Goth	Saddler	27	Sept. 6, 1861	3 yrs.	Mustered out June 29, 1862, by order of War Department.
Austin Hamett	Wagoner	30	Sept. 6, 1861	3 yrs.	Mustered out Oct. 6, 1864, on expiration of term of service.
Albright, John	Private	18	Feb. 23, 1864	3 yrs.	Mustered out Sept. 29, 1865, at New York City, by order of War Department.
Allen, Jasper J	do	21	Feb. 22, 1864	3 yrs.	Mustered out Sept. 13, 1865, by order of War Department.
Allen, William J	do	18	Sept. 20, 1861	3 yrs.	Mustered out Sept. 14, 1865, at Columbus, O., by order of War Department; veteran.
Anderson, L. D	do	21	Sept. 10, 1861	3 yrs.	Mustered out Oct. 9, 1864, on expiration of term of service.
Atherton, Joseph	do	28	Feb. 18, 1864	3 yrs.	Mustered out June 19, 1865, at Louisville, Ky., by order of War Department.
Baker, Conrad	do	20	Sept. 15, 1861	3 yrs.	Mustered out with company Sept. 13, 1865; veteran.
Barleon, George	do	43	Sept. 15, 1861	3 yrs.	Discharged June 12, 1862, on Surgeon's certificate of disability.
Bennett, Ira H	do	18	Feb. 27, 1864	3 yrs.	Mustered out with company Sept. 13, 1865.
Bentley, Levner C	do	25	Sept. 22, 1861	3 yrs.	Mustered out Oct. 6, 1864, on expiration of term of service.
Bentley, William J	do	24	Sept. 22, 1861	3 yrs.	Discharged April 2, 1863, to date Nov. 27, 1862, on Surgeon's certificate of disability.
Binkley, John E	do	19	Sept. 6, 1861	3 yrs.	Transferred from Co. E, 38th O.V.I., March 28, 1862; discharged May 27, 1862, at Corinth, Miss., on Surgeon's certificate of disability.
Bowers, Philip	do	22	Sept. 29, 1861	3 yrs.	Discharged Sept. 9, 1862, at Camp Chase, O., on Surgeon's certificate of disability.
Boyer, Marion	do	18	Oct. 12, 1864	1 yr.	Mustered out with company Sept. 13, 1865.
Braden, Andrew J	do	21	Sept. 22, 1861	3 yrs.	Turned over to civil authority Dec. —, 1861.
Bradley, James F	do	26	Sept. 6, 1861	3 yrs.	Reduced from Corporal May 1, 1862, at his own request; mustered out with company Sept. 13, 1865; veteran.

COMPANY M.

Mustered in Oct. 1, 1861, at Camp Chase, Ohio, by John R. Edie, Major 15th Infantry, U. S. A., Mustering Officer. Mustered out Sept. 13, 1865, at Hilton Head, S. C., by Leslie Smith, Brevet Major and Captain 1st U. S. Infantry, Commissary of Musters District of South Carolina.

Names.	Rank.	Age	Date of Entering the Service.	Period of Service.	Remarks.
James N. Scott	Captain	33	Aug. 30, 1861	3 yrs.	Appointed Oct. 1, 1861; promoted to Major April 1, 1864.
John D. Moxley	do	40	Aug. 30, 1861	3 yrs.	Appointed 1st Lieutenant Oct. 1, 1861; appointed Regt. Commissary of Subsistence Nov. 1, 1862; promoted to Captain from 1st Lieutenant of Co. B April 1, 1863; transferred to Co. H ——.
Alfred D. Lutz	do	20	Aug. 8, 1861	3 yrs.	Promoted from 1st Lieutenant of Co. E Sept. 13, 1864, to date May 25, 1864; transferred to Co. G Oct. 1, 1864.
Joseph T. Reynolds	do		Sept. 25, 1861	3 yrs.	Promoted to 2d Lieutenant from private of Co. F to date March 23, 1864; 1st Lieutenant Dec. 14, 1864; Captain March 18, 1865; commanded company since Nov. 28, 1864; mustered out with company Sept. 13, 1865.
Charles H. Schultz	1st Lieut.	21	Sept. 29, 1861	3 yrs.	Appointed 1st Sergeant from Sergeant Oct 1, 1862; promoted to 2d Lieutenant Dec. 30, 1862; 1st Lieutenant Dec. 31, 1862; Captain of Co. H May 25, 1864.
William G. Lawder	do	19	Aug. 21, 1861	3 yrs.	Promoted from 2d Lieutenant of Co. I to date March 31, 1864; transferred to Co. F ——.
Allen T. Overly	do	23	Sept. 5, 1861	3 yrs.	Mustered as private; appointed 1st Sergeant ——; promoted to 2d Lieutenant April 1, 1863; to 1st Lieutenant of Co. F to date March 31, 1864; transferred from Co. F ——; mustered out Nov. 25, 1864, at Louisville, Ky., on expiration of term of service.
William Davis	do	26	Sept. 15, 1861	3 yrs.	Appointed Sergeant from Corporal Oct. 18, 1862; 1st Sergeant Nov. 1, 1864; promoted to 1st Lieutenant March 18, 1865; resigned June 28, 1865; veteran.
Charles H. Goodrich	do	18	Aug. 5, 1861	3 yrs.	Promoted from 1st Sergeant of Co. D June 29, 1865, to date March 18, 1865; mustered out July 12, 1865, from hospital at Cincinnati, O., by order of War Department; veteran.
John M. Renick	2d Lieut.	28	Aug. 30, 1861	3 yrs.	Appointed Oct. 1, 1861; died May 28, 1862, at Corinth, Miss.
Arthur Watts	do	20	Aug. 30, 1861	3 yrs.	Also borne on rolls as "Arthur Watts, Jr.;" promoted to 2d Lieutenant from private May 28, 1862; discharged Dec. 29, 1862.
Abraham Gunther	1st Sergt.	23	Sept. 5, 1861	3 yrs.	Appointed Sergeant from Corporal Oct. 18, 1862; 1st Sergeant May 18, 1865; mustered out with company Sept. 13, 1865; veteran.
Thaddeus Scott	Q. M. S.	31	Sept. 4, 1861	3 yrs.	Appointed Sept. 19, 1861; appointed Act. Hart. Q. M. Sergeant May 2, 1862; promoted to 1st Lieutenant of Co. G Dec. 14, 1864.
John Featherstone	do	22	Sept. 15, 1861	3 yrs.	Mustered as private; appointed Sergeant June 14, 1863; Q. M. Sergeant March 23, 1864; mustered out with company Sept. 13, 1865; veteran.
Andrew M. Bard	Com. Ser.	29	Sept. 29, 1861	3 yrs.	Mustered as private; appointed Sergeant Dec. 1, 1862; Com. Sergeant Jan. 4, 1864; promoted to 1st Lieutenant and Regt. Commissary of Subsistence March 18, 1865.
John R. Woodall	do	27	Sept. 5, 1861	3 yrs.	Appointed Corporal ——; Sergeant June 13, 1863; Com. Sergeant ——; mustered out with company Sept. 13, 1865; veteran.
Thomas G. Trimbath	Sergeant	31	Oct. 2, 1861	3 yrs.	Captured Aug. 6, 1862; paroled Aug. 8, 1862; discharged Feb. 13, 1864, on Surgeon's certificate of disability.
Levi Knoderer	do	23	Sept. 5, 1861	3 yrs.	Appointed from Corporal March 23, 1862; mustered out Oct. 6, 1864, on expiration of term of service.
William H. Myers	do	23	Sept. 25, 1861	3 yrs.	Appointed Corporal Jan. 4, 1864; Sergeant July 1, 1864; mustered out with company Sept. 13, 1865; veteran.
Charles E. Levy	do	23	Sept. 24, 1861	3 yrs.	Appointed Bugler ——; Corporal Jan. 4, 1864; Sergeant Nov. 1, 1864; mustered out with company Sept. 13, 1865; veteran.
George W. Adams	do	26	Sept. 6, 1861	3 yrs.	Appointed Corporal Jan. 28, 1864; Sergeant Feb. 15, 1865; mustered out with company Sept. 13, 1865; veteran.

FIRST REGIMENT OHIO VOLUNTEER CAVALRY.

Names.	Rank.	Age.	Date of Entering the Service.	Period of Service.	Remarks.
Parker, James S	Private	25	Sept. 16, 1861	3 yrs.	Discharged June 14, 1863, on Surgeon's certificate of disability.
Parks, Miles	do	32	Jan. 4, 1864	3 yrs.	Mustered out with company Sept. 26, 1865.
Pattin, Thomas	do	21	Sept. 16, 1861	3 yrs.	Mustered out Sept. 17, 1864, on expiration of term of service.
Phillips, Lyman	do	28	Sept. 16, 1861	3 yrs.	Mustered out Sept. 17, 1864, on expiration of term of service.
Prior, Nathan	do	29	Sept. 16, 1861	3 yrs.	Mustered out with company Sept. 25, 1865; veteran.
Quinby, Daniel	do	26	Jan. 4, 1864	3 yrs.	Mustered out with company Sept. 26, 1865.
Reckard, Wesley J	do	24	Sept. 16, 1861	3 yrs.	Discharged June 22, 1862, on Surgeon's certificate of disability.
Reed, Stephen W	do	18	Sept. 16, 1861	3 yrs.	Died Jan. 3, 1862.
Reese, William	do	23	Sept. 16, 1861	3 yrs.	Mustered out Sept. 17, 1864, on expiration of term of service.
Reigney, Milton	do	22	Sept. 16, 1861	3 yrs.	Discharged May 1, 1862, on Surgeon's certificate of disability.
Rice, William W	do	23	Sept. 16, 1861	3 yrs.	Mustered out Sept. 17, 1864, on expiration of term of service.
Riley, John	do	24	Sept. 16, 1861	3 yrs.	Discharged Nov. 14, 1862, on Surgeon's certificate of disability.
Riley, Judson R	do	18	Jan. 14, 1864	3 yrs.	Mustered out with company Sept. 26, 1865.
Ripley, John	do	20	Sept. 16, 1861	3 yrs.	Died Oct. 1, 1862.
Rood, David R	do	18	Jan. 14, 1864	yrs.	Mustered out with company Sept. 26, 1865.
Schaffer, John M	do	22	Sept. 16, 1861	3 yrs.	Discharged Dec. 10, 1862, on Surgeon's certificate of disability.
Schawb, Peter	do	22	Sept. 16, 1861	3 yrs.	Died April 24, 1862.
Sheets, Isaac	do	46	Jan. 4, 1864	3 yrs.	Mustered out with company Sept. 26, 1865.
Slicker, Daniel	do	19	Sept. 16, 1861	3 yrs.	Mustered out with company Sept. 26, 1865; veteran.
Smith, Henry	do	22	Jan. 5, 1864	3 yrs.	Mustered out June 9, 1865, at Covington, Ky., by order of War Department.
Smith, John H	do	25	Sept. 16, 1861	3 yrs.	Died Oct. 4, 1862.
Smith, John W	do	20	Sept. 16, 1861	3 yrs.	Discharged March 27, 1863, on Surgeon's certificate of disability.
Snodgrass, William H	do	18	Sept. 16, 1861	3 yrs.	Appointed Corporal Sept. 29, 1864; reduced July 18, 1865, at his own request; mustered out with company Sept. 26, 1865; veteran.
Stewart, Ira A	do	19	Sept. 16, 1861	3 yrs.	Died Feb. 23, 1862.
Stewart, Joseph H	do	32	Sept. 16, 1861	3 yrs.	Mustered out Sept. 17, 1864, on expiration of term of service.
Stiles, Benjamin F	do	46	Jan. 5, 1864	3 yrs.	Mustered out with company Sept. 26, 1865.
Stotts, Alfred	do	21	Sept. 16, 1861	2 yrs.	Mustered out with company Sept. 26, 1865; veteran.
Strample, Henry	do	28	Jan. 5, 1864	3 yrs.	Mustered out with company Sept. 26, 1865.
Thornley, Thomas R	do	28	Sept. 16, 1861	3 yrs.	Died Aug. 23, 1864, in hospital, at Nashville, Tenn.
Tunnicliff, William	do	27	Sept. 16, 1861	3 yrs.	Mustered out with company Sept. 26, 1865; veteran.
Waldec, Simon	do	19	Sept. 16, 1861	3 yrs.	Mustered out with company Sept. 26, 1865; veteran.
Warren, George	do	34	Sept. 16, 1861	3 yrs.	Mustered out Sept. 17, 1864, on expiration of term of service.
Wells, William	do	18	Sept. 16, 1861	3 yrs.	Discharged Dec. 17, 1862.
Wheatley, Isaac	do	22	Jan. 14, 1864	3 yrs.	Mustered out with company Sept. 26, 1865.
Wilson, Aman	do	18	Jan. 16, 1864	3 yrs.	Mustered out with company Sept. 26, 1865.
Wilson, Joseph	do	21	Aug. 15, 1864	1 yr.	Mustered out June 12, 1865, by order of War Department.
Wood, Alfred S	do	18	Jan. 28, 1864	3 yrs.	Mustered out with company Sept. 26, 1865.
Wood, William	do	18	Sept. 16, 1861	3 yrs.	Discharged Oct. 20, 1863, on Surgeon's certificate of disability.
Wright, Luther	do	23	Sept. 15, 1861	3 yrs.	Discharged Nov. 17, 1862, at Cincinnati, O., on Surgeon's certificate of disability.
Yantiss, Francis M	do	18	Sept. 13, 1864	1 yr.	Mustered out May 29, 1865, by order of War Department.
Zimmerman, Lorenzo	do	21	Sept. 16, 1861	3 yrs.	Discharged Nov. 8, 1862, at Cincinnati, O., on Surgeon's certificate of disability.